palgrave macmillan law masters

Series editor: Marise Cremona

Company Law (6th edn)   Janet Dine and Marios Koutsias
Constitutional and Administrative Law (6th edn)   John Alder
Contract Law (7th edn)   Ewan McKendrick
Conveyancing (3rd edn)   Priscilla Sarton
Criminal Law (5th edn)   Jonathan Herring
Employment Law (6th edn)   Deborah J. Lockton
Evidence (3rd edn)   Raymond Emson
Family Law (5th edn)   Kate Standley
Housing Law and Property   David Cowan
Intellectual Property Law (4th edn)   Tina Hart, Linda Fazzani and
   Simon Clark
Land Law (5th edn)   Kate Green and Joe Cursley
Landlord and Tenant Law (5th edn)   Margaret Wilkie, Peter Luxton,
   Jill Morgan and Godfrey Cole
Law of the European Union (3rd edn)   Jo Shaw
Law of Succession   Catherine Rendell
Legal Method (6th edn)   Ian McLeod
Legal Theory (3rd edn)   Ian McLeod
Social Security Law   Robert East
Torts (3rd edn)   Ken Oliphant and Alastair Mullis
Trusts Law   Charlie Webb and Tim Akkouh

palgrave macmillan law masters

employment law

deborah j lockton *LLB MPhil*

Professor of Employment Law
De Montfort University

Sixth edition

Series editor: Marise Cremona
Professor of European Law
European University Institute
Florence
Italy

palgrave
macmillan

First edition 1994
Second edition 1996
Third edition 1999
Fourth edition 2003
Fifth edition 2006

Sixth edition 2008 published by
PALGRAVE MACMILLAN
Houndmills, Basingstoke, Hampshire RG21 6XS and
175 Fifth Avenue, New York, N.Y. 10010
Companies and representatives throughout the world

PALGRAVE MACMILLAN is the global academic imprint of the Palgrave Macmillan division of St. Martin's Press, LLC and of Palgrave Macmillan Ltd. Macmillan® is a registered trademark in the United States, United Kingdom and other countries. Palgrave is a registered trademark in the European Union and other countries.

ISBN-13: 978-0-2305-3748-4
ISBN-10: 0-230-53748-0

This book is printed on paper suitable for recycling and made from fully managed and sustained forest sources. Logging, pulping and manufacturing processes are expected to conform to the environmental regulations of the country of origin.

A catalogue record for this book is available from the British Library.

10   9   8   7   6   5   4   3   2   1
17   16   15   14   13   12   11   10   09   08

Printed and bound in China

Contents

Preface to the Sixth Edition

As is the case with Employment Law, this edition comes in the wake of considerable change. Since the fifth edition there has been the introduction of protection against discrimination on the grounds of age, by the Employment Equality (Age) Regulations 2006. The Transfer of Undertakings (Protection of Employment) Regulations 1981 have been replaced by Regulations of the same name introduced in 2006 and now give protection to a wider group of employees. The Equal Opportunities Commission, Commission for Racial Equality and the Disability Rights Commission have been abolished and their duties are now undertaken by a new Commission for Equality and Human Rights which came into existence in October 2007. Maternity leave and maternity pay have been increased, with intentions to increase them further in 2010, and from October 2007 the length of paid holiday that a worker is entitled to receive was increased, with again a further increase planned for October 2008. Perhaps the most interesting potential change in this area is the abolition of the statutory disciplinary and dismissal procedures. The Gibbons Review recommended their abolition, but at the time of writing they are still in existence although they will probably be abolished during the currency of this text.

In addition to new legislation noted above, there have been a number of cases, both in the national courts and the ECJ, which have developed and refined the law. Where appropriate they have been added to the text.

As usual, there are many people to thank for their patience and understanding. My students and colleagues continue to support me. Keith, as usual, has provided food and caffeine throughout and James is still thrilled to see his name in a book. Despite all of this support, any mistakes are my own.

The law is as I understand it to be on 1 December 2007.

Deborah J. Lockton

Table of Cases

Table of Legislation

Part I

Introduction

Chapter 1

Sources and Institutions of Employment Law

The law governing the relationship between an employer and employee has become increasingly complex over the last 50 years or so as more and more provisions have been introduced. In addition, employment law comes not only from common law and statute but also from a variety of additional sources such as codes of practice. Over the years, specific institutions have also been introduced into the area, some with an adjudicative function, such as the employment tribunals and Employment Appeal Tribunal, and some, such as the various Commissions, which have a variety of functions including overseeing legislation and helping applicants. All of these factors can appear to make the subject somewhat daunting but together they make it dynamic and one which is constantly changing. This changing nature of the subject is, in reality, very important, as the relationship between an employer and employee does not stand still but evolves over the years. Most employers nowadays do not regard their employees as their property and the law has changed with changing attitudes, introducing basic employment rights and providing specialised forums in which those rights can be quickly and cheaply enforced. As such, it is necessary to spend some time looking at the different sources and institutions of employment law today. At the time of writing, the impact of the Human Rights Act 1998 on the institutions and on employment law generally is difficult to assess.

1.1 Common Law

Although the area of employment law contains a great many statutory provisions, a large number of statutes are recent in that they came onto the statute books in the past 35 years. Before then, there were very few pieces of legislation governing the employment relationship and it was up to judges to interpret contractual provisions and to imply terms into a contract where the document was silent. While many older cases would not be followed today – given the changing nature of the employment relationship – judges are still required to interpret terms that the parties may, or may not, have included in the contract.

But this implies that judges have no function in the many areas of the employment relationship that is governed by statute. This is misleading.

The employment relationship is a fluid, ever-changing one and statutes, to some extent, reflect this. The most common phrase in the Health and Safety at Work Act 1974 is 'as far as reasonably practicable'; when considering whether an employee has been unfairly dismissed, a tribunal is required to consider whether the 'employer acted reasonably or unreasonably in treating the reason relied on as a sufficient reason for dismissing the employee; and that question shall be determined in accordance with equity and the substantial merits of the case' by s.98(4) Employment Rights Act (ERA) 1996. Such words as 'reasonably' or phrases such as 'as far as reasonably practicable' lead to a wealth of law on interpretation and as such the common law is an important source of employment law.

1.2 Legislation

Given the large amount of legislation enacted in the last 35 years, governing every facet of employment relationship, statutes are a primary source of employment rules. In addition to statutes, there is a wealth of delegated legislation. Statutory instruments may amend existing statutory provision, where existing authority is in place, because of a change in government policy, or UK legislation may be amended to comply with European Directives – the Equal Pay (Amendment) Regulations 1983 and the Transfer of Undertakings (Protection of Employment) Regulations 2006 being two examples.

1.3 Codes of Practice

A code of practice is not legally binding. It is intended to provide guidance for employers and to promote good industrial relations. Although not legally binding, however, a code may be used in evidence. The *ACAS Code on Disciplinary Powers and Grievance Procedures* 2004, which gives flesh to the statutory disciplinary and grievance procedures, for example, is often raised in evidence in an unfair dismissal claim. An employer who has not complied with the code will find it difficult to argue that he has acted reasonably unless he can show good reason why he departed from the code. Various bodies have the authority to issue codes of practice – the Secretary of State for Employment, the Advisory, Conciliation and Arbitration Service (ACAS), the Commission for Equality and Human Rights (incorporating since October 2007 the Commission for Racial Equality, the Equal Opportunities Commission and the Disability Rights Commission) and the Health and Safety Commission. There are codes covering a variety of areas including discipline, trade union ballots, picketing and discrimination.

1.4 European Community Law

The United Kingdom joined the European Community by the European Communities Act 1972. This provides that any treaty shall have legal effect in the United Kingdom without further enactment, as such Treaty Articles are directly applicable and will override national law. This means that individuals in Member States have rights under certain treaties in addition to rights created by national statute. This is seen, for example, in the area of equal pay. In addition to the three routes to equal pay provided by the Equal Pay Act 1970, all individuals have an additional route under Article 141 (formerly Art 119) of the Treaty of Rome which provides that men and women shall receive equal pay for equal work.

In addition to Treaty Articles, the Council of Ministers (or in rare circumstances the European Commission) may issue Directives. These are binding as to the result that Member States must achieve but not proscriptive as to the method by which such states achieve that result, for example the Equal Pay Directive (75 / 117) reiterates the principle of equal pay for equal work. The original UK Equal Pay Act did not achieve that result, and after action against the UK by the Commission (*Commission of the European Communities* v. *United Kingdom* [1982] IRLR 333) the Act was amended by the Equal Pay (Amendment) Regulations 1983. As it is the responsibility of the Member State to bring the purpose of the Directive into its law, an individual within a Member State has no right to sue a private employer for a breach of a Directive. The employer is only, after all, complying with national law. It has been decided, however, that a state should not profit from its own wrongdoing, and therefore an individual may sue the state (or an organ of the state) if that body employs the individual. This means that public employees have the additional right to sue the state or the organ of the state *qua* employer for a breach of the relevant Directive (*Marshall* v. *Southampton & South West Hampshire Area Health Authority* [1986] QB 401; *Foster* v. *British Gas plc* [1991] ICR 84).

The European Court of Justice (ECJ) has the jurisdiction to give rulings on the interpretation of Treaty Articles, Directives and Regulations. The Commission or any Member State may take another Member State to the court for a breach of Treaty obligations or a breach of the obligations under a Directive. In addition, a court in a Member State may refer a case to the ECJ for guidance on interpretation and the ECJ will give a ruling after which the national court will give its decision.

1.5 The European Convention on Human Rights 1950 and the Human Rights Act 1998

The European Convention on Human Rights was signed by the then Member States of the Council of Europe in 1950 and came into force in 1953. Until the passing of the Human Rights Act 1998 the only challenge under the Convention was against the state, and any claim for a breach of Convention rights had to be pursued in the European Court of Human Rights – a costly and lengthy process. Such challenges were successfully made and had an impact on UK practices, and in some cases legislation was introduced as a result of such challenges. For example, in *Smith and Grady* v. *UK* [1999] IRLR 734 there was a successful challenge against the questioning of members of the armed forces about their sexuality, such being an infringement of Article 8 which guarantees the right of respect for an individual's private life. The challenge led to the removal of the ban against employing homosexuals in the armed forces. Similarly in *Halford* v. *UK* [1997] IRLR 471 Halford successfully challenged the practice of monitoring employees' telephone calls as an infringement of Article 8. Such monitoring, and the use of information gained that way, is now covered by the Data Protection Act 1998, the Regulation of Investigatory Powers Act 2000 and the Telecommunications (Lawful Business Practice) (Interception of Communications) Regulations 2000 which give employers power to monitor employee communications as long as employees are aware of such monitoring. A further major change in UK law was as a result of *Young, James and Webster* v. *United Kingdom* [1983] IRLR 35 which successfully challenged the closed shop (a device whereby a union could insist an employer only employed members of that union) as an infringement of Article 11 which creates, *inter alia*, a right to be or not to be a member of a union.

The Human Rights Act 1998 effectively incorporates the Convention into UK law. It came into force in 2000. By s.3 of the Act all courts and tribunals, in determining questions which arise in connection with a Convention right, must take into account judgements from the European Court of Human Rights. In addition, by ss.6–8 all public authorities must act in a way which is in compliance with the Convention. Both courts and tribunals are deemed to be public authorities.

While the full impact of the Human Rights Act (HRA) 1998 on tribunal proceedings has yet to be seen, there have been a number of cases at the time of writing. In *De Keyser Ltd* v. *Miss Wilson* EAT 438/00 the complainant had presented a complaint to the tribunal of constructive dismissal arising from stress. The respondent had asked for a doctor to examine the complainant and his subsequent report gave a great deal of detail about the complainant's personal life, which both the doctor and the respondent felt was the cause of the stress. The complainant asked the tribunal for a fresh expert to be appointed because she felt that the original doctor was prejudiced against her. The tribunal, however, took the unprecedented step of striking out the ET3 (employer's response) as a breach of Article 8 (right to private life). The Employment Appeal Tribunal overturned the decision for a number of reasons. First, the letter of instruction from the respondent to the doctor was sent a week before the Human Rights Act came into force. Second, the report did not contain any information given in confidence. Third, the employer was not a public authority. Fourth, the tribunal could have directed that another expert be appointed. Fifth, the tribunal had not considered whether a fair trial of the issues was still possible and lastly, the right to privacy is qualified by the right of both parties to a just trial of the issues between them. Thus, even if the Act had been in force at the time of the respondent's instructions, it would appear from the decision that it would have made no difference to the outcome. The decision would suggest, moreover, that Article 6 (right to a fair trial) qualifies Article 8. This will be particularly important in cases of dismissal on health grounds discussed in Chapter 9.

The application of Article 6 was also discussed in *Tehrani v. UK Central Council for Nursing, Midwifery and Health Visiting* [2001] IRLR 208. The case confirmed that disciplinary proceedings before the Council's Professional Conduct Committee fell within Article 6 as they could result in Ms Tehrani's removal from the register of nurses and were thus a determination of her civil rights. However, although she was entitled to a hearing before an impartial and independent tribunal, the internal tribunal did not have to meet all of the necessary requirements as there was a statutory right to appeal to a court of law, which itself complies with Article 6. In *X v. Y* [2004] IRLR 625 the Court of Appeal considered the application of s.98(4) ERA 1996 where there had been alleged breaches of the employee's rights under the HRA 1998. In this case the employee, who worked with 16–25 year old young offenders, had failed to reveal to his employers that he had a conviction for gross indecency with another man in a public toilet. When his employers discovered the conviction he was dismissed. The employee argued that his employers were in breach of Articles 8 and 14 (rights against discrimination). While the Court of Appeal recognised that s.98 must be interpreted to give effect to the European Convention on Human Rights, in this case the act which gave rise to the dismissal did not take place in his private life and the employee had received a caution which was highly relevant to his employment. The fact that the employee wished to keep the act private did not prevent it from being public. Finally in *McGowan v. Scottish Water* (2004) IDS 771 EAT, McGowan was suspected of falsifying his time-sheets over call-outs, so his employer, a public authority, undertook covert surveillance of his home. The surveillance confirmed the employer's suspicions and McGowan was dismissed. He alleged a breach of Article 8. The EAT held that there was a breach of Article 8 but that the employer's actions were justified as it was protecting its assets.

1.6   Employment Tribunals

Industrial tribunals were renamed employment tribunals on 1 August 1998 by the Employment Rights (Dispute Resolution) Act 1998 and any reference to industrial tribunals in existing legislation changed to employment tribunals on that date. Employment tribunals became part of the legal system of the UK by the Industrial Training Act 1964 and at that time they had very little jurisdiction. Their functions have grown and they now have the jurisdiction to hear claims arising out of breaches of most aspects of the employment relationship. Most commonly they will hear claims for unfair dismissal, redundancy payments, equal pay and discrimination claims, breach of employment protection rights and claims in relation to unlawful deductions from wages. Until 1994 they were excluded from hearing claims for breaches of contract which had to be heard in the ordinary civil courts. This lack of jurisdiction caused problems for an applicant who had both a breach of statute claim and one of breach of contract. In *Treganowan* v. *Robert Knee & Co Ltd* [1975] IRLR 247 an applicant was found to be fairly dismissed but the tribunal felt that she should have been given notice and not dismissed instantly. She was entitled to six weeks' notice by her contract and as such was entitled to six weeks' wages as damages for the employer's breach of contract. The tribunal, however, had no jurisdiction to hear the breach of contract claim or award damages for that breach. Ms Treganowan had to go to the civil courts. The anomaly created by this lack of jurisdiction was often commented upon by the courts.

Breach of contract jurisdiction was given to the tribunals by the Employment Tribunals (Extension of Jurisdiction) (England and Wales) Order 1994. This order is now to be read in conjunction with the Employment Tribunals Act 1996. The changes create concurrent jurisdiction in the tribunals and the courts. Tribunal jurisdiction is, however, limited. First, it only arises when the contract is terminated (see *Capek* v. *Lincolnshire County Council* [2000] IRLR 590 and *Miller Bros and PF Butler* v. *Johnson* [2002] IRLR 386). Second, the type of claim that a tribunal can hear is also restricted. A tribunal can hear claims for a breach of the employment contract or any other contract connected with employment; claims for a sum due under such a contract or claims for recovery of such a sum in pursuance of any enactment relating to the terms of performance of such a contract (s.3(2) Employment Tribunals Act 1996). Breach of contract includes a breach of a term implied in a contract or under any enactment or otherwise; a term modified by or made under any enactment or otherwise; and a term which, although not contained in the contract, is incorporated into the contract by another term of the contract (s.3(6)). Certain claims are specifically excluded from the tribunal jurisdiction:

(a) damages or sums due in respect of personal injuries;
(b) breach of a term requiring the employer to provide living accommodation for the employee, or imposing an obligation on the employer or employee in connection with the provision of living accommodation;
(c) breach of a term relating to intellectual property (including copyright, rights in performances, moral rights, design rights, registered designs, patents and trade marks);
(d) breach of a term imposing an obligation of confidence;
(e) breach of a term which is a covenant in restraint of trade.

In all of the above cases only the courts have jurisdiction.

A claim is brought by issuing an originating application normally within three months of the effective date of termination of the contract. If there is no effective date of termination because, for example, the contract has been frustrated, then within three months from the last day that the employee worked an employer cannot originate a claim for a breach of contract in the tribunal but can issue a counter claim. Such a claim must be lodged within six weeks of the employer receiving a copy of the originating application. The tribunal has the discretion to extend both time periods if it feels that it was not reasonably practicable to present the claim or the counter claim in time.

Breach of contract claims are heard by the chair of the tribunal alone, unless the chair considers that a full tribunal should hear the case (s.4(3)(d) and s.4(5)). In making the decision as to whether the case should be heard by a full tribunal, the chair must consider the likelihood of a dispute arising on the facts or over an issue of law; any views of the parties as to whether the case should be heard by one person; and whether there are proceedings which might be heard at the same time which cannot be heard by the chair alone. The maximum damages a tribunal can award in a breach of contract claim is, at present, £25,000.

ACAS conciliation is available (s.18) and parties may also reach their own agreement to settle by a compromise agreement (see later). Appeals lie to the Employment Appeal Tribunal on a point of law.

The tribunal consists of a legally qualified chairperson and two lay members, one of whom is a nominee of an employer's organisation and the other a nominee of a trade union. The Tribunals, Courts and Enforcement Act 2007 received royal assent in July 2007. This inserts s.3A into the Employment Tribunals Act 1996 which renames tribunal chairpersons employment judges; implemented on 1 December 2007. By s.4(3) Employment Tribunals Act 1996, in addition to breach of contract claims certain other claims may be heard by the employment judge alone. Originally these included claims in relation to deductions from wages, claims on the insolvency of an employer, and claims in relation to interim relief pending determination of an unfair dismissal complaint or revocation or variation of an order arising from such a complaint. However, by s.3 Employment Rights (Dispute Resolution) Act (ER(DR)A) 1998 the type of claim which can be heard by the chair of the tribunal alone has been augmented as follows:

(a) the right not to suffer unauthorised or excessive deductions in respect of trade union subscriptions;
(b) the employer's failure to pay remuneration under a protective award;
(c) the right to receive written particulars, a statement of changes to the particulars or an itemised pay statement;
(d) the right to guarantee payments;
(e) the right of remuneration for suspension on medical grounds;
(f) the right to a redundancy payment;
(g) an application for an employer's payment against the Secretary of State for Employment;
(h) the appointment of an authorised person to conduct certain proceedings under the ERA 1996 where an employee has died and has no personal representative;
(i) a failure to pay compensation for failing to inform or consult over a transfer of an undertaking.

In addition, the employment judge alone may hear any claim, if the parties agree in writing, and may sit with one other member only if the parties present or represented at the hearing agree (s.4 ER(DR)A). The 1998 Act also provides that the tribunal may dispense with an oral hearing where the parties have given their written consent (even if they subsequently withdraw it) and may determine a case hearing only evidence from the applicant where:

(a) the party against whom proceedings are brought has not contested the case; or
(b) the applicant is not seeking relief that the tribunal has the power to grant or the applicant is not entitled to any such relief.

Section 2 also allows for tribunal rules to provide that the tribunal can determine a case hearing only the parties where the tribunal is, on undisputed facts, bound by a court decision to dismiss the case or the proceedings relate only to a preliminary issue.

The role of the tribunal has been described as that of an industrial jury and as such it is more informal than a court, with no requirement of legal representation, although such representation is allowed. Legal aid is not available for an employment tribunal claim. When a claim is presented, a conciliation officer from the Advisory, Conciliation and Arbitration Service (ACAS) will attempt to conciliate between the parties, and because of the success of this procedure the majority of cases are settled without reaching the tribunal. Should the parties reach an agreement with the help of ACAS, that agreement is binding between the parties. Until recently, this was the only way a claim could be settled without going to a hearing. Section 203 Employment Rights Act 1996 generally renders void any agreement which purports to oust the jurisdiction of the tribunal. It is now possible, however, for the parties to reach an agreement without the help of ACAS. The section now provides that an agreement to settle will be binding provided that it is in writing, the employee has received advice from a relevant independent adviser who has explained the effect of the agreement, and the adviser is insured and has been identified by the agreement (s.203(3)). Section 9 of the 1998 Act has extended the category of persons who may be advisers for the purposes of compromise agreements by amending s.203 ERA. Prior to the Act only lawyers could be advisers, but the category now includes trade union officials, employees and advice workers.

In addition, either party can apply for a pre-hearing review. At such a review, the tribunal will assess the strength of the claim and advise the parties accordingly. Reviews are conducted by the employment judge, and a party to such a review may be required to pay a deposit of up to £500 if he wishes to continue with what the tribunal decides is a weak case. The aim is to weed out weak cases as parties may think twice about continuing their action if to do so could mean the loss of £500.

Tribunal regulations introduced in 2001 have given employment tribunals more teeth and created a statutory duty for the tribunal to consider awarding costs in some circumstances. Prior to these regulations, tribunals had a discretion to award costs. The Employment Tribunals (Constitution and Rules of Procedure) Regulations 2001 create an overriding objective that tribunals deal with cases 'justly' (Regulation 10). This means that tribunals must ensure that parties are on an equal footing, keep down expense, deal with cases in ways that are proportionate to the complexity of the issues and deal with cases expeditiously and fairly. This will allow tribunals to move parties on where the issue argued is not difficult and allow the parties to argue more fully where the issues are more complex. Tribunals can now strike out any claims or proposed defences on the grounds that they are scandalous, misconceived or vexatious. 'Misconceived' replaces the word 'frivolous' under the old regulations and appears to give tribunals a much broader category of claims which can be struck out.

The greatest change in the 2001 Regulations is in relation to the costs that a tribunal can award. Prior to 2001, tribunals had a discretion to award costs of up to £500, where the claim was considered to be frivolous or vexatious. Under these regulations, tribunals for the first time may award costs where either a party, or a party's representative, has acted improperly. A second major change is that the tribunal must consider awarding costs where parties or their representatives have acted 'vexatiously, abusively, disruptively or otherwise unreasonably, or the bringing of the proceedings by a party has been misconceived' (Regulation 14). 'Misconceived' includes having no real prospect of success (Regulation 2). The costs a tribunal can award have been increased from £500 to £10,000. While these powers will certainly deter those claimants who have weak cases, tribunals will have to be circumspect in the exercise of their new powers to avoid genuine claimants being afraid to pursue legitimate claims through the tribunal system.

In addition to the changes introduced by the 2001 Regulations, the Employment Act 2002 gave the Secretary of State the power to issue further regulations covering a number of issues. Amendments were made by the Employment Tribunals (Constitution and Rules of Procedure) (Amendment) Regulations 2004 (later amended in 2004 to introduce new rules of procedure in equal value claims, see Chapter 6). First, tribunals will have the power to award costs against an applicant's representative because of the way he or she conducted the proceedings. For these purposes 'representative' only includes those who charge for their services. Costs are awarded on the same grounds as above and are limited to a maximum of £10,000. This can include an award in respect of the respondent's representative's time in preparing the case. Second, there are new powers for tribunals to determine cases without a hearing, where both parties consent in writing and waive their right to a hearing. Third, there is a power for tribunals to strike out weak cases at the pre-hearing review stage. Until 2004 tribunals could only order that an applicant paid £500 into the tribunal if he or she wished to pursue a weak case to a full tribunal. Cases where such a power may be exercised are: cases which have already been litigated and there is no fresh evidence; cases where the facts are not in dispute but the interpretation placed on the facts by one party is clearly wrong; and cases where the application is not sufficient to lead to a successful outcome and there is no further evidence. In April 2007 the Compensation Act 2006 came into force. This requires that any representative of an employee in an employment claim must be authorised by a Regulator who is formally the Secretary of State for Constitutional Affairs. Such authorised persons must comply with rules regulating their conduct. It is hoped that the introduction of such rules will reduce the number of costs orders in tribunals.

In addition, the 2002 Act introduced statutory disciplinary and grievance procedures (see Chapter 9). The introduction of these procedures has led to a change in the time limits for the presentation of certain claims before the tribunal, to allow time for the statutory procedures to be completed, and regulations will prevent the presentation of claims until the procedures have been gone through. Tribunals will have the power to vary compensation for failure to use the new procedures. By Employment Tribunals (Constitution and Rules of Procedure) Regulations 2005 new 'claim' and 'response' forms have been introduced from October 2005, replacing the old 'IT1' and 'IT3' which were mandatory.

Potential problems may arise out of the new procedures. In *Grimmer* v. *KLM Cityhopper Ltd* [2005] IRLR 596 an employment tribunal rejected a claimant's claim on refusal to consider flexible working on the basis that she did not provide details of the claim as required by Rule 1(4)(c). She had put on her form that her employer had refused her request based on the assumption that if she was allowed to work flexibly others would apply. Judge Prophet in the Employment Appeal Tribunal held that the new rules should not be interpreted to deny a claimant the right to pursue a claim that primary legislation provides. He said that in determining whether a claims form has sufficient detail is 'whether it can be discerned from the claim as presented that the claimant is complaining of an alleged breach of an employment right which falls within the jurisdiction of the employment tribunal'. In the case it was clear that the claimant was pursuing a claim in respect of the refusal of her request for flexible working and that was sufficient.

The Employment Tribunals Service in its annual report for 2004–5 showed a drop in the claims registered (86,181 compared with 115, 042 for 2003–4); this is a decrease of 25 per cent but is mainly due to fewer multiple claims. There were 1,038 cost orders made compared with 976 for the previous year. At the end of 2006, the government announced its intention to review the statutory discipline and grievance procedures (the Gibbons Review). Prior to the announcement of the review's findings the Employment Tribunals Service's annual report for 2005–6 showed an increase in tribunal claims of more than 25 per cent and in its annual report for 2006–7 showed a further increase of 15 per cent. This suggests that the introduction of the statutory discipline and grievance procedures, designed to encourage workplace resolution of disputes and thus reduce tribunal applications, were not fulfilling this function. Shortly afterwards the Gibbons Review recommended the abolition of the statutory procedures. At the time of writing the government has indicated that they will be abolished and greater emphasis placed on the *ACAS Code*.

1.7   The Employment Appeal Tribunal

The Employment Appeal Tribunal hears appeals on a question of law or a question of law and fact from the employment tribunal. It consists of the president, who is a High Court judge or a Lord Justice of Appeal, and two or four lay members. The lay members are again drawn from employers' representatives and trade unions. With the consent of the parties, a judge may sit with only one lay member and by s.28(4) Employment Tribunals Act 1996, if the case has been heard in the employment tribunal by the chairperson alone, an appeal will be heard by the judge alone unless the judge decides otherwise. In addition, a Minister of the Crown can direct in proceedings, on the grounds of national security, that the president alone hears the case (s.28(5)). Furthermore, by s.33, if on the application of the Attorney-General, the Appeal Tribunal is satisfied that a person has persistently and without reasonable cause instituted vexatious proceedings or made vexatious applications in either the employment tribunal or the Appeal Tribunal, a restriction of proceedings order can be made. This order prevents any proceedings being initiated or continued by the person in question without the consent of the Appeal Tribunal and can be for a specified period or can remain in force indefinitely. There is no appeal against the making of such an order. In *Attorney-General* v. *Wheen* [2001] IRLR 91 the Court of Appeal decided that the power under s.33 does not breach the right to a fair trial under the Human Rights Act 1998, Sch 1, Art 6.

The decisions of the Employment Appeal Tribunal are binding and an appeal lies to the Court of Appeal and from there to the House of Lords. As already discussed in relation to employment tribunals, the Employment Act 2002 gave the Secretary of State power to introduce regulations giving the Employment Appeal Tribunal similar powers to award costs against an applicant's representative and to give more flexibility in case management. These were introduced by the Employment Appeal Tribunal (Amendment) Rules 2004. In *Barke* v. *Seetec Business Technology Centre Ltd* [2005] IRLR 633 the Court of Appeal said that the EAT has a discretionary power in the exercise of case management, to adjourn an appeal and ask an employment tribunal to amplify its reasons for a decision.

1.8   The Civil Courts

In addition to the appellate function of the ordinary courts, both the civil and criminal courts have jurisdiction in the area of employment law. Even though the tribunals have the jurisdiction to hear breach of contract claims, they do not have the jurisdiction to hear claims for damages for personal injury and these claims are heard by the civil courts. The High Court additionally has the jurisdiction to issue injunctions to restrain unlawful industrial action.

Breaches of the Health and Safety at Work Act 1974 may involve civil and criminal claims. Criminal prosecutions are brought in the magistrates' court or, on indictment, in the Crown Court.

1.9 Advisory, Conciliation and Arbitration Service (ACAS)

ACAS came into existence in 1974 and was placed on a statutory footing by s.1 Employment Protection Act 1975. It was originally given the general duty to promote 'the improvement of industrial relations, and in particular the duty of encouraging the extension of collective bargaining and the development and, where necessary, reform of collective bargaining machinery'. This duty, however, has been taken away by the Trade Union Reform and Employment Rights Act 1993 and ACAS is now charged with the duty of improving industrial relations; the words 'in particular by exercising its functions in relation to the settlement of trade disputes' (s.209 Trade Union and Labour Relations (Consolidation) Act 1992) were removed by s.26 Employment Relations Act 1999. It consists of a Council which comprises a chairperson and up to nine members appointed by the Secretary of State. Three are appointed after consultation with employers' organisations, three after consultation with workers' organisations and three are neutral members. As its name suggests, ACAS has a variety of functions:

(a) *Advice* By s.213 Trade Union and Labour Relations (Consolidation) Act 1992, ACAS may give advice, on request or by its own volition, to employers or workers or their associations on any matter concerned with, or likely to affect, industrial relations. It may also publish general advice. The Trade Union Reform and Employment Rights Act 1993 amended the 1992 provisions, and removed its power to give advice on employment policies. In addition, s.251A of the 1992 Act allows ACAS, on the direction of the Secretary of State, to charge a fee for the exercise of any of its functions. Prior to 1993, it was not allowed to charge for its services.

(b) *Conciliation* By s.210 Trade Union and Labour Relations (Consolidation) Act, ACAS can conciliate where a trade dispute exists or is apprehended. Again ACAS may go in by its own volition or at the request of any party. Also, since 1993 a charge may be made for this service. ACAS also appoints conciliation officers who conciliate when a claim is presented to an employment tribunal (s.211).

(c) *Arbitration* At the request of one or more parties to a trade dispute, but with the consent of them all, ACAS may refer any matter to an arbitrator or to the Central Arbitration Committee. Such referral may only take place after the parties have exhausted all agreed procedures unless there is a special reason why those procedures should not be followed (s.212). Sections 7 and 8 Employment Rights (Dispute Resolution) Act 1998 set out a framework within which ACAS may establish a scheme whereby parties can submit their case to binding voluntary arbitration rather than take their claim to an employment tribunal. The Act states that such arbitration may cover unfair dismissal complaints although the Secretary of State may extend the category of claims.

The new ACAS arbitration scheme came into existence in May 2001. At present it only covers unfair dismissal. Arbitration is an alternative to a tribunal claim and thus should the parties agree to arbitration they must sign an agreement (a COT3 or a compromise agreement) taking the claim out of the tribunal system. That is arbitration is in place of a tribunal claim, not in addition to it. An arbitrator's finding is enforceable in the same way as a tribunal decision and the powers to award reinstatement, re-engagement or compensation are almost identical to those applicable in a tribunal.

The new scheme, however, has its limitations which has led to criticism. Although arbitration is quicker and less formal, this can lead to some parties feeling a sense of injustice. There are no procedural rules and parties cannot cross-examine witnesses. Arbitrators are not bound by existing law or precedent and can only decide if a dismissal is fair or unfair, although they must have regard to the *ACAS Code of Practice on Disciplinary Powers and Grievance Procedures* and the *Discipline at Work Handbook*. This means that provisions in the Employment Rights Act 1996, which render dismissals automatically unfair in certain circumstances (see Chapter 9), will not bind an arbitrator, neither will the 'band of reasonable responses test' which allows a tribunal to find a dismissal is fair if dismissal would be one of the sanctions a reasonable employer would have used in the circumstances. Further an arbitrator cannot decide any jurisdictional points such as whether the claimant is an employee or has sufficient service. An arbitrator can only decide whether the dismissal was fair or not.

The limits of the jurisdiction of the arbitrator may mean that few parties will chose to go to arbitration, preferring instead to take their claims to a tribunal. The limits mean that any case involving dismissal and another claim can only partially be decided by arbitration. Where a claim involves, for example, unfair dismissal and an unlawful deduction from wages, the issue in respect of whether there has been an unlawful deduction can only be heard by a tribunal. Further, if there is an issue regarding whether a dismissal has actually occurred, for example in a constructive dismissal situation, this must first be decided by a tribunal before the claim can be arbitrated. It is inconceivable that in such cases parties will use both the tribunal and arbitration in respect of the claim and they are likely to only use the tribunal system.

A further criticism surrounds appeals. There is no right of appeal from the decision of an arbitrator except in cases where there has been a serious irregularity, such as in the conduct or the process of the hearing. The logic behind this is that arbitrators are not bound by existing law, but must only have regard to the *Code* and the *Handbook*. However, while tribunals must have regard to the *Code*, there are circumstances where an employer may successfully argue he has fairly treated an employee in breach of the *Code*. It is unlikely that such an argument would be successful in arbitration, particularly as arbitrators do not have to be legally qualified and would appear to raise the status of the *Code* and the *Handbook* to the equivalent of near binding legal status.

At the time of writing the scheme has been operating for six years and has heard less than 100 cases. All arbitration hearings and awards are confidential and so until detailed research has been carried out, the success or otherwise of the scheme cannot be measured.

Section 24 Employment Act 2002 has introduced a fixed period for conciliation. Section 7 Employment Tribunals Act 1996 has been amended to enable the postponement of setting a time for a hearing to enable conciliation to take place. ACAS will be able to extend the fixed period if it believes that a settlement can be reached in a short time scale. Once the fixed period has expired, ACAS's duty to conciliate will become a power, in other words the conciliation officer can decide whether to continue to conciliate or pass the case to the tribunal service to fix a date for a hearing. These changes, along with the changes to tribunal powers noted above and the new ACAS arbitration scheme, are intended to reduce the number of tribunal hearings in a system which has become overloaded. Only time will tell if the changes will have this effect.

(d) *Enquiries* By s.214 ACAS may enquire into industrial relations generally, or any particular industry or undertaking. The findings may then be published after taking into account the views of the parties involved.

(e) *Codes of Practice* ACAS is one of the bodies empowered to issue Codes of Practice by s.199 of the 1992 Act. There are three ACAS *Codes* covering disciplinary powers and grievance procedures, disclosure of information for collective bargaining purposes and time-off for trade union duties and activities.

1.10 Central Arbitration Committee (CAC)

The Central Arbitration Committee was established by the Employment Protection Act 1975 (s.259 of the 1992 Act). It consists of a chairperson and members from both sides of industry. It has the jurisdiction to hear complaints from trade unions of failure on the part of an employer to disclose information for collective bargaining purposes. Should the employer fail to comply with a declaration of the CAC, the union may present a claim to the Committee that certain terms should become part of individual contracts of employment, and if the CAC finds the claim well-founded the award it makes automatically becomes a term of each individual contact (s.185 of the 1992 Act). In addition, the CAC has seen two major developments to its jurisdiction. By the Employment Relations Act 1999 it has jurisdiction to adjudicate on disputes arising from the statutory recognition procedure, and by the Transnational Information and Consultation of Employees Regulations 1999 and the Information and Consultation of Employees Regulations 2004 it now has jurisdiction in respect of certain issues such as confidentiality of information.

1.11 Certification Officer

Until recently, the Certification Officer had one main function which was the issuing of certificates of independence to trade unions. Throughout the rest of this book, readers will note that many rights which accrue to trade unions and their members are given to independent trade unions. By s.5 Trade Union and Labour Relations (Consolidation) Act 1992 an independent trade union is one which is 'a) not under the domination or control of an employer or group of employers or of one or more employers' associations and b) is not liable to interference by an employer or any such group or association (arising out of the provision of financial or material support or by any other means whatsoever) tending towards such control'. A trade union applies to the Certification Officer for a certificate of independence. He must decide whether the trade union is independent and issue a certificate if it falls within the statutory definition. If he feels that the union is not independent, he must give reasons for his refusal to issue a certificate. In coming to a decision, he can make any inquiries he sees fit and can take into account any information given by other trade unions which may wish to challenge the assertion of independence.

In addition to the power to grant certificates of independence, the Certification Officer was granted additional powers by the abolition of two posts under the Employment Relations Act 1999. Prior to 1999 there were two additional Commissioners: the Commissioner for the Rights of Trade Union Members and the Commissioner for Protection Against Unlawful Industrial Action. The 1999 Act abolished both of these posts, but the jurisdiction of the Commissioner for the Rights of Trade Union Members passed to the Certification Officer. The Certification Officer now has the jurisdiction to hear complaints brought by individuals on infringement of the laws relating to balloting for the political fund, union amalgamations and the appointment of union officers. He may also hear complaints from individual trade union members of breaches of a trade union's own rules such as disciplinary rules. His powers have been strengthened in that he can now issue enforcement orders to ensure compliance with his decisions. An appeal from his decision lies to the EAT on a point of law.

1.12 The Commissions

There are a two commissions established to oversee and advise on specific areas of legislation. The commissions and their particular functions are:

(a) *The Heath and Safety Commission (HSC)*   The HSC was established by the Health and Safety at Work Act 1974. Its duties are the supervision of the promotion of health and safety at work. It consists of a chairperson and nine members, three from either side of industry and three appointed after consultation with local authorities. Like the other commissions it has a duty to oversee the legislation and submit proposals for reform, to give advice and assistance, to disseminate information and to carry out research. The enforcement of the statutory provisions is carried out by the Health and Safety Executive. This consists of a director and two assistant directors.

(b) *Commission for Equality and Human Rights (CEHR)*   The CEHR was established by the Equality Act 2006. From October 2007 it took over the responsibilities of the Commission for Racial Equality, the Equal Opportunities Commission and the Disability Rights Commission. Its powers are wider than those of its predecessors in that in addition to responsibilities in respect of sex, race and disability discrimination, it also has responsibilities in respect of religion or belief, sexual orientation and age. The CEHR has similar powers to its predecessors in that it can conduct inquiries, investigations and assist litigation. It can also issue an unlawful act notice which is similar to the old power to issue a non-discrimination notice although, unlike the old power, it also has the jurisdiction to require a person to develop an action plan and it has the power to enter an agreement not to take legal action if the person agrees to stop committing the discriminatory act and take such steps as specified by the Commission.

Summary

1. There is a variety of sources of employment law, ranging from statutes to non-legally binding codes of practice.

2. European law has had a major impact on UK employment law, particularly in the areas of transfer of undertakings, health and safety, discrimination and equal pay.

3. In addition to the ordinary courts, employment law has specialised adjudicative forums in the form of employment tribunals and the Employment Appeal Tribunal.

4. The Health and Safety Commission is responsible for monitoring the operation of the Health and Safety at Work Act. Since October 2007, the Commission for Equality and Human Rights replaced the Equal Opportunities Commission, the Commission for Racial Equality and the Disability Rights Commission, and has a duty to monitor anti-discriminatory legislation in the areas of sex, disability, sexual orientation, religion or belief and age, thus creating a single commission with responsibility for promoting equal opportunities.

Further Reading

Baker *Access vs Process in Employment Discrimination: Why ADR Suits the US but not the UK* (2002) 31 ILJ 113.

Browne-Wilkinson J *The Role of the Employment Appeal Tribunal in the 1980s* (1982) 11 ILJ 69.

Burton *The Employment Appeal Tribunal: October 2002–July 2005* (2005) 34 ILJ 273.

Ewing *The Human Rights Act and Labour Law* (1998) 27 ILJ 275.

Lightman J and Bowers *Incorporation of the ECHR and its Impact on Employment Law* (1998) EHRLR 560.

MacMillan *Employment Tribunals: Philosophies and Practicalities* (1999) 28 ILJ 33.

McKee J *A Personal View of the Work of Industrial Tribunals* (1986) 49 MLR 314.

Morris *The Commissioner for the Rights of Trade Union Members: A Framework for the Future?* (1993) 22 ILJ 104.

Further reading cont'd

Palmer   *Human Rights: Implications for Labour Law* (2000) 59 CLJ 168.

Skidmore   *Labour Law in the Courts: National Judges and the European Court of Justice* (2003) 32 ILJ 334.

Vickers   *Unfair Dismissal and Human Rights* (2004) 33 ILJ 52.

Wood J   *The Employment Appeal Tribunal as it Enters the 90s* (1990) 19 ILJ 133.

Part II

The Employment Relationship

Chapter 2

The Nature of the Relationship

2.1 Distinction between Employees and Independent Contractors

It may seem a fairly obvious statement, but the two parties who make up an employment relationship are an employee and an employer. Such a distinction may not be so obvious, however, if the word 'worker' is used instead of 'employee'. Often lay people use the words interchangeably, but for a student of employment law the definition of employee is vitally important and must be distinguished from that of a self-employed person or an independent contractor. This is because a variety of legal and economic consequences flow from the distinction. An employee works under a contract of service whereas an independent contractor works under a contract for services. The major differences between the two types of contract are as follows.

Insurance and welfare benefits

Employees are entitled to jobseeker's allowance, statutory sick pay, and a state retirement pension as long as they have paid Class 1 National Insurance Contributions. Such contributions are assessed on the employee's earnings and should be deducted at source by the employer. In addition the employer also makes a contribution. By contrast independent contractors are responsible for their own contributions and pay the lower-rate Class 2 payments. These payments only give limited rights to certain welfare benefits and do not entitle the contributor to jobseeker's allowance or statutory sick pay.

PAYE

Employers must deduct tax at source from the wages of those of their employees who are so liable. It is very often because of tax liability that problems occur in this area. To take an example, a taxi driver may be given the option of having tax deducted at source or being responsible for his own payments and receiving his wages gross. He decides to take the latter option. At first sight this choice may seem perfectly reasonable, but it will be seen below that the law decides on the status of a person and not the parties themselves and should the law decide that our taxi driver is an employee, despite being paid gross, that leads to a variety of legal complications, not least that the employer may be committing a criminal offence for failing to deduct tax at source.

In *Jennings* v. *Westwood Engineering* [1975] IRLR 245 a person was given the option of receiving his pay net or gross. He chose the latter. Some time later he was dismissed. He sued for an unfair dismissal, arguing that despite the situation he was in fact an employee. (Independent contractors have no protection against unfair dismissal as will be seen below.) The court held, looking at the realities of the relationship, that Mr Jennings was indeed an employee. However, as Mr Jennings had not had tax deducted at source and had not paid any tax, the purpose of his contract had been illegal because there was an intention to defraud the Inland Revenue. As all students of contract will be aware, a contract set up for an illegal purpose is void and no rights can arise from it. As such Mr Jennings could not rely on his rights not to be unfairly dismissed. *Jennings* should be distinguished from *Hewcastle Catering Ltd* v. *Ahmed* [1992] ICR 626 where the Court of Appeal distinguished between contracts which were formed for an illegal purpose and contracts which were legal at their inception but which were performed illegally. The Court held that in the latter case, the innocence of the employee would be a defence and the contract would be saved. Thus in the case, waiters who were dismissed and where it was later discovered that the employer was committing VAT fraud could still sue for unfair dismissal. The cases of *Enfield Technical Services* v. *Payne/Grace* v. *BF Components Ltd* [2007] All ER 394 may, however, throw some doubt on *Jennings*. In the joined cases the EAT held that to defeat an unfair dismissal claim on the grounds of an illegal contract there must be some misrepresentation or hiding of the true relationship. A mislabelling of the relationship or an arrangement which deprives the Inland Revenue of monies is not enough to render the contract illegal. Note, however, that leave has been given to appeal to the Court of Appeal.

Vicarious liability

Employers can be made vicariously liable for the torts of their employees committed during the course of their employment. As a general principle there is no such liability for independent contractors.

Safety

The standard of care employers must exercise in relation to their employees' safety, both at common law and under statute, is generally higher than that owed to independent contractors.

Terms in the contract

In addition to the terms the parties themselves have negotiated the law implies a host of terms into the employment relationship. The law will rarely interfere in a contract between an employer and an independent contractor.

Employment protection rights

An employee enjoys a large number of employment protection rights. These include the right not to be unfairly dismissed, the right to redundancy payment, statutory maternity pay, statutory sick pay, security of employment after maternity leave, protection of the right to belong or not to belong to a trade union and time-off rights. Independent contractors have no such protection with one notable exception. Everyone is protected under anti-discriminatory legislation where they are providing personal services (*Quinnen* v. *Hovells* [1984] IRLR 227 and see also *BP Chemicals* v. *Gillick* [1995] IRLR 128).

2.2 Tests for Determining Status

It can be seen from the discussion above that it is important for both parties to know at the outset whether the relationship is that of employer/ employee. It has also been noted that it is the courts who determine that status and the name the parties give to the relationship is, normally, irrelevant. The courts over the years have devised a series of tests to apply to a relationship to determine the status of the parties within it.

Control test

The early cases, where the courts began looking at the nature of the relationship, arose in the context of vicarious liability and in some ways it was obvious to look at the control the employer exercised over the worker. In *Performing Rights Society* v. *Mitchell and Booker* [1924] 1 KB 762, McCardie J said that 'the final test, if there is to be a final test, and certainly the test to be generally applied, lies in the nature and degree of detailed control over the person alleged to be a servant.' The basis of the test was whether the employer not only controlled when a job was done, but also how it was done. If a large amount of control existed in relation to the method and content of the work, the person was in an employment relationship.

The control test, as a single test, worked well where there were unskilled workers but fell down when workers became more skilled than the persons employing them. The control test taken to its logical conclusion was shown not to work in *Hillyer* v. *Governors of St Bartholomew's Hospital* [1909] 2 KB 820 where it was held that nurses were not employees of a hospital when carrying out operating-theatre duties. Although the courts took the realistic approach in *Cassidy* v. *Minister of Health* [1951] 2 KB 343, increased technology meant that in a large number of cases control did not determine the true nature of the relationship and a more realistic test was needed.

Organisation test

As it became obvious that the control test, on its own, was inadequate for a modern industrial society, the judiciary tried to develop a new test which took into account industrial reality. To this end Denning LJ developed what became known as the organisation or integration test in 1952 in a case called *Stevenson, Jordan & Harrison Ltd* v. *Macdonald and Evans* (1952) 1 TLR 101. In the case he said: 'under a contract of service a man is employed as part of the business and his work is done as an integral part of the business but under a contract for services his work, although done for the business, is not integrated into it but only accessory to it.' Although as a test it overcame the problems with the control test, Denning did not explain what he meant by 'integration' or 'organisation' and as such the test was never widely used.

Multiple test

Over the years, the courts have realised that no one factor can be identified to denote an employment relationship. Such a relationship is complex and consists of a variety of factors depending on the nature of the job and the relative skills of the employer and the employee. It is this multiplicity of factors that the judges now look to and as such the predominant test used is known as the multiple test, indicating that one factor alone cannot identify the type of relationship. The test began in the case of *Ready Mixed Concrete (South East) Ltd* v. *MPNI* [1968] 2 QB 497. The appellants were arguing that the lorry drivers they employed were independent contractors and as such the appellants were not liable for National Insurance Contributions. McKenna J looked at a variety of factors to determine the status of the lorry drivers. On the facts there were some factors indicating an employment relationship and others indicating that the drivers were self-employed, as shown below:

Employee factors	*Self-employed factors*
1. Lorry painted in company colours	1. Bought lorry by company loan
2. Lorry for exclusive company use	2. Maintained own lorry
3. Had to obey orders	3. Could delegate driving duties

4. Minimum payment of £1,500 per year

4. After the minimum payment, paid on amount of concrete carried

McKenna then identified three conditions which must be present for the relationship to be one of employment. First, the employee agrees to provide his skill in consideration of a wage. Second, there is an element of control exercised by the employer and, third, provisions in the contract are consistent with its being a contract of service. On the basis of this final condition McKenna decided that the lorry drivers were self-employed because they could delegate driving duties and the basis of an employment relationship is that the duties within cannot be delegated. The decision has since been criticised but not the essence of the test. Later cases have seen judges looking at a host of factors within a relationship and balancing them to identify whether there are more factors indicating a person is self-employed rather than an employee or vice versa. Cooke J summarised the approach of the courts in the case of *Market Investigations Ltd* v. *MSS* [1969] 2 QB 173 when he said that the question to be determined by the court was whether a person was in business on his own account. If so, then there was a contract for services and not a contract of service.

These pronouncements by judges, however, in many ways are not helpful as they leave the question: what factors indicate that a person is an employee rather than self-employed?

Certainly, it is the law that decides on the status of a person and not the parties themselves, although the fact that the parties think that a person is an independent contractor will be one of the factors the court will take into account. In *Ferguson* v. *John Dawson Ltd* [1976] IRLR 346 a builder's labourer agreed to work as a self-employed worker. He was injured when he fell off a roof. No guard-rail had been provided, which was in breach of a duty owed to employees under the Construction (Working Places) Regulations 1966. The employer argued that the plaintiff was self-employed and consequently no duty was owed to him. The Court of Appeal disagreed. In reality the plaintiff was an employee and a statement as to the status of a person was a factor but not a conclusive factor. It appears, however, that if there is ambiguity as to whether the relationship is one of employment, the courts will resolve such ambiguity by looking at what the parties consider the relationship to be. This comes from a statement by Lord Denning MR in the case of *Massey* v. *Crown Life Insurance Co* [1978] ICR 590 although this has been doubted in later cases, particularly by Stephenson LJ in *Young & Wood Ltd* v. *West* [1980] IRLR 201 when he said: 'It must be the court's duty to see whether the label correctly represents the true legal relationship between the parties.'

The courts, therefore, decide the status of the relationship by looking to see if a person is really in business on his own account. This involves looking at a variety of factors such as investment, ownership of tools, who bears the risk of loss and who stands to make a profit. Whereas in a large number of cases, these questions are easily answered, in some situations it is difficult to come to any firm conclusions. Homeworkers are a group of persons who, on the face of it, appear to be self-employed. In *Airfix Footwear Ltd* v. *Cope* [1978] IRLR 396 it was held that homeworkers were employees because work was provided on a regular basis and in reality the employer decided on the way in which the job was to be done, and the time and place of performance. In *Nethermere (St Neots) Ltd* v. *Taverna and Another* [1984] IRLR 240 the Court of Appeal again decided that homeworkers were employees because although there was no legal obligation on the employer to provide work, a mutuality of obligations existed in reality based on the long-standing relationship between the employer and the workers concerned. This mutuality of obligations – that the employer will provide the work and the employee will provide his services – is the essence of an employment relationship and if it is lacking then the court will decide there is a contract for services. In *O'Kelly and Others* v. *Trusthouse Forte plc* [1983] IRLR 369 the plaintiff was a regular casual worker who was given preference when work was available. In a claim for unfair dismissal the tribunal held that the casuals were self-employed, even though they worked solely for one employer because of the long hours they had to work. The most important factor for the tribunal, in reaching this conclusion, was that there was no obligation on the employer to provide work and no obligation on the casuals to offer their services. This lack of mutuality was the clear reason for the decision, despite the fact that the employer had total control over the workers while they were there and it would be difficult to describe a casual worker as in business on his own account. Again, in *Carmichael and Leese* v. *National Power plc* [2000] IRLR 43 the House of Lords decided that guides employed on a 'casual as required' basis were self-employed because of the lack of mutuality.

Lack of mutuality has led to decisions that agency temporaries are self-employed (*Wickens* v. *Champion Employment* [1984] ICR 365) although the case of *McMeechan* v. *Secretary of State for Employment* [1997] IRLR 353 has said that this is not a general proposition. In the case the fact that there was a weekly wage, obligations of fidelity and confidence, a power of dismissal and a grievance procedure led the court to conclude that the agency worker was an employee of the agency. In *Serco Ltd* v. *Blair* (1998) IDS Brief 624 the Employment Appeal Tribunal held that agency workers who had a written agreement with the client company in which they were placed by the agency did not have an employment relationship with the client. The Appeal Tribunal held that the test in *Ready Mixed Concrete* was not satisfied in that the client did not exercise a sufficient degree of control over the agency workers; the workers were free not to accept the placement and the agency could terminate the agreement. However, in *Motorola Ltd* v. *Davidson* [2001] IRLR 4 an agency worker who had a written agreement with the client, Motorola, to comply with all reasonable instructions, was held to be employed by Motorola because there was a sufficient degree of day-to-day control. *Dacas* v. *Brook Street Bureau (UK) Ltd* [2004] IRLR 358 seemed to potentially give protection for agency workers when the Court of Appeal suggested that, because of mutuality of obligations and the control exercised by the client over the worker, Ms Dacas was an employee of the client and not the agency. While this would appear clear-cut in the later case of *Bunce* v. *Postworth Ltd and Skyblue* [2005] EWCA Civ 490 CA the court found that as there was no mutuality nor any real control exercised by the agency over Mr Bunce, he was not an employee of the agency. The same conclusion was reached in the race discrimination case of *Mingeley* v. *Pennock and Ivory t/a Amber Cars* [2004] IRLR 373 where the Court of Appeal held that where someone is free to work when it suits him and does not have an obligation to work, then he cannot be an employee. After *Dacas* there was a spate of cases involving agency workers. In *James* v. *Greenwich Borough Council* [2007] All ER 12 Mrs James was an agency worker who had worked for Greenwich Council for five years. The EAT upheld the tribunal decision that there was no implied contract of employment between Mrs James and the Council. The EAT said it was inappropriate to imply a contract when the end user could not insist on the agency supplying a particular worker, and went on to say that implying mutuality of obligations between the worker and the end user is inconsistent with a normal agency arrangement and that a tribunal can only infer a contract between the worker and end user if, after the relationship has commenced, there are words or conduct which would entitle the tribunal to conclude that the agency arrangements no longer reflect how the work is performed. Elias P also said that such circumstances would be rare and that the passage of time does not justify the implication of a contract. This was followed in *Craigie* v. *London Borough of Haringey* [2007] All ER 82, *Heatherwood & Wexham Park Hospitals NHS Trust* v. *Kulubowlia* (2007) UKEAT 0633/06 and *Astbury* v. *Gist* (2007) UKEAT 0619/06, all EAT decisions. The President of the EAT has stated that all agency cases are to be suspended pending the Court of Appeal hearing *James*. The EAT has also held that volunteer workers do not have contracts of employment in *South East Sheffield Citizens Advice Bureau* v. *Grayson* [2004] IRLR 353.

The position of agency workers is therefore not clear-cut, as tribunals are bound by the Court of Appeal and, as such, if *Dacas, McMeechan* or *Davidson* applies such workers are employees of either the agency or the client, and if none of those cases is applicable such workers are self-employed under *Bunce, Wickens, Blair* and the EAT decisions above and thus have limited employment protection. Some protection will exist. The Working Time Regulations 1998 (see Chapter 4) specifically provide that workers who are supplied by an agency to do work for a principal and who would not otherwise be covered by the Regulations because of the absence of a contract with the agent or principal, are taken to be employed, for the purposes of the Regulations, by whoever is paying them (Regulation 36). Similar provisions are also included in the National Minimum Wage Act 1998. Certain rights introduced by the Employment Relations Act 1999 and anti-discrimination legislation apply to workers or those who agree to personally provide services. Without the protection of an employment relationship, however, protection in respect of unfair dismissal and redundancy is not available. The government originally intended to introduce measures amending the Employment Agencies Act 1973, to make the contractual position of agency workers more clear. The Conduct of Employment Agencies and Employment Businesses Regulations 2002, however, do not do this completely. The Regulations give increasing differentiation between employment agencies and employment businesses. An agency provides a work-finding service for work-seekers and provides workers for employers, thus creating a contractual relationship between the work-seeker and the employer. This may or may not be an employment relationship depending on the factors in *Davidson* or *Blair* above. In a case prior to the regulations a contractor who hired himself out, through an agency, was not regarded as an employee of third party because there was no contractual relationship between him and the hirer (*Hewlett Packard Ltd* v. *O'Murphy* [2002] IRLR 4). An employment business, on the other hand, engages its own workforce which it supplies to hirers. Regulation 15 states that the agreement between the employment business and the worker must state whether the relationship is one of a contract of service, a contract for services or apprenticeship. If it is a contract for services, certain basic terms must apply relating to pay and holidays but it leaves the worker taken on by an employment business on a contract for services little protection in a dismissal situation. In February 2007 the DTI issued a consultation paper which proposed new measures to protect agency workers, however it does not propose to extend the same protection to agency workers as that enjoyed by part-time workers or fixed term employees, but focuses on the bad practices of certain employment agencies. As Bean J said in *Craigie*, the law on agency workers is unsatisfactory.

A similar lack of protection exists in certain types of employment. In *Hellyer Brothers Ltd* v. *McLeod* [1987] 1 WLR 728 trawler men who entered separate crew agreements for each voyage were found to be self-employed and therefore not entitled to a redundancy payment, despite the fact that they invariably returned to the same employer year after year. Lack of mutuality was the key factor.

The Privy Council highlighted the factors the courts take into account in the case of *Lee v. Chung & Shun Chung Construction and Engineering Co Ltd* [1990] IRLR 236. In this case the worker was a mason who suffered an injury while working on a building site. The court looked back to the judgement in *Market Investigations* and asked themselves the question whether the plaintiff was in business on his own account. The court continued: 'Other matters which may be of importance are whether the worker provides his own equipment, whether he hires his own helpers, what degree of financial risk he takes, what degree of responsibility he has for investment and management and whether and how far he has the opportunity to profit from sound management in the performance of his task.' By looking at all these factors the court decided that the plaintiff was an employee. In *Hall (Inspector of Taxes) v. Lorimer* [1994] IRLR 171 the court, however, stressed that the factors should not be gone through mechanically. Here the employee worked as a vision mixer. He used the equipment of the television company that employed him and was paid a lump sum plus travelling expenses for each job he did. He was registered for VAT, had his own pension and sickness policies, took bookings from home and had no long-term contracts with any single company. None of his own money was used in the production of any of the programmes he mixed nor did he stand to make a profit or loss from any of the programmes. The special commissioners had found that Lorimer was self-employed. The Inland Revenue appealed against this decision, arguing that it was the production company who controlled when and where he worked, provided the equipment and had the financial stake in the programme. The court held it could not run through a checklist of items to determine if a person was self-employed: 'The whole picture has to be painted and then viewed from a distance to reach an informed and qualitative decision in the circumstances of the particular case.' The special commissioners, on the evidence before them, had reached a conclusion and there was no evidence that their decision was unsustainable on the facts. As such, the court would not interfere with that decision.

More recent cases have talked about the irreducible minimum needed to constitute a contract of employment. In *Carmichael and Leese*, mutuality was seen as the irreducible minimum, while in *Express Echo Publications Ltd v. Tanton* [1999] IRLR 367 the Court of Appeal regarded personal service by the employee as the irreducible minimum, so that a power to delegate job duties was fatal to an employment claim. This was also the case in *Staffordshire Sentinel Newspapers Ltd v. Potter* [2004] IRLR 752, where a contract which allowed substitutes with company approval (and where such substitutes had been used) was held not to be a contract of employment because it did not require personal service. This would seem to go against *Macfarlane* v.

Glasgow City Council [2001] IRLR 7 however, where an earlier EAT stated that a limited or occasional power of delegation is not inconsistent with a contract of employment. This was supported by *Byrne Brothers (Formwork) Ltd* v. *Baird* [2002] IRLR 96. The issue in this case was slightly different in that it considered the definition of 'worker' for the purpose of the statutory rights introduced by the 1999 Act. Section 230 Employment Rights Act 1996 defines a worker as working under a contract of employment or 'any other contract . . . to do or perform personally any work or services for another party to the contract . . .'. In *Baird* the issue was whether a building contractor, who was permitted in his contract, with the express permission of the employer, to engage another person to do the job when he was unable to do it himself, fell within the definition in s.230. The court held that he was a worker and distinguished *Tanton* on the basis that in *Tanton* the person could delegate not only when he was unable to do the job but also when he was unwilling to do the job. Thus, in *Baird* a limited power to delegate was not inconsistent with an obligation of personal service. So too in *Redrow Homes (Yorkshire) Ltd* v. *Wright* [2004] IRLR 721 the Court of Appeal decided that bricklayers were workers, not self employed, even though their contracts permitted substitution and although substitutes had never been used. A useful decision in this area is the case of *Ministry of Defence Dental Services* v. *Kettle* [2007] All ER 301. Dr Kettle responded to an advertisement issued by the Ministry of Defence. The Ministry was looking for a part-time dentist and, according to the tribunal chair, the advertisement was worded in such a way as to indicate that the successful applicant would be employed under a contract of employment. Dr Kettle was successful in her application. The documentation she signed described her as a contractor and explicitly allowed her to delegate her services to a suitably qualified substitute, although she pointed out that she would never be able to find a substitute and when she was on holiday the Ministry provided cover. She paid her own tax and insurance. Although the contract was to run from March to September it was abruptly terminated in June. The tribunal held that she was an employee, despite the substitution clause in the contract, on the basis of the wording of the advertisement and the conduct of the parties. The Ministry appealed to the EAT. Richardson J looked at the decision in *Carmichael* and said that where there is a document said to be contractual, it is a question of fact for the tribunal whether the parties intended the document to be an exclusive record of their agreement. If it is, then generally a tribunal can only look at the document and interpret such, but if the tribunal decides that the parties do not intend the document to be exclusive then the tribunal can look at other materials, oral exchanges and conduct. The EAT concluded that it was clear from the advertisement and the conduct of the parties that the documentation did not reflect the intention of the parties. It did not, for example, state how many hours Dr Kettle was to work, although this was stated in the advertisement and agreed between the parties. It also talked about Dr Kettle as an organisation, which clearly she was not, and Dr Kettle when she questioned the appropriateness of the documentation pointed out it would be impossible for her to provide a substitute. As such there was both mutuality of obligations between the parties and control exercised by the Ministry, and as such Dr Kettle was an employee. It would appear therefore that a clause allowing substitution may not prevent a person being an employee if, in reality, such substitution is impossible.

It may appear that this is a grey area of the law and that no situation is clear-cut. What we can glean from the cases, however, is that the courts, when using the multiple test, look at a wide range of factors, of which control, mutuality of obligations, personal service and financial risk seem to be the most important.

Summary

1. An employee has far greater rights than an independent contractor and so it is important to determine the status of the parties in the relationship.

2. The consequences of a wrong analysis can be criminal liability and the contract rendered void on the basis of illegality.

3. The courts decide the nature of the relationship and not the parties.

4. The courts have used various tests over the years to help them to decide the true nature of the relationship before them.

5. The present test used by the courts is the multiple test. This involves the court looking at a variety of factors, of which the most important are control, personal service, financial investment and risk, and mutuality of obligations.

Exercises

1. What are the differences between an employee and an independent contractor?

2. What are the three tests used by the courts over the years to determine the nature of the relationship?

3. Florence works from home. Her employers, Roundabout Products, sell Christmas crackers. Florence has worked for the company, making up crackers, for six years. She receives no holiday or sick pay and is paid per 100 crackers she assembles. She uses no machinery in her work. Although

Exercises cont'd

she can work when she wishes, over the past four years she has worked constantly from October to January averaging 500 crackers per week, and then when demand has dropped, she has worked intermittently throughout the rest of the year when work has been available, averaging 200 crackers per week. Roundabout Products has informed Florence that they are closing their operation and they will no longer require her services. Florence wishes to claim a redundancy payment. Advise Florence whether she will be entitled to make a claim for a redundancy payment.

Further Reading

Collins *Independent Contractors and the Challenge of Vertical Disintegration to Employment Protection Law* (1990) 10 OJLS 353.

Davidov *Who is a Worker?* (2005) 34 ILJ 57.

Ewing *Homeworking: A Framework for Reform* (1982) 11 ILJ 94.

Fredman *Labour Law in Flux: The Changing Composition of the Workforce* (1997) 26 ILJ 337.

Freedland *From the Contract of Employment to the Personal Work Nexus* (2006) 35 ILJ 1.

Hakim *Employment Rights: A Comparison of Part-time and Full-time Employees* (1989) 18 ILJ 69.

Jones *Temporary Agency Labour: Back to Square One?* (2002) 31 ILJ 183.

Pitt *Law Fact and Casual Workers* (1985) 101 LQR 217.

Reynolds *The Status of Agency Workers: A Question of Legal Principle* (2006) 35 ILJ 320.

Chapter 3
Terms of the Contract

3.1 Express Terms

The employment relationship is a contractual one and as such must have all the basic elements of an enforceable contract to make it legally binding. In strict contractual terms, the offer is made by the employer and formally or informally accepted by the employee. This acceptance may be verbal or in writing, or conversely the employee may signify his acceptance by merely turning up for work on the appointed day. The consideration within the contract is the promise to pay wages on the part of the employer, and the promise to provide his services on the part of the employee. Once the acceptance has taken place, there is a legally binding agreement and an action will lie against the party who breaches that agreement, even though it may only just have come into existence. In *Taylor* v. *Furness, Withy & Co Ltd* (1969) 6 KIR 488 a dock worker was sent by the Dock Labour Board to a new employer. The employer sent him a letter welcoming him and an identity card to sign. When the employee arrived to begin his employment, the employer discovered that he had let his union membership lapse and under the terms of the Dock Labour Scheme the employer could not employ him. The employee was therefore sent home. He sued the employer for a week's wages, the notice he was entitled to under the contract. The employer argued that as the plaintiff had never worked, the contract had not come into existence. It was held that, by signing the identity card, the plaintiff had accepted the employer's offer, and at that time a legally binding contract came into existence. The plaintiff was thus legally entitled to one week's notice which he did not receive and the court awarded a week's pay as damages. More recently in *Sarker* v. *South Tees Acute Hospitals NHS Trust* [1997] IRLR 328 Sarker was offered a job by the Trust which she accepted, but the job offer was withdrawn before the start date. It was held that the Trust was in breach of contract.

The essence of any contract is the terms within it, for they show what the parties intended. An employment contract, however, is unlike most other contracts. Although the parties will have negotiated the main terms, we shall see that a large number of terms will be implied into the agreement from all sorts of different sources and will not have been individually negotiated by the parties at all. This is what makes an employment contract so different from other contracts.

Express terms are the terms agreed by the parties. The employee is unlikely to have accepted the job without knowing his salary and hours of work, and therefore these will have been agreed by the parties before the commencement of the relationship. From an employer's point of view it is better to have agreed as many terms as possible. It ensures certainty so that both parties know where they stand at the outset. Express terms, however, may cause problems. If the term itself is ambiguous, the courts will interpret the term should a dispute arise. Many an employer has discovered that his idea of 'reasonable overtime' differs greatly from both his employee's interpretation and that of the court (see for example *Johnstone* v. *Bloomsbury Area Health Authority* [1991] ICR 269). Likewise, because the express terms do show the parties' intentions, if the term is inaccurate, that can lead to problems. In *Stubbes* v. *Trower, Still & Keeling* [1987] IRLR 321 a firm of solicitors, in offering articles, omitted to provide expressly that the applicant had to pass the Law Society Final Examination before he could begin. The Court of Appeal held that this was not a requirement of the articles.

In addition to pay and hours, often the parties will have stated the details of the job. This means that should an employee refuse to perform duties he has agreed to, the employer will have an action for breach of contract. In *Wiluszynski* v. *London Borough of Tower Hamlets* [1989] IRLR 259 there was a NALGO dispute and, as part of industrial action, some employees were refusing to answer councillors' questions. These duties constituted about half an hour of a 37-hour week. Before the action started, the council informed the employees that if they did not perform the full range of their duties they would be held to be in breach of contract and would not be paid. The plaintiff took part in industrial action for five weeks and the council refused to pay him for any of the other duties he had performed. The Court of Appeal upheld the council's action. Answering councillors' questions was a material part of the employee's duties and he had refused to perform that material part. As such, the employee had committed a repudiatory breach of contract. In such circumstances the employer has the choice of accepting the breach as terminating the contract, or waiving the breach. In the case the council had made it clear that it considered the breach would terminate the relationship. Furthermore, by allowing the employee to continue working, the employer had not waived the breach and affirmed the contract. It was unrealistic to expect the employer of large numbers of employees to identify and physically eject those taking industrial action. Therefore, when the employee was working during the industrial action, he was doing so voluntarily and was not entitled to payment.

Wiluszynski should be distinguished from the earlier cases of *Sim* v. *Rotherham Metropolitan Borough Council* [1986] IRLR 391 and *Miles* v. *Wakefield Metropolitan District Council* [1987] IRLR 193, in both of which employees were refusing to perform part of their duties as part of industrial action. In *Miles* superintendent registrars were refusing to perform weddings on Saturdays, in *Sim* teachers were refusing to cover for absent colleagues. In both cases the employer deducted a proportion of pay, representative of the non-fulfilment of contractual duties, and the action was upheld by the court. The three cases demonstrate two important points. First, if the employee refuses to perform some of his duties, that is a breach of contract and the employer is entitled to assess his damages and withhold the pay which represents the duties not performed. This is the decision in *Miles* and *Sim*. Second, if the employer feels that the employee is refusing to perform a material part of his duties, and he informs the employee that this is the case and that he regards the employee's breach as repudiatory, then the employer is entitled to withhold all the employee's wages until he is prepared to fulfil all the terms of his contract. The employer must ensure, however, that he does nothing to waive the breach and if possible should prevent the employee from doing any work. This is the decision in *Wiluszynski*. Whereas the court seems to be prepared to accept the employer's contention that certain duties are a material part of the employee's contract, there may be a challenge if the employer is deducting a proportion of wages for non-performance, if the employee feels that the deduction is not truly representative of the amount of lost work.

Apart from the above, express terms usually cause no problems and can help both parties because they cannot be ousted by implied terms. In *Deeley* v. *British Rail Engineering Ltd* [1980] IRLR 147 an advertisement was displayed for a sales engineer (export). The plaintiff applied for and was given the job, but his contract described him as a sales engineer. He argued that his job was limited to export because of the advertisement and applied to the court to clarify the position. The court held that the contract prevailed. The express term was clear and it could not be overridden by an implied term. It should be noted, however, that the interpretation of an express term may be subject to the implied duties discussed in Chapter 4 (see *Johnstone* v. *Bloomsbury Area Health Authority* [1991] ICR 269 and *St Budeaux Royal British Legion Club Ltd* v. *Cropper* (1995) IDS Brief 552).

The law, to a large extent, allows parties to negotiate any terms they wish, subject to the restrictions noted below, and a clear agreement showing both sides' intentions can save a lot of trouble. There are four main statutory restrictions on the express terms in an employment contract. These are:

1. The employer cannot restrict his liability for the death or personal injury of his employees caused by his negligence. Further he may only restrict or limit his liability for damage to his employees' property, if such a term is reasonable in the circumstances (s.2 Unfair Contract Terms Act 1977).

2. Certain express terms must not infringe the Equal Pay Act 1970 and the Sex Discrimination Acts 1975 and 1986.
3. Certain express terms must not infringe the Race Relations Act 1976.
4. No term of the contract can take away an employee's right to take action in the courts or the employment tribunal (s.203 Employment Rights Act 1996).

Variation of terms

The employment relationship is an ever-changing one, particularly with the introduction of new technology which will often change the way the employee performs his job. One of the problems with express terms in the contract is that, if they are very specific, they may not allow for the flexibility inherent in the relationship. On contractual principles, any changes in the terms of the contract must be mutually agreed, and the employer who attempts a unilateral variation may find a constructive dismissal claim against him. In some situations, the courts may be prepared to agree that the employee's conduct shows that he has accepted the variation if, for example, he has continued to work, without protest, after the change has been made. In all cases, however, it is a question of fact as to whether the employee's conduct does indicate acceptance of the change. In *Jones* v. *Associated Tunnelling Co Ltd* [1981] IRLR 477 the Employment Appeal Tribunal stressed that continuing to work is not necessarily an implied assent to a unilateral variation by the employer, particularly where the variation does not have immediate effect. In *Marriott* v. *Oxford & District Co-operative Society Ltd* [1970] 1 QB 186 the Court of Appeal held that the fact that an employee worked for three weeks under protest, after the unilateral change by his employer, in no way constituted implied consent to the variation in the contractual terms.

Minor changes may be possible within the contract itself. In *Cresswell* v. *Board of Inland Revenue* [1984] IRLR 190 the court held that a change from manual calculation of tax codes to computerised calculation was not a breach on the part of the employer, provided the employer gave the necessary training to the staff. The basis of this decision is an implied term in all contracts of employment that employees will adapt to new methods of doing their job. As will be shown below, an employee is also expected to do tasks which are incidental to his job duties and asking that such tasks be performed is within the employer's contractual rights. These situations, however, are not variations, but the courts recognising the necessary flexibility within the express terms themselves. Where the employer wishes to have the right to make more radical changes from time to time, he should have an express term in the contract allowing such changes to be made. The two most common ways these terms appear are in the form of flexibility clauses and mobility clauses. The former give flexibility in the area of the employee's job duties and the latter in the place of work. In the case of flexibility clauses, the courts have been less willing to grant that they allow the employer a great deal more scope than the implied term that an employee can be asked to perform tasks which are reasonably incidental to his main job duties (see *Haden Ltd* v. *Cowan* [1982] IRLR 314).

In relation to mobility clauses the courts are more generous as long as the employer exercises his rights reasonably in the circumstances by, for example, giving sufficient notice before requiring a person to move halfway round the country (*United Bank* v. *Ahktar* [1989] IRLR 80). What is reasonable conduct on the part of the employer will depend on the circumstances, and a short move will not require notice. In *White* v. *Reflecting Roadstuds Ltd* [1991] ICR 733 the Employment Appeal Tribunal said that they would not imply a term that the employer would exercise his rights under the express terms of the contract reasonably if this was not needed to make the contract work properly. They distinguished *Ahktar* on the basis that, without the implication of reasonableness on the part of the employer, the contract would have been impossible to perform. In other words, expecting Mr Ahktar to start a job in a branch at the other end of the country without giving him sufficient time to sell his house and move his family made it impossible for the employee to perform his side of the bargain. In Mr White's case, the move to another department did not involve extra travelling or relocation. The contract allowed the employer to make such a move and it was not necessary to imply a term that such a right would be exercised after giving notice. It should be noted, however, that the enforcement of mobility clauses, even through express terms in the contract, could be potentially discriminatory on the grounds of sex following the Court of Appeal decision in *Meade-Hill* v. *British Council* [1997] IRLR 522. If the employer wishes to have the ability to make changes in areas other than job duties or place of work, he will need an express provision to do so unilaterally, although the exercise of such a right is subject to the implied duty of trust and confidence, and an employer cannot exercise the right in such a way so as to render performance of the employee's contractual duties impossible (*St Budeaux Royal British Legion Club Ltd* v. *Cropper*, above). A blanket term allowing an employer to introduce any change he wishes may not find favour with the courts and it is more likely that flexibility within each individual term will be deemed more acceptable.

3.2   Collective Agreements

Collective agreements are the result of joint negotiation between two sides of industry, that is, the union and employer or employer's association. They are defined by s.178(1) Trade Union and Labour Relations (Consolidation) Act 1992 as 'any agreement made by or on behalf of one or more trade unions and one or more employer or employer's association and relating to one or more of the matters specified below'. The section continues to give a list of the specified matters which include terms and conditions of employment, engagement or termination of engagement of workers, allocation of duties and so on. Such agreements have two major functions. On one level they deal with issues pertinent to the union as an entity and the employer. They will deal with matters such as negotiation rights, when the agreement will be renegotiated and so on. Such issues are not important to the relationship of the individual employee and his employer and as such do not bind the individual parties. On the other hand, many terms of the agreement will be relevant to the individual employee, terms such as pay rises and hours of work. It is therefore important to see how such terms become part of an agreement that binds the individual parties.

Enforceability between the collective parties

A collective agreement operates on two levels. It is first an agreement between the union and the employer or employer's association. For certain purposes the union is treated as if it were a body corporate (s.10 Trade Union and Labour Relations (Consolidation) Act 1992) and as such it is the union independent from its human members and officers which makes the agreement at this level. Apart from a short period during the currency of the Industrial Relations Act 1971, collective agreements are not legally enforceable between the collective parties (s.179(1) Trade Union and Labour Relations (Consolidation) Act 1992). While the Industrial Relations Act was in force, agreements were presumed to be legally binding, unless there was a clause to the contrary. Many agreements of the time contained such a clause, which became known as a TINA LEA clause (this is not a legally enforceable agreement). This means that between employer and union, agreements have no legal force and are little more than 'a gentleman's agreement'. In *British Leyland UK Ltd* v. *McQuilken* [1978] IRLR 245 the company agreed to close down a department. Skilled employees were to be given the option of redundancy or retraining. Some employees who had originally chosen redundancy wanted to change their minds, but were not allowed to by the company. They sued for a breach of the collective agreement which, they argued, had become part of their contracts of employment. The court held that the agreement was a policy plan rather than an agreement giving individual rights and, therefore, could not be enforced individually. In addition, because a collective agreement is not a legally binding contract, it could not be enforced by the union.

Enforceability between the individual parties

In addition to being an agreement between the collective parties, the negotiations with the union are likely to affect individual employees. Pay rises, for example, will affect all of the employer's workers. The problem that arises, however, is how the individual worker can enforce the pay rise against his employer. It is the union who is the other party to the agreement, and not the employees. Even if the agreement is legally binding at the collective level, on the basis of privity of contract the individual employee cannot enforce an agreement to which he is not a party, even if the agreement is for his benefit. This means that the only way the individual can enforce the relevant provisions against his employer is if those provisions have become part of the employment contract between them. This however is not as straightforward as it seems. Before looking to see whether a term has become incorporated, a court must first decide whether the term is appropriate for incorporation. Thus it is a two-stage process: is the term appropriate for incorporation into an individual contract of employment?; if 'yes', has the term been incorporated?

The issue of the appropriateness of the term for incorporation has caused what appear to be conflicting decisions. Deakin and Morris (*Labour Law*; Butterworths) say that it is necessary to distinguish between those terms which are procedural in nature (such as redundancy selection policies) and those which are substantive, laying down rights for employees such as pay and hours. While this appears to be clear-cut, in reality this is not so. *McQuilken* (above) decided that a policy allowing employees to choose redundancy or retraining was exactly that and inappropriate for incorporation. In *Alexander* v. *Standard Telephones and Cables Ltd* [1990] ICR 291, while Aldous J rejected an application for an injunction he was prepared to say that a redundancy selection policy of 'last in first out' could be capable of incorporation into an individual's contract. (This was later rejected in *Alexander* v. *Standard Telephones and Cables Ltd (No. 2)* [1991] IRLR 286). However in *Anderson* v. *Pringle of Scotland* [1998] IRLR 64 the Court of Session held not only that 'last in first out' had been incorporated into the individual contract but also restrained his dismissal in breach of the term. Despite this, and it is argued that a term which takes seniority into account is substantive and not procedural as it does confer rights on individuals, the most recent case at the time of writing has yet again decided that a redundancy policy is inappropriate for incorporation (*Rover Group plc* v. *Kaur* [2005] IRLR 40).

Once it has been decided that the term is appropriate for incorporation, there are a variety of ways in which terms at the collective level can become incorporated into the individual's contract.

Implied incorporation

This is the most complex way of incorporating the terms of a collective agreement. The basis of such incorporation is that there is evidence that both parties have accepted the agreement as binding. On the part of the employer this is not difficult as he is usually one of the parties who negotiated the agreement at the collective level and obviously agrees to be bound by it. The problem lies with the individual employee. What evidence is needed to show that he intends certain parts of the agreement to bind him? At one time it was thought that if the employee continued working once the collective agreement had been negotiated, this indicated acceptance on his part of the relevant provisions. More recently, however, the courts have argued that that may be a dangerous route to follow as taken to its logical conclusion it could mean that an employee is bound by provisions in an agreement he did not know existed. In *Joel* v. *Cammell Laird* [1969] ITR 206 it was decided that before an employee can be bound by a collective agreement, there must be:

(a) specific knowledge of the agreement;
(b) conduct on the part of the employee which shows that he accepts the agreement; and
(c) some indication of incorporation into the contract.

Further, in *Duke* v. *Reliance Systems Ltd* [1982] IRLR 347 it was held that the employee should have knowledge of the existence of the term if not its content. This may still work unfairly as an employee may know of the existence of a term relating to pay. He may mistakenly assume the term covers a pay rise, whereas in fact it covers a reduction in pay. From the decision in *Duke* he will be bound. He knows of the existence of the term; it is irrelevant that he does not know its content.

While the courts have tried to restrict implied incorporation, one point should be made. The above principles only apply to union members. The courts have long held that provisions of a collective agreement cannot be impliedly incorporated into a non-unionist's contract and that the only way a non-unionist can be bound is by express incorporation. In *Singh* v. *British Steel Corporation* [1974] IRLR 131 the plaintiff had left the union. Some time later the union negotiated a change in the shift system. Singh refused to accept the change and was eventually dismissed. It was held that the union agreement did not alter the terms of his contract. As a non-union member, the only way his contract could be altered was by express agreement on his part which he obviously had not given. He was still bound by his original terms and conditions, that is, the old shift system. It should also be added, however, that given that all the rest of the workforce had accepted the new system, it was held to be a fair dismissal under some other substantial reason.

The decision in *Singh* has been taken a step further and has been held to apply to an employee who is a member of a union other than the one which negotiated the collective agreement. In *Miller* v. *Hamworthy Engineering Ltd* [1986] IRLR 461 the plaintiff's union, along with the other union on the site, had negotiated a reduction in the working week. Some time later, the second union negotiated a further reduction on its own. The plaintiff refused to accept the new hours that had not been negotiated by his union. The Court of Appeal held he was not bound by the new hours. For the purposes of a collective agreement negotiated by a union other than his own, he was to be treated as a non-union member and as such he had to expressly incorporate the second agreement into his contract. The more recent case of *Henry* v. *London General Transport Services Ltd* [2002] IRLR 472 may, however, limit *Singh* and *Miller*. In that case, changes to contractual terms made by way of collective agreement were incorporated into individual contracts by virtue of custom (see below). Thus if a custom can be established, whereby collectively agreed variations (in this case a pay reduction) are implied into both union and non-union members' contracts, this will be upheld by the courts.

Express incorporation

The major problem with implied incorporation is evidence that the employee has accepted the change in his terms and conditions of employment. Express incorporation of the agreement provides such evidence. Such incorporation is a simple process and merely requires a statement in the contract or the statutory statement to the effect that the relevant negotiations by union X shall be part of the individual's contract. In 1993 the contents of the statutory statement were amended. These amendments are now contained in ss.1–6 Employment Rights Act 1996 which state the items which must be included in the statutory statement of terms and conditions (see below) and specifically provide that the employee must be given particulars about collective agreements which directly affect terms and conditions. This means that, from a practical point of view, in the future the relevant provisions of the collective agreement will be expressly incorporated through the statutory statement. Sometimes the whole of the agreement will be expressly incorporated, at other times it may only be part of the agreement. In *NCB* v. *Galley* [1958] WLR 16 the employee, by his contract, agreed to be bound by 'such national agreements for the time being in force'. This was held to incorporate the relevant collective agreement.

The provisions should prevent problems arising out of the fact that the agreement provides employees with certain rights but the employee is unaware of the existence of those rights. In *Scally and Others* v. *Southern Health & Social Services Board and Another* [1991] 3 WLR 778 doctors employed in Northern Ireland had made contributions to the statutory superannuation scheme. By collective agreement they had the right to improve their pension entitlement by buying added years, but this right had to be exercised within a certain time limit. None of the doctors were aware of this right. They claimed damages against the health boards for breach of an implied term, that is, the employer had a duty to tell them such a right existed. The House of Lords said that in a modern world it is common for people to have contracts negotiated collectively. They could not be expected to know all the details unless these were pointed out to them. In this situation, if the agreement gave a valuable right to the employee of which the employee had to take advantage and the employee could not, in all the circumstances, reasonably be aware of the right unless it was drawn to his attention, the employer was under a duty to make that right known to the employee. By providing the employee with the particulars about any collective agreement which affects his terms and conditions of employment, the onus will be on the employee to take up any rights the agreement confers upon him.

Once the provision has become part of the individual's contract, contractual principles apply. This has three consequences for the employer. First, the fact that the collective agreement is stated to be binding in honour only has no effect on the legal enforceability at the individual level. Once the provision becomes a contractual term it is legally binding and has no reliance on the legal enforceability of the collective agreement. This is obviously the case and is supported by the judgements in *Marley* v. *Forward Trust Group Ltd* [1986] IRLR 369. Second, if either party at the collective level withdraws from the agreement, this has no effect on the terms incorporated into the individual's contract. In *Burrough's Machines Ltd* v. *Timmoney* [1977] IRLR 404 the employer was a member of an employer's association which had negotiated a lay-off procedure. Some time later the employer left the association, but it was held that he was still bound by the procedure in relation to his employees because his leaving the association did not affect the employment contracts. In *Whent* v. *T Cartledge* [1997] IRLR 153 employees were transferred to a new employer. The Transfer of Undertakings (Protection of Employment) Regulations 1981 applied and therefore the employees were transferred on their existing terms and conditions. One of the terms of the contract incorporated a collective agreement between the old employer and the GMB that the National Joint Council (NJC) pay rates applied. After the transfer, the new employer derecognised the GMB and told the employees that the NJC rates would no longer be paid and froze the employees' pay despite an NJC rise. It was held that the provision to pay NJC rates was a term of the contract and the new employer's refusal to pay the rate, despite derecognising the union, was a breach of that contract. Any other conclusion in either of the above cases would, of course, give either party the right to unilaterally alter the terms of the contract. (See *Gibbons* v. *Associated British Ports* [1985] IRLR 376.) Third, the incorporation may affect the interpretation of the provision. Collective agreements tend to be loosely drafted but once certain parts become contractual terms, they are interpreted as such. In *Hooper* v. *British Railways Board* [1988] IRLR 517 a sick-pay term was incorporated into the employee's contract from an agreement made with the Railway Staff Joint Council. It was, however, badly drafted and did not reflect what happened in practice. The Court of Appeal held that the term had to be interpreted in the normal contractual way, objectively as it stood and without reference to the subsequent behaviour of the parties. The application of contractual rules was also seen in *Ali* v. *Christian Salvesen Food Services Ltd* [1997] IRLR 17. In this case, a collective agreement which had been incorporated into the employees' contracts provided for annual hours based on a notional 40-hour week. The annual hours were 1,824 and once these hours were worked overtime rates applied to the excess hours. Some employees were made redundant before the year was out. They had worked more than 40 hours a week but had not reached the total annual hours by the time of their redundancy. They sued for an unlawful deduction from their wages when they were not paid overtime for the weeks they had worked in excess of 40 hours. At first instance the employment tribunal held that overtime was not payable until the employees had worked 1,824 hours and that a term could not be implied that overtime would be paid for hours in excess of 40 per week where there was an early termination of the contract. The employees appealed arguing that such an implied term was needed on business efficacy grounds. This argument was upheld by the EAT but rejected by the Court of Appeal which stated that as the contract did not mention early termination the omission must have been deliberate and a term did not need to be implied for the contract to work.

Agency

As seen from the above, there are problems in incorporating the relevant provisions of a collective agreement into an individual contract. Whereas express incorporation is the simplest way, in practice implied incorporation is the most common, leading to a wealth of law on what type of conduct implies acceptance and what knowledge the employee must have before it can be said that his conduct represents acceptance of this agreement or this term. The courts at one time did try to make their task easier by arguing that when the union negotiated, it was doing so as an agent of its members. The attractiveness of this argument is undeniable. It avoids the problems seen above and means that any agreement negotiated collectively automatically binds the member as the union's principal, whether he knows of the negotiation or not. The proposition has major flaws, however. First, it would only apply to members at the place of work when the agreement was negotiated; employees taken on after the negotiation would have to separately accept the agreement when starting their employment. Second, the proposition does not address the issue of non-union members. How would the union act as their agent? Would non-union members have to appoint the union as agent, and would the appointment be general, for a particular item such as pay, or for a particular agreement? Last, what is the basis of the agency in the case of a union member? Is it the contract of membership which would give unfettered authority in any negotiation or would the member have to give authority each time negotiations started or, conversely, is authority presumed unless the member withdraws it before negotiations begin? The problems, as can be seen, are numerous. While some judges feel agency is a neat way of dealing with the issues, most have recognised the inherent problems. While agency as a concept will work where there is a small unionised workforce, it becomes impractical where there are large numbers of employees, some unionised and some not, with perhaps two or more unions operating on one site. The present state of the law on this issue was voiced by Arnold J in *Burton Group Ltd* v. *Smith* [1977] IRLR 191 when he said: 'There is no reason at all why, in a particular case, union representatives should not be the agent of an employee – But that agency does not stem from the mere fact that they are union representatives and that he is a member of the union; it must be supported in the particular case by the creation of some specific agency.'

Conflicting collective agreements

A further problem exists when there are two collective agreements, perhaps a locally negotiated agreement and a nationally negotiated one, and the agreements conflict. Which one prevails? In *Clift* v. *West Riding County Council* (1964) The Times, 10 April the court held that a local agreement prevailed over an earlier national agreement because the local one was later in time. This decision, however, was not followed by the Court of Appeal in the later case of *Gascol Conversions Ltd* v. *Mercer* [1974] IRLR 155. In that case the court held that a national agreement prevailed over a later local one. Given this authority, it is probable that this is the position of the law at the moment.

No-strike clauses

The law is very specific on how a 'no-strike' or 'peace' clause in a collective agreement becomes part of an individual's contract. The law is found in s.180 Trade Union and Labour Relations (Consolidation) Act 1992. This provides that such a clause will become part of the individual contract if the following five conditions are met:

1. The collective agreement is in writing.
2. The agreement expressly states that the terms are to be incorporated into the individual's contract.
3. A copy of the collective agreement is reasonably accessible to the employees concerned.
4. The agreement is made by an independent trade union.
5. The individual contract expressly or impliedly incorporates the terms of the collective agreement.

If all the above apply, the provision becomes part of the employment contract. It must be remembered, however, that a strike is a repudiatory breach by the employee. While the 'peace' clause may make an employer feel safer, it gives him no more rights than he already has and, as such, the effect of the statutory provision is minimal.

3.3 Incorporation of Other Documents

In addition to collective agreements, the employer will often have other documents around the workplace to which he wishes his employees to adhere. He will be able to enforce such documents, however, only if they have become part of the individual contract. The two most common documents around a workplace will be the works rules and the employer's disciplinary and grievance procedures.

Works rules/staff handbooks

The status of the works rules is a somewhat grey area at the moment. Certainly, they do not appear to be contractual *per se*, and therefore must be incorporated into the individual's contract. If they are not incorporated they are orders from an employer to his employees. In the leading case in this area – *Secretary of State for Employment* v. *ASLEF (No. 2)* [1972] 2 QB 455 – Denning MR expressed the view that the rules were in 'no way terms of his contract. They are only instructions to a man on how he is to do his work.' Other cases have adopted this approach. In *Peake* v. *Automotive Products* [1978] QB 233 it was held that the rule-book was non-contractual and merely set out administrative arrangements for running the factory. Such an interpretation means that the employer has the right to alter the rules unilaterally, without consultation with his employees. Further, the employer does not lose a remedy against his employees who refuse to comply with the works rules if they are defined as non-contractual. It is an implied duty on the part of the employee that he obeys all lawful, reasonable orders issued by his employer. Failure to do so is a breach of contract. Whatever the status of the works rules, the employer will have the ultimate remedy of dismissal. While that may seem to paint a black picture for employees, even if the courts and tribunals do decide that the rules in a particular case are merely instructions from the employer, they will use the test of reasonableness to curb excesses of management power and they will not allow an employer to act autocratically. In *Talbot* v. *Hugh M. Fulton Ltd* [1975] IRLR 52 an employee was dismissed for wearing his hair long, which was in breach of the works rules. It was held that his dismissal was unfair. The rule did not state the exact length of hair considered to be acceptable and in addition such a rule would only be reasonable if there was a safety or hygiene risk.

The above comments, however, do not mean that works rules are never contractual. Just as collective agreements can become incorporated into the contract, so can the works rules. Where the rule-book is given or referred to when the contract of employment is formed and the employee acknowledges the rule-book as part of his conditions of employment, it is likely that the courts would hold that the rules had contractual effect. This will certainly be the case where the employee signs a document agreeing to be bound by the rules. In these cases, however, not all the rules will necessarily become contractual terms. Rule-books, like collective agreements, will often be vague and certain parts of the rules may be inappropriate for inclusion in the contract. In *Cadoux* v. *Central Regional Council* [1986] IRLR 131 the employee's contract was subject to the Conditions of Service laid down by the National Joint Council for Local Authorities' Administrative, Technical and Clerical Services, as supplemented by the Authorities Rules, as amended from time to time. The issue that arose out of this rather complicated clause was whether the employer would unilaterally withdraw a non-contributory life assurance scheme for staff. It was held that, given that the Joint Council could unilaterally alter the rules from time to time, the parties could not have intended them to have contractual effect. However in *Keeley* v. *Fosroc International Ltd* [2006] EWCA Civ 1277 the Court of Appeal held that where a staff handbook contains details of an enhanced redundancy payment, there is a presumption that it has contractual status.

The importance of the status of the works rules is demonstrated by

Cadoux. While the remedy for breach of the rules may be the same whatever the definition given to them, the power of the employer is restricted once they are classified as contractual. Then the employer may only alter his rules by mutual agreement. An example of how crucial the definition may be is given by Norman Selwyn in his book *Law of Employment* (published by Butterworths). What if the employer introduces, into the rules, a search policy? If the employee refuses to be searched, is he in breach of an express term in the contract, or is he refusing to obey an order and, if the latter, is the order reasonable? If the rules are non-contractual, the employer will have to show his order is both lawful and reasonable before he can compel an employee to obey it. Clearly there is a variety of issues arising out of this area which still need addressing by the courts.

Disciplinary and grievance procedures

By s.3 Employment Rights Act (ERA) 1996 the employer must give details of the disciplinary and grievance procedures to all of his employees at the start of their employment. While since October 2004 there are now minimum statutory discipline and grievance procedures which apply to all employees, many employers have procedures over and above the statutory ones. Despite originally being in the Employment Act 2002, the government decided not to implement s.30 which made the statutory procedures contractual. As such, failure to implement the statutory procedures will not give rise to a breach of contract claim, but will affect a finding of unfair dismissal and any subsequent compensation (see Chapter 9). In respect of disciplinary procedures however, some incorporation into the contract may be advantageous for an employer, particularly in relation to disciplinary sanctions. Should the employer wish to impose a sanction which will involve a reduction or loss of pay, for example, demotion or suspension without pay, he needs contractual authority or the employee's written consent. Failure to have this authority or consent will be a breach of s.13 ERA in relation to deductions from wages and will entitle the employee to sue for recovery.

Once procedures are in the contract they must be adhered to and this may be seen as a disadvantage for the employer, as all employees will be able potentially to claim a breach of contract, even those with insufficient continuity to present a claim for unfair dismissal, a thought presumably in the mind of the government when it failed to implement s.30. In *Jones v. Lee and Guilding* [1980] IRLR 67 the plaintiff was a headmaster who was dismissed when he divorced and remarried. His contract gave him a right to a hearing before the local education authority before the decision to dismiss was taken, but the plaintiff was not afforded this opportunity. The

Court of Appeal granted an injunction restraining the school managers from dismissing the employee before a hearing had taken place. In *Gunton* v. *London Borough of Richmond* [1981] 1 WLR 28 damages were assessed for wrongful dismissal to include a period of time the employee would have been employed if his contractual disciplinary procedure had been implemented. The House of Lords has decided in the case of *West Midlands Co-operative Society Ltd* v. *Tipton* [1986] IRLR 112 that failure to allow an employee to exercise his contractual right of appeal renders a dismissal unfair. All of the above show the different remedies available to an employee should the employer fail to comply with contractual disciplinary procedures.

Apart from compliance with s.3, however, it can be to an employer's advantage that the procedures are contractual. The procedures will not only lay down details about hearings and so on but will also give a list of examples of misconduct and the standards of behaviour and workmanship which the employer finds unacceptable. This will put the employer in a much stronger position in an unfair dismissal claim, for he will be able to show that the employee is in breach of contract.

Contractual grievance procedures can also be advantageous to an employer. In *Witham* v. *Hills Shopfitters* (unreported) the employee resigned after being at the receiving end of foul language. Without pursuing the company grievance procedure, the employee claimed unfair dismissal, arguing that the language constituted a constructive dismissal. It was held that the language was not unusual for the shopfloor and, furthermore, the employee should have pursued the company's internal procedures before resigning and presenting a claim to an employment tribunal. Furthermore, the Employment Appeal Tribunal in *W.A. Goold (Pearmak) Ltd* v. *McConnell* [1995] IRLR 516 held that the failure on the part of the employer to provide a grievance procedure was a breach of the duty of mutual respect which entitled the employee to resign and claim constructive dismissal.

Since October 2004, when the new statutory disciplinary and grievance procedures were introduced, a tribunal must increase or decrease compensation by up to 50 per cent for failure to use the procedures. In addition the time limits to present tribunal claims have been amended to allow the procedures to be completed before a claim is presented to the tribunal. In some cases failure on the part of an employee to lodge a grievance will prevent the employee from lodging a tribunal claim. Note also the provisions relating to dismissal procedures agreements (s.110 ERA as amended) and the new rights to be accompanied at disciplinary and grievance hearings introduced by s.10 Employment Relations Act 1999. For further discussion see Chapter 9.

3.4 Statutory Statement of Terms and Conditions

By s.1 Employment Rights Act 1996 every employee should receive a statement of the basic terms and conditions of employment within eight weeks of the commencement of relationship. The detailed requirements of s.1 were brought in to implement EC Directive 91/533 which requires employers to inform employees of the essential elements of the contract of employment. Certain employees are excluded from s.1, including employees who work for less than four weeks. The matters the statement must contain are as follows:

(a) identification of the parties;

(b) the date on which the period of continuous employment began, stating whether any continuous employment with a previous employer counts and, if so, when the continuous period began;

(c) the scale and rate of remuneration or the method of calculating the remuneration;

(d) the intervals at which remuneration is paid;

(e) any terms and conditions relating to hours of work;

(f) any terms and conditions relating to entitlement to holidays, including public holidays and holiday pay;

(g) the title of the job the employee is employed to do or a brief description of the work he is employed to do;

(h) either the place of work or, if there is more than one place, an indication of such and the address of the employer.

The terms above must be set out in one document, known as the principal statement. In addition, the following additional information must be given to employees, but can be given in instalments so long as this is done by the end of the eighth week:

(a) terms relating to incapacity for work due to sickness or injury, including any provision for sick pay;

(b) pensions and pension schemes;

(c) period of notice the employee must give and is entitled to receive;

(d) if the employment is temporary the period it is expected to last, or the termination date of a fixed term contract;

(e) any collective agreements which directly affect the terms and conditions of employment and, if the employer is not a party, the persons by whom they were made;

(f) where the employee is required to work outside the United Kingdom for a period of more than one month, the length of the period, the currency in which he is to be paid, any benefits or extra remuneration paid because he is working outside the United Kingdom and any terms and conditions relating to his return;

(g) details of the disciplinary and grievance procedures.

The employer may, by the statement, refer the employee to the provisions of another document, for items not in the principal statement, which the employee has reasonable opportunities to read during the course of his employment or which is made reasonably accessible to him. This means that the employer can put items in, for example, a staff handbook which he either gives to the employee or makes accessible. If there are any changes in any of the items the employer must inform the employee of the change, in writing, within one month of the change happening.

The statement is not contractual. In *System Floors Ltd (UK)* v. *Daniel* [1981] IRLR 475 Browne-Wilkinson J said about the statement that: 'It provides very strong *prima facie* evidence of what were the terms of the contract between the parties – Nor are the statements of the terms finally conclusive: at most they place a heavy burden on the employer to show that the actual terms of the contract are different from those which he had set out in the statutory statement.'

The importance of the statement above is demonstrated by the case of *Robertson and Jackson* v. *British Gas Corporation* [1983] IRLR 302. The statutory statement was silent regarding a bonus which had been incorporated into the plaintiffs' contracts from a collective agreement. It was held that where there is a conflict between the statement and the contract, the contract prevails. This approach has been confirmed by the ECJ in *Kampelmann* v. *Landschaftsverband Westfalen-Lippe* [1998] IRLR 333 and demonstrated by the ECJ decision in *Lange* v. *Georg Schünemann GmbH* [2001] IRLR 244 where it was held that the fact that the obligation to work overtime was not reduced to writing did not nullify a contractual term agreed verbally by the employee.

If the employee does not receive his statement, he may apply to an employment tribunal. The tribunal will then determine what particulars should be included. If the tribunal does not have sufficient evidence to determine what the parties would have agreed, they must determine what should have been agreed according to Stephenson LJ in *Mears* v. *Safecar Security Ltd* [1982] IRLR 183. This has since been doubted in another Court of Appeal decision, *Eagland* v. *British Telecom* [1993] ICR 644, where Parker LJ pointed out that Stephenson LJ's remarks were *obiter* and he doubted that a tribunal had the power to invent terms if the intentions of the parties were not discoverable. The Court of Appeal further decided in *Mears* that, given that a tribunal will hear a complaint because of the employer's breach of statutory duty, any doubt as to content should be resolved in favour of the employee.

It has already been noted above that the Employment Act 2002 introduced statutory disciplinary and grievance procedures which were implemented by the Employment Act 2002 (Dispute Resolution) Regulations 2004. To ensure employees are aware of these procedures, the Act changed the statutory statement to include details of an employer's disciplinary and grievance procedures and to increase tribunal powers where the statement is inaccurate, incomplete or non-existent. Tribunals have the power to award compensation where the lack of, incompleteness of or inaccuracy of the statutory statement becomes evident in certain tribunal claims such as unfair dismissal or discrimination. It is important to note that this allows a tribunal to look at the statement in a number of statutory claims and not only in claims relating specifically to the statement or lack of one. Compensation where there is an incomplete or inaccurate statement can be increased by two to four weeks' pay. Where a statement has not been issued, compensation can also be increased by two to four weeks' pay. In addition, where the remedy for the original complaint is not financial compensation, the tribunal can award two to four weeks' pay.

While these changes seem particularly harsh for employers, changes in unfair dismissal discussed in Chapter 9 will, to some extent, mitigate this harshness.

3.5 Custom

It is sometimes argued that the terms of a contract of employment can be found in the custom and practices of a particular industry. In the old case of *Sagar* v. *Ridehalgh* [1931] 1 Ch 310 a custom allowing the employer to deduct from workers' wages for bad workmanship was held to be a term of the contract. In *Marshall* v. *English Electric Ltd* [1945] 1 All ER 653 an established practice of using suspension as a disciplinary sanction was held to be a term in the employee's contract. It is fair to say, however, that custom as a source of contractual terms *per se* is used less and less, although working practices within an industry may be used to interpret an ambiguous express term. For a custom to become a contractual term, it must be certain, well-known and reasonable; a deduction for bad workmanship today would probably not be upheld as a term of the contract because of the uncertainty in the phrase itself. What constitutes 'bad'? Even if the courts do accept a custom as a contractual term, there seems to be judicial uncertainty as to exactly when the custom becomes part of the contract. Is it once it has become certain, well-known and reasonable, or does the individual employee have to know of the custom and accept it as part of his contract? The cases can perhaps be summarised as deciding that normally the employee should know of the custom and have accepted it, and evidence of this must be brought before the courts before the employee will be contractually bound. It is important to note that merely working, knowing of the custom, may not be sufficient to show the employee's acceptance of it into his contract. In *Samways* v. *Swan Hunter Shipbuilders Ltd* [1975] IRLR 190 the employee had been a labourer and was given the job of charge-hand with a consequent rise in pay of £4 per week. Because of a reduction in work, the employers withdrew his additional money and offered him his old job of labourer. The employee sued for a redundancy payment, but the employers argued that the extra money was temporary by virtue of custom and practice within the industry, and gave evidence of other workers who had been made up to charge-hands and reverted to labouring work with the reduction in pay. The tribunal held that the fact that men had reverted to labourers in the past was not sufficient to establish a custom. Furthermore, their conduct was not an indication that they were contractually bound to accept the change in status, but could be explained by the fact that they wished to remain in employment. However, in the more recent case of *Henry* v. *London General Transport Services Ltd* (above) the Court of Appeal upheld a custom which was 'reasonable, certain and notorious' incorporating a pay reduction agreed collectively into all contracts of employment. The Court of Appeal stated that incorporation could not be undermined by showing some individuals did not know of the practice or did not intend or wish it.

3.6 Implied Terms

Although many individual contracts will have covered all eventualities by express terms, in some situations circumstances may arise which have not been envisaged by the parties and therefore there is no term to cover the situation. In these cases the court 'fills in the gaps' and tries to establish what term the parties would have provided if they had thought about it. This function of the court to imply terms on an individual basis should be distinguished from the function to imply common law duties discussed in the next chapter. The duties discussed later are implied into every contract of employment by the common law. The implied terms discussed below are terms specific to an individual contract and to individual parties.

The courts rely on two old contractual tests to determine the content of the missing term:

1. The term is necessary to give the contract business efficacy (the test from the old case of *The Moorcock* (1889) 14 PD 64).

2. The term is so obvious that it goes without saying, so that if you asked an officious bystander if the term should be in, he would answer 'Oh, of course'. This test comes from the case of *Shirlaw* v. *Southern Foundries Ltd* [1939] 2 KB 206.

It is true to say that the business efficacy test lost favour after the case of *Lister* v. *Romford Ice and Cold Storage Co Ltd* [1957] AC 555 and that the preferred test is the obvious consensus one. While the courts will profess that they are merely putting into the contract what the parties would have intended this is obviously a legal fiction, as presumably if the parties knew the term they wanted, there would be no need to use the court in the first place! The tests are merely an aid to the courts to fill in the blanks. The problem with both tests, however, is that although they tell the court that a particular term should be included in the contract they do not tell the court what the content of that term should be. In *Shell UK Ltd* v. *Lostock Garage Ltd* [1977] 1 All ER 481 Lord Denning said that where an employment contract was silent, the courts should ask what would be reasonable in the circumstances. Although this view has been followed since, there is a vast difference between what is obvious and what is reasonable.

To establish the content of the term, the courts will start with how the parties have worked the contract in the past. In *Mears* v. *Safecar Security Ltd* (above) the Court of Appeal refused to imply a term that the employee was entitled to sick pay, because sick pay had never been paid in the past. If there is no evidence of past conduct, the courts will imply a term they feel is necessary and one the parties would have agreed if they were being reasonable (*Courtaulds Northern Spinning Ltd* v. *Sibson* [1988] IRLR 305). Finally, the courts may imply particular terms into the contract of a professional employee by reference to the nature of the profession. In *Sim* v. *Rotherham Metropolitan Borough Council* (above) the High Court implied a term that teachers should cover for absent colleagues as this would be seen by people outside the profession as part of the duties of a teacher. Note, however, that the court will not imply a term to distort the meaning of a clear express term (*Ali* v. *Christian Salvesen Food Services*, above).

Summary

1. Normal contractual rules apply to the employment relationship and the contract becomes binding as soon as the offer by the employer is accepted, expressly or impliedly, by the employee.

2. The terms of the contract come from a variety of sources.

3. Express terms in the contract should be clear and unambiguous.

Summary cont'd

4. Partial performance by the employee of the express terms relating to job duties may allow the employer to deduct a proportional amount of pay or, if the duties are deemed to be a material part of the contract, the employer may treat the contract as repudiated.

5. Express terms cannot be ousted by implied terms.

6. Certain statutory provisions restrict the content of express terms.

7. The law recognises the inherent flexibility needed within the relationship and a variation in working methods is within the employer's contractual rights. Any other variation must be mutually agreed and even if such variation is allowed by the contract, the courts may imply that the employer should exercise his rights reasonably.

8. Collective agreements are a major source of employment terms. Their provisions need to become part of the individual's contract to become enforceable against the employer. This is normally done by express or implied incorporation. In the case of non-unionists it must be done by express incorporation, unless a custom exists which varies all contracts.

9. A no-strike clause must comply with the statutory requirements to be enforceable.

10. Works rules and disciplinary and grievance procedures may become part of the contract. The court will see if they are appropriate for incorporation and whether the documents were given at the time the contract was made or whether reference was made to the documents within the contract. Since 2004 there are minimum statutory disciplinary and grievance procedures. A tribunal can increase or decrease compensation for failing to use the procedures and failing to implement the statutory disciplinary procedures results in a finding of automatically unfair dismissal.

11. The statutory statement is non-contractual but gives evidence of the contractual terms.

12. Certain customs may become part of the contract if they are certain, well-known and reasonable.

13. The courts may use the old contractual tests to imply terms into the contract to cover situations the parties have not envisaged. The content of such terms is decided on past conduct and reasonableness.

Exercises

1. To what extent is the contract of employment an individually negotiated agreement between two parties?

2. How far is it true to say that the rights of an employee come from status rather than contract?

3. Engineers working for Heavy Engineering Ltd have received a Christmas bonus every year for the past 10 years. This year the company has told the employees that no bonus will be paid.

   The company has recently issued a new rule which has been posted on the notice board. The rule states that the management reserves the right to require any employee to submit to a body search on leaving company premises in order to check that company property is not leaving the premises.

   Advise the company on the contractual implications of these changes.

Further Reading

Barmes   *The Continuing Conceptual Crisis in the Common Law of the Contract of Employment* (2004) 67 MLR 435.

Dolding and Fawlk   *Judicial Understanding of the Contract of Employment* (1992) 55 MLR 562.

Honeyball   *Employment Law and the Primacy of Contract* (1989) 18 ILJ 97.

Kenner   *Statement or Contract? – Some Reflections on the EC Employee Information (Contract or Employment Relationship) Directive* (1999) 28 ILJ 205.

McLean   *An Employer's Right to be Unreasonable* (1992) 49 CLJ 23.

Napier   *Incorporation of Collective Agreements* (1986) 15 ILJ 52.

Napier   *Computerisation and Employment Rights* (1992) 21 ILJ 1.

Wilson   *Contract and Prerogative: A Reconsideration of the Legal Enforcement of Collective Agreements* (1984) 13 ILJ 1.

Wynn-Evans   *Implication and Omission in Collectively Negotiated Contracts* (1997) 26 ILJ 166.

Chapter 4

Implied Duties in the Contract of Employment

4.1 Personal Nature of the Contract

It has already been seen that the courts have power to impose terms on the parties where the contract is silent. The power previously discussed applies on a contract-specific basis and as such the courts are implying terms into an individual contract only, not every contract of employment. By contrast, over the years, the courts have decided that some terms are so important that they should be in every contract, and if the parties have omitted them the courts will insert the relevant provision. These terms have been called implied duties to distinguish them from those discussed earlier. The nature and the content of the duties have changed over the years as the law has moved away from the attitude that the relationship is one of master and servant and towards the idea that it is a relationship between two equals. The law, however, will not go too far down the equality line. While the law has recognised an inequality of bargaining power between the parties it has only gone some way towards balancing that inequality. It will be seen that statute law has moved in to give employees minimum rights which cannot normally be contracted out of. For example, women generally have a right to equal pay with men, and certain employees have a right not to be unfairly dismissed and a right to redundancy pay. In addition to statute, the common law has developed the implied duties to protect employees during the performance of the contract. It would be unwise, however, to imagine that the courts have created a charter of employment rights. While there are duties imposed upon the employer, likewise the law imposes duties upon the individual employee. Breach of these duties on either side will create a potential claim for a breach of contract.

The duties discussed below are duties imposed during the performance of the contract and which limit how either side exercises its rights. To some extent, this is an unusual function of the law and demonstrates the unique nature of a contract of employment. On its most basic interpretation, a contract of employment is a personal contract. Both parties agree to provide personal services for each other. This aspect has already been seen in *Ready Mixed Concrete* v. *MPNI* where McKenna J refused to hold that lorry drivers were employees because they could delegate their driving duties under the contract. Given the fact that an employment contract is one where each party is chosen for individual attributes, such a term in the lorry drivers' contracts demonstrated that the relationship could not be one of employment. It has also been seen in *Express Echo Publications* v. *Tanton* where the Court of Appeal regarded personal service as the irreducible minimum in a contract of employment.

Given that the contract is unique to the two parties within it, it follows that, from basic contractual principles, the courts cannot force the parties to continue the contract should they no longer wish to do so. This has been recognised by statute and is at present s.236 Trade Union and Labour Relations (Consolidation) Act 1992, which provides that no court by an order of specific performance shall compel the parties to continue the contract, or, likewise, no court shall order an injunction to prevent a breach or threatened breach of a contract by an individual employee, if either order would have the effect of compelling an employee to work or attend a place for the purpose of doing work. In *Whitwood Chemical Co* v. *Hardman* [1891] 2 Ch 416 a manager's contract contained a clause that he agreed to devote the whole of his time to company business. He intended to work for a rival in his spare time and the employer sought specific performance of the clause. It was held that the action did not lie. Likewise if an injunction would have the effect of specific performance, in that it would compel the parties to continue the contract, it will not be granted. In *City & Hackney Health Authority* v. *National Union of Public Employees* [1985] IRLR 252 a shop steward obtained an injunction to restrain his employers from preventing him entering the premises when he was suspended. The employers appealed to the Court of Appeal who lifted the injunction. To allow it to stand would have forced the employer to allow the employee to attend the place of work and would therefore have the effect of an order of specific performance.

There is, however, one situation where the court will compel the parties to continue the contract. This is where the employer is blatantly ignoring the employee's contractual rights and preventing him from pursuing a remedy provided by the contract itself. The court will only exercise its power in exceptional circumstances, and in the majority of situations will decide that a better remedy is damages for a breach of contract. In *Hill* v. *C.A. Parsons & Co Ltd* [1972] Ch 305 an employee refused to join the union when there was a closed shop in existence. The employers gave him one month's notice of dismissal. The court felt that, given the employee's position as a senior engineer, he was entitled to six months' notice and granted an injunction restraining the employers from treating the contract as terminated until after that date. The court conceded, however, that there were exceptional circumstances in that there was no loss of confidence between the parties and the employers had dismissed him because of union pressure. In *Jones*

v. *Lee and Guilding* (above) an injunction was granted to prevent a dismissal taking place until the contractual disciplinary procedures had been observed. In *Irani* v. *Southampton & South West Hampshire Health Authority* [1985] IRLR 203 a similar decision was reached. Here the employer had not lost confidence in the employee, the procedures were contractual and damages would have been an inadequate remedy. Given this decision, it can be seen that the normal remedy will be damages and only if that is inadequate will an order to continue the contract be granted. It should be noted, moreover, that in most cases where an injunction has been granted, this has only been to continue the contract for a relatively short space of time. One exception to this is the case of *Powell* v. *Brent London Borough Council* [1988] ICR 176. In this case an employee was promoted. The council then feared that the appointment was in breach of their equal opportunities policy and rescinded the promotion and readvertised the post. Meanwhile the plaintiff continued to do the job and sought an injunction to restrain the council from treating her as demoted. There was nothing to show that she was unable to do the new job, or that the council did not have confidence in her. The injunction was granted. The later case of *Hughes* v. *London Borough of Southwark* [1988] IRLR 55 supports this decision. In that case the court granted an injunction to prevent the employers from requiring the employees to temporarily staff community areas and so stop their normal hospital work. All of these cases show that the court will compel the employer to continue the contract if there has been no loss of confidence in the employee (see also *Wadcock* v. *London Borough of Brent* [1990] IRLR 223 and *Alexander* v. *Standard Telephones and Cables Ltd* [1990] ICR 291). Courts, however, cannot grant an order in favour of the employer because of s.236 of the 1992 Act.

4.2 Duties of the Employer

Duty to provide work

Very often you hear lay people and the media talk about the right to work. If, however, there is a right to work, jurisprudentially there must be a corresponding duty on the employer to allow the employee to exercise that right, as for every right there must be a corresponding duty. If my neighbour has a right of way over my property, I must be under a corresponding duty to allow him to exercise his right. In the area of employment, it has been emphatically stated by the majority of judges that there is no right to work and therefore no duty of the employer to provide work. The clearest exposition of the law was by Asquith J in *Collier* v. *Sunday Referee Publishing Co Ltd* [1940] 2 KB 647 when he said: 'Provided I pay my cook her wages regularly, she cannot complain if I choose to take all or some of my meals out.'

Since Asquith's judgement, Lord Denning in particular seemed anxious to establish that there was a right to work. In *Nagle* v. *Fielden* [1966] 2 QB 633 a woman argued that a rule of the Jockey Club, which prevented women from holding licences to train horses, prevented her from earning her living. Denning MR held that such a rule was in restraint of trade and void. In the later case of *Langston* v. *Chrysler United Kingdom* [1974] 1 All ER 980 which was referred to the Court of Appeal by the National Industrial Relations Court, Lord Denning said: 'We have repeatedly said in this court that a man has a right to work which the courts will protect – I would not wish to state the decided view, but merely state the argument.' The case was referred back to the National Industrial Relations Court where Sir John Donaldson P decided that suspension of an employee on full basic pay was a breach of the contractual term to earn extra payment for night-shift and overtime working.

It seems, therefore, that despite attempts by Lord Denning, the courts have been reluctant to establish a general right to work. The courts have always recognised, however, that there is a duty to provide work in certain types of cases. Two exceptions to the general rule were given in the case of *Turner* v. *Sawdon* [1901] 2 KB 728 and since then the courts have expanded the group of situations where the employer is under a duty to provide work for his employee as the opportunity to work is seen to be as important as the salary received. The exceptions are as follows:

1. The work is needed to maintain the employee's publicity and reputation. In *Herbert Clayton & Jack Waller Ltd* v. *Oliver* [1930] AC 209 the employee, who was playing the lead in a play, was given a lesser part at the same salary. It was held that the employer was in breach of contract as the nature of the job was as important as the salary in terms of the publicity the employee needed.
2. The work is needed to enable the employee to earn the wage. This covers the situation of piece-workers or workers on a commission-only basis, where the failure to provide work will mean that the employee receives no pay (*Devonald* v. *Rosser & Sons* [1906] 2 KB 728). This will only apply, however, if the commission is the only way of earning the salary. In *Turner* v. *Sawdon* a salesman was on a fixed salary plus commission. He was given no work to do but still received the fixed salary. It was held that the employer was not in breach of contract.
3. There are *dicta* in *Langston* to suggest that if the nature of the job is such that the employee needs the work to develop or maintain his skills, the employer will be in breach of contract if he fails to provide it. This would cover the situation of apprentices or trainees, although the extension of the principle to the maintenance of skills does extend the potential situations.

4. Later cases seem willing to accept that *Turner* v. *Sawdon* did not lay down a definitive list. In *Pedersen* v. *London Borough of Camden* [1981] ICR 674 it was suggested that it may be a breach of contract to deprive an employee of a substantial proportion of his job, based on the view that a man does not work for wages alone. This view was relying on the earlier case of *Breach* v. *Epsylon Industries Ltd* [1976] IRLR 180 where an employer moved a large part of his operation to Canada, leaving the employee with little to do. On appeal to the Employment Appeal Tribunal, Phillips J said that *Turner* v. *Sawdon* envisaged exceptions to the general principle but the case was old and in more modern times there may be facts where it is easier to imply that there is an implied obligation to provide work. In other words the courts seem prepared to extend the exceptions first laid down in the case if they feel the circumstances are appropriate. This can be seen in the Court of Appeal decision in *William Hill Organisation Ltd* v. *Tucker* [1998] IRLR 313. In the case, Tucker had to give six months' notice to his employer. When he resigned to take up a job with a competitor, William Hill told him that they required six months' notice from him but that he would not be expected to work during that period. In other words Tucker had been put on garden leave. William Hill then sought an injunction to prevent Tucker working for a competitor during his notice period. The High Court found that there was no express clause in Tucker's contract which allowed the employers to require him to take garden leave and therefore they were obliged to provide him with work during the notice period. Failure to do so amounted to a breach of contract and thus Tucker was entitled to terminate his contract immediately. The employers appealed. The Court of Appeal noted that social conditions had changed since the older cases on the area and that the courts had been increasingly ready to recognise the importance to an employee of work as well as pay. Looking at Tucker's contract, the Court felt that it created an obligation on William Hill to provide Tucker with work during his notice period. This was because the skills the job required had to be exercised frequently, which was supported by a clause in the contract which stated that the employer would ensure that the employee had every opportunity to develop his skills; the employee had to work such hours as were necessary to carry out his job duties, which appeared inconsistent with the employer's contention that the employee could draw his wages but not be required to work; and finally the employer had a contractual right to suspend in disciplinary cases. The Court felt such a specific power would be unnecessary if the employers could put employees on garden leave. As such, the Court dismissed the employer's appeal. It would appear, however, that if the employer had had a specific contractual provision allowing garden leave, then the

employer's appeal would have been upheld, although the Court pointed out that the issue of an injunction to prevent the employee working during the notice period (in other words the injunction would restrain competition) should be justified on similar grounds to those necessary in relation to a covenant in restraint of trade.

Duty to pay wages

Although there is no general duty on the employer to provide work, his duty to pay wages is fundamental to the bargain and if persistently broken will entitle the employee to sue for a repudiatory breach of contract. Normally the contract itself will state the amount of pay the employee is entitled to receive. This will either come from individual negotiation between the employer and the employee or from a collective agreement. If the contract is silent as to the amount of pay, the law will imply that reasonable remuneration should be paid. The court will assess the value of the employee's services on an action for *quantum meruit* – literally suing for what the service was worth.

Since April 1999 the amount of pay an employee is entitled to receive is governed by the National Minimum Wage (NMW) Act 1998 and Regulations issued thereunder. The Act, by s.1 covers workers, which is wider than the traditional definition of employee in employment law. In *Redrow Homes (Yorkshire) Ltd* v. *Wright* (above) the Court of Appeal confirmed an earlier EAT decision that bricklayers were covered by the term 'worker' under Regulation 2(1)(b) in that they worked under a contract, they undertook to perform personally the work, and the other party to the contract was not a client or customer of a business undertaking carried on by the individual. The definition, however, does not cover pupil barristers (*Edmunds* v. *Lawson QC* [2000] IRLR 391). The power to issue regulations is found in s.2 and to extend the coverage of the legislation by regulations in s.41. Essentially the NMW applies to a worker's gross standard pay, which includes incentive payments based on output or performance, but certain benefits are excluded from the calculation such as: tips paid directly by the customer to the worker (but not tips distributed through the pay-roll); premium payments for shift and overtime working (but not standard pay for such working); and other benefits in kind such as company cars and private health insurance, although there are permitted offsets for certain benefits in kind. In *Leisure Employment Services* v. *HM Revenue and Customs* [2007] EWCA Civ 92 the employer provided accommodation for the employee. While the employee received a wage, £3 per week was deducted for the cost of gas and electricity, which took the wage received below the NMW. The Court of Appeal held that the employer could not count the £3 a week towards the NMW and the employer was in breach of the legislation. The definition of working time for the purposes of calculating the worker's hourly rate is based on the definition used in the EU Working Time Directive (93/104/EC), that is any period when a worker is working at the employer's disposal and carrying out his duties. The NMW is also payable when a worker is required to be at his place of work, even if no work is available. By Regulation 15 of the National Minimum Wage Regulations 1999, if workers sleep on the premises, the NMW applies when they are awake and required to be available for work. In *Wright* v. *Scottbridge Construction Ltd* [2001] IRLR 589 a night watchman was allowed to sleep during his hours of employment. His contract required him to be on site to respond to any alarm calls. It was argued that, on interpretation, his working time was only the time he was awake. The Employment Appeal Tribunal, however, said that Regulation 15 applies specifically to the situation where an employer allows an employee an allocated period of time for sleep. In the situation where the employee is required to be on site and is permitted to sleep at any time if he wishes, he is entitled to receive the NMW for the whole of the period he is required to be at the site (*Anderson* v. *Jarvis Hotels* (2006) UKEAT 0062/05).

The hourly rate is determined by calculating the average pay over the normal pay period, as agreed between the worker and employer, up to a maximum of one calendar month. Homeworkers and others paid by output must be paid no less than the NMW on average for the pay reference period. By the National Minimum Wage Regulations 1999 (Amendment) Regulations 2004, workers below the age of 18 who have ceased to be of compulsory school age qualified from October 2005. The rate is £3.40 per hour from October 2007. Workers aged 18–21 are paid less than the NMW but are entitled to a minimum 'development rate' of £4.60 per hour from October 2007. The NMW for other eligible workers is £5.52 per hour from October 2007.

The 2004 Regulations also ensure that home and piece-workers must be paid a rate linked to the NMW. From October 2004 an employer could no longer set the rate of pay at four-fifths of the time it takes an average worker to complete a set piece of work; and must pay home workers the minimum wage for all hours worked or 100 per cent of the NMW for the number of hours it takes an average worker to complete an agreed block of work. This increased to 120 per cent of the NMW from April 2005.

Enforcement of the NMW is through a variety of procedures. Workers have contractual rights (s.17 National Minimum Wage Act), plus enforcement via Part 11 of the Employment Rights Act 1996 (unlawful deductions from wages). In addition there is a national minimum wage statement as part of the itemised pay statement (s.12), and a right not to suffer a detriment or unfair dismissal as a result of enforcing the NMW (ss.23, 24 and 25). Employers are required to keep records (s.9) to which the worker has a right of access (ss.10 and 11). Officers have the power to issue enforcement and penalty notices and to take proceedings on behalf of workers (ss.19–22). There are also criminal sanctions for non-compliance (ss.31–33).

Itemised pay statement

If the pay is stated in the contract, then few disputes arise. By s.8 Employment Rights Act 1996 every employee who works eight hours a week or more has the right to an itemised pay statement at or before every payment of salary. It must state the gross and the net amount of pay, the amount of any variable or fixed deductions and the purposes for which those deductions are made. If different parts of the net payment are paid in different ways, the statement must give details of the amount and method of each part-payment. Where there are fixed deductions, for example union contributions, the employer need not give a statement each time a deduction is made, but may give a general statement covering those deductions for a period of 12 months. Such a general statement should include the amount of the deduction, the intervals at which it is paid and its purpose (s.9(5)). The statement should also include the NMW rate (see above). If the employer fails to give an itemised pay statement, or there is a dispute as to its contents, the employee may apply to an employment tribunal (s.11). The tribunal can declare the particulars which should have been in the statement (*Coales* v. *John Wood & Co* [1986] IRLR 129) and order the employer to make up any unnotified deductions from the employee's pay in the 13 weeks preceding the tribunal hearing.

Normal working hours/weekly pay

In addition to issues relating to the NMW, another problem which may arise is in relation to statutory compensation should the relationship come to an end. Statutory compensation is based on the concept of the employee's weekly pay and this may not be clear from the statement itself, particularly where the employee is paid hourly and the wage usually includes some provision for overtime. In *Tarmac Roadstone Holdings Ltd* v. *Peacock* [1973] 2 All ER 485 Lord Denning MR stated that for overtime to be part of the normal working hours of the employee it had to be obligatory on both sides. There are therefore three possible situations:

(a) overtime is voluntary on both sides;
(b) overtime is voluntary on the part of the employer but a contractual obligation on the part of the employee;

(c) overtime is obligatory on both sides, that is, the employer is under a contractual obligation to provide it and the employee is under a contractual obligation to work it.

In the third situation only is the overtime part of the employee's weekly pay. The judgement in *Tarmac Roadstone Holdings Ltd* is further endorsed by s.234 Employment Rights Act 1996. Subsections 1 and 2 provide that the normal working hours are the number of hours to be worked before overtime becomes payable. In *Fox* v. *C. Wright (Farmers) Ltd* [1978] ICR 98 an agricultural worker was employed under a contract which did not specify a minimum number of hours a week, but which stated that overtime would be paid for hours worked in excess of 40. He regularly worked 50–60 hours a week, but the Employment Appeal Tribunal held that his normal working hours were 40. There is an exception, however, in s.234(3) where the contract lays down a minimum number of obligatory hours which includes a number of hours payable as overtime. In this situation, the normal working hours are the obligatory hours even though they include overtime. For example, if the contract states that the working week is 40 hours but that overtime will be paid after 35 hours, the normal working hours are 40.

Apart from the provisions relating to overtime in s.234, ss.221–224 give three different methods of calculation of the normal working hours/weekly pay:

1. If there are normal working hours and the remuneration does not vary, the weekly pay is the normal payment under the contract when the normal hours are worked. Any further payments made on a regular basis, for example a bonus, will be added to the weekly pay (*Donelan* v. *Kerby Constructions Ltd* [1983] IRLR 191) (s.221).
2. If there are normal working hours but the remuneration varies with the amount of work, for example in the case of piece-workers, the weekly pay is the pay for the normal working hours payable at the average hourly rate. The average hourly rate is calculated by working out the total number of hours worked in the preceding 12 weeks, the total pay received and thus the average pay per hour (*May Gurney Ltd* v. *Adshead* [2006] All ER 388) (s.222).
3. If there are no normal working hours, the weekly pay is calculated by establishing the average weekly pay received by the employee over the preceding 12 weeks (s.224).

Ignoring the problems which can arise in relation to overtime and which have already been discussed, two further points should be noted. First, as the tribunal is calculating the weekly pay based on the average hourly rate, although the provisions specifically exclude non-contractually binding overtime this does not exclude commission or contractually binding bonus payments (*Amalgamated Asphalt Companies Ltd* v. *Dockrill* (1972) ITR 198 and *Weevsmay Ltd* v. *Kings* [1977] ICR 244). In *Horkulak* v. *Cantor Fitzgerald International* [2004] IRLR 942 the Court of Appeal stated that a discretionary bonus can be contractual if it is mentioned in the contract. In that case the employee's contract provided that 'the company may, in its discretion, pay you an annual discretionary bonus'. The Court of Appeal held that if the bonus was something the employer could pay on a whim it would not be in the contract. The bonus was clearly intended to be part of the salary structure and the discretion exercised in a rational and *bona fide* way. Section 229(2) further provides that if the bonus or commission is payable outside the 12-week calculation period, it should be apportioned for calculation purposes. In simple terms, therefore, if the employee is entitled to an annual bonus of £1,040 this is translated as £20 a week and is part of the calculation. Indirect benefits should also be taken into account, but non-cash benefits are not part of the calculation, nor are benefits from persons other than the employee's employer, for example tips. A service charge which the employer is contractually bound to distribute among his employees is, however, part of the weekly pay.

Second, the provisions require the tribunal to look at the preceding 12 weeks to calculate the normal working hours and hence the weekly pay. This means that the tribunal must look to weeks where the employee actually worked and thus base its calculation on the preceding 12 working weeks (*Secretary of State for Employment* v. *Crane* [1988] IRLR 238). The law only protects those who do not work, however. If in the preceding 12 weeks the amount of work has decreased, then those weeks will still be used for the calculation, even though they do not reflect the employee's normal wage.

Deductions from pay

The original Wages Act 1986 was brought in to remedy deficiencies in the Truck Acts 1831–1940. The provisions in relation to deduction from wages are now contained in the Employment Rights Act 1996. The provisions have far-reaching consequences for many contractual terms in that there must be a statutory or contractual right to deduct from wages before any such deductions can be made. This has implications should an employer wish to impose a disciplinary sanction such as suspension without pay, demotion or a deduction for bad workmanship. Since the case of *Robertson* v. *Blackstone Franks Investment Management Ltd* [1998] IRLR 376, it appears that the provisions protect not only employees but those who personally provide services, given the definition of worker in s.230(3) Employment Rights Act 1996.

By s.13(1) of the Act, an employer must not make a deduction from the wages of an employee unless the deduction is:

(a) required or authorised by statute (for example PAYE.); or
(b) required or authorised by a provision in the contract of employment which has been given to the employee or notified to the employee previously in writing; or
(c) agreed to by the employee in writing before the making of the deduction.

There is a corresponding duty on the employer in s.15 not to receive payment from the employee apart from in the circumstances above.

The wording of the contractual provision or agreement must be precise, however. In *Potter* v. *Hunt Contracts Ltd* [1992] IRLR 108 when the employee joined Hunt he had to repay the cost of an HGV course to his previous employer. Hunt agreed to give him a loan for this purpose which provided that if he left within 24 months 'you shall be required to return the fee, less any repayments made'. When Potter left the company within 24 months he received no wages, because the sum owed exceeded his pay. The Employment Appeal Tribunal held that the employer had no right to deduct, only to receive repayment. Furthermore, any agreement to deduct from wages must have been entered into before the happening of the event which caused the deduction, according to the significant decision of the Employment Appeal Tribunal in *Tobacco and Confectionery Ltd* v. *Williamson* [1993] ICR 371. In this case the employee was the manager of a store where in December 1988 and February 1989 large stock deficiencies were found. In March 1989 he signed a document giving his employers the right to deduct £3,500 from his wages at £20 per week. In May 1989 there was a further deficiency and the employee was dismissed, the employer withholding all of his wages in reliance on the March document. Section 13(6) of the Act states that any agreement by the worker to deduct shall not operate to authorise a deduction before the agreement was signed. The employers argued that this meant that the agreement had to predate the deduction. The Employment Appeal Tribunal disagreed. The agreement had to predate the event that had led to the deduction, that is, deductions made in respect of deficiencies prior to March 1989 were unlawful and the employer had no right to withhold the employee's wages in respect of those deficiencies.

Section 14 then contains a list of exceptions. The provisions of s.13(1) do not apply to deductions in respect of:

(a) overpayment of wages or expenses;
(b) disciplinary proceedings held by virtue of any statutory provision;

(c) a statutory requirement to deduct from wages to pay over to a public authority;

(d) payments agreed to by the employee which are to be made over by the employer to a third party;

(e) a strike or other industrial action in which the employee took part; or

(f)   the satisfaction of a court or tribunal order requiring the employee to pay something to the employer.

Again there is a corresponding provision in relation to the acceptance of such payments by the employer (s.16).

The list in s.14 does not give the employer the right to deduct such payments, it merely means that such deductions do not infringe s.13(1). Such deductions cannot be heard by the tribunal and an action lies in the County Court, because the deduction may still be illegal. For example, an overpayment of wages is within s.14 but in some cases the employer will have lost the right to claim the overpayment back. In *Avon County Council v. Howlett* [1983] IRLR 171 the employee was a teacher who had been regularly overpaid while off sick following an accident. The overpayment amounted to £1,007. The council sought to reclaim the money. The Court of Appeal held that where the money was accompanied by an express or an implied representation that the recipient was entitled to treat the money as his own, the employer is prevented from recovery. In the case, the employee, without any idea that the overpayment had been made, or that the council would seek recovery, had changed his position so that repayment would be inequitable. The overpayment was a result of a mistake of fact on the part of the council, in that it had failed to realise that Mr Howlett had been off sick for more than six months. The employee had spent the money, believing it to be his and the court intimated that the decision may have been different if the defendant still had the money in his possession.

The question of a deduction being made owing to a strike or other industrial action arose in the case of *Sunderland Polytechnic v. Evans* [1993] IRLR 196. The employer had deducted a full-day's pay from the employee after the employee had taken part in a half-day strike. The employee argued that there had been an illegal deduction of half-a-day's pay since she had not agreed to the deduction in advance. In other words, the employee was arguing that deduction of half-a-day's pay was within s.14 but not the deduction of the other half-day's pay. The Employment Appeal Tribunal held that whether the deduction was lawful or not was a question to be determined. If the reason for the deduction was industrial action, then it fell within s.14 whether the deduction was lawful or not and therefore the tribunal had no jurisdiction. A similar decision in relation to overpayment was reached in *SIP (Industrial Products) v. Swinn* [1994] ICR 473. It is for the tribunal to decide whether it has jurisdiction. In *Gill* v. *Ford Motor Company Ltd* and *Wong* v. *BAE Systems* [2004] IRLR 840 the EAT rejected the employers' contention that a tribunal had no jurisdiction to hear the claims. In *Gill*, production stopped because of unofficial industrial action which meant no-one could work, but Gill contended he was not taking part in the action. In *Wong*, BAE deducted from his wages because of an overpayment of a bonus. In both cases the EAT said the facts were unclear and remitted them back to the tribunal to decide the facts.

In addition to s.13 deductions, the Act in ss.17–22 gives further protection to workers in retail employment. Where a deduction is made in respect of cash shortages or stock deficiencies, the maximum which may be deducted is 10 per cent of the gross amount of wages for that particular day. However, the deductions can continue over successive pay days until the full amount is recovered, and the 10 per cent limit does not apply to the final pay-day if the employee's contract is terminated (s.22).

The provisions have been widely criticised. They deal with the mechanics of how an employer collects money from his employees rather than his entitlement to do so. Prior to changes in the law relating to employment tribunal jurisdiction, the provisions led to a variety of cases in its relatively short life on questions of interpretation. The major problem was whether the provisions applied to given situations. If there was an illegal deduction within s.13, the employee could complain to an employment tribunal, normally within three months of the deduction being made. Any other deduction made had to be recovered in the normal courts. Before the tribunals had jurisdiction in breach of contract cases, many problems arose concerning the definition of 'wages' and 'deduction'.

The starting point for a tribunal when it heard a claim was given by the Employment Appeal Tribunal in the cases of *Barlow* v. *A.J. Whittle* [1990] IRLR 79 and *Alsop* v. *Star Vehicle Contracts Ltd* [1990] IRLR 83. A tribunal had to ask itself three questions:

1. What is the wage due?
2. Is there an entitlement to a deduction or repayment?
3. Was that deduction properly made?

The above questions, however, meant that the tribunal had to first decide whether there had been a deduction, and whether that had been from the employee's wages.

Section 27 of the Act lists payments which can be regarded as wages. In particular s.27(1)(a) refers to 'any fee, bonus, commission, holiday pay, or any other emolument referable to his employment, whether payable under his contract or otherwise'. A number of cases since the Act was passed have discussed whether wages in lieu of notice are wages for the purpose of the legislation. In the House of Lords' decision in *Delaney* v. *Staples (trading as De Montfort Recruitment)* [1992] 1 AC 687 their Lordships decided (confirming the Court of Appeal decision) that payment in lieu was a substitution for damages for breach of contract. Such payment did not arise out of employment, but as a result of the termination of employment, and as such could not fall within s.27 even if the employer had a contractual right to give wages in lieu. While the decision is undoubtedly correct, it left the employee who had had deductions made from a final payment in lieu in the situation where he had to take action in the normal courts. If, however, there was also a deduction of, for example, holiday pay, the employee could sue for this deduction in the tribunal. This meant that many employees were taking two separate actions against their employer in two different forums, and this was hardly a satisfactory state of affairs. In *Delaney* the House of Lords ended with a plea that the jurisdiction of the tribunals be extended to hear breach of contract claims, a plea which has been answered to some extent, but given that the tribunals only have breach of contract jurisdiction when the contract has been terminated, the above discussion is still pertinent for those deductions made while the contract is still subsisting. In *Coors Brewers* v. *Adcock* [2007] EWCA Civ 19, 600 employees claimed that they had not been given the correct bonuses under an implied contractual promise to carry on with a bonus scheme operated by a previous employer. As they were still employed, the tribunal could not hear a breach of contract claim and thus heard the action under the unlawful deductions jurisdiction. The Court of Appeal held that such claims are claims for unliquidated damages as unlawful deductions jurisdiction only applied to claims for a specific sum of money or an identifiable sum (per Wall LJ). As there needed to be an investigation into the amount of the underpayment, the proper route was a breach of contract claim which had to be taken to the County Court and not the tribunal, as the employees were still employed.

The position as regards deductions from sums due and payable after the termination of the contract has been decided by the Court of Appeal in the *Robertson* case above.

Further problems have arisen in relation to whether a payment which is stated to be *ex gratia* can be wages for the purpose of the provisions. An immediate reaction would probably be a resounding 'no', but this may not always be the case as demonstrated in *Kent Management Services Ltd* v. *Butterfield* [1992] ICR 272. In this case the ex-employee complained that on his dismissal the employers had refused to pay him outstanding commission. The employers argued that commission and bonus schemes were discretionary and *ex gratia* because a document attached to his letter of appointment stated that such payments would not be made in exceptional circumstances such as bankruptcy. The employer therefore argued that as such payments were discretionary they could not be contractual. The Employment Appeal Tribunal looked at the definition of wages in s.27(1)(a). Wood P said that such schemes must be fairly common and that while they were in being the anticipation of both parties must be that in normal circumstances the commission etc would be paid. This was the situation here. No exceptional circumstances existed to prevent payment, therefore the expectation of both the parties must have been that the commission would be paid. As such it was wages and there had been an unlawful deduction. This decision has been confirmed by *Bannerman Co Ltd* v. *Mackenzie* (1995) IDS Brief 552.

In relation to deductions the law is somewhat unclear. The Employment Appeal Tribunal has held that in cases where there is a non-payment (for example, where the employer has paid none of the money due because he feels that the employee owes him that money) this is not a deduction. The Court of Appeal, however, in the *Delaney* case held that non-payment was a 100 per cent deduction, and as such the tribunal had the jurisdiction to hear the complaint. The House of Lords did not hear this point on appeal and it therefore appears that this is still the law.

Payment during sickness

There is no presumption that an employee will be paid by his employer while he is sick. While an employee may be entitled to statutory sick pay, this will only give the statutory level of payment and will often be considerably less than the employee's wage. It is therefore important to see if there is a term in the contract providing for payment during sickness. Such a term may be express or implied, but before a court will imply a term that the employee will be paid during sickness, there must be evidence that the parties intended this to be the case. In the leading case of *Mears* v. *Safecar Security Ltd* [1982] IRLR 183 the employee was ill for six months. During that time he did not ask for payment, he did not send in medical certificates and when he asked his colleagues about sick pay, they told him it was not available and had never been paid in the past. The Court of Appeal held that as there was no express term on sick pay, it was necessary to see if there was an implied term. To see if there was such a term the court had to look at the conduct of the parties. Given that the employer had never paid sick pay in the past and given that the conduct of the employee indicated that he did not expect to receive sick pay, no term was implied.

The statutory sick pay scheme was introduced by the Social Security and Housing Benefits Act 1982. The aim of the scheme is to pass the administration of the old sickness benefit on to the employer. The employer pays the employee his statutory sick pay (SSP) and, until recently, then recouped those payments through his National Insurance Contributions. By the Statutory Sick Pay Act 1994, as amended, only those employers who pay less than £40,000 in National Insurance Contributions can now recoup such payments. In outline, the scheme provides that a qualifying employee is entitled to SSP for the first 28 weeks of sickness and after that period he will receive state sickness benefit. Certain employees are excluded from the scheme. These include pensioners, persons who do not pay National Insurance Contributions and employees who are not employed because of a trade dispute at their place of work, unless they have no direct interest in its outcome.

To claim, the employee must be suffering from some disease or physical or mental disability rendering him incapable of performing any work he could reasonably be expected to do under his contract of employment. In addition the employee must satisfy the following three conditions:

1. There must be a period of incapacity for work which is a period of four or more consecutive days of incapacity which may include Sundays and holidays. Two periods of incapacity are treated as one if they are not separated by more than two weeks.
2. The period of incapacity must fall within a period of entitlement, which commences with the start of the period of incapacity for work and ends with the occurrence of the first of the following:
   (a) the day the employee returns to work;
   (b) after 28 weeks during a three-year period;
   (c) the termination of the contract;
   (d) when a pregnant employee reaches the beginning of the eleventh week before the expected week of confinement;
   (e) the day the employee is detained in custody or leaves the EC.
3. SSP is only payable in respect of qualifying days. These are normally agreed with the employer and include all working days. The first three qualifying days are waiting days, SSP being payable on the fourth day.

The amount payable is a daily rate but depends on weekly earnings. The general rule is to take the last pay-day before the period of sickness and average the weekly earnings over a period of the preceding eight weeks. To claim entitlement the employee must inform the employer that he is unfit for work. The employer can fix a time limit in which he must be notified, but in the absence of a time limit the employee must inform the employer within seven days. The employer can specify the mode of notification. Disputes as to SSP are decided at first instance by an adjudication officer, with an appeal to the Social Security Appeal Tribunal and a final appeal to a Social Security Commissioner.

Pay during lay-offs or short-time working

The general rule at common law is that the employer must pay the wages of staff who are available for work even if no work is provided by the employer. There is no common law right of lay-off. If there is an interruption in the provision of work, the employee is still entitled to payment (*Devonald* v. *Rosser & Sons*, above). It appears, however, that if the failure to provide work is totally outside the control of the employer, the courts will imply a term that the employees are not entitled to be paid. In *Browning* v. *Crumlin Valley Collieries* [1926] 1 KB 522 a colliery had to close down when a serious land fault made the mine dangerous. It was held that the failure to provide work was totally outside the employer's control and, as such, the implied term that the employees were entitled to payment would not apply. Thus the situation at common law is that there is an implied duty that the employer will pay wages unless the failure to provide work is outside his control. It should be noted that if the employer finds it inconvenient to provide the work, not impossible, the common law term will apply.

Given that the above term is implied into the contract by the common law, it follows that such a term can be ousted by an express term to the contrary. In *Hulme* v. *Ferranti Ltd* [1918] 2 KB 426 an employee was employed on terms that if there was no work he would not be paid. He was laid off as the result of a strike at his place of work and it was held that he was not entitled to payment during the period of the lay-off. The law, however, will restrict the employer's exercise of such a contractual right and it appears from the more modern case of *Dakri (A.) & Co Ltd* v. *Tiffen* [1981] IRLR 57 that the right can only be exercised for a reasonable length of time. After such a time has elapsed, the employee is entitled to treat the non-payment by his employer as a repudiatory breach and may, if he has the continuity, sue for a constructive dismissal.

Although the common law position is still important in this area, it has to some extent been superseded by the right to a guaranteed payment given by ss.28–35 Employment Rights Act 1996 discussed in Chapter 7.

Duty to indemnify

There is some legal argument as to whether the common law implies a duty that the employer should indemnify his employee against expenses incurred during the performance of his contract. While the majority of contracts will expressly cover the situation of travelling and accommodation expenses, the problem arises when the expense has not been envisaged by the contract, for example, if a lorry driver is fined for overloading or a defective tyre. Selwyn argues that there is an implied duty to indemnify, but that the duty does not apply where the employee has the choice of performing the job in a lawful or unlawful way, and by choosing the unlawful way he incurs an expense such as a fine. Selwyn gives two cases as authority for his proposition that such a duty exists. The first, *Gregory* v. *Ford* [1951] 1 All ER 121, was a case where an employee injured a third party owing to his negligent driving. His employer did not have third party insurance as required by legislation. As a result, the employee was sued personally, and it was held that there was an implied term in the contract of employment that the employer would not require the employee to do an illegal act which in this case had been broken. The damages resulting from the employer's breach were the damages the employee had to pay to the plaintiff. The second case cited by Selwyn is *Re Famatina Development Corporation* [1914] 2 Ch 271. In this case a consulting engineer was asked to prepare a report on the conduct of the managing director and as a result the managing director brought an action for libel against the engineer. It was held that the engineer was entitled to be indemnified against the cost of defending the action. Of the two cases, *Re Famatina* is more directly related to the question of indemnity, however Hepple argues that in that case the position of the engineer was more akin to that of an agent, and there has always been a principle in the law of agency that an agent should be indemnified for expenses incurred during the performance of his agency. It is difficult to come to any firm conclusion. Taking the *Ford* case, it would appear that if the employee incurs expense by doing an unlawful act at the instruction of his employer, he is entitled to be reimbursed, but on the basis of an implied term that the employer will not ask the employee to commit an unlawful act. Apart from this situation, it appears that if the employee is in the position of an agent, he is entitled to be indemnified, but because of the agency relationship and not because of an employment relationship. The position does not appear to be as clear-cut as it may at first seem.

Duty in relation to references

While employers are under no duty to provide references (unless there is a contractual obligation to do so) in practice most employers do. The recent case of *Spring* v. *Guardian Assurance Co* [1994] 3 All ER 129 has imposed duties upon employers who provide references for their employees. In the case, Spring had worked for Guardian Assurance and left to sell policies for another insurance company. As required by LAUTRO, Guardian Assurance provided a reference for Spring, which doubted, among other things, his honesty and his selling tactics. The reference was described by the House of Lords as 'the kiss of death' to his future career. Although the writer of the reference honestly believed what he had written, he had been negligent in ascertaining the facts.

The majority of the House of Lords held that the writer of a reference owed a duty to the subject of that reference to exercise reasonable care. They applied the test in *Caparo Industries* v. *Dickman* [1990] 1 All ER 568 for establishing a duty of care: that the damage is foreseeable, there was a sufficient closeness of proximity between the parties and that it was fair and reasonable to impose such a duty. The argument that the imposition of such a duty would deter employers from writing references was not considered to be a serious enough risk to prevent the duty being imposed. While it was not established whether Spring worked under a contract of employment or a contract for services, the Court felt that this was irrelevant and the duty would apply in both situations. Furthermore, although the duty was imposed in tort, it was held that the duty could also be implied into some contracts.

Since *Spring* there have been a number of cases refining the duty. In *Bartholomew* v. *London Borough of Hackney* [1999] IRLR 246 the Court of Appeal held that a reference must be true, accurate and fair, not giving a misleading impression, although there is no duty that the reference must be full and comprehensive. This was expanded in *Kidd* v. *Axa Equity and Law Life Assurance Society* [2000] IRLR 301 when the High Court stated that the duty owed by a referee is 'not to give misleading information . . . whether as a result of the unfairly selective provision of information, or by the inclusion of facts or opinions in such a manner as to give rise to a false or mistaken inference in the mind of a reasonable recipient'. The import of this is seen in *TSB Bank* v. *Harris* [2000] IRLR 157. In this case the bank provided a reference containing mere factual information. This included the fact that a number of complaints had been made against the employee, some of which were upheld and some of which were outstanding. The reference made no assessment of the employee's ability. In accordance with the practice of the bank, the employee was unaware of the complaints against her. The employee did not get the other job and when she discovered the content of the reference she resigned and claimed constructive dismissal. The Employment Appeal Tribunal held that the bank was in breach of the duty of mutual respect (see below) by revealing complaints of which the employee was unaware in a reference to a prospective employer. Although the contents of the reference were accurate, the reference could not be said to be reasonable and fair (*Bartholomew*). There was a further breach of the duty since the employee had not been given the opportunity to answer the complaints. It has also been held in *Coote* v. *Granada Hospitality (No. 2)* [1999] IRLR 452 that refusal to provide a reference after the termination of the relationship, because the ex-employee had brought a discrimination case against her employers, was victimisation under the Sex Discrimination Act 1975 (see Chapter 5).

Duty of mutual respect/trust and confidence

At the beginning of the Industrial Revolution, the employment relationship was seen as a relationship of servitude and this was reflected in the names the law chose for the parties in the relationship. For many years the law thought of an employment relationship as being between a master and his servant rather than between an employer and an employee. In fact the law itself reflected the servile nature of the relationship in the judgements made some hundred years ago. In *Turner* v. *Mason* (1845) M & W 112, for example, it was held that an employer was entitled to sack a domestic servant who in breach of her contractual provision requiring her to be on duty 24 hours a day, took a day off to visit her dying mother. Fortunately, the law has moved forward somewhat since that decision, to the extent that the law now imposes a duty on the employer to treat the employee with respect. It is often referred to as the duty of mutual respect, but the word 'mutual' merely demonstrates that the duty now applies to both parties and not merely to the employee, as was almost certainly the case 30 years ago. While reflecting the change in attitude of the courts, the duty has really arisen in the context of unfair dismissal, where the employee will argue that the employer's treatment of him has destroyed the trust and confidence the parties need to maintain the relationship and as such the employee argues that there has been a constructive dismissal.

The idea that the relationship is one that can only be maintained if there is trust and confidence is not new. As long ago as 1888, in the case of *Boston Deep Sea Fishing and Ice Co* v. *Ansell* (1888) 39 Ch 339 the court talked of a breach of the confidential relationship between an employer and employee and continued to find that should an employee commit an act which destroyed that relationship, such a breach was repudiatory, entitling the employer to dismiss. It was not until the 1970s, however, that the law considered that such a breach could be on the part of the employer. The first time this was considered by a court was in the case of *Donovan* v. *Invicta Airways* [1970] 1 Lloyds Rep 486 when the Court of Appeal considered whether consistent complaints about the employee by the employer constituted a repudiatory breach, entitling the employee to resign and claim constructive dismissal. On the facts it was held that there was no breach by the employer, not because the duty did not exist, but rather because on the particular facts it had not been broken. Cases since *Donovan* have found a breach on the part of the employer and the duty was accepted as an implied term in the contract by the Court of Appeal in the case of *Woods* v. *W.M. Car Services* [1982] IRLR 413. Conduct such as telling an experienced employee before his subordinates that he is incapable of doing the job has been found to be a breach (*Courtaulds Northern Textiles Ltd* v. *Andrew* [1979] IRLR 84), as has describing a senior officer as wholly unsuitable for promotion without any evidence to support that finding (*Post Office* v. *Roberts* [1980] IRLR 515). Perhaps the leading case in this area is *Bliss* v. *South East Thames Regional Health Authority* [1987] ICR 700 where the Court of Appeal held that refusing to allow a doctor to return to work after he had been suspended, because he refused to submit to a psychiatric examination, was a repudiatory breach by the employer. There was no evidence of mental instability on the part of the doctor and thus no evidence that such an examination was necessary.

The fact that this is an ever-expanding duty has been demonstrated by a number of cases. In *W.A. Goold (Pearmak) Ltd* v. *McConnell* [1995] IRLR 516 it was held that failure to provide a grievance procedure, given that there is a statutory duty to do so by s.3 Employment Rights Act 1996, was a breach of the duty of mutual respect entitling the employees to resign and claim constructive dismissal. In *Malik* v. *BCCI* [1997] IRLR 462 an employer's fraudulent conduct was held to be a breach of the duty and as such the ex-employee was entitled to claim damages for his difficulty in finding alternative work because of the loss of reputation he suffered when it was known that he had been employed by the bank. *TSB Bank* v. *Harris* (above) decided that a failure to allow an employee to answer complaints made against him/her and listing those complaints in a reference, without any judgement as to the ability of the employee, is also a breach. Furthermore, in *Morrow* v. *Safeway Stores* [2002] IRLR 9 the Employment Appeal Tribunal held that any breach of the duty is repudiatory and thus a constructive dismissal. In *University of Nottingham* v. *(1) Eyett and (2) Pensions Ombudsman* [1999] IRLR 87 on the other hand, it was held that the duty of mutual respect does not, however, extend to a positive obligation on the part of the employer to warn an employee that he is not exercising his rights, in connection with the contract of employment (in the case the date at which to take early retirement) in the most advantageous way. However, in the later case of *BC plc* v. *O'Brien* [2001] IRLR 496 the Employment Appeal Tribunal upheld the decision of an employment tribunal that the singling out of an employee by not offering him a revised contract of employment, providing for enhanced redundancy payments, was a breach of the duty. Mr Recorder Langstaff QC said:

> 'it is difficult, if not impossible, to draw any satisfactory distinction between an obligation positively expressed: a requirement not to take a certain course of action may be, in effect, a requirement to permit another.'

Nevertheless, the tribunal emphasised that there is no implied duty that an employer will act reasonably towards his employees. In *London Borough of Waltham Forest* v. *Omilaju* [2004] EWCA Civ 1493 the Court of Appeal talked about the 'last straw' where a final act by an employer, after a series of other acts, causes the employee to resign and claim constructive dismissal on a breach of the duty of mutual trust and confidence. The court stated that the act which constituted the last straw did not have to be unreasonable or blameworthy, but a blameless act by an employer could not constitute a last straw. Thus the refusal of an employer to pay for attendance at a tribunal could not be the last straw as the employer was not contractually bound to pay him.

Duty to ensure the employees' safety

Extent of the duty

While the provisions in the 1996 Act protect an employee health and safety representative from unfair dismissal while pursuing his duties (see Chapter 9) the ordinary employee's safety is protected in two ways. First, he is protected by the common law of negligence. This derives from the case of *Donoghue v. Stevenson* [1932] AC 562 and requires that an employer take reasonable care to protect his employees who are reasonably foreseeable victims should the duty of care be broken. This duty is translated into an implied term in the contract of employment and if broken can be seen as a repudiatory breach of contract. In *British Aircraft Corporation v. Austin* [1978] IRLR 332 the employer did not investigate a complaint about the suitability of protective glasses. It was held that the conduct was a repudiatory breach of contract which entitled the employee to resign and claim constructive dismissal.

In addition to the common law implied term, statute protects employees in the form of the Health and Safety at Work Act 1974. Both statute and common law run side by side but their aims are different. The common law exists to provide the employee with compensation once he is injured. The Act exists to prevent the injury happening in the first place and creates criminal, not civil, liability. As such, the two systems complement each other and interrelate so that often an employee will allege both a breach of contract and a breach of statute. In *Smith v. Vange Scaffolding & Engineering Co Ltd and Another* [1970] 1 WLR 733 the employee was injured when he fell over a cable when walking back to work. It was held that the employers were in breach of their common law duty in failing to provide safe premises and, in addition, they were in breach of their statutory duty imposed by the Construction (Working Places) Regulations 1966 by failing to provide safe access and egress to and from the employee's place of work. In some situations the employer may have complied with his statutory duties, but still failed to come up to the standard of a reasonable employer. In *Bux v. Slough Metals* [1973] 1 WLR 1358 the employer complied with his statutory obligation to provide goggles, however the employee did not wear them because they misted up. The Court of Appeal held that while the employer had not broken his statutory duties he was negligent at common law for failing to insist that the goggles were worn. As a result of this negligence, the employee lost the sight of his eye when he was splashed with molten metal and thus the employer was liable.

Although only the common law duty is implied into the contract of employment, given the interrelationship of the common law and statute, it is proposed to discuss both aspects below.

The common law

The common law standard is a negligence standard, in other words the employer must do all he can to prevent foreseeable injury. The important word is 'foreseeable' however, in that an employer will not necessarily be liable for every injury that his employees incur. For example, it may be that the state of knowledge in an area is such that it is not known that a certain process can cause injury until that injury occurs. Such an injury will not be foreseeable and the employer will not be liable. In addition the law requires the employer to act reasonably in all the circumstances. In *Latimer* v. *AEC* [1953] AC 643 a factory was flooded by a heavy rainstorm. The employer asked his employees to return to work, warning them that the factory floor was dangerous in places. The employer had put sawdust on the floor, but could not get enough to do the whole factory and some areas of floor were uncovered. The employee was injured when he slipped on an uncovered area of floor. It was held that the employer had done all that was reasonable. The only other alternative would have been to close down the factory until the floor had dried out and it was unreasonable to expect the employer to do this. The employer is also entitled to assume the employee has a modicum of common sense. In *O'Reilly* v. *National Rail* [1966] 1 All ER 499 a group of workers found an unexploded bomb in a scrap-yard where they worked. They challenged Mr O'Reilly to hit it with a hammer. He did so, with the inevitable result. It was held that the employer was not liable for failing to tell his employees not to go around hitting unexploded bombs – he was entitled to assume that the employees would know the inherent dangers in such a practice! Likewise in *Vinnyey* v. *Star Paper Mills* [1965] 1 All ER 175 an employee was injured when he slipped while mopping a floor. It was held that the employer was entitled to assume that the employee knew how to mop a floor properly. The employer, however, owes his duty to each individual employee and not his employees as a whole. If he therefore knows that an employee is particularly susceptible to risk, he must take added precautions. In *Paris* v. *Stepney Borough Council* [1951] AC 367 the employee had one eye. He lost the sight of his only eye while chipping off rust from underneath a bus. Despite the fact that it was not normal to provide the employees with goggles, the court held that a reasonable employer would have provided this employee with goggles, given that any injury would leave him totally blind. The employer was therefore liable.

Given that the employer should only act to prevent foreseeable injury, it follows that if knowledge in the area has not advanced sufficiently to identify the injuries which can be caused, the employer cannot be liable. In *Down* v. *Dudley Coles Long* (1969) (unreported) the employee suffered partial deafness from using a hammer-assisted drill. The employer did not provide ear-defenders because, at the time, medical knowledge was such that it was not known that such drills could cause deafness. It was held that the employer was not liable. On the other hand, once the knowledge becomes available, the employer will not be acting reasonably if he does not act quickly. In *Wright and Cassidy* v. *Dunlop Rubber Co and ICI* (1972) 13 KIR 255 the employers had been informed by the manufacturers that certain chemicals they were using could cause cancer. The manufacturers advised that all employees involved with the chemical should be screened. The employers did not institute screening for some time. It was held that the employers had not acted reasonably. Once the injury was foreseeable, the employers should have taken immediate steps to protect their employees. Likewise in *Baxter* v. *Harland & Wolff plc* [1990] IRLR 516 the employee had been subjected to high levels of noise since 1937 which had resulted in appreciable hearing loss. In 1963 the Ministry of Labour published guidelines regarding levels of noise at work. The defendants took no precautions. The Court of Appeal held that the defendants were liable because there was sufficient medical and scientific information, post-1963, which the defendants had failed to address to see what precautions they should have taken. This was taken a step further in *Bowman* v. *Harland & Wolff plc* [1992] IRLR 349 where employees alleged that the employers were negligent in failing to recognise that they risked contracting vibration white finger from working with pneumatic drills and failing to take precautions. The Northern Ireland High Court held that by January 1973 a reasonable employer in the defendant's position would have appreciated the problem and instituted preventative action. Hence the employer was liable for damage sustained from that date.

The cases above raise two important issues. How far can the employer balance the cost of protecting his employees against the likelihood of injury occurring and its potential seriousness and how far should the employer keep up to date with knowledge in the area? These questions were considered by Swanwick J in the case of *Stokes* v. *Guest, Keen & Nettlefold (Bolts & Nuts) Ltd* [1968] 1 WLR 1776. He listed five factors which should be taken into account when looking at this area:

1. The employer should take steps to ensure his employee's safety in the light of the knowledge he has or ought to have.
2. The employer can follow recognised practice unless this is clearly unsound.
3. Where there is developing knowledge, the employer must keep up to date and apply it.
4. If the employer has greater-than-average knowledge of the risk he must take greater-than-average precautions.
5. The employer must weigh up the risk (in terms of the likelihood of the injury occurring and its potential seriousness) against the cost of taking precautions and the effectiveness of those precautions.

Perhaps the most ambiguous point is the last one. This enables the employer to balance the cost of precautions against the likelihood and seriousness of injury. It can be demonstrated by comparing *Latimer* (above) with the case of *Bath* v. *British Transport Commission* [1954] 2 All ER 542. In *Bath*, an employee was killed when he fell from the top of a high narrow dock. The employer provided no protection whatsoever for his employees. It was argued that the cost of taking precautions was prohibitive. The court, however, decided that, given injury was likely to occur and could be foreseen as very serious when it did happen, the employer was under a duty to protect his employees whatever the cost. In *Latimer*, by contrast, injury was not likely to happen, but if it should it was unlikely to be serious. Thus the employer was entitled not to incur the considerable cost of closing down the factory. The key points, therefore, are how likely it is that injury will occur and how serious it will be if it happens.

While the implied term is a general term to ensure the employee's safety, the House of Lords in *Wilsons and Clyde Coal Co* v. *English* [1938] AC 57 identified three specific aspects of the duty – competent staff, adequate plant and equipment, and safe system of work. To this list we can add a fourth – the provision of a safe place of work.

1. *Safe place of work*   It has been seen from *Latimer* (above) that the courts will take a variety of factors into account when looking to assess whether the employer has acted reasonably in the circumstances. When looking specifically at the maintenance of safe premises, the court will investigate whether the employer has an adequate reporting system, how he reacts when complaints are reported and whether he has effectively maintained his premises. Part of the employer's grievance procedure, therefore, should provide for complaints about the place of work, and the employer should investigate those complaints if and when they arise. In *Franklin* v. *Edmonton Corporation* (1966) 109 SJ 876 the employer stated that complaints had to be

in writing, but later accepted verbal complaints. An employee verbally complained that the brakes on his lorry were defective but the employer did nothing. Eventually the employee had an accident due to the defective brakes. It was held that the employer was liable for failing to act on the complaint when received. (The damages were reduced by two-thirds because of the employee's contributory negligence in that he did not put the complaint in writing and he continued to drive the lorry knowing the brakes were defective.) In addition to an effective reporting system, the court will look at the employer's maintenance system. In *Braham* v. *Lyons & Co Ltd* [1962] 3 All ER 281 an employee dropped a food substance on the floor. The floor supervisor immediately sent a maintenance man to clean it up, but before he reached the place another employee had slipped on the spilt substance and was injured. It was held that the employer was not liable; he had done all he reasonably could to protect his employees. More recently in *Lowles* v. *Home Office* [2004] EWCA Civ 985 a prison worker, while deep in conversation, tripped on a step while entering work and was injured. There was a sign saying 'Please Mind the Step' and she had used the entrance before. The Court of Appeal held the employers 50 per cent liable for the injury because it had failed to ensure the doorway was 'suitable for the purpose for which it was used'.

One aspect of ensuring a safe place of work which has come to the fore recently is that of smoking and the effects of passive smoking on employees. While *Dryden* v. *Greater Glasgow Health Board* [1992] IRLR 469 decided that there was no implied term in an employment contract that a worker has a right to smoke at work and *Waltons and Morse* v. *Dorrington* [1997] IRLR 488 established that employees have a right not to work in a smoky environment, no court or tribunal has stated that employees are entitled to a smoke-free working environment. The law does not appear to have grasped the nettle in respect of whether smoking at work is a health and safety issue. It was not raised in *Dorrington* since there was no evidence that the employee had suffered an injury to her health. The amount of evidence in respect of passive smoking does suggest, however, that it is a health and safety issue and that an employer who failed to protect his employees would be in breach of his common law safety duties and be in breach of s.2(2)(e) Health and Safety at Work Act 1974 discussed below. This issue has now been resolved by the introduction of the ban on smoking in public places in July 2007.

Given that the employer must provide a safe place of work for his employees, the question which now must be asked is how far that duty extends to ensuring that other premises where his employees may work are safe. Many employees work in other places, either in people's homes (for example, plumbers, electricians and so on), or they may go onto other employers' premises to service machinery and so on. It appears that while the employer's duty does extend to other premises where his employee may work, for obvious reasons the duty is reduced. What is important, however, is that the employer cannot leave it up to the employee to protect himself just because he is working on premises over which the employer has no control. In *General Cleaning Contractors* v. *Christmas* [1953] AC 180 the employer operated a window-cleaning company. He provided safety belts for his employees, but on one particular building there were no safety hooks on which to attach the belts. The employee was injured when working on that building and a defective window sash fell on his fingers, causing him to lose his grip. It was held that the employer was liable. He could not abdicate his responsibility to the employee on the spot to devise a safe way of doing the job. It was the responsibility of the employer, once he knew of the problem, to devise a way of making the job safe. This case was confirmed in the Court of Appeal in *King* v. *Smith and Another* (1994) The Times, 3 November.

Obviously, in these situations the employer will often only know of the problem once it has been brought to his attention, and therefore again the court will look closely at his system of reporting safety hazards and how he reacts to such complaints. In *Smith* v. *Austin Lifts Ltd* [1959] 1 All ER 81 the employee maintained lifts supplied by his employer to other premises. One day he reported to his employer that the doors on the machine house at particular premises were dangerous and his employer reported this to the occupier. On the employee's next visit, the doors had not been repaired, so he tied them together to prevent the doors from being used and again reported to his employer, who again told the occupier. On his third visit, the rope had been taken off the doors and they had jammed. The employee was injured when he fell off a ladder while trying to unjam the doors. Four out of five judges in the House of Lords held that his employer was liable for failing to check the premises to see if the hazard had been removed before sending his employee back there.

2. *Safe plant and equipment*   All machinery, tools and equipment used by the employee should be reasonably safe for use. In *Bradford* v. *Robinson Rentals Ltd* [1967] 1 All ER 267 a driver was required to drive on a long journey, in very cold weather, in a van which the employer knew had a broken heater. As a result the driver suffered frostbite. It was held that the employer was liable for his injury. In *Sherlock* v. *Chester City Council* [2004] EWCA Civ 201 a joiner severed his thumb and finger using a bench saw. The wood had been bending and rather than ask for help or move to another bench, the employee continued sawing with the injury being the result. It was held that the employer was liable for 40 per cent of the damages because the joiner

had not been trained in the use of the bench saw nor in carrying out a risk assessment. It was irrelevant that the employee was experienced and the employer could not rely on experienced and skilled workers to discharge the employer's duty.

In the past, if plant or equipment had a hidden defect which was totally unknown to the employer, and he had purchased from a reputable supplier, then the employer had acted reasonably and was not liable for any subsequent injury to the employee (*Davie* v. *New Merton Board Mills* [1959] AC 604). Once the defect had become apparent, however, the employer was liable if he failed to take immediate action. In *Taylor* v. *Rover Car Co* [1966] 2 All ER 181 the employer had purchased a batch of chisels. He was unaware that they were badly hardened until one shattered, without causing injury. The employer did not withdraw the chisels from use and a second one shattered, injuring an employee. It was held that the employer was liable. If injury had occurred when the first chisel shattered, there would have been no liability because, until then, the employer was unaware of any defect. Once a problem had occurred, a reasonable employer would have realised that potentially all the chisels were affected and withdrawn them from use.

The problem with the proposition that the employer was only liable if he knew of the defect is that it left the injured employee with no contractual action. He could, of course, sue the manufacturer of the tools or equipment in negligence, but this is frequently difficult to establish and therefore many injured employees are left with no compensation. As a consequence the Employer's Liability (Defective Equipment) Act 1969 was passed. In essence, this provides that if an employee is injured during the course of his employment as a result of a defect in equipment provided by his employer, and the defect is attributable to the negligence of a third party, then the injury will be deemed to be due to the negligence of the employer. In addition, at the same time the Employer's Liability (Compulsory Insurance) Act 1969 was passed requiring all employers to take out insurance to cover personal injury claims from their employees. Although this may seem hard on the employer who is not to blame for the employee's injury, he (or his insurance company) can, of course, sue the manufacturer of the defective equipment and so recover the compensation he has paid to his employee.

3. *Safe system of work* This essentially means that the employer should provide safe working methods. The court will look at a variety of factors including layout of the workplace, training and supervision, warnings and the provision of safety equipment. The court is basically looking at how the employer conducts his business and whether he does all he can to protect his employees. In *Goodchild* v. *Organon Laboratories Ltd* [2004] EWHC 2341

QB a sales representative, who had been told by her doctor not to lift heavy weights following an operation, had been lifting heavy boxes with a colleague. The colleague left for a short time and she lifted a heavy box on her own, causing back injury. The employer was held 90 per cent liable on the basis that the Manual Handling Operations Regulations 1992 state that an employer must avoid the need for employees to undertake manual handling which could cause injury.

Given that the benchmark is reasonableness on the part of the employer, two fairly obvious points should be noted. First, a reasonable employer tells his employees where the safety equipment is kept. This may seem like a blindingly obvious proposition but there have been cases where this has not happened. In *Finch* v. *Telegraph Construction & Maintenance Co Ltd* [1949] 1 All ER 452 the employee was a grinder and was injured when a piece of flying metal struck him in the eye. The employer provided goggles but had not told the employees where they were kept. It was held that the employer was liable for the employee's injury. Second, to some extent the employer can assume that the employee has some common sense and therefore does not have to warn him against clearly obvious dangers. It has already been seen in *O'Reilly* that an employer was not liable when his employee hit an unexploded bomb with a hammer! In *Lazarus* v. *Firestone Tyre and Rubber Co Ltd* (1963) The Times, 2 May an employee was injured when he was knocked down in the rush to get to the canteen. The employer was not liable for failing to tell him of the potential risk in trying to get lunch!

While the common law places a duty on the employer, the employee too has some responsibility for his own safety. In *Smith* v. *Scott Bowyers Ltd* [1986] IRLR 315 the employee was injured when he slipped on a greasy floor. The employer knew the risk and provided the employees with wellingtons which had ridged soles. Smith had been provided with such a pair of wellingtons, but they had worn smooth on the soles and had become dangerous. The employer renewed the wellingtons on request, but Smith had not asked for a replacement pair. It was held that the employer was not liable. He was not under a duty to inspect the wellingtons every day to see if they needed replacing and was entitled to assume that his employees would take some responsibility for their own safety.

The situations listed above are, however, extreme cases. Most situations fall between the two extremes of total non-protection and assuming that the employee has a modicum of common sense. The majority of cases, therefore, raise the issue of how far must the employer go to protect his employees. Ignoring the issue of balancing cost and likelihood of injury, does the employer fulfil his common law duty by merely providing the equipment and telling his employees where it is, or does he need to go further and insist that it is used?

The answer to this depends on the obviousness of the risk to the employee and the likely seriousness of the injury. If the risk of the injury is obvious to the employee and not likely to be serious if it occurs, then the employer will have fulfilled his duty by providing the equipment and telling the employee where it can be found, leaving the employee to use it if he wishes. In *Qualcast (Wolverhampton) Ltd* v. *Haynes* [1959] AC 743 the employee was injured when he was splashed on the legs with molten metal. The employer provided protective spats but the employee chose not to wear them. It was held that the employer was not liable. The risk of injury was obvious to the employee (who was an experienced workman) and the injury was not serious. On the other hand, if the risk is not obvious, or the injury would be serious, the employer should insist that safety precautions are taken and supervise the employees to ensure that they are following orders. In *Berry* v. *Stone Maganese Marine Ltd* (1971) 12 KIR 13 the employee was working in high noise levels. The employer provided ear-defenders but did nothing to ensure their use. The employee suffered a loss of hearing due to working without the defenders. The employer was held liable. The seriousness of the potential injury and the risk of it occurring would not be obvious to the employee. The employer should have alerted the employee to the dangers of what he was doing and insisted that ear-defenders be worn.

The law is realistic, however. There will be a stage where the employer has done all that can be done bar physically putting the safety equipment on employees and watching them every moment of the working day. If an employee will not wear the equipment, despite the entreaties of the employer, and is subsequently injured, the employer will have done all a reasonable employer would have done and will not be liable. The ultimate sanction the employer can impose will be dismissal. Although he does not have to use this sanction to protect the employee, dangerous practices by one employee can lead to others being injured and the employer may find himself in breach of the duty to provide competent employees. Many employers now make failure to comply with safety rules a disciplinary offence so that they can employ the sanction of dismissal should everything else prove ineffective.

The importance and scope of this aspect of the employer's duty can be seen in two cases. In *Johnstone* v. *Bloomsbury Area Health Authority* [1991] ICR 269 the number of hours that the employee was required to work was held to be a breach of the employer's duty. Browne Wilkinson LJ argued that the employer should interpret the express terms of the contract reasonably. Stuart-Smith LJ went further and stated that the express term relating to hours was subject to the implied duty of the employer to take reasonable care to ensure the health and safety of employees. In *Walker* v. *Northumberland County Council* [1995] IRLR 35 an employee who had suffered a nervous breakdown due to the pressure of work, returned and was given the same level and amount of work with little support being put in place by the employer. In the end the employee suffered another nervous breakdown and had to retire on the grounds of ill health. It was held that the employer was in breach of the safety duty he owed to his employee. Given the first nervous breakdown, it was reasonably foreseeable that without extra staff the plaintiff's health would suffer and there was no reason why the employer should not be liable for psychiatric damage to the employee as well as physical damage. This was followed in *Ratcliffe* (1998) The Times, 25 August where a primary school deputy head won a £100,000 out-of-court settlement after suffering two nervous breakdowns allegedly caused by bullying in the workplace. In *Waters* v. *Commissioner of Police of the Metropolis* [2000] IRLR 720 the House of Lords held that an employer could be liable for psychological harm, caused by failing to take a complaint of sexual assault by a fellow officer seriously, and by allowing the employee to be subjected to victimisation and harassment by other officers after she had made the complaint. (See also *Cross* v. *Highlands and Islands Enterprise* [2001] IRLR 336 and Chapter 5). However, *Sutherland* v. *Hatton* [2002] EWCA Civ 76 restricted the imposition of liability. In that case the Court of Appeal held that, for liability to arise, there must exist plain indications of impending harm arising from stress. Even then, the employer will only be liable for breach of the duty if he fails to take reasonable steps to overcome the risk of ill health. In determining what is reasonable, regard must be had to the gravity of the harm, the size of the risk and the cost to the employer in rectifying the situation.

Since *Sutherland* a number of other cases have reached the courts. In *Barber* v. *Somerset County Council* [2004] UKHL 13 the House of Lords said that employers had to take the initiative rather than wait and see as suggested by the Court of Appeal, and in *Simmons* v. *British Steel* [2004] ICR 585 their Lordships confirmed this, saying that while physical injury had to be reasonably foreseeable for employers to be liable, this was not essential in cases of psychiatric injury. Employers became liable to take action once they were aware of the employee's condition. In *Intel Corporation (UK) Ltd* v. *Daw* [2007] EWCA Civ 70 Daw had a nervous breakdown caused by an excessive workload. The employer was aware of her history of depression and the High Court found Intel to be negligent. Intel appealed, arguing that it had a confidential counselling service. The appeal was rejected on the grounds that offering such a service was insufficient to discharge the employer's duty of care. In *Hartman* v. *South Essex Mental Health and Community Care NHS Trust* [2005] EWCA Civ 6 the Court of Appeal stated that courts are still finding it difficult to apply the appropriate principles to stress claims. The court reiterated that the duty on employers is to prevent foreseeable injury and employers are liable if a failure to take action leads to an employee suffering foreseeable loss. An employer may be aware of this through the way work is organised or because the employee has a health problem, although it is the responsibility of the employee to make the employer aware of the health problem, and complaining about overwork or possible risk to health is not sufficient. In *Hartman* the employee had a breakdown. She had told the Occupational Health Department about problems and a previous breakdown, but because she was passed as fit to work this was not passed on to the Trust. When aware of potential problems, the Trust offered counselling and leave, both of which she refused. She suffered no difficulties at work and could not identify an event at work which had caused her breakdown. As such the Trust was not liable. The employer was also not liable in *Deadmen* v. *Bristol City Council* [2007] EWCA Civ 822. In the case the employee suffered from depression after an allegation of sexual harassment was made against him. He claimed damages for breach of contract arguing that the way the employer handled the complaint against him, in breach of contract, had led to him suffering stress. The Court of Appeal held that a policy to handle complaints of harassment 'sensitively' was aspirational and did not form part of the contract. Although having a panel of two rather than three members was a breach of contract, it was not reasonably foreseeable that the claimant would suffer stress as a result. Further, the employer was not in breach by leaving a letter stating its decision on his desk. It was the content of the letter and not the way that content was disclosed which was important. However in *Melville* v. *Home Office* [2005] EWCA Civ 6 the Court of Appeal stated that if the employer could foresee the risk of harm, because of the nature of the job, the employer did not have to foresee harm to a particular employee. Thus an employer was liable for the breakdown of a healthcare worker in a prison who had the job of removing the bodies of suicide victims. His illness was caused by the last suicide and the employer was held to be liable. These cases demonstrate that the law in this area is still unclear.

4. *Reasonably competent fellow employees* Apart from any vicarious liability which may arise should an employee injure one of his colleagues during the course of employment, the employer may also be primarily liable if it can be shown that he knew one of his employees was potentially dangerous and did nothing to protect the rest of the workforce. Competence obviously begins with the employee's ability to do the job safely, and if the employer has not provided sufficient training and while performing work-duties the employee injures someone, the employer will be liable. In *Hawkins* v. *Ross Castings Ltd* [1970] 1 All ER 180 an employee was injured following the spillage of molten metal. The injury was partly due to the fact that the

plaintiff was working with a 17-year-old Indian who spoke little English and who had not been trained in the task of carrying and pouring molten metal. It was held that the employer was liable as the failure to ensure that the employees were competent had been a cause of the accident.

Competence, however, is defined more widely than the employees having the ability and training to do the job safely. Practical jokes which go wrong can be just as dangerous and cause as serious an injury. In *Hudson* v. *Ridge Manufacturing Co Ltd* [1957] 2 QB 348 an employee, who was known to be a practical joker, injured an employee when one of his jokes went wrong. The employer was liable for the consequent injury. The important point from both *Hawkins* and *Hudson*, however, is the employer's knowledge. In both cases the employer knew the failings of the employee involved and should have taken steps to protect the rest of the employees. By contrast in *Coddington* v. *International Harvester Co of Great Britain Ltd* (1969) 6 KIR 146, the employee, as a joke, kicked a tin of burning thinners close to X. X kicked it away and it injured a third employee. The employer was not liable for the injury. The employee had never before played a practical joke and the employer had no knowledge that he was a source of potential danger to other employees.

Defences to a common law claim   If the employee is injured and sues his employer for breach of his common law duties, there are three defences the employer can raise. First, he can deny negligence. In other words, the employer is arguing that he has done all a reasonable employer would do to protect his employee and yet the injury still occurred. He may show, for example, that the costs of providing total protection outweighed the risk of injury and its likely seriousness, as seen in *Latimer* (above). Or he may argue that he is following expert advice or recognised current practice. In *Brown* v. *Rolls-Royce Ltd* [1960] 1 All ER 577 an employee contracted dermatitis from the use of oil. There was a barrier cream which could have been used, but the employer did not provide it on the advice of his medical officer who did not think that it worked. It was held that the employer was not liable.

The second defence the employer can raise is an admission of technical negligence, but that the injury was, in reality, solely caused by the employee's own negligence. This argument is often raised when the employer commits a breach of the Factories Act 1961. Under that legislation liability is strict and the mere fact that a provision has been broken establishes liability without the need to prove negligence. For example, s.14(1) Factories Act 1961 states: 'Every part of dangerous machinery shall be securely fenced unless it is in such a position or of such a construction as to be safe to every person employed or working on the premises as it would be if securely fenced.' In *Horne* v. *Lec Refrigeration Ltd* [1965] 2 All ER 898 an employee was killed when he failed to operate a safety procedure as he had been trained to do. His employers were in breach of s.14(1) Factories Act 1961 as the machine was not fenced at the time of his death. The lack of the fence was due to the employee who had removed it. It was held that, although the employers were in breach of their statutory duty, it was not this breach that was the cause of the employee's death but the removal of the fence by the employee. As such, the employee's own negligence had been the cause of the accident and the employer was not liable.

The two defences above extinguish liability. The third defence reduces rather than totally eliminates the employer's liability. This is the partial defence of contributory negligence under the Law Reform (Contributory Negligence) Act 1945. This provides that fault for the injury can be apportioned between the employer and the employee, where the negligence of the employee has been partially to blame for the injury (see *Sherlock, Lowles* and *Goodchild*, above). In the *Bux* case (above) it will be remembered that the employer was liable for failing to insist that goggles were worn. The employee, however, was found to be 40 per cent responsible for his own injury and his damages were reduced accordingly, the employer only paying 60 per cent. The raising of the defence of contributory negligence is quite common in this area, particularly where the employee has ignored the use of safety equipment but the employer has not checked to see if the equipment is being used. The percentage by which the employee's damages may be reduced depends on the extent of his blameworthiness, a matter which is decided by the court.

On normal contractual principles, an express term will override an implied term; this is one area, however, where an employer cannot exclude his common law liability by an appropriately worded term in the contract. The Unfair Contract Terms Act 1977 provides, by s.2, that a person cannot, by reference to a contractual term or notice, exclude or restrict liability for death or personal injury resulting from negligence.

Vicarious liability   While the law imposes the duty to employ reasonably competent workers upon the employer, this duty does not help the employee who may be injured by the negligence of one of his colleagues if the employer had no knowledge of the lack of competence (*Coddington*, above). Likewise, it does not help a third party who may be injured by the negligence of one of his employees. While the injured party may sue the original tortfeasor, it is unlikely in the majority of cases that the employee who caused the injury will have the funds to support a claim for compensation, or that he will be insured against such risks. Employers, on the other hand, will have insurance which can support a compensation claim. Really, as a result of these financial considerations the law has developed the principle of vicarious (substituted) liability. Although it arises in other situations, its most common application is in the area of employment where the employer can be made vicariously liable for the tortious wrongs of his employees committed within the course of their employment. The basis of the liability is control. In theory, while the employee is performing his job, he is under the control of his employer, and therefore, should he perform his duties negligently, the employer, who has the ultimate control, should be liable. As we have seen, in a modern-day industrial society, the issue of control by an employer over how employees perform their job is probably more of a legal fiction than industrial reality, but the basis of vicarious liability remains, almost certainly because of the financial considerations discussed above.

It would be easy to simply impose liability on the employer every time an employee commits a tortious act while at work. The law does not go that far, however. There is a limit on the employer's liability in that he is only vicariously liable for the torts of his employees committed within the course of employment. The phrase 'course of employment' has produced many interpretations by the court and does not mean committed while at work. At its simplest, the phrase means when the employee is doing an act authorised by his employer, in a manner authorised by his employer. The employer, however, will also be liable if the employee commits a tort while performing an authorised act in an unauthorised way, unless the employer has expressly forbidden the employee to do that act. For example, in the old case of *Limpus* v. *London General Omnibus Co* (1862) 7 LT 641 a bus driver injured a queue of passengers when he negligently drove into them. It was held that the employer was liable. The driver was authorised to drive. Once that authorisation was given, the employer could not argue that he wished the employee to drive in a certain way, that is, not negligently. The authorisation was to drive, and because when he was driving the employee injured third parties, he was within the course of his employment. By contrast, in *Beard* v. *London General Omnibus Co* [1900] 2 QB 530 the employee, a bus conductor, was expressly forbidden to drive. He injured a third party when he was reversing a bus in the depot. It was held that he was performing an unauthorised act at the time of the commission of the tort, as such he was not acting within the course of his employment and the employer was not vicariously liable. The issue of the commission of authorised acts in an unauthorised mode was discussed by the Privy Council in relation to industrial action in the case of *General Engineering Services Ltd* v. *Kingston & Saint Andrew's Corporation* [1989] IRLR 35. Can industrial action such as a go-slow be deemed to be performing an authorised act in an unauthorised way? In the case, action was brought against an employer when, as a result of a go-slow operated by the fire brigade, it took 17 minutes to reach a fire instead of three and consequently the plaintiff's business was burnt to the ground. The reason it had taken so long for the fire brigade to reach the fire was that they were stopping and starting for the whole of the journey. The Privy Council held that the firefighters were not performing an authorised act in an unauthorised way. The go-slow was an unauthorised and illegal act and had no connection with the authorised activity of reaching a fire as soon as possible. This decision is not surprising. The courts have, in the past, argued that although the employee's action appears to be authorised, in essence it is alien to his job duties and therefore outside the course of employment. Often this is because the employee has performed his duties excessively and the excess will take him outside the course of his employment. In *Keppel Bus Co* v. *Sa'ad Bin Ahmed* [1974] 1 WLR 1082 a bus conductor got into a fight with a passenger, who objected to the way the conductor had treated another passenger on the bus. To end the fight, the conductor hit the passenger over the head with his ticket machine. It was held that the employer was not vicariously liable. While the conductor could use reasonable force to prevent trouble on the bus, here he had started the trouble and used excessive force to make his point. Likewise in *Daniels* v. *Whetstone Entertainments* (1962) 106 SJ 284 an employer was not liable when a bouncer at a nightclub chased a customer after he had left the club peacefully and attacked him in the street. When the bouncer had originally hit the customer in the club, during the course of a fight he was trying to break up, he was within the course of his employment; however, by chasing the customer along the street after the fight had died down, the employee had taken himself outside the course of his employment. In the particularly nasty case of *Tower Boot Co Ltd* v. *Jones* [1995] IRLR 529 some employees had committed acts of extreme racial harassment including whipping the plaintiff and branding him with a hot screwdriver. The Employment Appeal Tribunal held that in no way could the attacks be described as part of the employees' duties and thus there was no vicarious liability. While this decision appears to be legally correct, it leaves the victim of such harassment with little or no chance of gaining financial compensation for his injuries. The Court of Appeal reversed the decision ([1997] IRLR 168) stating that the concept of employer's liability under the Race Relations Act 1976 was wider than the concept of vicarious liability at common law. As such the court plugged a serious loophole in the protection of employees.

   While the Court of Appeal in *Jones* decided that the common law definition of the 'course of employment' was too restrictive and did not apply in a statutory context, recently the House of Lords has redefined the common law definition. In *Lister* v. *Helsey Hall Ltd* [2001] IRLR 472 their Lordships held that the correct approach to determine whether an employee's wrongful act is committed during the course of his employment is to concentrate on the relative proximity between the nature of the employment and the act committed. As such, a boarding school was liable for the sexual abuse of boys by a school warden, because the nature of the employment meant that the employee had close contact with the boys and this created a sufficiently close connection between the acts of abuse and the work he had been employed to do to make it fair to hold the employers liable (see also *Dubai Aluminium Ltd* v. *Salaam* [2003] 2 AC 407). The decision overrules the earlier Court of Appeal decision in *ST* v. *North Yorkshire County Council* [1999] IRLR 98, in which the court held that indecent assault was not an unauthorised way of doing an authorised act. *Lister* brings the statutory and common law definitions more in line with each other. However, it also has the effect of creating vicarious liability for the criminal acts of employees.

A further development arising from *Lister* comes from *Majrowski* v. *Guy's and St Thomas's NHS Trust* [2005] EWCA Civ 251. In this case the employee claimed to have been bullied by his manager. He argued that his manager had subjected him to harassment within the Protection from Harassment Act 1997 for which his employer was vicariously liable. The Court of Appeal held that the House of Lords in *Lister* established that the test was the closeness of the connection between the employee's duties and his wrongdoing, not based on some fiction based on implied authority, and where the connection was established it was immaterial whether the employee's act was authorised or expressly forbidden by the employer, or civily or criminally illegal. As such, an employer could be vicariously liable for a breach of a statutory duty imposed only on his employee if there was sufficient connection with the employment that it was fair and reasonable to impose such liability.

Given that until recently the underlying basis of vicarious liability is the authorisation of the act by the employer, it followed that if the employer expressly forbids the act, there is no authorisation and thus no liability. In *Conway* v. *George Wimpey* [1951] 1 All ER 56 a driver was expressly forbidden to carry people in his van. The plaintiff was injured by the driver's negligent driving when travelling as a passenger in the van. It was held that there was no vicarious liability. The employee was doing a prohibited act and thus there was no authorisation from his employer. This principle needs qualification, however. It appeared that if the prohibited act benefited the employer, vicarious liability would still lie. In *Rose* v. *Plenty* [1976] 1 WLR 141 a milkman, contrary to an express prohibition, took a 13-year-old boy with him to help him deliver the milk. The boy was injured owing to the milkman's negligent driving. It was held that despite the prohibition, the employer was vicariously liable for the milkman's negligence. So too in

Stone v. *Taffe* [1974] 1 WLR 1575 the manager of a public house was held to be in the course of his employment when a customer was injured by falling down unlighted steps some two and a half hours after licensed closing time. It remains to be seen, however, after *Lister* and *Majrowski*, whether such a prohibition will end what the House of Lords described as the relative closeness of the connection between the nature of the employment and the employee's wrongdoing, or whether the prohibition will have no effect on the employer's liability.

The employee will not, however, be acting within the course of his employment if during working hours he goes off on a 'frolic of his own', in other words if he does something unconnected with his job duties which is of no benefit to his employer. In *Hilton* v. *Thomas Burton (Rhodes) Ltd* [1961] 1 WLR 705 the plaintiff's husband was killed by the negligent driving of one of his colleagues. The employer was not vicariously liable, as the accident occurred while the employees were driving back from a cafe – following an unauthorised break. The case raises the issue, however, of whether the employee will be in the course of his employment when on meal breaks or travelling. In *Smith* v. *Stages and Another* [1989] IRLR 177 the House of Lords considered the question of whether an employee was within the course of his employment when he was injured by a fellow employee while travelling from home to a workplace other than his normal one. In this case the driver was on duty while driving to the workplace at the request of his employer, thus the employer incurred vicarious liability for his actions. Normally, however, an employee travelling from home to work would not be in the course of his employment unless he was paid for that time or using the employer's transport. Once on the employer's premises, however, the employee is benefiting his employer, even if he has not yet started work, and is therefore within the course of his employment. In *Compton* v. *McClure* [1975] ICR 378 the plaintiff was injured when struck by a car on the employer's premises. The car was driven by a fellow employee who was late for work. It was held that the employer was vicariously liable for the negligent driving of his employee.

What is the situation when the employer lends his employees to another employer? In *Mersey Docks & Harbour Board* v. *Coggins & Griffith Ltd* [1947] AC 1 the primary employer had lent a crane and its driver to the secondary employer. The employee was negligent and an accident occurred. The House of Lords held that the primary employer was vicariously liable for the employee's negligent operation of the crane. The employee remained the employee of the primary employer and hence under his control. The primary employer was also liable, on a different basis, in *Morris* v. *Breaveglen* [1993] IRLR 350 where firm A lent an employee to firm B to use certain machinery, knowing the employee was not competent. The employee was subsequently injured when working for the secondary employer. It was held that the primary employer was liable in negligence, even though the employee was under the control of the secondary employer, because it was the negligence of the primary employer, in lending out an employee to do a job the primary employer knew him to be incapable of, which had caused the employee's injuries.

The *Morris* case above, however, is unusual and normally the question of control is used to determine liability. In *Sime* v. *Sutcliffe Catering Scotland Ltd* [1990] IRLR 228 the employee was injured when she slipped on some food dropped by a fellow employee. The management of the catering had been put out to Sutcliffe, but there was an agreement that Sutcliffe retained the existing catering staff, including the employee. The catering company then bought in additional staff. It could not be established whether the employee who had dropped the food substance and so started the chain of events was an employee of the catering company or of the primary employer. The question for the court was whether the catering company could be vicariously liable for an employee they did not employ. The Court of Session held that the issue turned not on who was the actual employer at the time, but who had sufficient control to be the effective employer at the relevant time. The day-to-day running of the canteen was the responsibility of the catering company who had complete control over how all the catering workers worked. As such they were vicariously liable, whether they were the legal employers of the negligent employee or not. However, a recent case questioned this. In *Viasystems (Tyneside) Ltd* v. *Thermal Transfer (Northern) Ltd* [2006] EWCA Civ 1151 a fitter working for a third defendant caused damage through his negligence. At the time he was supervised by the second defendant and the Court of Appeal held both defendants were vicariously liable for his negligence. The point has been clarified in *Hawley* v. *Luminar Leisure Ltd* [2006] EWCA Civ 18 where the issue was where vicarious liability lay in respect of a serious assault carried out by a doorman in a nightclub. The doorman's services were provided by a security firm, but he wore the uniform of the nightclub and was subject to the orders of the nightclub manager. The defendant argued that either the security firm should be solely vicariously liable, or under *Viasystems* liability should be split. The Court of Appeal said that although it was a heavy burden upon an employer to show that control had passed to the second employer, this was the case here and Luminar were solely vicariously liable.

The Working Time Regulations 1998

The Working Time Regulations 1998 have been brought in to implement the EU Working Time Directive (93/104/EC) and the Young Workers' Directive (94/33/EC). The Regulations came into force on 1 October 1998. The

Regulations cover workers as a wider group of individuals than employees. The definition of 'worker' is found in Regulation 2 and includes employees and anyone who works under an express or implied contract whereby the individual undertakes to do or personally perform any work or services. Special provision applies for agency workers. Domestic workers in a private household are excluded from the Regulations although they are entitled to rest breaks, rest periods and paid annual leave.

The Regulations limit working time. This is defined in Regulation 2 as:

▶ any period when a worker is working or at the employer's disposal and carrying out his activities or duties;
▶ any period during which the worker is receiving relevant training;
▶ any other periods treated as working time by a relevant agreement.

Agreements are the method by which the Regulations can be supplemented or derogated from. There are three types of recognised agreement in the Regulations. A collective agreement, a workforce agreement and a relevant agreement. A collective agreement has already been defined in Chapter 3. A workforce agreement, by Schedule 1 must be in writing, have effect for a specified period which does not exceed five years, must apply to all the workforce or all the relevant members of the workforce who belong to a particular group and the agreement must be signed by the workforce representatives or, if the employer employs fewer than 20 employees, either the appropriate representatives or a majority of the workforce, the workforce having been provided with a copy beforehand. A relevant agreement is either a workforce agreement which applies to the worker, a provision of a collective agreement which is part of the employment contract, or any other agreement between the employee and employer which is in writing and legally enforceable (presumably an express term in the contract itself or a separately negotiated contract).

The limit imposed by the Regulations on the working week is 48 hours. This must be expanded upon, however. First, the 48-hour limit is a limit on average working time. The average is calculated over a reference period of 17 weeks, although this may be derogated against and certain workers are excluded because they have unmeasured working time, for example family workers, managing executives and workers officiating at religious ceremonies. In addition an individual may opt out of the 48-hour week. This is covered by Regulation 5. For a valid individual opt-out there must be an agreement in writing; the agreement must specify its length or may be of indefinite length subject to the right of the employee to bring it to an end by giving notice which must not exceed three months; the employer must keep records of the workers who have opted out and the terms of their agreement and the records must be available for inspection by the relevant inspector appointed by the Health and Safety Executive or any other relevant authority.

In addition to regulating the working week, the Regulations cover rest breaks and periods, night work and annual leave. By Regulation 10 adult workers are entitled a daily rest period of at least 11 consecutive hours in each 24-hour period (12 hours for workers under 18). Shift workers are exempt when they change shift or the shifts involve periods of work split up over the day provided they are given equivalent periods of rest. Workers are also entitled to an uninterrupted weekly rest period of no fewer than 24 hours (48 hours if under 18) in each seven-day period averaged over 14 days (Regulation 11) and are entitled to rest breaks during the day where the working time is more than six hours. The break should be negotiated by collective or workforce agreement, but if none is in force, should be for an uninterrupted period of not less than 20 minutes (Regulation 12).

In respect of nightworkers (that is, workers working between 11 p.m. and 6 a.m.) Regulation 6 specifies that the normal working hours should not exceed an average of eight in any 24-hour period. The 17-week reference period is used to calculate the average. If the work involves special hazards or heavy strain, working hours must not exceed eight in any 24-hour period. In addition, the employer must give the worker the opportunity of a free health assessment before starting night work and regular assessments thereafter, and if a night worker is suffering from health problems which are connected with night work, he or she is entitled to be transferred whenever possible to suitable day work.

Originally, all workers were entitled to three weeks' (15 days) paid annual holiday. This was extended to 4 weeks (20 days) and from October 2007 the entitlement increased to 24 days and will further increase to 28 days in October 2008. Originally the right only arose after a qualifying continuity period of 13 weeks. This qualifying period was challenged before the ECJ in *R* v. *Secretary of State for Trade and Industry ex parte BECTU* [2001] IRLR 559. The ECJ ruled that the Working Time Directive did not permit restrictions to be imposed on the granting of annual leave. As such, after consultation, the government amended the Regulations and the qualifying period was removed. The Regulations state that to claim the right to annual leave the worker must give the employer twice the amount of notice as the leave they want to take, for example, four weeks' notice that the employee wishes to take a two week holiday, unless otherwise provided for by agreement. While the Directive lays down that there cannot be payment in lieu of annual leave unless the contract is terminated, it allows national legislation to lay down conditions for entitlement to leave (Article 7). Further, in *Gibson* v. *East Riding of Yorkshire Council* [2000] IRLR 598, the Court of Appeal held that the right to annual leave contained in the Directive was not sufficiently precise to have direct effect, since a worker's entitlement to leave could only be ascertained once their working time was known. Once the working time is known, however, the right to paid holiday cannot be contracted out of. In *Witley & District Men's Club* v. *Mackay* [2001] IRLR 595 the applicant was dismissed for dishonesty and his holiday pay withheld as provided by his contract. The Employment Appeal Tribunal upheld his complaint that the withholding of holiday pay was a breach of Regulation 35(1)(a) and any contractual term to the contrary was void in so far as it sought to avoid the employer's obligations under the Regulations. Furthermore, in *Leisure Leagues UK* v. *Maconnachie* (2002) The Times, 3 May the EAT held that pay for a day's contractual leave should be based on the number of working days in the year and not the calendar days (overruling *Thames Water Utilities* v. *Reynolds* (1996) IDS 561). However in *Inland Revenue* v. *Ainsworth* [2005] EWCA Civ 441 the Court of Appeal has decided that holiday entitlement does not accrue during periods of sick leave. Further where there is a failure to pay or an underpayment of holiday pay, a claim must be brought under the Regulations and not under the Employment Rights Act 1996.

There have been a number of cases on 'rolled-up' holiday pay; that is, pay which is not separate but paid as part of an hourly rate. In *Marshalls Clay Products Ltd* v. *Caulfield* [2004] ICR 436 the EAT gave the following advice so that employers could ensure that when they paid rolled-up holiday pay all the provisions of the Regulations were met:

- the rolled-up holiday pay must be clearly incorporated into the individual contract and expressly agreed;
- the percentage or amount of holiday pay must be identified in the contract and preferably the pay slip;
- it must be a true addition to the hourly rate;
- records of holiday taken must be kept;
- reasonably practicable steps must be taken to require workers to take their holiday before the end of the relevant holiday year.

In *Smith* v. *A J Morrisroes & Sons Ltd; J J Cafferkey & Co Ltd* v. *Bryne; Wiggins* v. *North Yorkshire CC* [2005] IRLR 72 Smith was paid a daily rate which included holiday pay. His employer told him that his holiday pay would be retained until he actually took his holiday. The EAT held that since there was no difference in the actual rate of pay before and after his employer told him his holiday pay would be withheld, there was no genuine provision for holiday pay in the contract and Mr Smith was entitled to sue for a deduction from wages. In Mr Byrne's case his rate of pay included holiday pay at 8 per cent, however as the employer offered no evidence that it had complied with the guidelines in *Marshalls Clay Products Ltd* the EAT found in his favour. Mr Wiggin's contract had no express provision for holiday pay but did contain a number of other documents which together complied with *Marshall Clay Products Ltd* and gave details of the calculations of amounts and the arrangements for payments. As such, the employer was compliant with the Working Time Regulations. However in *Clarke* v. *Frank Staddon Ltd* [2006] All ER 749 (ECJ); [2006] EWCA Civ 1470 (CA), both the ECJ and the Court of Appeal have held that rolled-up holiday pay is contrary to the Directive and unlawful, and that holiday pay must be paid in respect of the period when leave is actually taken, although an employer who has paid rolled-up holiday pay in a manner that clearly identifies the pay for holidays can offset amounts already paid against future payments. Thus rolled-up holiday pay is a breach of the Working Time Regulations.

Although the Regulations will cover a large number of workers, they allow for exclusions and derogations. By Regulation 18 certain workers are excluded. These include service activities such as the police or armed forces, and certain sector activities such as air, rail, road and sea. Regulation 21 also excludes certain workers or activities from the Regulations or parts of the Regulations. These include service providers such as gas, electricity and water; where there are foreseeable surges in activity such as tourism and agriculture, and security workers; or unforeseeable circumstances beyond the employer's control. However the Working Time (Amendment) Regulations 2003 extended the working time measures to all non-mobile workers in road, sea, inland waterways and lake transport, and to all workers in the railway and off-shore sectors. If Regulation 21 applies, then the workers are not covered by the provisions on length of night work, daily and weekly rest periods and rest breaks. Regulation 23 also allows the employer and employees to exclude or modify certain provisions by collective agreement. The 48-hour week cannot be modified in this way but the reference period for averaging hours can be increased to 52 weeks by a collective or workforce agreement.

Employees can enforce entitlement by complaint to an employment tribunal. However, in *Barber* v. *RJB Mining (UK) Ltd* [1999] IRLR 308 the High Court held that the right not to be required to work more than 48 hours a week was a term of the individual's contract of employment, and therefore the limits set down in the Regulations are enforceable as contractual rights by workers. The Regulations make it unlawful to subject an employee to a detriment because of refusal to work beyond the limits set in the Regulations, refusing to work during rest breaks, refusing to sign an agreement, being a candidate in an election of workplace representatives, alleging contravention of a right under the Regulations or taking proceedings. The same protection exists against dismissal, and dismissal for any of the above grounds is automatically unfair, with no continuity required. Enforcement is carried out by the Health and Safety Executive and Regulation 9 introduces an obligation on employers to keep records showing the limits on weekly working and night work, including the assessments of night workers.

The Regulations are complex. They were brought in to implement the Working Time Directive which was adopted under the health and safety provisions contained in Article 118a of the Treaty of Rome. As such, they are a valuable extension of an employee's health and safety rights and an addition to the employer's common law duties.

The Health and Safety at Work Act 1974

As with the Working Time Regulations the provisions of the Health and Safety at Work Act 1974 cannot be seen as implied duties in the contract of employment, therefore it would be incomplete to talk about the employer's liability in relation to the safety of his employees without a brief overview of the statutory provisions. Breach of the common law implied term can also lead to criminal prosecution for breach of the legislation and therefore the two areas are necessarily interlinked.

The 1974 Act was introduced as a result of the Robens Committee 1970 which reported in 1972. The Committee found that the law on health and safety was piecemeal and badly structured, with 11 pieces of major legislation supplemented by over 500 supplementary statutory instruments. The majority of the law based liability on occupation of premises.

The Committee proposed a unification of the law, basing liability on employment, not occupation of premises. It felt the aim of the law should be accident prevention, which should be underpinned by enforcement powers and criminal liability. It did not feel that the purpose of any changes should be to provide compensation for an employee who was injured as a result of a breach of the proposed legislation. This is why the common law duty on the part of the employer is so important today.

The Committee's recommendations were embodied in the Health and Safety at Work Act 1974. The aim of the Act is twofold – to lay down general duties applicable across the whole of the area of employment, and to provide a unified system of enforcement under the control of the Health and Safety Executive and local authorities. General duties are imposed upon various types of people, for example employers, suppliers and manufacturers, with the aim of ensuring, in so far as is reasonably practicable, a safe working environment.

Section 2(1) lays down the general duty on employers: 'It shall be the duty of every employer to ensure, so far as is reasonably practicable, the health, safety and welfare of all of his employees.' Subsection (2) then specifies particular duties which are as follows:

1. The provision and maintenance of plant and systems of work so that they are safe and without risk to health.
2. The making of arrangements for the use, handling, storage and transport of articles and substances.
3. The provision of information, instructions, training and supervision.
4. The maintenance of places of work under the employer's control in a safe condition, with safe and risk-free means of access and egress.
5. The provision and maintenance of a safe, risk-free working environment with adequate welfare facilities and arrangements.

The phrase to which all of these duties are subject is 'so far as is reasonably practicable'. This necessarily involves an examination of the common law to discover what action is deemed to be reasonably practicable in what circumstances, and the judgements, whether under the common law or the statute, come to similar conclusions. In *Associated Dairies* v. *Hartley* [1979] IRLR 171 the employer supplied safety shoes for which he charged £1 a week. An employee was injured when a truck went over his foot when he was not wearing the shoes. The employee argued he could not afford to pay for the shoes and an improvement notice was served on the employer, requiring him to provide the shoes free of charge. The employer appealed against the improvement notice. The Court of Appeal upheld the employer's appeal. The cost of providing the shoes was estimated at £20,000 in the first year and £10,000 per year thereafter. Comparing the cost of providing the shoes with the likelihood of injury occurring and its seriousness should it occur, it was not reasonably practicable for the employer to provide shoes free of charge. This is a similar decision to that of *Latimer* v. *AEC* (above) – a decision under the common law.

The basis of the duties under s.2(2) is that of employment – it covers duties owed by an employer to his employees; the duties, however, extend beyond the employment relationship. Section 3(1) provides that employers should conduct their business in such a way, 'in so far as is reasonably practicable to protect persons other than their own employees from risks to their health and safety'. The provision relates back to the specific duties in s.2(2). The interaction of the two sections can be seen in the case of *R* v. *Swan Hunter Shipbuilders Ltd and Telemeter Installation Ltd* [1982] 1 All ER 264. Eight men were killed by a fire caused by the failure of the subcontractor (Telemeter) to turn off the oxygen supply overnight. Both Swan Hunter and Telemeter were convicted under the Act and appealed against their convictions. The Court of Appeal held that the provision of a safe system of work in s.2(2) involved the provision of information and instructions. This provision of information and instructions should be to the employer's employees by virtue of s.2(1). In addition the same information and instructions should be available to other employees involved in the employer's undertaking by s.3(1). By failing to supply such information, the employers would be liable unless they could show that to do so was not reasonably practicable. Section 2(2) also covers the provision and maintenance of plant so that it is reasonably safe. This means that the employer will be in breach of his duty under s.3(1) if he lends out equipment which injures a third party. In *R v. Mara* [1987] 1 All ER 478 a company had a contract to clean International Stores on weekdays. The loading bay was in constant use during the week, so there was an agreement that the employees of International Stores would clean the bay using equipment provided by the cleaning company. On Saturday, an employee of International Stores was electrocuted when using the cleaning equipment. The cleaning company was convicted for a s.3 offence. An argument that was raised in the case was that the cleaning company did not work on a Saturday and was therefore not conducting its undertaking within the wording of s.3 when the accident occurred. The Court of Appeal rejected this argument. The court said that the company conducted its undertaking by cleaning on weekdays and by leaving its equipment for use by its client's employees at weekends. The company had therefore broken the duty it owed to its client's employees.

Previous legislation based liability on occupation of premises as has already been stated. Robens disagreed with liability based solely on occupation, but felt that such liability should go hand in hand with the general liability of employers. As such, s.4(1) places a general duty on those who occupy premises. They should ensure 'so far as is reasonably practicable the safety of premises, any means of access and exit from the place of work, and of any plant or substance provided for use on the premises'. This duty is owed to all persons and not just those employed by the occupier. In *Austin Rover Group Ltd* v. *HM Inspector of Factories* [1990] 1 AC 619 Austin Rover was prosecuted for a breach of s.4 when the employee of a contractor working on Austin Rover premises was killed by a flash fire. The House of Lords, hearing the appeal against conviction, said that when looking at the reasonableness of the precautions taken by the occupier to render his premises safe, account must be taken of the knowledge of, and control over, the use of his premises that the occupier has. An occupier cannot be made liable if the injury which occurs arises from totally unforeseen and unexpected events which could not be prevented. A flash fire was an unforeseen and unpreventable event and therefore the appeal was allowed.

Liability is imposed not only on those who physically occupy premises but also on those who are responsible for the maintenance of such premises, or the access to and exit from the premises (s.4(2)). In addition, liability is imposed against those responsible for safety and absence of risk concerning plant or substances used on the premises (s.4(3)).

Protection of those other than employees is continued in s.5. This imposes a general duty on those who control work premises to use the best means practicable to prevent the emission of offensive or noxious substances and to render harmless any such substances which are so emitted. This general duty overlaps with the more specific duties laid down by the Control of Pollution Act 1974.

The Act attempts to increase protection by imposing duties on designers, manufacturers. importers and suppliers. By s.6(1) designers should ensure, as far as is reasonably practicable, that an article's design is safe and without risk to health. By s.6(2) information must be available indicating the uses for which an article has been made and tested, stating the conditions for safe use. Duties are imposed upon designers and manufacturers to undertake research to identify and minimise the risks to health and safety, and similar duties are imposed on an importer or supplier.

The Act therefore imposes a chain of responsibility from the design and manufacture of an article to its installation, use and maintenance. It can be seen, however, that the duties under the Act overlap and this demonstrates the stated aim of the legislation of accident prevention. For example, if an employee of a subcontractor is injured when using a machine owned by an occupier, there may be a breach of duty by the designer of the machine, by the manufacturer, by the occupier of the premises and by the employee's own employer. The principle of the Act is that the more people entrusted with the duty to ensure safety, the less likely it is that an accident will happen. The fact that other people owe duties towards the employee will be no defence in an action for breach of statutory duty. In the *Swan Hunter* case (above), the employers argued that they had no duty to inform the employees of the subcontractor about the dangers of the build-up of oxygen since the subcontractor was under a duty to inform them because he employed them. It was held that this did not discharge Swan Hunter of their duties under the Act.

The duty owed to employees goes further in that by s.2 of the Act, if the employer employs five or more persons he should have a general policy on health and safety and bring this policy to the notice of his employees (s.2(3)). The policy should identify who is responsible for health and safety and should point out particular health and safety problems and the arrangements for dealing with them. The policy should also cover such matters as training, supervision, inspection procedures, safety precautions and consultative arrangements. In addition it should tell employees how they may complain about any health and safety risk to which they feel they are being exposed.

While the common law imposes no duty on employees to look after their own safety, failure to do so may mean that any damages could be wiped out by the employer raising the defence of contributory negligence. Given that the aim of the statutory provisions is not to provide compensation, the Act places a duty on the individual employee to have regard to his own safety and that of others around him. Any breach of this statutory duty will form the basis of the employer's common law defence of contributory negligence. By s.7 every employee, while at work, is under a duty (a) to take reasonable care for the health and safety of himself and other persons who may be affected by his acts or omissions at work; and (b) as regards any duty or requirement imposed on his employer or any other person by or under any of the relevant statutory provisions, to cooperate with him so far as is necessary to enable that duty or requirement to be performed or complied with. This places a clear duty on the employee to have regard for his own safety as well as that of his colleagues or third parties, and in addition imposes a duty of cooperation upon all employees to help all persons comply with their statutory duties. This reinforces the Robens' philosophy that health and safety should be a joint venture between employers and employees and gives the employer more leverage when trying to impose safety procedures on his workforce. Often employers will make breaches of safety procedures a disciplinary offence and in some cases it may be fair to dismiss the employee if the breach of procedure could have serious consequences. In *Roger* v. *Wicks and Wilson* COIT 228 90/97 wilful breach of a no-smoking policy imposed for safety reasons was held to be a justifiable reason for dismissal.

4.3 Duties of the Employee

Duty of cooperation

The law has always required that an employee should serve his employer faithfully and act in a loyal manner. More specific duties discussed below have been developed out of this proposition. The idea, however, that an employee should always cooperate with his employer was first expounded in detail by the Court of Appeal in the case of *Secretary of State for Employment* v. *ASLEF (No. 2)* [1972] 2 QB 455. The issue arose because under the Industrial Relations Act 1971, which was in force at the time, the Secretary of State could order a cooling-off period where the employees were acting in breach of contract. ASLEF was conducting a work-to-rule and argued that there was no breach of contract as the employees were merely following the rule-book to the letter and nothing more. All the judges in the Court of Appeal held that the employees were in breach of contract. Denning MR said that if the employee took steps to wilfully disrupt his employer's undertaking, he would be in breach of contract. Buckley LJ said that there was an implied term in all contracts that the employee should serve his employer faithfully and promote the employer's commercial interests.

While rarely specifically mentioned, the duty of cooperation again reared its head in the case of *Ticehurst* v. *British Telecommunications plc* [1992] IRLR 219. The employee was a BT manager and also a union official. The union instigated a number of one-day strikes and also a withdrawal of goodwill. British Telecommunications wrote to the employees saying that if they did not fully comply with the terms of their contracts, the company would consider them to be taking industrial action and that they would be sent home without pay until they were prepared to work normally. Ticehurst went on strike and when she returned to work she refused to sign an undertaking that she would work normally and take no further industrial action. As a result she was sent home. At the end of the dispute, she sued for the money BT had deducted for the time she had not been at work. At first instance it was held that as she was ready, willing and able to work, BT had no right to deduct her pay. BT appealed against that ruling to the Court of Appeal. The appeal court held that Ticehurst had demonstrated that if she returned to work she would withdraw her goodwill. This amounted to a breach of the implied term that she would serve her employer faithfully. It was necessary to imply such a term in a manager's contract because they are in charge of other employees and therefore must exercise judgement and discretion when they give orders. Managers were bound to exercise their discretion to further the employer's interests and as Ticehurst had indicated that she would withdraw her goodwill, she would not be promoting her employer's interests and the employers were entitled to refuse to accept this part-performance. While the principle of non-payment for part-performance has already been noted earlier, this case goes further. Yet again the Court of Appeal has implied a term of cooperation into employees' contracts and this, taken to its logical conclusion, will mean that any industrial action on the part of the employee, even if it is within the bounds of the contract such as a work-to-rule or a go-slow, will be a breach of contract. It is important to note, however, that the court appears to have restricted the *ASLEF* decision. In 1972 the court talked of such a term being in every contract of employment, whereas in *Ticehurst* the court went to great lengths to point out that Ticehurst was a manager and therefore the term should be implied. It may be that the term may not be implied so generally in the future.

Duty to obey reasonable lawful orders

The duty to obey the employer's orders is the most fundamental duty of the employee. Providing his services in the manner required by the employer is his consideration within the contract, just as providing wages is his employer's consideration. Given that the duty is fundamental, it follows that should the employee refuse to obey a legitimate order the common law entitles the employer to dismiss without notice. By refusing to obey orders the employee is essentially saying that he does not wish to be bound by the contractual terms any longer and is thus committing a repudiatory breach. The classic example of this is a strike. The employer, subject to unfair dismissal provisions discussed later, is entitled to accept the strike as a breach which terminates the contract. The modern statement of the law is by Lord Evershed MR in *Laws* v. *London Chronicle* [1959] 1 WLR 698:

> 'wilful disobedience of a lawful and reasonable order shows a disregard . . . of a condition essential to the contract of service, namely the condition that the servant must obey the proper orders of the master,' and that unless he does so the relationship is, so to speak, struck at fundamentally.'

The duty is not, however, to obey all orders of the employer, but only those that are reasonable and lawful. Furthermore, the duty is to obey orders and not requests. To establish whether the duty has been broken, it is necessary to first ask if the order is reasonable and this generally means asking whether the order is within the contractual obligations of the employee.

Very often the order will be in relation to the employee's job. The starting point is therefore what the contract states are the job duties, and a refusal to perform such duties will be, in the main, a breach of contract. The courts, however, recognise that the employee needs to be flexible and may decide that the duties are wider than those expressly listed in the contract. Certainly an employee will be expected to perform duties which are reasonably incidental to his main job duties and it has already been seen in the case of *Sim* v. *Rotherham Metropolitan Borough Council* that the courts may imply duties into particular types of contracts and will expect the employee to adapt to new methods of performing his job (*Cresswell* v. *Board of Inland Revenue*, above). Some employers try to foresee any future problems by the use of a flexibility clause in the contract. In essence, this is normally a wide clause requiring the employee to perform any task ordered by the employer. Taken to their logical conclusion, however, these clauses could mean that the employee could be asked to do anything and such an interpretation has fundamental consequences in the case of redundancy. As such, the Court of Appeal limited the application of flexibility clauses in the case of *Haden Ltd* v. *Cowan* [1982] IRLR 314 when it decided that such clauses had to be referred back to the employee's main job duties. This means that, even with the widest of flexibility clauses, a lecturer could not be told to clean his/her office as cleaning duties are totally unrelated to lecturing duties!

In addition to orders in relation to the job, there may be other areas where the employee refuses to obey, for example, mobility or overtime requirements. The starting point again is the contract, remembering that the courts may imply a term if they feel that would have been the parties' intention. In *Courtaulds Northern Spinning Ltd* v. *Sibson* [1988] IRLR 305 the employee was asked to transfer to another site which was within easy travelling distance of his home. The contract was silent as to mobility between sites, but the employee had worked on the site in the past. The Court of Appeal held that because of his past conduct, there was an implied term in the contract requiring him to move sites and refusal to do so was a breach of contract. Certainly, refusal to move where there is an express mobility clause will normally be, on the face of it, a breach of contract, as would be refusal to work contractually binding overtime. The courts may, however, decide that an employee has been fairly dismissed even though he is refusing to do something which is outside the ambit of his contract. In *Horrigan* v. *Lewisham London Borough Council* [1978] ICR 15 the employee was a driver who was contracted to work until 4.30 p.m. but in practice rarely finished at that time. He was paid overtime rates after 4.30 p.m. but there was no contractual requirement for him to work overtime. After 10 years of working overtime, the employee began working only his contractual hours and was eventually dismissed. It was held that his dismissal was fair given the difficulties that would be faced by the employer in not knowing from day to day whether the employee would be available to complete his round.

While the contract, therefore, is the starting point, the courts interpret the word 'reasonable' in a flexible way and this can mean that the employee will be required to do duties which are not within his contract. But this works both ways, and there have been situations where the courts have decided that even though the order is within the contractual authority of the employer, it is still unreasonable and the employee is not in breach of contract in refusing to obey it. In the old case of *Ottoman Bank Ltd* v. *Chakarian* [1930] AC 277 the employer ordered the employee, an Armenian, to stay in Constantinople where he had been previously sentenced to death. It was held that the order, although within the employer's contractual rights, was not reasonable in the circumstances and the employee was entitled to refuse to obey it.

In addition to the requirement that the order is reasonable, it must also be lawful and the employee can legitimately refuse to obey an order which requires him to act illegally, even if the order is within his contractual obligations. In *Morrish* v. *Henlys (Folkestone) Ltd* [1973] IRLR 61 an employee was dismissed when he refused to obey an order to falsify the account books at the garage where he worked. It was held that his dismissal was unfair as he was not in breach of contract by refusing to comply with the order.

Duty to exercise reasonable care and skill

In addition to the duty to obey reasonable, lawful orders the law imposes a duty on the employee that he will perform his work with reasonable care and skill. This duty can arise in three situations. First and at its simplest, the law requires the employee to take reasonable care of his employer's property (for example tools and equipment). In *Superlux* v. *Plaisted* (1958) The Times, 12 December a salesman negligently left his van unlocked and as a result a stock of vacuum cleaners was stolen. It was held that the employee was in breach of contract. In some cases the act of negligence may be so serious that it warrants dismissal, but minor acts of neglect will not justify the employer sacking the employee unless there is a series of such minor acts (*Lowndes* v. *Specialist Heavy Engineering Ltd* [1977] ICR 1). The second situation involves the skill part of the duty. An employee impliedly promises that he is able to do the job where he is not being trained and failing to reach an acceptable standard of performance is a breach of that implied promise. Under the common law, such a breach would entitle an employer to dismiss instantly (*Harmer* v. *Cornelius* (1858) 5 CBNS 236) but nowadays the procedural protection which arises from the statutory unfair dismissal will aid an incompetent employee to some extent.

The third situation when a breach of this implied duty can arise is when the employee performs his work negligently and in doing so injures a third party, who may be a fellow employee or nothing to do with the employer. In these cases, the employer may find himself liable to his injured employee for failing to provide a competent colleague or in either situation he may find himself vicariously liable. While in theory, the employer could, in either of these situations sue the employee who caused the injury for his breach of contract, it has been seen that in practice since the case of *Lister* v. *Romford Ice and Cold Storage Co Ltd* this rarely, if ever, happens where physical injury occurs and the injured party is another employee. In other cases, however, the courts have upheld an action for damages against the employee. In *Janata Bank* v. *Ahmed* [1981] IRLR 457 a bank manager performed his duties negligently and was dismissed. The bank sued him for its loss of £34,640 and the Court of Appeal upheld the claim. The employer's loss had been caused by the employee's failure to exercise proper care and skill, as implied by his contract.

Duty not to accept bribes or secret commission

The employee should only accept rewards from his employer and is under an implied duty not to accept payment from another source, even if the payment does not influence him. The basis of the duty is that the employee must serve his employer faithfully, and it is inconsistent with this duty that he should receive payment from another source for performing his job. In *Boston Deep Sea Fishing and Ice Co* v. *Ansell* (1888) 39 Ch 339 the employee was accepting payment for placing orders with a supplier and was receiving dividends from shares he owned in another supplier of his employer. It was held that his dismissal was justified. Breach of this duty is considered to be so serious by the courts that it will normally justify instant dismissal. The payment must be secret, however, and if the employer knows that the payment has occurred and accepts it, the duty is not broken, for example it is accepted in a number of jobs that employees will receive tips.

While the duty is a simple one to state, in practice it may be difficult to enforce. Many employees will receive gifts from customers or suppliers and will often receive free meals and drinks. While technically a breach of contract will have occurred few employers would pursue a remedy against the employee. In practice many employers will tell those employees likely to be put in the position what is and is not acceptable. Should an employee then step out of line, he will be in breach of contract.

Duty not to disclose confidential information

The law recognises that if the employee divulges confidential information he has acquired during the course of his employment, this may harm the employer's interests and therefore the duty not to disclose such information not only applies during the currency of the relationship, but also continues once the relationship has ended. The extent of the duty was discussed in detail in *Faccenda Chicken Ltd* v. *Fowler* [1987] Ch 117. Mr Fowler was a salesman who left Faccenda Chicken to set up a business in competition. He recruited a number of his ex-employer's staff and most of his customers had previously been customers of his ex-employer. Faccenda Chicken sued for damages for the misuse of sales information relating to prices and customers. The Court of Appeal dismissed the claim. The court laid down that as a matter of principle the duty of the employee once he had left the relationship is more restricted than during his employment. The court distinguished between two types of confidential information. The first is information of a highly confidential nature which should be treated as if it were a trade secret, and the employee can be restrained from divulging this information even though the relationship has ended. The second type of information is that which is confidential, so that it would be a breach of this duty to disclose it while in employment, but not a breach to use it after the relationship has ended. If the employer wants to protect himself after the relationship has terminated, he should insert a restraint covenant in the contract to bind the employee once he has left. Such covenants are discussed later. If there is no such covenant, then to see if a breach of duty has occurred, the court must look at:

(a) the nature of the employment;
(b) the nature of the information;
(c) whether the information can be isolated from other information which the employee is free to use;
(d) whether the employer impressed upon the employee the need for confidentiality.

In a large number of cases, it may be difficult to distinguish between the two types of information but the judgement means that, in relation to ex-employees the duty will not normally protect the employer in the majority of cases. In the few successful cases, a clear breach has occurred during the currency of the relationship and this has led the court to be more willing to find that the employee is liable. In *Robb* v. *Green* [1895] 2 QB 315 a manager copied his employer's customer list before leaving his employment. He then set up in competition and solicited the customers on the list. His ex-employer successfully obtained an injunction against him. Similarly in *Sanders* v. *Parry* [1967] 2 All ER 803 an assistant solicitor set up on his own, taking with him one of the practice's main clients whose affairs he had looked after. It was held that he was in breach of duty.

Although the duty may be restricted in relation to ex-employees, the only restriction in respect of existing employees is that the information must be confidential. This, however, leaves the question as to what information is deemed to be confidential. Certainly it includes information which the law allows an employer to protect by a restraint covenant. This means any information which the law regards as the employer's property and as such includes trade secrets, secret processes and customer lists. There may be other information, however, which the employer regards as confidential and which, if divulged, could injure the employer's business. In *Marshall (Thomas) (Exports) Ltd* v. *Guinle* [1979] Ch 227 the court identified certain factors which should be considered in deciding if the information is confidential and in need of protection:

1. The owner of the information must reasonably believe that the release of the information would benefit a competitor or cause harm to himself.

2. The owner must reasonably believe that the information is confidential and not already public knowledge.
3. The information must be judged bearing in mind the practice of the particular trade or industry.

Given the factors listed above, it is irrelevant if the item disclosed is simple or could be discovered by the person to whom the information is divulged with some research. In *Cranleigh Precision Engineering Ltd* v. *Bryant* [1965] 1 WLR 1293 the employee divulged the right type of clamp to use to keep the inner and outer skins of swimming pools together. The materials and type of clamp were common in the industry, but had not been used for that purpose before. It was held that the employee was in breach of contract. The courts feel that information which the employer regards as confidential and which, if divulged, would put the recipient in a stronger position than others should be protected. The attitude of the courts was summed up by Roxburgh J in *Terrapin Ltd* v. *Builders Supply (Hayes) Ltd* (1959) (unreported) when he said: 'a person who has obtained information in confidence is not allowed to use it as a springboard for activities detrimental to the person who made the confidential communication.'

One problem which exists in determining whether the employee is in breach of duty is separating out confidential information from the skills the employee has learnt during his employment and which he is entitled to use for the benefit of his new employer. For example, if the employee has learnt a process during his employment, is this a skill he has acquired or is it confidential information? In *Printers & Finishers Ltd* v. *Holloway* [1964] 3 All ER 731 the ex-employee, a manager, had knowledge of the employer's flock-printing process, skill in using a flock-printing plant, plus information from documents acquired from his ex-employer. His former employer successfully obtained an injunction only in respect of the information contained in the documents. The other information was skill he had acquired during his employment which he could use for the benefit of his new employer. In this case the dividing line was quite clear-cut, but in many cases it will not be.

Until recently, there was one exception when the duty not to disclose confidential information did not apply. This was where the information must be disclosed by law, or it was in the public interest that the information should become known. In *Initial Services Ltd* v. *Putterill* [1968] 1 QB 396 an ex-employee gave details of restrictive trade practices operated by his ex-employer to a newspaper. Such practices were in breach of the Restrictive Trade Practices Act 1968. It was held that the disclosure was not a breach of the employee's duty as the information should be divulged in the public interest. Likewise, employees are required to divulge information by certain statutes such as the Health and Safety at Work Act 1974. To do so will not be a breach of duty on the part of the employee.

The Public Interest Disclosure Act 1998 has now increased protection for employees who disclose information that their employer is likely to regard as confidential. The Act inserts new sections into the Employment Rights Act 1996. Employees are protected if they make a qualifying disclosure. In *Bolton School* v. *Evans* [2007] ICR 641 the Court of Appeal discussed what is meant by 'disclosure'. Evans was an IT teacher. He resigned and claimed constructive dismissal after he had been given a final warning when he disabled some of the service accounts on the school's computer network from a pupil's computer. He had done this to show flaws in the network's security. He argued he had suffered a detriment as a result of disclosing the school's breach of its data protection obligations. The school claimed he had been disciplined for his misconduct in hacking into the system. Buxton LJ said that the word 'disclosure' should be given its common meaning and this meant words spoken to the employer about the breach, and does not extend to the surrounding circumstances. As such Evans had not made a disclosure. Leave has been granted for an appeal to the House of Lords.

A 'protected disclosure' is defined by s.43B as any disclosure of information which, in the reasonable belief of the worker making the disclosure, tends to show one or more of the following:

(a) a criminal offence has been committed, is being committed or is likely to be committed;
(b) that a person has failed, is failing or is likely to fail to comply with a legal obligation;
(c) a miscarriage of justice has occurred or is likely to occur;
(d) the health or safety of an individual has been or is likely to be endangered;
(e) the environment has been or is likely to be damaged; or
(f) information showing any of the above has been or is likely to be deliberately concealed.

It is important to note that the standard used is subjective and the question for a tribunal will be whether the employee has a reasonable belief (*Babuld* v. *Waltham Forest* [2007] IRLR 346). There are also two exceptions when the disclosure is not protected. This is where the person making the disclosure commits a criminal offence by making it and where it is a disclosure in respect of which legal professional privilege would apply.

In order to qualify for protection there are specified procedures the employee must have followed. The aim of the legislation is to encourage the employee to go through appropriate channels first, and thus an employee will gain protection more easily if he discloses to a person within employment rather than go outside to, for example, the press. The provisions are:

- *Disclosure to employer or other responsible person (s.43C)* The aim of this provision is that the employee makes the disclosure to the person responsible for preventative action. This will normally be the employer but may be another person to whom the employer has delegated responsibility.
- *Disclosure to a legal adviser (s.43D)*.
- *Disclosure to a Minister of the Crown (s.43E)* This will apply when the employer is an individual appointed by a Minister of the Crown.
- *Disclosure to a prescribed person (s.43F)* The persons who fall within this category are defined by an order made by the Secretary of State.
- *Disclosure in other cases (s.43G)* If the worker makes the disclosure in good faith, believes the allegation to be true, the conditions in the section are met, the worker does not make the disclosure for personal gain and it is reasonable in all the circumstances to make the disclosure, then it will be protected. The conditions are that at the time he or she makes the disclosure, the worker reasonably believes that he or she will be subjected to a detriment if the disclosure is made to the employer or a prescribed person; if there is no prescribed person, the worker reasonably believes that evidence will be concealed or destroyed if the disclosure is made to the employer; or the worker has previously disclosed substantially the same information to the employer or a prescribed person. In deciding whether it was reasonable for the worker to make the disclosure the tribunal should take account of the identity of the person to whom the disclosure was made; the seriousness of the relevant failure; whether the failure is continuing or likely to reoccur; whether the disclosure is a breach of the employee's duty of confidentiality; any action the employer could have taken or could reasonably be expected to take as a result of the previous disclosure; whether when making the disclosure to the employer the worker complied with any procedure laid down by the employer.
- *Disclosure of exceptionally serious breaches (s.43H)* If the disclosure is serious enough to bypass the procedures, it will be protected if it is made in good faith, the worker reasonably believes the allegations are true, the worker does not make the disclosure for personal gain, the matter disclosed is of an exceptionally serious nature and in all the circumstances it was reasonable to make the disclosure. The identity of the person to whom the disclosure is made is a relevant factor when considering whether it was reasonable to make the disclosure.

Section 47B of the Employment Rights Act provides protection for the employee who has suffered a detriment because of a qualifying disclosure. Section 103A states that the dismissal of an employee in those circumstances shall be unfair and the employee has protection from selection for redundancy. Protection will not apply however if the disclosure is made in bad faith (*Street* v. *Derbyshire Unemployed Workers' Centre* [2004] IRLR 678). The normal continuity period does not apply. In *Kuzel* v. *Roche Products Ltd* [2007] IRLR 309 the Employment Appeal Tribunal stated that where a claimant has shown that the reason put forward by the respondent was not some other substantial reason but a reason falling within s.103A, the employer must either prove the real reason for the dismissal or disprove the s.103A reason. If he is unsuccessful, the dismissal is for the s.103A reason. Section 43J provides that any term in an employment contract preventing disclosure is void. In *Lucas* v. *Chichester Diocesan Housing Association Ltd* (2004) EAT 0713/04 Lucas reported concerns about financial irregularities in a project to a senior manager, who then informed the project manager. The manager cut Lucas's hours and after she raised further issues she was dismissed. She claimed a breach of s.103A. The employment tribunal found that her disclosures were motivated by her worsening relationship with her manager, but the EAT found that there were no relationship problems at the time of the first complaint and the employer had not raised bad faith. Furthermore, in *Miklaszewicz* v. *Stolt Offshore Ltd* [2001] IRLR 656 the Court of Appeal held that the Act can apply to protect a disclosure made before the Act was in force where an employee was dismissed as a result of that disclosure after the Act came into force.

Duty not to work for a competitor

Generally the employer cannot restrict what the employee does in his spare time and the employee can take on a second job without interference from his employer. There are, however, two exceptions to the rule. The first is that the employee cannot work for a competitor of his employer in his spare time. In *Hivac Ltd* v. *Park Royal Scientific Instruments Ltd* [1946] Ch 169 employees were working for a competitor in their spare time. Although the first employer sued the second employer and successfully obtained an injunction to restrain future employment of his employees, the court was in agreement that the employees were in breach of contract. Given that an employee may not work for a competitor, it also follows that he may not set up in competition in his spare time. In *Adamson* v. *B&L Cleaning Services* [1995] IRLR 193 a foreman at a contract cleaning firm was dismissed for seeking to obtain an existing contract when it came up for tender. The Employment Appeal Tribunal held that the dismissal was fair, in that intending to leave and set up in competition would not be a dismissable offence, but here the employee had overstepped the mark by breaching the duty of fidelity. The emphasis, however, is that spare-time employment must harm the employer, and without evidence of such harm the duty will not be broken.

The second situation which may arise is that the employee gets another job in his spare time which has nothing to do with his employer's business. In this situation there is very little the employer can do unless he has an express provision in the contract forbidding such employment. The only way this type of work could be a breach of an implied term is if the second job made the employee so tired he became incapable of performing his main job. He would then be in breach of the implied duty to perform his work with reasonable skill and care.

The cases above were all situations when the employee was under a contract of employment and still under a duty to work. If, however, the employer has relieved the employee of the duty to work, there is no breach on the part of the employee if, despite the fact a relationship still exists with the employer, the employee works for a competitor, unless the employer makes it clear that this is forbidden. In *Hutchings* v. *Coinseed Ltd* [1998] IRLR 190 the employee resigned, giving a month's notice. Her contract provided that during the notice period the employers were not obliged to provide her with work and could require her to stay at home and not work for a competitor. The employers on receipt of her letter of resignation replied stating that the employee was not required to work her notice and that she would be paid in lieu. On the same day the employee started work with a competitor and the employers withheld her lieu payment.

The Court of Appeal held that the employer's letter made it clear that the employee was not required to work for them nor did it say that she should not take up other employment. As such, she was free to work for a competitor, as the letter from the employer varied the terms of her contract. It would appear, however, that if the employer's letter had reiterated the garden leave clause, or stated that the employee could not work elsewhere until the end of the notice period, the employee would have been in repudiatory breach.

Inventions

At common law the duty of fidelity meant that any ownership of inventions made by an employee during the course of employment vested in the employer (*British Syphon Co Ltd* v. *Homewood* [1956] 1 WLR 1190). Often collective agreements modified the common law and protected the employee to some extent, to enable a share in any profits made from the invention but, without such an agreement, the invention was seen as part of the employee's general duty to promote his employer's interests. The position has now been changed by the Patents Act 1977 and the Copyright, Designs and Patents Act 1988.

Section 39 of the 1977 Act provides that in two circumstances the invention belongs to the employer. These circumstances are where the invention:

(a) was made in the course of the normal duties of the employee, or outside those normal duties but within the course of duties specifically assigned to him and in both cases the invention reasonably resulted from the carrying-out of those duties; or

(b) was made during the course of the duties of the employee and at the time of making the invention the employee had a special obligation to further the interests of his employer's undertaking.

In all other circumstances the invention is owned by the employee. In *Reiss Engineering Co Ltd* v. *Harris* [1985] IRLR 232 the court decided that the employee's normal duties are those he is actually employed to carry out. In the case the employee invented a valve while he was under notice of redundancy. It was held that the invention belonged to the employee because it did not arise out of his normal duties and he was under no obligation to further his employer's interests.

Even if the invention is owned by the employer, s.40 provides that the employee can apply to the Patents Court or the Patents Office for compensation, where the invention belongs to the employer under s.39 but is proved to be of outstanding benefit to the employer, or where the invention is owned by the employee, but he has assigned it to the employer for inadequate compensation in relation to the benefit obtained by the employer from the invention. The amount of compensation is determined by taking into account the criteria listed in s.41.

Copyright is covered by the 1988 Act. Section 11 provides that the copyright in any work is owned by the author unless it is written by the employee in the course of his employment and the employee was employed for the purpose of writing such work, in which case the copyright is owned by the employer, subject to any agreement to the contrary.

While the Acts simplify the position, they still provide problem areas in terms of what are the employee's normal duties, when is the employee under a special obligation to further his employer's interests and when is something produced in the course of the employee's employment. Many employers avoid these problems by providing specifically in the contract what type of work is deemed to be owned by the employer or conversely that the employee is under a special obligation to further the employer's interests.

Summary

1. A contract of employment is a contract for personal services and the law normally will not compel the parties to continue the contract by the use of specific performance or injunction.

2. The law implies duties into all contracts of employment and they will be imposed on the parties unless ousted by an express term.

3. The law imposes duties on both the employer and the employee.

4. The consideration by the employer is the payment of wages and therefore generally there is no duty on the employer to provide work, only pay.

5. The Employment Rights Act 1996 prevents unauthorised deductions from an employee's pay by the employer.

6. The law now recognises that both parties owe a duty of respect towards each other.

7. The common law imposes detailed duties on the employer to look after the employee's safety. These duties complement the duties imposed by the Health and Safety at Work Act 1974.

8. The employer will be vicariously liable for the acts of employees committed during the course of their employment if there is a sufficient connection between the act committed and their employment.

9. The duties imposed upon the employee come under the general heading of fidelity. This means that the employee owes duties of obedience, loyalty and care and skill to his employer.

Exercises

1. Paul is a weekly-paid production worker in an engineering factory. During the last six months he has been laid off on three separate occasions, but has received no wages during the course of any of the three periods of lay-off. On the first occasion, he was laid off when the factory was closed after a week-long rail strike made it impossible for half the workforce to get to work. On the second occasion, he was laid off for three consecutive weeks as a result of a fall in demand for the company's products, caused by the last-minute cancellation of a large order by an overseas customer. On the last occasion, he was laid off intermittently over a period of six weeks as a result of sporadic industrial action by other workers at the plant who forced the closure of certain parts of the plant at regular intervals. Paul is a highly skilled worker who had only been laid off once previously, last year, when again he received no wages, although he made no complaint. Now, however, he wishes to sue his employers for breach of contract. Advise Paul.

2. Bill and Ben work for Flowerpot Ltd as roofers. In winter the roofs are dangerous. Six months ago, Flowerpot provided safety belts for the roofers to wear. They showed the employees how to use the belts and where they were kept, and put up a notice saying belts should be worn at all times. Bill is illiterate and was away on a training course when the belts were first issued. Ben thinks it spoils his image to wear the belts because he likes impressing Weed, who works in the canteen, by dancing on the roof.

Last week both Bill and Ben were working on a roof. Neither of them was wearing belts. Ben was dancing about, trying to attract Weed's attention, when he distracted Bill. Both fell from the roof and were seriously injured. Consider the liability of Flowerpot Ltd.

Further Reading

Barnard   *The Working Time Regulations 1998* (1999) 28 ILJ 61.

Barnard   *The Working Time Regulations 1999* (2000) 29 ILJ 167.

Barrett   *Clarification of Employer's Liability for Work-related Stress* (2002) 31 ILJ 285.

Barrett   *Employer's Liability after Hatton v. Sutherland* (2005) 34 ILJ 182.

Brodie   *Beyond Exchange: The New Contract of Employment* (1998) 27 ILJ 79.

Brodie   *The Personal Employment Contract* (2004) 33 ILJ 87.

Brodie   *Health and Safety, Trust and Confidence and Barber v. Somerset County Council: Some Further Questions* (2004) 33 ILJ 261.

Clarke   *Breach of Confidence and the Employment Relationship* (2002) 31 ILJ 353.

Clarke   *Repudiation of Contract and Breach of Confidence: General Billposting v. Atkinson Revisited* (2003) 32 ILJ 43.

Freedland   *The Obligation to Work and to Pay for Work* (1977) Current Legal Problems 175.

Hepple   *A Right to Work?* (1981) 10 ILJ 65.

Holland and Chandler   *Implied Mobility Clauses* (1988) 17 ILJ 253.

Lewis   *Whistleblowers and Job Security* (1995) 58 MLR 208.

Lewis   *The Public Interest Disclosure Act 1998* (1998) 27 ILJ 325.

Lewis   *Freedom of Speech and Employment* (2003) 32 ILJ 72.

Lewis   *Providing Rights for Whistleblowers: Would an Anti-discrimination Model be more Effective?* (2005) 34 ILJ 239.

Lewis   *Whistleblowers, Reasonable Belief and Data Protection* (2006) 35 ILJ 324.

Middlemiss   *The Truth and Nothing but the Truth? The Legal Liability of Employers for Employee References* (2004) 33 ILJ 59.

Napier   *Judicial Attitudes Toward the Employment Relationship: Some Recent Developments* (1977) 6 ILJ 1.

Further reading cont'd

Simpson   *A Milestone in the Legal Regulation of Pay: The National Minimum Wage Act 1998* (1999) 28 ILJ 1.

Simpson   *Implementing the National Minimum Wage – The 1999 Regulations* (1999) 28 ILJ 171.

Simpson   *The National Minimum Wage Five Years On: Reflections on Some General Issues* (2004) 33 ILJ 22.

Weir   *Physician – Kill Thyself!* (1991) Cambridge Law Journal (50) 397.

Part III

Constraints on the Employment Relationship

Chapter 5
Discrimination

The Concept of Discrimination

The common law principle of freedom of contract applies equally to employment contracts and, as such, at common law the employer can employ, or refuse to employ, anyone for whatever reason he wishes, including reasons based on the sex or race of that person. Such a proposition nowadays, however, would offend most people's sense of fairness and over the past 30 odd years the law has sought to intervene to restrict an employer from exercising his common law rights.

The original impetus to bring in legislation in this area came from international law. The Universal Declaration of Human Rights 1948 states that everyone is entitled to all rights and freedoms 'without distinction of any kind, such as race, colour, sex, language, religion, political or other opinion, national or social origin, property, birth or status'. Such statements are reiterated by the International Labour Organisation's Conventions of 1958 and 1980. Without doubt, however, the most important influence on national law has been the UK membership of the European Community.

An EC Directive of 1976 (EEC 76/207) required the implementation of the principle of equal treatment for men and women in all aspects of employment. Article 189 of the Treaty of Rome states that Directives are binding on Member States as to the result, but the method of implementation is left up to the particular member. Failure to implement a Directive fully will lead to action against the Member State by the EC Commission. In relation to the United Kingdom this has happened twice in the area of equal opportunities, once in the area of equal pay, discussed later, and once in the area of sex discrimination, when the European Court of Justice (ECJ) decided that Britain had failed to comply with Article 4(b) of the Equal Treatment Directive in that legislation did not outlaw discriminatory treatment in collective agreements, internal rules of undertakings or rules governing independent occupations and professions. Furthermore, the ECJ has held that the Directive can be directly enforced where the employer is an organ of the state and the Directive is clear. This issue is discussed later.

To comply with its international and European obligations, the United Kingdom has introduced a series of legislation. The first of these was the Race Relations Act 1965 which was later replaced by the Race Relations Act 1976. The Equal Pay Act 1970 and the Sex Discrimination Act 1975 together were supposed to form a code to prevent discrimination in all aspects of employment, both contractual and non-contractual. Both pieces of legislation were challenged by the EC Commission in the ECJ and as a result the Equal Pay Act was amended by the Equal Pay (Amendment) Regulations 1983 and the Sex Discrimination Act was amended by the Sex Discrimination Act 1986. Further amendments to the Sex Discrimination Act have been made by the Sex Discrimination (Gender Reassignment) Regulations 1999 and the Sex Discrimination (Indirect Discrimination and Burden of Proof) Regulations 2001, the latter being enacted to implement the Burden of Proof Directive (97/80/EC). The Equal Pay Act covers discrimination within the contract of employment in relation to pay and is discussed in the next chapter. The Race Relations Act was amended in 2003 by the Race Relations Act 1976 (Amendment) Regulations 2003. The Sex Discrimination Act and the Race Relations Act cover contractual and non-contractual discrimination. Since December 1996, with the coming into force of the Disability Discrimination Act 1995 (amended by the Disability Discrimination Act 2005), it is also illegal to discriminate in respect of a person's disability. The Act covers areas other than employment, but only the relevant provisions will be covered in this text. Until recently, none of the legislation went as far as international law and therefore it was legal under UK law to discriminate on the grounds of age, religion, political persuasion and so on. The government, however, was required to legislate to prevent discrimination in most of these areas to implement the Anti-Discrimination Framework Directive (2000/78/EC). The Framework Directive also required significant changes to the Disability Discrimination Act 1995. Legislation prohibiting discrimination at work on the grounds of religion or sexual orientation was implemented by the Employment Equality (Religion or Belief) Regulations and the Employment Equality (Sexual Orientation) Regulations 2003, and legislation prohibiting discrimination on the grounds of age was implemented by the Employment Equality (Age) Regulations 2006.

The legislation is monitored and kept under review by a body which also has the power to issue codes of practice. The Commission for Equality and Human Rights (CEHR) took over the role of the Equal Opportunities Commission, the Commission for Racial Equality and the Disability Rights Commission, and in addition monitors the Employment Equality (Sexual Orientation) Regulations (SO Regulations), the Employment Equality (Religion or Belief) Regulations (RB Regulations) and the Employment Equality (Age) Regulations (Age Regulations).

The Race Relations Act (RRA) 1976 used the Sex Discrimination Act of the previous year as its model. While there were stark differences between the two pieces of legislation between 2001 and 2005, these were to a large extent eliminated by the Employment Equality (Sex Discrimination) Regulations 2005 and therefore it is appropriate to discuss both pieces of legislation together, noting the differences as we go along. Similar wording applies to the SO Regulations, the RB Regulations and the Age Regulations.

The Sex Discrimination Act (SDA) prohibits discrimination on the grounds of sex (s.1) or marital status (s.3) and applies equally to men and women (s.2). The Act did not, however, prevent discrimination on the grounds that a person is single – marital status means being married. In *Bick* v. *School for the Deaf* [1976] IRLR 326 the employee was dismissed just before her wedding day because of a policy operated by the school of not employing married staff. It was held that the applicant had no action for discrimination on the grounds of marital status, as she was still single at the date of her dismissal. However, a tribunal decision has now held that such action is discrimination on the grounds of marital status. In *Turner* v. *Stephen Turner* (2005) 138 EOR 31 the complainant was dismissed when it was announced that she was to marry her employer's son. The tribunal dismissed the complaint of sex discrimination as there was no evidence that the employer would not have treated a male employee, in similar circumstances, in the same way. The tribunal did, however, find that there was discrimination on the grounds of marital status. The tribunal found that there was no binding authority on the point and that Article 12 of the European Convention on Human Rights states: 'Men and women of marriageable age have the right to marry and to found a family according to the national laws governing the exercise of this right.' As such, the tribunal found that to give effect to the Human Rights Act 1998, s.3 SDA had to be interpreted as protecting those who were about to marry. To find differently would be contrary to the mischief at which s.3 SDA and the HRA was aimed. This only applies to a direct discrimination claim as the amended definition of indirect discrimination makes it clear that this protection only applies to married persons.

Since 1999 the Act also prohibits discrimination on the grounds that a person intends to undergo, is undergoing or has undergone gender reassignment (s.2A). Such an employee must not be treated less favourably than someone who is absent through sickness or injury.

The Race Relations Act prohibits discrimination on the grounds of colour, race, nationality or ethnic or national origins (s.3(1)). While this Act does not specifically include protection against discrimination on the grounds of religion, the persons who practise that religion may themselves form a racial group within the meaning of the Act. Thus in *Seide* v. *Gillette Industries* [1980] IRLR 427 the Employment Appeal Tribunal held that the term 'Jewish' can mean membership of a race or ethnic group as well as a religion. In *Mandla* v. *Dowell Lee* [1983] 2 AC 548 the House of Lords held that

Sikhs were a racial group and in *Commission for Racial Equality* v. *Dutton* [1989] IRLR 122 the Court of Appeal held that gypsies were within the definition of racial group given that the definition under the Act referred to ethnic origins, and gypsies have a long history, their own customs and a unique dialect. The Court of Appeal in *Dawkins* v. *Department of Environment* [1993] IRLR 284 has decided that Rastafarians, on the other hand, are not a racial group for the purposes of the legislation. Their history only goes back 60 years and there is nothing to distinguish them from others of Jamaican or Afro-Caribbean descent. Protection from discrimination on the grounds of religion is now specifically provided by the RB Regulations 2003 discussed below.

The Race Relations Act 1976 (Amendment) Regulations 2003 amended the RRA to implement the Race Discrimination Directive (200/43/EC); however, unlike the RRA, the Directive only applies to discrimination on the grounds of race or ethnic or national origin, unlike the wider RRA which also covers colour and nationality. This means that changes made by the Regulations in the areas of burden of proof, harassment and indirect discrimination do not apply where discrimination is on the grounds of colour or nationality and the original definitions apply. The impact of this is there are now in theory two different burdens of proof, and two definitions of indirect discrimination under the RRA.

Both pieces of legislation cover employees but the protection is wider. Both Acts apply to anyone who works under or applies for 'a contract to personally execute any work or labour' (s.82 SDA; s.78 RRA). In *Quinnen* v. *Hovells* [1984] IRLR 227 it was held that the legislation would protect the self-employed provided they are providing personal services. (See also *Harrods Ltd* v. *Remick and Others* [1997] IRLR 583.) Furthermore, as protection comes from statute and not from the contract, an illegality within the contract (for example, failing to pay tax and insurance contributions) will not prevent an action being brought under the Act (*Leighton* v. *Michael* [1996] IRLR 67). In addition, should an employer commit an act of discrimination and then transfer his business, liability for the act passes onto the transferee (*DJM International Ltd* v. *Nicholas* [1995] IRLR 76).

Burden of proof (discrimination on the grounds of colour or nationality)

When the ground for the claim is discrimination on the basis of colour or nationality, the burden of proof is on the party alleging discrimination. This can be a heavy burden, as most employers will not be silly enough to blatantly admit the reason for their actions. The courts are aware that the burden can be heavy and have eased it somewhat over the years so that if the action of the employer leads to an inference of discrimination, the burden may shift to him to show some other reason for his actions. In the case of *Khanna* v. *MOD* [1981] ICR 653 the fact that the applicant had been passed over for promotion 22 times and the person eventually appointed was less experienced than the applicant gave rise to a *prima facie* presumption of discrimination which the employer had to rebut. This approach was modified by the Court of Appeal in *Baker* v. *Cornwall County Council* [1990] IRLR 194 and *King* v. *Great Britain China Centre* [1991] IRLR 513 where Neil LJ said that a difference in treatment and a difference in gender will often point to the possibility of discrimination. In such circumstances the tribunal will look to the employer for an explanation and if one is not forthcoming or is inadequate, it is legitimate to infer that discrimination has occurred and come to a conclusion on the balance of probabilities. This approach and in particular the judgement of Neil LJ was cited with approval by the House of Lords in *Zafar* v. *Glasgow City Council* [1998] IRLR 36. It is, however, up to the tribunal to decide whether to draw the inference of discrimination. In *Quereshi* v. *London Borough of Newham* [1991] IRLR 264 the tribunal refused to infer discrimination from Newham's failure to follow its own procedure, to follow its equality policy and to provide the statistics for the Commission for Racial Equality's questionnaire. An appeal lies if the tribunal draws the wrong inference from the employer's action. In *Anya* v. *University of Oxford* [2001] IRLR 377 the Court of Appeal held that both the employment tribunal and the Employment Appeal Tribunal had failed to correctly analyse their findings of inconsistencies in the University's evidence and breaches of the equal opportunities policy in finding there was no discrimination, and had failed to follow *King*. Conversely, in *Zafar*, the original tribunal decided that the conduct of the employer in the treatment of Zafar was below that of a reasonable employer and this raised the presumption that the employee had been treated less favourably. In the absence of a non-racial explanation, the tribunal felt that it had to draw the inference that the reason for the less favourable treatment had been Mr Zafar's race. The House of Lords held that the tribunal had erred. The fact that the conduct of the employer was less than that of a reasonable employer was irrelevant. The tribunal had also erred in deciding that given the absence of a non-racial explanation it should infer that the less favourable treatment had been on the grounds of Mr Zafar's race – 'this put the matter too highly [and was] inconsistent with later Court of Appeal authority' (per Lord Browne-Wilkinson).

Burden of proof (sex discrimination, discrimination on the grounds of race or ethnic or national origins)

Until the enactment of the Sex Discrimination (Indirect Discrimination and Burden of Proof) Regulations 2001, the above text on the burden of proof in race discrimination claims applied equally in a sex discrimination case. The government, however, was required to implement the Burden of Proof Directive (97/80/EC) which only applies in sex discrimination claims. Article 4 of the Directive requires Member States to take such measures as are necessary to ensure that in complaints of sex discrimination the burden is on the complainant initially to establish facts from which the tribunal may presume there has been direct or indirect discrimination, and thereafter the burden shifts to the respondent to prove that there has been no such discrimination. The Regulations implement the Directive by inserting s.63A into the Sex Discrimination Act. This provides that where the complainant proves facts from which the tribunal could conclude, in the absence of an adequate explanation from the respondent, that the respondent has committed an act of discrimination, the tribunal shall uphold the complaint unless the respondent proves he did not commit the act. The Regulations only apply to sex discrimination in matters of employment, self-employment or vocational training. The Regulations thus impose a statutory duty on a tribunal to shift the burden of proof to the respondent where the facts establish a *prima facie* case of sex discrimination. By the Race Relations Act 1976 (Amendment) Regulations 2003 the same burden of proof now applies in claims of discrimination based on the grounds of race or ethnic or national origins. As noted, the old burden applies where the claim is on the basis of colour or nationality. It may be that in practice, however, cases such as *King* and *Zafar* mean in reality the differences between the two will be minimal.

There have been a number of cases on the burden of proof. In *University of Huddersfield* v. *Wolff* [2004] IRLR 534 the EAT held that the burden shifts once the tribunal has concluded that a *prima facie* case of less favourable treatment (on the grounds of sex or race) has been made out and has set out the relevant facts on which it has made its findings, so that the employer knows what it has to justify. Only at that stage must the tribunal consider the employer's explanations (see also *Sinclair Roche & Temperley* v. *Heard* [2004] IRLR 763). In *Rihal* v. *London Borough of Ealing* [2004] IRLR 642 the Court of Appeal stated that a tribunal is obliged to consider all the evidence about the conduct of the alleged discriminator before or after the event complained about and should not look at incidents in isolation where there are allegations of discrimination over a period of time, as to do so would give a fragmented picture. However, the same court in *Bahl* v. *Law Society* [2004] IRLR 799 has also stated that unreasonable treatment of the complainant alleging discrimination, if there is nothing else to explain it, cannot of itself lead to an inference of discrimination, even in the absence of evidence from the employer that it would treat a member of the opposite sex the same. In addition, the tribunal must find that subjectively racial or sexual considerations were in the mind of the discriminator. It appears, however, that, despite the above, the evidence needed to shift the burden is not that onerous. In *Webster* v. *Brunel University* EAT 0730/04 the complainant was employed as a help desk officer, providing IT support to administrative staff. She complained that while giving advice over the telephone to accommodation staff, she heard laughter in the background and heard someone say 'Paki'. The tribunal dismissed her complaint on the basis that the accommodation office was a public place and someone other than a member of staff could have said the offending word. The EAT, however, said that once the tribunal had established the facts, it had to ask itself if the employer could have been responsible. Once the complainant had shown the speaker could have been an employee, the burden shifted to the employer to prove it was not. This seems a very low threshold. Further in *Dattani* v. *Chief Constable of West Mercia Police* [2005] IRLR 327 the EAT pointed out that a tribunal may also find inferences of discrimination from evasive or equivocal replies from the employer to any questions from the complainant.

The Court of Appeal in *Igen Ltd* v. *Wong* [2005] IRLR 258 has refined previous EAT guidance to tribunals (in *Barton* v. *Investec Henderson Crosthwaite Securities Ltd* [2003] IRLR 332) on how to approach the burden of proof in discrimination claims as follows:

'(1) Pursuant to s.63A of the SDA, it is for the claimant who complains of sex discrimination to prove on the balance of probabilities facts from which the tribunal could conclude, in the absence of an adequate explanation, that the respondent has committed an act of discrimination against the claimant which is unlawful by virtue of Part 11 or which by virtue of s.41 or 42 of the SDA is to be treated as having been committed against the claimant. These are referred to below as "such facts".

(2) If the claimant does not prove such facts he or she will fail.

(3) It is important to bear in mind in deciding whether the claimant has proved such facts that it is unusual to find direct evidence of sex discrimination. Few employers would be prepared to admit such discrimination, even to themselves. In some cases the discrimination will not be an intention but merely based on the assumption that "he or she would not have fitted in".

(4) In deciding whether the claimant has proved such facts, it is important to remember that the outcome at this stage of the analysis by the tribunal will therefore usually depend on what inferences it is proper to draw from the primary facts found by the tribunal.

(5) It is important to note the word "could" in s.63A(2). At this stage the tribunal does not have to reach a definitive determination that such facts would lead it to the conclusion that there was an act of unlawful discrimination. At this stage a tribunal is looking at the primary facts before it to see what inferences of secondary fact could be drawn from them.

(6) In considering what inferences or conclusions can be drawn from the primary facts, the tribunal must assume that there is no adequate explanation for those facts.

(7) These inferences can include, in appropriate cases, any inferences that it is just and equitable to draw in accordance with s.74(2)(b) of the SDA from an evasive or equivocal reply to a questionnaire or any other questions that fall within s.74(2) of the SDA.

(8) Likewise, the tribunal must decide whether any provision of any relevant code of practice is relevant and if so, take it into account in determining such facts pursuant to s.56A(10) of the SDA. This means that inferences may also be drawn from any failure to comply with any relevant code of practice.

(9) Where the claimant has proved facts from which conclusions could be drawn that the respondent has treated the claimant less favourably on the ground of sex, then the burden of proof moves to the respondent.

(10) It is then for the respondent to prove that he did not commit, or as the case may be, is not to be treated as having committed, that act.

(11) To discharge that burden it is necessary for the respondent to prove, on the balance of probabilities, that the treatment was in no sense whatsoever on the grounds of sex, since "no discrimination whatsoever" is compatible with the Burden of Proof Directive.

(12) That requires a tribunal to assess not merely whether the respondent has proved an explanation for the facts from which such inferences can be drawn, but further that it is adequate to discharge the burden of proof on the balance of probabilities that sex was not a ground for the treatment in question.

(13) Since the facts necessary to prove an explanation would normally be in the possession of the respondent, a tribunal would normally expect cogent evidence to discharge that burden of proof. In particular, the tribunal will need to examine carefully explanations for failure to deal with the questionnaire procedure and/or code.'

This clearly establishes a two-part process whereby the claimant has to establish that there has been discrimination which has been committed by the employer or for which the employer is responsible. Once that is established, the burden passes to the employer to show that there was no discrimination.

Presentation of complaint

A complaint of discrimination must be presented within three months of the act of discrimination or the last act of discrimination. Any act done over a continuing period is treated as being done at the end of that period (s.68(7) RRA, s.76(6) SDA). This can cause problems, however. In *Calder* v. *James Finlay Corporation* [1989] IRLR 55 the employers operated a subsidised mortgage scheme which by an unwritten rule excluded women. The employee lodged a complaint five months after being refused the mortgage but within three months after leaving the employment. It was held that the refusal of the mortgage was a continuing act which continued during the whole of the time she was employed, and only ceased when she left her employment. The question of a continuing act arose again in *Littlewoods Organisation* v. *Traynor* [1993] IRLR 154. Here an employee had brought a grievance under the company procedure, complaining of discrimination by a supervisor. Remedial action was promised but never taken. In January 1990 the employee took voluntary redundancy and then entered a complaint of discrimination in the employment tribunal. The act had taken place more than three months before proceedings were commenced. The EAT, however, held that where remedial action was promised and never carried out, the possibility of further discrimination existed and that *per se* could constitute continuing discrimination. The complaint was therefore not out of time. In *Cast* v. *Croydon College* [1998] IRLR 318 it was held to be a continuing act of discrimination when an employer refused on three separate occasions to allow an employee to job share after returning from maternity leave, so that the three-month time limit started to run from the date of her resignation, prompted by the refusal. Conversely, in *Sougrin* v. *Haringey Health Authority* [1992] IRLR 416 the Court of Appeal held that the appointment of a nurse at a particular grade and the refusal of her appeal against that grade was a one-off act and not a continuing one. The fact that she continued to be paid at a lower salary than a white staff nurse was a consequence of a one-off act and not the act itself. Moreover, in *Tyagi* v. *BBC World Service* [2001] IRLR 465 the Court of Appeal distinguished *Calder* and *Cast* in respect of a complainant who claimed that a discriminatory recruitment policy, which resulted in a post not being offered to him, was a continuing act allowing him to claim out of time. The court held that there was a difference between a practice which prevented an existing employee from gaining promotion under s.4(2) RRA, and a policy which prevented a non-employee from gaining a job. The former would be a continuing act, whereas the latter was not and thus any claim had to be presented within three months of the refusal of the job.

Further problems with the three month rule can be seen in *Adekeye* v. *Post Office* [1997] IRLR 105. Adekeye was summarily dismissed on 8 June 1991. She appealed against her dismissal, the appeal being heard on 17 August 1991 and which confirmed her dismissal. The Employment Appeal Tribunal felt that although initially the dismissal had not been racially motivated, there had been racial discrimination in the way the appeal was handled and remitted the case back to the tribunal. At that hearing the Post Office argued that, given the date of termination was 8 June 1991, Adekeye was not an employee at the time of the appeal and therefore had no protection under the RRA. The tribunal argued that given s.4(1)(c) made it unlawful to discriminate by refusing or deliberately omitting to offer employment, this provision would cover employees who were dismissed and were awaiting an appeal against that dismissal. The EAT rejected this argument. The Appeal Tribunal said that Adekeye was an ex-employee at the time of the discrimination (the appeal) and therefore (under the legislation at the time) was not protected, a decision endorsed by the Court of Appeal.

The implications of this decision were far reaching and severely limited protection by creating a loophole in the law. It appeared, however, that this limit on the protection of ex-employees only applied in respect of race discrimination claims. In *Coote* v. *Granada Hospitality Ltd* [1998] IRLR 656 the ECJ held that Article 6 of the Equal Treatment Directive requires Member States to protect workers from discrimination after the employment relationship has ended. This led to the Employment Appeal Tribunal ([1999] IRLR 452) finding that an ex-employee could make a complaint of victimisation against her ex-employers who refused to provide her with a reference after she had brought a sex discrimination case against them. However, in the case of *Rhys-Harper* v. *Relaxion Group plc* [2001] EWCA Civ 634 the Court of Appeal applied *Adekeye* and distinguished *Coote*. The court said that the ECJ decision in *Coote* required a different interpretation to be placed on s.4 Sex Discrimination Act, because of Article 6 of the Equal Treatment Directive, and so provided protection for ex-employees who had been victimised on the ground of sex after the relationship had ended. This did not extend to protecting ex-employees under the provisions of s.6 of the 1975 Act or s.4 of the 1976 Act. In both sections there was a requirement for the employee to be employed when the discriminatory acts occurred and as such Rhys-Harper had no claim. However, the House of Lords in *Relaxion Group plc* v. *Rhys-Harper* [2003] IRLR 484 and *D'Souza* v. *Lambeth London Borough Council* [2003] IRLR 484 held that post-termination discrimination was covered by both the RRA and the SDA provided that there was a connection between the act and the employment. While the Sex Discrimination Act 1975 (Amendment) Regulations 2003 and the Race Relations Act 1976 (Amendment) Regulations of the same year both introduce protection against post-termination discrimination, this will not protect victims where the basis of the post-termination discrimination is on the grounds of colour or nationality, and as such *D'Souza* is still of importance.

5.2 Direct Discrimination

Direct discrimination occurs when a person is treated less favourably on the grounds of sex or race. The relevant provisions are s.1(1)(a) of both Acts. In *Sidhu* v. *Aerospace Composite Technology Ltd* [2000] IRLR 602 the Court of Appeal stated that to find direct discrimination under s.1(1)(a) of the 1976 Act the complainant must show that he has been treated less favourably than a person of another race and the reason for the less favourable treatment is the complainant's race. Therefore if an employee had been assaulted for non-racial reasons and had retaliated and subsequently had been dismissed, if this was because of a policy adopted by the employer which disregarded provocation and other mitigating circumstances, this was a non-race-specific policy and could not found a race discrimination claim without evidence that persons of a different race in the same circumstances had been treated more favourably.

One act is sufficient and the motive behind the action is irrelevant; there is no defence once the claim has been proved. In *Greig* v. *Community Industries* [1979] IRLR 158 the applicant was on a work experience scheme for painting and decorating. She was withdrawn from the scheme when the only other girl left 'for her own good'. It was held that she had suffered direct discrimination and the motive behind the action was irrelevant. Trivial differences in treatment are, however, not discriminatory, according to Denning MR in the famous (or infamous) case of *Peake* v. *Automotive Products* [1978] QB 233. In this case Mr Peake claimed direct discrimination on the basis that the women in his factory were allowed to leave five minutes earlier than the men. The employer argued that the reason was that the women would be trampled in the rush if they did not leave at a different time to the men. The Court of Appeal held that there was no discrimination on three grounds: first, rules for safety and good administration could not be discriminatory; second, 'it would be very wrong if this statute were to obliterate the chivalry and courtesy which we expect mankind to give to womankind'; third, the *de minimis* principle. The first reason was considered dangerous by later critics of the judgement because it suggested that motive was a valid consideration in deciding whether discrimination had occurred. This is clearly against the legislation. The second reason given quite frankly wipes out the whole purpose of anti-discriminatory provisions. While Denning admitted he may have gone too far in *Peake* in the later case of *MOD* v. *Jeremiah* [1980] ICR 13, he still supported the decision on the grounds of *de minimis*. While five minutes a day may not seem a lot, it adds up to 25 minutes a week which, taken over a 48-week year, is a lot of paid time to which the men were not entitled.

It has been decided that assumptions based on sex can also be direct discrimination. In *Horsey* v. *Dyfed County Council* [1982] IRLR 395 Mrs Horsey was denied a place on a training course by her employers because, under county council rules, she was required to remain in her job for two years after completing the course. Her employers discovered that her husband had recently obtained employment in London, and assumed that he was the breadwinner and his wife would resign and join him after completing the course. Mrs Horsey was never asked her intentions. It was held that she had been discriminated against. Likewise, assuming that a woman with young children will be an unreliable employee is sex discrimination (*Hurley* v. *Mustoe* [1981] IRLR 208). On the other hand, it is not discriminatory to take into account natural differences between the sexes. In *Schmidt* v. *Austicks Bookshops Ltd* [1977] IRLR 360 it was held not to be discriminatory to tell women they could not wear trousers to work when men were also subjected to rules on dress.

Section 1(1)(a) of both pieces of legislation talk about discrimination 'on the grounds of' a person's sex or race. The concept of a person's sex has been widened by the case of *P* v. *S and Cornwall County Council* [1996] IRLR 347. Here the applicant was dismissed when he informed his employer that he was about to undergo gender reassignment surgery and live his life as a woman. The employment tribunal considered that a claim did not lie under the Sex Discrimination Act but referred the question to the ECJ as to whether discrimination on the grounds of gender reassignment could be in breach of the Equal Treatment Directive. The ECJ held that P had been discriminated on the grounds of sex for two reasons. First, given that a fundamental principle of Community law is equality and the right not to be discriminated on the grounds of sex, it followed that a person was not only protected because of the sex they were born, but also because of the sex they chose to become. Second, the fact that P showed that she received less favourable treatment by comparison with persons of her former sex showed that the treatment she suffered was based on her sex. The Sex Discrimination Act now specifically prohibits less favourable treatment on the grounds of gender reassignment. In *A* v. *Chief Constable of West Yorkshire Police* [2004] IRLR 573 the House of Lords stated that EU law requires that a transsexual person must be recognised in her reassigned gender for the purposes of sex discrimination law. Thus in a case of a transsexual person, the complainant's treatment must be compared to the treatment afforded to the sex to which he/she used to belong.

After *P* v. *S* it was thought that logically the principle of equality would also protect against discrimination on the grounds of sexual orientation. On this basis two cases were referred to the ECJ. In *Grant* v. *South-West Trains Ltd* [1998] IRLR 206 Grant argued that a policy of paying benefits only to heterosexual partners of employees was in breach of the Equal Pay Directive. While the Advocate-General gave the opinion that there was such a breach, the ECJ declined to follow that opinion and ruled that Community law, as it then stood, did not cover discrimination based on sexual orientation. In a similar case, *R* v. *Secretary of State for Defence ex parte Perkins* [1998] IRLR 508, the High Court originally referred the same issue to the ECJ in respect of the forces' ban on homosexuals. Again the Advocate-General gave the opinion that such a ban was contrary to the Equal Treatment Directive but that whether the ban could be justified on the basis of ensuring combat effectiveness was outside the scope of both the EC Treaty and the Directive. Following the ruling in *Grant*, however, the ECJ asked Lightman J in the High Court whether he wished to withdraw the reference. Lightman J, in considering the issue, said it must be reasonably inferred that the word 'sex' in both the Equal Pay and the Equal Treatment Directives was intended to have the same meaning and thus, albeit reluctantly, he was bound to withdraw the reference. However, there appeared to be some protection from the case of *Smith* v. *Gardner Merchant* [1998] IRLR 510. Smith, who was gay, was employed as a barman. Following a complaint about his conduct from a female member of staff, Smith was subjected to disciplinary proceedings, during which he alleged that the member of staff had made offensive remarks about his homosexuality and had punched him on one occasion. The company upheld the female member of staff's complaint, choosing not to believe the applicant's complaints and dismissed Smith for gross misconduct. Smith complained of sex discrimination to an employment tribunal which decided it did not have the jurisdiction to hear the complaint, a position upheld by the Employment Appeal Tribunal. Smith appealed to the Court of Appeal. The Court of Appeal held that the tribunal had understandably but wrongly come to the decision that it did not have jurisdiction. The tribunal had concluded that Smith was being treated differently from a man who was not gay and that but for his homosexuality the less favourable treatment would not have happened. As such, there would be no protection. However, the Court of Appeal held that the proper question to ask was whether Smith was treated differently from a woman in similar circumstances and, if so, was this different treatment on the grounds of his sex. The correct comparator in Mr Smith's case, therefore, was a lesbian. If it could be shown that the member of staff who subjected the applicant to harassment would have treated a lesbian in the same way, there was no discrimination. If, however, she would not have harassed a lesbian, Mr Smith had been treated less favourably on the grounds of his sex. Likewise, if Mr Smith could show that the decision in not believing his allegations taken by his employers was predominantly because he was a man, and not because he was gay, again he had suffered less favourable treatment because of his sex. On the basis of the decision, the Court of Appeal remitted the case back to the tribunal. It should be noted that this case did not conflict with *Grant* or *Perkins*. There was still no protection against discrimination on the grounds of sexual orientation, but if it could be argued that the less favourable treatment was directed at gay men and the treatment of a gay woman would be different (or vice versa) then the complainant would be protected by the Sex Discrimination Act.

In *Governing Body of Mayfield School* v. *Pearce* [2001] IRLR 669 CA a teacher complained of homophobic abuse by pupils. The Court of Appeal held that no action lay under the Sex Discrimination Act because there was no evidence that a gay man would not have suffered the same sort of abuse

(*Smith*, above). However, the court went on to say that at the time of the complaint the Human Rights Act 1998 was not in force and thus there was no duty on the tribunal to interpret the 1975 Act in a way to ensure compatibility, but if the complaint had arisen after the Act had been in force, the abuse would have been a breach of Sch 1, Part 1, Arts 8 and 14 and the complainant would have been able to seek redress. In addition to potential protection under the HRA, the Employment Equality (Sexual Orientation) Regulations 2003 now provide specific protection in the area of sexual orientation and are discussed in more detail below.

In the important case of *James v. Eastleigh Borough Council* [1990] 2 AC 751 the House of Lords discussed the interpretation of the words 'on the grounds of (sex or race)' in s.1(1)(a) of both pieces of legislation. In the case, Mrs James was entitled to free admission to the local swimming pool because at 61 she had reached the state pension age for women which is 60. Her husband, on the other hand, who was the same age as his wife, could not get free admission until he reached the state retirement age for men, that is 65. There was no intention to discriminate on the part of the council, it was merely giving concessions to pensioners and Mr James did not become a pensioner by the state rules until he reached 65. The House of Lords established what has become known as the 'but for' test. The House affirmed that the test for discrimination is objective and motive or intention is irrelevant. If the reason for the less favourable treatment is the complainant's sex (or race) then there is discrimination. In other words but for Mr James's sex would he have received the concession? The answer is 'yes'. It was because he was a man that the concession did not apply. Second, they held that to use a criterion to decide an advantage, which is itself discriminatory, means that the action resulting from the use of that criterion must also be discriminatory. In other words, the state retirement age is discriminatory because it gives men less favourable treatment. To give someone a concession based on the state retirement age therefore perpetuates the discrimination. In the employment field, many employers give concessions based on length of service. This is not discriminatory, provided that when calculating length of service, time women have out for maternity leave is counted in the calculation. If it is not, then women will have to be employed longer to acquire the concession. This is less favourable treatment and is based on a selection criterion which is discriminatory because it puts women at a disadvantage. From the *James* case, if the criterion is discriminatory, so too is any action flowing from the use of that criterion.

The application of the 'but for' test can be seen in *Coyne v. Home Office* [2000] ICR 1443. In that case Coyne complained of sexual harassment by a member of staff. Her supervisor told her manager that Coyne was to blame and that she should be relocated. Her complaint was not dealt with for over two years and she was subsequently dismissed. Coyne argued that the failure to deal with her complaint of sexual harassment constituted sex discrimination. The Court of Appeal held that in order for a claim to lie, Coyne had to show that but for her sex the complaint of harassment would have been investigated. Here, however, there was no evidence that the Home Office would have treated a complaint by a man in a more favourable way. The detriment she suffered was the failure of the Home Office to investigate her complaint but the evidence did not show that this failure was due to her sex.

While both Acts use similar wording in s.1(1)(a) there is an important difference. The Sex Discrimination Act talks about less favourable treatment on the grounds of her sex, whereas the Race Relations Act talks about less favourable treatment on racial grounds. The importance of the distinction is seen in the case of *Showboat Entertainment Centre* v. *Owens* [1984] 1 WLR 384 where an employee was dismissed for failing to obey an order not to admit young black men into an amusement arcade. The Court of Appeal held that, on the wording of the Act, discrimination had occurred if the reason for the less favourable treatment was race – the Act did not specify that it had to be the complainant's race. The employee had been dismissed because he refused to obey an order which was racially discriminatory, therefore he had been dismissed on racial grounds (see also *Weathersfield Ltd t/a Van Truck Rentals* v. *Sargent* [1999] IRLR 94). While the judgements are to be welcomed, the basis of them leads to the question of whether the same decision would have been reached if Mr Owens or Mrs Sargent had been dismissed or had suffered for refusing to obey an order not to discriminate against women.

Pregnancy

Both Acts talk of direct discrimination consisting of less favourable treatment. To discover if the treatment of the complainant is less favourable, a comparison must be made with the treatment of other persons either of the opposite sex, or from another racial group, where 'the relevant circumstances in one case are the same, or not materially different, in the other' (s.5(3) SDA; s.3(4) RRA). Therefore a comparison must be made with another person whose circumstances are the same, or not materially different (note the *Smith* case, above). In most cases, the comparison exists between people in the same circumstance (or a hypothetical comparator in unidentical but not wholly dissimilar circumstances – *Chief Constable of West Yorkshire* v. *Vento* [2001] IRLR 124) but the wording of the section has caused major problems when the reason for the less favourable treatment is pregnancy. This is important as a report published by the EOC in 2005 entitled '*Greater Expectations*' found that up to 30,000 jobs a year are lost as a result of pregnancy discrimination.

When the Sex Discrimination Act first came onto the statute books, the law argued that as a man could not get pregnant, there was no comparison when looking at the treatment of a pregnant woman and thus there could be no claim for sex discrimination. While such women would be protected by unfair dismissal provisions (see later), until 1993 this meant that any pregnant woman without the relevant continuity would not be protected by the law and this was clearly an unsatisfactory state of affairs. The position was rectified in the case of *Hayes* v. *Malleable Working Men's Club & Institute* [1985] IRLR 367 when the Employment Appeal Tribunal held that a comparison could be made between a pregnant woman and a man with a long-term health problem. Thus if the employer could show, for example, that he would have dismissed a man if he needed extended time off for sickness, it would not be discrimination to dismiss the pregnant woman. This should be qualified by saying that there had to be an objective reason why those dismissals would take place, such as business necessity – in other words, the employer could not continue to keep the job open for the employee.

While this interpretation was infinitely better, it still leads to the situation of the employer hypothesising as to his likely conduct should one of his male employees go on long-term sick leave. It is also an incorrect analogy. Pregnancy is not an illness, it is often planned and normally people do not plan when to be sick. A better way of looking at this area would be to argue that if an employer dismisses a pregnant woman he is imposing a condition that, to remain in employment, a person should not become pregnant. This condition will obviously only affect women and can therefore form the basis of an indirect discrimination claim discussed below. This reasoning was, however, rejected by the Employment Appeal Tribunal in the case of *Webb* v. *EMO Air Cargo (UK) Ltd* [1990] IRLR 124 (EAT). In this case, Webb had been taken on by the employer as a replacement for a woman going on maternity leave. Just after she obtained the post, Webb discovered she too was pregnant, and would need maternity leave at virtually the same time as the woman she had replaced. The employer therefore sacked her and successfully argued that he would have sacked a man in similar circumstances, because he needed someone who could cover the 40-week maternity period. Webb appealed against the decision and before her case came before the Court of Appeal, there was a series of cases in the European Court of Justice on pregnancy dismissals. The leading case in the ECJ was *Dekker* v. *VJV Centrum* [1991] IRLR 27 where a woman was offered a job and then the offer was withdrawn when she informed her new employers that she was pregnant. The employers argued that they could not afford to employ her, because under Dutch law they would have to pay her salary for the period of her maternity leave and the salary of a replacement. The ECJ stated that there was no valid comparison with a man with a long-term illness, because pregnancy is not an illness. Only women can get pregnant, therefore to treat a woman less favourably than a man because she is pregnant is treating her less favourably because of her sex. Less favourable treatment because of pregnancy must therefore be direct discrimination on the grounds of sex, to which there is no defence. It followed, therefore, that VJV were liable as they could not raise a defence of economic circumstances. A similar conclusion was reached in *Handels- og Kontorfunktionaererernes Forbund i Danmark* v. *Dansk Arbejdsgiverforening* [1992] ICR 332.

The basis of all the law against sex discrimination, in all the Member States of the EC, is the Equal Treatment Directive. While a Directive is only binding on Member States as to the result and not the method of implementation, it can become binding if the terms are precise and do not leave the Member State with any discretion in its application. In *Marshall* v. *Southampton & South West Hampshire Area Health Authority* [1986] QB 401 the ECJ ruled that a policy requiring women to retire at 60, while men could continue until 65, was contrary to the Equal Treatment Directive even though it was (then) permissible under national law. The court ruled, however, that a Directive does not have horizontal effect. In other words, it binds the state and organs of the state but not private employers. The ECJ, however, has been generous on its interpretation of organs of the state, and cases like *Foster* v. *British Gas plc* [1991] ICR 84 ECJ show that nationalised industries are bound by the Directives but public limited companies are not (*Doughty* v. *Rolls-Royce plc* [1992] IRLR 126). The case of *Francovich* v. *State of Italy* [1992] IRLR 84 could lead to individuals suing the state for failure to implement a Directive fully, but will still not provide an action for the employee against her private employer. This was the situation that faced Mrs Webb when she took her appeal to the Court of Appeal. In the ECJ case of *Marleasing S.A.* v. *La Commercial Internacional de Alimentacion S.A.* [1992] 1 CMLR 305 the court decided that existing national law had to be interpreted in the light of the wording and purpose of a later Directive. The Court of Appeal in *Webb* felt that the Sex Discrimination Act was unambiguous in its necessity to have a comparator in the same or materially similar circumstances. As such, given that the employer had argued that he would have treated a man with a long-term illness in the same way, Mrs Webb was not the victim of sex discrimination. The court added, however, that if the interpretation of the statute was wrong, *Dekker* could be distinguished in that Mrs Webb's condition made her incapable of doing the job for which she was appointed, that is, cover for the duration of a maternity leave. The later Court of Appeal decision in *Shoner* v. B&R *Residential Lettings Ltd* [1992] IRLR 317 lent support to the approach adopted in *Webb*.

Mrs Webb pursued an appeal to the House of Lords and that court referred the case to the ECJ ([1993] IRLR 27). The ECJ made a ruling ([1994] ICR 770) and the case came back to the House of Lords ([1995] IRLR 645). The essence of the ECJ decision was that pregnancy is not comparable with a pathological condition. In the Court's view, the dismissal of a pregnant woman who had been appointed for an indefinite period could not be justified on grounds relating to her inability to fulfil a condition of her employment contract temporarily. The fact that Webb was recruited initially to replace another woman on maternity leave did not affect the question and the dismissal of a woman in Webb's situation was contrary to the Equal Treatment Directive. The House of Lords, Lord Keith giving the leading judgement, noted that the ECJ had considered it relevant that Mrs Webb had been appointed for an indefinite period and that the period during which she would be unable to do the job was limited in relation to the total length of the contract. The Court thought that there could be a distinction between Webb's case and a woman appointed for a fixed period who would not be able to work for a large proportion of that period because of pregnancy. The Court then considered whether it was possible to construe the Sex Discrimination Act in a way that complied with the ECJ's ruling. The problem for their Lordships was the requirement in s.5(3) to compare the treatment of the woman with that of a comparator of the opposite sex whose relevant circumstances are the same or not materially different. Lord Keith stated that the only way to reconcile the wording of the Act with the ECJ ruling was to hold that:

> 'In the case where a woman is engaged for an indefinite period, the fact that the reason why she will be temporarily unavailable for work, at a time when to her knowledge her services will be particularly required, is pregnancy is a circumstance relevant to her case, being a circumstance which could not be present in the case of a hypothetical man.'

It did not follow that pregnancy would be a relevant circumstance where the woman was denied employment for a fixed term during the whole of which her pregnancy would make her unavailable for work, nor in the situation where after her engagement for such a period the discovery of her pregnancy led to the cancellation of the engagement. To some extent, the outcome of the actual case was academic because s.99 Employment Rights Act 1996 (implementing the EC Pregnant Workers Directive 92/85/EC) makes it an unfair dismissal to dismiss a woman on the sole ground of pregnancy and no continuity is required. This means that in the future, women in Mrs Webb's position will pursue a claim for unfair dismissal and not a discrimination claim. This change in the law will not, however, help women who have action short of dismissal taken against them. For example, a company policy which requires women on maternity leave to return company cars where employees can keep the cars if they are on long-term sick leave will not be covered by the unfair dismissal provisions, and therefore the decision in *Webb* is still important. Unfortunately, however, the House of Lords did not really clarify the issue. To comply with the ECJ ruling, the Court ruled that where there is a dismissal of a pregnant woman on an indefinite contract, her pregnancy is not a relevant circumstance for the purposes of s.5(3). This still left the position unclear in the situation of a fixed term contract, or when action was taken against her short of dismissal. Is pregnancy a relevant circumstance? The decision left a great number of questions still unanswered, in particular whether any unfavourable treatment because of pregnancy is sex discrimination *per se*. The *Webb* decision was followed in *O'Neill* v. *Governors of St Thomas More RC Voluntary Aided Upper School* [1996] IRLR 372 in respect of a dismissal. However, the original decision in *Brown* v. *Rentokil* [1995] IRLR 211 was that the dismissal of a pregnant woman, who had exhausted her period of sick leave, was dismissal for sickness and not pregnancy. Mrs Brown appealed to the House of Lords who referred a number of questions to the ECJ, in particular whether it is contrary to the Equal Treatment Directive to dismiss a woman during her pregnancy as a result of absence through illness arising from that pregnancy and whether it was relevant that the dismissal occurred in accordance with a contractual provision entitling the employer to dismiss, irrespective of gender, after a stipulated number of weeks of absence.

The ECJ ([1998] IRLR 445) referred to the EC Pregnant Workers Directive (92/85/EC) and noted that Article 10 prohibited dismissal during the period from the beginning of the pregnancy to the end of maternity leave (save in exceptional circumstances not connected with the woman's condition). Hence the dismissal of a woman during pregnancy for absences due to such incapacity 'must therefore be regarded as essentially based on the fact of pregnancy'. Such a dismissal can only affect women and therefore constitutes direct discrimination on the grounds of sex. In respect of pathological conditions caused by pregnancy or childbirth which arise after the end of maternity leave, the question is whether the female worker's absences are treated in the same way as a male worker and if they are, then there is no sex discrimination. However, absences during the pregnancy and during maternity leave cannot be taken into account for the computation of the sickness period for dismissal under a contractual procedure. In deciding *Brown*, the ECJ went against their earlier decision of *Handels- og Kontorfunktionaerernes Forbund i Danmark (acting on behalf of Larsson)* v. *Dansk Handel & Service (acting on behalf of Fotex Supermarket A/S)* [1997] IRLR 643.

The decision is now embedded in s.3A SDA. It is interesting to note, however, that prior to the ECJ ruling in *Brown*, the Employment Appeal Tribunal decided that the dismissal of a woman suffering from post-natal depression and who thus failed to return to work after her 14-week maternity leave period was a pregnancy-related dismissal and therefore sex discrimination (*Caledonia Bureau Investment & Property* v. *Caffrey* [1998] IRLR 110). Note also *Patefield* v. *Belfast City Council* [2000] IRLR 664 where it was held that the replacement of a contract worker with a permanent employee while she was on maternity leave, and when the employer knew she wished to return, was sex discrimination.

In respect of actions other than dismissal, again the ECJ in the case of *Caisse Nationale d'Assurance Vieillesse des Travailleurs Salariés* v. *Thibault* [1998] IRLR 399 has held that a woman who was deprived of the right to an annual performance assessment, and consequently the possibility of qualifying for promotion, because she was on maternity leave, was discriminated on the grounds of sex. If she had not been on maternity leave she would have been assessed and could have qualified for promotion the following year. Furthermore, in *GUS Home Shopping Ltd* v. *Green* [2001] IRLR 75 it was held that an employer had discriminated on the grounds of sex when a discretionary bonus was not paid to Green when she was on maternity leave. The bonus was paid on the successful transfer of the marketing department in which she worked to another office. The transfer had occurred while she was on maternity leave and the only reason she was not paid it was because she had been absent at the relevant time. The Employment Appeal Tribunal held that the bonus scheme could not be divorced from the contract of employment as all it required was the proper performance of the employee's responsibilities under the contract.

It appears, therefore, that we have had a spate of cases discussing pregnancy and sex discrimination. The cases here must be read in conjunction with the protection of maternity rights afforded by the Court of Appeal decision in *Crees* v. *Royal London Mutual Insurance Society Ltd* and *Greaves* v. *Kwik Save Stores Ltd* [1998] IRLR 245), and demonstrate that at last the law is attempting to give adequate protection in respect of pregnancy and childbirth. This is further strengthened by the Employment Equality (Sex Discrimination) Regulations 2005, which amend the SDA. A new s.3A makes it clear that less favourable treatment of women on the grounds of pregnancy or maternity leave is sex discrimination.

5.3 Indirect Discrimination

The second type of discrimination recognised by the legislation is discrimination against a particular sexual or racial group which prejudices the complainant, hence the title 'indirect discrimination'. The definition of this type of discrimination is to be found in s.1(2)(b) of both Acts. While the definition is the same whether the claim is based on sex, marital status, race or national or ethnic origin, given that the 2003 Regulations do not cover discrimination on the grounds of colour or nationality, we have two definitions of indirect discrimination.

Indirect discrimination on the grounds of colour or nationality

For indirect discrimination on these grounds to be actionable, four conditions must be satisfied:

1. The employer imposes a condition or requirement which applies equally to all colours or nationalities.
2. The proportion of the complainant's national group who can comply with the condition or requirement is considerably smaller than the proportion of the other group who can comply.
3. The condition or requirement is not justifiable irrespective of colour or nationality.
4. It is to the complainant's detriment that he/she cannot comply with the condition or requirement.

This was the definition which used to apply to both sex and race discrimination prior to changes to the SDA and RRA and therefore the old cases will aid in interpretation. Thus in *Price* v. *CSC* [1978] IRLR 3 the imposition of an age requirement of 17½–28 for promotion to executive officer was held to be indirect discrimination as more women than men would be out of the labour market between those ages having children. Such age limits could also be indirect race discrimination, if potential applicants were immigrants who were unlikely to have the necessary qualifications for the job by the age of 28, because they had entered the educational system at a later age than the indigenous population. While examples are easy to state, it is necessary to examine those four conditions in more detail.

Condition or requirement imposed across the board

The definition of 'condition or requirement' has caused problems in this area. In the case of *Clarke* v. *Eley (IMI) Kynoch* [1982] IRLR 482 the Employment Appeal Tribunal suggested that the phrase be interpreted widely so as to include practices as well as express requirements. Thus a redundancy selection criterion which selected part-timers first was indirectly discriminatory towards women. However, in a case in the following year, the Court of Appeal restricted this interpretation by holding that something was only a condition or requirement if it was a necessity for the job (*Perera* v. *CSC* [1983] IRLR 166). This interpretation means that the employer who expresses a preference for certain experience or qualificatior.s is not imposing a condition or requirement for the purposes of indirect discrimination. It is submitted that this is an unfortunate decision – a view expressed by a later Court of Appeal in *Meer* v. *Tower Hamlets* [1988] IRLR 399 where the preference of a candidate who had previously worked for the local authority effectively excluded non-British applicants. However, in *Falkirk Council* v. *Whyte* [1997] IRLR 560, the Employment Appeal Tribunal gave a wide interpretation to the phrase 'condition or requirement' in the then s.1(1)(b) Sex Discrimination Act. In *Whyte*, the applicant had unsuccessfully applied for a managerial post at a prison. One of the selection criteria for short-listing was that managerial training and supervisory experience were desirable. Whyte argued that this indirectly discriminated against female applicants who were mainly in basic grade posts and who therefore did not have the training or experience. The employer argued that by saying that the training and experience were desirable they were stating a preference, not laying down a condition. The employment tribunal, however, said that as the factors in the particular case were decisive in the selection process, they were conditions or requirements and therefore the female applicants had been indirectly discriminated against as the employer could not objectively justify the requirements. This decision was upheld by the Employment Appeal Tribunal. It appears therefore that whatever the employer calls the offending provision, if the provision is in fact a deciding factor, it will be a condition or requirement for the purposes of indirect discrimination.

Given that to claim successfully, the complainant must show an unjustifiable requirement is being imposed, it is necessary for the courts to properly identify the offending provision. This has been demonstrated in equal pay claims where an argument can be raised that pay structures can create indirect discrimination. For example in the equal pay case of *Jenkins* v. *Kingsgate Clothing Productions Ltd* [1981] IRLR 228 ECJ it was held that a pay structure which paid less to part-timers could be justified if there was a sound economic reason for the difference and it was irrelevant that this created indirect discrimination. A similar case has been decided in the European Court in the form of *Enderby* v. *Frenchay Health Authority and Secretary of State for Health* [1994] 1 All ER 495. In this case, one of the arguments of the speech therapists, who were the complainants, was that by placing speech therapists on a lower salary scale there is indirect discrimination because speech therapists are predominantly female. In *Jenkins* the requirement was one of full-time working, and although there was no such identifiable requirement in *Enderby* the therapists won their claim. This is an important case because the real argument, of course, is that women tend to be concentrated in traditionally low-paid work and that the provisions of the Equal Pay Act 1970 are insufficient to deal with this problem. This will be discussed in the next chapter.

The comparative group

If the complainant can establish a condition or requirement, the next hurdle is to show that the proportion of his or her national group who can comply is considerably smaller than that of the comparative group who can comply. This suggests two questions; which is the comparative group and what is meant by 'considerably smaller'?

The issue of the comparative group is confusing. Is the comparison the workforce nationally, the workforce locally, or the workforce within the particular workplace? The problem rests on the fact that tribunals choose the relevant comparative group, which can lead to some confusing decisions, although the tribunals should look to the group that the employer is targeting, which may be national or local depending on the employer's business.

The case of *Clarke* has already been mentioned. The idea of imposing a requirement of full-time working as being discriminatory to women was also accepted in *Holmes* v. *HO* [1984] IRLR 260. The later case of *Kidd* v. *DRG (UK)* [1985] IRLR 190, however, seems to throw doubt on that general proposition and demonstrates the need to choose the relevant comparative group with care and the need for evidence to support the complainant's contentions. In the case the employer had a redundancy selection procedure which selected part-timers first. Within the workplace the majority of the women worked full time, but Mrs Kidd argued that nationally more women than men worked part time and therefore the selection policy was indirectly discriminatory. Unfortunately, Mrs Kidd assumed that this contention was self-evident, but the Employment Appeal Tribunal did not agree. It held that, in the absence of statistical evidence, it was no longer safe to assume that more women than men, or more married women than single women, work part time because of childcare responsibilities. However, in the case of *Meade-Hill* v. *British Council* [1997] IRLR 522 the Court of Appeal confirmed the decision of the Employment Appeal Tribunal and decided that the imposition of a mobility clause is indirectly discriminatory because it is common knowledge that women are secondary earners who would therefore find it difficult to comply with such a requirement to be mobile. Furthermore, in *Whiffen* v. *Oxfordshire CC* [2001] The Times, 3 April it was held that a redundancy selection policy selecting fixed term workers first was indirectly discriminatory to women. This decision is supported by the implementation of the Fixed Term Work Directive (99/70/EC) in October 2002.

Even if the complainant does bring forward statistical evidence to support the claim, the tribunal may reject the comparative group as being inappropriate. In *Pearse* v. *Bradford Metropolitan District Council* [1988] IRLR 379 one requirement of eligibility to apply for a post of senior lecturer was that the applicants had to work full time at the college run by the local authority. Pearse claimed that the requirement was discriminatory and produced statistics that out of the academic staff, 21.8 per cent of women could apply, compared with 46.7 per cent of men. The Employment Appeal Tribunal held that the comparative group was too wide. The group should have been those staff with the necessary qualifications to apply and not all academic staff. The complainant had therefore failed to show that the requirement was indirectly discriminatory. *Jones* v. *University of Manchester* [1993] IRLR 218 was the first case where the Court of Appeal was required to decide the relevant comparative group. In this case the university had advertised a post requiring a graduate between the ages of 27 and 35. Mrs Jones had been a mature student who graduated at 41. She argued that the job was asking for mature graduates, that is, those who had graduated after the age of 25, and as such the age limit of 35 was indirect discrimination against women because fewer mature women students than mature male students would complete their degree by that age. The Court of Appeal held that the applicant was choosing too narrow a comparative group. The advertisement was asking for graduates and not those who had graduated after the age of 25. To place any other interpretation would involve redrafting the advertisement. As such, there was no discriminatory effect on women.

While there are problems in identifying the pool for comparison, there are further problems in the meaning of the phrase 'considerably smaller'. In *Fulton* v. *Strathclyde Regional Council* [1986] IRLR 315 the council decided that certain posts should only be available for full-time staff. Statistics showed that 90 per cent of the women could comply with the requirement of full-time working and 100 per cent of the men. It was held that 90 per cent was not considerably smaller than 100 per cent. However, in *R* v. *Secretary of State for Employment ex parte Seymour-Smith and Perez* [1995] IRLR 464 the Court of Appeal granted a declaration that the then two-year qualifying period in unfair dismissal was indirectly discriminatory, despite the fact that the difference in proportion of men and women who could comply with the rule was less than 10 per cent. The case was appealed to the House of Lords ([1997] IRLR 315) which discharged the declaration, but adjourned the appeal pending a reference to the ECJ on a number of questions, including what is the legal test for establishing whether a measure adopted by a Member State has such a degree of disparate impact between men and women that it amounts to indirect discrimination. The Advocate-General gave an opinion which did not address the indirect discrimination point raised by the House of Lords. The ECJ ([1999] IRLR 253) on the indirect discrimination point said that the national court must verify whether the statistics available indicated that a considerably smaller percentage of women was unable to comply with the requirement and that it was not sufficient to consider the number of persons affected. The Court added that in the case the different percentage of men and women who could comply with the two-year rule did not on the face of it show indirect discrimination.

However, in the Court of Appeal decision of *London Underground* v. *Edwards (No. 2)* [1998] IRLR 364 it was decided that where 100 per cent of men could comply with the new rota operated by the employer and 95 per cent of women, the proportion of women who could comply was 'considerably smaller' even though the difference was only 5 per cent. Simon Brown LJ noted that parliament had not chosen to stipulate what difference in proportions would be sufficient to establish indirect discrimination and therefore must have intended the courts to adopt a flexible approach. Taking this into consideration, he looked at other factors, rather than merely regarding a comparison between 95 per cent and 100 per cent. Of the 2,023 men in the pool of comparison, not one was disadvantaged by the new rotas, whereas of the 21 women, one was disadvantaged. The employment tribunal was also entitled to take into account the large discrepancy in numbers between male and female train operators affected by the new rotas, which suggested that it was difficult or unattractive for women to take the jobs. Given the small numbers of women, if only one could not comply then this represented a larger proportion of the female group than if one of the males could not comply. The Court of Appeal therefore suggest that the difference in proportions is only one factor which should be examined when seeing if there is a disparate effect on one group. This is supported by the ECJ in *Seymour-Smith* where the court said that a small but persistent and constant disparity over a long period of time could indicate discrimination. The proportion of the groups who can comply, however, is still very important. In the USA, there is a rule that if the proportion of the complainant's group who can comply is 80 per cent or less there is discrimination. The Commission for Racial Equality has recommended the adoption of the same rule here, although to do so would lose the flexibility stated in *Edwards*. Whatever rules of thumb the tribunals adopt, it should be emphasised that the legislation talks of proportions and not numbers. This is important, because looking at the numbers within the group who can comply may lead to a wrong conclusion. For example, an employer employs 100 Scottish people who work full time and 200 English people, 100 who work full time and 100 who work part time. The employer introduces a redundancy selection policy which lays off part-time workers first. On numbers, 100 Scottish and 100 English can comply with the requirement of full-time working but when looking at proportions, 100 per cent of the Scottish can comply with the condition, but only 50 per cent of the English – hence there is indirect discrimination.

Justifiability

The third stage in the establishment of an indirect discrimination claim is that the requirement or condition is not justifiable irrespective of colour or nationality. In the early case of *Steel* v. *UPOW* [1978] ICR 181 the employers operated a rule which gave the choice of walks to the most senior post staff. Seniority was based on length of service as a permanent employee. Mrs Steel had been employed since 1961 but, because of Post Office rules, women could not hold permanent status until 1975. Mrs Steel lost her choice of walk to a man who had been employed since 1973, who on the rules had two years' seniority over Mrs Steel. The Employment Appeal Tribunal said that, in looking at the defence of justification, a tribunal had to distinguish between a requirement which was necessary and one which was merely convenient for the employer. In the case, it was not necessary to base seniority on permanent length of service but convenient because it had always been calculated in that way. Mrs Steel had therefore been the victim of indirect discrimination. This decision became blurred, however, after the Court of Appeal decision in *Ojutiku* v. *Manpower Services Commission* [1982] IRLR 418 when the court held that a requirement was justifiable if it 'would be acceptable to right thinking people as (having) sound and tolerable reasons for so doing'. In *Bilka-Kaufhaus* v. *Weber von Hartz* [1987] ICR 110 ECJ the European Court, in interpreting Article 141, stated that the employer would have to show 'objectively justified' grounds to make out the defence, in that the employer must show that any factors which have a disparate effect on one group 'correspond to a real need on the part of the undertaking, and are appropriate with a view to achieving the objectives pursued and are necessary to that end'. This interpretation has been supported in *Hampson* v. *DES* [1989] IRLR 69 where Balcombe LJ held that to show a condition is justifiable 'requires an objective balance to be struck between the discriminatory effect of the condition and the reasonable needs of the party who applies that condition'. This balancing is to be done by the tribunal as indicated by the Employment Appeal Tribunal in *Cobb* v. *Secretary of State for Employment and Manpower Services Commission* [1989]

IRLR 464 when it said: 'It is for the tribunal – to carry out the balancing exercise involved, taking into account all the surrounding circumstances and giving due emphasis to the degree of discrimination caused against the object or aim to be achieved – the principle of proportionality.' In *Allonby* v. *Accrington and Rossendale College* [2001] IRLR 364 the Court of Appeal gave guidance on the principle of proportionality. The court held that once the tribunal had identified what was the condition or requirement which had a disparate impact, the tribunal had to demonstrate that it had objectively weighed the justification for the condition or requirement against its discriminatory effect. At the minimum this meant conducting a critical evaluation of whether the employers' reasons demonstrated a real need. If there was a real need, the tribunal should consider the seriousness of the disparate impact and make an evaluation of whether those reasons were sufficient to outweigh it. If the tribunal gets the balance wrong, the Appeal Tribunal will intervene. Thus in *Saint Matthias Church of England School* v. *Crizzle* [1993] ICR 401 there was a condition that any applicant for the post of headteacher had to be a communicant (that is a Christian receiving Holy Communion). Crizzle was an Asian and a Christian but was not a communicant and therefore brought a claim of indirect racial discrimination. His complaint was upheld by the tribunal who decided that the requirement that the headteacher be a communicant was not necessary for efficient education and was therefore not justifiable. The Employment Appeal Tribunal disagreed. The Appeal Tribunal held that the school was concerned with spiritual worship as well as efficient education. This was a legitimate objective and the means of achieving it, that is, requiring the headteacher to be a communicant, was reasonable when weighed against the discriminatory effect.

Detriment to the complainant

The final hurdle in an indirect discrimination claim is that the complainant must suffer a detriment because he or she cannot comply with the condition or requirement imposed. By this last hurdle the Act limits the pool of complainants to those who actually apply for a job etc and are turned down because they cannot comply with the condition or requirement.

The Act talks of a complainant suffering a detriment because he or she cannot comply with the condition. The House of Lords, however, has made it clear in *Mandla* v. *Dowell Lee* [1983] 2 AC 548 that this does not mean that someone can theoretically comply, but whether it is reasonable to expect them to do so. In the case it was theoretically possible for a Sikh boy to comply with the condition of short hair, but not reasonable to expect him to.

The problem in this area is what exactly constitutes a detriment. In *MOD*

v. *Jeremiah* [1980] ICR 13 Lord Brandon described detriment as 'putting under a disadvantage' but in the later case of *De Souza* v. *AA* [1986] IRLR 103 it was held that suffering distress was not a detriment. In *Clymo* v. *Wandsworth London Borough Council* [1989] IRLR 241 the Employment Appeal Tribunal held that a refusal to allow a woman in a managerial post the opportunity of job sharing was not subjecting the complainant to a detriment. The tribunal accepted the argument that job sharing was not available for managers and if the facility was not available to others on her grade she had not suffered a detriment by being denied it. While the case also decided that full-time working was an inherent characteristic of the managerial job, rather than a condition or requirement and therefore there was no indirect discrimination, the discussion on the meaning of 'detriment' leads to a circular argument and creates loopholes in the legislation. The argument that there can be no detriment if the facility is not in existence must be fallacious.

Indirect discrimination on the grounds of sex or marital status

The Employment Equality (Sex Discrimination) Regulations 2005 introduced a new definition of indirect discrimination. The Regulations inserted a new s.1(2) and a new s.3 into the Sex Discrimination Act 1975 which redefined 'indirect discrimination' where there is an employment claim on the basis of sex discrimination or discrimination on the grounds of marital status. The definition now provides:

(a) that the employer applies a provision, criterion or practice which he applies or would apply equally to a man;
(b) which puts or would put women at a particular disadvantage when compared with men;
(c) which puts her at that disadvantage, and;
(d) which he cannot show to be a proportionate means of achieving a legitimate aim.

It will be noticed immediately that 'provision, criterion or practice' is not as proscriptive as 'condition or requirement', which was the earlier wording and still applies where discrimination is alleged on the grounds of colour or nationality. The words in the definition above do not connote something which is necessary for the job, although as stated earlier, the requirement that something is necessary for the job has been flexibly interpreted in *Falkirk Council* v. *Whyte*. In *British Airways plc* v. *Starmer* [2005] IRLR 863 a female pilot asked to reduce her hours by 50 per cent after having a baby. The employer refused on the basis that it would be difficult to reorganise schedules and it would be expensive to train replacements. After she sued for indirect sex discrimination the company introduced a policy saying that pilots could only reduce their hours by 25 per cent for safety reasons. The Employment Appeal Tribunal held that the decision not to allow her to go part time was a provision, criterion or practice even though the company argued that at the time of their refusal, there was no policy in place and the decision had been a one-off based on her request. This shows a liberal interpretation of 'provision, criterion or practice'.

The definition which was in force between 2001 and 2005 required the woman to show that a larger proportion of women compared with men was disadvantaged by the provision etc. In *Rutherford* v. *Secretary of State for Trade and Industry (No. 2)* [2004] IRLR 892 the Court of Appeal held that the sections of the Employment Rights Act 1996 which exclude those who have reached the age of 65 from unfair dismissal or redundancy compensation, do not have a disparate impact on men. The relevant pool of comparison was the entire workforce to which the requirement applied – that is, not just those disadvantaged by the age limit. On that comparison the differences were very small and did not show a disparate impact on men. The amended definition does not require the complainant to show proportions so it is debatable whether *Rutherford* would be decided the same way today. In *Hardys & Hansons* v. *Lax* [2005] EWCA Civ 846 the Court of Appeal held that the range of reasonable responses test does not apply to justification of indirect discrimination. Thomas LJ held that the principle of proportionality requires the tribunal to take into account the business needs of the business, but has to make its own decision as to whether the proposal (in this case for a full-time appointment) is reasonably necessary. A tribunal cannot only consider whether the employer's views are within a range of reasonable responses. He added that where the employer is relying on the economic needs of the business, it would be expected to adduce sufficient evidence to enable the tribunal to 'set out at least a basic economic analysis of the business and its needs'. A recent case, however, gives a broad interpretation of 'proportionate means of achieving a legitimate aim'. In *GMB* v. *Allen* [2007] All ER 497 GMB had encouraged its members to agree a pay settlement in equal pay litigation which seriously undervalued the women's claim. While the Employment Appeal Tribunal criticised the GMB's method of obtaining the members' agreement to the settlement, it held that the settlement of claims was a legitimate aim and the means adopted were appropriate. Elias P said: 'in short, the fact that the objective might be achieved by using unlawful, even dishonest practices does not necessarily mean that the means are disproportionate once it is accepted that the aim itself is legitimate' (para 89).

Indirect discrimination on the grounds of race or national or ethnic origin

The definition of 'indirect discrimination' under the Race Relations Act is the same as that of the Sex Discrimination Act when the basis of the claim is race or national or ethnic origin. The definition provides:

(a) that the employer applies a provision, criterion or practice which he applies or would apply equally to persons not of the same race or national or ethnic origins;

(b) which puts, or would put, persons of the same race or national or ethnic origins as that other at a particular disadvantage when compared to other persons;

(c) which puts that other at that disadvantage; and

(d) which the employer cannot show to be a proportionate means of achieving a legitimate aim.

5.4 Victimisation

Both Acts have a third type of discrimination known as victimisation. It is found in s.4 Sex Discrimination Act and s.2 Race Relations Act. Victimisation occurs when a person is treated less favourably because he or she has brought proceedings under either Act or the Equal Pay Act 1970, has given evidence in such proceedings, done anything under or by reference to any of the Acts, or has alleged that the discriminator has contravened one of the Acts unless the allegations were false and made in bad faith. The Court of Appeal in *Cornelius* v. *University College Swansea* [1987] IRLR 141 has said that it is the conduct listed in s.4 SDA and s.2 RRA which is the basis of a victimisation claim and not a person's sex or race. This means that the complainant must show that a person who has not done the act would be treated differently. In *St Helens MBC* v. *Derbyshire* [2007] UKHL 16 female catering staff argued that they were entitled to a bonus scheme operated for roadsweepers because their work was of equal value. While many claims were settled, some were not and those workers continued their claims. Before the hearing, they received letters from a senior council official stating that if their claims were successful it could lead to redundancies and deprive children of school dinners. The House of Lords held that this amounted to victimisation. In *Chief Constable of West Yorkshire* v. *Khan* [2001] IRLR 830 the House of Lords confirmed that the correct test was to see if a person who had not done the act would be treated differently. However, their Lordships rejected the 'but for' test applied by the Court of Appeal as they considered it too low a threshold. In the case the employee was not provided with a job reference because he was pursuing a race discrimination claim and the employer wished to preserve its position. If the 'but for' test was applied, 'but for' the race discrimination claim (the protected act) the references would have been provided. However the reason references were withheld was for the employer to preserve its position. Their Lordships therefore concluded that the correct interpretation of s.2 was that the less favourable treatment was 'by reason that' the applicant had carried out the protected act. In the leading case of *Aziz* v. *Trinity Taxis* [1988] ICR 534 a person was dismissed for making secret recordings to be used in discrimination proceedings. The employers showed that they would have dismissed anyone who had taped conversations, whatever the final purpose of the tapes. The Court of Appeal held that there was no victimisation. Aziz had been dismissed because he had recorded conversations and not because those recordings were to be used in any proceedings under the Act. By contrast in *London Borough of Lambeth* v. *D'Souza* [1999] IRLR 240 the applicant had brought several successful race discrimination complaints against his employer. He alleged further discrimination and was suspended by his employer as a troublemaker. He brought a victimisation complaint and was dismissed. His complaint of victimisation was upheld by the employment tribunal and the House of Lords (see above) The Court of Appeal, however, has stated that the concept of victimisation requires the discriminator to have a motive which is consciously connected with the legislation. In other words, it must be shown that the fact that a protected act was done or believed to have been done by the complainant at the very least influenced the alleged discriminator in his unfavourable treatment of the complainant (*Nagarajan* v. *London Regional Transport* [1998] IRLR 73). This interpretation of s.2, however, was rejected by the House of Lords ([1999] IRLR 572). Their Lordships said that it was not necessary for the applicant to show a conscious motivation, connected with the Race Relations Act, on the part of the discriminator, because motivation is irrelevant in respect of other areas of the legislation. It is sufficient to establish that the protected act was done and this was an important cause of, or significant influence on, the less favourable treatment. This, however, is now subject to *Khan*, as in *Khan* their Lordships appeared to be suggesting that motivation is important in that the less favourable treatment is in reaction to the protected act. This appears to create a difference between victimisation and other forms of discrimination where motive is irrelevant. It also appears, that to constitute victimisation, the act complained of must be legally actionable (*Waters* v. *Commissioner of Police of the Metropolis* [2000] IRLR 720, below).

Harassment

Harassment did not originally appear as a separate legislative head and was treated as direct discrimination by subjecting the victim to a detriment. This is still the case where harassment is on the grounds of colour or nationality. However, the 2003 Regulations introduced a form of discrimination called harassment into the RRA, and the 2005 Regulations introduced a similar definition into the SDA. Thus while a victim of harassment on nationality grounds will have to use the direct discrimination provisions of the RRA, with the problems such entail, a specific definition is now contained in the SDA and RRA where harassment is on the grounds of sex or race or ethnic or national origin. A similar definition can also be seen in the Employment Equality (Religion or Belief) Regulations 2003 and the Employment Equality (Sexual Orientation) Regulations 2003. The definition also appears in the Disability Discrimination Act 1995 as amended by the Disability Discrimination Act 1995 (Amendment) Regulations 2003. All of these regulations are discussed below.

Section 3A(1) RRA provides that harassment occurs when:

On the grounds of race or ethnic or national origin a person engages in unwanted conduct which has the purpose or effect of:

(a) violating that other person's dignity, or
(b) creating an intimidating, hostile, degrading, humiliating or offensive environment.

Section 3A(2) provides that:

Harassment occurs if in all circumstances, in particular the perception of the complainant, it should be reasonably considered as having that effect.

A similar definition is contained in a new s.4A SDA but with the following added:

(c) on the ground of her rejection of or submission to unwanted conduct (as mentioned above) he treats her less favourably than he would treat her had she not rejected, or submitted to, the conduct (s.4A(1)(c) SDA).

There are a number of things to note about this definition, which is replicated in other pieces of legislation, as noted above. First, it is clear that the harassment need not be intentional. Second, it is not confined to action based on the complainant's race or sex etc, therefore harassment can occur when, for example, jokes about the race of a friend of the complainant create an offensive environment. Third, the statute particularly directs the tribunal to take into account the perception of the complainant, introducing a subjective element, something which is not so clear-cut in a sexual harassment claim. However, it is important to note that this is qualified by an objective element, in that despite the perception of the complainant it will only be harassment if such perception is reasonable.

Until the introduction of the statutory definition of sexual harassment the victim had to pursue a direct discrimination claim arguing that the harassment had caused her to suffer a detriment. At one time it was thought that detriment had to mean a contractual detriment, therefore in *Porcelli* v. *Strathclyde Regional Council* [1985] ICR 177 the complainant pursued her claim because as a result of sexual harassment she had asked for a transfer; the Scottish Court of Session, however, held that the harassment was the detriment. However, following *Snowball* v. *Gardener Merchant Ltd* [1987] IRLR 397 the tribunals were prepared to accept that sexual harassment *per se* was a detriment within the legislation and in the case of *Bracebridge Engineering Ltd* v. *Darby* [1990] IRLR 3 the Employment Appeal Tribunal held that one act of harassment was a detriment within the meaning of the Act. This was applied in *Institu Cleaning Co* v. *Heads* [1995] IRLR 4. The Court of Session in *Porcelli* defined sexual harassment as unwelcome acts involving physical contact of a sexual nature and conduct falling short of such acts. The Code of Practice issued by the EC defines it as 'unwanted conduct of a sexual nature, or other conduct based on sex affecting the dignity of men and women at work. This can include unwelcome physical, verbal or non-verbal conduct.' In *Wadman* v. *Carpenter Farrer Partnership* [1993] IRLR 374 the Employment Appeal Tribunal held that a tribunal hearing a sexual harassment case would obtain useful guidance from EC material, especially the code. In *Wileman* v. *Minilec Engineering Ltd* [1998] IRLR 144 the Appeal Tribunal decided that whether the harassment was a detriment depended on subjective factors relating to the employee (see also *Reed and Bull Information Systems Ltd* v. *Stedman* [1999] IRLR 299). On more general ground, the case of *De Souza* (above) decided that to suffer a detriment 'a reasonable worker would or might take the view that he had been thereby disadvantaged in the circumstances in which he had thereafter to work'. As such, a racial insult of itself was not deemed to amount to a detriment. Furthermore, in *Stewart* v. *Cleveland Guest Engineering* [1994] IRLR 440 it was held that a woman who complained about nude pin-ups and who complained when her employer did nothing had not suffered a detriment because of her sex as a man might easily be offended by the same pin-ups. This decision, which fails to recognise that women are more vulnerable to such conduct than men, was then subject to *British Telecommunications plc* v. *Williams* [1997] IRLR 668 where the Employment Appeal Tribunal held that in sexual harassment cases there was no necessity for a male comparator, and further it was no defence in a sexual harassment case to argue that a person of the opposite sex would have been treated in the same way (approved in *Stedman*). The later case of *Driskel* v. *Peninsula Business Services Ltd* [2000] IRLR 151 went against this, however. In that case a later Employment Appeal Tribunal stated that in a sexual harassment claim a tribunal should objectively judge whether the facts disclose less favourable treatment of a woman as compared to a man. The Appeal Tribunal did go on to say that in coming to a decision, the applicant's subjective perception and the discriminator's intention should also be considered, and tribunals should be aware that sexual banter between two men cannot completely be equated to sexual banter between a man and a woman. The emphasis on the victim's perception was welcomed (and supported by *Shamoon*, below). This is also emphasised in the new statutory definition. The new s.4A also appears to remove the need for a male comparator and focuses on the effect of the conduct. However, it talks about such conduct being on the basis of her sex, suggesting that a male comparator will be needed, and if an employer can argue he would treat everyone in the same way a claim will not lie, so in the future, decisions such as *Stewart* will be decided in the same way.

While a claim for harassment should now be considerably easier to make, there are other avenues open to a victim. In *Waters* (above) the House of Lords stated that an employer could be liable in negligence if it could foresee harassment taking place and did nothing to stop it. More recently in *Majrowski* v. *Guy's and St Thomas's NHS Trust* [2006] IRLR 695 the House of Lords held that an employer could be vicariously liable for the harassment caused by an employee to another under the Protection from Harassment Act 1997.

5.5 Acts of Discrimination

Both pieces of legislation list a series of discriminatory acts which can be committed by an employer; these are found in s.6 Sex Discrimination Act and s.4 Race Relations Act.

Arrangements for the purpose of determining who shall be employed (s.6(1)(a) SDA; s.4(1)(a) RRA)

Jobs must be generally available to everyone unless there is a genuine occupational qualification for the job (see later). 'Arrangements' include interviews, advertisements (where the Commissions can take action) and application forms. In *Saunders* v. *Richmond-upon-Thames Borough Council* [1978] ICR 75 a woman applied for a job as a golf professional. She was asked certain questions not asked of the male applicants such as how did she feel men would react to a woman as a golf professional. It was held that these questions were pertinent to the job and not discriminatory. In

Gates v. *Wirral Borough Council* (1982) (unreported) however, it was held that it was discrimination to ask questions of a woman such as 'what will you do when the children are sick?' when such questions were not also asked of a man. To some extent, however, this judgement is not particularly helpful. While it establishes that these questions may be discriminatory when only asked of women, it suggests that asking men the same questions eliminates the discrimination. This, of course, is a nonsense because it is the answers to the questions that will affect an employer's decision. Even in today's more enlightened society, the majority of men are unlikely to take full responsibility for childcare and the bulk of the work will still fall on the women within a partnership. The Equal Opportunities Commission in its Code of Practice recommends that employers should be entitled to ask such questions, but only after they have appointed someone to the post. So far the courts have not adopted this approach.

Terms on which employment is offered (s.6(1)(b) SDA; s.4(1)(b) RRA)

Any terms offered to a person that are different from those offered to others of the opposite sex or a different race are *prima facie* discriminatory. The exception in relation to sex discrimination is pay, unless the woman's contract contains an equality clause by virtue of the Equal Pay Act 1970.

Refusing or deliberately omitting to offer employment (s.6(1)(c) SDA; s.4(1)(c) RRA)

An employer commits an act of discrimination if he refuses to employ a person solely because of their race or sex. In *Batisha* v. *Say* [1977] IRLR 6 a woman was turned down for a job as a cave guide because 'it was a man's job'. It was held that discrimination had occurred. Similarly in *Owen & Briggs* v. *James* [1982] IRLR 502 a woman was discriminated against on the grounds of race when she was rejected for a job (despite having a better shorthand speed than the successful applicant) when it was shown that the person who had interviewed her had said to the successful applicant, 'why take on a coloured girl when English girls are available?' The employer's argument, that there could only be discrimination where race was the sole factor involved, was rejected by the Court of Appeal. It is sufficient that sex or race is an important factor in the employer's decision.

A problem arises under these particular provisions where a person is rejected on the grounds of race or sex but no one is appointed to the job. The problem arose in earlier cases because of the requirement that the complainant had to show he or she had been treated less favourably than a person in the same or not materially different circumstances. In other words, if a woman applies for a job and is rejected because she is a woman, how can she argue she has been treated less favourably than a man when a man also does not get the job? Two early tribunal cases in this area are often cited as conflicting, although they can be reconciled. In *Roadburg* v. *Lothian Regional Council* [1976] IRLR 283 a man and a woman applied for a job. The woman was told she was unsuitable because she was a woman. The man was offered the job, but the post was then frozen and in fact the post was not filled. The tribunal held that there had been discrimination. In *Thorn* v. *Meggit Engineering Ltd* [1976] IRLR 241 again a woman was rejected for a job because she was a woman, but no one was appointed to the post. The tribunal held that there had been no discrimination. She had not been treated less favourably than a man because a man had not been appointed either. While these cases may appear to be in conflict they can be distinguished, as in *Roadburg* the man was offered the job while the woman was not. This still left the law in the ridiculous position that if no one was offered the job there could be no discrimination. The position has now been clarified by the Employment Appeal Tribunal decision in *Brennan* v. *Dewhurst Ltd* [1984] ICR 52. In this case a girl applied for a job as a butcher's assistant. She was not offered the job because she was female, but after her interview the post was frozen. It was held that the interview was the incident of discrimination and therefore her action was under s.6(1)(a). While this case will be of help where there is evidence from the interview stage of a job application, if that evidence does not exist, the fact that the post is not filled will make it very difficult to prove discrimination. However, in *BP Chemicals* v. *Gillick* [1995] IRLR 128 it was held that an agency worker, who, through the agency, had worked for the respondents, and who had then gone on maternity leave, had been discriminated against by the respondents when they told the agency they did not want her to return. This is an important case because obviously the plaintiff was already employed by the agency.

Access to opportunities for promotion, transfer or training, or any other benefits, facilities or services (s.6(2)(a) SDA; s.4(2)(b) RRA)

Promotion, transfer or training

It is a breach of the legislation to choose or not choose employees for the above because of sexual or racial factors and, as we have already seen, this will include rejecting a person because of an assumption made by the employer which has sexual or racial connotations (*Horsey* v. *Dyfed County Council*, above). In *R* v. *CRE ex parte Westminster City Council* [1985] IRLR 426 a black roadsweeper applied for the post of cleansing operative within the council. He was offered the job, but a representative of NUPE objected to his appointment, ostensibly on the grounds of his poor attendance record. The assistant director of cleansing felt that the union was objecting to the appointment on racial grounds but, because he feared industrial action if the appointment went ahead, he withdrew the offer of the job. It was held that a discriminatory act had been committed under s.4(2)(b) and the fact that the intention had been to preserve industrial peace was irrelevant.

There are two exceptions, however. By s.48 Sex Discrimination Act, an employer can encourage one sex if in the preceding 12 months the job has been done exclusively by members of the opposite sex, or the numbers of one sex doing the job are so small it creates a sexual imbalance. By s.38(2) Race Relations Act, an employer can encourage a racial group where there are no members of that group doing the work or the numbers are small within the establishment or in proportion to the population in the area in which recruitment normally takes place. The legislation is, however, encouraging positive action and not positive discrimination. In *Hughes and Others* v. *London Borough of Hackney* (1986) (unreported) the council advertised for gardeners, stating that applications from ethnic minorities would be welcomed. Three white applicants were told that the posts were only open to ethnic minorities. This was held to be unlawful discrimination. Furthermore, the legislative requirements for positive action did not exist, as although the number of ethnic minorities doing the work was small in relation to the mix in the population in the immediate area, the council often recruited from outside that area. Similarly, in *ACAS* v. *Taylor* (1998) IRLB 594 a written guidance exhorting regional directors to do more to ensure the reality of the claim that ACAS was an equal opportunity employer led some regional directors to positively discriminate in favour of women. The complaint of sex discrimination brought by an unsuccessful male applicant for promotion was upheld.

Benefits, facilities or services

While the first part of the sections is very specific, this second part is deliberately wide. 'Benefit' was given a broad interpretation by the Employment Appeal Tribunal in the case of *Peake* (above) when Phillips J said that benefit 'meant no more than advantage', and although the decision was overturned on appeal it is suggested that the definition is still pertinent. By s.1(2) Race Relations Act, to have separate facilities for different races is unlawful, even if they are equal in quality, although the decision in *Pel Ltd* v. *Modgill* [1980] IRLR 142 shows that the employer is under no duty to remove *de facto* segregation. Obviously different facilities can be provided for different sexes, although they should be equal.

Dismissing a person or subjecting them to any other detriment (s.6(2)(b) SDA; s.4(2)(c) RRA)

Unlike unfair dismissal provisions, there is no continuity requirement for pursuing a claim for a discriminatory dismissal and a complainant can pursue an action despite not having one year's service. The reason for the dismissal must be sex or race however. In *Gubala* v. *Crompton Parkinson Ltd* [1977] IRLR 10 an employer chose to select a woman for redundancy, despite the fact that she had longer service than her male counterpart, because the man was the breadwinner in his family. It was held that she had been discriminated against. By contrast, in *Goult* v. *Reay Electrical* [1977] IRLIB 80 a woman was dismissed when it was discovered that she had married an employee of a competitor of her employer. It was held that the reason for her dismissal was not her sex or marital status but rather whom she had married. This should be contrasted, however, with the later case of *Skyrail Oceanic Ltd* v. *Coleman* [1981] IRLR 398 where a woman was dismissed when she became engaged to an employee of a rival firm. The two employers decided that, given her husband would be the breadwinner, she should be the one to lose her job. The Court of Appeal decided that the reason for her dismissal was primarily an assumption based on her sex and she had therefore suffered discrimination. In *Derby Specialist Fabrications Ltd* v. *Burton* [2001] IRLR 69 the Employment Appeal Tribunal held that dismissal for the purposes of s.4(2)(c) Race Relations Act includes constructive dismissal.

The meaning of the phrase 'subjecting to a detriment' was given a broad interpretation in the case of *Burton* v. *De Vere Hotels* [1996] IRLR 596. Two waitresses were working at a function which had Bernard Manning as a guest act. The waitresses complained that Manning made racist jokes and comments about them, as did members of the audience. Both waitresses argued that the employer had subjected them to a detriment – that is racial harassment by a third party. The Employment Appeal Tribunal held that the words 'subjecting to' connoted control, therefore an employer subjected his employee to a detriment if he caused or allowed harassment to happen in circumstances where he could control whether it happened or not. It was not necessary to imply foresight on the part of the employer, although foresight might be relevant in determining the amount of control he could exercise. The question to ask was whether the event was sufficiently under the control of the employer that he could, by the application of 'good employment practice', have prevented or reduced the extent of the harassment. In the particular case the employer could have told the assistant manager to withdraw the waitresses from the function. He had not done so, therefore he subjected them to the detriment of harassment. This case had far-reaching implications in that the harassment was not by a person under the employer's control, but by a third party on the employer's premises. However in *Pearce* v. *Governing Body of Mayfield School* [2003] IRLR 515 the House of Lords disapproved of *Burton*. While the House of Lords upheld the Court of Appeal in holding that Ms Pearce had not been the victim of sex discrimination, it went further and stated that even if the conduct of the pupils had been sex discrimination, the school would not have been liable for their actions. Their Lordships stated that the school could only be liable if it could be shown that it had omitted to act on the grounds of her sex. While *obiter*, it signs the death knoll for *Burton* and the much wider liability of employers.

The definition of 'detriment' within the provisions has had a chequered history. In a direct discrimination claim the complainant has to show that one of the acts of discrimination in s.6 or s.4 has occurred. Therefore the concept of what constitutes a detriment is important. The Court of Appeal developed a test of whether a reasonable worker would feel placed at a disadvantage (*MOD* v. *Jeremiah*; *De Souza* v. *AA*, above) but this itself raises the question of what constitutes a reasonable worker. In *Shamoon* v. *Chief Constable of the Royal Ulster Constabulary* [2003] IRLR 285 while the House of Lords stated that there did not need to be any physical or economic consequence to constitute a detriment, they did reiterate the reasonable worker test, although stating that the victim's view is important.

5.6 Other Unlawful Acts

In addition to the specific acts of discrimination which can be committed by an employer during recruitment to, or in the course of, employment, both the Sex Discrimination and the Race Relations Acts list four other unlawful acts that can be committed. Should a breach of any of the following be alleged, action is taken by the CEHR only and cannot be pursued by an individual.

Discriminatory practices (s.37 SDA; s.28 RRA)

This is where an employer imposes a requirement or condition which is unlawful indirect discrimination, or would be unlawful if the persons to whom it is applied were not all of the same sex. In other words it is conduct which may not result in actual discrimination because there is no victim but is designed to have a discriminatory effect. For example, an employer may insist that all his workers have beards and so no women ever apply for a job. This is a discriminatory practice.

Discriminatory advertisements (s.38 SDA; s.29 RRA)

An advertisement is discriminatory if it indicates, or may reasonably be understood to indicate, that there is an intention to discriminate, unless a particular sex or race is a genuine occupational qualification for the job. Specifically mentioned in the legislation are terms such as 'salesgirl', 'postman', 'waiter' and 'stewardess' but many other examples spring to mind. In *Equal Opportunities Commission* v. *Robertson* [1980] IRLR 44 the respondent placed an advertisement stating he wanted 'a good bloke (or blokess to satisfy fool legislators)'. It was held that this might reasonably be understood to mean that women need not apply. The advertiser will not incur liability if there is an indication in the advertisement that there is no intention to discriminate, for example a statement that the employer is an equal opportunities employer. Furthermore, the publisher will not be liable if he can show he relied on a statement by the person who placed the advertisement that it was not unlawful and it was reasonable for the publisher to rely on that statement. Knowingly or recklessly making a false statement is a criminal offence.

Instructions to discriminate (s.39 SDA; s.30 RRA)

It is unlawful for an employer to instruct his employees, or any other person over whom he has authority, to unlawfully discriminate. In addition to any action taken by the commissions, an employee who refuses to obey an order to discriminate on racial grounds, and thus suffers a detriment, will also have an action, as seen from the cases of *Showboat Entertainment Centre* v. *Owens* [1984] 1 WLR 384 and *Weathersfield Ltd t/a Van Truck Rentals* v. *Sargent* [1991] IRLR 94. Because of the wording of the Sex Discrimination Act however, a person dismissed for refusing to obey an order to discriminate on sexual grounds may not have the same protection.

Pressure to discriminate (s.40 SDA; s.31 RRA)

It is unlawful to induce, or attempt to induce, a person to commit a discriminatory act by either offering a benefit or subjecting a person to a detriment. The act is committed even if the approach is not made by the discriminator directly, but is done in such a way that a person is likely to hear of the inducement.

Employer's liability

In addition to the acts listed above, an employer or principal will be liable for any unlawful act committed by his employees during the course of their employment, unless the employer can show he took all reasonable steps to prevent those unlawful acts being perpetrated (s.41 SDA; s.32 RRA). The interpretation of these two sections came to the fore in the infamous case of *Tower Boot Co Ltd* v. *Jones* [1997] IRLR 168. Jones was subjected to severe racial harassment by his colleagues. He was branded with a hot screwdriver, whipped with flex and had metal bolts thrown at him. Despite being moved to another part of the factory the harassment continued and he resigned having only been employed for one month. The Employment Appeal Tribunal held that the liability of the employer under s.32 Race Relations Act was that of vicarious liability. As such, Jones had to establish that the harassment occurred during the course of the employees' employment. This meant that the acts committed had to be authorised by the employer and performed in an authorised way, or acts authorised by the employer but performed in an unauthorised way. The Appeal Tribunal then held that the nature of the acts was such that they could not be described as authorised acts done in an unauthorised manner and thus the employer could not be liable under s.32. This was despite the fact that the employer knew about the harassment and had done little to prevent it. The judgement was severely criticised and left a very large gap in protection for employees against harassment from colleagues. On appeal to the Court of Appeal, the decision was reversed. The Court of Appeal held that there was insufficient similarity between vicarious liability and liability under s.32 to impose tortious principles on the statutory provisions. A purposive approach was needed and 'in the course of employment' in s.32 should be given its everyday meaning, that is during employment. As such, the employer was liable, as any other interpretation would seriously undermine the legislation. In *Canniffe* v. *East Riding of Yorkshire Council* [2000] IRLR 555 the Employment Appeal Tribunal held that to see whether an employer has taken reasonable steps to prevent the unlawful acts, the proper approach is to first identify whether the employer took any steps at all and, if steps were taken, to consider whether there were any further steps which it would have been reasonably practicable to take. Whether the steps would have been effective is irrelevant and an employer cannot argue that he has failed to take steps because, even if he had, the unlawful acts would still have taken place. Liability has since been extended. In *Chief Constable of Lincolnshire Police* v. *Stubbs* [1999] IRLR 81 the Employment Appeal Tribunal held that an employer could be liable for harassment which took place in a social situation if this could be regarded as an extension of work (in this case a leaving party). However, in *Sidhu* v. *Aerospace Composite Technology Ltd* [2001] ICR 167 the Court of Appeal held that the employer was not liable for racial harassment during a works outing, even though the employer had disciplined those concerned. Such conduct was not during the course of the perpetrators' employment.

Thus the more generous interpretation in *Jones* can still leave an employee unprotected. This is shown by *Waters* v. *Commissioner of Police of the Metropolis* (above) where the employer was not liable for a serious sexual assault committed outside working hours on the complainant by a fellow employee. The House of Lords held that as the assault took place outside working hours, it could not be held to have been committed during the employee's employment and thus the employer was not liable under s.41 Sex Discrimination Act. Furthermore, as the employer could not be liable, the complainant could not have been victimised under s.4 despite the fact that she had complained repeatedly about the assault and was taken off special duties following her complaints. As the employer could not be liable, her treatment could not constitute victimisation under the Act. Their Lordships did, however, find the employer liable at common law (see Chapter 4). This shows why the more generous interpretation in *Jones* is important, as if the employer is not liable then neither is the perpetrator, as the legislation only prevents discrimination by employers and not employees. Should the employer be liable, however, the perpetrator can be ordered to pay compensation.

Finally, it is also unlawful to aid a person in the commission of an unlawful act of discrimination unless the person has relied on a statement by the perpetrator of the act that the act is not unlawful and it is reasonable for him to rely on that statement (s.42 SDA; s.33 RRA). In *Anyanwu* v. *South Bank Student Union* [2001] ICR 391 the House of Lords considered the liability under s.33. The appellants were students of the university who were employed by the union after being elected to their posts. The university raised allegations of misuse of funds and bullying against them and, after instigating disciplinary proceedings, the university expelled them and banned them from university premises. As a result, the union sacked them. They claimed against the union as their employer, but also claimed against the university for a breach of s.33, arguing that the university had knowingly aided the union in committing an unlawful act. The House of Lords said that 'knowingly aids' in s.33 meant that the person had given 'some kind of assistance to the other person which helps him to do it . . . All that is needed is an act of some kind, done knowingly, which helps the other person to do the unlawful act' (per Lord Hope). In other words, there is no requirement that the person aiding should have any knowledge of the unlawful act or desire that it takes place and, as the expulsion by the university had helped the union in dismissing the appellants, the university were liable under s.33. However, in a case heard a week before (*Hallam* v. *Cheltenham Borough Council* [2001] ICR 408) the House of Lords upheld a trial judge's decision that there must be an element of joint enterprise when considering s.33. Thus there appears to be a conflict in the interpretation of the provision, a conflict which will not aid tribunals when dealing with s.33 claims.

5.7 Genuine Occupational Qualifications (GOQs)

The legislation recognises that in some cases a job must be done by a particular sex or race. If the employer can show that this is the case, he will have a defence to a discrimination claim. Both Acts, therefore, permit discrimination where the sex or race of the applicant is a genuine occupational qualification for the job and state the situations where the defence may be raised.

Sexual GOQs

Sexual GOQs are found in s.7 Sex Discrimination Act and are listed below. It should be noted that those situations where sex is deemed to be a necessary requirement for the job are considerably more numerous than those situations where race is a necessary requirement for a post.

1. The essential nature of the job calls for a man for reasons of physiology (excluding strength or stamina) or, in a dramatic performance or other entertainment, for reasons of authenticity.
2. The job needs to be held by a member of a particular sex as it involves physical contact with a person in circumstances where they may reasonably object to the job being carried out by a person of the opposite sex; or the job involves working in a private home and involves physical contact or the knowledge of intimate details of a person's life and that person might reasonably object to the job being performed by a person of the opposite sex; or a person would be in a state of undress or using sanitary facilities. For example, this would cover toilet attendants and so on. It must, however, be necessary to employ a particular sex. In *Wylie* v. *Dee & Co (Menswear) Ltd* [1978] IRLR 103 a woman was turned down for a job in a menswear shop. The employer argued that the job would require her to measure men's inside legs and therefore a GOQ existed. The tribunal found that the shop had changing cubicles and seven male assistants who could be called upon to do the appropriate measurements if required. A GOQ did not exist and there had been an act of discrimination. By contrast, there is the case of *Times* v. *Hodgson* [1981] IRLR 530 where a male supervisor, with longer service than his female counterpart, was chosen for redundancy. The reason was that all other female supervisors had left and the employers had to retain one to deal with the problems of the women workers, to take them to the first-aid

room and to take urine samples from them when they had been working with toxic substances. The tribunal held that the employer had discriminated against the man, but that a GOQ existed.

3. The job involves living on the employer's premises, there are no separate sleeping or sanitary facilities and it is not reasonable to expect the employer to provide separate facilities.

4. The job is in a single-sexed institution such as a prison or a hospital and, given the essential nature of the establishment, the job needs to be held by a person of the same sex.

5. The holder of the job provides individuals with personal services promoting their education or welfare and therefore can best be provided by a person of the same sex. For example an employer could employ a female social worker to run a centre for unmarried mothers.

6. There are statutory restrictions on the employment of women. Since the Sex Discrimination Act 1986 the majority of such restrictions have been removed.

7. The job involves duties outside Great Britain, in a country whose laws and customs are such that those duties could not be effectively carried out by a woman.

8. The job is one of two held by a married couple.

Gender reassignment GOQs

GOQs relating gender reassignment are found in ss.7A and B Sex Discrimination Act. Section 7A essentially reiterates the sexual GOQs as stated above and therefore applies when a person has completed the gender reassignment and is thus living in their new sex, so that, for example, a post-operative male-to-female transsexual could not be offered a job as an attendant in a male toilet.

Section 7B(2) creates supplementary GOQs in respect of gender reassignment:

1. The job involves the holder of the job being liable to be called upon to perform intimate physical searches pursuant to statutory powers.

2. The job is likely to involve the holder of the job doing his work, or living, in a private home and needs to be held otherwise than by a person who is undergoing or has undergone gender reassignment, because objection might reasonably be taken to allowing such a person –

   (i) the degree of physical or social contact with a person living in the home, or

   (ii) the knowledge of intimate details of such a person's life,

   which is likely, because of the nature or circumstances of the job, or of the home, to be allowed to, or available to, the holder of the job.

These two GOQs apply to anyone who intends to undergo, is undergoing or has undergone gender reassignment, so effectively excluding them from a number of jobs.

3. The nature or location of the establishment makes it impracticable for the holder of the job to live elsewhere than in premises provided by the employer, and –
   (i) the only such premises which are available for persons holding that kind of job are such that reasonable objection could be taken, for the purposes of preserving decency and privacy, to the holder of the job sharing accommodation and facilities with either sex while undergoing gender reassignment, and
   (ii) it is not reasonable to expect the employer either to equip those premises with suitable accommodation or to make alternative arrangements.
4. The holder of the job provides vulnerable individuals with personal services promoting their welfare, or similar personal services and, in the reasonable view of the employer, those services cannot be provided by a person while that person is undergoing gender reassignment.

These last two GOQs apply only where the person intends to undergo gender reassignment or is undergoing gender reassignment. Once the reassignment is complete, the person is recognised as their new sex, although will be prohibited from certain jobs permanently as indicated above.

Amendments made by the Employment Equality (Sex Discrimination) Regulations 2005 mean that these GOQs also apply where the person has not undergone gender reassignment but the employee's gender has become the acquired gender under the Gender Recognition Act 2004.

The GOQs in relation to gender reassignment seem very complex. The blanket exclusion of any transsexual from employment in a private home seems inappropriate in that the Act already exempts employment in a private household from its provisions (see below) and there is already a GOQ to prevent inappropriately sexed persons from working in single-sex institutions, as noted above. To also exclude them from jobs where there is a statutory power to conduct intimate searches again seems inappropriate once the gender reassignment is complete. These provisions have led to criticisms that transsexuals are seen as a third sex, being neither male nor female. The last two GOQs suggest the question of when does a transsexual intend to undergo gender reassignment and when is such reassignment complete? For many, the process may take years and for this period they will be excluded from a large number of occupations falling within the

GOQs. One final criticism of the amendments to the Sex Discrimination Act to include gender reassignment is that they were unnecessary since the decision of *P* v. *S* (above). It is arguable that the amendments have taken away rights of transsexuals established by the ECJ in *P* v. *S*. Whether this is the case has yet to be seen.

Racial GOQs

The circumstances constituting racial GOQs are in s.5 Race Relations Act:

1. The job involves participation in a dramatic performance or other entertainment and a member of a racial group is needed for authenticity.
2. The job involves participation as an artist's or photographic model and a member of a racial group is needed for authenticity.
3. The job involves serving members of the public with food and drink in a particular setting and a member of that racial group is needed for authenticity. For example, an employer could advertise for Chinese waiters to serve in a Chinese restaurant.
4. The holder of the job provides individuals with personal services promoting their education or welfare and these services can best be provided by a person of the same racial group. In *London Borough of Lambeth* v. *CRE* [1990] IRLR 231 the council advertised the post of group manager and assistant head of housing benefits for Asian or Afro-Caribbean applicants only. The council argued that over half the tenants were of Asian or Afro-Caribbean descent and that staff had to be sensitive to their problems. The Court of Appeal held that as the holders of the posts would have very few dealings with the public, the jobs did not fall under the personal services GOQ and the council was guilty of unlawful discrimination. By contrast, in *Tottenham Green Under Fives' Centre* v. *Marshall* [1991] IRLR 162, the Employment Appeal Tribunal held that caring for children was the provision of personal services and that as 84 per cent of the children were of Afro-Caribbean or African descent, a GOQ existed and the council could restrict the job to persons of the same racial group.

In the case of both Acts it is permissible to discriminate in filling a vacancy where the employer already has employees of one sex or race capable of carrying out the duties listed above whom it would be reasonable to employ on those duties and whose numbers are sufficient to meet the employer's requirements (s.7(4) SDA; s.4(4) RRA).

Racial genuine occupational requirements (GORs)

The Race Relations Act 1976 (Amendment) Regulations 2003 inserted s.4A into the Act and introduced the concept of genuine occupational requirements. These are now in a new 4A(2):

'This subsection applies where, having regard to the nature of the employment or the context in which it is carried out –

(a) being of a particular race or particular ethnic or national origins is a genuine and determining occupational requirement;

(b) it is proportionate to apply that requirement in the particular case; and

(c) either –

   (i) the person to whom that requirement applied does not meet it, or

   (ii) the employer is not satisfied, and in all the circumstances it is reasonable for him not to be satisfied, that that person meets it.'

Section 5 is amended so that a GOQ will only be available if a GOR is not. While this complies with the Directive and is replicated in the regulations protecting against discrimination on the grounds of religion or sexual orientation, until we have case law it is unclear how this section and s.5 will relate. It is important to note that the section is quite wieldy in that the race or ethnic or national origins has to be a determining occupational requirement and it has to be proportionate to apply the requirement in the particular case. Thus this provision, on paper, seems quite limited in its potential application and may only apply in a handful of cases.

5.8 Exceptions to the Legislation

There are areas under both pieces of legislation where the laws preventing discrimination do not apply. Some of the areas are common to both Acts while others are specifically under one or the other.

General exceptions

National security is exempt from both pieces of legislation as is employment in private households. The latter exemption, however, is narrower under the Sex Discrimination Act where the only exemption is that of close physical contact with a person of the opposite sex who might reasonably object to that contact, as above in s.7. The exemption under the RRA is much wider; it applies to any act apart from victimisation although no exemption applies to contract workers. Charitable trusts are exempt from both Acts, therefore in *Hugh-Jones* v. *Saint John's College, Cambridge* [1979] ICR 848 it was held that a senior common room could exclude women as it had charitable status. There is also a territorial exemption in that under the present SDA and the original RRA, to be protected an employee had to be employed in Great Britain (amendments to the RRA now widen this to whether the employee 'does his work wholly or partly in Great Britain' and also provide that a claim can be brought if the employer carries on business in Great Britain and the employee is ordinarily resident in Great Britain at any time during the employment). In *Saggar* v. *Ministry of Defence* [2005] IRLR 618, a case under the original RRA, the claimant worked mainly in Great Britain for 16 years, but the alleged discriminatory act took place in Cyprus where he was posted for just over three years. Lord Justice Mummery held that it could not be the intention of parliament, that the claimant would lose all protection he had gained by working in Great Britain, by being posted outside Great Britain towards the end of his employment. In other words it is the whole of the employment which must be considered and not just where the employment is at the time of the alleged act.

Specific exemptions under the Sex Discrimination Act

Certain occupations are still excluded from the operation of the Act, such as ministers of religion, and police and prison officers in respect of height and so on. Special provisions in relation to the treatment of women in connection with pregnancy or childbirth are also exempt. The Act appears to give an exemption in relation to provisions relating to death or retirement. This needs qualification however. The exemption does not apply in relation to training, transfer, promotion, dismissal or demotion. Furthermore, it does not apply to benefits, facilities or services under an occupational pension scheme. While this would appear to mean that although retirement ages must be the same, pension ages can be different; this is now subject to the decision of *Barber* v. *Guardian Royal Exchange Assurance Group* [1990] IRLR 240 in which the ECJ ruled that a pension was pay within the meaning of Article 141. This effectively means that both retirement and pension ages must be the same.

Specific exemptions under the Race Relations Act

The Act does not apply to immigration rules or civil service regulations restricting employment. Seamen recruited abroad are not protected and it is lawful to discriminate in the selection for national or local sports teams on the basis of nationality, birthplace or length of residence.

5.9 Enforcement and Remedies

Enforcement by an individual

When an individual presents a complaint of discrimination to an employment tribunal a conciliation officer will attempt to conciliate. If this fails, the tribunal has three main remedies that it may award the complainant:

(a) an order declaring the complainant's rights;
(b) financial compensation;
(c) a recommendation of action to be taken by the respondent to reduce the adverse effect of the discrimination.

In addition, s.6(4)(A) Sex Discrimination Act 1986 provides a further remedy. This provides that where a term in a contract or collective agreement or in the rules of an undertaking contravenes the Sex Discrimination Act 1975 it shall be void. The amended section allows an individual to apply to an employment tribunal for a declaration that a term will have effect in relation to him some time in the future and that the act which the term permits is unlawful by the 1975 Act. If the tribunal finds the complaint well-founded, it can make a declaration that the term is void.

If the respondent fails to comply with a recommendation, compensation can be increased. In *D'Souza* (above), the council refused to comply with an order to reinstate the complainant. He was originally awarded £358,289 in compensation. This included loss of pension and future loss of earnings that he would sustain in the four years and 10 months he had left until he retired. This was later reduced however by the Court of Appeal. If the complaint is one of indirect discrimination and the respondent shows that there was no intention to discriminate, until 1996 no compensation could be awarded, although the courts gave a broad interpretation to intention (*London Underground* v. *Edward (No. 1)* [1995] IRLR 355; *JH Walker Ltd* v. *Hussain* [1996] IRLR 11). In July 1996, the Sex Discrimination and Equal Pay (Miscellaneous Amendments) Regulations 1996 were introduced which allow a tribunal to award compensation where indirect sexual discrimination was unintentional.

General principles on the award of compensation can be found in the judgement of May LJ in the case of *Alexander* v. *Home Office* [1989] IRLR 190. The purpose of an award is restitution but, given the difficulties of quantification in this area, awards should be restrained. Awards can be made for injury to feelings. In *Vento* v. *Chief Constable of West Yorkshire Police (No. 2)* [2003] IRLR 102 the Court of Appeal reiterated the guidance given in *Alexander* saying that damages have some similarity to those awarded in personal injury cases. The maximum award should be in the region of £25,000 for serious cases and the lowest should be £500 for isolated incidents. Awards below £500 should not be made.

Damages are not confined to pecuniary loss and sometimes aggravated damages may be appropriate if the defendant has behaved in a high-handed, malicious, insulting or oppressive manner when compared to the conduct, character and circumstances of the complainant. For example, in *McLaughlin* v. *London Borough of Southwark* (1997) The Times, 11 December the total award of £234,000 included a sum for aggravated damages because the council refused to disclose certain documents. The award of aggravated damages was considered appropriate in the case of *City of Bradford Metropolitan County* v. *Arora* [1989] IRLR 442 but it was held by the Court of Appeal that the award of aggravated damages in discrimination cases was only appropriate in the event of outrageous conduct on the part of the employer. This statement on the award of aggravated damages was, however, subject to doubt from the later Court of Appeal decision in *AB* v. *South Western Water Services Ltd* [1993] 1 All ER 609. The court held that the effect of the decision in *Rookes* v. *Barnard* [1964] 1 All ER 367 was that aggravated damages could only be awarded for torts recognised at that time (1964). Legislation on sex and race discrimination came into force after 1964. Consequently, in *Deane* v. *Ealing London Borough Council* [1993] ICR 329 Wood P decided that aggravated damages could not be awarded for a breach of anti-discriminatory legislation. However, this is now subject to *Kuddus* v. *Chief Constable of Leicestershire Constabulary* (2001) IDS Brief 690. While the case is not an employment case, it is of importance to issues of compensation in discrimination cases. Briefly, Kuddus was asking for aggravated damages when he discovered that a police constable had forged his signature on a document withdrawing a complaint about the police. The Chief Constable, while accepting that there had been a forgery, successfully argued in both the High Court and the Court of Appeal that aggravated damages could not be awarded because the tort of misfeasance in public office was not a tort for which aggravated damages could be awarded prior to 1964, the date of the *Rookes'* decision. Kuddus appealed to the House of Lords. Lord Slynn, giving the leading judgement, stated that he did not think that anything in Lord Devlin's analysis in *Rookes* required that in addition to the categories of conduct for which aggravated damages can be awarded, there was an additional requirement that the claim should amount to a tort for which aggravated damages were available before 1964. He concluded on this basis that the Court of Appeal in *AB* v. *South Western Water Services Ltd* had not been justified in restricting an award in such a way. Such a limitation would affect the future development of the law. Thus, Kuddus's claim for aggravated damages was not precluded on the basis that the claim was not a tort for which aggravated damages were available prior to 1964. The issue of whether aggravated damages are now available for statutory torts such as those created by anti-discrimination legislation was not resolved by their Lordships. Lord Mackay was of the view that such damages would only be available if expressly authorised by statute, Lord Scott, on the other hand, felt that such a claim would lie if the conduct fell within one of the categories laid down by Lord Devlin in *Rookes*. In *Scott* v. *Commissioners of Inland Revenue* [2004] IRLR 713, however, the Court of Appeal accepted that aggravated damages could be awarded and stressed that they were intended to deal with cases where the injury was inflicted by conduct that was 'high-handed, malicious, insulting or oppressive' and should be awarded separately to damages for injury to feelings.

Commonly, tribunals make substantial awards against an employer and only a small award against the discriminator. However in *Way & IntroCate Chemicals* v. *Crouch* [2005] IRLR 603 the Employment Appeal Tribunal held that it was proper to make both the employer and discriminator liable for the full amount on a joint and several basis, as this will allow the complainant to sue the discriminator in the case of employer bankruptcy. In the case, the EAT made an award against the employer and its managing director after the claimant was dismissed for refusing to have a relationship with the director. The EAT held that a tribunal should apportion the share of the award between the respondents. This apportionment should be on the basis of culpability and not on the basis of financial strength. Whether in reality this decision helps complainants is debatable, as it is highly unlikely an employee will have the finances to pay the compensation and a complainant could end up with little or nothing. It is hoped that in these situations a claimant will be advised to pursue the employer for the full amount and thus place the burden on it to pursue a claim against the discriminator.

The statutory maximum which can be awarded was, until 1993 in sex discrimination claims and 1994 in race discrimination claims, £11,000, although the ECJ ruled that such a limit conflicted with EC law in the *Marshall* case (below). The actual amount awarded will depend on the detriment which is caused and the injury to the complainant's feelings. In *Wileman* v. *Minilec Engineering Ltd* (above) the compensation awarded was £50, whereas in *Noone* v. *North West Thames Regional Health Authority* [1988] IRLR 195 £3,000 was awarded. The large award made in *McLaughlin* is unusual and the average award is much lower.

Two major problems lie with the available remedies. First, the normal detriment suffered in these cases will be the loss of a job or a promotion. The Court of Appeal in *Noone* held that the health authority could not be ordered to offer the next available vacancy to the complainant and this has been followed by the Employment Appeal Tribunal in the later case of *British Gas plc* v. *Sharma* [1991] IRLR 101. Second, the tribunal has no power to award interest. Given the low level of compensation which could be awarded, this was a serious deficiency in the legislation, particularly where the complainant may have lost considerably more than the statutory maximum. If the complainant has the locus to sue under the Equal Treatment Directive, European law has no compensation limits. In the famous case of *Southampton and South West Area Health Authority* v. *Marshall (No. 2)* [1991] ICR 136 Mrs Marshall originally received an award in excess of the statutory maximum then operating. Despite the fact that the award was made applying European law however, the Employment Appeal Tribunal overturned the employment tribunal's award of interest although the ECJ restored the award. After the ECJ restored Mrs Marshall's award, various employment tribunals applied the no-limit rule and in December 1993 the compensation limit of £11,000 in sex discrimination cases was removed by statutory order, and removed in race discrimination cases in 1994.

Enforcement by the commission

The functions of the Commission for Equality and Human Rights were discussed in Chapter 1. In addition to the specific acts contained in the legislation which only the commission can take action on, such as discriminatory advertisements, the commission has wide powers to carry out formal investigations and issue non-discrimination notices.

Formal investigations are a vital part of the commission's functions. They are the means by which discrimination in large areas of employment can be investigated. It has extensive powers to order the production of documents and to require witnesses to give evidence, and a person who wilfully alters, suppresses or destroys a document may be fined. On completion of an investigation, the commission will produce a report in which there may be recommendations for changes applicable to an individual or organisation, or it may recommend changes in the law to the Secretary of State. After the investigation is complete, the commission may decide to issue a non-discrimination notice. To do so it must have found a discriminatory practice, a discriminatory advertisement, an instruction to discriminate, pressure to discriminate or a breach of an equality clause under the Equal Pay Act. The body on which the notice is served will then have the opportunity to make representations to the commission and may appeal against any requirement in an industrial tribunal. The notice can be enforced by a county court injunction if within five years of its issue the respondent commits an unlawful act. Before the whole process begins, however, the commission must be sure it has grounds to begin an investigation and allow the body investigated to make representations. In *CRE* v. *Prestige Group* [1989] IRLR 166 the House of Lords declared an investigation by the Commission for Racial Equality unlawful and the subsequent non-discrimination notice *ultra vires* and void. The investigation had started without a belief that a discriminatory act had occurred or without giving the company the opportunity to make representations.

In addition to their role in relation to investigations, the commission has the power to provide legal assistance to an individual. Given that the commission does not have an unlimited purse, such assistance is only given in a few cases deemed to be of importance, where the commission may want to test the Acts for future complainants.

5.10 Part-Time Workers

While many part-time workers are women and therefore have protection under the Sex Discrimination Act as seen in the cases noted above, in addition to such protection the government implemented the Part Time Work Directive (97/81/EC) by the Part Time Workers (Prevention of Less Favourable Treatment) Regulations 2000. These Regulations give part-time workers the right not to be treated less favourably in terms and conditions of employment than a full-time comparator, unless the employer can justify the less favourable treatment on objective grounds. Objective grounds are that the less favourable treatment is necessary and appropriate to achieve a legitimate business objective (Regulation 5(2)). As with a lot of recent legislation, the Regulations apply to workers and not just employees, and therefore apply to anyone who has agreed to perform personally any work or services. The definition of 'full-time' and 'part-time' is by reference to the practice of the employer.

A part-time worker must compare his or her treatment to that of a full-time comparator. That comparator must be:

(a) employed by the same employer and under the same type of contract;
(b) engaged in the same or broadly similar work, having regard where relevant to qualifications, skills and experience; and
(c) based at the same establishment or another establishment operated by the employer and employed at the same time as the part-time worker (Regulation 2(4)).

There is no requirement that the comparator must be of the opposite sex to the part-time worker because the basis of the less favourable treatment is that the worker works part time and is not based on the worker's sex. However, unlike other anti-discriminatory legislation, the comparator must be an actual full-time worker and not a hypothetical one. In *Matthews* v. *Kent and Medway Towns Fire Authority* [2006] IRLR 367 part-time firefighters took an action to gain access to the same benefits as full-time firefighters. There were two issues for the House of Lords to address. First, whether the part-time workers were on the same contract as the full-time workers, which the House of Lords stated in the affirmative. Second, whether the two groups were on work which was broadly similar. The employer argued this was not the case as the full-time firefighters had extra duties over and above fighting fires, which was the only duty required of the part-time workers. The House of Lords stated that if both groups spent a large proportion of their time pursuing the core activities of the organisation, the work was broadly similar.

If a full-time worker becomes part time or returns to work part time after an absence of less than twelve months, the worker can choose her former full-time post as comparator (Regulations 3 and 4). However, the Regulations do not give a full-time worker the right to return to work part time nor do they give a woman returning from maternity leave the right to return to work part time, although a refusal in respect of the latter may be the basis of a claim under the Sex Discrimination Act.

A part-time worker has the right not to be treated less favourably than a comparable full-time worker as regards the terms of contract or being subjected to a detriment by any act, or deliberate failure to act, by her employer (Regulation 5(1)). In *McMenemy* v. *Capita Business Services Ltd* [2007] IRLR 400 McMenemy worked Wednesdays, Thursdays and Fridays. The employer allowed people to have bank holidays off but only if they actually worked on the bank holiday. McMenemy claimed this amounted to less favourable treatment on the grounds of his part-time status as most bank holidays fell on a Monday. The Court of Session held that the treatment must be solely on the grounds of part-time status. As the employer would have treated a full-time worker who did not work on Mondays in the same way, there was no discrimination.

Regulation 5(1) is subject to a defence of justification on objective grounds. In *Gibson* v. *Scottish Ambulance Service* (2004) EAT S0052/04 the Employment Appeal Tribunal had to determine whether rostering a part-time worker for a greater number of stand-by hours, *pro rata*, than a full-time worker was less favourable treatment. While the EAT found that it was, it found that the reason for the stand-by hours was need and varied between region. As such, there was objective justification.

In determining whether there is less favourable treatment the *pro rata* principle applies. This is defined in Regulation 1:

> 'where a comparable full-time worker receives or is entitled to receive pay or any other benefit, a part-time worker is to receive or be entitled to receive not less than the proportion of that pay or other benefit that the number of his weekly hours bears to the number of weekly hours of the comparable full-time worker.'

Regulation 5(4) specifically states that it is not less favourable treatment to pay a part-time worker a lower hourly rate for overtime than a comparable full-time worker for hours which, added on to the part-time worker's normal hours, constitute less than the full-time worker's normal hours excluding overtime. This merely adopts the ECJ decision in *Stadt Lengerich* v. *Helmig* [1995] IRLR 216 and has been applied in *Jones* v. *Great Northern Railways* (2005) IDS 780.

Where the less favourable treatment is not dismissal, the worker can request in writing that the employer provides her with written reasons for the less favourable treatment within 21 days. The statement is admissible in any tribunal hearing. Failing to do so, or providing an evasive statement, allows a tribunal to draw an adverse inference against the employer, including an inference that the employer has discriminated against the part-time worker (Regulation 6).

The part-time worker has a right not to suffer a detriment by any act, or deliberate failure to act, by her employer, on the grounds that:

(a) she has brought proceedings under the Regulations;
(b) she has requested a written statement from her employer;
(c) she has given evidence or information in connection with such proceedings brought by another worker;
(d) she has otherwise done anything under the Regulations;
(e) she has alleged that the employer has infringed the Regulations, unless the allegation is false and not made in good faith;
(f) she has refused or proposed to refuse to forgo a right under the Regulations; or
(g) the employer believes or suspects that the worker has done one of the above (Regulations 7(2) and (3)).

Dismissal on any of the above grounds is automatically unfair (Regulation 7(1). No continuity is needed (Sch, para 2(2)).

An employee may complain to a tribunal within three months of the act or last act. Where the complaint is of less favourable terms, the less favourable treatment takes place on each day during which the terms are less favourable. Where the employee goes from full time to part time, the three month period starts to run with the first day of the varied contract and where the employee returns from an absence to part-time work, the three months starts on the day of the employee's return (Regulation 8(4)).

The tribunal, if it finds the complaint well-founded, can make a declaration as to the employee's rights, compensation which the tribunal considers just and equitable, or order the employer to take steps to obviate or reduce the adverse effect on the worker (Regulation 8(7)). Compensation can be reduced for contributory conduct and the worker is under a duty to mitigate her loss (Regulations 8(12) and (13)). Failure to comply with a tribunal order can lead to an increase in compensation (Regulation 8(14)).

While in the vast majority of situations part-time workers who are women would already have protection under the Sex Discrimination Act 1975 and the Equal Pay Act 1970 (see Chapter 6), the Regulations will provide a quick and speedy remedy for all part-time workers, including men, suffering less favourable treatment which cannot be objectively justified. In some cases, however, the worker may wish to use the Sex Discrimination Act rather than the Regulations as it is likely that any financial compensation awarded under that legislation will be higher.

5.11 Fixed Term Employees

Draft Regulations to implement the Fixed Term Work Directive (99/70/EC) were put to consultation in March 2001. The Directive prohibits discrimination of fixed term employees as compared to permanent employees, unless there is objective justification. The deadline for implementation was 10 July 2001, but the DTI stated that it needed more time to analyse responses to the draft and was taking advantage of the 'special difficulties' provision in the Directive which allows Member States to delay implementation for up to a year. As such, from October 2002 the Fixed Term Employees (Prevention of Less Favourable Treatment) Regulations 2002 came into force.

Regulation 1(2) defines a fixed term contract as one which expires after a specific time, expires after a specific task or expires on the occurrence or non-occurrence of an event, other than retirement. The comparator is the same as under the Part Time Worker Regulations, that is a permanent employee employed by the same employer, at the same establishment, or different establishment operated by the employer and employed on the same or broadly similar work (Regulation 2). The comparator must be an actual employee and cannot be someone who used to be employed.

A fixed term employee has a right not to be treated less favourably as regards:

(a) terms of the contract;
(b) being subjected to any other detriment by any act or deliberate failure to act;
(c) period of service qualification relating to any condition of service;
(d) the opportunity to receive training;
(e) the opportunity to secure permanent employment.

All the above is subject to justification on objective grounds (Regulation 3). The *pro rata* principle applies and the employee has the right to be informed of vacancies (Regulations 3(5) and (6)). Objective justification exists if the fixed term employee's terms, taken as a whole, are at least as favourable as the comparator's terms (Regulation 4). In *Cure and Another* v. *Coutts and Co plc and Another* (2004) The Times, 25 October fixed term employees at the bank were not awarded a discretionary bonus which had been awarded to permanent employees. The Employment Appeal Tribunal held that a detriment under the Regulations 'will occur when a reasonable worker might take the view that he had been disadvantaged in the circumstances in which he had, thereafter to work'. However, in *Webley* v. *Department for Work and Pensions* [2005] IRLR 288 the Court of Appeal held that the non-renewal of a fixed term contract did not amount to less favourable treatment, pointing out that it 'was of the essence of a fixed term contract that it came to an end at the expiry of the fixed term'.

Where a fixed term employee has been employed on a fixed term contract for four years, or a succession of shorter fixed term contracts which together amount to four years, then the employee will become permanent, unless the continuation of fixed term employment can be objectively justified (Regulation 8). Where the employee satisfies the test for permanent status, there is a right to a written statement of variation within 21 days of a request being made (Regulation 9).

As with the Part Time Worker Regulations, a fixed term employee has the right to receive written reasons for the less favourable treatment (Regulation 5) and has the same protection from unfair dismissal and detriment (Regulation 6). The same remedies are available on application to an Employment Tribunal within three months of the act complained of (Regulation 7). In *Cure* the EAT decided that the three months ran not from the time when the employer decided not to pay the bonus to fixed term employees, but when it had decided on the detail and application of the bonus to relevant employees.

The Regulations also remove the right to waive entitlement to redundancy rights in fixed term contracts. While the Regulations seem extensive, two points should be noted. First, they only apply to employment under a fixed term contract from 10 July 2002. Second, unlike the previous Regulations, these only apply to employees and not the wider class of workers.

5.12   Discrimination on the Grounds of Sexual Orientation

The Employment Equality (Sexual Orientation) Regulations 2003 were introduced to implement the Employment Directive (2000/78/EC) and provide protection from discrimination and harassment on the grounds of sexual orientation. Sexual orientation covers homosexual, heterosexual and bisexual behaviour (Regulation 2). The Regulations protect against direct and indirect discrimination, victimisation and harassment, and also protect against post-termination discrimination. They came into force on 1 December 2003.

Direct discrimination

By Regulation 3(1)(a) a person discriminates against another if on the grounds of sexual orientation he treats that person less favourably than he treats or would treat other persons. The comparison is with a person whose relevant circumstances are the same or not materially different (Regulation 3(2)). Note this is the same definition as in the Race Relations Act so that treating someone less favourably because the employer believes they are gay, or because they associate with gay people, is covered. The actual sexual orientation of the complainant is irrelevant.

Indirect discrimination

By Regulation 3(1)(b) indirect discrimination occurs when:

A applies to B a provision, criterion or practice which he applies or would apply equally to persons not of the same sexual orientation as B, but –
(i)   which puts or would put persons of the same sexual orientation as B at a particular disadvantage when compared with other persons,
(ii) which puts B at that disadvantage, and
(iii) which A cannot show to be a proportionate means of achieving a legitimate aim.

You will note that this is the same as the definition in the amended RRA and SDA and presumably will be interpreted in the same way.

Victimisation

Victimisation has the same definition as that in the SDA and RRA and thus by Regulation 4 victimisation occurs where a person treats another less favourably by reason that the person has:

(a) brought or intends to bring proceedings against the employer or any other person under the Regulations;
(b) given or intends to give evidence or information in connection with any proceedings against the employer or another;
(c) otherwise done or intends to do anything under or by reference to the Regulations in relation to the employer or another;
(d) alleged or intends to allege that the employer or another has contravened the Regulations, unless the allegations were false and not made in good faith.

It is sufficient that the employer suspects that a person has done the above and this is the reason for the less favourable treatment.

Harassment

Harassment occurs where, on the grounds of sexual orientation, a person engages in unwanted conduct which has the purpose or effect of violating a person's dignity 'or creating an intimidating, hostile, degrading, humiliating or offensive environment for that person' (Regulation 5(1)). As with the definition under the RRA and SDA, conduct shall be regarded as having that effect if, in all the circumstances, including in particular the perception of the victim, it should reasonably be considered as having that effect (Regulation 5(2)). As with the RRA, note that it is not the person's sexual orientation which is the crux of the complaint and therefore, for example, if a father with a gay son is offended by gay jokes made by other employees, he may make a claim. Note also that the conduct, although unwanted, does not have to intend to violate a person's dignity etc.

Acts of discrimination

By Regulation 6 it is unlawful for an employer to discriminate in:

(a) the arrangements for determining who to employ;
(b) the terms on which employment is offered;
(c) refusing or deliberately not offering employment;
(d) the terms during employment;
(e) opportunities for promotion, transfer, training or any other benefit;
(f) refusing to afford or deliberately not affording him such opportunity;
(g) dismissing him or subjecting him to any other detriment.

Dismissal includes the expiry of a fixed term contract which is not renewed (Regulation 6(5)(a)) and constructive dismissal (Regulation 6(5)(b)).

Genuine occupational requirements

Regulation 7 introduces the concept of a genuine occupational requirement (GOR). By Regulation 7(2) where, having regard to the nature of the employment or the context in which it is being carried out, being a particular sexual orientation is a genuine and determining occupational requirement and it is proportionate to apply that requirement, an employer can discriminate if the person does not meet that requirement or the employer is not satisfied he meets that requirement. For example, it would probably be a GOR for the head of a gay organisation to be gay.

More controversially, Regulation 7(3) provides that where the employment is for the purposes of an organised religion, the employer may apply a requirement as to sexual orientation, to either comply with the doctrines of the religion or to avoid conflicting with the strongly held religious convictions of a significant number of the religion's followers. Parliamentary debate indicated that this was only intended to apply to priests, but the wording is much wider and as such a challenge was mounted arguing that Regulation 7(3) did not comply with the Directive. In *R (on the application of Amicus – MSF section)* v. *Secretary of State for Trade and Industry* [2004] IRLR 430 the High Court held that Regulation 7(3) is compatible with the Directive. It is narrow and when interpreted to ensure compatibility with the Directive it can be seen to afford an exception in very limited circumstances. This is because of the words 'for the purposes of an organised religion' which is narrower than the wording in the Regulations relating to discrimination on religious belief (see below) which use the words 'for the purposes of a religious organisation'. As such, the employment of, for example, a teacher in a faith school, would not be employment for the purposes of an organised religion. The fact that the employer must apply the requirement to comply with the doctrines of the religion is an objective test so that the employer must show that the employment of a person not meeting the requirement would be incompatible with the doctrines of the religion. This is very narrow in scope. Further, to apply a requirement to avoid conflicting with the strongly held religious convictions of a significant number of the religion's followers requires precise examination of the precise nature of the employment and is an objective test which will be difficult to satisfy. As such, Regulation 7(3) is not incompatible with the Directive.

While the challenge was unsuccessful, only case law will determine how Regulation 7(3) will be interpreted.

Post-termination protection

By Regulation 21 there is protection against harassment or suffering a detriment after the relationship has ended where the discrimination or harassment arises out of and is closely connected to the relationship.

Liability of employers

By Regulation 22 an employer is liable for the acts of its employees, done with or without the employer's knowledge or approval, unless it can prove that all steps were taken that were reasonably practicable to prevent the employee doing the act complained of. By Regulation 23 a person who knowingly aids another to commit an act unlawful under the Regulations shall be treated as committing the act, unless the employer can show that it relied on a statement that the act was not unlawful and it was reasonable to rely on such a statement. It is likely that these two Regulations will be interpreted in the same way as the corresponding provisions in the SDA and the RRA.

Enforcement and remedies

A complaint must be lodged in a tribunal normally within three months of the alleged act (Regulation 34). The burden of proof is the same as that in other anti-discriminatory legislation, that is the complainant must establish a *prima facie* case and the burden shifts to the employer to show the reason for the act was something other than the complainant's sexual orientation (Regulation 29). Where a tribunal finds the complaint well-founded, it can make an order declaring the complainant's rights; an order of compensation or a recommendation of action for the employer to take within a specified period of time, to obviate or reduce the adverse effect on the complainant. Failure to comply with the recommendation, without reasonable justification, can lead to an increase in compensation (Regulation 30).

5.13 Discrimination on the Grounds of Religion or Belief

At the time of introduction of protection against discrimination on the grounds of sexual orientation, the government, in accordance with its obligations to implement the Employment Directive, also introduced protection against religious discrimination by the Employment Equality (Religion or Belief) Regulations 2003 which also came into force in December 2003. These Regulations are almost identical in wording to the Sexual Orientation Regulations and thus reference should be made to any discussion above.

The Regulations protect against discrimination on the grounds of religion, religious belief or philosophical belief (Regulation 2). The definition was amended by s.77 Equality Act 2006. Originally the philosophical belief had to be similar to a religious belief but the word 'similar' has been removed. The original wording led to the decision in *Baggs* v. *Fudge* (2005) (unreported) that there was no protection under the Regulations for a person who was a member of the BNP as political beliefs were not protected. The change in wording may mean *Baggs* would be decided differently today. The protection, however, is against discrimination on the basis of the complainant's religion etc and not that of the discriminator. Whether this will prove to limit the protection has yet to be seen. There is no definition in either the Directive or the Regulations as to the meaning of religion, religious belief or philosophical belief, but they will encompass a wide range of beliefs and tribunals will be required to have regard to

Strasbourg jurisprudence in applying Article 9 (freedom of religion). Under the European Court of Human Rights case law, Article 9 protects druidism (*Campbell* v. *UK* (1987) 53 DR 241); pacifism (*Arrowsmith* v. *UK* (1978) 19 DR 5); veganism (*X* v. *UK (Commission)* Appl 18187/91); the Divine Light Zentrum (*Omkarananda and the Divine Light Zentrum* v. *Switzerland* (1981) 25 DR 105); and the Church of Scientology (*X and the Church of Scientology* v. *Sweden* (1979) 16 DR 68). The European Court of Human Rights has also said that Article 9 is a 'precious asset for atheists, agnostics, sceptics and the unconcerned' (*Kokkinakis* v. *Greece* (1994) 17 EHRR 397). Thus the Regulations protect not only those who hold religious beliefs but equally those who do not. This has now become explicit by an amendment to the Regulations by s.44 Equality Act 2006. While the European Court case law gives tribunals guidance, the lack of definitions in the Regulations could lead to a lot of litigation.

Apart from problems of exactly what is protected, the Regulations are similar to those relating to sexual orientation. Thus a complainant is protected against direct discrimination, indirect discrimination, victimisation and harassment (Regulations 3, 4 and 5) and against post-termination discrimination or harassment (Regulation 21). All of these have the same definition as that in the Sexual Orientation Regulations and the Race Relations Act. In *Azmi* v. *Kirklees MBC* [2007] All ER 484 the Employment Appeal Tribunal held that a Muslim teaching assistant had not been directly discriminated against on the ground of religion or belief by a requirement that she remove her veil when teaching. While it concluded that the requirement was indirectly discriminatory, it was justified as a proportionate means of achieving the legitimate aim of raising the educational achievements of the pupils. The same acts of discrimination can be committed (Regulation 6) and the same burden of proof applies (Regulation 29). Likewise, employers are liable for the acts of employees (Regulation 22) and there is liability for aiding unlawful acts (Regulation 23). There is specific protection for Sikhs from discrimination in connection with requirements to wear safety helmets (Regulation 26).

A recent unfair dismissal case shows the interface between the Regulations, Article 9 and other UK law. In *Copsey* v. *WWB Devon Clays Ltd* [2005] EWCA Civ 932 a claim of unfair dismissal was brought by a Christian employee who refused to accept shift changes requiring Sunday working, and was dismissed as a result. The Court of Appeal held that the dismissal was fair, but for different reasons. Mummery LJ held that the employer was bound by jurisprudence of the European Court of Human Rights ending with *Stedman* v. *UK* [1997] 23 EHRR CD that Article 9 does not apply because an employee is always free to resign. Rix LJ felt that this was not what the European Court cases said, but held on the facts that the employer had tried to accommodate the employee when changing his hours, and although Article 9 did apply, it was not breached. Neuberger LJ dealt with UK law and held that a dismissal is fair if an employer strikes a reasonable balance between the needs of the business and the employee's religious beliefs. Thus it is unclear at present how the different pieces of law interlink.

Genuine occupational requirements

This is one area where the Regulations differ. By Regulation 7 it is permissible to appoint a person to a job if one of the following apply:

1. Being of a particular religion or belief is a genuine and determining occupational requirement and it is proportionate to apply that requirement in the particular case.
2. The employer has an ethos based on religion or belief and having regard to that ethos, and the nature of the employment and the context in which it is carried out:
   (i) being a particular religion or belief is a genuine occupational requirement for the job;
   (ii) it is proportionate to apply that requirement in that particular case.

It is important to note the differences in the two. In the first, religion must be a genuine and determining occupational requirement whereas in the second, the word 'determining' is omitted, suggesting it will be easier for an employer to successfully argue the second compared with the first. Commentators have argued that the first will only cover ministers of the church and the second would cover employees such as teachers in faith schools or medical staff in a hospital with a religious ethos, but would not, for example, cover catering or cleaning staff in such establishments. Without case law it is difficult to predict how Regulation 7 will be interpreted.

Enforcement and remedies

By Regulation 30 the same remedies apply as those in the Employment Equality (Sexual Orientation) Regulations 2003.

5.14 Discrimination on the Grounds of Disability

The meaning of disability

In 1995 the Disability Discrimination Act was passed and came into force in December 1996. The original Act had a small employer exemption and bore little relation to then other then existing pieces of anti-discriminatory legislation, namely the Sex Discrimination Act 1975 and the Race Relations Act 1976. The EU Employment Directive (2000/78/EC) had discrimination as part of its content and thus the Disability Discrimination Act 1995 (Amendment) Regulations 2003, which came into force in October 2004, radically altered the existing legislation.. The Disability Discrimination Act 2005 further amended the 1995 Act. In addition, *Notes of Guidance* and a *Code of Practice* help on interpretation. It should be noted that an action only lies if a person is discriminated against because they are disabled. Therefore, unlike the Sex Discrimination Act and the Race Relations Act, it allows the employer to positively discriminate in favour of a disabled person.

To be protected against discrimination an individual must be a person who has a disability (s.1(2)) or a person who has had a disability (s.2). A 'disability' is defined as either a physical or mental impairment, which has a substantial and long-term adverse effect on the person's ability to carry out normal day-to-day activities (s.1(1)). In other words, the physical or mental impairment must be the cause of the substantial and long-term adverse effects. There is no definition of physical impairment, but Sch 1, para 1(1) qualifies the term 'mental impairment'. Until amendments made by the 2005 Act a person with a mental illness was only to be regarded as having a mental impairment if the mental illness was clinically well-recognised. For example, in *Goodwin* v. *Patent Office* [1999] IRLR 4 the Employment Appeal Tribunal held that an employee dismissed because of paranoid schizophrenia had been dismissed on the grounds of disability. However, many critics of the original definition felt that this placed too many hurdles on a claimant who was clearly mentally ill but the precise condition had not been diagnosed. As such, the 2005 amendments remove this qualification so that a person with a long-term mental illness is now protected. It is still important, however, to note the case of *Dunham* v. *Ashford Windows* [2005] IRLR 608. In this case the EAT emphasised that a tribunal hearing a mental impairment case based on learning difficulties should always seek expert evidence of an identified condition. While the new definition removes the requirement that a mental impairment is clinically well-recognised, a claimant will still have to establish that he or she has a mental impairment and its effect on normal day-to-day activities, hence the need for expert evidence.

The impairment must have an adverse effect on the ability to carry out normal day-to-day activities. There is a list in Sch 1, para 4 of day-to-day activities: mobility; manual dexterity; physical co-ordination; continence; ability to lift, carry or otherwise move everyday objects; speech; hearing or eyesight; memory or ability to learn or understand; the ability to concentrate; and the perception of risk of physical danger. What constitutes 'substantial' is not defined in the Act. Schedule 1, para 2 defines what is meant by 'long term', however. The effect must have lasted at least 12 months or be expected to last either 12 months or for the rest of the person's life.

In some cases the disability will be well-recognised, such as blindness, and the employee will be registered as disabled. Problems arise, however, when the situation is not so obvious. In *O'Neill* v. *Symm & Co Ltd* [1998] IRLR 233 an Employment Tribunal considered that chronic fatigue syndrome and ME (myalgic encephalomyelitis) could be a disability for the purposes of the Act. This finding was upheld by the Employment Appeal Tribunal, but the appeal tribunal went on to say that nothing in its judgement, nor that of the employment tribunal, should be taken as establishing that chronic fatigue syndrome is generically a disability which falls within the ambit of the Act. A tribunal must consider each case in relation to the particular complainant and the impairments relative to that complainant. In *Tarling* v. *Wisdom Toothbrushes Ltd t/a Wisdom* (1997) IDS Brief 597 the employee had a club foot which resulted in progressive deterioration of her bone structure. As a result she had sciatica which made it difficult for her to stand for the long periods of time which her job required her to do. The employment tribunal found that she was disabled for the purposes of the Act, and in *Clark* v. *Novacold Ltd* [1998] IRLR 420 the employment tribunal and the Employment Appeal Tribunal accepted that an applicant who did manual work and who, after injuring his back at work could not walk short distances or lift heavy loads, a condition which would last more than 12 months, also had a disability for the purposes of the Act. Conversely, in *Foord* v. *JA Johnston & Sons* (1998) IDS Brief 611 an employment tribunal considered that an applicant with fallen arches which meant that she was unable to stand or be on her feet for prolonged periods of time was not disabled. She was able to cope with her normal working hours of 8 a.m. to 2 p.m. and she only experienced difficulties when on one occasion she worked an extra two hours. In *Goodwin* v. *Patent Office* (above) the employment tribunal held that the applicant who suffered from paranoid schizophrenia was not disabled within the meaning of the Act. Although recognising the applicant had a mental illness, his work was of a satisfactory standard and he could carry out domestic activities without assistance. The reason for his dismissal was not his inability to work to the required standard but complaints from female staff that he stared at them and made unwelcome social advances. It was questionable whether the decision was correct given that paragraph C3 of the *Guidance* issued under the Act suggests that a tribunal should not judge the question of whether a person has a disability by what he or she is able or not able to do at work. On appeal the Employment Appeal Tribunal reversed the decision and emphasised that the fact that a disabled person can carry out certain day-to-day activities does not mean that their ability to do so has not been impaired. Disabled persons often adjust their lives and circumstances to enable them to cope.

This does not mean that their condition is not a disability. In *Hewett* v. *Motorola Ltd* [2004] IRLR 545 the Employment Appeal Tribunal said that 'understand' as a normal day-to-day activity is not limited to an ability to understand information, knowledge or instructions. Someone who has difficulty in understanding normal social interaction, such as someone with Asperger's Syndrome, should be regarded as having their understanding affected. Further, in *Kapadia* v. *London Borough of Lambeth* [2000] IRLR 14 the Employment Appeal Tribunal allowed an appeal against a tribunal decision that the applicant was not disabled. The tribunal had ignored medical evidence and come to an opinion based on how the applicant had given evidence.

The Disability Discrimination Act 2005 has inserted a new paragraph 6A into Schedule 1 which deals with progressive conditions. Paragraph 6A(1) provides that a person who has certain cancers, HIV infection or multiple sclerosis is to be deemed to have a disability. This protects persons who have progressive conditions in that there is no longer a need to show an effect on the ability to perform normal day-to-day activities and thus they will be protected from the time of diagnosis. Certain cancers are excluded, for example those cancers such as most cervical cancers which can be treated successfully and fully by cone biopsy.

In *Swift* v. *Chief Constable of Wiltshire Constabulary* [2004] IRLR 540 the Employment Appeal Tribunal considered the position in relation to recurring conditions. This is an important decision where the condition does not fit the definition of 'progressive conditions' above. The EAT said that a tribunal had to ask itself four questions. First, was there at some stage an impairment which had a substantial adverse effect on the complainant's ability to carry out normal day-to-day activities? Second, did the impairment cease to have such an effect and if so when? Third, what was the substantial adverse effect? Fourth, is that substantial adverse effect likely to recur? A substantial adverse effect is likely to recur if it is more probable than not that the effect will recur, although the tribunal does not need to be satisfied that the recurrence will last twelve months. The tribunal must look to see if the effect will recur and not the illness, which may run its course but leave behind an impairment.

In relation to employment, applicants and employees are protected against discrimination. By s.68 'employment' is defined as 'employment under a contract of service or of apprenticeship, or a contract personally to do any work'. In *South East Sheffield Citizens Advice Bureau* v. *Grayson* [2004] IRLR 353 it was held that volunteer advisers were not employees within the meaning of s.68 as there was no contractual obligation on the bureau to provide work for the volunteer, or on the volunteer to personally perform any work.

Disability related discrimination

Discrimination is defined in s.3A. By s.3A(1) an employer discriminates against a person with a disability if, for a reason which relates to that person's disability, he treats that person less favourably than he would treat a person to whom that reason does not or would not apply and he cannot show that the less favourable treatment is justified. In *Reedman* v. *Fresh Connection Ltd* (1997) (unreported) the employment tribunal stated that there was no need for any ill intention or improper motive on the part of the employer, but there had to be a causal connection between the less favourable treatment and the disability. According to the Employment Appeal Tribunal in *O'Neill*, to establish this causal connection it is necessary for the employer to know about the complainant's disability at the time of the less favourable treatment. This, however, was rejected by a later Employment Appeal Tribunal in *Heinz Co Ltd* v. *Kenrick* [2000] IRLR 144. The Appeal Tribunal stated that it was not necessary for an employer to have knowledge of the disability in order to have acted for a reason 'which relates' to the disability. A person's work may be affected because of a disability they have concealed from the employer. If the employer then dismisses them, for example, this is because of poor work which is poor because of their disability and thus the employer is acting for a reason which relates to that disability. This decision – that is the test is objective, not subjective – is consistent with the Court of Appeal decision in *Clark* (see below). Furthermore, the reason for the less favourable treatment must relate to the person's disability and not to some other factor. For example in *Hanlon* v. *University of Huddersfield* (1998) (unreported) a disabled employee was suspended because of his refusal to perform a contractual duty. By contrast in *Clark* v. *Novacold* the employee was dismissed because of his absence from work, which was caused by his disability and in *Cox* v. *Post Office* (1998) IDS Brief 609 an employment tribunal found that a postman had been dismissed because of his disability since his absences were caused mainly by his asthma, and if these absences had been ignored when invoking the irregular attenders' procedure he would only have received an informal warning. However, in *O'Hanlon* v. *HM Revenue and Customs* [2007] IRLR 404 the claimant, who was off work with clinical depression, argued that the employer had discriminated against her for a disability related reason when it adhered to the normal sick pay policy of six months on full pay and six months on half pay. Her argument was that as her absence was disability related, the employer should have paid her 12-months' full pay. The EAT (confirmed by the Court of Appeal) held that the reduction in pay because of sick absence when the employee was disabled was disability related discrimination but that it was justified, as to pay full pay would go against the policy of the Disability Discrimination Act which is to assist the integration of disabled persons into the workplace and would also be a disincentive for disabled people to return to work.

In *Reedman* the employment tribunal said that once it is shown that the applicant is disabled and a *prima facie* case of less favourable treatment has been established, the tribunal should look to the employer for an explanation. If that explanation is inadequate, it is reasonable to infer that the reason for the less favourable treatment is the applicant's disability. This now has statutory authority in that by s.17A(1A) the burden of proof is the same as the Sex Discrimination Act and Race Relations Act, that is if the complainant establishes a *prima facie* case, the burden shifts to the employer to prove the reason for the treatment was not related to the person's disability.

Until the 2003 amendments there was no statutory definition of a 'comparator'. In *O'Neill* the Employment Appeal Tribunal discussed the relevant comparator. The Tribunal said: 'An employer can be held to have treated a disabled employee, for a reason related to that disabled employee's disability, less favourably than in comparable circumstances he would treat an otherwise comparable employee, without knowing of the fact of the disability.' Therefore in *Clark*, the employment tribunal compared the employee's treatment with that of a non-disabled long-term sick employee who had had the same amount of absence and like the applicant was unlikely to return in the foreseeable future. Clark appealed to the Employment Appeal Tribunal arguing that the employment tribunal had used the wrong comparator. He argued that as his inability to attend work was because of his disability it was inappropriate to compare him with someone who was also absent for a non-disability reason, the comparator should be someone at work and able to carry out the normal functions of the job. The Employment Appeal Tribunal, however, rejected Clark's argument and upheld the employment tribunal decision that the correct comparator was a non-disabled employee who was off sick for the same length of time as Clark and who was unlikely to return in the foreseeable future. The Appeal Tribunal itself, however, said that it was 'without great confidence' that they rejected Clark's arguments.

Clark appealed to the Court of Appeal ([1999] IRLR 318). That court reversed the decision of the Employment Appeal Tribunal. The Court of Appeal said that the test for less favourable treatment is based on the reason for the treatment of the disabled person and not on the fact of his disability: 'It does not turn on a like for like comparison of the treatment of the disabled person and of others in similar circumstances.' Thus the correct comparator is a person who has not been absent from work or who has the same absence record when any disability related absences are ignored. This was also the decision of the Employment Appeal Tribunal in *British Sugar plc* v. *Kirker* [1998] IRLR 624 which did not consider its earlier decision in *Clark*. Section 3A(5) discussed below now gives a statutory definition of a comparator.

Section 3A(1)(b) provides the employer with a defence if he can show that the less favourable treatment is justified. Section 3A(3) provides that for the purposes of s.3A(1)(b): 'treatment is justified if, but only if, the reason for it is both material to the circumstances of the particular case and substantial.' The Employment Appeal Tribunal in *Morse* v. *Wiltshire County Council* [1998] IRLR 352 said that in deciding whether or not the employer has shown that the treatment was justified the tribunals should apply an objective test. In other words, it is the tribunal which decides whether the treatment is justified and whether the reason for it is material to the particular case and substantial, not whether the employer feels it is so. The employment tribunal in *Terry* v. *Sheldon School* (1998) (unreported) stated that the test of justification under the Act was much stricter than the concept of reasonableness under s.98(4) Employment Rights Act 1996, and in *Kenrick* the Employment Appeal Tribunal stated that a dismissal which was unlawful under the Act is not automatically unfair under the Employment Rights Act. However, in *Jones* v. *Post Office* [2001] IRLR 384 the Court of Appeal held that, when looking at justification, the task facing tribunals is 'not very different to the task which they have to perform in cases of unfair dismissal', in which they have to adopt a 'range of reasonable responses approach'. The court said that in both cases the tribunal may come to a different conclusion from the employer, but it must 'respect the opinion of the employer in the one case if it is within the range of reasonable responses and in the other if the reason given is material and substantial'. According to the employment tribunal in *Holmes* v. *Whittingham & Porter Ltd* (1998) IDS Brief 609 this strict test of justification is because the aim of the Disability Discrimination Act is not to promote equality for disabled employees but to require the employer to take steps to protect disabled employees. Thus, in the case, although the tribunal found that Holmes had been fairly dismissed for the purposes of the Employment Rights Act in that the employer had acted reasonably within the provisions of s.98(4), the employer had not justified his less favourable treatment. Health and safety reasons have been held to justify dismissal in a number of employment tribunal cases (for example, *Smith* v. *Carpets International UK plc* (1998) IDS Brief 611 and *Reilly* v. *EXI Ltd* (1997) (unreported)). Furthermore in *Fozard* v. *Greater Manchester Police Authority* (1997) Personnel Management, Jane a disabled applicant who was not shortlisted for a job as a word processor because of her inability to produce accurate written work, was not discriminated against as although some of the errors were due to her disability, others were due to carelessness and the employer's need for accuracy was material to the particular case and substantial. Conversely, in *Holmes*, while reliance on a company medical report, prepared by a general practitioner, was sufficient to defeat an unfair dismissal claim, it was not sufficient to satisfy the test of justification in the Disability Discrimination Act. The employers should have obtained a specialist's report before acting and therefore the dismissal of the disabled applicant was unjustified less favourable treatment (see also *Vickary* v. *British Telecommunications plc* [1999] IRLR 680).

Direct discrimination

While the discussion of s.3A(1) above appears to give a definition of direct discrimination with a defence of justification, this is not the case. Section 3A(5) creates direct discrimination which occurs when:

> 'on the ground of the disabled person's disability, an employer treats the disabled person less favourably than he treats or would treat a person not having that particular disability whose relevant circumstances, including his abilities, are the same as, or not materially different from, those of the disabled person.'

Furthermore, s.3A(4) provides that the treatment of a disabled person cannot be justified if it is direct discrimination under s.3A(5). This means that an employer will never be able to justify discrimination solely on the grounds of a person's disability, rather than a consideration of his abilities to do the job.

Harassment

A second way the employer can discriminate is by harassment. This is the same as under the amended Race Relations Act and the Sexual Orientation Regulations and those on religion or belief. By s.3B a person harasses a disabled person where, for a reason related to that person's disability, he engages in unwanted conduct which violates the disabled person's dignity, or creates an intimidating, hostile, degrading, humiliating or offensive environment for him. As with the RRA etc, a tribunal must have regard in particular to the perception of the disabled person.

Victimisation

A third way an employer can discriminate is by victimising a disabled person. This is found in s.55. The definition of 'victimisation' is the same as under the SDA and RRA but with the added protection that an employer can victimise a non-disabled person who has taken action under the Act (s.55(5)).

Duty to make reasonable adjustments

A fourth method by which an employer can discriminate against a disabled person is found in s.4A (1) which states:

Where –
(a) a provision, criterion or practice applied on or behalf of an employer, or
(b) any physical feature of premises occupied by the employer,
places the disabled person at a substantial disadvantage in comparison with persons who are not disabled, it is the duty of the employer to take such steps as it is reasonable, in all the circumstances of the case, or him to have to take in order to prevent the provision, criterion or practice or feature, from having that effect.

The above applies in relation to both job applicants and employees (s.4A(2)) but the duty does not arise if the employer does not know, and could not be reasonably expected to know, that the person is disabled and likely to be affected (s.4A(3)). By s.3A(6) if an employer is under a duty to make reasonable adjustments and fails to comply with that duty, the defence of justification cannot apply unless his treatment of the disabled person would have been justified even if he had complied with the duty.

There was a similar duty under the old Act but the new duty is described in the same way as indirect discrimination in other legislation. However, the duty arises when the employer knows, or could be reasonably expected to know, that the person has a disability and, as a result, is placed at a substantial disadvantage. In *Archibald* v. *Fife Council* [2004] IRLR 651 Mrs Archibald had been a roadsweeper when a complication after surgery left her virtually unable to walk. As such, she undertook administrative work and was assessed as 'more than capable of carrying out work in an office environment'. The Council's office jobs were on a higher grade than manual ones and it was the Council's policy that all employees seeking redeployment on a higher salary had to go through competitive interviews. Mrs Archibald went through a number of interviews and was unsuccessful and was eventually dismissed. Mrs Archibald argued disability discrimination on the basis that she should not have to go through interviews for a job she was qualified to do. The House of Lords held that the duty to make an adjustment is triggered where an employee becomes so disabled she can no longer meet the requirements of her job description. The arrangements employed by her employer in selecting for the jobs fell into the definition of 'provision, criterion or practice'. She was placed at a substantial disadvantage when she could no longer meet a requirement of her job description that she was physically fit as she was liable to be dismissed. The duty to make reasonable adjustments arises even if there is nothing an employer can do to prevent the disabled person being placed at a disadvantage, and the duty may require an employer to treat a disabled person more favourably to remove the disadvantage. This necessarily involves a measure of positive discrimination. The comparator in this case is not confined to non-disabled persons doing the same job, and thus a measure the employer can take is transferring to another job. As such, a reasonable adjustment would be a transfer without competitive interview and such a transfer could be sideways, upwards or downwards. However, in *NTL Group* v. *Difolco* [2006] EWCA Civ 1508 the employee, who was partially paralysed and could only work part time, was made redundant. She was given the opportunity to apply for another job which was advertised as full time but was told if she got the job the employer would consider making it part time. She refused to apply for the job unless it became part time before she applied and claimed that her employer had failed to make reasonable adjustments. The Court of Appeal stated that the employer had not failed in its duty. Until the claimant applied for the job, the duty did not arise. In *Spence* v. *Intype Libra Ltd* [2007] All ER 261 an employee, who had become disabled, argued that his employer had failed to make reasonable adjustments by not obtaining and consulting on a medical report before dismissing him. The Employment Appeal Tribunal held that the employer was not in breach of the duty but gave leave to appeal to the Court of Appeal.

There is no duty on employers to be proactive, merely to react once the substantial disadvantage is known or could reasonably be known. In *Ridout* v. *TC Group* [1998] IRLR 628 the applicant stated on her application form that she had photosensitive epilepsy which was controlled by medication and that she was disabled. She was interviewed in a room lit by fluorescent lighting and when she entered she commented that she may be affected by the lighting. She was not offered the job and claimed under the Act that the employer had failed to make reasonable adjustments. The Employment Appeal Tribunal held that she had not been discriminated against. The Act did not require a disabled person to go into detailed explanations about the adjustments required, nor require the employer to ask questions as to what adjustments should be made. The employment tribunal was entitled to conclude that a reasonable employer would be unaware of the effect of fluorescent lighting on the applicant's rare form of epilepsy. Whether this decision is now right in the light of *Kenrick* (above) is debatable. Furthermore, the duty only arises when the person with a disability is placed at a substantial disadvantage.

By s.18B(2) examples of adjustments an employer may be required to make include:

(a) making adjustments to premises;
(b) allocating some of the employee's duties to another person;
(c) transferring him or her to an existing vacancy;
(d) altering his or her working hours;
(e) assigning him or her to a different place of work;
(f) allowing time off for rehabilitation, assessment or treatment;
(g) arranging training;
(h) acquiring or modifying equipment;
(i) modifying instructions of reference manuals;
(j) modifying procedures for testing or assessment;
(k) providing a reader or interpreter;
(l) providing supervision.

In *Kenny v. Hampshire Constabulary* [1999] IRLR 76 the Employment Appeal Tribunal held that the duty only applies to job-related arrangements and does not require the employer to provide a carer to deal with an employee's personal needs. It is suggested that this interpretation is outwith the spirit of the Act in that if a disabled person cannot use a toilet without help they cannot work.

In deciding whether it is reasonable to expect the employer to take steps, s.18B(1) provides a list of factors to be taken into account. These are:

(a) the extent to which the step would prevent the effect in question;
(b) the extent to which it is practicable for the employer to take the step;
(c) the financial and other costs which would be incurred by the employer and the disruption to his business;
(d) the extent of the employer's financial and other resources;
(e) the availability to the employer of financial or other assistance;
(f) the nature of his activities and the size of his undertaking;
(g) where it is a private household, the extent to which taking the step would disrupt that household or disturb a resident.

Under the original Act, the Employment Appeal Tribunal in *Morse* held that there are a number of steps that an employment tribunal must go through when dealing with a complaint. First, it must decide whether or not the provisions impose a duty on the employer. Second, if such a duty exists, the tribunal must decide whether or not the employer has taken such steps as are reasonable to prevent the disabled person being placed at a substantial disadvantage. This involves the tribunal looking at any steps the employer could have taken, including those in (now) s.18B(2), having regard to the factors in (now) s.18B(1). Third, if the tribunal finds that the employer has failed to comply with the duty, the tribunal has to decide whether the employer has shown that such a failure is justified (now ss.3A(3) and (6)).

The new section 3A(3) provides that a failure to comply with a s.4A duty is justified if the reason for the failure is material to the circumstances of the particular case and substantial. In *Tarling* v. *Wisdom* (above) the employee could have worked with the provision of a special chair. The employer had sought advice from the DfEE, a medical opinion and the Shaw Trust which provides financial support for employers with disabled employees. The DfEE advised that two special chairs were available, one at a cost of £1,000, but which was available on a four-week free trial and another at a cost of £500. The employer thought both chairs would be difficult to move between workstations and gave the applicant a number of ordinary chairs. Eventually the applicant was dismissed on the grounds of poor performance. The tribunal found that the employer had failed in the duty to make reasonable adjustments, particularly as the most expensive chair would have cost the employer about £200 with assistance from the Shaw Trust. In *Williams* v. *J Walter Thompson Group Ltd* [2005] IRLR 376 the complainant needed special equipment and training in Lotus notes because she was blind. The employer claimed its failure to provide this was justifiable because of the costs involved. The Court of Appeal rejected this, stating that the company knew she was blind when it employed her, but did no investigation and made no plans to deal with this before or after her employment started. The decision in *Archibald* has already been noted. In *Nottinghamshire County Council* v. *Meikle* [2004] IRLR 703 Mrs Meikle had a visual impairment and mobility problems. She argued that her employer had failed to make reasonable adjustments since 1993 in respect of, *inter alia*, providing large print documents, adjusting the timetable so she did not have to walk too far to classrooms and she had classrooms with proper equipment, and giving her additional non-teaching time to complete paperwork in daylight. She started proceedings, then was off sick with eye strain. As such, she was put on half pay. She eventually resigned and claimed constructive dismissal, in addition to failure to make reasonable adjustments. The Court of Appeal, upholding the Employment Appeal Tribunal, said that there had been a breach by the employer of the duty to make reasonable adjustments. It also held that putting Mrs Meikle on half pay was a failure to make a reasonable adjustment, which placed Mrs Meikle at a substantial disadvantage. It further held that a persistent failure to carry out reasonable adjustments amounted to a fundamental breach of the obligation of trust and confidence, and was therefore a constructive dismissal.

Acts of discrimination

By s.4 of the Act it is unlawful for an employer to discriminate against a person with a disability in relation to:

(a) the arrangements for appointing employees;
(b) the terms on which the employment is offered;
(c) by refusing to offer the employment (s.4(1)).

It is also unlawful to discriminate:

(a) in the terms of the employment;
(b) in the opportunities offered for training, promotion, transfer or any other benefit;
(c) by refusing to offer such opportunities;
(d) by dismissing him or subjecting him to any other detriment (s.4(2)).

There were problems in relation to the interpretation of some of the provisions of the original s.4, most particularly the definition of dismissal. Section 82(1A)(b) Sex Discrimination Act expressly incorporates the concept of constructive dismissal into the Act and thus 'dismissal' in s.6(2)(b) includes constructive dismissal. Neither the Race Relations Act nor the Disability Discrimination Act had an equivalent of s.82(1A)(b), but it has been seen above that the EAT in *Derby Specialist Fabrications Ltd* v. *Burton* decided that constructive dismissal was implicitly contained in the meaning of dismissal in the Race Relations Act on the basis that whether an employer dismisses someone on racial grounds or is guilty of racially discriminating conduct, which is repudiatory and causes the employee to resign, the effect is still the same, that is the contract is terminated. It was thought that since *Burton* the same argument would apply to claims under the Disability Discrimination Act, however in *Commissioner of the Police of the Metropolis* v. *Harley* [2001] IRLR 263 the EAT held that the constructive dismissal of an employee did not amount to a dismissal under the Disability Discrimination Act. The EAT highlighted the fact that the original Act did not expressly include constructive dismissal, unlike the SDA. This has now been rectified with a new s.4(6) specifically providing that dismissal includes constructive dismissal.

Post-termination discrimination

Section 16A provides protection against detriment or harassment where there has been discrimination or harassment during the course of the employment relationship. By s.16A(4) such protection also arises where a provision, criterion or practice, or physical feature of the premises, places the ex-employee at a substantial disadvantage, unless the employer did not know, and could not be reasonably expected to know, that the person was placed at a substantial disadvantage. This will protect persons who, for example, need to access premises after employment to, for example, talk to potential witnesses.

Other unlawful acts

There are enforcement duties on the Commission for Equality and Human Rights in respect of the following:

Discriminatory advertisements

Section 16B provides that it is unlawful for a person in relation to a relevant appointment or benefit, to publish or cause to be published, an advertisement which indicates or might be reasonably understood to indicate, that a non-disabled person will be preferred or that the employer is unwilling to make reasonable adjustments. This includes, for example, employment, promotion or transfer, membership of a pension scheme and membership of a trade association (s.16B(3)). It includes not only public advertisements but notices whether public or not, and internal advertisements (s.16B(4)).

Instructions and pressure to discriminate

Section 16C renders it unlawful for a person who has authority over another to instruct that person to do anything unlawful under the Act or induce or attempt to induce a person to do an unlawful act, by offering a benefit or subjecting or threatening to subject that person to a detriment.

Aiding an unlawful act

Section 57 provides that a person who knowingly aids an act unlawful by the Disability Discrimination Act shall be treated as if he or she had committed the act and by s.58 an employer is liable for discriminatory acts by his employees, whether or not done with his knowledge or approval, unless he can show that he took such steps as were reasonable to prevent such discrimination (s.58(3)).

Enforcement and Remedies

Section 17A provides that a tribunal can award compensation against the employer, stating that the amount of compensation shall be calculated by applying the principles applicable to the calculation of damages in claims in tort. While many of the awards to date have been low, in *Kirker* (above) the award was £103,146.49. This included past loss of earnings and interest, estimated future loss of earnings less disability living allowance, loss of enhancement of accrued pension and the loss of being able to take early ill health retirement; £3,500 was included for injury to feelings. This took into account the fact that the dismissal had substantially undermined the employee's confidence and the fact that he had lost congenial work and would find it very hard to replace it.

Monitoring

Monitoring of the legislation is done by the Commission for Equality and Human Rights.

It can be seen from above that many of the Act's provisions have been based on existing anti-discriminatory legislation, however the Court of Appeal has warned that a direct comparison between the Acts may be misleading. In *Clark*, Mummery LJ said:

> 'Contrary to what might be reasonably assumed, the exercise of interpretation is not facilitated by familiarity with the pre-existing legislation prohibiting discrimination in the field of employment . . . on the grounds of sex . . . and race. Indeed, it may be positively misleading to approach the 1995 Act with assumptions and concepts familiar from experience of the workings of the 1975 Act and the 1976 Act.'

While noting the above, *Reedman* (above) has stated that motive and intention are irrelevant to establish a claim under, and the same applies in a direct discrimination claim under, the 1975 and 1976 Acts (*Grieg* v. *Community Industries*, above). Further similarities may be seen as case law develops.

5.15 Discrimination on the Grounds of Age

The Employment Equality (Age) Regulations 2006 came into force in October 2006. The Regulations use the same format as we have seen above and have the concepts of direct and indirect discrimination, victimisation and harassment (Regulations 3, 4 and 6). Note, however, unlike other pieces of anti-discriminatory legislation, an employer may have a defence of objective justification in respect of a direct discrimination claim. In addition, there is an exception to the legislation where age is a genuine and determining occupational requirement (Regulation 8). There is also employer liability for instructions to discriminate and aiding unlawful acts (Regulations 5 and 25) and employers will be liable for unlawful acts committed by their employees (Regulation 24). The same burden of proof applies as seen elsewhere (Regulation 40). In brief, the Regulations:

(a) ban age discrimination in terms of recruitment, promotion and training;
(b) ban all retirement ages below 65, except where objectively justified;
(c) require employers to inform employees in writing, at least six months in advance, of their intended date of retirement;

(d) remove the current upper age limits on unfair dismissal and redundancy;

(e) impose a duty on employers to consider employee requests to work beyond retirement.

5.16 The Future

In October 2007 the government abolished the Equal Opportunities Commission, the Commission for Racial Equality and the Disability Rights Commission, replacing them all with the single Commission for Equality and Human Rights. The Commission also has powers in respect of sexual orientation, religion or belief, age discrimination and human rights.

Following on from this, in June 2007 the government issued a consultation paper entitled *Discrimination Law Review*. The paper seeks views on the implementation of a single Equality Act covering all bases of discrimination and extending its present scope to include, for example, equal pay.

Summary

1. While international law protects against discrimination in a large number of areas, national law at present only protects against discrimination on the grounds of sex, race, marital status, disability, gender reassignment, sexual orientation, religion or belief, and age.

2. The Sex Discrimination Act, Race Relations Act and Equal Pay Act together form a code to provide equal treatment for both sexes and all races.

3. All the legislation recognises four types of discrimination: direct, indirect, victimisation and harassment.

4. Direct discrimination is treating someone less favourably on one of the prohibited grounds. Apart from age and disability discrimination, there is no defence to a direct discrimination claim.

5. Indirect discrimination is imposing a provision, criterion or practice, which applies to all, but places a particular group at a disadvantage. The defence to an indirect discrimination claim is that of objective justification.

6. Victimisation is treating someone less favourably because they have taken part in proceedings under the legislation or alleged breaches of the legislation.

7. Harassment is violating a person's dignity or engendering an intimidating, hostile, degrading, humiliating or offensive environment. The perception of the victim is important and no intention is necessary.

8. EC law has had a major impact in this area, particularly in the implementation and interpretation of the Equal Treatment Directive and the Framework Employment Directive.

Summary cont'd

9. There are specific acts of discrimination that an employer can commit against a person.

10. The Sex Discrimination Act and the Race Relations Act have the concept of a genuine occupational qualification when discrimination is permitted. In addition the RRA, the Sexual Orientation Regulations, the Religion or Belief Regulations and the Age Discrimination Regulations have a concept of genuine occupational requirements.

11. The remedy for discrimination is financial compensation or a declaration of the complainant's rights. In addition, the Commission for Equality and Human Rights may undertake an investigation and may issue a non-discrimination notice against an employer.

Exercises

1. What do you consider to be the main deficiencies in the present laws on discrimination?

2. Ms Brown applied for a temporary social work post in an old people's home in the county of Anglesey in Wales. Her application was turned down because she could not speak Welsh. In Anglesey itself, 62 per cent of the population are Welsh-speaking. In all other respects, Ms Brown was qualified for the job. In fact all social work posts in Anglesey were advertised on a 'Welsh essential' basis. In the event no one was actually appointed to the post because no suitable applicant applied. Ms Brown has now entered a complaint of discrimination against the council in Anglesey. Advise Ms Brown.

3. Hilda and Annie work for Mike's Fashions Ltd, a firm producing ladies' wear. The firm also has a factory shop. Hilda has worked in the factory for six years on a part-time basis. The majority of the women in the factory work part time. Women make up 30 per cent of the workforce. Today the firm has announced that it will be making 25 per cent of the workforce redundant, laying off part-time workers first.

Annie has been working in the factory shop for six months. The shop is run by a manageress who has a firm policy that, as it is a ladies' wear shop, men should not be served. She tells Annie not to serve men, arguing that they always buy the wrong things and create extra work when the goods are returned. Annie thinks this is a ridiculous order and today serves Terry, who bought a set of lingerie for his wife. His wife returned the goods this afternoon and the manageress was tied up for one hour sorting out all the paperwork involved in returned goods. She has now sacked Annie for refusing to obey orders. Advise Annie.

Further Reading

Bowers, Moran and Honeyball *Justification in Direct Sex Discrimination: A Reply* (2003) 32 ILJ 185.

Buckley *Vicarious Liability and Employment Discrimination* (1997) 26 ILJ 158.

Collins *Discrimination, Equality and Social Inclusion* (2003) 66 MLR 16.

Connolly *Discrimination Law: Requirements and Preferences* (1998) 27 ILJ 133.

Connolly *Discrimination Law: Victimisation* (2002) 31 ILJ 161.

Cunningham *Sex Discrimination: Equal but Different?* (1995) 24 ILJ 177.

Cunningham *Discrimination through the Looking Glass: Judicial Guidelines on the Burden of Proof* (2006) 35 ILJ 279.

Davies *A Cuckoo in the Nest? A 'Range of Reasonable Responses', Justification and the Disability Discrimination Act 1995* (2003) 32 ILJ 164.

Docksey *The Principle of Equality Between Men and Women as a Fundamental Right Under Community Law* (1991) 20 ILJ 258.

Doyle *Enabling Legislation or Dissembling Law? The Disability Discrimination Act 1995* (1997) 60 MLR 64.

Fredman *European Discrimination Law: A Critique* (1992) 21 ILJ 119.

Freedland *Equal Treatment, Judicial Review and Delegated Legislation* (1994) 23 ILJ 338.

Gill and Monaghan *Justification in Direct Sex Discrimination Law: Taboo Upheld* (2003) 32 ILJ 115.

Gooding *Disability Discrimination Act 1995* (Blackstones, 1995).

Honeyball *Pregnancy and Sex Discrimination* (2000) 29 ILJ 43.

James *The Meaning of Disability: Physical and Mental Impairment* (2002) 31 ILJ 156.

Lockton *Disability Discrimination: Where We Are Now* (1999) SLPQ vol. 4, no. 4, 261.

Lustgarten *Racial Inequality and the Limits of Law* (1986) 49 MLR 68.

Manknell *Discrimination on the Grounds of Sexual Orientation, Harassment and Liability for Third Parties* (2003) 32 ILJ 297.

McColgan *The Fixed Term Employees (Prevention of Less Favourable Treatment) Regulations 2002: Fiddling While Rome Burns?* (2003) 32 ILJ 194.

McCrudden *Rethinking Positive Action* (1986) 15 ILJ 219.

McGinley *Judicial Approaches to Sex Discrimination in the United States and the United Kingdom – A Comparative Study* (1986) 49 MLR 413.

Oliver *Sexual Orientation Discrimination: Perceptions, Definitions and Genuine Occupational Requirements* (2004) 33 ILJ 1.

Rubenstein *The Law of Sexual Harassment at Work* (1983) 12 ILJ 1.

Sargeant *Age as an Equality Issue: Legal and Policy Perspectives* (2004) 33 ILJ 208.

Sargeant *The Employment Equality (Age) Regulations 2006: a Legitimisation of Age Discrimination in Employment* (2006) 35 ILJ 209.

Further reading cont'd

Sinclair *Harassment: Discrimination and Interpretation* (1998) Web Journal of Current Legal Issues.

Skidmore *Sex, Gender and Comparators in Employment Discrimination* (1997) 26 ILJ 51.

Skidmore *Anti-Discrimination Law and the European Union* (2003) 32 ILJ 132.

Swift *Justifying Age Discrimination* (2006) 35 ILJ 228.

Vickers *The Employment Equality (Religion or Belief) Regulations 2003* (2003) 32 ILJ 188.

Vickers *Is All Harassment Equal? The Case of Religious Harassment* (2006) CLJ 579.

Watt *Goodbye But For Hello But Why* (1998) 27 ILJ 121.

Wells *The Impact of the Framework Employment Directive on UK Disability Discrimination Law* (2003) 32 ILJ 253.

Whittle *New-isms: Transsexual People and Institutionalised Discrimination in Employment Law* (1999) CIL vol. 4, issue 1, 31.

Wintermute *When is Pregnancy Discrimination Indirect Discrimination?* (1998) 27 ILJ 23.

Chapter 6

Equal Pay

6.1 Introduction

Equal pay for women did not become a relevant issue in the law of the United Kingdom until 1975. The Equal Pay Act (EPA) was introduced in 1970, but employers were given five years in which to implement equality, and so the Act came into force in 1975. While the normal applicant for equal pay will be a woman, obviously the rules of statutory interpretation apply and a man can sue for equal pay with a woman.

The Act was brought in to adopt the European principle of equal pay which is found in Article 141 of the Treaty of Rome. This not only states the principle but, in addition, gives a wide definition of pay:

> 'pay means the ordinary, basic or minimum wage or salary and any other consideration, whether in cash or in kind, which the worker receives, directly or indirectly, in respect of his employment from his employer.'

By virtue of the European Communities Act 1972 the Article is directly applicable in UK law and creates, in addition to the EPA, an independent right to equal pay as was established in the case of *Defrenne* v. *SABENA* [1976] CMLR 98 and *McCarthy* v. *Smith* [1981] QB 15, Furthermore, the Equal Pay Directive, which expands the principle of equal pay in the Article, outlines the law that Member States of the Community should adopt and, as will be seen, the Directive creates a right for certain employees to sue under European law, expanding their rights under the Article. These employees are those employed by an emanation of the state. This means that in relation to equal pay the nature of the employer determines how many routes there are to claim equality:

National law	*European law*
EPA (all employees)	Article 141 (all employees)
	Equal Pay Directive (public employees)

6.2 Equal Pay Act 1970

National law provides three methods of claiming equal pay – like work, work rated equivalent and work of equal value. The way in which a woman's pay will change, should she be successful in her claim, is novel. By s.1(1) of the Act all contracts of employment are deemed to include an 'equality clause'. If she proves her right to equal pay, the equality clause will be activated. This means that on a term-by-term comparison between her contract and a man's, any term in her contract which is less favourable than the terms in his becomes as favourable and any term in his contract which is not included in hers will become incorporated (s.1(2)). The tribunal does not look at her pay package as a whole but at each individual term – this is the principle from *Hayward* v. *Cammell Laird Shipbuilders* [1988] AC 894. It is important to note that if she has a term which is more favourable than his, she will retain it and it will not go into the man's contract unless he pursues an equal pay case using her contract as a comparison!

Obviously, as can be seen from above, a woman needs a contract with which to compare terms. Her claim will start, therefore, by finding herself a man! Such a man is known as her male comparator.

6.3 The Male Comparator

A male comparator is defined in s.1(6) of the Act. Her comparator must be:

(a) employed by her employer or an associated employer (that is, an employer over whom her employer has control, or her employer and his employer are under the control of a third); and
(b) employed at the same establishment; or
(c) employed at a different establishment in Great Britain and common terms and conditions are observed for that class of employee.

It will be seen that there must be a common employer plus a common workplace or, if that is not the case, common terms and conditions observed for that class of employee. It was observed by the Employment Appeal Tribunal in *Scullard* v. *Knowles* [1996] IRLR 344 that the need for a common employer means that the definition of a comparator under s.1(6) is much more restrictive than the comparator under Article 141. In *Scullard*, the Appeal Tribunal, overturning the employment tribunal, held that the broader definition applied by virtue of the doctrine of direct effect. Thus a manager of a training unit, which was one of a number of units run by a regional education council, could compare herself to male managers of other units run by another regional education council, even though neither the organisation nor the units were limited companies, as all of the councils were funded by the Department of Employment and there was a common collective agreement applying to the employees. (See also *South Ayrshire Council* v. *Morton* [2002] IRLR 256). However, in *Lawrence* v. *Regent Office Care Ltd* [2002] IRLR 822, Mrs Lawrence was transferred to Regent Office Care after North Yorkshire County Council put their catering services out to tender. Her pay was reduced and she claimed equal pay with her former male council employees. While Morison J in the Employment Appeal held that it was only necessary for an applicant to establish that she and her comparators were employed at the same establishment in a loose and non-technical sense, he went on to say that he did not consider the principle wide enough to cover Mrs Lawrence's case. She appealed to the Court of Appeal and that court referred the case to the European Court of Justice to determine whether Article 141 allowed Mrs Lawrence to compare herself to employees of her former employer with whom her work had previously been rated equivalent in *Ratcliffe* v. *North Yorkshire County Council* [1995] IRLR 439 (see below). The ECJ stated that comparisons under Article 141 were not confined to men and women who work for the same employer, but there had to be a single source, such as a common collective agreement, which caused the discrepancies, so that one body was responsible for the discrimination and had the power to prevent it. In Lawrence's case there were different arrangements for negotiating terms and a comparison could not be made. The Court of Appeal also referred the case of *Allonby* v. *Accrington and Rossendale College* [2004] IRLR 224 to the European Court. In *Allonby* the issue referred was whether a man employed by a college was in the same employment as a woman employed by a company which supplied services to the college. Again the ECJ stressed that although Article 141 is wider than the Equal Pay Act, where differences cannot be attributed to a single source, there is no body responsible for the inequality that could restore equal treatment and thus it does not come within the scope of Article 141. Applying these principles, in *Robertson and Others* v. *Department of Environment, Food and Rural Affairs* [2005] IRLR 363 the Court of Appeal held that male civil servants could not use female civil servants working for another government department as comparators. Mr Robertson's claim that there was a common source of payment – the Crown – was dismissed. The Court held that following the Civil Service (Management Functions) Act 1992, each government department was authorised to agree the terms and conditions of employment of its civil servants, therefore the source of the anomalies was the individual departments and not the Crown; there was no common source. Likewise in *Armstrong* v. *Newcastle upon Tyne NHS Hospital Trust* [2006] IRLR 124 the Court of Appeal held that although there were some common terms across the different hospitals, others were determined at a local level and thus a comparison could not be made across hospitals. However in *South Tyneside Council* v. *Anderson and Others* (2007) (unreported) female school support staff were paid at a rate determined by their contractual grades set out in a collective agreement known as the White Book. Their male comparators were employed by the local authority doing identical work, although none worked in schools. The employment tribunal and the Employment Appeal Tribunal upheld the equal pay claims but the council appealed in respect of employees who were employed on the recommendation of the governing body of a community school (as opposed to being directly employed by the local authority). The local authority argued that the women and their comparators were not in the same employment because it was open to each governing body to establish terms and conditions of employment. The Court rejected the argument and held that the women were employed by the same employer as their comparators and were paid by reference to the White Book to which governing bodies referred and thus they were entitled to equal pay.

Furthermore, the Court of Appeal has held that a woman cannot limit her choice of comparator artificially. In *Cheshire and Wirral Partnership NHS Trust* v. *Abbott* [2006] IRLR 546 a group of domestic staff which was predominantly female sought an equal value claim using as their comparators hospital porters who were all male, in respect of a bonus scheme which applied to porters but not domestic staff. The Court of Appeal upheld the employer's argument that the comparative group should also contain catering staff, who were on work of equal value to the porters – a group which was predominantly female and which also had access to the bonus scheme. As such, the domestic staff could not show the scheme had an adverse effect on women.

While the above cases seem to limit the definition of comparator, in *Alabaster* v. *Woolwich plc* [2004] IRLR 486 the ECJ stated that the principle of non-discrimination required that a woman who still has an employment relationship during maternity leave must benefit from any pay rise awarded during that leave, and that should be taken into account in the calculation of the earnings related element of her statutory maternity pay. On hearing the case after the reference, the Court of Appeal in *Alabaster* v. *Barclays Bank and the Department of Work and Pensions* [2005] EWCA Civ 508 held that s.1 Equal Pay Act, insofar as it requires a woman to cite a male comparator, should be disapplied if the reason for not paying a pay increase is based on the woman's pregnancy, so bringing the Equal Pay Act in line with the Sex Discrimination Act and the House of Lords' approach in *Webb* v. *EMO Cargo* (see Chapter 5). While limited, this shows a loosening of the requirement to show a male comparator.

The issue of common terms and conditions has also been subjected to wide judicial interpretation. In *Leverton* v. *Clwyd County Council* [1989] IRLR 28 a nursery nurse sought to compare herself with higher-paid clerical workers employed by the county council at a different establishment. The Court of Appeal originally held that the clerical workers were not valid male comparators. The complainant worked 32 hours a week and had 70 days' holiday. The comparators worked a 37-hour week with 20 days' holiday. The court held that although common terms and conditions did not mean identical terms, there had to be a sufficient amount of commonality to enable a proper comparison to be made. In Leverton's case two fundamental terms – hours and holidays – were different and as such the clerical workers were not valid comparators within s.1(6). The House of Lords, however, held that the clerical workers were valid comparators, Lord Bridge holding that where there was a common collective agreement as in Leverton's case, then that would 'seem to represent the paradigm, though not necessarily the only example, of the common terms and conditions contemplated by the Act'. In *O'Sullivan* v. *Sainsbury plc* (1990) IRLIB 393 although some terms were different, hours, holidays, maternity and sick provisions were the same. It was held that there was sufficient commonality for s.1(6) to apply. In *British Coal Corporation* v. *Smith* [1996] IRLR 404 the House of Lords decided that common terms and conditions meant terms and conditions 'that were on a broad basis substantially comparable rather than identical'.

It is for the woman to choose her male comparator and not the tribunal (*Ainsworth* v. *Glass Tubes and Components* [1977] IRLR 74) and there is no requirement that her choice must be fairly representative of a group of workers (*Thomas* v. *National Coal Board* [1987] IRLR 451). In addition, from the case of *McCarthy* v. *Smith* (see above) she may choose a man who used to do her job before being promoted, but not a hypothetical man. She may also choose her successor (*Diocese of Hallam Trustee* v. *Connaughton* [1996] IRLR 505). This means that the woman can choose whom she wishes and is not constrained because a man does the same job as she does. Her choice of comparator determines her avenue for an equal pay claim, from *Pickstone and Others* v. *Freemans plc* [1988] IRLR 357, not vice versa. This prevents an employer from putting a token man into women's work. While *Pickstone* has alleviated some of the problems women have in choosing a comparator, it should be noted that there is still a problem when a woman has gone on maternity leave. Given the ECJ in *Webb* v. *EMO Cargo* (see Chapter 5) decided that you cannot compare a pregnant woman with a man on long-term sick leave, a claim that maternity pay is less than an employee's sick pay is unsustainable according to the Northern Ireland Court of Appeal in *Todd* v. *Eastern Health and Social Services Board* [1997] IRLR 410. In *Gillespie* v. *Northern Health and Social Services Board* [1996] IRLR 214, the ECJ held that although statutory maternity pay fell within the definition of pay in Article 141 of the Treaty of Rome, it was not a breach of the Article to set a level of maternity pay which was less than that earned normally by the woman, as this was not unequal treatment based on the sex of the individual (see also *Edwards* v. *Derby City Council* (1998) IDS Brief 624). Furthermore, the Northern Ireland Court of Appeal in *Gillespie* v. *Northern Health and Social Services Board (No. 2)* [1997] IRLR 410 held that statutory maternity pay which was higher than statutory sick pay could not be classed as inadequate for the purposes of Article 11(3) Pregnant Workers Directive (92/85/EC), which requires that maternity pay should not be less than statutory sick pay.

Once a woman has chosen her comparator that will then determine her route to equal pay. The route will either be like work, work rated equivalent or work of equal value.

6.4   Like Work

'Like work' is defined by s.1(4) Equal Pay Act. A woman is employed on like work with a man if: 'her work and theirs is of the same or broadly similar nature, and the differences (if any) between the things she does and the things they do are not of practical importance – regard shall be had to the frequency or otherwise with which such differences occur in practice as well as to the nature and extent of the differences.' Two things should be noted. First, the work does not have to be identical, merely broadly similar. Second, an employer cannot insert differences in the man's contract if in practice these differences never arise. In *Capper Pass* v. *Lawton* [1977] ICR 83 the Employment Appeal Tribunal explained how the section should be applied. In that case Mrs Lawton was employed in the director's dining room, on her own, cooking 10–20 meals a day. She sought equal pay with the assistant chefs in the staff canteen who cooked 350 meals a day. The assistant chefs were supervised. Phillips J said that in applying s.1(4) the job should not be dissected minutely. First, the tribunal should consider if the work is the same or broadly similar by looking at the duties and responsibilities and, second, the tribunal should look to see what in practice is done, whether there are differences and whether these are of practical importance. What is done and when are therefore important, and a job can be split into three basic areas – duties, responsibilities and hours.

Different duties

In *Electrolux* v. *Hutchinson* [1977] ICR 252 there was a contractual obligation in the men's contracts to work overtime, at weekends or at night if so required. In other respects the work was broadly similar. In practice the men rarely performed those extra duties and it was held that the women were entitled to equal pay. Likewise in *Coomes (Holdings) Ltd* v. *Shields* [1978] IRLR 263 Mrs Shields was paid 62p an hour, her male counterpart £1.06 an hour. The employers argued that the men had the extra duties of removing unruly customers and carrying cash between different shops. The Court of Appeal, however, discovered that in practice there were few unruly customers and the court decided that transporting cash between the shops was not a difference of practical importance. Mrs Shields was entitled to equal pay. By contrast in *Thomas* v. *National Coal Board* [1981] IRLR 451 the fact that the male comparator worked permanent nights unsupervised was a difference of practical importance and Ms Thomas was therefore not on like work.

Different hours

In *Dugdale* v. *Kraft Foods* [1977] ICR 48 men and women were doing the same work but the men had to work compulsory overtime. It was held that the fact that the men worked overtime did not justify a higher hourly rate for all the working hours, merely those which were unsociable, as long as overtime was available to women should they wish to do it. See also *Kerr* v. *Lister* [1977] IRLR 259.

Different responsibilities

If a man has more responsibility than a woman doing broadly similar work, this is a difference of practical importance and again will justify a difference in pay. In *Eaton Ltd* v. *Nuttall* [1977] IRLR 71 a man and woman were doing the same work but the woman handled items valued at less than £2.50 whereas the man handled items valued between £5 and £1,000. It was held that the man had more responsibility in that if he made a mistake the loss to the company would be much greater. Ms Nuttall was not entitled to equal pay. A similar conclusion was reached in *Capper Pass* v. *Allan* [1980] IRLR 236.

On the wording of the section, however, the different responsibility must exist for the whole of the working year and not just at particular times. In *Redland Roof Tiles* v. *Harper* [1977] ICR 349 a man and a woman were doing similar jobs but the man was paid more because he deputised for the transport manager for five weeks a year. It was held that this did not justify a difference in pay for the whole year – he could be given additional pay when he had the extra responsibility.

6.5 Work Rated Equivalent

A second route to equal pay is where the woman's job and the man's job have been rated equivalent under a job evaluation scheme (JES). Section 1(5) states that a JES is a study undertaken with a view to evaluating jobs to be done by all or any employees in an undertaking or group of undertakings and an equal value has been determined in terms of the demand made on the worker under various headings, for example effort, skill and decision-making.

The Act does not lay down detailed requirements for such a scheme but, once it has been carried out, s.2A(2A) creates a presumption of upholding the JES unless the tribunal has reasonable grounds for suspecting it is discriminatory (*Green* v. *Broxtowe DC* [1977] IRLR 34; *Neil* v. *Ford Motor Co* [1984] IRLR 339).

Guidance on the nature of such a scheme was given by the Employment Appeal Tribunal in *Eaton* v. *Nuttall* (see above). It was said that the scheme had to be:

'thorough in analysis and capable of impartial application. It should be possible ... to arrive at the position of a particular employee at a particular point in a particular salary grade without taking other matters into account except those unconnected with the nature of the work.'

In other words, subjective views on the value of work are not permissible but objective factors such as seniority are relevant. Relative weightings on 'whole job' comparisons are thus inadequate for this purpose, according to the Court of Appeal in *Bromley* v. *H & J Quick* [1988] IRLR 249. In *Redcar* v. *Cleveland Borough Council* (2007) The Times, 21 September the Court of Appeal held that the woman is entitled to equal pay with her comparator when the JES gives her job a higher rating than his.

Once both sides have accepted the validity of the scheme it comes into effect and operates the equality clause (*Arnold* v. *Beecham Group Ltd* [1982] IRLR 307). In *O'Brien* v. *Sim-Chem Ltd* [1980] IRLR 373 a JES was carried out by the company but before they paid Mrs O'Brien her increased salary the government announced a voluntary incomes policy and so the implementation of the scheme was postponed. The House of Lords ruled that once the scheme had been completed, the comparison of the respective terms in the man's and woman's contracts could be made, thus the equality clause was operated. Note, however, that claims for back pay only go back to the date of the JES and not six years, as is the case of a like work or equal value claim (*Bainbridge* v. *Redcar and Cleveland Borough Council* [2007] IRLR 494).

6.6 Work of Equal Value

The original unamended Equal Pay Act had only like work and work rated equivalent as the routes to equal pay. As such, it did not comply with EC Directive 75/117 on Equal Pay which has the concept of equal pay for equal work. This was because an employee could not compel her employer to carry out a JES. In *Commission of the European Communities* v. *United Kingdom* [1982] IRLR 333 the European Court of Justice held that the Act did not satisfy the principle of equal pay for equal work. As a result the Equal Pay (Amendment) Regulations 1983 were introduced to amend the existing legislation and thus introduce the third route to equal pay under national law: that of equal value.

A specific procedure was introduced for equal value claims. This procedure was amended by the Equal Pay Act 1970 (Amendment) Regulations 2004 and the Employment Tribunals (Constitution and Rules of Procedure) (Amendment) Regulations 2004. The changes are designed to reduce the lengthy delays that were a main criticism of the original procedure. The new procedures are contained in Schedule 6 of the 2004 Rules.

Rule 8(5) authorises the Presidents of Employment Tribunals to establish specialist panels of chairmen and members. The Rules also contain an indicative timetable for dealing with claims which envisage that where no independent expert is appointed the claim should take 25 weeks, and if one is appointed a claim should take 37 weeks. The Rules also provide for standard orders at each stage of an equal value hearing and give extensive powers to tribunals to make case management orders. These include the power to order that no new facts shall be admitted unless disclosed to all parties in writing by a specified date; that parties send copies of documents to all parties and the expert; the employer should grant access to its premises to the expert; where there is more than one expert they must provide a statement to the tribunal stating areas where they agree and disagree.

Stage 1 hearing

The stage 1 hearing will take place in all equal value claims and will decide if there is a claim. The Equal Pay Act has been amended so that the no reasonable grounds defence has been removed, particularly the part of the defence which required a tribunal to strike out a claim where a JES had determined that the woman's work was of a different value, unless the woman could show the JES was discriminatory. This now means that the tribunal must decide whether the claim should proceed and, if so, whether to hear the claim itself or appoint an independent expert. It also means that a tribunal can no longer strike out a claim purely because it considers there are no reasonable grounds to determine that the complainant's work is of equal value to her comparator. If a JES has given the complainant's work a different value, a new s.2A(2A) creates a presumption of upholding the evaluation unless the tribunal has reasonable grounds for suspecting that the evaluation is discriminatory or is otherwise unreliable. What difference in practice this will make has yet to be seen.

The standard orders require that within 28 days of the stage 1 hearing, the parties shall provide each other with written job descriptions for the complainant and comparator and identify any relevant facts. Within 56 days the parties must provide the tribunal with a joint statement covering job descriptions and relevant facts. At least 28 days before the hearing the parties must produce a joint statement for the tribunal stating the facts on which they agree and those on which they disagree, giving reasons for the disagreement. The tribunal can order an employer to grant access to its premises to the independent expert if appointed (Rule 3(1)(d)) or, if no expert is appointed, to the complainant and her representative to enable them to interview any comparator (Rule 5(1)(C)). If no expert is appointed the next stage is a full hearing. If one is appointed, there is a stage 2 hearing.

Stage 2 hearing

The aim of a stage 2 hearing is to resolve disputed facts so that the expert can evaluate the jobs. The tribunal must make a determination on facts upon which the parties disagree and require the expert to prepare a report based on the agreed facts and those determined by the tribunal. The Rules provide that the tribunal sets a date by which the report is to be produced (normally within 8 weeks of the stage 2 hearing). The amended Equal Pay Act also provides that the tribunal can withdraw the requirement for an expert report and decide the case itself.

Full hearing

This will occur within 18 weeks after the stage 1 hearing if no expert is appointed and 20 weeks after the stage 2 hearing if there is an independent expert. The tribunal hears the case along with the expert's report, if there is one, and the employer's defence.

It is hoped that these new powers will prevent the long and tortuous claims of the past.

Since the introduction of the equal value route, there have been some important rulings on the interpretation of the relevant provision in the amended Equal Pay Act.

The first of these was the House of Lords' decision in *Hayward* v. *Cammell Laird Shipbuilders* (above). Ms Hayward was a canteen assistant in a shipyard and claimed her work was of equal value to the shipyard workers who were paid as skilled tradesmen. The independent expert ruled that her job was of equal value, but the tribunal, the Employment Appeal Tribunal and the Court of Appeal held that she was not entitled to extra cash as she had free luncheons and two days' additional holiday compared to her male comparator and, taking the pay package as a whole, her non-cash benefits equalised her pay. This decision was reversed by the House of Lords. Their Lordships said that s.1(2) states that if the equality clause operates, any term in her contract which is less favourable shall become as favourable and any favourable term in his contract shall become a term of her contract. Thus:

Woman	Man
£99	£150
20-days' holiday	18-days' holiday

The term in the woman's contract above which is less favourable is the pay, therefore her pay becomes the same as his, £150. All her other terms remain because they are more favourable than his. This is an important case on the interpretation of the legislative provisions; it does, however, leave the way open for the men to claim equal pay with Ms Hayward!

A further important House of Lords' decision in this area is *Pickstone and Others* v. *Freemans plc* [1988] IRLR 357. Mrs Pickstone was employed as a warehouse operative and claimed her work was of equal value to that of a male warehouse checker. Unfortunately, there was one man doing the work of a warehouse operative and the employers argued that Mrs Pickstone could not claim equal value under s.1(2)(c) EPA as that route only applied where s.1(2)(a) (like work) or s.1(2)(b) (work rated equivalent) does not apply. Freemans were therefore arguing that as Mrs Pickstone had a like work comparison with a man doing her job, she could not take an equal value comparison with another man doing a different job. This interpretation of the legislation was rejected by the House of Lords. The House agreed that s.1(2) gave mutually exclusive routes to equal pay, but this was only after the applicant had chosen her male comparator. Had Mrs Pickstone chosen a man doing similar work as her comparator she would have had to choose a like work claim. As her male comparator did a totally different job she could use the equal value route. This is an important decision as it prevents employers from placing a 'token' man in women's work to prevent equal value claims.

Some critics of the new route were concerned that equal value would be interpreted strictly. In other words, if the woman's job was assessed at a higher value than that of her male comparator, she would lose her equal value claim. The case of *Murphy* v. *Bord Telecom Eireann* [1988] IRLR 267 has now decided that a woman is entitled to equal pay if her work is of at least equal value to that of her comparator. However, although a woman may choose a comparator who is less than her equal she is only entitled to equal pay with that comparator and not more. In *Evesham* v. *North Hertfordshire Health Authority* [2000] IRLR 257 a speech therapist successfully compared herself to a clinical psychologist. The Court of Appeal held that she should have been on the same pay scale as her comparator and should receive the same rate of pay, but stated that she was not entitled to be further up the scale because of her longer service. There was no requirement in the legislation that the employer modify an individual term so that it became more favourable than that of her comparator. While this is a correct interpretation of the Act which talks about the term of the woman's contract becoming as favourable as that of her comparator, it fails to remedy the injustice that Mrs Evesham would have been higher up the scale if the employer had not discriminated against her in the first place.

6.7   Defences

The defence for an employer to an equal pay claim in s.1(3) is that of genuine material factor. In the case of a claim of like work or work rated equivalent, that factor must be a genuine material difference between her case and his. In the case of an equal value claim, the factor may be a genuine material difference between her case and his. It is clear, therefore, that the Act envisages two different defences depending on the basis of the claim, and for ease they will be called the genuine material difference defence and the genuine material factor defence. The Employment Appeal Tribunal in *Financial Times Ltd* v. *Byrne (No. 2)* [1992] IRLR 163 held that the burden is on the employer to show both that the difference in pay is genuinely due to a material factor and that the factor is not due to a difference in sex.

Genuine material difference

In like work or work rated equivalent claims, the difference between her case and his must be a genuine material difference which is not based on sex. The defence was initially given a narrow interpretation by the Court of Appeal in the case of *Clay Cross (Quarry Services)* v. *Fletcher* [1979] ICR 1. Mrs Fletcher was earning £35 per week and her employer appointed a man, doing the same job, at £43 per week. The employer argued that he had to offer the man this salary because that was the salary in his old job, therefore market forces dictated he should pay the man more than Mrs Fletcher. The Court of Appeal rejected the employer's claim that there was a genuine material difference between his case and hers. The court stated that, on interpretation, the difference had to be in the 'personal equation', in other words, something different in the people doing the job, other than sex. As such, more experience or better qualifications would be a defence, but not the fact that men traditionally are paid more in an industry. As Lord Denning remarked, if an employer could pay men more because they asked for more the legislation would be rendered impotent.

Since the *Fletcher* decision, however, the defence has been widened considerably, and it can now be argued that this widening has allowed what are essentially market forces arguments to be used as a defence.

If the man's salary has been 'red circled', that is, his higher salary has been protected because for health or other reasons he has had to take a lower-paid job, then this is a genuine material difference (*Methven* v. *Cow Industrial Polymers Ltd* [1980] IRLR 289). Likewise a difference in pay based on the difference in the cost of living between certain geographical areas is also permitted (*NAAFI* v. *Varley* [1976] IRLR 408). Perhaps two more controversial areas where the defence has been permitted are in the case of part-time workers and situations where there is an approved pay body which has decided the scales, such as the Whitley Council. In *Jenkins* v. *Kingsgate Clothing Productions Ltd* [1981] IRLR 388 the employer offered a lower hourly rate to part-time workers. This was for economic reasons as machinery lay idle for part of the week when operated by part-time workers and there was a higher rate of absenteeism among his part-time workers. The employer therefore hoped to encourage full-time working by paying the higher rate. The EAT, after a reference to the European Court, held that economic necessity was a genuine material difference defence as long as there was evidence that this was the valid reason for the difference in pay, that reason existed and the employer did not intend to discriminate. In *Rainey* v. *Greater Glasgow Health Board Eastern District* [1987] AC 224 Mrs Rainey was a prosthetist working in the National Health Service. The Health Board needed to attract extra prosthetists into the service and offered jobs to practitioners in the private sector, but on their existing salaries, not on NHS rates. This created a pay difference between Mrs Rainey and her male comparator of £2,790 per year. The House of Lords 'regretted' the narrow interpretation given to the defence in *Fletcher* (which Rainey's case resembled on the facts). Their Lordships held that the defence allowed an employer to take into account circumstances outside the personal equation and argue that the difference was necessary to achieve a result such as economic necessity or administrative efficiency. This decision adds a further genuine material difference to the list – that of administrative efficiency. The case of *Ratcliffe* v. *North Yorkshire County Council* [1995] IRLR 439 suggests that there may be a limit to how far the defence will be extended however. In the case, the females employed by the council's direct service organisation had successfully claimed equal pay with male comparators. The organisation, however, cut the pay rate in order to make their bid competitive when a contract was put out for tender. The Court of Appeal upheld the employer's defence under s.1(3) but this was rejected by the House of Lords. Lord Slynn, echoing the words of Lord Denning in *Fletcher*, stated that reducing women's wages below that of their male comparators 'was the very kind of discrimination in relation to pay which the Act sought to remove'. In other words, the courts will not allow the market forces defence to become too wide. A limit imposed by the House of Lords in *Rainey* was that the factor raised by the employer had to be objectively justified, however a later House of Lords' decision in *Strathclyde Regional Council* v. *Wallace* [1998] 1 WLR 259 suggests that where the woman cannot show that the difference in pay is due to a practice which has an impact on a particular group, the employer merely has to show why the difference exists but does not have to objectively justify it. In the case, women who were acting up as principal teachers but not getting the pay rate of permanent principal teachers, claimed equal pay on a like work comparison. Of the group acting up, 81 were men and 53 were women. The applicant could not therefore establish that there was discrimination and therefore the employer's explanation, that of financial constraint, did not have to be objectively justified (see the Employment Appeal Tribunal in *Tyldesley* v. *TML Plastics* [1996] IRLR 395 and *Parliamentary Commissioner for Administration* v. *Fernandez* [2004] IRLR 22). The approach was recently endorsed again in *Armstrong* (above).

Genuine material factor

In equal value claims the defence is wider, in that the difference between her case and his may be a material difference. This was clearly an attempt by the legislature to avoid the *Fletcher* decision in equal value claims and allow market forces to be an available defence. In *Reed Packaging Ltd* v. *Boozer* [1988] IRLR 333 it was held that different pay structures were a genuine material factor defence as long as these were non-discriminatory and the employer was required by law to comply with the pay differentials (*R* v. *Secretary of State for Social Services and Others ex parte Clarke and Others* [1988] IRLR 22). In *Barber* v. *NCR (Manufacturing)* [1993] IRLR 95, however, a reduction in hours bargained for by the union representing women workers brought about an inequality in the hourly rate of the women and another group of workers. There was no intention to produce this result and the employment tribunal upheld a genuine material factor defence because the difference in pay had been caused by a different history of collective bargaining. The Employment Appeal Tribunal held that the tribunal had posed the wrong question. It was insufficient to isolate the cause of the pay differential and see if it was tainted by discrimination. It was necessary to go further and decide if the cause constituted a material factor justifying a difference in pay on objective grounds. This interpretation is supported by the ECJ decision of *Enderby* v. *Frenchay Health Authority and Secretary of State for Health* [1994] 1 All ER 495. The case was brought by a speech therapist alleging that her work was of equal value to that of principal grade pharmacists and clinical psychologists. Under the NHS Whitley Council negotiating procedures, the pay rates of speech therapists, who are predominantly women, were negotiated by a different committee from that of clinical psychologists, who are predominately men. The same is true for pharmacists, who are predominately male. Enderby was therefore on £10,106 per year whereas a clinical psychologist with the same experience was on £12,527 per year and a pharmacist on £14,106 per year. The Authority argued on three points. First, Enderby's pay was negotiated by a separate bargaining unit from that of her comparators on a non-discriminatory basis. This was a genuine material factor defence. Second, the agreements arising out of the negotiations were non-discriminatory, so Enderby could not complain of direct discrimination. Finally, she could not complain of indirect discrimination as there was no barrier to her becoming a pharmacist or clinical psychologist.

The ECJ rejected all three arguments. It decided that when bringing an equal pay claim, a woman employed in a female-dominated profession could compare herself to a male-dominated profession, even where there was no barrier between the two, where on statistical evidence there was a significant difference in pay. The burden then fell to the employer to show that the differential is objectively justified irrespective of sex. The ECJ further held that different non-discriminatory bargaining procedures or collective agreements did not necessarily amount to an objective justification, otherwise employers could avoid equal pay claims by using separate bargaining procedures. Finally, the fact that part of the pay differential is justified for genuine economic reasons, such as recruitment difficulties, will not justify the whole of the differential and the claimant is entitled to receive the balance. This will involve tribunals in identifying the part of pay the differential relates to. The case has established important points and should affect the defence as a whole and not just in equal value claims. Further, it has made severe inroads into one major criticism of the Equal Pay Act – that it does not protect women employed in female-dominated work. The application of Enderby can be seen in British Road Services v. Loughran [1997] IRLR 92. In the case the applicant was a clerical officer in an office of nine women clerical officers and seven men. In respect of all the employees employed by her employer, 75 per cent of clerical staff were women. The applicant sought equal pay with warehouse operatives whose pay was covered by a different collective agreement. The employer argued that the different bargaining structures created a defence under s.1(3) unless the principle in Enderby applied. The employer, however, argued that Enderby would only apply if the group including the applicant is exclusively or almost exclusively composed of women. The Northern Ireland Court of Appeal held that the phrase used in Enderby that the applicant's group was 'almost exclusively' women referred to the facts of the particular case. In the present case, 75 per cent of clerical workers were women and the employment tribunal was entitled to conclude that the proportion compared to 100 per cent of the warehouse operatives being male provided a reliable indication of unequal treatment and that the different bargaining structures on their own did not justify the pay difference. While the difference in *Loughran* was considerable, the Court of Appeal decision in *Home Office* v. *Bailey* [2005] IRLR 369 shows that a much smaller difference can still establish a claim. In that case the Employment Appeal Tribunal held that prison administrators could not put in an equal pay claim comparing themselves with prison officers and support staff because the group consisted of 49 per cent men and 51 per cent women, and as such the women could not show that they were paid less because of their sex. The Court of Appeal, however, overturned the EAT saying that as long as the number of women exceeded the number of men that established a *prima facie* case and so the claim could proceed.

All the differences discussed above which are genuine material differences will also be genuine material factors.

Prior to *Enderby*, if either defence was raised, the employer did not have to justify every penny of the pay differential. In *Calder* v. *Rowntree Mackintosh Confectionery* [1993] IRLR 212 male employees worked a rotating shift system. Male and female employees received the same basic pay but the men received a shift premium. The female applicants, while not working rotating shifts, did work unsocial hours. The employers accepted that part of the shift premium paid for the rotating shifts was for unsocial hours but not all. The women therefore argued that as the whole of the shift premium was not for working unsocial hours, the defence in s.1(3) was not made out. The Court of Appeal held that the tribunal was entitled to find that there was a genuine material difference because of the different shift patterns and the fact that some of the premium covered unsocial hours did not negate the defence. This must now be subject to the *Enderby* decision.

One of the problems experienced by women pursuing an equal pay claim is gaining information about her employer's pay structures in order to establish whether she has a claim. Section 42 Employment Act 2002 remedied this by the introduction of an equal pay questionnaire, similar to those used in other discrimination claims, by a new s.7B Equal Pay Act. Questions or replies are admissible as evidence and a tribunal can draw any inference it considers to be just and equitable if the respondent deliberately fails to respond without reasonable excuse or if the tribunal feel that the respondent's response is evasive or equivocal.

6.8   European Law and Equal Pay

In addition to the three routes to equal pay under national law, European law gives two further ways in which a complainant may achieve equal pay.

Article 141

Article 141 of the Treaty of Rome states:

'Each Member State shall . . . ensure and subsequently maintain the application of the principle that men and women should receive equal pay for equal work.'

In *Defrenne* v. *SABENA* [1976] CMLR 98 the European Court of Justice held that Article 141 was directly effective in the national courts but only where there is direct and overt discrimination. As such, all employees in Member States have the right to sue under the Article for equal pay for equal work.

The definition of 'pay' within the Article is also wide. It is defined as:

'the ordinary, basic or minimum wage or salary or any other consideration, whether in cash or in kind, which the worker receives, directly or indirectly, in respect of his employment from his employer.'

As such, it not only covers a weekly or monthly wage but also any benefit which the worker receives as a result of the employment relationship, whether the contract is still subsisting or not. The ECJ has therefore ruled that payment of wages during sickness is covered by Article 141 (*Rinner-Kuhn* v. *FWW Spezial Gebaudereinigung GmbH* [1989] IRLR 493), as are concessionary travel benefits for retired employees (*Garland* v. *British Rail Engineering Ltd* [1982] IRLR 257, although note the important decision in *Grant* v. *South-West Trains Ltd* [1998] IRLR 206) and occupational pension schemes (*Vroege* v. *NCIV Instituut voor Volkshuisvesting BV* [1995] ICR 635 and *Fisscher* v. *Voorhuis Henglo BV* [1994] IRLR 662).

There have been a number of cases in respect of part-time employees. It is not a breach of the Article, however, to only offer overtime to those working 39 hours a week so long as the same overtime rates are paid to part-time and full-time workers (*Stadt Lengerich* v. *Helmig* [1995] IRLR 216). In *Barry* v. *Midland Bank* [1999] IRLR 581 an employee who had worked full time for eleven years returned to work part time after maternity leave. She took voluntary redundancy after two years. The redundancy package was based on her final salary and thus took no account of her eleven years of full-time working. She claimed this had an adverse impact on women. The House of Lords held, however, that as full-time and part-time workers were treated the same (that is, redundancy package was based on final salary) there was no discrimination. This, however, seems hard to justify after the case of *Elsner-Lakeburg* v. *Land Nordrhein Westfalen* [2005] IRLR 209. In this case both full-time and part-time teachers were treated as working overtime after they had worked their contractual hours (unlike *Stadt Lengerich*, above). Under German law, however, workers were paid for overtime only if they worked at least three additional hours a month. A part-time worker complained that this meant that she had to work 5 per cent more than her usual hours whereas a full-time worker had to work only 3 per cent over the normal hours, and as such the rule had a disparate impact on women. The ECJ upheld the complaint, showing that the same treatment of full- and part-time workers can create discrimination.

Given the above, the case of *Cadman* v. *Health and Safety Executive* [2006] IRLR 969 seems a surprising decision of the ECJ. In 1989 the ECJ stated in *Handels- og Kontorfunktionaerernes Forbund i Danmark* v. *Dansk Arbejdsgiverforening ex parte Danfoss A/S* [1989] IRLR 532 that length of service is an acceptable criterion for determining pay, even if it had an adverse effect on women. Given *Elsner-Lakeburg* (above), it was to be hoped that this position would have moved forward but it was confirmed in *Cadman*, the ECJ arguing that the legitimate objective achieved was that the worker performed better.

Perhaps the most important decision in this area is *Barber* v. *Guardian Royal Exchange Assurance Group* [1990] IRLR 240. Mr Barber was made redundant at 52. Under the provisions of his non-contributory pension scheme, a man, if made redundant before the age of 62, could claim an immediate pension at 55; women, however, if made redundant, could claim a pension at 50. Mr Barber alleged sex discrimination, but under the then present Sex Discrimination Act, retirement and pension provisions were excluded from its operation. The Court of Appeal, however, asked the ECJ to give a preliminary ruling on certain issues – in particular whether a pension payable under a redundancy scheme could be pay within the meaning of Article 141. The ECJ ruled:

1. Benefits paid by an employer under a compulsory redundancy constitutes pay and fall within Article 141 whether paid under a contract of employment, by virtue of a statutory provision or on a voluntary basis.
2. Private pensions are pay within Article 141.
3. It is contrary to Article 141 for a man who has been made redundant to be entitled to a deferred pension, whereas a woman would be entitled to an immediate pension: 'the application of the principle of equal pay must be ensured in respect of each element of remuneration.'
4. Article 141 may be relied upon in the national courts.
5. The direct effect of Article 141 on entitlement to pensions may not be relied upon for entitlement arising prior to 17 May 1990 (the date of the decision) unless legal proceedings have already been initiated.

The effect of the decision has been dramatic. At first sight it creates a discrepancy between state pension ages and private pension ages. Existing legislation allows for different pension ages but this must now be subject to the *Barber* decision. A problem arose, however, in relation to 5 above. The implications were not clear and as such the government supported the firm Coloroll in a reference to the ECJ for an interpretation of the point – in particular if back pension was payable only to 17 May 1990 or to the date of the original act of discrimination. At Maastricht in 1991 all Member States signed a protocol limiting the effect of *Barber* to cases initiated before the judgement or those arising after the judgement, and limiting back pension to the date of the decision. A protocol, however, is not legally binding. In *Ten Oever* v. *Stichting Bedriffspensionfunds voor het Glazenwassers* [1993] IRLR 601, however, the ECJ gave a narrow interpretation to the *Barber* decision. The court ruled that benefits have to be equal only if they are earned by periods of employment falling after 17 May 1990; thus the court has confirmed the result required by the protocol. The limitation was further tested in the recent case of *Quirk* v. *Burton Hospitals NHS Trust and Secretary of State for Health* [2002] EMP LR 469. In this case, until *Barber* the rules of the health service pension allowed women to retire at 55 but men could not retire until 60. After *Barber*, the ages were aligned but women who retired before 60 were entitled to receive benefits calculated by reference to all of their pensionable service whereas men retiring before 60 were only entitled to benefits calculated by reference to service after 17 May 1990, the date of the *Barber* decision. The Employment Appeal Tribunal held that this was a correct interpretation of *Barber* but has given leave to appeal to the Court of Appeal.

While *Barber* decided that statutory redundancy pay was pay for the purposes of Article 141, the position in relation to unfair dismissal compensation was unclear until the decision in *R* v. *Secretary of State for Employment ex parte Seymour-Smith and Perez* [1999] IRLR 253 where the ECJ decided that unfair dismissal compensation constituted pay within the meaning of Article 141.

Equal Pay Directive

The Equal Pay Directive (75/117) states that the principle of equal pay in Article 141 means:

> 'for the same work or for work to which equal value has been attributed, the elimination of all discrimination on grounds of sex with regard to all aspects and conditions of remuneration.'

A Directive establishes a result it wishes Member States to achieve through national legislation. As such, should national legislation fail to give that result, an individual who is employed by a government authority acting in the capacity of an employer may sue under the Directive in the national courts, as long as the Directive is sufficiently precise. In other words the government, acting as an employer, should not benefit from its wrongdoing in failing to fully implement the Directive. Private employers, however, should not be punished for merely complying with inadequate national law. The concept of the government as an employer is wide. It covers area health authorities (*Marshall* v. *Southampton & South West Hampshire Area Health Authority* [1986] QB 401) and nationalised industries (*Foster* v. *British Gas plc* [1991] ICR 84). It does not, however, include public limited companies (*Doughty* v. *Rolls-Royce plc* [1992] IRLR 126). This means, in effect, that public employees have an additional route to claim equal pay – that of the Directive – which is not available to private employees. The Directive, however, may assist private employees in so far as the courts will look to the Directive when interpreting provisions of national law and should seek to interpret the Equal Pay Act in line with the Directive and Article 141.

Time limits and retrospective claims

Recent cases necessitate a discussion of time limits and retrospective claims. It has been seen from the discussion above that the ECJ has decided that more and more benefits fall within the definition of pay. *Vroege* and *Fisscher* held that the exclusion of part-time workers from occupational pension schemes was potentially contrary to Article 141. Those cases also decided that the time limits placed by *Barber* did not apply to the right to join an occupational pension scheme. This means potentially that part-time workers have claims going back to 1976 when *Defrenne* held that Article 141 had direct effect.

However, there is a distinction between those employees who have left their employment and those employees still employed. In respect of those employees whose contracts have terminated, there is the issue of the relevant time limit for bringing claims. In relation to employees in the private sector, this was extensively discussed in *Biggs* v. *Somerset County Council* [1996] IRLR 203, a case involving a retrospective unfair dismissal claim after the decision of *R* v. *Secretary of State for Employment ex parte EOC* [1994] IRLR 176 (see Chapter 9). In the case the applicant was dismissed in 1976, two years before the implementation of the Equal Treatment Directive. She was not protected at the time of her dismissal by unfair dismissal provisions because she was a part-time worker. The issue was whether she could pursue a retrospective claim given that the House of Lords had decided that the limitations relating to part-time workers were contrary to the Equal Treatment Directive and Article 141. Given the date of her dismissal, her claim was relying on Article 141. The Court of Appeal held that a claim under Article 141 should be seen as a claim under the relevant domestic law, the Court having the ability to disapply the offending provisions. As such, the relevant time limit under national law applied in relation to the presentation of a claim. In Biggs' case this was three months from the effective date of termination of her contract and it was not impossible for the applicant to present her claim in time, given that the right to claim unfair dismissal arose from Article 141 which had direct effect since the decision in *Defrenne* in 1976. This decision has an impact on part-time workers claiming access to occupational pensions retrospectively after their contract has terminated. This is because, on the basis of *Biggs*, their claim will lie under the Equal Pay Act 1970. Section 2(4) of that Act states that claims must be brought within six months of the last act complained of, that is within six months of the effective date of termination of the contract, with no discretion on the part of the tribunal to extend the time limit. This interpretation was upheld by the Court of Appeal in *Preston* v. *Wolverhampton Healthcare NHS Trust* [1997] IRLR 233, effectively wiping out the claims of 60,000 part-time workers who were excluded from pension schemes because of their part-time status. An alternative argument is that it would be impossible for the applicant to enforce her European law rights until the date of *Vroege* and *Fisscher* and that the time limits run from that date. *Preston* was appealed to the House of Lords. That Court decided to refer a number of questions to the ECJ ([1998] IRLR 197). First, were the time limits in the Equal Pay Act compatible with European law? Second, what were the criteria for determining whether the time limits are compatible? Lastly, did the six-month time limit run from the end of the individual contract? In making the reference, the House of Lords was mindful of the European Court's decision in *Margorrian* v. *Eastern Health and Social Services Board* [1998] IRLR 86.

The argument in relation to employees in the public sector is different. There is an argument that until the passing of the Occupational Pension Schemes (Equal Access to Membership) Regulations 1995 came into force (amending s.118 Pension Schemes Act 1993), the Equal Pay Directive had not been properly implemented and therefore on the basis of *Emmott* v. *Minister for Social Welfare and Attorney-General* [1991] IRLR 387, the time limit did not start to run until the Regulations came into force. The principle in *Emmott* is that time limits do not start to run until the Directive is fully implemented.

A second issue was whether the (then) s.2(5) Equal Pay Act applied and thus restricted back pensions to two years. The section talked about 'arrears of remuneration or damages' and there was an argument that any applicant would not be claiming remuneration or damages and thus s.2(5) did not apply. An alternative argument, which had wider implications, was that, since *Marshall* (above), limits on compensation for discriminatory acts were inconsistent with the Equal Treatment Directive and thus the two-year rule should be disregarded. The ECJ in other areas has held that it is not a breach of EC law to place a restriction on how far back the award can be made (see, for example, *Johnstone* v. *Chief Adjudication Officer (No. 2)* [1995] IRLR 157), although those cases were based on the implementation of the Social Security Directives. In a reference from the Northern Ireland Court of Appeal in *Magorrian* (above), the ECJ decided that similar time limits in Northern Ireland's legislation were contrary to EC law, both in the restriction on an application to six months after the termination of the contract and on the two-year limit in respect of back pay, however the decision related specifically to pension claims, which is why the House of Lords in *Preston* referred wider questions to the ECJ. The Employment Appeal Tribunal referred the more general question to the ECJ in *Levez* v. *T H Jennings (Harlow Pools Ltd)* [1996] IRLR 499. The ECJ decided [1999] IRLR 36 that a limit which operates in the field of equal pay, where limits do not apply in respect of other claims, for example recovery of arrears of pay in breach of contract claims, and where the national legislation gives the court no discretion to increase the two-year limit, is contrary to Article 141.

The long awaited ECJ ruling in *Preston* came in the millennium year. The European Court ruled ([2000] All ER 714) that the statutory limitation period which restricted compensation for the unlawful exclusion of women from the membership of occupational pension schemes to two years is incompatible with EC law. The House of Lords ([2001] 2 WLR 448) confirmed therefore that the two-year recovery rule in the Occupational Pension Schemes (Equal Access to Membership) Regulations 1995 was incompatible with the Directive and Article 141, and future pension benefits had to be calculated using both full- and part-time periods of service arising after 8 April 1976 (the date of *Defrenne*). Their Lordships went on to say, however, that the six-month time period in which to present a claim was not unreasonable and it could not be said to be less favourable than the rules existing in contract. Where there were intermittent contracts, with no stable employment relationship existing, the six-month period ran from the date each contract ended but where there was employment in the same employment, interrupted at regular intervals, the six-month period ran from the end of the last contract.

The Equal Pay Act 1970 (Amendment) Regulations 2004 took into account the ECJ decisions and provide that where an employee is employed on a series of contracts, the six-month time limit for bringing a claim runs from the end of the employment relationship, gives discretion to the tribunal to extend the six-month limit and extends the period for recovery of arrears from two years to six.

The Act, however, only entitles the complainant to claim arrears. In *Degan* v. *Redcar and Cleveland Borough Council* [2005] IRLR 504 and *Council of*

Newcastle upon Tyne v. *Allan* (2005) IDS 781 the Court of Appeal (*Degan*) and the EAT (*Allan*) held that the Equal Pay Act does not provide for a tribunal to award compensation for injury to feelings. Claims under the Act are based on contract law where damages are restricted to financial loss.

Summary

1. The Equal Pay Act introduces the European concept of equal pay into national law.

2. The Act implies an equality clause in a woman's contract which if activated makes any term in the woman's contract relating to pay as favourable as the equivalent term in a man's contract.

3. In order to claim equal pay the woman must find a male comparator within the definition in s.1(6) of the Act, although Article 141 gives wider protection.

4. A woman is on like work if her work is the same or broadly similar and the differences between her case and the man's are not of practical importance. The tribunal will look at duties, hours and responsibilities.

5. A woman is entitled to equal pay if a JES has given her job an equal rating to that of the man.

6. Equal value is the third route to equal pay. An independent expert may be appointed by the tribunal who will evaluate her job and that of her male comparator. If an expert is not appointed, the tribunal will assess whether the jobs are of equal value.

7. The defences to an equal pay claim are genuine material difference in a like work or work rated equivalent claim, and genuine material factor in an equal value claim.

8. In addition to national law, all employees have a European route to equal pay under Article 141 Treaty of Rome. In addition, public employees can claim under the Equal Pay Directive.

Exercise

Hilda works in the Sales Office at Coronation Products Ltd as a Grade 2 clerical worker. She earns £310 per week. Two months ago the company took on Mike as a clerical worker. In order to attract him to the job, they offered it to him at Grade 3 with a salary of £350 per week. Mike was one of a group of men who came from a local firm which had closed down, and Coronation was anxious to attract them into employment. All were offered jobs at higher grades. There is no difference between the job Hilda does and Mike's job, but the company argues that to regrade Hilda's job, and that of the other 60 Grade 2 clerical workers (all of

Exercises cont'd

whom are women), would involve a great deal of administrative work in restructuring the grading system and would prove to be very expensive. Advise Hilda whether she can claim equal pay with Mike.

Further Reading

Carty *Equal Pay for Equal Work* (1984) JSWL 1620.

Collins *CCT, Equal Pay and Market Forces* (1994) 23 ILJ 341.

Fredman *Equal Pay and Justification* (1994) 23 ILJ 37.

Fredman *Marginalising Equal Pay Laws* (2004) 33 ILJ 281.

Gregory *Dynamite or Damp Squib – An Assessment of Equal Value Law* (1997) 2 IJDL 167.

Kilpatrick *Deciding When Jobs of Equal Value can be Paid Unequally* (1994) 23 ILJ 163.

Lester and Rose *Equal Value Claims and Sex Bias in Collective Bargaining* (1991) 20 ILJ 630.

McColgan *Just Wages for Women* (Oxford: Clarendon, 1997).

Ross *Equal Pay and Sex Discrimination Law in the UK and Europe: the Need for Coherence* (1996) JSWFL 18(2) 147.

Ross *Justifying Unequal Pay* (1997) 26 ILJ 171.

Steele *Tracing the Single Source: Choice of Comparators in Equal Pay Claims* (2006) 35 ILJ 338.

Szyszczak *Pay Inequalities and Equal Value Claims* (1985) 48 MLR 1390.

Thomas *Equal Pay and Redundancy Schemes* (2000) 29 ILJ 68.

Chapter 7

Employment Protection

Introduction

Over the past 40 years, there has been a transformation in employment law. Until 1963, the rights of employees were contained almost exclusively within an individual contract of employment, with very little statutory intervention other than in the areas of health and safety and the payment of wages. However, 1963 saw the introduction of the Contracts of Employment Act which introduced minimum notice periods and the right to written particulars, and since then various pieces of legislation have given employment protection rights which are enforced through the tribunals rather than the ordinary courts. Many of these rights, such as the right not to be unfairly dismissed and the right to redundancy payments, are discussed more fully later on. In addition to these major rights, however, there are a variety of disparate individual rights which were created by the Employment Protection Act 1975 and the Employment Relations Act 1999 and which can now be found in the Employment Rights Act 1996. It is these rights that the following will discuss.

Guaranteed Week

The provisions relating to a guarantee payment are contained in ss.28–35 Employment Rights Act 1996. The original provisions were intended to ensure that when an employer temporarily laid off workers, those employees would be entitled to a minimum payment from the employer for a limited period of time. Section 28 lays out the general entitlement and provides that where an employee is not provided with work by his employer because of a diminution in the requirements of the employer's business for work of the kind the employee is employed to do or any other occurrence affecting such work, the employee shall be entitled to a guarantee payment. To claim, the employee must have at least one month's continuous employment. The employee is entitled to a payment where there is a workless day, that is a day when he would normally have worked, and therefore holidays are not included.

Section 29 goes on to deal with the exclusions from payment. Where the employee is on a fixed term contract of three months or less, or on a contract for a specific task which was not expected to last for more than three months, the entitlement only arises if the employee has more than three months' continuity. In addition, an employee loses entitlement if the workless day is due to a strike, lock-out or any other industrial action affecting his employer or an associated employer (s.29(3)) or where the employer has offered suitable alternative work which the employee has unreasonably refused, whether the employee is contractually obliged to perform the work or not (s.29(4)(a)). Furthermore, the employee will not be entitled if he fails to comply with reasonable requirements imposed by his employer with a view to ensuring that his services are available (s.29(5)). There are rather complicated provisions in s.31 as to the amount and limits on a guarantee payment. In essence, these mean that an employee is entitled to a maximum of five one-day payments in any three-month period at the statutory daily rate. In other words, the employee is entitled to one normal working week's pay at the statutory rate. If normally he only works four days, that is the extent of his entitlement in any three-month period (s.31(3)). If normally he works for six days, the statutory maximum applies and he will only receive payment for five of those days. The employee is not entitled to jobseeker's allowance for the days he receives a guarantee payment nor do such days count as waiting days for the purpose of such benefit. A collective agreement, however, which gives better rights than the statute, will take precedence over the statutory entitlement. The right to a guarantee payment is enforced through the employment tribunals within three months of the day in question.

7.3 Medical Suspension Pay

Under s.64 Employment Rights Act 1996, an employee who is suspended from work on certain specified medical grounds is entitled to receive medical suspension pay for up to 26 weeks of suspension. This applies where the employee is suspended because of a requirement imposed by statute or due to any provision in a code of practice issued under s.16 Health and Safety at Work Act 1974 (s.64(2)). In other words, the provisions are not another form of sick pay but are providing an employee who is suspended because, for example he has been dealing too long with a particular chemical, with a salary during his suspension. In such cases the employee is entitled to be paid his normal week's pay by his employer. The same exclusions to a medical suspension payment apply as in the case of a guarantee payment, with the added exclusion that the employee will not be entitled to medical suspension pay in respect of any period during which he is incapable of work by reason of disease or bodily or mental disablement (s.65(3)).

By ss.66–68 if a woman who is pregnant has recently given birth or who is breast-feeding would otherwise be suspended from work under these provisions and there is no suitable alternative work, she is entitled to her full remuneration. Similar provisions apply if the woman is suspended from work on health and safety maternity grounds. In other words, if because she is pregnant she is suspended because of health and safety considerations it is treated in the same way as any other medical suspension on those grounds.

7.4 Maternity Rights

Apart from the important protection from unfair dismissal because of pregnancy discussed in Chapter 9, the Employment Rights Act (ERA) 1996 as amended by the Employment Relations Act 1999, the Maternity and Parental Leave Regulations (MPLR) 1999 and the Work and Families Act 2006 provide three further protections in relation to pregnancy – the right to maternity leave, the right to time off for ante-natal care and the right to maternity pay.

Right to maternity leave

All pregnant employees since April 2007 are entitled to 52-weeks' maternity leave, regardless of length of service. Such leave is continuous and consists of ordinary maternity leave (OML) and additional maternity leave (AML).

Compulsory maternity leave

All employees are entitled to a period of two-weeks' compulsory maternity leave which is part of OML and which commences on the day childbirth occurs (s.72 ERA and Regulation 8 MPLR). An employer must not allow an employee to work during this period and commits a criminal offence if he or she does so.

Ordinary maternity leave

The amended s.71 ERA and the Maternity and Parental Leave Regulations implement the EC Pregnant Workers Directive (92/85/EC). This section refers to the first 26 weeks of maternity leave as 'ordinary maternity leave'. Leave may not begin until the eleventh week before the expected week of childbirth or the first day of the beginning of the sixth week before the expected week of childbirth if the employee is absent wholly or partially because of pregnancy (Regulation 6(1)(b)). The latest day that leave can commence is the day of childbirth (Regulation 6(2)). During ordinary maternity leave the employee is entitled to all the terms and conditions of her contract excluding pay, and all her benefits will continue (s.71). In *Hoyland* v. *Asda Stores Ltd* [2006] CSIH 21 the Scottish Employment Appeal Tribunal held that a *pro rata* reduction of a bonus for absence on maternity leave was not sex discrimination nor pregnancy related detriment, as such a bonus was remuneration and therefore not a benefit to which the claimant was entitled during her maternity leave. She was, however, entitled to be made a bonus for the two week compulsory maternity leave period. This is obviously a complex area. If there is no contractual right to pay, she will be entitled to statutory maternity pay if she meets the qualifying conditions (see below). Ordinary maternity leave will count as continuous service when assessing pension rights or other benefits based on length of service.

To be entitled to ordinary maternity leave the employee must comply with certain notification provisions. She must inform her employer no later than the end of the fifteenth week before the expected week of childbirth (EWC) of the fact that she is pregnant and the date she intends to start taking leave (Regulation 4(1)(a)). She must also provide a certificate from a midwife or general practitioner stating the expected week of childbirth (Regulations 4(1)(b) and 4(2)). Failure to comply with the notification provisions may mean she loses her right to statutory maternity pay and to start her leave on her intended date. If her maternity leave starts at the beginning of the fourth week before the expected week of childbirth because of a pregnancy related absence, she does not have to notify the employer of the expected week of childbirth or the date on which her leave starts (it will have started by Regulation 6(1)(b)). She will, however, lose her rights if she does not inform her employer as soon as reasonably practicable that she is absent wholly or partly because of pregnancy (Regulation 4(3)). If the illness is not related in whole or in part to her pregnancy, she can remain off work on sick leave up to the date of birth or the date she has notified.

Once she has informed her employer of the date she intends to start ordinary maternity leave she can change the date if she notifies the employer (in writing if so requested) by whichever is the earlier of 28 days before the date she originally intended to start her leave or 28 days before the new date she wishes to start her leave, unless it is not reasonably practicable to do so in which case she should notify the employer as soon as it is reasonably practicable.

Additional maternity leave

All employees, regardless of length of service, are entitled to additional maternity leave (s.73 ERA and Regulation 5 MPLR). Additional maternity leave is 26 weeks starting from the end of ordinary maternity leave (Regulation 7(4)). This means that the total maternity leave which could be taken is 52 weeks, although it could be longer if there is a late birth. During additional maternity leave the employee is entitled to the benefit of the implied obligation of trust and confidence, and terms in the contract relating to notice, redundancy compensation and disciplinary and grievance procedures. She is bound by terms relating to notice and good faith (Regulation 17). Unlike OML, AML does not count as continuous service for pensions or other benefits based on length of service, but does count as continuous service for the purpose of qualifying for statutory employment rights. She is entitled to return to her previous job or, if that is not reasonably practicable, another job which is suitable for her to do and appropriate for her to do in the circumstances (Regulation 18(2)).

Return from leave

Unlike under the previous provisions, the employee does not need to inform her employer about her date of return. The employer, after he has received notification of the start date of her leave, should inform the employee within 28 days of the date. If she has not been properly informed of when her leave is due to end, and does not return on time, she is protected against victimisation and dismissal. If she wishes to return before the end of the 52-week period, she must give at least eight-weeks' notice of her intention to do so. If she intends to return immediately after the 52 weeks there are no notification requirements. At the end, she is entitled to return to her previous job with her seniority and all other benefits in place as if she had not been absent (s.71(7)). If when her leave ends it is no longer practicable to continue to employ her because of redundancy, she is entitled to be offered suitable alternative employment (s.74 ERA and Regulation 10 MPLR). If her contract gives her more favourable rights than the statutory provisions, she is entitled to choose the more favourable rights (Regulation 21). If she wishes to return to different working conditions, she has no statutory right to do this, although she does have the right to request flexible working (see below).

Contact during maternity leave and keeping in touch days

During maternity leave, employers and employees may make reasonable contact with each other. What is reasonable will depend on the nature of the job and the nature of information which may need to be communicated. It is useful if, before leave commences, the parties discuss what contact should be made, how frequently, how contact should be made and the type of information to be communicated. The Maternity and Paternity Leave etc and the Paternity and Adoption Leave (Amendment) Regulations 2006 allow women or adopters to work for up to 10 mutually agreed keeping in touch days, during their leave, without losing entitlement to statutory maternity or adoption pay for those days. The type of work undertaken is a matter of agreement between the parties. An employer may not require an employee to work during maternity leave nor does an employee have the right to keeping in touch days if the employer does not agree to them. Any amount of work on one day counts as a day and the employer cannot, for example, ask an employee to work 20 half days. There is no legal requirement that the employee is paid for the keeping in touch days, although government guidance suggests that she should be paid.

Time off for ante-natal care

To qualify for this right the employee must have made an appointment for ante-natal care on the advice of a doctor, midwife or health visitor (s.55(1)). The employer may not refuse time off for the first appointment, but for succeeding appointments, the employer may ask for a certificate certifying that she is pregnant and an appointment card or some other document showing that the appointment has been made (s.55(2)). She is entitled not to be unreasonably refused time off with pay to keep such appointments. Any complaint in relation to refusal of time off or refusal to pay for the time taken must be made to a tribunal within three months of the date of the appointment.

Statutory maternity pay (SMP) and maternity allowance

The Social Security Act 1986 and the Statutory Maternity Pay Regulations of the same year (as amended) entitle certain employees to statutory maternity pay. If the employee does not have the qualifying conditions to claim SMP, she is entitled to maternity allowance. If the employee has been working for the employer for 26 weeks by the fifteenth week before the expected week of confinement, she is entitled to SMP for 39 weeks. This is now (2008) due to be extended to 52 weeks by the end of parliament. Maternity allowance is also payable for 39 weeks, again with an intended increase to 52 weeks. The rate of SMP is fixed by the Regulations. The employee is entitled to nine-tenths of her pay for the first six weeks of the 39 and the flat rate of SMP for the further 33 weeks.

To claim, the employee's earnings in the last eight weeks ending with the qualifying week must not be less than the lower earnings limit for the payment of National Insurance Contributions. She must produce a certificate (not earlier than the fourteenth week before her expected week of confinement) stating her expected week of confinement, and inform her employer 28 days before her absence begins that she is stopping work because of pregnancy. The maternity pay period starts when she wishes it to. The employer recoups the payments he has made on the 12-week element by making deductions from his National Insurance Contributions. Restrictions on recoupment which exist in relation to statutory sick pay also apply to SMP. A woman who does not qualify for SMP is entitled to a maternity allowance from the state. This is payable to women who have been employed or self-employed for at least 26 weeks in the 66 weeks ending with the EWC, who have paid 26-weeks' National Insurance Contributions and have earned on average £30 per week. It is a weekly benefit paid by the government rather than the employer and is paid at a flat rate or 90 per cent of weekly earnings if this is less than the flat rate. It continues for 39 weeks (52 in the future) and stops if the woman returns to work before the end of the maternity allowance period.

Amendments made to the Equal Pay Act 1970 by the Employment Equality (Sex Discrimination) Regulations 2005 provide (ss.1(2)(d) and (e)) that it is discriminatory to pay a woman less than she would otherwise have been paid because of her pregnancy or maternity leave. In other words, any pay increase or bonus achieved while on maternity leave must be reflected in her maternity pay.

7.5 Parental Leave

The Parental Leave Directive (96/34/EC) was implemented by the UK in December 1999. The rights are contained in ss.76–80 Employment Rights Act 1996, and the details of the rights are in the Maternity and Parental Leave Regulations 1999. The rights contained in the Regulations are a fall-back position, the legislation encouraging employers to develop workplace arrangements. As such, the statutory provisions only apply if no workplace agreement exists. Originally the right to parental leave applied to parents of children born on or after 15 December 1999, the date that the provisions came into force. This excluded parents with young children born before that date. The TUC mounted a legal challenge arguing that under the Directive the right should apply to all parents of children who were under the age of 5 when the Regulations came into force (*R* v. *Secretary of State for Trade and Industry ex parte TUC* [2000] IRLR 565). The Divisional Court referred the question to the ECJ as a result of which the government in April 2001 extended the right to parents of children who were under 5 on 15 December 1999, and thus the legal challenge was withdrawn.

The Regulations provide that an employee with one-year's continuous employment can take up to 13-weeks' unpaid parental leave in respect of each child for which the employee has responsibility (Regulations 13 and 14). The leave may be taken up to the child's fifth birthday. In respect of disabled children, 18-weeks' leave can be taken up to the child's eighteenth birthday. Where a child has been adopted, leave may be taken up to the five-year anniversary of the placement, or the child's eighteenth birthday, whichever is the earlier (Regulation 15). During parental leave an employee is entitled to the benefit of the same contractual terms as an employee on additional maternity leave, and is bound by the same contractual terms (Regulation 17). If an employee returns to work after her additional maternity leave followed by parental leave, she is entitled to return to the same job, unless it would not have been reasonably practicable to return to the same job after AML; if this is not possible, then she has a right to a similar job.

The Regulations encourage workplace agreements and have default provisions which are applicable if such agreements do not exist (Regulation 16). Schedule 2 lists the default provisions and provides for leave to be taken in blocks of multiples of one week, with a maximum of four-weeks' leave a year. Any leave amounting to less than a week is classed as a whole week for the purposes of entitlement. The employee must give 21-days' notice before taking leave and the employer can postpone leave for up to six months if the leave required by the employee would unduly disrupt his business. The employer, however, must agree alternative dates on which the leave can be taken.

To prevent the default provisions operating, the employer must have a collective or workforce agreement governing parental leave which is incorporated into the contracts of employment of his employees. A collective agreement is one made with an independent trade union. A workforce agreement may only be made if there is no collective agreement governing terms and conditions of employment. It must be made in consultation with workforce representatives, be in writing and be effective for a period not exceeding five years. The employer must send written copies of the agreement, together with guidance, to relevant employees.

7.6 Paternity Leave and Pay

New fathers are entitled to two-weeks' paternity leave paid at the same rate as statutory maternity pay. This is in addition to parental leave. Eligibility for paid paternity leave will be the same as for SMP. The right is lost unless the father has informed his employer of his intention to take leave by the fifteenth week before the expected week of childbirth, and he will have to give 28-days' notice if he wishes to change the start date. To qualify for the right, the employee must have 26-weeks' service before the expected week of childbirth and he must have, or expect to have, responsibility for the child's upbringing or be the mother's husband or partner. This applies in relation to natural or adopted children. The leave period will start on or after the onset of labour and leave will have to be taken in a single block within the first 56 days of the child's life (unless otherwise agreed with the employer). There is protection from detriment and dismissal for taking paid paternity leave and a father will be able to take unpaid parental leave immediately afterwards.

The Work and Families Act 2006 proposes to increase this right so that fathers would benefit from leave and statutory pay if the mother returns to work after six months but before the end of her maternity leave period. The Regulations implementing these provisions have proved complex but are now (2008) expected by the end of parliament.

7.7 Adoption Leave and Pay

Couples who have a child placed with them for adoption are able to choose which of them is entitled to take 52 weeks of adoption leave. The first 39 weeks is paid at the same rate as the flat rate of SMP. The other adoptive parent is able to take two-weeks' paid paternity leave at the time of the adoption. Parental leave may also be taken in addition to adoption leave. The right is available to adoptive parents who have 26-weeks' continuous service. Adoptive parents have to inform their employer when they have been approved for adoption and the indicative matching time given by the adoption agency. Adoption leave starts as soon as the child is placed with the parents. There is a right of return which is the same as the right to return after additional maternity leave. As with maternity leave, should an employee wish to return before the end of the 52 weeks, the employee must give the employee at least eight-weeks' notice of the date on which they intend to return. In addition there is protection from detriment or dismissal. The right is not available to step adoption or adoption by foster-parents.

7.8 Right to Request Flexible Working

Originally the Employment Act 2002 introduced a right to request flexible working, in order to care for a child under the age of six, by the insertion of a new s.80F into the Employment Rights Act 1996. This right was extended by the Work and Families Act 2006 to include an employee who cares for a spouse or partner, adult relatives or an adult living at the same address as the employee. The right allows a qualifying employee to apply to his employer for a change in his terms and conditions of employment in relation to: the hours he is required to work; the times he is required to work; as between his home and place of work, the place he is required to work; or any other such aspect of his terms and conditions. A qualifying employee is an employee who has been employed for 26 weeks. If an employee has already made an application to his employer he may not make a further application for twelve months.

An employer can only refuse an application on specified grounds which are: costs; detrimental effect on ability to meet customer demand; inability to reorganise existing staff; inability to recruit additional staff; detrimental impact on quality; insufficiency of work during the periods the employee proposes to work; and planned structural changes. Such refusals should be in writing.

An employee has two weeks in which to appeal against a decision not to allow flexible working, setting out the reasons for the appeal. The appeal should be part of the ordinary company procedures and the employer must respond in writing within two weeks of the appeal.

The procedural steps are:

(a) an employee should make a request in writing setting out the work pattern he or she wants and how it could work;
(b) the employer should consider the business case for accepting or rejecting the request;
(c) there should be a meeting within four weeks to consider the request;
(d) the employer should respond in writing within two weeks of the meeting either accepting the request, putting forward the compromise agreed at the meeting, rejecting the request with the business reasons for doing so and informing the employee of the procedure for an appeal.

There is a right to apply to a tribunal that the employer has failed to comply with the statute or that he has rejected the application on incorrect facts. Such a complaint must be made within three months of either the date the employee was informed of the employer's decision, or the date the employer committed a breach of the statute. A tribunal, should it find the complaint well-founded, may either make an order that the employer reconsider the application or make an award of compensation it considers to be just and equitable in the circumstances.

7.9 Right Not to Suffer a Detriment

Sections 43M–47 Employment Rights Act 1996 create the right not to suffer a detriment in certain cases. 'Detriment' is an act or any deliberate failure to act by the employer. These rights complement the protection against unfair dismissal in these situations discussed in Chapter 9.

Jury service

The Employment Relations Act 2004 inserts a new s.43M into the ERA 1996. This provides that an employee has the right not to suffer a detriment by any act, or deliberate failure to act, on the grounds that he or she has been summoned to attend as a juror or has been absent because of such a summons. Detriment does not include non-payment of salary during such service unless the contract gives an entitlement to payment.

Health and safety cases

Section 44(1) ERA provides that an employee has the right not to be subjected to any detriment by an act, or a failure to act, on the grounds that as a health and safety representative he was carrying out his duties; or he was or proposed to carry out his duties as a health and safety committee member; or, where there was no such representative or it was not reasonably practicable to raise the matter with such, he brought to his employer's attention safety risks; or, in circumstances of danger he could not reasonably avert, which he reasonably believed to be serious and imminent, he left or proposed to leave his place of work or took steps to protect himself and others from danger. Whether the action is reasonable is up to the tribunal, taking all the circumstances, including the employee's knowledge and the advice available, into account; however, the Employment Appeal Tribunal in *Kerr* v. *Nathan's Wastesavers Ltd* (1995) IDS Brief 548 stressed that tribunals should not place too onerous a duty on the employee to make enquiries to establish if his belief was reasonable. In *Barton* v. *Wandsworth Council* (1995) IDS Brief 549 an employee was disciplined when he voiced concerns over the safety of patients as a result of what he considered to be the lack of ability of newly introduced escorts. The tribunal held that he had been unlawfully disciplined, showing that the legal protection is triggered when the employee raises concerns.

The employee may complain to an employment tribunal within three months of the act, or failure to act, complained of (s.48(3)) unless this is not reasonably practicable. The burden is on the employer to show why he acted as he did. If the tribunal finds the complaint well-founded, it may make a declaration and an award of compensation. The amount of compensation is what is just and equitable in the circumstances, taking into account any loss sustained by the complainant. The complainant is under a duty to mitigate his loss and the tribunal may reduce the award for contributory conduct (s.49).

Sunday working for shop and betting workers

An employee who is a protected shop or betting worker, or an opted-out shop or betting worker, has the right not to suffer a detriment on the ground that he refused or proposed to refuse to work on Sundays (s.45). 'Protected', under this provision, means that the worker was under a contract, at the date of the commencement of the provision, which did not require him to work on Sundays (s.36). An 'opted-out' worker is a worker who by his contract is required to work on Sundays and who has given his employer written notice that he objects to Sunday working (s.40). Such workers are not protected in relation to acts on the part of the employer during the opted-out notice period. The remedies are the same as in relation to health and safety cases (s.49).

Working time cases

By s.45A a worker has the right not to be subjected to a detriment on the grounds that he refused to comply with a requirement imposed upon him by his employer in contravention of the Working Time Regulations 1998; he refused or proposed to refuse to forgo a right conferred on him by the Regulations; he failed to sign a workforce agreement or vary or extend any other agreement provided for by the Regulations; he was a workforce representative for the purposes of the Regulations, or a candidate in a representative election, and performed or proposed to perform activities in relation to that role; or he brought proceedings against the employer under the Regulations or he alleged that the employer had infringed a right under the Regulations. For the purpose of the last protection it is irrelevant whether the worker has the right or whether it has actually been infringed as long as the worker's claim is made in good faith. It will be noted that the section brings together a number of rights listed in the other sections but relates them particularly to breaches of the Working Time Regulations.

Trustees of occupational pension schemes

By s.46 an employee has the right not to suffer a detriment by his employer on the ground that, being a trustee of a relevant occupational pension scheme which relates to his employment, he performed or proposed to perform any of his functions as a trustee. A relevant pension scheme means an occupational pension scheme as defined in s.1 Pension Schemes Act 1993.

Employee representatives

By s.47 an employee has a right not to suffer a detriment by his employer on the ground that being an employee representative for the purposes of the Trade Union and Labour Relations (Consolidation) Act 1992 or the Transfer of Undertakings (Protection of Employment) Regulations 2006, or a candidate in elections for such a representative, he performed or proposed to perform any functions or activities.

Employees exercising the right to time off work for study or training

By s.47A employees who have exercised rights under s.63A to take paid time off for study or training are entitled not to suffer a detriment because they have exercised such rights.

Protected disclosures

By s.47B an employee who has made a protected disclosure under the Public Interest Disclosure Act 1998 has a right not to have action short of dismissal taken against him. *Bolton School* v. *Evans* [2007] ICR 641 discusses what is meant by a 'disclosure'.

Leave for family and domestic reasons

Sections 47C and D create a right not to suffer a detriment, by any act or deliberate failure to act, for a prescribed reason. A prescribed reason is one prescribed by the Secretary of State that relates to:

(a) pregnancy, childbirth or maternity leave;
(b) ordinary, compulsory or additional maternity leave;
(c) parental leave, paternity leave or adoption leave;
(d) time off for dependants; or
(e) an application (or proposed application) made for flexible working, a right to flexible working exercised or proceedings brought for breach of such rights.

Disciplinary and grievance hearings

Section 12 Employment Relations Act 1999 creates the right not to suffer a detriment (which is defined as an act or a failure to act) on the grounds that as a worker he exercised his right to be accompanied at a disciplinary or grievance hearing or he acted as a representative at such a hearing.

Collective agreements

The Employment Relations Act 2004 inserts two new sections into the Trade Union and Labour Relations (Consolidation) Act 1992. Section 145B protects a worker from being offered an inducement to come out of collective bargaining and a new s.146(2C) protects a worker from being subjected to a detriment on the grounds that he has refused to enter a contract which includes terms which differ from the terms of a collective agreement which applies to him. Again, 'detriment' means an act or a failure to act (for example, by not granting a pay rise). This amendment is as a result of *Wilson* v. *UK* (2002) 35 EHRR 20 in which the ECJ held that an essential part of the right given in Article 11 ECHR (freedom of association) was the fact that an employer could not offer financial inducements to persuade an employee to give up his rights. As such, the government amended the Trade Union and Labour Relations (Consolidation) Act.

Recognition

Schedule 1 Employment Relations Act 1999 gives details on statutory recognition of trade unions and inserts a new Schedule A1 into the Trade Union and Labour Relations (Consolidation) Act 1992. These are discussed in Chapter 12. Paragraph 156 of the Schedule protects a worker from suffering a detriment by an act or failure to act because he has taken action or refused to take action in respect of trade union recognition. The provisions complement similar protection against unfair dismissal contained in para 161 which are discussed more fully in Chapter 9.

7.10 Time-off Provisions

In addition to the time-off provisions for ante-natal appointments, the law creates other rights to time off in respect of specified duties or activities. These are discussed below. Any complaint in relation to refusal of time off or refusal to pay for the time taken (if relevant) must be made to a tribunal within three months of the alleged act.

Trade union duties

By ss.168 and 169 Trade Union and Labour Relations (Consolidation) Act 1992 an employee who is an official of an independent trade union recognised by the employer is entitled to reasonable time off with pay during working hours to carry out those duties and undergo training. If an employer refuses to allow such time off the official may complain to an industrial tribunal and obtain a declaration and compensation. 'Official' is defined in s.119 as any officer of the union or branch or any other person elected under union rules to represent members. The statute creates the right to reasonable time off. The *ACAS Code of Practice* gives factors to be taken into account when assessing what is reasonable, such as the amount of time already allowed. In *Wignall* v. *British Gas Corporation* [1984] IRLR 493 it was held not to be unreasonable to refuse an employee 10 days off when he had already been granted and taken 12 weeks to pursue union duties.

Time off for union learning representatives

Section 43 Employment Act 2002 has introduced a new type of trade union representative called a 'union learning representative' (ULR). By a new s.168A Trade Union and Labour Relations (Consolidation) Act 1992, such a representative is a member of a recognised independent trade union who has been elected or appointed, in relation to members of the union, to analyse learning or training needs, provide information or advice about learning or training matters, arrange learning or training or promote the value of learning or training. The ULR is entitled to reasonable time off with pay but only if the union has given the employer written notice that the person is the ULR and that the ULR has undergone sufficient training to fulfil the role or will have undergone relevant training within six months of the notice. If the employer is required to give the ULR time off to perform his role, he is also required to give him time off to undergo training. Members of the union are entitled to unpaid time off during working hours to access the services of a ULR (s.170(2B)).

Trade union activities

By s.152 of the 1992 Act, a member of an independent recognised trade union is entitled to reasonable time off without pay but during working hours to take part in trade union activities.

Health and safety duties

The Safety Representatives and Safety Committees Regulations 1977 made under the Health and Safety at Work Act 1974 provide that an employer shall allow an employee who is a safety representative time off with pay during normal working hours to perform his statutory functions and undergo training.

Public duties

An employee has the right to reasonable time off, without pay, to perform specified public duties. These duties are found in s.50 Employment Rights Act 1996 and include magistracy, membership of a local authority, membership of a statutory tribunal, membership of a health authority, school governor or membership of a water authority. The right to time off extends to attendance at meetings and doing anything approved by the body for the purpose of discharging its functions. Criteria for establishing reasonable time off include how much time the employee has already had, the effect of the employee's absence and so on. In *Walters* v. *British Steel Corporation* IDS Brief 150 the employee was transferred to another job and agreed that his public duties would take second place. Safety considerations meant that there had to be certain manning levels and his colleagues refused to cover for him. It was held that, taking into account the circumstances of his employer's business, he was not entitled to time off. In *Emmerson* v.

Inland Revenue Commissioners [1977] IRLR 458 the employee had already had 18-days' paid leave for public duties and his request for further unpaid leave of absence was refused by his employers. The tribunal held that as the applicant was prepared to use some of his own holidays, a further 12-days' unpaid leave was not unreasonable. Conversely, in *Borders Regional Council* v. *Maule* [1992] IRLR 199 the Employment Appeal Tribunal reiterated that a tribunal has to achieve a balance in the situation of an employee claiming time off in relation to several public commitments. In the case the employee, who was a member of a social security tribunal, sought a day off to attend a training session. The employers refused to allow her the time off. The employment tribunal upheld her complaint under s.50 on the basis that, as the employers had allowed her the time off to sit on the tribunal, they also had to allow her the time off to attend training sessions. The Employment Appeal Tribunal disagreed. The Appeal Tribunal said that the tribunal should look at all factors, including time off taken for other purposes. Lord Coulsfield added that where an employee had a variety of public duties, the employee had a responsibility to scale the level of duties to one which can be regarded as reasonable in all the circumstances. In other words, the fact that the employer has allowed an employee time off to participate in certain public duties does not mean that he is acting unreasonably if he sometimes refuses time off in relation to those duties. All the circumstances must be taken into account. The employee must be allowed time off, however, and it is insufficient for the employer to alter times of the employee's work to fit in with his public commitments (*Ratcliffe* v. *Dorset County Council* [1978] IRLR 191).

Time off to look for work

By s.52 of the 1996 Act, an employee who is under notice of redundancy is entitled to reasonable time off with pay during working hours to look for new employment or make arrangements for training, before the expiry of his notice. This right, however, only applies to employees who have been continuously employed for two years on the date the notice is due to expire. The employee does not need to provide his employer with proof of appointments and so on, but if the employer feels that the request is not genuine, it may not be unreasonable to refuse the time off (*Dutton* v. *Hawker Siddeley Aviation Ltd* [1978] IRLR 390).

Time off for occupational pension scheme trustees

A trustee of an occupational pension scheme is entitled to time off during working hours to perform any of his duties as trustee or to undergo training (s.58 of the 1996 Act). Such time off is what is reasonable in the circumstances having regard to the effect of the time off on the employer's business. Such time off is with pay (s.59). Failure to comply with the section entitles the trustee to apply to a tribunal within three months of the refusal. The tribunal, if it finds the complaint well-founded, can award such compensation as it considers just and equitable (s.60).

Time off for employee representatives

By s.61 an employee who is an employee representative, or a candidate in an election for such a representative, is entitled to reasonable time off during working hours in order to perform his functions as a representative or candidate. Since 1999 such a representative is also entitled to reasonable time off for training. Time off is also provided to accompany a worker in a disciplinary or grievance hearing. The time off must be with pay (s.62). By s.63, a complaint in relation to a breach of the provisions can be presented within three months of the breach and the tribunal can award the remuneration the employee would have received if the time off had been allowed (s.63).

Time off for study or training

Section 63A gives an employee who is 16 or 17 years old and who is not receiving full-time secondary or further education, the right to time off with pay, during working hours, in order to undertake study or training leading to a relevant qualification. If an employee is 18 years old and was undergoing such study or training prior to commencing employment with the employer, he is entitled to paid time off during working hours to complete that study or training.

Time off for dependants

The Employment Relations Act 1999 inserted a new s.57A into the Employment Rights Act 1996 and created a right to reasonable time off for dependants. There is no requirement that such time off be paid. Reasonable time off should be given to allow an employee to provide assistance to a dependant because of illness, injury or giving birth; to make arrangements for the provision of care for a dependant who is ill or injured; in consequence of the death of a dependant; because of the unexpected disruption or termination of arrangements for the care of a dependant; or to deal with an incident involving the child of the employee which occurs unexpectedly at an educational establishment which the child is attending (s.57(1)). In *Qua* v. *John Ford Morrison Solicitors* [2003] ICR 482 the Employment Appeal Tribunal heard the case of a single mother claiming automatically unfair dismissal for taking dependant leave 17 times in a nine-month period. The Appeal Tribunal held that the right did not entitle an employee to take more time off than what would be reasonable to deal with an immediate crisis. Similarly, in *Forster* v. *Cartwright Black* [2004] IRLR 781 the EAT held that an employee was entitled to time off under these provisions to deal with the funeral arrangements following the death of a relative, but not time off to grieve. From this it can be seen that an employee has the right to reasonable time off to make care arrangements, but not to deal with the dependant themselves. The employee is not entitled to exercise the right to time off unless he tells his employer the reason for his absence as soon as reasonably practicable and tells his employer his expected length of absence (unless it was not possible to tell the employer before the incident occurred) (s.57(2)). In *MacCulloch and Wallis Ltd* v. *Moore* EAT 51/02 the EAT stated that where an employee had given the reason and the length of the absence to the employer, there would be a breach of the provisions if circumstances changed and the employee did not inform the employer of the changes. 'Dependant' means, in relation to the employee, a spouse, child, parent or any person who lives in the same household other than by reason of being an employee, tenant, lodger or boarder of the employee (s.57(3)). In *Truelove* v. *Safeway Stores plc* (2005) IDS 774 an employee who frequently worked Saturdays asked for a day's leave one particular Saturday when his baby-sitting arrangements fell through. Leave was refused, but he took it anyway. He was disciplined and lost a £250 bonus. The tribunal held that the employer did not have enough information to decide if the request was reasonable. The EAT disagreed. It was sufficient that the employer knew that the request was because of childcare. This was an unforeseen eventuality and reasonableness was not applicable, although it would be applicable when considering the number of times the employee had taken time off for childcare.

Where the incident requires the employee to provide assistance or make provision for the care of a person because of illness or injury, the definition of dependant also includes any person who reasonably relies on the employee (s.57(4)). Where the incident is the unexpected disruption or termination of arrangements for care, the definition of dependant also includes any person who reasonably relies on the employee to make such arrangements (s.57(5)).

Summary

1. There are various employment protection rights which apply to employees.

2. These rights apply independently from any contractual provision, unless the contract gives more favourable rights.

3. The rights divide into: right to a guarantee payment, right of pay for medical suspension, maternity rights, paternity rights, adoption rights, parental rights, rights not to suffer a detriment in certain cases and leave and time-off rights.

Exercise

Martin, Ronnie and Phil work as teachers for Middlewich School. The recognised union in the school is the National Union of Teachers.

Martin has been a member of the governing body of the local university for the past four years. During that time he has had, on average, 14 days off a year to attend meetings during term time. Because of a recent scandal involving the university vice-chancellor, the governing body has met frequently in the past three months and Martin has had 21 days off to date. The chair of the governing body has just informed him that he will be required to attend meetings on at least another 15 days during the rest of the academic year. Martin's headmaster has refused to allow him any more time off saying that it is unfair to other colleagues who cover his classes. Martin has never been paid for his time off.

Ronnie is the union health and safety representative at the school. Given that the school has just opened a chemistry department, Ronnie has had three weeks off in the past six months to attend training courses in the handling of chemicals. He now requires a further seven days off to train the chemistry teachers. The headmaster has refused to allow Ronnie the time to train the teachers and has said that he must train them during the vacation. In addition, Ronnie's class size has doubled recently and he has been given extra classes to teach to make up for the time he has been away from the school on courses.

Phil is a member of the NUT. The union has held regional meetings in the past to discuss action against Curriculum 2008. These meetings are normally held at lunchtime, or in the evenings, and Phil has always attended them. He has just been informed that the next two regional meetings will be held on two mornings during term time when Phil has classes. The union also wishes him to be a member of a party which is being sent to London for a week, again in term time, to lobby parliament. The headmaster has refused to allow Phil to attend the meetings or join the lobby.

Advise Martin, Ronnie and Phil.

Further Reading

Anderson *Sound Bite Legislation: The Employment Act 2002 and New Flexible Working 'Rights' for Parents* (2003) 32 ILJ 37.

Dickens *Equality and Working Life Balance. What's Happening in the Workplace?* (2006) 35 ILJ 445.

Evans and Lewis *Anti-Union Discrimination: Practice, Law and Policy* (1987) 16 ILJ 88.

Ewing *The Implications of Wilson and Palmer* (2003) 32 ILJ 1.

James *The Work and Families Act 2006: Legislation to Improve Choice and Flexibility?* (2006) 35 ILJ 272.

Mortimer *Strengthening Workers' Rights: A New Agenda* (2003) 32 ILJ 129.

Vallely and Quinn *The Family Friendly Workplace: A Right For All Or A Prize For Few?* (2001) 12(5) PLC 43.

Part IV

Termination of Employment

Chapter 8

Termination at Common Law

Termination by Operation of Law

Although the most common way the contract of employment will come to an end is by an act of the parties, in some circumstances the law will operate to end the relationship automatically on the happening of an event. Should the contract terminate in this way, there will be no liability on either side. The ways in which the contract will terminate by operation of law are discussed below.

Frustration

Frustration occurs when, without the fault of either party, the contract becomes either impossible to perform or fundamentally different from what the parties originally intended. The recognition that an employment contract could be frustrated happened over 100 years ago in the case of *Poussard* v. *Spiers & Pond* (1876) 1 QBD 410 where an opera singer caught a cold and as a result was unable to take part in a week of rehearsals and the first few performances. The replacement hired by the management was only prepared to perform if she was given a month's contract. The opera singer sued the management for breach. It was held that the contract had been frustrated and there was no breach by the management. The circumstances were unusual, in that a few days' illness would not normally frustrate an employment contract which would normally last for some years. In the *Poussard* case, however, the opera was not due to run for a long period of time and the only replacement the management could get insisted on a contract exceeding the period of illness of the original singer.

The two major events that will frustrate an employment contract are illness and imprisonment. Normally it is only when these events strike the employee that frustration can occur, because often, in today's employment relationships, the employer is not a person but a company, although there is special protection for an employee if a company is wound up or a partnership is dissolved (see below).

The original test in employment cases to see if illness had led to a frustration was formulated by Donaldson P in *Marshall* v. *Harland & Wolff Ltd* [1972] 1 WLR 899 when he said that the tribunals had to ask whether the nature of the employee's incapacity was such that further performance of his obligations was impossible or radically different from that originally intended when he entered the contract. He then gave a list of factors the tribunals should consider when looking to see if a frustration had occurred. These factors were added to in the later case of *Egg Stores Ltd* v. *Leibovici* [1977] ICR 260 by Phillips J and have now been summarised and approved by the Employment Appeal Tribunal in the case of *Williams* v. *Watsons Luxury Coaches Ltd* [1990] IRLR 164:

(a) the court must be careful not to use the doctrine too easily, as it may mask a dismissal for disability;

(b) it is useful to decide the date on which frustration occurred to determine whether it is a true frustration;

(c) there are a number of factors that should be considered, which include the length of the employment prior to the event and the length of future foreseeable employment, the nature of the job and the terms of the employment, the nature, length and effect of the illness and the prospect of recovery, the employer's need for a replacement, the risk of the employer's acquiring statutory obligations to a replacement, the conduct of the employer, whether wages or sick pay have been paid and whether in all the circumstances a reasonable employer would have waited longer;

(d) the frustrating event has not been caused by the party seeking to rely upon it.

The operation of the doctrine can be demonstrated, perhaps, by the comparison of two cases. In *Hart* v. *A R Marshall & Sons (Bulwell) Ltd* [1977] IRLR 51 a night service fitter, who was described as a key worker by his employer, was ill for 20 months. He sent in regular sick notes and on his return was informed that he had been replaced. The Employment Appeal Tribunal held that, given he was such an important employee, the contract had been frustrated by the illness. By contrast there is the case of *Hebden* v. *Forsey & Sons* [1973] IRLR 344. Here the employee was one of two sawyers employed by the employer. In total he was away from work for almost two years after an operation. During that time he was in contact with his employer, his employer had agreed to his taking the time off and there was insufficient work for him to do until he had fully recovered. It was held that the contract had not been frustrated.

Imprisonment is another event which may frustrate the contract, but the courts' attitude towards this has changed over the years. The problem that has arisen is that it will normally be the employee's fault that he is serving a prison sentence and a self-induced frustration is no frustration because it is caused by the fault of one of the parties. In *Hare* v. *Murphy Brothers* [1974]

IRLR 342 imprisonment was held to frustrate the contract, Lord Denning pointing out that an opera singer sitting in a draught may lose her voice and it could be said that she had induced this, but her contract would still be frustrated. In *Norris* v. *Southampton City Council* [1982] IRLR 141, however, the Employment Appeal Tribunal decided that as the imprisonment had been caused by the employee's own misconduct there could be no frustration, and the employee was guilty of a repudiatory breach which, if accepted by the employer, would lead to a dismissal. This fails to recognise, however, that the employee did not commit the offence with the intention of breaking the contract and could have received a fine rather than a prison sentence. The position has now been clarified by the Court of Appeal in *Shepherd (FC) & Co Ltd* v. *Jerrom* [1986] 3 WLR 801. The court decided that a six-month prison sentence could frustrate a four-year contract of apprenticeship. However, in *Four Seasons Healthcare Ltd* v. *Maughan* [2005] IRLR 324 a care worker who was suspended and unpaid for eleven months while police investigated complaints of patient abuse, claimed wages for the period. The employer argued the contract was frustrated because the care worker was banned from entering the care home as part of his bail conditions. The EAT held that the contract was only frustrated when the worker was convicted and imprisoned and as the contract only allowed for seven days unpaid suspension, he was entitled to wages for the rest of the period. This pushes an employer to make an early decision to dismiss.

Although illness and imprisonment are the commonest forms of frustrating events in an employment relationship, there have been other events that have led to a frustration. In *Morgan* v. *Manser* [1948] 1 KB 184 a 10-year management contract entered into in 1940 was frustrated by the call into the army of the employee. In *Tarnesby* v. *Kensington, Chelsea & Westminster AHA* [1981] IRLR 369 suspension from medical practice for 12 months was deemed a frustration. Although, by contrast, in *Gryf-Lowczowski* v. *Hinchingbrooke Healthcare NHS Trust* [2006] IRLR 100 it was held that the contract of a consultant was not frustrated when he was suspended for two years following allegations of incompetence. The High Court held that there was a likelihood he would return after retraining and, given his length of service, there was no frustration. This was despite the fact that the suspended employee was one of only two consultants in the field.

Note that as the contract terminates on the frustrating event and without fault on either side, any rights under the contract cease. Therefore in *G F Sharp & Co Ltd* v. *McMillan* [1998] IRLR 632 it was held that where the contract of an employee had been frustrated by the employee's injury, he was not entitled to a payment in lieu of notice, despite the fact that the employer had 'kept him on the books' in order to ensure that he received enhanced pension benefits. This did not keep the contract alive after the frustrating event.

Liquidation of the employer or dissolution of a partnership

At common law the liquidation of a company or dissolution of a partnership is clearly a frustration because the contract becomes impossible to perform. The common law rules are, however, superseded by statute. By s.139(4) Employment Rights Act 1996 the death or liquidation of an employer or the dissolution of a partnership shall be treated as a dismissal for redundancy, unless the business is taken into new ownership and the employee's contract is renewed. If there is a transfer of an undertaking and the employee objects to being transferred, his contract terminates and there is no dismissal (Regulation 4(8) Transfer of Undertakings (Protection of Employment) Regulations 2006).

8.2 Termination by Agreement

If the parties mutually agree that the contract should come to an end, then neither party has ended the agreement and as such there will be no dismissal (employer termination) or resignation (employee termination). If there is a genuine agreement there is no problem, but it is important to discover whether the 'agreement' to end the relationship has been brought about by employer pressure, in which case it will be a dismissal. Donaldson J in *McAlwane* v. *Boughton Estates Ltd* [1973] ICR 470 said that tribunals should be careful when finding a mutual agreement to terminate and ensure that the employee was aware of the financial implications in so agreeing. Thus if there is some financial consideration the tribunals will be more prepared to accept a genuine agreement. In *Scott* v. *Coalite Fuels and Chemicals Ltd* [1988] IRLR 131 the employees took early voluntary retirement while under notice, in order to claim a lump sum under a pension scheme. It was held that there was a mutual agreement to terminate. In *Birch and Humber* v. *University of Liverpool* [1985] IRLR 165 the employees were invited to volunteer for early retirement. Two employees volunteered and received a reply from the university that the institution confirmed 'that it is in the managerial interests for you to retire and requests that you do so'. The vacancies created by the retirement were not filled and the two employees argued that they had been dismissed for reasons of redundancy and were entitled to a redundancy payment in addition to any payment for early retirement. The Court of Appeal disagreed and held that there was no dismissal but a mutual agreement to terminate. *Scott*, however, was distinguished in the case of *Gateshead Metropolitan Borough Council* v. *Mills* (1995) IDS Brief 551. The case on its facts was similar to *Scott* in that the employee was under notice of redundancy, although the employer had stated that there may be alternative employment and therefore the notice may not be acted upon. Mills applied for a variety of other jobs within the council, but was unsuccessful, and so he successfully applied for early retirement. He then applied to a tribunal for a redundancy payment. The employer argued, on the basis of *Scott*, that the subsequent agreement to take early retirement had impliedly withdrawn the notice of dismissal, and that Mills' contract had terminated by agreement. The Employment Appeal Tribunal disagreed. Any withdrawal of the dismissal notice had to have the consent of the recipient. There was no evidence that Mills had so consented and the fact that he agreed to take early retirement did not indicate that he had impliedly consented. As such, Mills was dismissed and entitled to a redundancy payment. While the cases seem difficult to reconcile it could be argued that a distinction can be made, however, between the situations where redundancy would be inevitable should the employee not volunteer and those where it would not. In *Morton Sundour Fabrics* v. *Shaw* (1966) 2 KIR 1 the employee had been warned of the possibility of redundancy and therefore found himself another job. It was held that he had resigned and not been dismissed as his redundancy was not inevitable. By contrast in *Morley* v. *C T Morley Ltd* [1985] ICR 499 the employees were a father and two sons who had incorporated their family business. The father volunteered for redundancy, and afterwards the sons decided to wind up the business. It was held that there had been a dismissal. Furthermore, the courts will be unsympathetic to an employer who tries to force his employees to leave because of the threat of redundancy, as a cheap way of reducing his workforce. In *Caledonian Mining Co Ltd* v. *Bassett and Steel* [1987] IRLR 165 the employer had told his employees that there would be a reduction in manpower on the site and asked his employees if they were interested in alternative employment. The men expressed interest in alternative employment, but the employer failed to respond and eventually the men were offered work by the National Coal Board which they accepted. They informed their employer who then argued that they had resigned and as such were not entitled to redundancy payments. The Employment Appeal Tribunal held that there had been a dismissal. The men had been encouraged to take other jobs by their employer with the intention of avoiding redundancy payments. The employer had caused the men to resign and therefore the employer had terminated the contract. As such, the men had been dismissed.

Some years ago, it was possible for the employee to agree that his employment would automatically terminate on the happening of an event, and as such there would be no dismissal or resignation. The authority for such a proposition was the case of *British Leyland (UK)* v. *Ashraf* [1978] IRLR

330 where the employee was given five-weeks' unpaid leave to visit his family in Pakistan. He signed a document that if he failed to return on a due date, for whatever reason, his contract would terminate immediately. When he did not return at the appointed time the employers treated the contract as terminated as per the agreement. The Employment Appeal Tribunal held that there had been a consensual termination and no dismissal. This decision, however, is very hard, and takes no account of the reasons for failure to return. As such, later decisions tried to mitigate the harshness. In *Midland Electric Manufacturing Co Ltd* v. *Kanji* [1980] IRLR 185 the employee's leave of absence was granted with the warning that if she failed to return the company would consider that she had terminated her employment. Talbot J distinguished *Ashraf* on the basis that the wording in *Kanji* was ambiguous and was merely a statement of intention by the employer that she would be dismissed. In *Tracey* v. *Zest Equipment Co* [1982] IRLR 268 the Employment Appeal Tribunal stressed that very clear words were needed to constitute a mutual agreement to terminate.

These cases must now be read subject to the Court of Appeal decision in *Igbo* v. *Johnson Matthey Chemicals Ltd* [1986] IRLR 215. In this case there was an agreement similar to that in *Ashraf*. Both the tribunal and the Employment Appeal Tribunal held that there was no dismissal despite the fact that the employee had failed to return because of illness and had a medical certificate. The Court of Appeal held that *Ashraf* was wrong. It did this by applying s.140(1) Employment Protection (Consolidation) Act 1978 (now s.203 of the 1996 Act) to automatic termination clauses. This section renders any agreement to restrict the operation of any provision of the Act void. As such, any agreement purporting to exclude the provisions on unfair dismissal or redundancy has no effect and this is precisely what automatic termination clauses purport to do. This decision means that in situations such as *Ashraf* the employer makes the decision that the contract has terminated and therefore there is a dismissal. This does not mean that the dismissal is unfair, merely that the tribunal then has the jurisdiction to look at the fairness or otherwise of the employer's decision.

The decision in *Igbo*, however, only applies to agreements where the termination occurs on the happening or non-happening of an event. It does not restrict the freedom of the parties to negotiate a separate agreement to terminate if that is supported by consideration. In *Logan Salton* v. *Durham County Council* [1989] IRLR 99 the employee had been redeployed as a result of disciplinary proceedings. Further disciplinary proceedings were to be initiated and there was a recommendation that at the conclusion of the proceedings the employee should be summarily dismissed. Prior to those proceedings, his union representative negotiated with the employer that the employment be terminated and an outstanding car loan of £2,750 be wiped out. Both parties signed an agreement to that effect. The employee subsequently claimed unfair dismissal on the basis that the agreement was void because of s.203. The Employment Appeal Tribunal held that the case could be distinguished from *Igbo* in that here there was a separate agreement to terminate which did not depend on the happening of some future event and which was supported by consideration. The parties had thus mutually terminated their contract.

8.3 Repudiation

A repudiatory breach may terminate the contract if the innocent party so decides. If the innocent party is the employee and the employee decides to end the contract, then unless the employee has one-year's continuous service, the contract will have come to an end by resignation, leaving the employee with a claim for damages. If, however, the employee has one-year's continuity and is protected by unfair dismissal provisions, the law steps in to protect him and the resignation will be treated as a dismissal because it was caused by the employer's conduct. This is known as a 'constructive dismissal' and will be discussed in detail later. If the employee commits the repudiatory breach and the employer decides to end the contract, then the contract has terminated by dismissal. Such a situation is always a dismissal irrespective of the length of employment of the employee as the law has no concept of a constructive resignation.

One of the problems that has exercised the judges in this area is the precise time at which the contract comes to an end. A breach which is repudiatory rejects the original contract and may produce a variety of results. It may reject the original contract and bring into play new terms. The innocent party has two options in this case: he can reject the new terms or he can accept them and continue the relationship. In the latter case, he has decided not to treat the action by the other party as terminating the contract but has agreed to waive the breach and treat the contract as varied (see, however, *Hogg* v. *Dover College* [1990] ICR 39 and *Alcan Extrusions* v. *Yates* [1996] IRLR 327 in Chapter 9). On the other hand, the breach may be a rejection by one party of the contract with no alternative terms offered. Again, the innocent party has the two options, but in reality his choice may be an illusory one if, for example, performance of the contract has been made impossible by the party in breach. If the employer locks out his employees, for example, in practical terms the employees have no real choice as to whether they continue to work or not. The question of deciding at what precise time the contract comes to an end when there is a repudiatory breach is not a purely academic one. The answer will have implications for both parties in terms of whether the employee has the continuity to claim an unfair dismissal should the employer be in repudiatory breach, what compensation he may claim if he has been unfairly dismissed and what damages either party may claim at common law for the breach.

The normal contractual doctrine is that a repudiatory breach will not operate to terminate a contract until the innocent party accepts it as so terminating (*Howard* v. *Pickford Tool Co Ltd* [1951] 1 KB 417). While many cases have decided that the normal doctrine applies in employment law, this can cause difficulties in that often the choice given to the innocent party is no real choice at all, for example in a strike or a lock-out, and further, as has already been seen, the courts cannot award the normal contractual remedy of specific performance in an employment contract, to compel the parties to continue the contract.

As a result of the unique nature of an employment contract and the remedies available to the parties, judges originally argued that the normal doctrine did not apply and that repudiation terminated the relationship automatically. Megarry VC rejected this argument in the case of *Marshall (Thomas) (Exports) Ltd* v. *Guinle* [1979] Ch 227 because this gave the guilty party the right to decide when the contract would come to an end and would allow the wrongdoer to profit from his wrongdoing. (An employer could, for example, commit a repudiatory breach just before the employee had the continuity to claim unfair dismissal and so exclude the employee's rights.) To argue that the innocent party should always accept the breach as terminating before the contract ends is somewhat false where the party has no choice, and therefore the court in the later case of *Gunton* v. *Richmond-upon-Thames London Borough Council* [1980] IRLR 321 tried to find a middle ground between the automatic termination theory and the acceptance theory. Shaw LJ said that in some situations the nature of the repudiatory act was such that it automatically destroyed the contract and acceptance is therefore unnecessary, for example a dismissal by the employer. In other situations, however, the repudiation is not so straightforward, for example a change of contractual terms, and in these situations an acceptance of the termination would be needed by the innocent party before the contract came to an end. The House of Lords, while accepting this argument in *Rigby* v. *Ferodo Ltd* [1988] ICR 29, declined to comment on situations such as a wrongful dismissal by the employer or a walk-out by the employee who then fails to return. In *Smith* v. *Phil's TV Service* (1991) IDS Brief 447 the employee walked out after a dispute with the employer. When he did not return for work the next day, the employer assumed he had resigned and wrote a letter to that effect. The Employment Appeal Tribunal held that the repudiatory breach by the employee would only terminate the contract when the employer accepted it as such. Here the employer had accepted it by his letter and therefore the employer had terminated the contract. It was up to the tribunal to decide if the dismissal was fair (see also *Boyo* v. *Lambeth London Borough Council* [1994] ICR 727). Thus a strike by an employee is a repudiatory breach, but it will not end the contract until the employer treats it as so doing by dismissing the strikers. This position is confirmed by statute in that by s.238 Trade Union and Labour Relations (Consolidation) Act 1992 unfair dismissal protection is afforded to strikers where there are selective dismissals for striking. Such protection would not be available if the fact of the strike terminated the contract automatically, as there would be no action by the employer needed to end the relationship.

It follows from the proposition that in the majority of situations the breach will not end the contract until it is accepted as such by the innocent party, that is if the breach is rectified before the acceptance then the contract continues as normal. In *Norwest Holst Group Administration Ltd* v. *Harrison* [1985] IRLR 240 the employee worked for the employer in a post which included a directorship. The contract was renewed every year. On 14 June he was told that he was to be transferred to another post which did not include a directorship. He replied by a letter headed 'without prejudice' that he assumed his contract had been terminated and asked if the employer wanted a meeting to sort out the matter amicably. The meeting was held on 24 June where he was offered his original post plus directorship. He purported to accept the original repudiatory breach by the employer and claimed unfair dismissal. It was held that there had been no dismissal. A repudiatory breach terminates the contract when it is unequivocally accepted as such by the innocent party. Here the employee had not unequivocally accepted the breach because his letter had been headed 'without prejudice'. It therefore followed that the employer could rectify his breach up to the time of the employee's acceptance and this is what had happened in this case. The employee had therefore resigned and there had been no breach by the employer entitling him to do so.

While the elective theory appears to have prevailed, it has to be said that it has prevailed with reluctance on the part of the judges. Lord Oliver, in *Rigby*, stated that he could see no reason in law why a contract of employment should be treated differently from any other contract and, in *Boyo*, Staughton LJ said that the principles decided in *Gunton* 'were distinctly lacking in rhyme or reason'. Even so, that court felt bound to apply *Gunton*. However, Ralph Gibson LJ gave clear support for the automatic theory. Further doubt has been cast on the elective theory by Sedley LJ in *Cerebus Software Ltd* v. *Rowley* [2001] IRLR 160. It may be that the days of the elective theory are coming to an end.

8.4 Resignation

An employer termination of the contract is called a 'dismissal'. An employee termination of the contract is a 'resignation' and, unless he has the statutory protection of constructive dismissal, the tribunal will have no jurisdiction in relation to unfair dismissal or redundancy. It follows, therefore, that if an employee accepts a repudiatory breach by the employer and terminates the contract, if he has less than one-year's continuity he may only claim damages for the breach.

If the words used by the employee are clear and unambiguous, then there is no problem legally. If, however, the words are ambiguous, then the test is that of a reasonable employer and his interpretation of the employee's intention. If the employee is given the option of resigning or being dismissed and chooses the former, he is treated as dismissed in law (*Robertson* v. *Securicor Transport Ltd* [1972] IRLR 70) but if the employee chooses to resign for other reasons, for example to avoid disciplinary procedures or because a financial inducement has been given, then that is a resignation and not a dismissal. In *Sheffield* v. *Oxford Controls* [1979] IRLR 133 the director of a small company fell out with the owner who asked him how much money he wanted to leave. They agreed on £10,000 and the director resigned. He then claimed unfair dismissal. It was held that there had been no dismissal. The offer of £10,000 had induced his resignation and not the fear of dismissal.

To be effective, the resignation must have an ascertainable date. If an employee states that he is resigning without the date of the resignation being clear, either expressly or impliedly, it is merely a statement of an intention to perform an act sometime in the future. Where there is such ambiguity, however, the employer would be better advised to insist on confirmation in writing before assuming the contract is at an end. This is also the safest course of action when the employee resigns in the heat of the moment because of an argument with the employer or because he is upset, even if the words are clear and unambiguous. In *Kwik-Fit (GB) Ltd* v. *Lineham* [1992] IRLR 156 Lineham was a manager. One night on his way home from the pub he used the depot toilet. This was not contrary to any rules and he reactivated the alarm. The security staff reported the visit and a director of the company felt that Lineham had committed a disciplinary offence and gave him a written warning in the presence of a junior employee. Lineham threw his keys on the counter and walked out. When he did not return the next day, the employer sent a letter confirming the termination of employment. In the claim for unfair dismissal the employer argued that the employee's actions constituted a resignation. The tribunal found that where there was an ambiguous resignation, the onus was on the employer to establish the true intention of the employee. The Employment Appeal Tribunal held that the employer was not under such a heavy burden unless there were special circumstances. Where these existed the employer should allow a reasonable period of time before accepting the resignation on face value. Here, special circumstances existed and the employer should have not assumed that there was a resignation. Lineham was unfairly dismissed.

8.5 Common Law Dismissal

The common law only recognises one act which can constitute dismissal and that is a termination by the employer with or without notice. It will be seen in the next chapter that where the employee has the protection of unfair dismissal or redundancy, that statute recognises two other situations where dismissal is deemed to have occurred. These situations will only normally come into effect, however, if the employee has one-year's continuous service and until then employees only have the protection of the common law. Once employees gain the required continuity, however, the statutory protection is in addition to the protection at common law and thus an employee may be able to claim for unfair dismissal in the tribunal and sue for a wrongful or unlawful dismissal. Given that termination by the employer is recognised by the statutory provisions on dismissal, it follows that the discussion below on what constitutes a dismissal is also relevant in the context of an unfair dismissal.

If the contract is terminated by the employer, this is a dismissal at common law, but this leaves the question: when is the action by the employer deemed to be an intention to terminate the contract? Just as the employee may use ambiguous words which may appear to be a resignation, so too the employer may use ambiguous words which the employee construes as a dismissal but that was not the intention of the employer. In *Futty* v. *Brekkes Ltd* [1974] IRLR 130 the tribunal was asked to interpret language used in a disagreement which took place on Hull docks. During the disagreement a fish filletter was told: 'If you don't like the job you can fuck off.' The employee did so and presented a claim for unfair dismissal. The employer argued that what the words meant were that if he did not like the job he was doing he could clock off and come back tomorrow. The employer also pointed out that colourful language was a normal occurrence within the context of the employment. The tribunal agreed with the employer and held that the words did not constitute a dismissal. The same conclusion with the same choice of words was also reached in the case of *Davy* v. *Collins Builders Ltd* [1974] IRLR 324. It should be noted that the industry is relevant as is the type of employee. In some cases such language will be construed as a dismissal (for example, if used to a secretary) and the use of swear words themselves may also be the basis of a claim for a constructive dismissal, if the employee has the correct continuity, on the basis of a breach of the implied duty of mutual respect.

If the words used do not display such dialectal originality as those above, then normally a dismissal will have occurred, therefore the more common phrases such as 'You're fired' or 'Collect your cards' or 'You are dismissed' will all constitute a dismissal. The tribunals, however, will again look to see the circumstances in which the words are spoken and deduce the intention of the employer. In *Tanner* v. *Kean* [1978] IRLR 110 the employer lost his temper with an employee who had taken the company van without consent. He ended a barrage of abuse with the words: 'That's it, you're finished with me.' The Employment Appeal Tribunal decided these words were spoken in anger and were not intended to be a dismissal. Likewise in *Martin* v. *Yeoman Aggregates Ltd* [1983] IRLR 49 the employer told the employee to leave after the employee had refused to perform a task. Within five minutes, however, the employer had recanted his words and suspended the employee instead so that a more rational decision could be made. The employee insisted on treating himself as dismissed. Kilner Brown J said that it was a matter of common sense vital to industrial relations that either party should be able to retract words spoken in the heat of the moment.

Summary dismissal

At common law the employer is required to give notice of termination to his employee, however the law has always been of the opinion that in some cases the employee's conduct justifies dismissal without notice, and should the situation arise the employer will not be in breach of contract. Such dismissals are known as 'summary' or 'instant' dismissals. While earlier cases gave the employer considerable latitude in this area, Edmund Davies J in *Wilson* v. *Racher* [1974] IRLR 114 said that the older cases treated the employee/employer relationship as akin to the relationship of czar and serf and would be decided differently today. This demonstrates that the attitude of the judges in relation to the type of conduct which allows the employer to dismiss without notice is constantly changing, as is the attitude towards the relationship itself.

Certain things do remain constant, however, and the law has always regarded dishonesty within the employment as gross misconduct justifying summary dismissal. In *Sinclair* v. *Neighbour* [1967] 2 QB 279 a manager took £15 from a till and left an IOU. He intended to replace the money, but his employer regarded his actions as dishonest and instantly dismissed him. His dismissal was held to be lawful. Serious breaches of duty will justify dismissal without notice (*Ross* v. *Aquascutum Ltd* [1973] IRLR 107), as will a refusal to obey a lawful and reasonable order and gross neglect. In relation to the last category, however, the consequences of the neglect and the position of the employee will be considered when the courts look to see if the dismissal is lawful. One single act of neglect is unlikely to justify instant dismissal unless the consequences are very serious. The employer will often in his own procedures lay down instances of conduct he considers will justify instant dismissal. While the court will allow an employer to lay down his own rules, it will not allow him to act in an autocratic manner. It is the court which eventually decides whether the conduct was serious enough to warrant instant dismissal and not the employer. Should the employer instantly dismiss in circumstances where he is not entitled to do so, the dismissal is wrongful or unlawful and the employee is entitled to damages for the employer's breach of contract. These damages will normally be the wages he would have received if he had been given notice.

Dismissal with notice

The protection given to employees at common law is that terminations by the employer should normally occur with notice. The notice the employer is required to give will be found in the contract, but this can be ousted if the employer is giving less than the statutory minimum periods of notice laid down by s.86 Employment Rights Act 1996, in which case the statutory minimum notice periods will apply. Those notice periods are as follows:

(a) employees with between four-weeks' and two-years' continuity – one week;
(b) employees with more than two-years' continuity – one week for every year of service subject to a statutory maximum of 12 weeks;
(c) employees should give a minimum of one-week's notice.

Should the contract give greater rights than the statute, the contract prevails; on the other hand, if the contract gives lesser rights than the statute, the contractual term is void and the statutory term is the one to be applied. If the contract is silent as to the notice period, the common law imposes a reasonable period which could be in excess of the statutory minimum. The fact that the statutory minimum will override lesser contractual periods can be important for the employee who is dismissed shortly before acquiring continuity for unfair dismissal or redundancy. (See next chapter on effective date of termination.) The Employment Appeal Tribunal has held that where the employee is dismissed by letter, the date of dismissal is the date that the employee reads the letter and not the date of delivery. There is no such concept as 'constructive knowledge' of the contents of the letter (*McMaster* v. *Manchester Airport plc* [1998] IRLR 112).

There are two situations where the contract will terminate before the expiry of the notice given. First is when the employee accepts payment in lieu of notice. This will terminate the contract immediately on the receipt of the wages. The employee will lose any rights to payment in lieu if the right to notice has been waived or lost (*Trotter* v. *Forth Ports Authority* [1991] IRLR 419 and *Baldwin* v. *British Coal Corporation* [1995] IRLR 139) given that the payment is in place of the notice the employee has the right to receive. The employee cannot insist on working his notice and refuse to accept payment in lieu (*Marshall (Cambridge) Ltd* v. *Hamblin* [1994] IRLR 260) given that there is no duty to provide work. The case of *Abrahams* v. *Performing Rights Society* [1995] IRLR 486 has stated, however, that if the contract gives the employer a right to pay in lieu, such a payment is not damages for a breach of contract (because there has been no breach), but the employer exercising a contractual right to make a lump sum payment. As such, although the employee will not gain the tax advantages associated with receiving contractual damages, as he is receiving a payment he is entitled to under the contract it is not subject to the rules of mitigation and therefore the employer cannot reduce the amount because the employee has failed to mitigate his loss. The second situation comes from the EAT decision in *Palfrey* v. *Transco plc* [2004] IRLR 916. In this case Palfrey was given notice of redundancy, his contract terminating on 19 May. He asked to leave on 31 March and Transco agreed and confirmed this would be his final day of employment. The EAT held that, on the facts, this was a withdrawal of the original notice date and a new date agreed. It would appear, however, that each case will depend on its own particular facts as in this case the effect of the decision was that Palfrey was out of time to claim unfair dismissal as his date of termination was 31 March and not 19 May. Clear evidence has to be available that any change is mutually agreed.

The amount of wages the employee is entitled to receive during his notice period is laid down by s.87 Employment Rights Act 1996. The employer must pay the normal week's pay even if the employee does not work because no work is provided, or because he is sick, or because he is on holiday. The employee is not entitled to payment, however, if he takes time off, he breaks his contract during the notice period or he goes on strike.

8.6 Reasons for Dismissal

The common law does not require that the employer has a fair reason to dismiss the employee, only that if the employee has been instantly dismissed, gross misconduct or gross neglect should have occurred. In relation to dismissals with notice, the reason for the dismissal is irrelevant. This has repercussions in relation to a dismissal which is originally wrongful in that if before the employee leaves the employment the employer discovers a reason which would justify instant dismissal, that reason can retrospectively legalise an original unlawful act. This is the complete reversal of the law on unfair dismissal when the reason for the dismissal is investigated by the tribunal at the time the dismissal occurred. While it may affect the issue of compensation, if the employer had no reason to dismiss at the time he made that decision, it is irrelevant to the issue of fairness if he discovers a reason during the employee's period of notice or after the employee has left. This means that the employee who is only protected by the common law may lose his right to damages depending on his reaction to hearing of his dismissal. In the old case of *Ridgeway* v. *Hungerford Market* (1835) 3 Ad & El 516 the employee was dismissed in the morning and told that his employment would terminate at the end of the day. This dismissal at the time was wrongful as the employee had not been given the correct amount of notice. The employee was asked to take notes at a meeting just before his employment ended and the meeting discussed the appointment of his successor. He wrote what the report describes as a protest on the minute book. It was held that although the original dismissal had been unlawful, his subsequent conduct was gross misconduct which justified instant dismissal and thus the original unlawful act had been rendered lawful retrospectively. This is also the case at common law where the employer only discovers the gross misconduct after he has unlawfully dismissed the employee. Again, the discovery will render the dismissal lawful retrospectively (*Boston Deep Sea Fishing and Ice Co* v. *Ansell* (1888) 39 Ch 339). It should be emphasised again, however, that this is the position at common law. Once the employee is protected by unfair dismissal provisions, the employer must have a statutory fair reason to dismiss and that reason must exist and be known to the employer at the time he dismisses, otherwise the dismissal will be unfair.

8.7 Procedure for Dismissal

At common law, unlike statute, there is normally no laid-down procedure for dismissal and as long as the employer gives the correct amount of notice the employee will have no claim. This position is vastly different once the employee is protected by unfair dismissal provisions in that a fair employer will have certain procedures laid down to deal with discipline, including dismissal, and if he has no procedures, the law will expect him to comply with the *ACAS Code of Practice on Disciplinary and Grievance Procedures*. In two situations, however, even though the employee only has common law protection, his employer may be required to comply with a procedure before dismissal. These situations are, first, where a disciplinary procedure has become part of the employee's contract and, second, where the employee is an office-holder or an occupant of a statutory position.

Contractual procedures

If the employee has had the employer's disciplinary procedures incorporated as part of his contract, then a failure to observe those procedures is a breach of contract. This may affect the remedy available to the employee, as we have already seen that while the courts are reluctant to force the parties to continue the contract, they have, on occasion, awarded an injunction against an employer to protect an employee and ensure that the contractual procedures are adhered to before the termination takes effect. It is unusual for the court to grant an injunction however. In *Marsh* v. *National Autistic Society* [1993] ICR 453 the employee was the principal of a special school. By his contract he was entitled to three-months' notice of termination. After an internal disagreement, the employee was dismissed with three-months' wages in lieu of notice. He sought an injunction restraining the employers from treating him as dismissed and requiring them to continue paying his wages on the basis that he had not accepted their repudiatory breach of contract and so the contract continued. Ferris J refused the injunctions on the basis that although there was authority for the acceptance theory at common law, those cases which supported the theory had the caveat that if the employment had *de facto* ceased, the employee could no longer perform his part of the bargain and therefore no action lay in debt for wages – there lay only an action for damages for breach of contract. The measure of damages was the wages due under the notice period, which in this case had been paid. In some cases the damages awarded for any breach may also include a sum to cover the period when the employee would have remained in employment had the contractual procedures been complied with (see Chapter 4).

Public law

In addition to any contractual procedures, if the employee is an office-holder or occupies a statutory position the law provides further protection in that the employer must comply with the rules of natural justice. Breach of the rules of natural justice will render any decision void and so leave the innocent party in the position he was in before the decision to dismiss was taken, that is, still employed, and he can seek a declaration to that effect. In the famous case of *Ridge* v. *Baldwin* [1964] AC 40 the dismissal of a chief constable was declared void because he had not been given the opportunity to make representations before the dismissal took place. While it will be seen that in employment cases the elements of natural justice which must be adhered to are similar, if not identical, to the rules of a fair hearing under unfair dismissal provisions, it is important to note that the consequences of breach are vastly different. If the rules of a fair hearing are broken in an unfair dismissal situation, normally the dismissal will be found to be unfair and compensation awarded as a remedy. The decision to dismiss is still a valid one although it has been found to be unfair in law. If the rules of natural justice are broken, the decision to dismiss is void and therefore, legally, never happened and the employee is still employed. The rules of natural justice, however, do not apply in a normal employment situation. As Lord Wilberforce said in the case of *Malloch* v. *Aberdeen Corporation* [1971] 1 WLR 1578:

> 'One may accept that if there are relationships in which all requirements of the observance of rules of natural justice are excluded – these must be confined to what have been called pure master and servant cases, which I take to mean cases in which there is no element of public employment or service, no support by statute, nothing in the nature of an office or status which is capable of protection.'

The elements of the rules which apply in employment cases are the right of a person to know the case against him, the right to an unbiased hearing, the right to put his side of the case and the right to an unbiased appeal. While this may seem to give the office-holder greater remedies than the employee, recent cases have limited the application of the rules. Certainly it appears that mere employment by a public authority does not mean that the employee holds a statutory position and thus he will only be protected by the normal unfair dismissal rules and not the rules of natural justice (*R* v. *East Berkshire Health Authority ex parte Walsh* [1984] IRLR 278) and it appears that only if the relationship is excluded from the normal statutory provisions, leaving the employee with no other protection, will natural justice apply (*R* v. *Secretary of State for the Home Office ex parte Benwell* [1985] IRLR 6). Many Crown employees are now on contracts of employment and on the basis of *Walsh* will thereby be protected by unfair dismissal provisions only in relation to their employment.

Having stated the above, should an office-holder fall within the ambit of public as opposed to private law his remedies are considerable. In addition to a declaration that his employment continues because of a breach of natural justice, other public law remedies of judicial review are open to him. Judicial review will lie on the basis of illegality, unreasonableness or procedural impropriety (*Council for the Civil Service Unions* v. *Minister for the Civil Service* [1985] AC 374) giving the availability of *certiorari* to quash the decision.

8.8 Remedies for Wrongful Dismissal

While the employment relationship is contractual, it has already been noted in Chapter 4 that because it is a personal contract the courts are unwilling to grant an injunction which would force the parties to continue the contract and are prevented by statute from issuing an order of specific performance. This means that, apart from in the circumstances where contractual procedures are broken and the court may issue an injunction, by far the most common remedy is damages. The measure of damages is limited to the amount of notice the employee would have received had the contract been adhered to and no account is taken of any prospective periods of unemployment he may have to endure as a result of the loss of his job. In *Janciuk* v. *Winterite Ltd* [1998] IRLR 63 the Employment Appeal Tribunal held that although damages may be awarded for failing to comply with a contractual disciplinary procedure, these damages will only reflect the period of time the employee's contract would have continued had the procedure been followed and cannot take into account the fact that had the procedure been adhered to, the employee may have not been dismissed. Furthermore, no account is taken of the manner of the dismissal, for example, a dismissal because of a false allegation of theft, or injury to feelings, even if the dismissal has affected the employee's future job prospects (*Addis* v. *Gramophone Co Ltd* [1909] AC 488 and *Meatyard* v. *St Edmunds College* (1998) IDS Brief 624). In *Malik* v. *BCCI* [1997] IRLR 462, however, the House of Lords held that where the employer conducts his business in a dishonest manner, and the employment relationship comes to an end, damages for breach of contract may include financial losses where the former employee's future job prospects are prejudiced by the damage to his reputation caused by the stigma of having worked for a dishonest employer. While it was thought that *Malik* may lead to a challenge to *Addis*, the House of Lords has affirmed the principle in *Johnson* v. *Unisys Ltd* [2001] IRLR 279, confirming that no damages are available in wrongful dismissal for any distress caused by the unfair manner of the dismissal or the damage caused to the employee's reputation. Furthermore their Lordships decided in *Johnson* that an employee claiming wrongful dismissal could not also bring a claim for a breach of mutual trust and confidence based on the same facts. This is explained by the Court of Appeal in *McCabe* v. *Cornwall CC* [2003] IRLR 87 as meaning that if there is identifiable damage caused by the breach which is separate from the damage caused by the dismissal it will be compensated (endorsed by *Dunnachie* v. *Kingston upon Hull City Council* [2004] EWCA Civ 84). *Eastwood* v. *Magnox Electric* [2004] IRLR 733 has extended this principle to unfair dismissal claims, thus an employee cannot use facts for the basis of an unfair dismissal claim and use the same facts to support a claim of a breach of mutual trust and confidence. These rules reflect the contractual position that damages for breach of contract should reflect the actual loss sustained. Note, however, the unusual case of *Gregory v. Wallace* [1998] IRLR 387 where the contract provided for two-years' notice and allowed the employee not to attend during the notice period and take other full-time employment. The Court of Appeal held that, given the clause in the contract allowing the employee to take on other work during the notice period, he was entitled to full contractual damages for a breach of the notice provision and no account would be taken of his earnings from his new employment.

Apart from lost wages, extra damages may be claimed where the contract envisages more than merely the pay, for example publicity or reputation, or where there are other contractual benefits such as a car (*Shove* v. *Downs Surgical plc* [1984] ICR 532), and it was stated *obiter* in *Robert Cort* v. *Charman* [1981] IRLR 437 that damages may include a sum to cover the loss of unfair dismissal compensation if the nature of the dismissal was such that the employee had been excluded from such protection, for example by the employer insisting on payment in lieu to avoid the employee gaining continuity for unfair dismissal (*Raspin* v. *United News Shops Ltd* [1999] IRLR 9). In addition, given that the damages reflect actual loss, should the employee be on a fixed term contract with no notice provision, the damages will reflect the loss of earnings for the rest of the unexpired term.

As with all contractual claims for damages, the employee is under a duty to mitigate his loss and therefore will be expected to look for other work, although he is entitled to look for work of a similar kind and at a similar level (but note *Gregory* v. *Wallace*, above). In *Yetton* v. *Eastwoods Froy* [1967] 1 WLR 104 a dismissed managing director had turned down the offer of a job as a junior manager. It was held that he had not failed to mitigate his loss by his refusal. However, if there is a contractual right to pay in lieu, there is no duty to mitigate on the part of the employee (*Abrahams*, above).

Again, because contractual damages are paid for actual loss, the court will deduct from the award the amount the employee would have paid in income tax and National Insurance Contributions. In addition, any benefits the employee may have received during his period of unemployment, such as jobseeker's allowance or income support, will also be deducted. Note the decision in *Fraser* v. *HLMAD* [2007] 1 All ER 383 where the Court of Appeal has held that where the loss exceeds the £25,000 limit on breach of contract jurisdiction in the employment tribunal, but the claimant chooses to take a claim to a tribunal, a claim for the remainder cannot be brought in the High Court.

Summary

1. Although the most common way that an employment relationship ends is an act of the parties, the law can operate in some circumstances to end the relationship automatically without liability on either side.

2. The most common way the relationship ends automatically is by frustration and the usual frustrating event is long-term sickness.

3. The parties may seek to end the relationship by agreement. The courts will protect an employee by ensuring that there is genuine agreement and an employee cannot contract out of his rights to sue in the tribunals or courts unless the employer has given consideration for such an agreement.

4. Breach by either party which goes to the root of the contract is repudiatory. The contract ends when the innocent party accepts the breach as a termination.

5. If the employee has less than one-year's continuity and accepts a repudiatory breach by the employer as terminating the contract, he can only sue for damages for a breach of contract. After one year the law calls such a breach a 'constructive' dismissal.

6. A repudiatory breach can be withdrawn before acceptance by the innocent party.

7. If the employee ends the relationship it is called a 'resignation'. If he is forced to resign or be dismissed, the law will treat his resignation as a dismissal.

8. Words of resignation or dismissal spoken in the heat of the moment may not be construed as such by the courts. The law looks to the intention of the party.

9. If the employer ends the relationship it is a dismissal, and in some situations the common law allows the employer to dismiss instantly.

10. Apart from the situations of instant dismissal at common law, the only right of the employee is the right to notice. Contractual notice which is less than the statutory minimum is void and the statutory notice will apply.

11. Acceptance of wages in lieu of notice terminates the contract on the date of acceptance and not when the notice expires.

12. At common law, information discovered by the employer during the notice period or after the employee has left is relevant to the issue of whether the dismissal was lawful or not.

13. If the employee is deemed to be an office-holder or the occupant of a statutory position, he will have increased protection in the form of the rules of natural justice and the availability of judicial review.

Exercises

1. Mary and Kath work for Keith's DIY shop. Both have been employed for 6 months.

    Mary was given three-days' notice of termination of contract last week. After she left, the employer discovered that for the last six weeks the till in the shop had been down by £50 per week. Mary is one of seven shop assistants.

    Kath was told last Friday morning that her employment would finish that afternoon. She shouted abuse at the manager and stormed off the premises shouting 'I'll get in first, I'm going and you know what you can do with your job.'

    Both Mary and Kath now wish to sue for a breach of contract. Advise them.

2. Bill has worked for Fred's Fashions for 51 weeks operating a machine that cuts out patterns. Last week he was told that because the manager's son needed a job he was being given two-days' notice as per his contract. He has never had any complaints about his work. He worked his notice and now wishes to know if he can claim unfair dismissal.

    Would your answer differ if, after he had left, Fred's Fashions discovered that because of Bill's negligent use of his machine they had to spend £1,500 on repair costs?

Further Reading

Brodie   *Specific Performance and Employment Contracts* (1998) 27 ILJ 79.

Brodie   *Wrongful Dismissal and Mutual Trust* (1999) 28 ILJ 260.

Carty   *Dismissed Employees: The Search for a More Effective Range of Remedies* (1989) 52 MLR 449.

Fodder and Freer   *The Effect of Contractual Provision for Payment in Lieu of Notice* (2001) 30 ILJ 215.

Forest   *Political Values in Individual Employment Law* (1980) 43 MLR 361.

Fredman and Lee   *Natural Justice for Employees: The Unacceptable Face of Proceduralism* (1986) 15 ILJ 15.

Fredman and Morris   *Public or Private? State Employees and Justicial Review* (1991) 107 LQR 298.

Halson   *Claims for Non-Pecuniary Loss in Employment Tribunals Following Johnson v. Unisys* (2003) 32 ILJ 214.

Kerr   *Contract Doesn't Live Here Anymore* (1984) 47 MLR 30.

McMullen   *Extending Remedies for Breach of the Employment Contract* (1997) 26 ILJ 245.

Sargeant   *Protecting Employees with Insolvent Employers* (2003) 32 ILJ 53.

White   *Repudiatory Breach and the Definition of Dismissal* (1997) 26 ILJ 252.

Chapter 9
Unfair Dismissal

Introduction

The concept of unfair dismissal was introduced into British law by the Industrial Relations Act 1971 as a result of the International Labour Organisation's Recommendation 119, which Britain accepted in 1964. The provisions within the Industrial Relations Act were the only ones to survive when the Labour government came into power in 1974 and were re-enacted in the Trade Union and Labour Relations Act of the same year. The present law relating to unfair dismissal is to be found in the Employment Rights Act 1996.

The reason for its introduction was that by 1970 there were a great number of unofficial strikes, many of which were a protest against dismissals. The common law has always provided inadequate remedies against dismissal, in that provided the employer complies with the relevant notice provisions within the contract, the employee has no protection against arbitrary dismissal. The introduction of the concept of an unfair dismissal was intended to give protection against the harshness of the common law and thus give rights in addition to the common law. These rights, however, do not apply to all employees but only to those who satisfy the qualifying criteria to make a claim. In essence, this means that all employees have the minimal protection of the common law and some employees have the additional protection of statutory unfair dismissal provisions.

Created by statute, unfair dismissal bears no relation to a common law breach of contract claim and thus a dismissal may be lawful, in that the contract has been complied with, and still be unfair. Conversely, a dismissal may be unlawful, in that a breach of contract has occurred, but be fair according to the statute. In *Treganowan* v. *Robert Knee & Co Ltd* [1975] IRLR 247 Ms Treganowan had been fairly dismissed but had been given insufficient notice. Her dismissal was therefore fair but unlawful (wrongful). Unfair dismissal does not look for a breach of contract on the part of the employer but a breach of the statute and the remedies which lie against an employer are not remedies which rely on a contractual claim, but rather recognise that the dismissed employee has a property right in his job. This means that the first remedy the tribunal should consider is reinstatement, that is, giving the employee his job back, and the second is re-engagement, that is, giving the employee an alternative job; and if those remedies are not practicable, financial compensation should be awarded based on age, years of service and, to some extent, actual loss.

It has already been noted, however, that not all people have the statutory protection. First, only employees are protected and not the self-employed. The distinction between an employee and an independent contractor has already been discussed. For these purposes the definition of 'employment' is found in s.230(1) Employment Rights Act 1996 which defines an employee as an individual who works under a contract of employment and which defines a contract of employment as a contract of service or apprenticeship, whether express or implied, oral or in writing. Employees must have been continuously employed for one year generally before they get the statutory protection, although there are certain exceptions where no continuity is needed. It used to be the case that part-time employees had to work for longer periods before they gained protection and part-time workers who worked less than eight hours a week had no protection at all. These restrictions were challenged in *R* v. *Secretary of State for Employment ex parte EOC* [1994] IRLR 176 where the House of Lords issued declarations that such restrictions on part-time workers were contrary to the Equal Treatment Directive, the Equal Pay Directive and Article 141 Treaty of Rome. As a result, the Employment Protection (Part-Time Employees) Regulations 1995 were enacted, removing all such restrictions from the right to claim unfair dismissal and redundancy, and now all employees need one-year continuity whatever their number of working hours. Originally the continuity period which applied in unfair dismissal cases was two years. The two-year rule was challenged in *R* v. *Secretary of State for Employment ex parte Seymour-Smith and Perez* [1997] IRLR 315 (HL). The Court of Appeal issued a declaration that at the time of the applicants' dismissals, the two-year requirement was indirectly discriminatory against women and contrary to the Equal Treatment Directive. On appeal to the House of Lords, that court discharged the declaration but referred various questions to the European Court of Justice. First, was unfair dismissal compensation pay for the purposes of Article 141? Second, if so, did the continuity requirements fall within the scope of Article 141 or the Equal Treatment Directive? Third, what was the legal test for establishing whether a measure adopted by a Member State has such a degree of disparate impact between men and women as to amount to indirect discrimination unless objectively justified? Fourth, when must this legal test be applied to the measure – when the measure is adopted, when it is brought into force, when the employee is dismissed or at some other time? Finally, what were the legal conditions for establishing objective justification for the purposes of indirect discrimination under Article 141 and in particular what material must the Member State adduce in support of its argument of justification? As has been noted, the decision of the European Court impacted not only on this area but also on discrimination generally. After the reference three things happened. In *Davidson* v. *City Electrical Factors Ltd* [1998] IRLR 108 the Scottish Employment Appeal Tribunal held that unfair dismissal complainants with between one and two-years' service had an enforceable right to a stay of application in order to preserve their position pending the outcome of *Seymour-Smith*. This led the president of the Employment Tribunals (England and Wales) to issue guidance to all regional employment tribunals ([1998] IRLR 351). The guidance stated that all new applications for unfair dismissal, where it appeared that the applicant had less than two-years' service, should be referred to the tribunal chair 'with a view to the case being stayed pending clarification from the higher courts on whether the merits of the complaint can be considered in the light of the length of service'. Thus all cases of between one and two-years' service were stayed pending the European Court ruling. Shortly after *Davidson* and the guidance, the Advocate-General gave his opinion in *Seymour-Smith* (1998) IRLB 599. It has to be said, however, that the opinion did not clarify the position at all. The opinion started by accepting that unfair dismissal compensation is pay for the purposes of Article 141, but nevertheless concluded that the conditions governing the right not to be unfairly dismissed fall to be considered in the context of the Equal Treatment Directive rather than Article 141. After this, however, the Advocate-General appeared to go off at a tangent. He argued that the basis on which the case was considered to date was wrong. He stated that because the two-year rule allowed an employer to dismiss an employee on grounds relating to her sex, the rule was directly contrary to the Directive, regardless of whether the percentage of women affected was greater or smaller than that of male employees. This was because it allowed an employer to dismiss a person with less than two-years' service on the grounds of her sex and she had no remedy. On the further questions referred, the Advocate-General expressed the opinion that in the actual case the difference in the proportions of men and women who could comply with the two-year continuity requirement was not sufficient to establish indirect discrimination. He thought that the point in time to assess the disparate impact was the duration of the qualifying period, and finally he noted that in the case there appeared to be no specific grounds and evidence capable of objectively justifying the measure.

The ECJ gave its decision in *Seymour-Smith* on 9 February ([1999] IRLR 253). In respect of the questions referred, the court decided first, that unfair dismissal compensation is pay for the purposes of Article 141. Second, the conditions determining whether an employee was entitled, where he had been unfairly dismissed, to obtain compensation fell within the scope of Article 141, but the conditions determining whether he could claim reinstatement or re-engagement fell within the scope of the Equal Treatment

Directive. Third, it was for the national court to determine the point at which the legality of the two-year rule was to be assessed. Fourth, in order to establish whether the rule was indirectly discriminatory to women, the national court must determine whether the statistics indicated that a considerably smaller percentage of women than men were able to comply with the rule. Lastly, if the rule was discriminatory, it was for the Member State to show that the rule reflected a legitimate aim of its social policy, that that aim was unrelated to any discrimination based on sex and that it considered that the means chosen were suitable for attaining that aim.

The court further stated that it was insufficient to consider the number of persons affected since that depended on the number of working people in the Member State, the national court had to look at the proportions of the relevant groups to determine whether the rule had a disparate effect. It further stated that on the relevant percentages in 1985 when the rule was introduced (77.4 per cent of men and 68.9 per cent of women could comply with the rule at that date) there did not appear to be a disparate impact. However, the court added that a lesser difference may indicate indirect discrimination if it showed 'a persistent and relatively constant disparity over a long period'. It would, nevertheless, be up to the national court to determine the conclusions to be drawn from such statistics.

The House of Lords decided the case in the light of the ECJ ruling ([2000] IRLR 263). Their Lordships seemingly appeared to disagree with the ECJ which appeared to be saying that the difference in the proportion of men and women who could comply with the two-year rule was not sufficiently great to constitute indirect discrimination. Lord Nicholls, with whom Lords Goff and Jauncey agreed, appeared to adopt the second test of indirect discrimination advocated by the ECJ by saying:

> 'I find myself driven to the conclusion that a persistent and constant disparity . . . in respect of the entire male and female labour forces of the country over a period of seven years cannot be brushed aside as insignificant or inconsiderable . . . I think these figures are adequate to demonstrate that the (two-year) qualifying period had a considerably greater adverse impact on women than on men.'

Their Lordships went on to say, however, that the government had introduced the two-year rule to increase employment (the argument being that employers were more likely to take on staff if they had a reasonable length of time during which they could dismiss without penalty) and it was not unreasonable for the government to wait a period of time to assess whether the introduction of the two-year service requirement had achieved the goal of increased employment. As such, although the two-year rule was indirectly discriminatory to women, the government had objectively justified its introduction.

The present government, when it came to power in 1997, had stated that it would reduce the qualifying period from two years to one year. It did this in 1999, prior to the House of Lords' decision and the relevant statutory provision is now s.108(1) Employment Rights Act 1996.

In addition to the restrictions above, certain classes of employee are excluded from the legislation. If the employee shows that he has the required continuity and he is not an excluded employee, he must prove that he has been dismissed and Chapter 8 has already shown the variations that can occur there! He must also present his claim to the tribunal within three months of the effective date of the termination of his employment, unless the tribunal feels that it was not reasonably practicable for the employee to present a claim within that time period (s.111(2) Employment Rights Act 1996). In *London International College* v. *Sen* [1993] IRLR 333 the employee had been dismissed on 9 July 1990 and having gone through the internal appeal procedures, he asked a solicitor the time limit for bringing an unfair dismissal complaint. He was told that he should submit his complaint on or before 9 October 1990. He also contacted the Central Office of Industrial (Employment) Tribunals where a member of staff confirmed that the relevant date was 9 October. In fact 9 October was a day late and his complaint should have been submitted by 8 October. The employment tribunal found that it was not reasonably practicable for Sen to present his claim within three months of the effective date of termination of his contract. The employer appealed, arguing on the basis of *Jean Sorrel* v. *Rybak* [1991] IRLR 153 that as Sen had consulted a solicitor the exception to the three-month rule did not operate. (The *Rybak* case is authority for the proposition that professional advice from a solicitor, which is wrong, does not make it impracticable to present a claim in time and that therefore the claim should not be heard and the employee must sue his solicitor for negligence. Incorrect advice from the tribunal office, on the other hand, will allow the exception to operate.) The Employment Appeal Tribunal held that the employment tribunal was entitled to find that the substantial cause of Sen failing to present his case in time was advice from the tribunal and not the solicitor. The employer appealed to the Court of Appeal which upheld the Employment Appeal Tribunal, adding that there was no cut-and-dried rule that consulting a skilled adviser will always prevent an employee from presenting a claim outside the three-month limit. These cases are now subject to *Chohan* v. *Derby Law Centre* [2004] IRLR 685 and *Marks and Spencer plc* v. *Williams-Ryan* [2005] EWCA Civ 70. In *Chohan* the EAT ruled that extending the time limit can be just and equitable where a claimant can show that the failure to lodge in time was the result of a legal adviser giving the wrong advice. In *Williams-Ryan* the claimant contacted the Citizens Advice Bureau (CAB) after being dismissed for gross misconduct. The CAB told her to complete the company's internal appeal procedure, but did not tell her of her right to complain to a tribunal. Her letter of dismissal outlined her right of appeal and told her of her right to lodge a complaint of unfair dismissal, but did not mention the three-month time limit. The claimant thought she had to go through the procedures before lodging a claim. The internal appeal took 3.5 months and she lodged her claim four months after her dismissal. The Court of Appeal reviewed the authorities and ruled that although a claimant cannot have a time limit extended where a solicitor has given negligent advice (*Rybak*) the situation is less clear where the negligent advice is given by the CAB. However, the Court of Appeal did not deal with the issue that it was the negligent failure of the CAB to tell her of her right to claim, nor the fact that the employer had told her of such a right but did not mention the time limits. The Court of Appeal found that as there was no authority on advice from the CAB, the original tribunal had not given a perverse decision when holding it was not reasonably practicable to present her case in time. It is debatable whether this is a softening of the law as if the employer had not delayed in the appeal, Williams-Ryan would have presented her claim in time and this influenced the Court of Appeal. Note also that this decision will be affected by the statutory disciplinary and grievance procedures (see below).

Account now has to be taken of technology. In *Tyne and Wear Autistic Society* v. *Smith* [2005] IRLR 336 Smith submitted his claim via the Employment Tribunal Service's website on the last day of the time limit. He received a receipt from the website but the claim did not reach ETS until the next day because the website was hosted by a commercial provider. The Employment Appeal Tribunal held that because the claim had reached the website and been accepted there, the claim had been presented in time.

In *Aniagwu* v. *London Borough of Hackney* [1999] IRLR 303 it was held that it was just and equitable to extend the three-month time limit when the complainant had delayed presenting his claim until he knew the outcome of an internal grievance procedure or appeal, and in *Schultz* v. *Esso Petroleum Company Ltd* [1999] IRLR 488 the Court of Appeal held that an employment tribunal had erred in finding that it was reasonably practicable for an applicant to bring his claim in time when, although well for the first seven weeks after his dismissal, he had been too ill to contact his solicitor in the last six weeks. The court held that the tribunal should take account of events at the end of the three-month period and not the beginning, and take all the circumstances into account (in that case, the fact that the applicant was hoping the employers would settle without recourse to a tribunal). A similar conclusion was reached in *Harris* v. *Towergate London Market Lt*d (2007) IDS 832 where, on selection for redundancy, Harris made a grievance complaint during which there were further discussions about her selection. The Employment Appeal Tribunal held that the discussions meant it was reasonable for Harris to assume that the dismissal procedure was still continuing and thus the time limit ran from the date the procedures ended and not the date of dismissal. However, the Court of Appeal took a much stricter approach in *London Underground Ltd* v. *Noel* [1999] IRLR 621. In this case the applicant was dismissed but then offered a lower grade job on a reduced salary within the three-month period. She accepted the offer which was withdrawn shortly after the limitation period had expired. The Court of Appeal held that it was reasonably practicable for her to present her complaint in time and the offer of re-employment did not make it reasonably impracticable. This seems to be a harsh decision which could be abused by unscrupulous employers.

Once the employee has surmounted these hurdles the burden shifts to the employer, who must prove that his reason for dismissal was one of the statutory fair reasons, and during the whole of the hearing the tribunal must consider whether the employer acted reasonably in how he handled the dismissal and whether dismissal was an appropriate sanction in the light of the employee's 'offence'. While all of this may seem complex, it means that any unfair dismissal case nicely divides itself into certain questions:

▷ Has the employee the required continuity?
▷ Is the employee excluded from the statute?
▷ Has the employee been dismissed?
▷ Has the employer got a statutory fair reason for dismissal?
▷ Has the employer acted reasonably?

9.2 Continuity of Employment

Most employment protection rights require a period of continuous employment before the right can be claimed. In most cases of unfair dismissal, the necessary period of continuous employment is one year. Continuity is defined in ss.212–218 Employment Rights Act 1996 and the aim is to exclude the common law rules that a change of terms means a new contract comes into force. Such a rule operating would mean that, for example, every time an employee received a pay rise, a new contract would come into being and the old contract would cease to exist. Given that many employees receive annual pay rises, to acquire rights based on the length of the contract would mean that employees who received annual pay rises would never acquire the protection from unfair dismissal. The provisions, therefore, base eligibility on the length of employment and not the contract. In *Wood* v. *York City Council* [1978] IRLR 228 the employee had a variety of jobs with the city council for three years and then he resigned to take up a position with the council's York Festival Office. He was made redundant one year later. It was held that he had sufficient continuity to claim redundancy pay. His employment was with the same employer even though there had been a change of job, a change of location and a change in the terms of employment. *Wood* has been followed in *Cranston* v. *Harwich Dock Co Ltd* [1998] IRLR 567. In this case the employee resigned on Friday and was re-engaged on the following Monday to take advantage of a pension scheme. He agreed with his employer that his resignation would break his continuity. When he was dismissed some months later and claimed unfair dismissal, the employers argued that he did not have the continuity to claim. The Employment Appeal Tribunal, overturning the employment tribunal stated that s.203 Employment Rights Act 1996 states that it is not generally possible for employers and employees to enter a contract which deprives the employee of his statutory rights. *Morris* v. *Walsh Western UK Ltd* [1997] IRLR 562 confirms that this means that the parties cannot agree to disapply the continuity rules. As such, Cranston had the requisite continuity to claim unfair dismissal.

Continuity starts when the contractual employment starts and not the actual employment (*General of the Salvation Army* v. *Dewberry* [1984] IRLR 222) and will normally continue until the employment comes to an end. As will be seen, certain breaks in the period will not stop the running of the continuity and will be counted in the final computation. Other breaks will not stop the running of the period but will be discounted in the final computation. In one case, continuity will stop altogether. This is when the contract involves an illegal act. In *Hyland* v. *J H Barker (North West) Ltd* [1985] IRLR 403 a lorry driver who had been employed for 16 years received a tax-free lodging allowance for one month in the 12 months prior to his dismissal. It was held that he did not have the continuity to claim unfair dismissal because the illegality wiped out the period when the contract was legal and continuity started from scratch once the illegality ceased. (Note, however, *Hewcastle Catering Ltd* v. *Ahmed* [1992] ICR 626.) The recent cases of *Enfield Technical Services* v. *Payne/Grace* v. *BF Components Ltd* [2007] All ER 394 may throw doubt on this. In the cases the Employment Appeal Tribunal held that to defeat an unfair dismissal claim on the grounds of an illegal (and therefore void) contract, there must be some misrepresentation or some attempt to hide the true nature of the relationship and the fact that the parties have wrongly labelled the relationship or have an arrangement which has the effect of depriving the Inland Revenue of monies is not enough to render the contract illegal and void. This is an important decision and leave has been given to appeal to the Court of Appeal.

Weeks which do not break continuity and count towards the final computation

The provisions envisage situations where the employee will not be at work but his continuity will continue. Section 212(3) Employment Rights Act 1996 states that where there is:

(a) incapability due to sickness or injury;
(b) a temporary cessation of work; or
(c) an absence due to an arrangement or custom;

these absences shall not break the continuity and shall count in the final computation.

In relation to sickness or injury, the employee will retain continuity for 26 weeks of illness. In *Donnelly* v. *Kelvin International Services* [1992] IRLR 496 the Employment Appeal Tribunal discussed whether the incapability is in relation to the employee's particular work or any work. It opted for the former interpretation and thus Donnelly, who while ill had taken a less demanding job for a month and then returned to his employer when his health improved, had not lost his continuity. It must be the illness which is the cause of the absence for the provisions to apply, however; if after the illness the employee remains off work for some other reason, if that reason does not fall within s.212(3), there will be a break in the continuity period (*Pearson* v. *Kent County Council* [1993] IRLR 165).

A temporary cessation of work envisages situations where, not because of the fault of the employee, no work is available for him. It is work for the particular employee which must have temporarily ceased and not work in the factory itself. In *Fitzgerald* v. *Hall, Russell & Co Ltd* [1970] AC 984 the employee, a welder, was laid off temporarily, even though others of his colleagues were still employed to weld. The House of Lords decided that the section required the court to look at the situation of the individual employee, and not the situation of the employer as a whole. If, however, the work of the employee is given to someone else, there is no cessation for the purposes of the section (*Bryan* v. *Birmingham City District Council* [1987] IRLR 191).

The section will only operate if the cessation of work is temporary and this leaves the question of how long is 'temporary'. The aim of s.212 was to protect workers in particular industries where lay-offs are common, but the effect has been much wider. In *Bentley Engineering Co Ltd* v. *Crown* [1976] IRLR 146 a period of absence of two years was held to be temporary as it was a relatively short period in the context of the whole employment history. This means that the decision as to whether the cessation is temporary takes place at the end of the break, when all factors are taken into account. What the parties intend is, to a large extent, superfluous as circumstances may change during the absence. If the employee resigns or is dismissed during the absence, it ceases to be a temporary cessation, even if the employee resumes employment with the same employer (*Wessex National Ltd* v. *Long* (1978) 13 ITR 413). In the important decision of *Ford* v. *Warwickshire County Council* [1983] 2 AC 71 the employee was a teacher who was employed on a session basis. Her contracts ended in July and were renewed in September. This arrangement continued for eight years. The House of Lords stated that the holidays were a temporary cessation of work and that the employee had eight years' continuity, given the length of the employment and the length of the holidays. 'Temporary', according to the House of Lords in the case, means transient. Although the Employment Appeal Tribunal has stated that a strict mathematical approach is wrong (*Flack* v. *Kodak Ltd* [1986] IRLR 255), in *Berwick Salmon Fisheries Co Ltd* v. *Rutherford* [1991] IRLR 203 the same tribunal held that it would not be possible to call a cessation temporary when the periods of lay-off were longer than the periods of working.

Where the absence is by arrangement or custom, again s.212(3) will preserve continuity, although for the section to apply the agreement or custom must be that continuity is so preserved. In *Lloyds Bank Ltd* v. *Secretary of State for Employment* [1979] IRLR 41 an employee worked one week on, one week off, for five years. When she became pregnant, the employers paid her statutory maternity pay and sought to recover from the Maternity Fund. It was held that she had been continuously employed for five years and her employers were entitled to recover. From *Morris* v. *Walsh Western UK Ltd* (above) the arrangement with the employer must be in place when the employee is absent, it cannot be entered into retrospectively when the employee returns to work. The most common example under this provision is that of secondment to another employer or where the employee is allowed time off for personal reasons. Continuing to pay the employee is strong evidence that there is an arrangement that continuity should continue.

In addition to the situations listed in s.212, if a person is reinstated or re-engaged after an unfair dismissal or redundancy, he can count the period between his dismissal and reinstatement or re-engagement for continuity purposes (s.219).

Weeks which do not break continuity, but which do not count in the final computation

Any period during which the employee is on strike or locked out by his employer does not break his continuity, but such weeks will be deducted from the final computation of his continuity period (s.216). The question of when an employee is deemed to be on strike is discussed later in this chapter. Likewise, periods spent in the armed forces do not break the continuity but are not part of the final calculation (s.217).

Should the employee not fall within the paragraphs above, any break in employment will break the continuity period and a new period will begin when the employment next starts. Any illegality in the contract may stop continuity running, and a new period will start when the illegality ceases (*Hyland* v. *J H Barker (North West) Ltd*, above, although note *Enfield Technical Services* v. *Payne/Grace* v. *BF Components Ltd*, above).

Change of employer

Under the common law, only service with the same employee is calculated for continuity purposes. This means that should the employee change his job, the continuity he acquired with his old employer is ignored and a new period commences with the start of his new employment. This is also the situation when his employer sells his business to another employer. Again the employer has changed and therefore continuity is broken. This can be hard on the employee, who, through no decision of his own, may lose years of continuous service and with it a great deal of statutory protection. The law, therefore, protects certain employees when a business is sold as a going concern. The protection, however, will not apply when only the assets of a business are sold, even if the new employer takes on the old employees. In that case, the employees must claim a redundancy payment from their old employer and start continuity afresh with their new employer.

Protection for employees comes from two sources – s.218 Employment Rights Act 1996, and the Transfer of Undertakings (Protection of Employment) Regulations 2006. While two sources exist, it should be noted that in fact the Act and the Regulations overlap and often a transfer will be covered by both.

Employment Rights Act 1996

Continuity will be preserved in the following circumstances:

(a) a trade, business or undertaking is transferred (s.218(2));
(b) a body corporate is substituted for another body corporate by statute (s.218(3));
(c) an employer dies and the employee is retained by his personal representatives or trustees (s.218(4));
(d) there is a change of partners, personal representatives or trustees (s.218(5));

(e) the employee is taken on by an associated employer of his employer (s.218(6)).

For s.218(2) to apply the business must be transferred as a going concern. If only the assets are transferred, this does not fall within the section and continuity will not be preserved. In *Woodhouse* v. *Peter Brotherhood Ltd* [1972] 2 QB 520 the employers manufactured diesel engines and on moving part of their operation to Manchester, sold the factory and machinery to Peter Brotherhood who manufactured spinning machines, compressors and steam turbines, although they completed four engines begun by the original employer before engaging in their own work. Woodhouse was employed on the engines before being made redundant. The Court of Appeal held that there was not a transfer of a business but only of physical assets as the business of the new employer, while using the same machinery, was totally different from that of the old. A similar conclusion was reached in *Melon* v. *Hector Powe Ltd* [1981] ICR 43 where despite the fact that the new employers finished the work of the old employers before starting their own business, there was not a relevant transfer for the purposes of s.218(2). How different the new business must be to prevent the operation of the provision is up to the court. In *Crompton* v. *Truly Fair (International) Ltd* [1975] IRLR 250 the old employers manufactured children's clothes while the new employers manufactured men's trousers. It was held that there had been no transfer of the business. Likewise it has been held that the transfer of a franchise is not within the section.

For s.218(2) to operate, the business and physical assets must be transferred to the new employer, along with the goodwill. In *Blumestead* v. *John Cars Ltd* (1967) 2 ITR 137 the employee worked for successive owners of a concession at a petrol station. It was held that he did not have continuity because only the right to sell petrol had been transferred and no physical assets.

The section states: 'the period of employment of an employee . . . at the time of the transfer counts as a period of employment with the transferee' but this leads to the question: when does the transfer actually take place? The question is a perplexed one as shown by the Court of Appeal decision in *Teesside Times Ltd* v. *Drury* [1980] IRLR 72 where the employee was dismissed during negotiations for a transfer when a verbal agreement had been reached, but before the contract was signed. The court held that continuity continued with the new employer. While Stephenson LJ thought that the transfer is not necessarily the actual transfer but also the processes which are part of it, Goff LJ thought that transfer meant the moment when the transaction of transfer was effected. The later Employment Appeal Tribunal decision of *Macer* v. *Abafast Ltd* [1990] IRLR 137 has said that tribunals should lean in favour of that interpretation which best gives effect to the preservation of continuity of service. In *Clark Tokesley Ltd t/a Spell Brook Ltd* v. *Oakes* [1998] IRLR 577 the Court of Appeal interpreted the phrase to mean during the course of the transfer given that two out of three judges in *Drury* interpreted transfer as the date of the actual transfer and so created ambiguity. The purpose of the provision was to provide a period of continuous employment for the purposes of the Act even though the person at the particular time might not be in employment.

While the rest of s.218 is, to a large extent, self-explanatory, some explanation of subsection 6 is needed. This states that continuity will be preserved if the employee is employed by an associated employer of the original employer. The definition of associated employer is found in s.231 Employment Rights Act 1996. In essence, employers are associated if one has control over the other or both are under the control of a third. Control means legal control rather than ownership of shares and therefore the voting power of the shares is important (*South West Launderettes Ltd* v. *Laidler* [1986] IRLR 305) and does not include negative control, so that a person who holds 50 per cent of the voting shares does not have control because he can thwart the other shareholders. Singular denotes the plural, therefore control can be exercised by a group of individuals, however, to be associated employers, the same group must be present in both companies (*Poparm Ltd* v. *Weeks* [1984] IRLR 388). Thus if a husband and wife own 60 per cent of the shares in X Ltd and the husband and his brother own 80 per cent of the shares in Y Ltd, they are not associated employers for the purposes of paragraph 18. The subsection is, however, wide enough to include overseas companies. In *Hancill* v. *Marcon Engineering Ltd* [1990] IRLR 15 the employee had worked abroad for an American firm and then in England for a British company which dismissed him. Both were wholly owned subsidiaries of a Dutch company. The employee sought to include his time worked for the American company in his continuity period. At first instance his claim was dismissed because the tribunal argued that an American company could not be a limited company under s.231. The Employment Appeal Tribunal overruled the decision. In perceiving the intention of parliament, the Employment Appeal Tribunal said: 'It seems to us here that a coach and four could easily be driven round a few corners and then straight through the provision of this legislation if the word company (in s.231) were only to include a UK Ltd company when the overseas vehicle is to all intent and purposes identical.'

Transfer of Undertakings (Protection of Employment) Regulations 2006

Further rights are contained in the above Regulations. The original Regulations, which were enacted in 1981, were brought in to give effect to

EC Council Directive 77/187 (the Acquired Rights Directive). This Directive has now been codified by the Acquired Rights Directive 2001 (2001/123/EC) and transposed into UK law by the Transfer of Undertakings (Protection of Employment) Regulations 2006. The aim of the Directive is to ensure that on the transfer of an undertaking the contractual rights of the employees are maintained.

The history of the Regulations

Some detail about the original Regulations, and the case law thereunder, is necessary to understand the 2006 Regulations. Until amendments introduced by s.33 Trade Union Reform and Employment Rights Act 1993, the original Regulations defined an undertaking as any trade or business and did not include an undertaking which was not in the nature of a commercial venture. This meant that undertakings which had a charitable status did not fall within the Regulations (*Woodcock* v. *Committee of the Friends School* [1987] IRLR 98), nor did the transfer of services in local government to private contractors. It could be argued, however, that there is no requirement that the business must be a commercial venture under the Employment Rights Act 1996 when looking at the interpretation provisions in s.235. Therefore, even if the employee was not protected by the Regulations, his continuity could still be preserved by s.218. The Employment Appeal Tribunal in *Stirling* v. *Dietsman Management Systems Ltd* [1991] IRLR 368 held, however, that the definition of business within the (now) Employment Rights Act 1996 could not be used to widen the definition of a commercial venture under the Regulations. Further, what was or was not a commercial venture was a question of fact for the tribunal.

The restriction of the Regulations to commercial ventures did not fully implement the EC Acquired Rights Directive. The amendments made by the 1993 Act were by no means in the original bill and were introduced during the parliamentary process after the ECJ decision of *Dr Sophie Redmond Stitchting* v. *Bartol* [1992] IRLR 366. In this case the Sophie Redmond Foundation carried out certain local council functions in relation to drug addicts. The local authority decided to switch the functions to another foundation and some of the employees from Sophie Redmond were transferred to the second foundation. The issue for the ECJ was whether the Dutch provisions implementing the Directive applied to the transfer of the functions between the two foundations. The ECJ held that a legal transfer was wide enough to include the situation when a public body terminated a subsidy to one body and transferred it to another with similar aims. Second, the court held that there would be a transfer of an undertaking as long as whatever unit was being transferred retained its factual identity, thus qualifying as a business or part of a business.

Bartol (above) and other cases show that the ECJ, in the early years of the Directive, took a broad view of what constituted a business. In *Watson Rask and Christiansen* v. *ISS Kantineservice A/S* [1993] IRLR 133 the issue came before the ECJ again. When deciding whether a business had been transferred, previous UK decisions had looked for some transfer of ownership (for example *Stirling*, above) and therefore had decided that the contracting out of a service which was peripheral to the main activity of the organisation, such as catering or security, was not the transfer of an undertaking. In *Watson Rask*, Philips A/S contracted out its canteen service to ISS. The terms of the contract were that ISS would receive a fee from which labour, management and administrative costs would be met. Philips would provide the premises, equipment, refuse collection and cleaning products. ISS would offer employment to Philip's employees. ISS made minor changes to the terms of employment and two employees complained. ISS argued that there was no contract involving a change in ownership, merely a transfer of an internal service to an outside contractor. That contractor had so many restrictions placed upon him that there was no change in the ownership of the service. ISS also argued that no assets were transferred, no customers were transferred and there was no profitable objective because ISS was merely providing a service to Philip's staff.

The ECJ rejected all the arguments and held that the Directive applied where, following a legal transfer or merger, there is a change in the legal or natural person who is responsible for carrying on the business and who by virtue of that fact incurs the obligation of an employer *vis-à-vis* the employees of the undertaking, regardless of whether or not ownership of the undertaking is transferred. The court continued that it was necessary to consider all the factual circumstances, including:

- the type of business or undertaking concerned;
- whether the business's tangible assets are transferred;
- whether or not the majority of the employees are transferred;
- the value of the intangible assets at the time of the transfer;
- whether or not customers are transferred;
- the degree of similarity of activities before and after the transfer;
- the period, if any, for which those activities are suspended.

These were all questions which an earlier ECJ in *Spijkers* v. *Gebroeders Benedik Abattoir CV* [1986] CMLR 296 stated must be asked when looking to see if there was a relevant transfer under the Directive. Furthermore, the court in *Spijkers* stated: 'the decisive criterion for establishing the existence of a transfer within the meaning of the EU Acquired Rights Directive is whether the entity in question retains its identity.'

Watson Rask was followed in the UK by the cases of *Dines v. Initial Health Care Services* [1994] IRLR 336 and *Kelman v. Care Contract Services* [1995] ICR 260 and was applied to first or second generation contracting out. In addition, the Directive was held to apply where there was a transfer of one employee (*Schmidt v. Spar- und Leihkasse der Fruheren Amter Bordesholm, Keil und Cronshapen* [1995] ICR 237 (ECJ), but does not apply where there is a transfer to complete a one-off contract (*Ole Rygaard v. Dansk Arbejdsgiverforening* [1996] ICR 333, although see below).

The cases above established that the Directive and hence the original Transfer of Undertakings (Protection of Employment) Regulations applied to the contracting out of local authority services under the Compulsory Competitive Tendering policies of the previous government. There were attempts by a number of European countries to restrict the scope of the Directive in these situations but all met with opposition from the European Parliament. However, an unexpected decision from the European Court of Justice led to a restriction in the application of the Directive and created uncertainty once again. In *Suzen v. Zehnacker Gebaudereinigung GmbH Krankenhausservice and Lefarth GmbH* [1997] ICR 662 Suzen was a cleaner working for a company that had a contract to clean a school. When the contract came to an end, Suzen, along with seven of her colleagues, were dismissed. The school entered a contract with another company to provide cleaning services but that company did not take on Suzen and she commenced legal proceedings in the national court which referred a number of questions to the European Court, the most pertinent being whether the circumstances gave rise to the transfer of an undertaking. The court stated that the question was to be determined by reference to the criteria laid down in *Spijkers*. The court, however, went on to say:

> 'the mere fact that the service provided by the old and the new awardees of a contract is similar does not therefore support the conclusion that an economic entity has been transferred. An entity cannot be reduced to the activity entrusted to it. Its identity also emerges from other factors such as its workforce, its management staff, the way in which its work is organised, its operating methods or indeed, where appropriate, the operational resources available to it. The mere loss of a service contract to a competitor cannot therefore by itself indicate the existence of a transfer within the meaning of the Directive. In those circumstances, the service undertaking previously entrusted with the contract does not, on losing a customer, thereby cease to exist, and a business or part of a business belonging to it cannot be considered to have been transferred to the new awardee of the contract.'

The court further stated that the Directive only applied where the transfer involved the transfer of significant tangible or intangible assets or a major part of the workforce who provided the service prior to the transfer. *Suzen* was followed in the UK courts in *Betts v. Brintel Helicopters* [1997] ICR 792 and *Superclean Support Services plc* v. *Lansanna and Wetton Cleaning Services* (1997) IDS Brief 596. However, there were cases where the contracting out of services has been held to be covered by the Directive and thus the Regulations, despite *Suzen*. In *Highland Council* v. *Walker* (1998) IDS Brief 606 the Employment Appeal Tribunal refused to overturn the decision of the employment tribunal that the transfer of dog warden services from a contractor back to the local council, which involved the transfer of one employee, was a transfer under the Regulations. Although the employment tribunal had decided on the basis of *Schmidt* and prior to *Suzen*, the Employment Appeal Tribunal said that the employment tribunal, after careful consideration of the facts, had decided that the lack of transfer of assets did not preclude the transfer of an undertaking and such an approach was not precluded by *Suzen*. Similarly, in *Holmes* v. *Sita (GB) Ltd & FM Conway* (1998) IDS Brief 606 the transfer of 10 out of 15 employees, with no transfer of any assets, was deemed to be a transfer under the Regulations. Indeed, the Court of Appeal in *Betts* acknowledged that where there is a labour intensive undertaking, there can be a relevant transfer where a major part of the workforce is transferred even though no physical assets are transferred. The potential loophole this can create has hopefully been closed by the recent Employment Appeal Tribunal decision in *ECM (Vehicle Delivery Services) Ltd* v. *Cox* (1998) IRLB 596 where the tribunal decided that a transferee could not avoid the operation of the Regulations by refusing to take on the transferor's workforce. In the case, the transferor had lost a business and not merely a customer, therefore the decision is consistent with *Suzen*.

It can be seen that what constituted the transfer of an undertaking was therefore highly complex. On 4 June 1998 the EU Social Affairs Committee reached an agreement on a Directive amending the original Acquired Rights Directive. The new Directive (98/50/EC) amended Articles 1–7 of the 1977 Directive and was implemented by the UK in 1999. Article 1 of the new Directive stated that:

> 'there is a transfer within the meaning of this Directive where there is a transfer of an economic entity which retains its identity, meaning an organised grouping of resources which has the objective of pursuing an economic activity, whether or not that activity is central or ancillary.'

The amendments made to the original Directive gave a clearer definition of what was meant by a transfer. As such, how far *Suzen* remained sound was questioned by the Employment Appeal Tribunal in *RCO Support Services and Aintree Hospital Trust* v. *UNISON* [2000] IRLR 624. In this case there was a change in the cleaning and catering contractors following a change in hospitals providing in-patient care. None of the staff were taken on by the new contractors. The employment tribunal, however, found that there was a transfer under the Transfer of Undertakings (Protection of Employment) Regulations because the cleaning and catering activities were economic entities which retained their identity after the transfer. The EAT stated that *Suzen* could no longer be safely relied upon and the absence of a transfer of significant assets or of a major part of the workforce did not necessarily mean that a transfer has not occurred. The appeal tribunal stated that it was bound to follow *ECM* in preference to *Betts* and refused to limit *ECM* to cases where the transferee refuses to take on the transferor's workforce to avoid the application of the Transfer of Undertakings (Protection of Employment) Regulations. (See also *Cheesman* v. *R Brewer Contracts Ltd* [2001] IRLR 144 and *ADI (UK) Ltd* v. *Willer* [2001] IRLR 542.) In *Argyll Training Ltd* v. *Sinclair and Argyll & The Islands Enterprise Ltd* [2000] IRLR 630, the Scottish Employment Appeal Tribunal also held that *Suzen* could not be relied upon to establish that there was no transfer if significant assets or a major part of the workforce were not transferred. Furthermore, in *Argyll* the appeal tribunal held that the decision in *Ole Rygaard* (above), that there can be no transfer within the meaning of the Directive where the transfer is to complete a one-off contract, would, if given a broad interpretation, 'give rise to many doubts and difficulties' and thus refused to accept that a transfer of an entity whose activities were limited to one specific contract could not be a protected transfer under the Transfer of Undertakings (Protection of Employment) Regulations.

As seen above, there was still confusion where there were service provision changes. The Transfer of Undertakings (Protection of Employment) Regulations 2006 specifically cover such transfers.

What is a 'relevant transfer'?

Regulation 3 of the 2006 Regulations gives two situations which constitute a relevant transfer. Regulation 3(1)(a) is very similar to the wording in the 1981 Regulations and states that a 'relevant transfer' is:

> 'a transfer of an undertaking, business or part of an undertaking or business situated immediately before the transfer in the United Kingdom to another person where there is a transfer of an economic entity which retains its identity.'

Regulation 3(2) defines an 'economic entity' as an 'organized grouping of resources which has the objective of pursuing an economic activity whether or not that activity is central or ancillary'. Regulation 3(4)(a) states that the Regulations apply to both private and public bodies whether or not they are operating for gain. As such, it is clear that the Regulations are picking up on the old case law discussed above such as *RCO Support Services*, *Argyll Training Ltd* and *Cheesman*.

Regulation 3(1)(b) defines the second type of relevant transfer which is called a 'service provision change'. This applies where:

'(i) activities cease to be carried out by a person (a client) on his own behalf and are carried out instead by another person on the client's behalf (a contractor);

(ii) activities cease to be carried out by a contractor on a client's behalf (whether or not those activities had previously been carried out by the client on his own behalf) and are carried out instead by another person (a subsequent contractor) on the client's behalf; or

(iii) activities cease to be carried out by a contractor or subsequent contractor on a client's behalf (whether or not those activities had previously been carried out by the client on his own behalf) and are carried out instead by the client on his own behalf.'

The above will only fall within the regulations if Regulation 3(3) is satisfied. This states:

'(a) immediately before the service provision change –
(i) there is an organized grouping of employees situated in Great Britain which has as its principal purpose the carrying out of activities concerned on behalf of the client;
(ii) the client intends that the activities will, following the service provision change, be carried out by the transferee other than in connection with a single specific event or of a short-term duration; and
(b) the activities concerned do not consist wholly or mainly of the supply of goods for the client's use.'

Again, it can be seen that the Regulations are picking up on the case law discussed above such as *ECM* and *RCO Support Services*. The Regulations would also seem to endorse *Ole Rygaard*.

The effect of a transfer

If there is a transfer which falls under the Regulations, employees have certain rights. Employee is defined by Regulation 2(1) as an individual who works under a contract of service or apprenticeship or otherwise. In *Cowell v. Quilter Goodison Co Ltd and QG Management Services Ltd* [1989] IRLR 392 the Court of Appeal held that an equity partner in a firm which had transferred its business was not an employee for the purposes of the Regulations as he worked under a contract for services and not a contract of service.

The effect of the transfer on the relevant employees' contracts is found in Regulation 4. This states that the transferee takes over 'all rights, powers, duties and liabilities under or in connection with any such contract'. There was an exception relating to occupational pension schemes and invalidity and survivors' benefits (Regulation 10). While the effect of the original exception was called into question in the case of *Perry* v. *Intec Colleges Ltd* [1993] IRLR 56, it was overruled by the Employment Appeal Tribunal decision in *Walden Engineering* v. *Warner* [1993] IRLR 420 where the EAT held that the Regulation meant what it said and should not be given a gloss. As the Regulation was worded, it did not require the new employer to provide equivalent provision. The Court of Appeal confirmed this interpretation in *Adams* v. *Lancashire County Council and BE Catering Services* [1997] IRLR 436. However, in *Beckman* v. *Dynamco Whicheloe MacFarlane* ECJ Case C-164/00 the ECJ held that although benefits paid at the end of a working life under a pension scheme were excluded, early retirement benefits paid in the event of redundancy were not, even if they were calculated using normal pension benefit rules. As such, the relevant provision under the superannuation scheme operated by her old employer transferred and Beckman was entitled to an early retirement pension and lump sum on being made redundant.

While old age, invalidity and survivors' benefits do not automatically transfer because of Regulation 10, the Transfer of Undertakings (Pension Protection) Regulations 2005, which came into effect in April of that year, create an obligation on transferees to make provision for transferred employees in respect of old age, invalidity and survivors' benefits in that the transferee must match the contributions of employees of up to 6 per cent of salary.

Regulation 4 therefore means that the contract transfers lock, stock and barrel to the new employer, including any continuity which has been acquired. In *MITIE Managed Services Ltd* v. *French* [2002] IRLR 512 a question arose on the application of the Transfer of Undertakings (Protection of Employment) Regulations and the liability of a transferee where the transferor provided a profit-sharing or share-option scheme. The employment tribunal stated that under Regulation 4 the clause in the contract transferred and the transferee had to honour it. The EAT, however, allowed the employer's appeal stating that in a case like this, the entitlement of the transferred employees is to 'participation in a scheme of substantial equivalence but one that is free from unjust, absurd or impossible features'. It is suggested that this does little to clarify the law. Regulation 11 imposes a duty on the transferor to notify the transferee of the transferring employees and of all the associated rights and liabilities which will transfer. This information has to be given by the completion date, even if the transferor is unaware that Transfer of Undertakings (Protection of Employment) Regulations apply, and transferees can sue defaulting transferors. Tribunals can award compensation if the claim is well-founded, which it considers just and equitable, although it cannot be less than £500 per employee unless the tribunal feels a lesser sum is just (Regulation 12).

While Regulation 4 states that all rights and liabilities transfer, Regulation 4(3) states that the Regulations only protect those persons employed immediately before the transfer or who would have been so employed if they had not been dismissed in the circumstances described in Regulation 7. This wording is again picking up on existing case law. In *Secretary of State for Employment* v. *Spence* [1987] QB 179 the Court of Appeal held that employees who were dismissed at 11 a.m. one morning when the business was transferred at 2 p.m. the same day were not employed immediately before the transfer according to the wording of the Regulations. The question of interpretation came before the House of Lords in *Litster* v. *Forth Dry Dock and Engineering Co Ltd* [1989] IRLR 161. In this case, Forth Dry Dock was in receivership and another company had agreed to buy the business. The transferee did not want to take on the employees of Forth Dry Dock because some redundant employees from another company had agreed to accept lower wages. The transferee therefore arranged with the receivers that the employees were to be dismissed an hour before the transfer took place. The transferee then argued that Regulation 4 did not apply, and liability for the dismissals lay with the transferor, who was, of course, in receivership. The House of Lords held that, in order for the purpose of the Directive to be fully realised, it was necessary to imply into the Regulations the words 'or would have been so employed but for being unfairly dismissed under Regulation 7'. Regulation 7 provides that a dismissal will be fair if for an economic, technical or organisational reason requiring a change in the nature of the workforce. Thus if the employees have been dismissed for a reason other than those in Regulation 7, they will be deemed to have been employed immediately before the transfer.

While *Litster* and the new Regulation 7 are to be welcomed, in *Ibex Trading* v. *Walton* [1994] IRLR 564 the Employment Appeal Tribunal held that the dismissal of employees of an insolvent company by the receiver, when there was no purchaser on the scene, was not a dismissal connected with a transfer and thus the Regulations did not apply. Furthermore, it should be noted that *Litster* only deals with the question of liability for compensation (that is, the transferee is liable) and does not render the dismissal void. This would seem to go against the ECJ decision of *Bork (P) International A/S* v. *Foreningen af Arbejdsledere i Danmark* [1989] IRLR 41, which made it clear that the Acquired Rights Directive was meant to prevent dismissals before the transfer. The case of *Celtec Ltd* v. *Astley* (2005) ECJ Case C-478/03, however, has implications for employees. The case concerned civil servants seconded to Training and Enterprise Councils during the 1990s and subsequently employed by them. Astley was seconded in 1990 and employed from 1993. The issue was whether his continuity of service was protected by either s.218 Employment Rights Act 1996 or the Transfer of Undertakings (Protection of Employment) Regulations. The ERA, as seen, protects those employed at the time of the transfer, the Regulations protect those employed immediately before the transfer, so the question for the court was whether the transfer took place at one point in time, 1990, or over a period of time ending when the last secondee was employed (in the case, 1996). The EAT held that it was at one point in time, 1990, while the Court of Appeal held that a transfer could happen over a period of time. The House of Lords referred the issue to the ECJ. The ECJ held that the use of the word 'date' in the Directive meant that a transfer could not happen over a period of time. As such, the House of Lords ([2006] UKHL 29) when it heard the case, concluded that the transfer took place in 1990. However, Regulation 4(3) states that an employee employed immediately before the transfer includes where the transfer is effected by a series of two or more transactions. Whether this has a impact in situations such as *Astley* remains to be seen.

The ECJ also stressed the automatic effect the Directive had on the date the transfer takes place irrespective of the parties' wishes, in line with its decision in *Rotsart de Hertaing* v. *Benoidt* [1996] IRLR 127. This may well have implications on the duty on transferors to inform transferees of all employees and rights and liabilities which are transferring, discussed above. Regulation 11 provides that this information should be given not less than 14 days before the transfer. The ruling in *Astley* is that the transfer takes place when the new employer assumes responsibility for the transferred employees, which will obviously be some time after the contracts, and thus a transferee could find that he only receives important information after he is legally committed to the transfer and the transferor will not be in breach of his duty.

While the Regulations are discussed further below and in Chapter 10, two further points should be made at this point. If liability has transferred and the new employer changes the terms of the contract, the employee may argue that he has been constructively dismissed, but only if there are changes in terms 'which involve a substantial change in working conditions to the material detriment of a person' (Regulation 4(9)). In *Berriman* v. *Delabole Slate Ltd* [1985] IRLR 305 the Court of Appeal held that a reduction in salary to bring the transferred employees' pay in line with that of the transferee's employees was a substantial change and not an economic reason within Regulation 7, but in the *Watson Rask* case (above) the changes to terms were minor, and the ECJ still upheld the employees' complaint, suggesting that Regulation 4(9) does not comply with the Directive, which talks of a 'significant' change, not 'substantial'. However, in the later case of *Rossiter* v. *Pendragon plc* [2001] IRLR 256 the Employment Appeal Tribunal held that s.95(1)(c) Employment Rights Act 1996 (see below) had to be construed purposively to give effect to the Acquired Rights Directive and while the section may be construed differently in the context of domestic law, this did not preclude a broader construction to give effect to the Directive. Therefore a tribunal was not required to find a fundamental breach of contract in order to give rise to a claim of constructive dismissal under the Transfer of Undertakings (Protection of Employment) Regulations. It was sufficient for the applicant to show that there had been a substantial and detrimental change to his working conditions. The Court of Appeal, however, in the joined appeals of *Rossiter and Air Foyle Ltd* v. *Crosby-Clarke* [2002] IRLR 483, overruling the EAT, has held that a change to employees' terms and conditions following a transfer does not automatically amount to a constructive dismissal, and the employee still has to establish a fundamental breach of pre-transfer rights. In *Rossiter* the contract allowed changes in commission which the transferee instigated, resulting in a loss of £3,000 per year. In *Crosby-Clarke* the transferee moved the business to Belgium which allowed pilots to work for 11 days without a break, whereas in the UK the maximum was four days. Both the employees' contracts allowed the changes and as such there was no fundamental breach. Thus, the transferee can vary terms in the same way as the original employer, as long as the variation is allowed by the contract. In *Power* v. *Regent Security Services* [2007] ICR 970 the Employment Appeal Tribunal held that the principle that any changes to contracts made as a result of transfers under the Transfer of Undertakings (Protection of Employment) Regulations are void does not apply where the change is to the benefit of the employee, but only when the change is to the employee's detriment. This ruling was confirmed by the Court of Appeal ([2007] EWCA Civ 1188). However, *Jackson* v. *Computershare Investor Services* [2007] All ER 448 shows that there are limits to this. In the case Mrs Jackson was transferred to Computershare in 2004 and was dismissed for redundancy in 2005. Computershare had an enhanced severance scheme which it paid to employees who had joined the firm before 2002. The Court of Appeal held that Mrs Jackson was not entitled to the enhanced severance pay, stating that Regulation (4) does not give a transferred employee access to benefits other than those to which the employee was entitled before the transfer.

The Advocate-General in *D'urso* v. *Ecole Marelli Elettro-meccanica Generale SpA* [1992] IRLR 136 expressed an opinion that a constructive dismissal caused by a change in terms would only be fair if such a change would have occurred despite the transfer. This appears to raise doubts as to the validity of Regulation 7, however the Court of Appeal in *Wilson* v. *St Helens Borough Council* and *Meade and Baxendale* v. *British Fuels Ltd* [1997] IRLR 505 decided that where an employee is dismissed by the transferor for a reason connected with the transfer and is taken on by the transferee on less favourable terms, the dismissal is ineffective and the original terms still apply. This does not, however, apply to dismissals for an 'economic, technical or organisational reason entailing changes in the workforce'

(Regulation 7(2)). The argument of the Court of Appeal was that Regulation 7 states that a dismissal before or after a relevant transfer is unfair unless it is for an economic, technical or organisational reason. The Court then concluded that if it is unfair within the Regulation it must therefore be void. The Court went on to hold that in *Meade* the dismissal was void and thus the change of terms by the transferee was ineffective, despite the fact that the employees had agreed to the change and had worked under them. Conversely, in *Wilson* the dismissal was for an economic, technical or organisational reason and therefore effective, leaving the employees free to agree a change in terms. After the decisions, the Employment Appeal Tribunal in *Cornwall County Care Ltd* v. *Brightman* [1998] IRLR 228, while acknowledging it was bound by *Wilson* and *Meade*, held that, in certain cases, the employee may be taken to have accepted his dismissal and that if the employee worked under the new terms for some time, he could be said to have accepted his dismissal, albeit the dismissal is unfair by Regulation 7(1), and should be paid compensation to buy out his old terms.

It must be said that the above cases left the law in a confused state. *Wilson* and *Meade* were appealed to the House of Lords. That court in its decision ([1998] 3 WLR 1070) reviewed the views of both the Employment Appeal Tribunal and the Court of Appeal in the cases. In the Employment Appeal Tribunal, *Foreninggen a.f. Arbejdsledere i Danmark* v. *Daddy's Dance Hall a/s* [1988] ECR 739 was cited, in which the ECJ said that the employment relationship may be changed by a transferee, provided it was done lawfully, but that the relationship could not be altered if the transfer itself was the reason for the change. Similarly in *Watson Rask* (above), the employees successfully argued that the transferee could not change their pay day from the last Thursday of the month to the last day of the month. The ECJ held that if a term is altered to the employee's detriment because of a transfer, the alteration is invalid. In *Meade*, the Employment Appeal Tribunal held that as the employees had been made redundant by the transferor and offered new terms by the transferee which they accepted, there had been an effective dismissal and the employees could not argue that they were employed under their original terms. *Daddy's Dance Hall* as a variation case was irrelevant but was relevant on the facts as presented to the Appeal Tribunal in *Wilson*. In the Court of Appeal, it was discovered that the facts relied on by the Employment Appeal Tribunal in *Wilson* were incorrect as the employees had been made redundant and offered new contracts by the transferee.

The House of Lords upheld the Court of Appeal decision in *Wilson*, stating that although the dismissal was transfer related it was for an economic, technical or organisational reason. In respect of *Meade*, however, the House of Lords felt that there was nothing in the Regulations which rendered a dismissal ineffective, even if it was connected with the transfer. The dismissal was therefore effective but unfair. The employees' claim, however, fell outside the three-month time limit required. This leaves the law in the curious position that if the employer dismisses the employees and then offers new terms, the dismissal will be effective but unfair unless it is for an economic, technical or organisational reason affecting changes in the workforce. The new terms, however, will be valid. If, on the other hand, the employer takes on the transferred employees and negotiates a change in terms, such a change will be invalid (*Daddy's Dance Hall* and *Watson Rask*, above) and the old terms will continue. Note however *Power* v. *Regent Security Services* (above).

Recently, however, the ECJ appears to be relaxing its position. In *Boor* v. *Ministre de la Fonction Publique et de la Reforme Administrative* ECJ Case C-425/02, Boor was transferred when a non-profit organisation in the private sector transferred to the State of Luxembourg. Public sector rates were set by legislation and lower than the private sector. The ECJ said there was nothing to prevent the new employer reducing Boor's salary to comply with national laws relating to public sector employees. However, if the change was substantial, the employee could resign and claim constructive dismissal. This seems to allow for some harmonisation of terms and supports the Court of Appeal findings in *Rossiter*.

It can be seen that the law in this area still lacks clarity and whether the 2006 Regulations will improve this has yet to be seen.

Effective date of termination

For the purposes of unfair dismissal (and redundancy) it is necessary to know the exact date when the employment relationship ended. There are two reasons for this: (1) to calculate the period of continuous employment, and (2) because the complainant has a short time period after the termination of the employment in which to present his claim (three months for unfair dismissal, six months for redundancy). For unfair dismissal purposes the date the relationship is deemed to end is known as the 'effective date of termination'. The date which applies is given in ss.97(1) and (4) Employment Rights Act 1996:

(a) if the contract is terminated by notice on either side, the date that notice expires whether it is of the proper length or not;
(b) if the contract is terminated without notice, the date on which the termination takes effect;
(c) if a fixed term contract expires without being renewed, the date on which it expires;

(d) if the employee gives counter-notice which is shorter than the employer's notice, the date the counter-notice expires.

The only problem area is (b) above. Two problems can arise in this area. First, the employer may instantly dismiss the employee to prevent him acquiring the continuity for unfair dismissal. The Court of Appeal in *Stapp* v. *Shaftesbury Society* [1982] IRLR 326 confirmed that the actual date of termination is the effective date of termination, and this has since been supported in *Batchelor* v. *BRB* [1987] IRLR 136. Second, if the employee accepts wages in lieu of notice then again the date of termination is when the employee leaves and not when the notice expires unless there is some ambiguity, for example the employee being given written notice but verbally agreeing to accept wages in lieu (*Robert Cort* v. *Charman* [1981] IRLR 437).

If the employee is given contractual notice which is shorter than the statutory minimum to which he is entitled then the date of termination is the date when the statutory notice expires for certain purposes by s.97(2) of the Act. These are:

(a) calculation of the qualifying period for unfair dismissal;
(b) calculation of the basic award in unfair dismissal;
(c) calculation of the period of continuous employment on which the award is based.

9.3 Excluded Employees

The legislation excludes certain employees from protection from unfair dismissal. We have already seen that the employee must normally have the requisite amount of continuity of employment to claim and unless the reason for the dismissal is one where no continuity is required, employees without the minimum amount of service will not be protected. In addition, certain other classes of employee are excluded. The main areas of exclusion are discussed below.

(a) *An employee who has agreed to waive his rights to unfair dismissal*
Normally an employee cannot sign away his rights to unfair dismissal or redundancy compensation and any such agreement which purports to exclude such rights is void by s.203 Employment Rights Act 1996 (*Igbo* v. *Johnson Matthey Chemicals Ltd* [1986] IRLR 215). There are two exceptions to s.203. The first is where an officer of ACAS has promoted an agreement between the parties and the employee accepts that agreement in full settlement of his claim. The normal procedure is for the parties to sign an

ACAS agreement but the fact that the form has not been signed by the employee although his agreement has been registered is sufficient (*Gilbert* v. *Kembridge Fibres Ltd* [1984] IRLR 52). If the employee's representative signs on the employee's behalf this may be insufficient if the tribunal does not recognise the authority of the representative to so sign. While solicitors, barristers and members of the Citizens Advice Bureau will have that authority (*Freeman* v. *Sovereign Chicken Ltd* [1991] IRLR 408) trade union representatives may not and this could render the agreement void.

The second exception is in s.203(2)(f). This allows an employee to enter a compromise agreement which is legally binding provided that:

(a) the agreement is in writing;
(b) the agreement relates to the particular complaint;
(c) the employee has received independent advice from a relevant independent adviser (the list of those who may be an independent adviser is discussed earlier in this text);
(d) the adviser has a contract of insurance or an indemnity provided for members of a profession or professional body in force covering the risk of loss by the employee;
(e) the agreement identifies the adviser; and
(f) the agreement states that the conditions regulating compromise agreements under the Act are satisfied (s.203(3)).

It appears that a problem with compromise agreements is that they have to be particularly well-worded to be effective. In *Bank of Credit and Commerce International SA* v. *Ali* [2001] IRLR 292 a compromise agreement expressed to be 'in full and final settlement of all or any claims whether under statute, common law or in equity of whatsoever nature that exists or may exist' did not bar an action for stigma damages which the parties could not have contemplated when drawing up the agreement. The House of Lords said that clear language would be needed, leaving no room for doubt that the employee intended to surrender rights and claims he could not have been aware of when signing the agreement. In *Hinton* v. *University of East London* [2005] EWCA Civ 532 a more detailed 'catch all' phrase was used. The compromise agreement contained the statement that the agreement 'was in full and final satisfaction of all claims in all jurisdictions (whether arising under statute, common law or otherwise) . . . arising out of or in connection with his employment with the university, the termination of his employment or otherwise, including in particular the following claims which have been raised by or on behalf of the employee as being claims he may have'. The list which followed contained eleven different kinds of claims but did not include a claim of continuing detriment arising from whistle blowing, despite Hinton having raised this in correspondence. The Court of Appeal held that the statutory claims to which the agreement related must be identified. Generic words such as 'unfair dismissal' will suffice, as will referring to a particular section of a relevant statute, but a general phrase such as 'all statutory rights' or naming the statute without identifying the relevant sections is not sufficient and an employee is free to pursue a claim. As such, Hinton had not compromised his detriment claim and was free to pursue it. The case shows that employers should specify all claims mentioned by the employee in some detail and a general compromise agreement, used for all employees, is likely to leave an employer exposed. This is definitely not a case of one size fits all!

The fact that s.203(2)(f) talks of an agreement relating to a particular complaint does not mean that it is limited to complaints that have been presented to the tribunal, according to the Employment Appeal Tribunal in *Lunt* v. *Merseyside TEC Ltd* [1999] IRLR 458, although parliament did not intend to permit a blanket compromise agreement compromising claims which had never been indicated in the past. Therefore, in the case, it included claims the applicant had indicated by letter she would not pursue if a settlement was reached. This is endorsed by *Hinton*.

If a compromise agreement does not comply with s.203(2)(f) it is void and the claim has not been settled. This for example would, at present, be the case if a compromise agreement purported to be in final settlement of any claim, as it must relate to a particular complaint. However, according to the Employment Appeal Tribunal in *Sutherland* v. *Network Appliance Ltd* [2001] IRLR 12 this will not invalidate the whole of the agreement but only renders it void in respect of statutory claims as it falls foul of the restrictions in s.203(1). Thus it is still enforceable in settlement of any breach of contract claims.

It can be seen that compromise agreements have to be worded very specifically to achieve their aim. One problem is the fact that the agreement has to relate to a particular complaint. A proposed amendment to s.203(2)(f), originally in the Employment Bill, did not survive the parliamentary process and, as such, the problems remain.

There are two further exceptions where an employee may agree to exclude his rights to go to an employment tribunal. The Employment Rights Act 1996 introduced the concept of dismissal procedures agreements in s.110. Such an agreement, if recognised by the Secretary of State, is in substitution of the right to claim unfair dismissal in a tribunal. To date only one industry, the electrical contracting industry, has a designated dismissal procedures agreement which has now lapsed. This was thought to be because of the many hurdles that had to be surmounted under the original Act. As such, the Employment Rights (Dispute Resolution) Act 1998 amended s.110. The new section provides for a greater number of reasons for dismissal to be covered by a dismissal procedures agreement, provides that such agreements include provision for arbitration and provides for legal enforcement of any award made under the procedures. These changes may encourage more industries to set up agreements and prevent unfair dismissals being heard in the employment tribunals.

A further method whereby an unfair dismissal will not be heard by a tribunal is if the parties use the new arbitration scheme established by ACAS and discussed in Chapter 1.

(b) *An employee who falls within the category of excluded persons*   Certain classes of employee are excluded by ss.198–200 Employment Rights Act. These include share fisher persons, employees employed for less than a month, members of the police and mariners. Police includes the British Transport Police Force (*Spence* v. *British Railways Board* [2001] ICR 232).

(c) *An employee whose dismissal is to safeguard national security and the Minister has issued a certificate to that effect.*

(d) *An employee outside the territorial scope of UK labour legislation*   Section 196 Employment Rights Act had a further restriction where the employee ordinarily worked outside Great Britain, but this section was repealed by the Employment Relations Act 1999. However, the Rome Convention (Convention on the Law Applicable to Contractual Obligations) 1980 was incorporated into UK law by the Contracts (Applicable Law) Act 1990. Territorial limits are seen in other legislation, but the removal of s.196 apparently removed such restrictions from unfair dismissal. However, the Court of Appeal has held in *Crofts* v. *Cathay Pacific Airways Ltd* [2005] EWCA Civ 599 that in order to gain protection, an employee must be employed in Great Britain. However, in the case a liberal interpretation was given to the phrase. The court had to decide whether there was jurisdiction to hear unfair dismissal claims from international airline pilots who were employed by a UK subsidiary of a Hong Kong registered company, to fly aircraft operated by Cathay Pacific. The pilots had Hong Kong licences, contracts subject to Hong Kong law, were paid in Hong Kong dollars into a Hong Kong bank, but their contracts required them to be based in England. The Court said that where the contract bases the employee is likely to shed light on where the employment is when the job is international and mobile. As such, there was jurisdiction to hear the claim.

The House of Lords has now discussed the issue in *Lawson* v. *Serco Ltd* [2006] UKHL 3. In the case their Lordships heard three joined appeals involving a security officer working for a British company at an RAF base on Ascension Island, a youth worker employed by the Ministry of Defence at British Army bases in Germany and an air crew member, based in the UK but employed by a company resident in Hong Kong. In all three cases the House of Lords held that the employee had the right to claim unfair dismissal. The House of Lords said that in three situations an employee working abroad may be protected from unfair dismissal:

(a) peripatetic employees who are based in Britain;
(b) employees working in a British enclave abroad;
(c) an employee posted abroad by a British employer 'for the purposes of a business carried on in Great Britain'.

While the last example was *obiter*, as it covered none of the employees in question, the Employment Appeal Tribunal has applied it in the case of *Williams* v. *University of Nottingham* UKEAT 0124/07/RN. The case concerned a Nottingham University lecturer who was employed to work for the University of Nottingham in Malaysia, which was a totally separate company. He resigned and claimed unfair dismissal. The EAT held that he was unable to claim but confirmed that employees posted abroad would have such a right if they fitted the House of Lords' description.

(e) *An employee who has not complied with the statutory dispute procedures* At the time of writing the relevant provisions of the Employment Act 2002 and the Employment Act 2002 (Dispute Resolution) Regulations 2004 are still in force, although, by the Employment Bill 2007, both the statutory dismissal and grievance procedures are to be abolished, and it is thought this will happen in 2009. As such, until their abolition, an employee who fails to go through the statutory grievance procedure will normally be unable to present a claim of unfair dismissal as s.32 of the Act states that in such cases the tribunal has no jurisdiction to hear a claim. The tribunal may also not hear a complaint until 28 days have elapsed from the presentation of the grievance letter (s.32(3)). Where a claim exists, the time limit for its presentation to a tribunal is extended to six months by Regulation 15 Dispute Resolution Regulations 2004.

There is a standard and a modified grievance procedure set out in the 2002 Act, Sch 2 paragraphs 6–8. In the standard procedure, the employee must set out his grievance in writing and send a copy to the employer, the employer must then set up a meeting at which the employee has the right to be accompanied, and the third stage is an appeal. Under the modified procedure there are two steps, a letter from the employee stating the grievance and the basis for it and the employer's response.

Cases to date have focused on what constitutes a written form of grievance. In *Shergold* v. *Fieldway Medical Centre* [2006] ICR 304 the employee resigned and complained of unfair dismissal. After a meeting with the employer she was advised to put in a formal grievance but she did not do so. The Employment Appeal Tribunal held that her letter of resignation constituted the grievance. Burton J stated that the statutory requirements were minimal and that all that was required was that the grievance should be in writing, hence a letter of resignation was sufficient. Similarly in *Commotion* v. *Rutty* [2006] ICR 290 a letter requesting flexible working which had not been allowed was also held to be a written grievance, and in *Galaxy Showers* v. *Wilson* [2006] IRLR 83 the EAT held that the grievance letter merely had to set out the grievance, it did not need to state that the employee wished to take things further. However in *City of Bradford Metropolitan District Council* v. *Pratt* [2007] IRLR 192 the EAT stated that when using the modified procedure, as there is no meeting, the employee must put the grievance and the grounds for it in writing, to comply with the statute. In the case, Pratt put in a post-employment grievance concerning equal pay. Her written grievance did not include the grounds for her complaint because it did not name her comparators, information she sent to the employer later. The EAT held that she had not complied with the procedure and was barred from bringing a claim.

9.4 Has There Been a Dismissal?

In order to claim unfair dismissal the employee must obviously show that he has been dismissed. The different types of termination of the contract at common law have already been discussed in the previous chapter. For the purposes of unfair dismissal there is a statutory definition of dismissal in s.95 Employment Rights Act 1996. This states that dismissal will occur in the three situations discussed below.

Employer terminating with or without notice

This is, of course, the classic termination at common law. It is the employer ending the relationship and the question of whether the dismissal is wrongful or not is irrelevant to the issue of fairness. Thus a lawful dismissal may be unfair and likewise a wrongful dismissal may be fair. All the situations discussed in the previous chapter which are a dismissal at common law will be a dismissal under s.95.

Fixed term contract which expires and is not renewed

Section 95(1)(b) states this specifically as a dismissal.

Constructive dismissal

While the previous two situations are more or less self-evident, this third category is not. It picks up on the common law situation of a repudiatory breach by the employer which forces the employee to resign, therefore, on the face of it, there appears to be a resignation. The law is aware, however, that this construction can leave employees with little protection against an unscrupulous employer who makes life so bad as to force them out, therefore statute calls this situation a dismissal. The breach by the employer must have caused the employee's resignation and not some other reason (*Jones* v. *F. Sirl & Son (Furnishers) Ltd* [1997] IRLR 493). It should be noted, however, that statute has created this concept and therefore two very important points should be noted. First, the concept only arises if the statutory protection applies, therefore the concept only protects those with the requisite continuity and, until the employee has been employed for one year by his employer; if he (the employee) ends the relationship for whatever reason, it will be construed as a resignation. While resignation by the employee is the normal position in constructive dismissal, two cases suggest that this might not always be the case. In *Hogg* v. *Dover College* [1990] ICR 39 a full-time member of staff received a letter following an illness offering him part-time work on a reduced salary. He lodged a complaint of unfair dismissal while still working under the new terms under protest. The Employment Appeal Tribunal held that the letter from the employer terminated the contract even though the employment continued. Alternatively, there was a new contract, the old one terminating by Hogg's acceptance of the employer's repudiatory breach. *Hogg* was followed in *Alcan Extrusions* v. *Yates* [1996] IRLR 327 where the imposition of a new shift system, which also involved changes in pay and holidays, was a repudiation which the employee accepted as terminating the old contract even though he worked to the new terms under protest. The Employment Appeal Tribunal held that whether the change in terms is radical enough to amount to a termination of the original contract and the substitution of a new contract is a question of fact for the tribunal. While the cases protect employees without the need to resign, they create uncertainty as each case must be decided on its own facts. *Edwards* v. *Surrey Police* [1999] IRLR 426 makes it clear, however, that there must be some communication, by words or conduct, to inform the employer that the existing contract has ended. In the absence of such communication the relationship continues.

Second, statute has created the concept of a constructive dismissal but has chosen not to create the corollary – a constructive resignation. This means that if the employee commits a repudiatory breach and the employer chooses to end the relationship, as the employer has terminated the contract, it is a dismissal, although the reasons for the dismissal will obviously be relevant when looking at the issue of fairness.

Section 95(1)(c) says that it is a dismissal if the employee terminates the contract, with or without notice, in circumstances in which he is entitled to do so because of the employer's conduct. This leads to the question of what conduct entitles the employee to leave and claim constructive dismissal.

In the early days of the concept, judges argued that any unreasonable behaviour on the part of the employer could form the basis of a constructive dismissal claim, but Denning MR decided that the test was a contractual test in *Western Excavating (ECC) Ltd* v. *Sharp* [1978] IRLR 27. Here the employee was suspended without pay as a disciplinary sanction. As he had no money, he asked his employer for his holiday pay, which was refused, and then asked for a loan, which was also refused. He then resigned, claiming constructive dismissal because of unreasonable conduct on the part of his employer. The Court of Appeal held that there was no dismissal and that he had resigned because the employer had committed no breach of contract. Denning MR said:

> 'If the employer is guilty of conduct which is a significant breach going to the root of the contract of employment or which shows that the employer no longer intends to be bound by one or more of the essential terms then the employee is entitled to treat himself as discharged from any further performance. If he does so, then he terminates the contract by reason of the employer's conduct. He is constructively dismissed.'

While other cases have since tried to subtly reintroduce the reasonableness test, the Court of Appeal has reiterated the contractual importance in *Courtaulds Northern Spinning Ltd* v. *Sibson* [1988] IRLR 305 where the employee had resigned when his employer told him to move sites. The employee argued that, as there was no contractual mobility clause, the order was unreasonable and that therefore he had been constructively dismissed. The court rejected this argument, first on the basis that unreasonable conduct on the part of the employer was not the test for constructive dismissal and second because, as the employee had moved sites in the past, there was an implied mobility clause in his contract.

The breach must be fundamental, and minor changes in terms would not set up a constructive dismissal claim. In *Irving* v. *Thwaite Holme Kitchens* (1995) IRLB 518 a persistent breach of a contractual right to a pay rise entitled the employee to resign and claim constructive dismissal. Likewise, reducing pay, fundamentally altering hours and a major alteration of job duties have all been successful constructive dismissal claims. A breach of the duty of trust and confidence will also found a constructive dismissal claim, as we have already seen in Chapter 4. Although sometimes a one-off act is the breach, very often it is a series of acts where the final act is the last straw.

In *London Borough of Waltham Forest* v. *Omilaju* [2004] EWCA Civ 1493 the Court of Appeal stated that the last straw did not have to be an unreasonable or blameworthy act but it could not be a blameless act. The act has to contribute, however slightly, to the breach of trust and confidence. In the case, the claimant resigned and claimed constructive dismissal, claiming that the last straw was the fact that the council did not pay him for his attendance at tribunal proceedings that he brought against his employer. The Court of Appeal held that it could not be the last straw as the Council, under its rules, was not entitled to pay him in such circumstances.

A strange situation arose in *Warnes* v. *Trustees of Cheriton Oddfellows Social Club* [1993] IRLR 58. Warnes was employed as a steward and secretary of a social club. There was a resolution to remove his secretarial duties at the club's Annual General Meeting. On learning of this, Warnes wrote a letter claiming he had been constructively dismissed. The employment tribunal found that, while taking away the secretarial duties could be a constructive dismissal, the resolution by which it was done was invalid under the club rules because it had not been submitted 14 days prior to the AGM. The tribunal concluded that the resolution therefore did not take away Warne's secretarial duties and his claim for constructive dismissal failed. The Employment Appeal Tribunal allowed Warne's appeal. It held that if an officer of the employer dismissed an employee where, as a matter of contract, he did not have the power to do so, in general it would not be open for the employer to rely on the abuse of power. Therefore, the fact that the resolution was invalid did not prevent a finding of constructive dismissal.

A constructive dismissal may arise out of an anticipatory breach as long as the breach has not been withdrawn (*Norwest Holst Group Administration Ltd* v. *Harrison* [1985] IRLR 240 but also see *Kerry Foods Ltd* v. *Lynch* [2005] IRLR 680) but there can be no claim if the terms of the contract are in dispute and the employee argues that the employer has broken a disputed term. In *Frank Wright & Co (Holdings) Ltd* v. *Punch* [1980] IRLR 217 the employee resigned when he did not receive cost of living increases. His original contract said he was so entitled but his statutory statement said he was not. The Employment Appeal Tribunal said there could be no constructive dismissal when the employer genuinely believed that he was complying with the contract, however erroneous that belief was. This shows that intention is important in this area, but leaves the somewhat unsatisfactory position that it is up to the employee to prove that the employer was not mistaken and knew what the terms were.

If the employee wishes to treat the employer's breach as terminating the contract, he must do so quickly or he may find that he has, by his conduct, accepted the variation in his terms. In *Jeffrey* v. *Laurence Scott & Electromotors Ltd* [1977] IRLR 466 the employee waited some three and a half months after the breach before he resigned and it was held that there was no constructive dismissal. Note, however, *Hogg* and *Yates* (above) and *El-Hoshi* v. *Pizza Express Restaurants Ltd* (2004) IDS 768 where a restaurant worker, who made a public interest disclosure to management about employing illegal workers, was transferred to kitchen work which he found humiliating and went off sick as a result. He asked for the manager to be disciplined but nothing was done, so after two months he resigned and claimed unfair dismissal. The Employment Appeal Tribunal held that the delay was understandable in the light of his illness and allowed his constructive dismissal claim.

It does not follow that, because the employer is in breach of contract, the constructive dismissal is unfair. In *Hall* v. *Lodge* (1977) IRLIB 76 an employee was promoted, but it soon became apparent that she was unable to do the job. The employers demoted her to her original grade at another shop and she resigned and claimed unfair dismissal. While there had clearly been a breach by the employer and therefore a constructive dismissal, it was fair in the circumstances. On the other hand, if the breach by the employer is an excessively harsh sanction imposed after a disciplinary offence, then the employer is not acting within the band of reasonable responses as a reasonable employer would do and this will be unfair. This is because, for a dismissal to be fair, the employer must have a fair reason and act reasonably in the circumstances, as will be shown below. If he has acted as no reasonable employer would do and this is the repudiatory breach, logic dictates that the dismissal must be unfair (*Cawley* v. *South Wales Electricity Board* [1985] IRLR 89).

9.5 Reasons for Dismissal

In any unfair dismissal claim the employee must show that he is eligible to claim and that he has been dismissed. This means that the burden of proof starts with the employee to show that a dismissal has taken place. Of course, in practice, in the majority of cases this is obvious, and normally the employee will only have the burden of proof when he alleges constructive dismissal or when the situation is ambiguous and the employee is alleging that the words of the employer constituted a dismissal and the employer alleges that he did not intend to dismiss. The burden is always on the employer, however, to prove he had one of the statutory fair reasons to dismiss and this means that in any tribunal hearing the employer must bring forward evidence that the reason existed. From the famous case of *British Home Stores* v. *Burchell* [1978] IRLR 1379 the employer must show that he had a genuine belief, based on reasonable grounds following a reasonable investigation, that the employee was guilty. This was approved by the Court of Appeal in *Weddel* v. *Tepper* [1980] IRLR 96. This means that although, in theory, the employer does not have to prove he acted as a reasonable employer (see below), in practice reasonableness and the reason for the dismissal are closely linked and an employer who has not investigated will find it hard to prove a reason existed. Furthermore, it is only the reason known to the employer at the time of the dismissal which is relevant (*Devis and Sons Ltd* v. *Atkins* [1977] IRLR 314). This means that should the employer have no reason at the time of the dismissal, but before the case comes before the tribunal a reason emerges, the dismissal must be unfair, although compensation may be reduced. This is interpreted strictly. In *Alboni* v. *Ind Coope Retail Ltd* [1998] IRLR 131 the employer gave notice to a pub manageress after the pub manager resigned. The reason for the notice given to the manageress was that the employer did not think that she could do the job single-handedly, but the employer was prepared to keep an open mind until the end of the notice period. During the notice period, the employer received no application from her to do the job alone nor did she submit a business plan and so the dismissal went ahead. The Employment Appeal Tribunal held that the dismissal was unfair because the employer had taken into account events after the notice had been given. The Court of Appeal held that this was a misinterpretation of *Devis* v. *Atkins* which holds that if a reason becomes known to the employer after the employment has actually terminated that cannot be used retrospectively to justify the dismissal. It should be noted that the position is totally the opposite when looking at common law dismissal, as seen in *Ridgeway* v. *Hungerford Market* (see Chapter 8). In addition, the tribunal will ignore any pressure put upon the employer to dismiss the employee (for example, the threat of industrial action) although should the union put pressure to bear on the employer, either the employer or the employee may join the union as a party to the unfair dismissal proceedings and the tribunal may apportion compensation between the employer and the union so that the union may end up paying the whole of the award to the employee (s.160 Trade Union and Labour Relations (Consolidation) Act 1992).

The list of statutory fair reasons is to be found in ss.98(1) and (2) of the Act. These will be discussed in detail below.

Capability and qualifications

Capability

Inherent incapability Capability is defined as 'capability assessed by reference to skill, aptitude, health, or any other physical or mental quality'. This indicates that the statute envisages that the capability reason can be based on inability to do the job, that is, failing to reach acceptable standards for whatever reason, or that illness or accident can render a person who was once capable unable now to do the job. A tribunal will expect an employer to handle the two categories in different ways, for while it is reasonable to warn an employee that he should improve his standards it may not be so reasonable to warn a genuinely sick employee that he must get well or else. In addition, there is a difference between the employee who is inherently incapable and the one who is incapable because of negligence, laziness or just sheer bloody-mindedness! The latter categories fit more neatly into the second reason, that is conduct.

The skill part of the section includes both managerial and manual skills, but obviously the expectations of the employer need to be communicated to the employee. Failing to reach a standard he does not know about is hardly a fair reason to dismiss an employee. In *Davison* v. *Kent Meters Ltd* [1975] IRLR 145 an employee was dismissed for assembling the majority of 500 components wrongly. She said that she was merely following the instructions laid down by the charge-hand. The charge-hand gave evidence that he had never shown her how to assemble the components. Not surprisingly it was held that her dismissal was unfair. She could hardly be expected to do something if no one had shown her how to do it. This does not mean, however, that the standard must remain static, although a reasonable employer will train and allow a reasonable length of time for the employee to adjust. The incapability, however, must relate to the job he is employed to do, that is the job and duties laid down by his contract.

Aptitude may mean that the employee is unsuited to the particular job because of a facet in his character. He may, for example, lack interpersonal skills – hardly a good point for a salesman! Aptitude can also cover aptitude tests, although it will be unfair if the employer dismisses before the employee has completed all the attempts allowed. In *Blackman* v. *Post Office* [1974] IRLR 46 a telegraph officer was dismissed when he failed an aptitude test after the maximum number of attempts. It was held that his dismissal was fair.

The employer will have to prove that the employee was actually incapable of doing the job he was employed to do. The *Burchell* test means that the employer must show he genuinely believed, on reasonable grounds, that the employee was incapable. This means that he must produce evidence for the tribunal that the employee was failing to meet standards. Such evidence will come from a comparison with employees doing the same work, or with results such as sales figures.

The tribunal will look to see whether the employee knew that he was failing to achieve the correct standards or whether he was left in blissful ignorance. Just as it will be unfair not to lay down the standards, it will be unfair not to warn the employee that his standards are dropping or not reaching an acceptable level. In other words, the tribunal will look to see if the employee has been warned. As Donaldson J pointed out in *Winterhalter Gastronom* v. *Webb* [1973] IRLR 120, many do not know they are capable of jumping the five-barred gate until the bull is close behind them. This means that in the majority of cases, dismissals for incapability will only be fair if there is a period of inability, with evidence of warnings and evidence of the employee's lack of improvement. In some cases, however, a one-off act will justify dismissal if the consequences are serious. In *Alidair* v. *Taylor* [1978] IRLR 82 a pilot was dismissed after a bad landing in fair weather conditions. The landing caused damage to the plane but the passengers were uninjured. It was held that his dismissal was fair.

Ill-health   Incapability because of ill-health requires different considerations on the part of the employer because no amount of training or warnings will make the employee get well again. In situations of sickness the starting point is the reason for the illness. If the sickness is caused by the working conditions then the employer must try to take steps to alleviate the conditions or provide alternative employment, and only if neither of these are possible will a resultant dismissal be fair. A risk of illness may result in a fair dismissal if the employee is in an important position and a sudden illness could be potentially dangerous. In *Converform (Darwen) Ltd* v. *Bell* [1981] IRLR 195, however, it was held unfair to dismiss the works director who had had a heart attack when the employer discovered he had been warned that he was in great danger of having another.

The law distinguishes between persistent short-term illness and a single long-term illness. In relation to the former, the Employment Appeal Tribunal has said that in such cases the procedure to be adopted is akin to that adopted in misconduct cases (*International Sports Co Ltd* v. *Thomson* [1980] IRLR 340). In such cases a warning as to the consequences of persistent absence will normally be reasonable as well as a review of the employee's attendance record. There is usually no point in requiring a medical investigation although should the review reveal an underlying cause for the absences the tribunal will expect a medical investigation to have been carried out.

In relation to long-term sickness the situation and procedure are different. First, the nature and length of the illness may frustrate the contract, in which case issues of dismissal and fairness are irrelevant as there has been no termination, but rather the contract has come to an end by operation of law rather than by the actions of either party (see Chapter 8). Where the illness does not frustrate the contract the tribunal will look for sympathetic treatment by the employer, including consultation with the employee.

The starting point is again evidence. Reliance on medical certificates is unlikely to suffice and consultation with the employee's doctor and a company doctor or an independent specialist is normally essential. As the reason for the dismissal is that the employee's illness makes him incapable of doing the job, it is necessary that the doctors know the nature of the job that the employee is employed to do. The employee's doctor cannot give information to an employer without the employee's consent and by the Access to Medical Reports Act 1988, the employee has a right to see any report prepared by his doctor and can veto its transmission to his employer. Furthermore, an employer does not have an implied right to require his employees to undergo a medical examination by a company doctor or a specialist (*Bliss* v. *South East Thames Regional Health Authority* [1987] ICR 700). If the employee refuses however, a tribunal may well find any subsequent dismissal fair. Should the medical evidence conflict, the employer should normally seek the opinion of a third doctor, although this may be unnecessary where there is a conflict between the employee's general practitioner and the company doctor who will be more aware of the nature of the employee's job.

Once the medical evidence has been obtained, the employer should consult with his employee. In *Luke* v. *Navy, Army & Airforce Institutes* (1990) EAT 223/90 the employee worked for NAAFI, installing and maintaining billiard tables. On 31 October 1988 he had a road accident in which he sustained a severe whiplash injury. In February 1989 NAAFI's medical officer examined him and concluded that he could not resume the work for which he was employed but that he could do alternative lighter work. The employee's own doctor agreed with this assessment. In June 1989 the employee was warned that if he did not return to work within three months his contract would be terminated. Meanwhile the employer had looked for alternative work but could find none and in September the employee was dismissed. The Employment Appeal Tribunal held that while there was sufficient evidence of incapacity to do the job, the employer had failed to adequately consult with the employee and the dismissal was unfair. On the other hand, if the employer can show that there was good reason not to consult, he may escape a finding of unfair dismissal but only if the circumstances are exceptional. By contrast with *Luke* there is the case of *Eclipse Blinds Ltd* v. *Wright* [1992] IRLR 133. In this case the employee's health had gradually deteriorated. In 1987 she had been made part time and in 1989 she was off for a long period. Her General Practitioner considered that her health was not good and that she would not return to work in the near future. The company decided that a permanent replacement was needed. The manager did not consult with the employee but wrote to her instead. He thought it would be difficult to talk to her as, unlike her doctor, she thought she was improving. The tribunal found that on the circumstances the failure to consult was not unfair and the decision was supported by the Employment Appeal Tribunal.

The different treatment of long-term illness and persistent short-term sickness is well illustrated by comparing two Employment Appeal Tribunal decisions. In *Mitchell* v. *Arkwood Plastics (Engineering) Ltd* [1993] ICR 471 Mitchell was absent from work after fracturing his shin as a result of an accident at work in May 1990. For four months, apart from sick certificates, there was no communication between Mitchell and his employers. On 27 September the employers wrote to him and asked when he would be fit to return to work. Mitchell went to see his doctor and replied on 5 October, stating that he did not know his date of return as he was due to see a consultant. One week later Mitchell was dismissed. The employment tribunal held that the dismissal was fair as the employee had a duty to keep his employer informed as to his progress. The Employment Appeal Tribunal, allowing Mitchell's appeal, held that the employee was under no such duty. The employers should have discovered the true medical position before dismissing on health grounds and should have considered the possibility of Mitchell undertaking light duties until he was fully recovered. By contrast, in *London Borough of Tower Hamlets* v. *Bull* (1993) Personnel Today, 10 August, Bull was absent from work for a total of 110 days between October 1987 and February 1990 with a variety of unconnected illnesses. In February 1990 he was called in to see the council's doctor who reported that Bull was not suffering from any underlying medical condition. In May 1990, after another period of absence, Bull was warned that unless his attendance improved he would be dismissed. In June he was absent for a further four days and was sacked. After his dismissal, Bull's trade union representative told the council that Bull had a drinking problem and that that was the reason for his absences. The council, however, refused to reconsider its decision and did not activate its special procedure for dealing with alcohol-related problems. The employment tribunal found that Bull had been unfairly dismissed because the council had not consulted Bull's doctor. The Employment Appeal Tribunal disagreed. There was no duty to consult the employee's doctor in these circumstances in the light of the absence record. Furthermore, the council was entitled to ignore Bull's alcohol problem as it had not been raised until after the dismissal.

Employers should also be aware of the impact of the Disability Discrimination Act. If the illness falls into the definition of disability, as discussed in Chapter 5, then a dismissal may be discrimination.

Qualifications

Qualifications are defined as any degree, diploma or other technical or professional qualification relevant to the employee's job. This has been interpreted in *Blue Star Ship Management Ltd* v. *Williams* [1979] IRLR 16 as qualifications which have a bearing on ability or aptitude, such as an HGV licence, and not merely permits or authorisations and so on. It should, however, be a contractual requirement to hold such a qualification. In *Lister* v. *Thom & Sons Ltd* [1975] IRLR 47 the employee was employed as a fitter/driver. He was required to hold an HGV licence if he drove heavy goods vehicles, but he failed the necessary test. He continued in employment, however, as a fitter. His contract did not require him to hold a licence. After a disagreement with his employer, he was told that if he did not obtain his licence he would be sacked. He tried again and failed and was dismissed. It was held that his dismissal was unfair. The requirement to hold the qualification, however, may be implied into the contract. In *Tayside Regional Council* v. *McIntosh* [1982] IRLR 272 the employers advertised for a vehicle mechanic, saying that a driving licence was essential. The applicant was appointed to the post but no mention was made of a driving licence. He subsequently lost his licence and was dismissed. It was held that his dismissal was fair as the nature of the job clearly required a driving licence.

Conduct

Conduct, or more correctly misconduct, is one of the most common reasons for dismissal. Yet again it is up to the employer to provide evidence that the reason exists and so an investigation is essential. In relation to this reason in particular, the procedure used by the employer will be closely scrutinised by the tribunal, particularly how far the employer's procedure complies with or adopts the principles of the *ACAS Code of Practice on Disciplinary and Grievance Procedures*. The code, the statutory disciplinary and dismissal procedures and the employer's procedures will be discussed below when looking at aspects of reasonableness. While the statute lays down no guidelines as to the type or seriousness of misconduct that can justify dismissal, some principles seem to have emerged from the cases. First, the conduct does not have to be gross, only substantial in relation to the circumstances of the case, so that relatively minor acts may, in certain circumstances, justify dismissal. Second, the conduct does not have to be blameworthy. In *Jury* v. *EEC Quarries Ltd* [1980] EAT 241/80 the employee refused to retrain as a Class 2 HGV driver when all Class 3 vehicles went out of service, and he was dismissed. It was held that although he was in no way to blame, his dismissal was fair. Third, if the employer has a number of suspects and after an investigation cannot discover which one is guilty, but knows at least one must be, it appears that it is fair to dismiss all. This was stated by the Court of Appeal in *Monie* v. *Coral Racing Ltd* [1981] ICR 109 and has been applied to the dismissal of four employees in *Parr* v. *Whitbread plc t/a Threshers Wine Merchants* [1990] IRLR 39. Care must be taken, however, to ensure that the employer has narrowed the group down to only those who could have done it and his investigation must show how he has discounted other potential suspects.

For the purposes of looking simply at the reason for dismissal for the moment, by an analysis of the cases we can see the type of conduct which can justify dismissal. The tribunal usually will be looking at misconduct committed within employment, but in some circumstances conduct committed outside the employment situation can justify dismissal.

Conduct inside employment

Absenteeism and lateness As a general rule, absenteeism and lateness are not gross misconduct and therefore the employer cannot fairly dismiss for a first offence. If, however, the consequences are serious, such as the loss of a big order, dismissal may be fair (*Galloway* v. *K. Miller (Contractors)* (1980) COIT 243/80). In the majority of situations the employer must warn his employee and investigate the reasons for the lateness or absenteeism before dismissing.

Disloyalty We have already seen that the employee owes a duty of loyalty to his employer and should he act disloyally, he will be in breach of contract. Disloyalty may take a number of forms. The employee may disclose confidential information to an unauthorised person, he may be working for his employer's competitor in his spare time or actually conducting a rival business. In all of these situations, provided the employer has the evidence that the employee is guilty, then dismissal, in some cases instant dismissal, will be fair. In *Carson* v. *John Lewis & Co* (1977) EAT 266/77 a manager failed to tell her employers that she was working in competition to them in her spare time (she was required to inform them of outside work by the works rules) and then lied about her activities when she was found out. It was held that she was fairly dismissed. The outside work must be potentially damaging to the employer however. In *Nova Plastics Ltd* v. *Froggatt* [1982] IRLR 146 an odd-job man did work for a competitor of his employer in his spare time and was dismissed when this was discovered. It was held that, given his position in the firm, he was unlikely to know or pass on information which could damage his main employer and his dismissal was unfair. Dismissing for working for a non-rival in his spare time will almost certainly be unfair unless it affects the employee's performance.

One major problem in this area is when the employee intends to leave and does preparatory work to setting up on his own. In *Marshall* v. *Industrial Systems and Control Ltd* [1992] IRLR 294 the employee was the managing director of a company which distributed software. The company's major customer was a large American plane-maker. The employee had been warned of poor performance in autumn 1990 although not actually threatened with dismissal. In December 1990, the company discovered that the employee and another manager intended to set up in competition and had approached the American customer and had sought to induce another employee to join them. The managing director was dismissed. The employee argued that his dismissal was unfair because it was obvious that the respondents were waiting to dismiss him on poor performance and it was reasonable for him to take steps to secure his own future. He relied on the previous decision of *Laughton and Hawley* v. *Bapp Industries Supplies Ltd* [1986] IRLR 245 where it was held that writing to suppliers and asking for price lists was not a breach of duty, even though it indicated the employee was going to set up in competition when he left. The Employment Appeal Tribunal so decided because there was no evidence of an intention to abuse confidential information, and no evidence that the employee had not devoted the whole of his time to the employer's business before leaving. The Employment Appeal Tribunal rejected the analogy in *Marshall*, the important distinction between the two cases being that it is not a breach of duty to hold an intention to set up in competition or to find out prices from suppliers, but it becomes a breach of duty when key employees are approached to leave, and direct and definite approaches are made to the employer's customers. From *Marshall* it appears that such conduct will justify dismissal even if there is no evidence of a danger of future misuse of information or connections; in other words, it is irrelevant if the customers approached would not leave the existing employer. It is the approach which is the breach of duty, not the consequences. This is supported by *Tithebarn Ltd* v. *Hubbard* (1992) (unreported) where the employee was dismissed for trying to entice other employees to join him when he set up in competition. The Employment Appeal Tribunal held that this conduct did not amount to a breach of duty and his dismissal was unfair.

Disobedience   It has been seen that another duty in the employment contract is that the employee shall obey the lawful, reasonable orders of his employer and thus refusal to do so is a breach of contract and misconduct. Chapter 4 has already demonstrated that not all orders are reasonable even if they are within the employee's contract and, likewise, some orders will be deemed reasonable even though they go outside the employee's contractual duties. What constitutes a reasonable order is often a question of fact for the tribunal, looking at the circumstances of the case. In any case of dismissal for disobedience, therefore, the tribunal will look to see if the order is lawful and reasonable and whether the employee had valid grounds for refusing to comply with it.

The starting point will be the contractual duties. As a rule of thumb, refusal to obey a contractually binding order will normally be fair unless the employee has very good reasons for his refusal. In *Osborn Transport Services v. Chrissanthors* (1977) EAT 412/77 a driver refused to pick up a load from a customer with whom he had had a bad experience. He was dismissed for disobedience and the tribunal ruled that his dismissal, in the circumstances, was unfair. Conversely, refusal to do something which is outside the contract may still constitute disobedience. We have already seen in *Horrigan v. Lewisham London Borough Council* (Chapter 4) that refusal to do non-contractual overtime can justify a dismissal if there are no valid reasons for the refusal.

Many refusals will come from employees whose duties or hours have changed because of a business reorganisation. In *Ellis* v. *Brighton Co-operative Society Ltd* [1976] IRLR 419 the employee, after returning to work following an illness, discovered that the employer had agreed a reorganisation with the union which involved the employee working additional hours. He refused to work over his contractual hours and was dismissed. The Employment Appeal Tribunal held that, while the employee was not bound to work those hours, the employer, having consulted with the union, could not be expected to make an exception for one employee and therefore the dismissal was fair under some other substantial reason (see below).

Refusal to relocate may amount to misconduct if there is a mobility clause in the contract, although the tribunal may imply a provision of reasonable notice depending on the extent of the move and the circumstances of the employee (*United Bank* v. *Ahktar*, see Chapter 3). Even without an express mobility clause, if the move will not affect the employee's travelling time or expenses the order will be reasonable. In some circumstances, the court may imply a mobility clause if that is the way the parties have operated the contract in the past (*Courtaulds Northern Spinning Ltd* v. *Sibson*, above).

Breach of company rules may also amount to disobedience even though they are not contractual, although just because the rules state that certain conduct will result in dismissal it does not necessarily follow that the dismissal will be fair. In *Laws Stores Ltd* v. *Oliphant* [1978] IRLR 251 it was held to be unfair to dismiss an employee with eight-years' service for till irregularities even though the works rules stated that such irregularities constituted gross misconduct. This was supported by the Court of Session in *Ladbroke Racing Ltd* v. *Arnott and Others* [1983] IRLR 154 when three employees broke the company rule against placing bets at their own place of work. While such conduct was stated in the rules to be a dismissable offence, the court held that the dismissals of the employees were unfair. To apply the rule rigidly, without taking all the circumstances into account, was unreasonable. Where the rule broken is one of the company's health and safety rules, the tribunal is more likely to find that the dismissal is fair, given the employer's safety duties towards his employees. In *Lindsay* v. *Dunlop Ltd* [1980] IRLR 93 a group of employees refused to work in an area which contained hot rubber fumes which were believed to cause cancer. The employer was waiting for a report from the Health and Safety Executive to see what changes were necessary and asked the employees as a temporary measure to wear masks. All the employees agreed apart from Lindsay. It was held that his subsequent dismissal was fair. It was reasonable for the employer to wait for a specialist report before making major changes.

Dishonesty   Although dishonesty is a criminal matter, the employer does not have to produce evidence that establishes beyond a reasonable doubt that the employee is guilty. As with all of the reasons, he merely has to show that he has a genuine belief in the employee's guilt. The fact that the employee is charged, however, is not sufficient to establish a genuine belief without investigation by the employer (*Scottish Special Housing Association* v. *Cooke and Others* [1979] IRLR 264). The major problem in this area is that the employer needs to investigate to discover the evidence he needs to establish his reason, but often the police are also investigating and the employee will have been instructed by his solicitor to say nothing during the employer's investigation. It appears that if the employer has enough evidence without the employee's statement to come to a reasonable belief, the dismissal will be fair even if the employee is subsequently acquitted of criminal charges. In *Harris and Shepherd* v. *Courage* [1981] IRLR 153 two drivers loading stolen beer were identified by witnesses. The police later charged them with theft and on the advice of their solicitor, the employees refused to take part in the employer's investigation. The employer dismissed them and they were later acquitted. It was held that the dismissals were fair because the employer had enough evidence to form a reasonable belief in their guilt. It is the employer's belief at the time of the dismissal which is important, not what happens afterwards.

Violence and fighting   In relation to fighting the employer must gather all the evidence available before he can establish his reason. Interviewing only one or two witnesses will be insufficient. Again, many employers will class fighting as gross misconduct within the works rules, but as in other areas, rigid enforcement of the rules without taking all the circumstances into account will render a dismissal unfair. Issues such as the status of the employee, where the fight took place, provocation and past work record should all be considered.

Other misconduct   While it is impossible to go through every act of misconduct which could justify dismissal, a general point should be noted. Dismissal will be fair if it is within the range of reasonable responses that a reasonable employer would adopt (*Rolls-Royce Ltd* v. *Walpole* [1980] IRLR 342), therefore it is not within the remit of the tribunal to find that a dismissal is unfair because it would not have dismissed in those circumstances. If a reasonable employer would have dismissed, the dismissal is fair. In *East Berkshire Health Authority* v. *Matadeen* (1992) The Times, 1 July the employee, a charge nurse in a hospital for the mentally and physically handicapped, admitted to making a number of nuisance telephone calls to members of the nursing staff. The health authority found this to be gross misconduct and dismissed him. The employment tribunal felt that his conduct was not serious misconduct and found that his dismissal was unfair. The Court of Appeal found the tribunal's decision to be perverse. The question is whether a reasonable employer would have dismissed him, not whether the tribunal would have acted in that way.

Conduct outside employment

As a general rule, conduct outside the employment hours has nothing to do with the employer and he cannot therefore discipline his employee. In some circumstances, however, the conduct may reflect on the relationship in that the employer loses all trust and confidence in the employee. In these situations, dismissal may be fair if the employer can show that the conduct outside working hours has a direct effect on the employment relationship. For example, if a lorry driver is convicted of a drink-driving offence and loses his licence, it will be fair to dismiss him if there is no alternative work he can do. But whereas that example is fairly self-explanatory, others are not. It appears that if the conduct is such that it makes the employee unsuitable for his job, or unacceptable to other employees, or could cause potential harm to the employer's business, dismissal will be fair. In *Moore* v. *C&A Modes* [1981] IRLR 71 a section leader was dismissed after 20-years' service after being convicted of a shop-lifting offence in another store. It was held that her dismissal was fair. In *Gardiner* v. *Newport Borough Council* [1974] IRLR 262 a lecturer of boys aged 16–18 was convicted of committing an indecent act with another man in a public toilet. His subsequent dismissal was fair and in *Whitlow* v. *Alkanet Construction Ltd* [1975] IRLR 321 the dismissal of an employee who was sent to do work in one of his director's houses and who used the opportunity to begin an affair with the director's wife was also held to be fair. The director felt that if he could not trust him with his own wife, he certainly could not trust him with customers' wives! On the other hand, in *Bradshaw* v. *Rugby Portland Cement Ltd* [1972] IRLR 46 the dismissal of an employee after his conviction for incest was held to be unfair. The conduct had no bearing on his work and there was no evidence that his colleagues found him unacceptable to work with (see also *Securicor Guarding Ltd* v. *R* [1994] IRLR 633).

Redundancy

Redundancy is the third fair reason that can be pleaded by an employer. If the employee claims a redundancy payment there is a presumption that the dismissal was due to redundancy by s.163(2) Employment Rights Act 1996 but the presumption will not apply if the employee claims unfair dismissal (*Midland Foot Comfort Centre* v. *Moppett* [1983] All ER 294). In this case the employer must show that redundancy was the reason for the dismissal. Even if redundancy is the reason, if the employee shows that he was chosen for a reason which is automatically unfair, or there was lack of consultation or warning, he will win his claim for unfair dismissal. In addition, the law requires that the employer has a fair procedure when dealing with redundancies and even though the employer may show that the reason exists and that there was fair selection, he may still find himself at the end of a ruling of unfair dismissal if he has not handled the redundancies reasonably. Aspects of reasonableness in respect of redundancies are discussed below.

To establish the reason, the employer must show that a redundancy situation exists within the statutory definition in s.139(1) Employment Rights Act 1996. While the definition will be discussed fully in Chapter 10, at present it is sufficient to state that this means that the employer must show that he is ceasing business, moving his place of business or that work of the particular kind which the employee was employed to do has ceased or diminished or expected to cease or diminish. Even though the reason may exist however, there will be an unfair dismissal if the employee can show that he falls within the provisions relating to an automatically unfair redundancy. The provisions are contained in the Employment Rights Act 1996 and the Trade Union and Labour Relations (Consolidation) Act 1992. The Employment Rights Act provides: where the circumstances constituting the redundancy applied equally to one or more other employees in the same undertaking who held positions similar to that held by him and who have not been dismissed by the employer and he was selected for dismissal because he was carrying out health and safety duties; he was a shop worker or betting shop worker who refused to work Sundays; he asserted a statutory right; he was an employee representative; he was a trustee of an occupational pension scheme; he made a protected disclosure; he asserted working time rights; he asserted rights under the National Minimum Wage Act 1998; he asserted tax credit rights; the assertion of part-time worker rights; the assertion of fixed term employee rights; he took leave for family reasons (including parental leave, dependant leave and maternity leave); he was absent on jury service; he requested flexible working or, in the case of a female employee, she was selected because of her pregnancy or because she had recently given birth. The 1992 Act adds further reasons: that selection was for membership or non-membership of a trade union, participation in the activities of an independent trade union at the appropriate time, use of trade union facilities or services at an appropriate time, refusing an inducement to come out of collective bargaining and certain dismissals in connection with statutory recognition and certain dismissals during industrial action.

All the above provisions show that there are three stages involved: the employees must be in the same undertaking, similar employees must have been retained and selection must have been on the basis of one of the reasons above.

The same undertaking

The meaning of 'undertaking' is not clear, but it is probably wider than an establishment at a particular location and could mean the whole of the employer's business if run in a unified way. A common management will be a relevant factor but flexibility of labour and different skills could also affect the decision. Thus departments could be considered in isolation in some circumstances.

Similarly placed employees

At least one other employee must remain employed in a similar position to that of the dismissed employee. The tribunal will look at the type of work as well as the status of the employee, his skills and the terms and conditions of employment (*Simpson* v. *Roneo Ltd* [1972] IRLR 5). If others are capable of doing the work of the redundant employee, they will only be in similar positions if they have covered the work in the past or there is a great deal of interchange of labour at the workplace (*Dorrell* v. *Engineering Developments Ltd* [1975] IRLR 234).

Automatically unfair reasons

Once the employee has established that similarly placed employees in the same undertaking were not selected, he must then show that the reason for his selection was one of the automatically unfair reasons listed above. These reasons are discussed later. In all of the cases of automatically unfair reasons for selection the normal continuity does not apply (s.108) and neither does the normal age limit (s.109).

Statutory restriction

The penultimate potentially fair reason for dismissal is that the employee could no longer continue to work in the position which he held without contravention by himself or his employer of a duty or restriction imposed by or under any enactment. The provision is objective and there must be potential contravention of a legislative provision – an employer's misguided belief in such a contravention will not suffice. In *Bouchaala* v. *Trusthouse Forte Hotels Ltd* [1980] IRLR 382 the employer was mistaken as to the legality of a work permit obtained by the employee and dismissed him. It was held that it was not a dismissal for statutory contravention. The statutory provision must specifically relate to the work the employee was actually employed to do. Thus if an employee is employed solely or substantially to drive a vehicle, he might be fairly dismissed should he be disqualified from driving. In *Appleyard* v. *Smith (Hull) Ltd* [1972] IRLR 19 a mechanic in a small garage was banned from driving. A substantial part of his job was road-testing vehicles and after his ban the employer could not find him sufficient work to do which did not involve driving. It was held that his dismissal was fair. An employer must show, however, that the prohibited part of his duties constituted a significant part of his job and that the employer considered whether he could continue to employ him until the disqualification ceased. By contrast in *Mathieson* v. *W.J. Noble & Son Ltd* [1972] IRLR 76 a travelling salesman was disqualified from driving and had arranged for a driver to drive him for the period of his ban. The employer dismissed him without seeing if the arrangement would work and it was held that the dismissal was unfair.

Some other substantial reason

The final potential fair reason in s.98(1)(b) Employment Rights Act 1996 seems almost to be a catch-all reason in that if the reason does not fall within the first four it will be caught by this one, bearing in mind that almost anything will fall under this heading. While cases do show that a variety of different situations will fall within s.98(1)(b), the two most common situations which arise in the tribunals and courts are business needs and pressure from third parties.

Business needs

This is the situation where the employer is changing the terms of the employee's contract and thus is in breach, and the employee refuses to accept the change. It should be stressed that the fact that the employee has a right to refuse to accept the change has no bearing on the fairness or otherwise of the dismissal and in many cases the needs of the business will be overriding. In *RS Components* v. *Irwin* [1973] IRLR 239 the employer was losing business because his sales staff were leaving and working for competitors. The employer unilaterally imposed restrictive covenants on the existing sales staff and the employee was dismissed when he refused to accept the change in his contractual terms. It was held that his dismissal was fair. Originally, to justify a change in terms and conditions, the employer had to show that the business was in serious danger of being brought to a standstill (*Ellis* v. *Brighton Co-operative Society Ltd* [1976] IRLR 419), but the standard is not so high today and the employer must only show that there is a sound business reason for the reorganisation. It is not sufficient, however, for the employer to show merely that the change was a good idea. He must show what advantages or benefits the policy will bring. The tribunal does not need to be convinced that it would have taken similar measures, only that a sound business reason existed, necessitating changes, and that the changes could reasonably have either alleviated the problem, improved the business or maximised its potential. In *Hollister* v. *National Farmers' Union* [1979] ICR 542 the union reorganised its insurance business so that the terms of the employees who sold the insurance changed. In deciding that the dismissal of one who refused to accept the changes was fair, the Court of Appeal said that a tribunal only had to ask 'whether the reorganisation was such that the only sensible thing to do was to terminate the employee's contract unless he would agree to a new arrangement'. The decision as to what reorganisation takes place is therefore a management decision alone. In *McGibbon and McCoy* v. *O.I.L. Ltd* (1995) IDS Brief 541 the Employment Appeal Tribunal said that it was for the tribunal to carry out a balancing exercise, whereby the disadvantages to the employee and the advantages to the employer in the offer of new contracts have to be weighed up.

A dismissal arising from a change in terms is more likely to be fair if:

- many or all the other employees have agreed to the change (*Robinson* v. *Flitwick Frames Ltd* [1975] IRLR 261);
- the union has agreed to the change (*Bowater Containers Ltd* v. *McCormack* [1980] IRLR 50);
- the change is trivial (*Baverstock* v. *Horsley Smith & Co* COIT 910/112).

While reorganisation is the most common business need, the tribunals do accept others. In *Farr* v. *Hoveringham Gravels Ltd* [1972] IRLR 104 the employee, who was on 24-hour call-out, moved to a house some 40 miles from his place of work. It was held that his subsequent dismissal was fair. In *Foot* v. *Eastern Counties Timber Co Ltd* [1972] IRLR 83 the employee was dismissed when it was discovered that she was married to an employee of a rival firm. Again the dismissal was fair.

Pressure from third parties

Where other employees refuse to work with a colleague or customers put pressure on the employer, it may be fair to dismiss even though the employee has done nothing wrong. In *Scott Packaging Ltd* v. *Paterson* [1978] IRLR 465 the Employment Appeal Tribunal held that it would be justifiable to dismiss an employee in response to an ultimatum from the company's major customer. In *Dobie* v. *Burns International Security Services (UK) Ltd* [1984] ICR 812 the employee was employed by the company which provided the security service at Liverpool Airport and was based at the airport as a security officer. Following two incidents for which he was not to blame, the airport refused to have him working there. The employers offered him alternative work at a lower rate of pay which he refused and he was dismissed. The Court of Appeal held that his dismissal was fair. This decision, while within the statutory provisions, seems particularly harsh as the customer's reasons for their reaction is never brought to question and it means that the employee, who may be blameless, can be fairly dismissed because of a whim of a person outside the employment relationship. If work colleagues refuse to work with the employee, this too can constitute some other substantial reason (SOSR). In *Treganowan* v. *Robert Knee & Co Ltd* [1975] IRLR 247 a woman upset other staff she worked with by describing in detail her affair with a younger man. Eventually they refused to work with her and it was held that her consequent dismissal was fair.

In one situation, however, pressure put upon the employer will be ignored for the purposes of determining whether the dismissal is fair or not. This is where the pressure is brought by a union in the form of the threat of a strike or other industrial action (s.107 Employment Rights Act 1996). Furthermore by s.160 Trade Union and Labour Relations (Consolidation) Act 1992 either the employer or the employee may join the union as a party to the unfair dismissal proceedings, and the tribunal may apportion any compensation to be paid between the employer and the union so it may be that the union pays all of the award to the complainant.

9.6 The Concept of Reasonableness

Although the employer only has to prove that he has a fair reason for dismissal, in some ways this is deceiving. Section 98(4) Employment Rights Act 1996 states:

> 'Where the employer has fulfilled the requirements of subsection (1) . . . the determination of the question of whether the dismissal was fair or unfair, having regard to the reasons shown by the employer, shall depend on whether in the circumstances (including the size and administrative resources of the employer's undertaking) the employer acted reasonably or unreasonably in treating it as a sufficient reason for dismissing the employee; and that question shall be determined in accordance with equity and the substantial merits of the case.'

In other words, having a fair reason to dismiss is only one step. The employer must show the tribunal that he acted reasonably in dismissing the employee and he can only do that by ensuring that the members of the tribunal have considerable information before them as to how he dealt with the employee and how he has dealt with similar cases in the past. Thus, while the employer does not have to prove that he acted reasonably in the circumstances, he will certainly have to bring forward much evidence of his conduct in the particular case before the tribunal and of his conduct in previous cases, to allow the tribunal to come to a decision. It must be stressed, however, that just because the tribunal would not have dismissed in those circumstances, this does not make the dismissal unfair. This was pointed out by Browne-Wilkinson J in *Iceland Frozen Foods* v. *Jones* [1983] ICR 17. In that case he pointed out the correct approach for an employment tribunal when considering the question of reasonableness and he gave a five-stage approach that tribunals should adopt:

'(1) the starting point should always be the words of section (98(4)) themselves; (2) in applying the section an industrial tribunal must consider the reasonableness of the employer's conduct, not simply whether they (the members of the industrial (employment) tribunal) consider the dismissal to be fair; (3) in judging the reasonableness of the employer's conduct an industrial (employment) tribunal must not substitute its decision as to what was the right course to adopt for that employer; (4) in many, though not all, cases there is a band of reasonable responses to the employee's conduct within which one employer might reasonably take one view, another quite reasonably take another; (5) the function of the industrial (employment) tribunal, as an industrial jury, is to determine whether in the particular circumstances of each case the decision to dismiss the employee fell within the band of reasonable responses which a reasonable employer might have adopted.'

The oft-quoted phrase 'band of reasonable responses' is the essence of any unfair dismissal case and you would be forgiven for thinking that this allows employers considerable latitude and that only the most unreasonable dismissals will be judged to be unfair. While this would perhaps be overstating the situation, it is only later cases laying down principles in relation to consistency and fair procedure that have perhaps limited total autocratic action on the part of the employer. The employment tribunals are kept in check by the higher courts and should they substitute their own decision for that of the employer, their decision will be perverse and an appeal will lie. In the case of *East Berkshire Health Authority* v. *Matadeen* (above) the Court of Appeal discussed the issue of perverse decisions. The applicant was a charge nurse and in 1988 he admitted to making nuisance calls to other members of nursing staff. The health authority found this to be gross misconduct and dismissed him. The tribunal upheld his complaint of unfair dismissal because they did not feel that his conduct constituted serious misconduct and therefore dismissal was not in the band of reasonable responses which the employer was entitled to make. The health authority appealed against the decision and eventually the case came before the Court of Appeal. In *Neale* v. *Hereford & Worcester County Council* [1986] ICR 471 the Court of Appeal said that an employment tribunal's decision could be said to be perverse if the appeal tribunal could say of the decision, 'My goodness, that was certainly wrong'. However, in *Piggott* v. *Jackson* [1992] ICR 85 a later Court of Appeal urged caution when applying this definition because it allowed the appeal tribunal to take the impermissible step of substituting its own decision for that of the tribunal. A finding of perversity had to be supported by other evidence, that is, that the tribunal had misdirected itself in law or had reached a conclusion which was unsupported by the facts. In the *Matadeen* case, the Court found that the Employment Appeal Tribunal could not find the employment tribunal's decision to be perverse simply because it would have reached a different decision. However, the employment tribunal had found the employer's decision to be irrational and to defy logic. It was therefore wrong in law and thus perverse.

Section 98(4) talks of the tribunal deciding whether the employer acted reasonably in treating the reason as sufficient cause to justify dismissal 'in accordance with equity and the substantial merits of the case'. In practice, this means that a tribunal will look at two aspects when looking at reasonableness – the actual fairness of the decision, that is whether dismissal was outside the range of reasonable responses for this type of conduct, and procedural fairness, that is whether the employer used a fair procedure before the employee's eventual dismissal. In looking at the employer's procedures, the tribunal must take into account the size and administrative resources of the employer's undertaking, so that a larger employer may be expected to reach different standards from those of a smaller one. In practice, of course, the two aspects are invariably interlinked.

Fairness of the decision

It has been noted already that the decision of the employer must be within the band of reasonable responses that a reasonable employer would choose, but this leaves the question of what is a reasonable employer and what does he take into account when making his decision. The tribunal will look at a variety of factors such as how the employer has treated such cases in the past, whether he has taken the employee's past work record into account, whether he has taken the length of the employee's service into account and whether he has looked to see if there is an alternative to dismissal in appropriate circumstances.

Consistency

An employee must know where the goal posts are and what penalty he can expect for certain conduct. If the employer is inconsistent in the way he applies his sanctions, employees will not know where they stand and this in itself may render a dismissal unfair. If the employer treats employees differently, or has treated certain conduct leniently in the past and then decides to raise standards, this will leave employees not knowing where they stand and feeling a sense of injustice when they are treated differently for the same act. In *Post Office* v. *Fennell* [1981] IRLR 221 an employee was instantly dismissed after assaulting a colleague in the staff canteen. He argued that other workers who had committed the same offence in the past had not been dismissed. The Court of Appeal held that his dismissal was unfair. In *Hadjioannou* v. *Coral Casinos Ltd* [1981] IRLR 352 the Employment Appeal Tribunal limited the operation of *Fennell* by saying that consistency was only relevant where employees had been misled into thinking that certain conduct would be overlooked or that dismissal would not be the sanction. This has now been followed in *Levenes Solicitors* v. *Dalley* [2007] All ER 52. The Employment Appeal Tribunal reviewed consistency in the case of *Proctor* v. *British Gypsum* [1991] Personnel Today, 3 December. In the case Proctor was a foreman of a team of vehicle loaders who were paid a bonus which depended on the rate of loading. When one of the team refused to resume work after a break, Proctor began arguing with him and eventually hit him. During the disciplinary hearing, the company looked at sanctions it had imposed in the past for similar conduct. While it had imposed lesser sanctions than dismissal previously, the company took the decision to dismiss Proctor. The employment tribunal dismissed his claim of unfair dismissal and he appealed to the Employment Appeal Tribunal which upheld the earlier decision on the basis that the decision could not be faulted, but at the same time took the opportunity to review the law surrounding inconsistency and comparability. From *Wilcox* v. *Humphrey & Gasgow Ltd* [1975] IRLR 211 it was established that before making a decision to dismiss, the employer should consider truly comparable cases which he knew about or ought reasonably to have known about. However, small companies may not keep records and there was no requirement to do so. The Employment Appeal Tribunal then stressed that situations within an undertaking may change. Dishonesty or fighting, for example, may have increased, in which case the employer would only have to go back a few years and not since records began because the policy may have changed. In each situation, however, the comparison must be a true one where the circumstances of the relevant employees were the same. An untrue comparison was as dangerous as no comparison at all. In simple terms, the employer is under a duty to review past sanctions but only by comparing like with like. One thing that is clear, however, is that it is the employer's policies which are relevant and not the policies of individual managers who work for the employer. Consistency within a department but not within an undertaking will not satisfy the requirement of reasonableness (*Cain* v. *Leeds Western Health Authority* [1990] IRLR 168). If the employer considers the case not to be comparable, however, the tribunal cannot substitute its own opinion and say that it is (*Paul* v. *East Surrey Health Authority* [1995] IRLR 305).

Past work record and length of service

In misconduct cases in particular, failure to take account of the employee's past record and length of service may render a dismissal unfair. In *Johnson Matthey Metals Ltd* v. *Harding* [1978] IRLR 248 the employee, who had been employed for 15 years with an unblemished record, was dismissed when a colleague's watch, which had gone missing some time before, was found in his possession. The Employment Appeal Tribunal held that his dismissal was unfair given the length of his previous good service. A good work record can also justify different treatment of employees who have committed the same act of misconduct. In *Sherrier* v. *Ford Motor Co* [1976] IRLR 146 two employees were caught fighting and despite an investigation by the employer, the instigator could not be established. One of the employees had a 15-year unblemished record and the employer suspended him for five days without pay. Sherrier, on the other hand, had been employed for two years and had six disciplinary offences on his record, and the employer dismissed him. His claim for unfair dismissal was dismissed.

Alternative employment

In some cases a reasonable employer will look to see if there is alternative work for the employee to do. This is particularly so in the case of illness or redundancy but the principle can be applied to almost any situation bar serious misconduct. An employee, for example, may have been over-promoted and demotion back to his original grade is a possibility (*Hall* v. *Lodge* [1977] IRLIB 76), however a tribunal will not expect an employer to demote a person who is clearly incompetent at any level. On the other hand, a tribunal will expect an employer to have actively considered alternative employment where the dismissal is for illness, and failure to do so may well render the dismissal unfair, particularly if there is light work that the employee can do (*Todd* v. *North Eastern Electricity Board* [1975] IRLR 60). In *McAdie* v. *Royal Bank of Scotland* [2007] EWCA Civ 806 McAdie was dismissed after being on long-term sick leave as a result of stress caused by bullying and mismanagement at work. The Court of Appeal held that the fact that the employer had caused the incapacity in question did not preclude the dismissal being fair. However, the question for the tribunal was had the employer acted reasonably in the circumstances and the tribunal had to include in its considerations that the employer was to blame for the absence. Where the employer was responsible for an employee's incapacity, it should normally be expected to 'go the extra mile' in finding alternative employment or put up with a longer period of absence than would be otherwise reasonable. On the facts of the case, given she was adamant that she did not want to return to work, her dismissal was fair, although the judgement is clear as to the responsibilities of an employer when incapability is caused by the working environment.

In relation to redundancy, the Employment Rights Act 1996 envisages alternative employment being offered and by s.138 allows the employee a trial period in the new employment without the loss of redundancy compensation should it prove to be unsuitable (see Chapter 10). Certainly, refusing to allow an employee a trial period if alternative employment is offered in a redundancy situation is an unfair dismissal (*Elliot* v. *Richard Stump Ltd* [1987] IRLR 215).

The Court of Appeal has looked at the question of alternative employment in conduct dismissals in the case of *P* v. *Nottinghamshire County Council* [1992] IRLR 362. In that case, P was employed as an assistant groundsman at a school. After a complaint by his 14-year-old daughter, he was arrested and charged with indecent assault and released on bail. The council suspended him on full pay until the outcome of the criminal case. At his trial he pleaded guilty and asked for other offences to be taken into account. At the subsequent disciplinary hearing, P argued that he had only pleaded guilty to prevent his daughter from having to attend court. The council was concerned about the risk to school children and told P he would be dismissed with 12-weeks' notice, but that an attempt would be made to find him alternative employment in the highways department. He was not required to attend for work during his notice period and during his notice he received a letter saying that the highways department would not consider him because of his sickness record. P claimed unfair dismissal. The employment tribunal found that P had been unfairly dismissed. The Employment Appeal Tribunal held that the tribunal had erred in law in its answers to certain questions and remitted the case back to the tribunal for a rehearing. The Court of Appeal held that the tribunal had erred in relation to certain questions, but concentrated on the issue of alternative employment. The employment tribunal had found that the council had not reasonably investigated the possibility of alternative employment but the Employment Appeal Tribunal had found that because the tribunal's answers to questions it had asked itself were wrong, this could have coloured their view on this issue. The Court of Appeal held that where an employee's conduct rendered him unsuitable to continue in employment in a particular capacity, in an appropriate case and where the size and resources of the company permitted, it may be unfair to dismiss without first considering if the employee could be offered an alternative job. This does not have to occur before notice of dismissal is given however, it is dismissal which is the operative act.

Fair procedure

While the tribunals will have regard to the factors listed above, without doubt one of the most important aspects of fairness is the procedure the employer uses before dismissing the employee. Failing to use a procedure or using a procedure unfairly will almost certainly mean that a dismissal is unfair. A reasonable employer has a fair procedure and adheres to it. While there are certain basic principles which apply to any of the reasons for dismissal, the tribunal will look for different procedures applying in different cases. A reasonable employer does not invoke disciplinary procedures against an employee who is long-term sick, for example. The following discussion will therefore look at procedural fairness in relation to each reason for dismissal, in order to highlight both the differences and the similarities.

(a) Statutory procedures

Schedule 2 Employment Act 2002 introduced minimum statutory disciplinary and grievance procedures which impact on procedural fairness. These were given flesh by the Employment Act 2002 (Dispute Resolution) Regulations 2004 and came into force in October 2004. These procedures apply to all of the reasons for dismissal discussed above except for collective redundancies and constructive dismissal. A failure to follow the mandatory statutory dismissal and disciplinary procedure (DDP) will result in a finding of automatically unfair dismissal and compensation can be increased by between 10 and 50 per cent. Likewise, failure on the part of the employee to follow the statutory grievance procedure will, in most cases, prevent a tribunal claim being presented.

Essentially both the statutory discipline and grievance procedures envisage a standard three-step procedure and a modified two-step procedure.

Dismissal and disciplinary procedures (DDPs)

These are given in the Employment Act 2002, Sch 2, Part 1, and the Employment Act 2002 (Dispute Resolution) Regulations 2004. At the time of writing, the Employment Bill 2007 abolishes the procedures and it is likely that this will happen in 2009. The intention behind the procedures was to resolve more disputes in the workplace and thus reduce the number of claims being heard in employment tribunals.

However figures issued by the Tribunal Service in September 2007 showed that tribunal claims 2006/7 were up 15 per cent when compared to 2005/6 figures.

The procedures apply in all situations apart from collective redundancies and constructive dismissals. For action short of dismissal, the DDP applies in the areas of conduct and capability and does not apply when the sanction is a warning.

The standard DDP consists of:

- notifying the employee in writing of the alleged misconduct, characteristics or other circumstances which lead the employer to contemplate dismissal or disciplinary action and inviting the employee to a meeting;
- holding a meeting before deciding on any action (except in the case of a disciplinary suspension) and then informing the employee of the outcome and the right to appeal;
- holding an appeal meeting if required and informing the employee of the final decision.

In *Alexander* v. *Brigden Enterprises Ltd* (2006) UKEAT 010/06 the Employment Appeal Tribunal discussed the information which must be made available to the employee. Schedule 2 Employment Act 2002 states that a meeting should not be held 'unless the employer has informed the employee what the basis was for including in the statement . . . the ground or grounds given in it'. In *Alexander* the dismissals were for redundancy. The EAT held that the employer not only had to tell the employee why redundancies were happening by also why the particular employee was being selected. In *YMCA Training* v. *Stewart* [2006] All ER 69 the Employment Appeal Tribunal held that although the employer did not have to detail all the evidence against the employee, the employee should be given enough information to be able to answer the case against him.

The modified procedure applies in cases of gross misconduct and is the two-step procedure. This consists of:

- notifying the employee in writing of the alleged misconduct which has led to dismissal and informing him of the right to appeal;
- holding an appeal and informing the employee of the final outcome.

In other words, in cases of gross misconduct, the DDPs do not require a hearing before dismissal. The Explanatory Notes to the Act make it clear that the two-step procedure should only be used in exceptional circumstances and suggest that not all gross misconduct should be dealt with by this route. It has to be said that dismissal without a hearing, prior to October 2004, would in almost all circumstances have been unfair, only situations where the employee was caught red-handed being fair dismissals. It has yet to be seen whether this is the way the DDPs are to be interpreted. The government originally intended to make the procedures an implied contractual term in all employees' contracts, but decided against this. Of course, a consequence of making them contractual is that failure to comply would also set up a breach of contract claim, something without doubt which influenced the government's decision. The case of *Scott-Davies* v. *Redgate Medical Services* [2007] ICR 348 makes it clear that there is no free standing right to claim a breach of the statutory procedures if the employee does not have the necessary continuity to claim unfair dismissal. This does not apply in the case of an automatically unfair dismissal where no continuity is needed (*RKS Services* v. *Palen* [2007] All ER 115).

The procedures are regarded as a minimum and apply to all employers, whatever their size. However, many large employers will have procedures which are over and above the minimum, for example an investigative hearing prior to a disciplinary one and two rights of appeal. Section 98A Employment Rights Act 1996 now provides that if an employer has complied with the statutory DDP, any failure to comply with his own procedures which are over and above the statutory minimum shall not render a dismissal unfair, if the failure has made no difference to the final outcome. This is the statutory overruling of the famous House of Lords' decision in *Polkey* v. *A E Dayton Services Ltd* [1987] IRLR 503. In *Polkey* the House of Lords overturned the infamous decision of *British Labour Pump Co Ltd* v. *Byrne* [1979] IRLR 94 and the notorious 'no-difference' rule which allowed an employer to show that even if he had followed his procedures he would still have dismissed the employee, and thus his failure had made no difference to the final outcome. The House of Lords in *Polkey* stated that this was a misinterpretation of the statute, which looked at the reasonableness of the employer's behaviour and not the unfairness to the employee, thus, except in very few cases, a failure to follow a laid down procedure would render a dismissal unfair. Section 98A resurrects the 'no-difference' rule which has caused some disquiet, particularly from Judge Prophet, an ex-President of Employment Tribunals, who feels that employers will become lax in their procedures. It is suggested that this statutory reversal of *Polkey* is unnecessary and will leave employees vulnerable. The Employment Bill 2007 proposes to resurrect the *Polkey* decision.

One issue which has now been resolved is the impact of the procedures on the revised *ACAS Code on Dismissal and Disciplinary Procedures*, much of which has been embedded in case law, as discussed below. We have already seen above that Schedule 2 of the 2002 Act specifies that an employee should be told the basis for the allegation. Schedule 2 further states that the employee, before the meeting, should have a reasonable opportunity to consider his response. In *Premier Foods plc* v. *Garner* [2007] All ER 337 the claimant was one of three employees who received a final written warning after disciplinary proceedings. All three denied the allegations and appealed, and at the appeal two of the employees stated that they had been covering for Garner. Garner was suspended and at a hearing two days later was dismissed. The Employment Appeal Tribunal held that the dismissal was automatically unfair because the employer had failed to follow the statutory DDP. The employer should have started the procedures again when the new evidence was presented. Garner had not been given enough information to know the case against her or enough time to consider her response. In *Bowen* v. *Millbank Estate Management Organisation* [2007] All ER 143 Bowen was suspended and invited to a disciplinary hearing. It was postponed to allow her to arrange to be accompanied and it was only at the hearing that she was given details of the investigation. The allegations were discussed and the hearing adjourned at her request to enable her to make further representations. At the reconvened hearing Bowen was dismissed. Again it was held that the dismissal was automatically unfair as there was a breach of the statutory DDP in that she had been given insufficient information at the initial hearing to enable her to know the case against her or prepare a response. It was irrelevant that the hearing was reconvened. Further, in *Stewart* (above) the Employment Appeal Tribunal made it clear that an employer should not make a decision until he has heard the employee's side. These cases show that the case law built up prior to 2004 and discussed below is still relevant.

In the case of both the disciplinary and grievance procedures, there is a requirement that meetings should be held within a reasonable time. In addition, employees are entitled in both sets of procedures to be accompanied by a companion. This right was introduced by s.10 Employment Relations Act 1999 and applies to workers. The right in relation to disciplinary hearings is to be accompanied to any meeting which may result in the administration of a warning, confirmation of a warning or other disciplinary action. In relation to grievance hearings, the right arises in relation to hearings which are about a 'duty by an employer in relation to a worker' (s.13(5)). The companion is entitled to paid time off to prepare for and attend the hearing. Originally under the 1999 Act the companion had a right to address the hearing on the worker's behalf but could not answer questions. The Employment Relations Act 2004 has extended the right of a companion. A new s.10(2B) allows a companion to put the worker's case; sum up that case and respond on the worker's behalf to any view expressed in the hearing; however by s.10(2C) an employer is not required to permit the companion to answer questions on behalf of the worker. It is submitted that the distinction between responding to a view expressed by the hearing and answering questions, may, in reality, be difficult to distinguish.

As seen above, failure to follow the DDP will result in a finding of automatically unfair dismissal. In addition, the tribunal may increase compensation by between 10 and 50 per cent.

(b) Common law procedures

In order to distinguish the procedures discussed below with the new statutory procedures, I have called the ones about to be discussed 'common law procedures'. These are a set of principles, many coming from the original *ACAS Code of Practice*, which have built up over the years. A number of points should be noted before discussing the procedures in any detail. First, case law has established that different procedures apply for different reasons. Second, in almost all cases, case law has established that an employer should conduct a thorough investigation before conducting a disciplinary hearing. Third, there are established rules in relation to fair hearings and fair appeals. All of these points are contained in the revised *ACAS Code* and it has been seen above that they are part of the DDPs. As noted, case law envisages different procedures applying to the fair reasons, therefore it is proposed to discuss each reason separately.

Capability and qualifications

Inadequate work The starting point for the employer is to decide whether this is deliberate incapability, that is laziness or deliberate negligence or inherent incapability. The former case is really misconduct and should be treated as such. Where the reason appears to be inherent incapability, the tribunal will normally look for three stages in the employer's procedure – an investigation, reasonable opportunity to improve and warnings.

Investigation Instant dismissal without an investigation will almost always be unfair. When the employee is the subject of an investigation, he should be told the scope of the investigation and the facts and the matters alleged against him (*British Midland Airways Ltd* v. *Gilmore* [1981] EAT 173/81). The employer should normally give the employee the opportunity to explain, particularly if the incapability is sudden after years of acceptable work. It may be, for example, that the nature of the job has changed and the employee needs training, or something may have happened in his personal life which is affecting his work. In *Davison* v. *Kent Meters Ltd* (above) the employee had never been shown how to assemble the components. Not surprisingly, her dismissal was found to be unfair. A proper investigation by the employer would have revealed her lack of training.

Reasonable opportunity to improve   If after the investigation the employer can detect no reason for the incapability, for example lack of training, a failure to allow the employee opportunity to improve will often render a dismissal unfair (*Mansfield Hosiery Mills Ltd* v. *Bromley* [1977] IRLR 301). The employee must know, however, where his standards fall down and what he must do to improve. In other words, the employer must tell him specifically what standards to reach – a general comment that he must improve is not likely to get either of them anywhere. The length of time given to the employee will depend on a variety of factors, such as the employee's seniority, length of service and past performance. The employee should be told the date by which he has to improve and be warned that his job is in jeopardy.

Warnings   Normally, the employer should warn the employee before dismissal, but failure to do so may not always render the dismissal unfair. The Employment Appeal Tribunal pointed out in *Littlewoods Organisation Ltd* v. *Egenti* [1976] IRLR 334 that there is a distinction between disciplinary procedures and capability procedures. Whereas disciplinary procedures should always be followed strictly, this is not necessarily the case in relation to capability. The aim of a warning in capability cases is to improve the employee's performance and if the warning would not have this effect one does not have to be given. Thus in *Lowndes* v. *Specialist Heavy Engineering Ltd* [1977] ICR 1 the employee was dismissed after five serious and expensive mistakes. He was not warned and was given no opportunity to make representations. It was held that his dismissal was fair. Having said that, the employer must ensure that his evidence shows that a warning would not have improved the employee. If the tribunal feels that a warning would have made a difference, failing to warn will render the dismissal unfair.

Sickness and injury   The aim of a fair procedure in these cases is the gathering of sufficient information to form an accurate picture of the employee's present and future health and his ability to do the job. This will involve the employer in the gathering of medical evidence and consultation with the employee, giving the employee the opportunity to bring forward his own evidence. Failure to obtain evidence or consult will normally render the dismissal unfair.

Medical evidence   Reliance on medical certificates is unlikely to suffice as evidence. The employer should gain as much evidence as possible from the employee, the employee's doctor and, if appropriate, the company doctor (*East Lindsey District Council* v. *Daubney* [1977] IRLR 191). To ensure that the evidence is pertinent, the employer should inform the doctor of the nature of the employee's job, although the decision to dismiss will ultimately be a managerial and not a medical one. Any fresh evidence which comes to light after the employer has taken the decision to dismiss but before the notice period has expired should be taken into account, and the employer should review his initial decision (*Williamson* v. *Alcan (UK) Ltd* [1977] IRLR 303). The employer must get the employee's permission to obtain evidence from the employee's own doctor under the Access to Medical Reports Act 1988 and the employee can refuse or veto part of the report before it reaches the employer. In such circumstances it will probably be fair to dismiss the employee if the veto is unreasonable and the employer reasonably believed the employee was and would be incapable of performing his job. If there is a conflict between the employee's own evidence and that of the company doctor, the employer will normally be expected to obtain a third opinion, although this may not be necessary where, for example, the company doctor's report is likely to be more accurate because of his knowledge of the nature of the job.

Consultation with the employee The employer should consult with the employee before making his decision and the *Daubney* case (above) says that only in exceptional cases will dismissal where there has been no consultation be fair. Consultation does not mean warnings however, because you cannot warn a person to get well. Consultation means treating the employee with sympathetic consideration, although this does not mean keeping the job open for an unreasonable length of time or creating a job for him if one does not exist. An employer should also not dismiss the employee because of the risk of a recurrence or future illness without strong evidence that a recurrence is likely. In *Converform (Darwen) Ltd* v. *Bell* [1981] IRLR 195 the employee had suffered a heart attack and his employers refused to allow him to return on his recovery because they feared he would have another attack. It was held that in the circumstances his dismissal was unfair. If, however, it was the work environment which had caused the illness, subject to the possibility of alternative employment, it may be fair to dismiss (*Taylorplan Catering (Scotland) Ltd* v. *McInally* [1980] IRLR 53).

Some firms place employees in a holding department and the employees will return when they are fit and a suitable vacancy occurs. The exact position of such an employee will depend on the arrangements made. If the effect is to terminate the contract, with the employer under a moral obligation to provide work when the employee is fit again, there is a dismissal and the employee may sue (*Marshall* v. *Harland & Wolff Ltd* [1972] 1 WLR 899), however it has been held that if the employee agrees to such action there is no dismissal. In *Parker* v. *Westland Helicopters Ltd* IDS Supp 15 an employee was put into a holding department with her consent until a suitable vacancy occurred. It was held that no dismissal had taken place.

Conduct

Every employer must give his employees a copy of the disciplinary procedures which apply to them or refer them to a document stating the procedures. In practice, where an employer has his own disciplinary procedures they will break down into three constituent parts: the rules, the procedures and the sanctions.

Rules Disciplinary rules will either be part of the employer's disciplinary procedures or contained in a separate document such as the works rules or a company handbook. Wherever they are contained they must be communicated to the employee so he knows exactly what conduct is or is not acceptable to the employer. Given that this is the purpose of the rules, it follows that a lack of communication of the rules to the employee or insufficient communication can render a dismissal unfair. In *Brooks & Son* v. *Skinner* [1984] IRLR 379 the employer had agreed with the union that any employee who, as a result of overindulgence at the Christmas party, failed to turn up for work the next day would be dismissed. This agreement was not communicated to the employees and Skinner was dismissed when he failed to show up the next day. It was held that his dismissal was unfair as he would not have realised, without being told, that such conduct could lead to dismissal. This leads to the question, however, of how far must the employer communicate obvious rules, for example that theft is gross misconduct. In *Parsons (C.A.) & Co Ltd* v. *McLoughlin* [1978] IRLR 65 a dismissal for fighting was fair even though it was not included in the employer's rules as gross misconduct, because everyone would know that such conduct would be looked upon gravely by management. It should be stressed, however, that in the particular case the fighting took place by dangerous machinery on the shopfloor, and where the potential consequences are not so serious, failure to communicate the rule may lead to the dismissal being unfair (see, for example, *Meyer Dunmore International Ltd* v. *Rogers* [1978] IRLR 167).

In addition, the employee must understand that what is being communicated to him is a standard to which he must conform. Vague and badly drafted rules which could be misunderstood by an employee could again lead to a finding of unfair dismissal. Even if the rule has been adequately made known to the employee and has been broken, the employer may still be acting unreasonably if the rule breached has no relevance to the employment. The law will not allow an employer to act in an autocratic manner and will always question whether the punishment fits the crime. In *Talbot* v. *Hugh M. Fulton Ltd* [1975] IRLR 52 the employee was dismissed for having long hair contrary to the rules. It was held that his dismissal was unfair. There was no safety risk involved and no definition of what was meant by 'long'. On the other hand, in *Higham* v. *International Stores* [1977] IRLIB 97 there was a company rule requiring employees to wear a tie and proper shoes and socks. The employee was dismissed for continually wearing clogs and sandals and failing to wear a tie. It was held that his dismissal was fair. The shop had a middle-class clientele in a conventional town and it was reasonable for the employer to lay down standards of dress.

Procedures Even if the rule is clear and well-communicated but has still been broken, the employer will lose the case if he has not gone through the correct procedure before dismissing the employee. Normally, if the employer has followed his own procedures the dismissal will be fair, although if the tribunal feels that the procedures themselves are unfair it will lead to a finding of unfair dismissal. In *Vauxhall Motors Ltd* v. *Ghafoor* [1993] ICR 370 the employee was dismissed for fighting. Under the disciplinary procedure agreed with the union, he could only appeal against his dismissal with the consent of the union convenor, who in this case refused his consent. The Employment Appeal Tribunal held that this constituted procedural unfairness because the right to appeal is the right of every individual and such a right should not be taken away without the individual's express consent. The fact that the employee was a union member did not mean he had given this consent.

In the majority of cases the tribunal will look for a thorough investigation, a fair disciplinary hearing and an appeal. At one time it was thought that failing to follow a fair procedure would not render the dismissal unfair if the employer could show that the breach of procedure had made no difference to the employee, that is if the procedure had been followed, the employee would have been dismissed anyway so that the breach of procedure had made no difference to the final outcome (*British Labour Pump Co Ltd* v. *Byrne* [1979] IRLR 94). This so-called 'no-difference' rule was deemed to be a misinterpretation of s.98(4) Employment Rights Act 1996 by the House of Lords in *Polkey* v. *A.E. Dayton Services Ltd* [1987] IRLR 503, their Lordships arguing that the rule concentrated on the unfairness of the decision to the employee rather than the reasonableness of the employer's action. In the case, the employers decided to make three out of four van drivers redundant. Polkey was asked to drive two of the drivers home after they had been given the news of their redundancies and when he returned to his place of work he was called into the office and told that he was the third! The employee claimed unfair dismissal on the basis that he had never been warned or consulted about his redundancy (see below). The employers pleaded the 'no-difference' rule, arguing that even if they had warned and consulted, Polkey would have been made redundant anyway. The House of Lords said that that was irrelevant. A reasonable employer would have warned and consulted whether the redundancy was inevitable or not, and by failing to do so the employer had not acted reasonably. The dismissal was unfair. Since this decision, even greater emphasis was placed on fair procedures and adherence to such by the tribunals, although in *Cabaj* v. *Westminster City Council* (1996) IDS Brief 567 where the procedure allowed for an appeal to be heard by a three-member panel but in *Cabaj* only two turned up and the appeal was heard anyway, the Employment Appeal Tribunal held that this was a fundamental defect and as such rendered the dismissal unfair. The Court of Appeal overturned the decision on the basis that the panel reached a majority decision. As noted above, *Polkey* has now been partially reversed by s.98A so while the employer may now plead the no-difference rule, it may still be the case that failing to follow more detailed procedures, if a tribunal feels that to do so may have prevented the dismissal, will lead to a finding of unfair dismissal. It should be noted, however, that *Polkey* is resurrected in the Employment Bill 2007.

Investigation We have already seen that the employer must have a genuine belief based on reasonable grounds after a reasonable investigation that the employee is guilty. In other words, the employer must gather all the evidence he can so that he can make a reasoned and fair decision (*Scottish Daily Record & Sunday Mail (1986) Ltd* v. *Laird* [1996] IRLR 665). This means, for example, that if the employee has been caught fighting, the employer should investigate who started the fight, whether there was any provocation, whether it was a subordinate who started the fight against someone more senior or vice versa, whether the fight was in potentially dangerous circumstances, and whether it was in work time on work premises. All of these factors will be relevant and the employer cannot discover the answers without an investigation, that is making sure he has questioned anyone who saw the fight.

Normally an employer will suspend the suspected employee pending the outcome of the investigation. This suspension should be with pay, unless there is a contractual right to suspend without pay, otherwise the employer will be in breach of his common law duty to pay wages. Having said that, even if such a contractual right exists, a person is innocent until proved guilty and to suspend without pay almost seems like a punishment and prejudging the issue, and this could be seen as unreasonable in the circumstances by a tribunal. As soon as an employer suspects an employee he should suspend and begin his investigation. Memories fade quickly and witnesses may not remember everything if there is too long a delay between the event and the investigation. In *Marley Home Care Ltd* v. *Dutton* [1981] IRLR 380 a delay of one week before the start of the investigation made the dismissal unfair because the employee could not remember the incident clearly. A delay may also lead the employee to think that the incident is being ignored or that it has blown over.

Although normally an employer should conduct as thorough an investigation as possible, in one set of circumstances this may not be possible, that is where the conduct is a criminal offence and the police are also investigating. In this case the employee will often remain silent on the advice of his solicitor and therefore the employer does not hear the employee's version of events. In these circumstances, as long as the employer has enough evidence to form a reasonable belief in the guilt of the employee, the dismissal will be fair. In *Harris and Shepherd* v. *Courage* (above) it was held that the dismissals were fair, because the employer had enough evidence to form a reasonable belief that the employees were guilty. If the employee does confess, he may retract his confession when he knows that criminal proceedings are being brought. In this situation the employer is entitled to rely on the original confession if it is reasonable to do so (*University College of Buckingham* v. *Phillips* (1981) EAT 608/81).

While there has been authority stating that a dismissal may be fair even when the employee is dismissed without an investigation in cases of admitted dishonesty (*Royal Society for the Protection of Birds* v. *Croucher* [1984] ICR 604) this should be treated with caution. In *John Lewis plc* v. *Coyne* (2001) The Times, 5 January, it was discovered that the employee had made two to three personal telephone calls a week. She had a thirteen-year unblemished work record. On the discovery she was interviewed without warning and, on admitting the allegation, was dismissed. The Employment Appeal Tribunal upheld the employment tribunal that the dismissal was unfair. The appeal tribunal distinguished *Croucher* on the basis that the dishonesty in that case was on a far greater scale and the dismissed employee was a director. Furthermore, although the employer in *Coyne* considered that making personal telephone calls fell within the dishonesty policy, the appeal tribunal did not agree that the employee's actions satisfied the test for dishonesty.

Hearing Once the employer has gathered the evidence he must conduct a disciplinary hearing to make a decision as to the sanction he will impose. The procedures will normally lay down who will conduct the hearing. Many books state that the hearing must comply with the rules of natural justice. While the principles of a fair hearing are similar if not identical to the rules of natural justice, it should be noted, as stated in the previous chapter, that the consequences of a breach are not the same. If natural justice applies and its principles are breached, the decision is void. If the rules of a fair hearing are broken the decision to dismiss still stands, but the dismissal without doubt will be found to be unfair. The rules of a fair hearing are as follows:

(1) The employee must know the case against him to enable him to answer the complaint (*Hutchins* v. *British Railways Board* [1974] IRLR 303). Given that the aim of this rule is that the employee should have a chance to prepare his case, he should be told the basis for the hearing in sufficient time for him to adequately prepare. It has also been held in *A* v. *Company B Ltd* [1997] IRLR 405 that as well as knowing the allegations against him, an employee must know the identity of his accuser. However, in *Hussain* v. *Elonex plc* [1999] IRLR 420 the Court of Appeal held that there was no obligation on the employer to show witness statements to the employee during the disciplinary hearing. It would be unfair not to tell the employee of the existence of the statements but not unfair not to show those statements to him.

(2) The employee should have the opportunity to put his side of the case, that is the employer should listen to the employee's side of the story and allow him to explain his conduct or put forward mitigating circumstances. In *Budgen & Co* v. *Thomas* [1976] IRLR 174 the employee was dismissed after she signed a confession that she had stolen a sum of money. She was dismissed after the security officer had sent his report to the head office which took the dismissal decision without allowing the girl an opportunity to put her side of the case. She was a diabetic and claimed that she was confused at the time she made the confession and that the confession was untrue. It was held that her dismissal was unfair. She had not been given a hearing and, in view of her circumstances, had she been given the hearing the decision to dismiss may not have been taken. The employee's right to put his side of the case arose again in the case of *Clarke* v. *Trimoco Motor Group Ltd* [1993] IRLR 148. Here, Clarke and another employee were accused by a customer of billing for petrol which had not been put into the customer's lorries. In the course of the investigation, Clarke denied fraud but admitted that he had postdated some fuel vouchers at the request of drivers. He was given a written warning, but told that the employers might take further action if the police came up with new evidence. Two lorry drivers confessed to fraud to the police and implicated Clarke. The employers therefore suspended Clarke pending the outcome of the court case against him and the lorry drivers. After the case was adjourned twice, Clarke was dismissed for the original offence of altering fuel vouchers. The tribunal found that the real reason for the dismissal was the suspicion that Clarke was involved in the fraud, although this was not the reason given, and the dismissal was fair because Clarke knew that this was the reason. Furthermore, the employer had not acted unfairly in not giving Clarke an opportunity to answer the allegation of fraud as Clarke could have raised it in the grievance procedure between his suspension and dismissal. The

Employment Appeal Tribunal, while agreeing with the employment tribunal that Clarke knew the real reason for his dismissal, held that the dismissal was unfair. The fact that Clarke could have used the grievance procedure was no excuse for the employer's failure to allow Clarke to answer the allegations of fraud.

(3) The employee must be allowed representation at the hearing if he wishes. Denying the employee this right may well render the dismissal unfair (*Rank Xerox Ltd* v. *Goodchild and Others* [1979] IRLR 185) although the employer can specify the type of representation he will allow and there is no right to legal representation. The right to be accompanied at both disciplinary and grievance hearings has been enhanced by the Employment Relations Act 1999. Sections 10–13 create rights for workers to be accompanied at a disciplinary or grievance hearing by a single representative who may address the hearing and confer with the worker but who cannot ask questions on behalf of the worker. Such a representative may be a trade union official or a worker employed by the employer. There is a complaint to an employment tribunal for denial of this right within three months of the denial and, if the tribunal finds the complaint well-founded, it can award compensation of up to two-weeks' pay. A worker who exercises the right to be accompanied or who accompanies a fellow worker is protected from suffering a detriment or dismissal. Note that the provisions protect workers as defined in s.13. This definition is wider than employee and includes, for example, agency and home workers.

(4) The hearing should be unbiased, that is, the employer should approach the hearing with an open mind and not prejudge the issue. It would clearly be unfair if the employee was accused of hitting a manager and that manager chaired the hearing to decide whether to dismiss him or not. Without doubt the manager will have already decided before the hearing starts! In *Moyes* v. *Hylton WMC* [1986] IRLR 482 two witnesses to an act of sexual harassment also conducted the investigation and one chaired the disciplinary hearing which decided to dismiss the employee. It was held that the dismissal was unfair. In *BOC Ltd* v. *McConnon* (1989) EAT 613/89 an employee had been to the pub and was found drunk and asleep in his truck by the foreman. The foreman reported him to the acting branch manager who sent the employee home and told him to return the following Monday. The Friday before McConnon's return the foreman, the branch manager and the personnel officer discussed the case and held a further meeting on Sunday to discuss the evidence. On Monday the branch manager conducted the disciplinary hearing which dismissed McConnon. The Employment Appeal Tribunal held that the branch manager should not have

conducted the investigation and the hearing. There was another branch manager on the site who could have chaired the hearing. To ensure there is no bias, if possible the person who conducts the investigation should not be the person taking the decision to dismiss. Mr McConnon was unfairly dismissed (see also *Whitbread plc t/a Whitbread Medway Inns v. John Hall* [2001] ICR 699).

(5) The employee should be informed of his right to appeal to a higher level of management who have not been involved in the previous decision to dismiss. Should an employee fail to exercise his right to an appeal, he will not have failed to mitigate his loss and it will not contribute to the finding of the tribunal in any way (*William Muir (Bond 9) Ltd v. Lamb* [1985] IRLR 95), however by s.13 Employment Rights (Dispute Resolution) Act 1998, inserting s.127A into the Employment Rights Act 1996, where an employee fails to make use of an internal appeals procedure, the employment tribunal has the power to reduce the compensation awarded by up to two-weeks' pay where the effective date of termination of the contract is after 1 January 1999. On the other hand, refusing to allow the employee to exercise a contractual right of appeal will almost always render the dismissal unfair (*West Midlands Co-operative Society Ltd v. Tipton* [1986] IRLR 112). By s.127A, the tribunal may increase the employee's compensation in this case where the effective date of termination is after 1 January 1999 and in addition the court may place an injunction upon the employer to prevent the contract being treated as terminated until the appeal has taken place (*Jones v. Lee and Guilding* [1980] IRLR 67).

Appeals   The tribunal is required to consider if the employer has acted reasonably, taking into account the resources of the employer and the size of his undertaking. This means that the tribunal will expect the employer to have provided an appeal against the original dismissal decision. All the principles which apply to a fair hearing also apply to an appeal. Three further points should be noted, however. First, given the rule against bias, a person cannot chair the disciplinary hearing and also chair the appeal. Second, given that the employee should know the case against him, it follows that the appeal cannot endorse the decision to dismiss for another reason. If therefore the employee has originally been dismissed for theft and the appeal feels that there is insufficient evidence, it cannot confirm the dismissal because the employee failed to report theft by fellow employees (*Monie v. Coral Racing Ltd* [1981] ICR 109). Finally, given that the aim of the law is to provide that the employee has a fair hearing before dismissal, an appeal which is a total rehearing of the case, rather than a review of the evidence, can rectify previous breaches of procedure at the disciplinary hearing stage (*Whitbread & Co plc* v. *Mills* [1988] IRLR 501 and *Adivihalli* v. *Export Credits Guarantee Department* (1998) IDS Brief 620).

It has already been noted that the Human Rights Act 1998 has impacted on this area. In *Tehrani* v. *UK Central Council for Nursing, Midwifery and Health Visiting* [2001] IRLR 208 the Court of Session looked at the impart of Schedule 1, Part 1, Article 6. It held that disciplinary proceedings before the council's professional conduct committee fell within Article 6 because the proceedings fell within the determination of the complainant's civil rights since they could result in the removal of Tehrani's name from the register of nurses. As such, she was entitled to 'a hearing before an independent and impartial tribunal' (Article 6). The court went on to state, however, that it is not necessary for a professional disciplinary tribunal to meet all of the requirements of an independent and impartial tribunal, if the disciplinary procedure provides a statutory right of appeal to a court of law. Case law from the European Court of Human Rights establishes that there is no breach of the European Convention on Human Rights if the disciplinary tribunal is subject to control by a court which itself complies with Article 6. Further case law will determine what impact, if any, the 1998 Act has on proceedings of non-professional bodies.

Sanctions The employer will normally have a variety of sanctions he may impose for misconduct, the ultimate sanction being dismissal. The variety of the employer's sanctions will be an important consideration for the tribunal in seeing if the decision is a fair one and if the punishment fits the crime. Imposing too harsh a sanction short of dismissal may in itself be a repudiatory breach of contract, justifying the employee resigning and claiming constructive dismissal. The procedures themselves must be clear as to the sanctions which can be applied.

Warnings Generally, apart from serious or gross misconduct, an employee should receive a warning before being dismissed. The *ACAS Code* recommends three warnings before dismissal, the first verbal, the second and the third written, although these are only guidelines and clearly it depends on the circumstances of the case and the type of misconduct. Whereas it may be unreasonable to depart from that sequence in relation to, for example, an employee being five minutes late on one occasion, it would not be unreasonable to circumvent the earlier stages of the procedure for serious acts of misconduct and issue a final warning. A warning is an indication to the employee that his behaviour is disapproved of and to give him an opportunity to improve that behaviour, although a warning for different misconduct may be considered when looking at later misconduct (*Auguste Noel Ltd* v. *Curtis* [1990] IRLR 326). The *ACAS Code* urges that, apart from gross misconduct, no one should be dismissed for a first breach of discipline and recommends that warnings should only remain on the employee's record for a set time (often 6–12 months). After the warnings have expired they will not be taken into account when looking to see if the procedure has been followed in later cases of misconduct, but they can be considered when the employer is looking at the employee's work record when considering what sanction to impose. Employers should take care, however. In *Airbus Ltd* v. *Webb* (2007) UKEAT 0453/06 Webb and his colleagues were disciplined for taking a break when they should have been working. Webb's colleagues had clean records and were given final written warnings but Webb had had a warning for a similar act which had expired three weeks earlier. As a result Webb was dismissed. The Employment Appeal Tribunal held that the dismissal was unfair and that once the warning had expired the slate was wiped clean.

Fines or deductions The Employment Rights Act 1996 provides that the employer must have contractual authority to make such deductions or get the written consent of the employee before such deductions are made (see Chapter 4). Failure to obtain the permission of the employee, either through the contract or before the deduction is made, will lead to a possible claim under the 1996 Act and a potential claim for constructive dismissal. In *Lethaby* v. *Horsman, Andrew & Knill Ltd* [1975] IRLR 119 a deduction was made from the employee's salary to cover the loss of company property. There was no contractual authority to deduct and the employee resigned. It was held that the employee had been constructively dismissed.

Suspension without pay It follows that if deduction from wages without contractual authority or written agreement is a breach of the Employment Rights Act and a potential constructive dismissal, so too will be a suspension without pay.

Demotion Given that the employee is employed in a certain capacity to perform certain duties, any alteration in either without the consent of the employee is a fundamental breach by the employer and again a potential constructive dismissal. The same is true if the employer imposes a disciplinary transfer on the employee without his consent or the contractual authority to do so.

One thing should be noted about all the above sanctions which, if there is no contractual authority to impose such sanctions, may lead to a constructive dismissal claim. It does not necessarily follow that because the employee has been constructively dismissed the dismissal is unfair. In *Hall*

v. *Lodge* (1977) IRLIB 76 an employee was promoted from supervisor to manager. Within a short time, however, it was apparent that she had been promoted too soon and she was unable to do the manager's job. The employer therefore offered her another supervisor's job at a different branch at her old salary. She refused, resigned and claimed constructive dismissal. It was held that, although the employer had constructively dismissed the employee, in the circumstances the dismissal was fair. Where the demotion is out of proportion to the misconduct committed, even if there is a contractual right to demote, the excessiveness of the employer's actions could lead to a constructive dismissal claim and the dismissal is likely to be unfair. As a contrast, in *Cawley* v. *South Wales Electricity Board* [1985] IRLR 89 an employee was demoted when he was seen urinating from a moving van. Although the employer had a contractual right to demote, it was held that demotion for a first act of misconduct was too harsh a sanction. It therefore followed that the employer had committed a repudiatory breach which meant that the resignation of the employee was a constructive dismissal. Given that the repudiatory breach was the employer's unreasonable action, it followed that the constructive dismissal was unfair. In other words, if the sanction is too harsh the consequent dismissal must be unfair.

Statutory restriction

There are no real procedural issues involved when dismissing for this reason. The fairness of the dismissal will turn on the fairness of the decision, for example whether the employer has considered alternative employment, rather than the procedure he adopted.

Redundancy

We have already seen above that in certain circumstances a redundancy will be unfair if the employee is selected for particular reasons (s.105 Employment Rights Act 1996 and s.153 Trade Union and Labour Relations (Consolidation) Act 1992). Even if these sections have not been infringed, a redundancy may still be unfair if the employer has not acted reasonably. In particular the tribunal will look at the unit of selection used, the criteria chosen for selection, the reasonableness of the procedure and the efforts made to find alternative employment.

Unfair unit of selection   The employer should define his pool of employees in a reasonable manner before using his selection criteria. If work is interchangeable between groups of workers, for example, the broader unit of selection should be adopted (*Gilford* v. *GEC Machines* [1982] ICR 725). If the union has agreed the selection unit it is more likely to be held that the unit of selection was reasonable.

Unfair selection criteria The selection criteria should be objective and not subjective. Criteria such as employees who in the opinion of management will keep the company viable was frowned upon by the Employment Appeal Tribunal in *Williams* v. *Compair Maxam Ltd* [1982] IRLR 83 as being too heavily reliant on individual opinion. A good starting point is last in first out (LIFO) and a selection based on LIFO is unlikely to be unfair. The employer may depart from LIFO as long as he uses other objective criteria such as experience, skill, attendance and so on. The employer must ensure that any criterion he adopts is not discriminatory and we have already seen that a criterion selecting part-time workers first may constitute sex discrimination (see Chapter 5).

Reasonable procedure The case of *Williams* v. *Compair Maxam* (above) laid down guidelines for a fair procedure where there is a recognised trade union. Although the guidelines only apply in an unionised situation and may be inappropriate for a small business (*Simpson & Son (Motors)* v. *Reid and Findlater* [1983] IRLR 401) some of the principles are appropriate to any business. The guidelines are as follows:

1. The employer should give as much warning as possible of the impending redundancies to the union and employees concerned.
2. The employer should seek the agreement of the union regarding selection criteria and the best means of achieving the necessary result, causing as little hardship and unfairness as possible.
3. The employer should consider any representations made by the union as to the selection.
4. The employer should consider whether, instead of dismissing the employee, he could offer alternative employment.

Warning and consultation Consultation should be the normal rule whether the employee is a member of a recognised union or not. In *Hough* v. *Leyland Daf* [1991] IRLR 194 failing to consult with the employee, despite consulting with the employee's union, was held to render a redundancy unfair. (See also *Rolls-Royce Motor Cars Ltd* v. *Price* [1993] IRLR 203.) Consultation, however, requires positive action on the part of the employer and merely informing the employees of impending redundancies and then telling them the selection procedure is not consultation (*Rowell* v. *Hubbard Group Services Ltd* [1995] IRLR 195. Furthermore, the duty to consult applies to all employees, even those on fixed term contracts which have expired (*University of Glasgow* v. *Donaldson and McNally* (1995) IDS Brief 543). In some circumstances, however, lack of consultation may not affect the fairness of the dismissal if the tribunal accepts that the ensuing publicity could damage the business or result in a loss of faith in the company's products. Failure to consult the union, of itself, is unlikely to make the dismissal unfair, but it will do if accompanied by other procedural shortcomings. There is a statutory duty to consult with a recognised trade union or an elected employee representative in redundancy situations by s.188 Trade Union and Labour Relations (Consolidation) Act 1992.

Alternative employment We have already noted above that the employer should consider whether there is alternative employment he can offer the employee, although he is not required to create vacancies.

Some other substantial reason (SOSR)

As with statutory restriction, there are few, if any, procedural issues in relation to SOSR. The only relevant issue is in relation to pressure from third parties when the employer must show he has adequately investigated and has sufficient evidence on which to base his decision.

Retirement dismissals

The Employment Equality (Age) Regulations 2006 inserted ss.98ZA–G into the Employment Rights Act 1996 providing for retirement dismissals. If the dismissal is not a retirement dismissal, the normal rules on unfair dismissal apply.

The new sections detail the following:

Section 98ZA: there is no normal retirement age and the date of termination is before the date on which the employee reaches 65. This is not a retirement dismissal.

Section 98ZB: there is no normal retirement age and the date of termination takes place on or after the employee is 65 and the employer has notified the employee of his right to request to continue working. In this situation there is a retirement dismissal.

Section 98ZC: there is a normal retirement age and the date of termination is before the employee reaches normal retirement age. This is not a retirement dismissal.

Section 98ZD: the normal retirement age is higher than 65 and the date of termination is on or after the employee reaches that age and the employer has informed the employee of his right to request to continue in employment. This is a retirement dismissal.

Section 98ZE: the normal retirement age is below 65 and the date of termination is on or after the date on which the employee reaches that age and the employer has informed the employee of his right to request to continue in employment. This is a retirement dismissal.

The Employment Equality (Age) Regulations 2006 create a default retirement age of 65. Should the employer have a normal retirement age which is below 65 he must objectively justify it (Regulation 3). Prior to the 2006 Regulations, employees lost the right to claim unfair dismissal once they had reached the normal retirement age for the job or 65. A number of cases laid down principles for determining what was the normal retirement age for the job. Section 98ZH of the 1996 Act defines normal retirement age as 'the age at which employees in the employer's undertaking who hold, or have held, the same kind of position as the employee are normally required to retire'. It is submitted, given the wording in the Act, that previous case law will still be relevant, and this is discussed below

In *Notham* v. *London Borough of Barnet* [1980] IRLR 65 the House of Lords held that normal retirement age was the age at which the employee was supposed to retire under the terms and conditions of employment. However, although the contractual test is logical, it can cause injustice where the contract gives a retirement age but in practice employees work beyond it. As such, in *Waite* v. *GCHQ* [1983] IRLR 341 the House of Lords qualified *Notham* and said that the normal retirement age is the age at which the employee expects to be compelled to retire. The starting point to determine this is the contract, but evidence can be adduced to show that, in practice, employees in the same position as the complainant retire at a later age. In *Brooks* v. *British Telecommunications plc* [1992] IRLR 66 the Court of Appeal stated that the court should look at the age at which an employee might reasonably expect to retire. On the facts, employees in the same position as Brooks had a contractual retirement age of 60 but had been allowed to work beyond that age. The company wished to stop the practice and sent a letter to all employees reaffirming that the retirement age was 60. The court held that Brooks could reasonably expect to retire at 60 and that was the normal retirement age for the job.

Schedule 6 Employment Equality (Age) Regulations 2006 sets out a procedure that an employer must follow in order for a retirement dismissal to be fair. The employer must inform the employee, in writing, of the intended date of retirement and of the right to request to work beyond that date. This notification must be given between one year and six months before the intended retirement date. If the employee wishes to work beyond the retirement date, he must so request in writing three months before the intended retirement date. The request must state if the employee wants to work indefinitely, for a fixed period or until a stated date. If the employer agrees then there is not a problem; if not, the employer must hold a meeting to consider the request. If the request is refused, the employer must provide an appeal. The employer does not have to give reasons why a request is rejected.

Thus if retirement is the reason for the dismissal, it takes place on or after the normal retirement date or 65 and the employer has complied with the procedure above, the dismissal will be fair. Failing to comply with the above in some cases will render the dismissal automatically unfair. By paragraph 4 of Schedule 6, if the employer has failed to inform the employee within the time limits above of his intended date of retirement and his right to request to continue to work, the employer is under a continuing duty to give this information to the employee at least two weeks before the date of retirement. By s.98ZG, failure to do so renders the dismissal automatically unfair. The dismissal will also be unfair where a request has been made and the employer has not considered it or has failed to hold a meeting with the employee.

9.7 Automatically Unfair Reasons for Dismissal

In certain cases of dismissal the issue of reasonableness is irrelevant and, should the employee show the reason for dismissal, the dismissal will be automatically unfair. In all the cases below (with the exception of a transfer under the Transfer of Undertakings (Protection of Employment) Regulations 1981) the normal continuity rules are disapplied.

Leave for family reasons

A dismissal for pregnancy, a reason connected with pregnancy or for taking family leave is automatically unfair. By s.99 Employment Rights Act 1996 an employee dismissed for these reasons needs no continuity to claim unfair dismissal. There must, however, be a causal link between the dismissal and the exercise of the rights. Therefore if the employee can no longer do her job because of pregnancy or it would be a breach of a statutory provision to keep on employing her, the dismissal will not be automatically unfair but the question of reasonableness may still mean that the tribunal finds the dismissal unfair in the circumstances, because, for example, there is alternative work she could do. Where a woman is selected for redundancy because of her pregnancy, this is a dismissal for pregnancy and not redundancy (*Brown* v. *Stockton-on-Tees Borough Council* [1988] IRLR 263 and s.105 ERA). Leave covered by s.99 is maternity leave, parental leave, paternity leave, adoption leave, and s.57A covers time off to look after dependants.

Spent convictions

The Rehabilitation of Offenders Act 1974 was enacted to ensure that those convicted of a criminal offence who had genuinely tried to rehabilitate themselves should not be handicapped by having to disclose their past. Consequently, under the Act, certain rehabilitation periods are laid down, at the end of which the conviction is deemed to be spent. The rehabilitation period depends on the seriousness of the offence, but generally when a conviction is spent the employee does not have to reveal it. For employment purposes s.4(3)(b) states that a spent conviction or failure to disclose such shall not be grounds for dismissing or excluding a person from any office, profession, occupation or employment or for prejudicing him in any way in any occupation or employment.

The main rehabilitation periods are:

Sentence	Rehabilitation period
Imprisonment of more than 6 months and up to 2.5 years	10 years
Imprisonment of 6 months or less	7 years
Youth custody	7 years
Fine or community service order	5 years
Detention centre	3 years
Probation order, conditional discharge, binding over, care order or supervision order	1 year, or when order expires, whichever is the longer
Absolute discharge	6 months

The rehabilitation period runs from the date of conviction, not the expiry of the sentence. The periods of imprisonment are the sentence imposed and not the time served. Certain professions are exempt from the Act by the Rehabilitation of Offenders (Exception) Order 1975, such as nurses, solicitors and accountants.

The Act provides no remedy if a person is refused a job because of a spent conviction or if a person is discriminated against because of such a conviction. However, a dismissal for a spent conviction is unfair within the meaning of s.98 Employment Rights Act 1996. In *Hendry* v. *Scottish Liberal Club* [1977] IRLR 5 the employee was dismissed when it was discovered he had a spent conviction for possession of cannabis. It was held that the reason for his dismissal did not fall within the fair reasons for dismissal and was therefore unfair.

Transfer of undertakings

The Transfer of Undertakings (Protection of Employment) Regulations 2006 by Regulation 7 render a dismissal automatically unfair if the transfer or a reason connected with it is the reason or the principal reason for the dismissal. In *Milligan* v. *Securicor Cleaning Ltd* [1995] IRLR 288 the Employment Appeal Tribunal held that as Regulation 7 rendered such a dismissal unfair, normal continuity rules did not apply. The last government swiftly reacted and amended then Regulation 8 (now Regulation 7) by the Collective Redundancies and Transfer of Undertakings (Protection of Employment) (Amendment) Regulations 1995. Regulation 7(6) now makes it clear that an employee must have one year's continuity to claim. *Milligan* has also now been overruled by the Court of Appeal in *MRS Environmental Services Ltd* v. *Marsh* [1997] ICR 995. There is an exception in Regulation 7(2) when the dismissal will not be automatically unfair. This is where the reason was economic, technical or organisational (ETO) entailing changes in the workforce of either the transferor or transferee before or after the relevant transfer, in which case it is a fair dismissal. The ETO defence appears to be wide and could defeat the purpose of the Regulations. As such, the courts have tried to keep the defence as narrow as possible. In *Whitehouse* v. *Blatchford & Sons Ltd* [1999] IRLR 492 Whitehouse was a prosthetic technician employed by a company providing services for a hospital. At the end of the contract the new contract was awarded to another company which agreed to take on the existing employees, although a condition of the contract inserted by the hospital was that the number of employees was reduced by one to reduce the contract price. As such, Whitehouse was made redundant after the transfer by the transferee. The employment tribunal held that the dismissal was fair on the ETO defence and Whitehouse appealed. The Employment Appeal Tribunal reviewed the authorities in this area, namely *Berriman* v. *Delabole Slate Ltd* [1985] IRLR 305 and *Wheeler* v. *Patel* [1987] ICR 631. In *Berriman*, there was not an ETO defence when the transferee dismissed an employee for failing to accept a reduction in pay so standardising the pay of all the transferee's employees. The action did not involve changes in the workforce and therefore the ETO defence did not apply. In *Wheeler*, the dismissal of all the staff prior to the transfer to achieve an enhanced price similarly was not an ETO defence as it did not relate to the conduct of the business. In *Whitehouse*, the majority of the Employment Appeal Tribunal found that the employment tribunal was entitled to find an ETO defence existed because the reduction in the number of employees had been at the insistence of the hospital and the transferee would not have obtained the contract without that reduction, a decision upheld by the Court of Appeal. It does seem on the facts, however, that *Whitehouse* is difficult to distinguish from *Wheeler*, in that in *Wheeler* the business would not have been sold without the dismissal of the employees.

Trade union membership or activities

By s.152(1) Trade Union and Labour Relations (Consolidation) Act 1992 a dismissal is automatically unfair if the reason for the dismissal was that the employee:

(a) was, or proposed to become, a member of an independent trade union; or

(b) had taken, or proposed to take, part in the activities of an independent trade union at an appropriate time; or

(c) was not a member of any trade union, or of a particular trade union, or of one of a number of particular trade unions, or had refused, or proposed to refuse, to become or remain a member.

For the purposes of (c) above, this includes the refusal of a non-union member to make payments in lieu of union dues or his objection or proposed objection to such payments (s.152(3)). Dismissal on this ground does not require any continuity as a prerequisite to any claim.

The tribunals have given a wide interpretation to the provisions. In *Discount Tobacco and Confectionery Lt*d v. *Armitage* [1990] IRLR 14 the employee enlisted the help of her trade union representative to secure a written contract from her employer. She wished to raise certain discrepancies between the written terms and the terms originally offered, but the employer dismissed her. She argued her dismissal was for her trade union membership and this was confirmed by the Employment Appeal Tribunal who ruled that dismissal for using the services provided by a trade union fell within s.152 (see also *O'Dea* v. *ISC Chemicals* [1995] IRLR 599).

There is also protection for taking part in trade union activities at an appropriate time. This leads to two questions: what are trade union 'activities' and what constitutes an 'appropriate time'? 'Activities' is given its normal meaning so that union meetings, recruitment and so on are all union activities. In *Controlled Demolition Group Ltd* v. *Lane and Knowles* (1991) EAT 418/91 the employees were employed as asbestos strippers. Lane was a member of the union and took an active part in its activities. Knowles was not a member of the union. The union held a meeting to recruit new members, but neither employee attended. Shortly afterwards both were given notice of redundancy and both claimed unfair dismissal despite the fact that neither had the requisite continuity. The tribunal found that there was a genuine redundancy situation and that the employer needed to reduce the workforce by 13. However, 20 employees were made redundant and seven new employees were taken on. The tribunal found that the employer was antagonistic towards the union and had taken the opportunity of redundancy to rid itself of those involved in trade union activities. In Lane's case it was because of his membership and participation, in Knowles's case it was because the employer thought he had intended to join the union. The Employment Appeal Tribunal confirmed the finding. The tribunal was justified in concluding that the principal reason for the dismissal was the membership or proposed membership of the union and not the redundancy. If the principal reason had been redundancy, and the reason for selection had been union activities, then the employees would have needed two-years' service, but that was not the case here. The evidence showed that the employer knew of Lane's activities and mistakenly thought that Knowles had attended the meeting, and these were the reasons for their selection. On the other hand, the employee must be indulging in those activities by or on behalf of the union. In *Chant* v. *Aquaboats* [1978] ICR 643 the employee was dismissed for organising a petition about an unsafe machine. Although he was a union member, he was not an official nor was he organising the petition on behalf of the union. It was held that his dismissal was not for union activities. However, in *Fitzpatrick* v. *British Railways Board* [1990] ICR 674 the dismissal of a union activist when her employer discovered that she had been dismissed by her previous employer because the previous employer had found her activities disruptive was a dismissal within the section.

To gain protection, the activities must have taken place at the 'appropriate time'. By s.152(2) this means outside working hours or within working hours in accordance with arrangements with or with the consent of the employer. In *Zucker* v. *Astrid Jewels Ltd* [1978] IRLR 385 the employee tried to persuade her colleagues to join the union at every available opportunity while she was working. It was held that she was taking part in union activities at the appropriate time as the employer could hardly restrict topics of conversation. Conversely, in *Marley Tile Co Ltd* v. *Shaw* [1980] ICR 72 a union meeting was not held with the consent of the employer who merely remained silent when informed it was to take place. It should be noted that striking or other industrial action is not taking part in trade union activities for the purposes of the section.

Dismissal for the use of trade union services or refusal of an inducement

The Employment Relations Act 2004 amended s.152(1) Trade Union and Labour Relations (Consolidation) Act 1992 to increase protection to employees who are dismissed if the reason or principal reason is that they had made use of, or proposed to make use of, trade union services at an appropriate time, or that they have failed to accept an inducement to come out of collective bargaining. Trade union services are defined in s.152(2A) as being services made available to an employee by an independent trade union by virtue of his membership of the union and includes 'consenting to the raising of a matter on his behalf by an independent trade union of which he is a member'.

Dismissal in connection with recognition

The Employment Relations Act introduced a new right to be protected against unfair dismissal in respect of recognition disputes. The Act added Schedule A1 into the Trade Union and Labour Relations (Consolidation) Act 1992. Paragraph 161 renders a dismissal of an employee automatically unfair if the reason for the dismissal was that:

- the employee acted with a view to obtaining or preventing recognition of a union;
- the employee indicated that he supported or did not support recognition of a union;
- the employee acted with a view to securing or preventing the ending of bargaining arrangements;
- the employee indicated that he supported or did not support the ending of bargaining arrangements;
- the employee influenced or sought to influence the way in which votes were to be cast by workers in a ballot in connection with recognition;
- the employee sought to influence other workers to vote or not to vote in such a ballot;
- the employee voted in such a ballot;
- the employee proposed to do, failed to do, or proposed to decline to do, any of the above.

Dismissal in health and safety cases

By s.100 Employment Rights Act 1996, a dismissal will be unfair if the reason for the dismissal was that:

(a) the employee was a health and safety representative and performed or proposed to perform any of the functions of such; or

(b) there is no such representative and the employee brought to his employer's attention circumstances which the employee reasonably believed were harmful or potentially harmful to his health and safety; or

(c) in circumstances of danger he reasonably believed to be imminent and which he could not avert he left or proposed to leave his workplace, or refused to return to his workplace while the danger continued; or

(d) in circumstances of danger he reasonably believed to be imminent he took or proposed to take steps to protect himself and others from danger.

Such a dismissal will not be unfair if the employer can show that it was or would be so negligent for the employee to take those steps that a reasonable employer would have dismissed him.

Selection for redundancy for any of the above reasons is an automatically unfair redundancy.

Dismissal of shop workers or betting workers who refuse Sunday work

By s.101 of the 1996 Act, when a shop or betting worker is protected or has opted out it is an automatically unfair dismissal to dismiss him for refusing to work on Sundays. A protected worker is one who was not contracted to work on Sundays unless he has given his employer written notice that he does not object to Sunday working (s.36). An opted-out worker is one who has given written notice to his employer that he objects to Sunday working (s.40). The dismissal is not, however, automatically unfair if the reason for the dismissal was the employee's refusal to work on a Sunday during the opted-out notice period (s.101(2)).

Dismissal in working time cases

Section 101A of the 1996 Act provides that it is an automatically unfair dismissal if the reason or principal reason for the dismissal was that: the employee refused or proposed to refuse to comply with a requirement which the employer imposed or proposed to impose in contravention of the Working Time Regulations 1998, he refused or proposed to refuse to forgo a right under those Regulations, failed to sign or enter into, vary or extend an agreement under the Regulations or as a candidate or representative under the Regulations performed or proposed to perform any functions or activities.

Dismissal of trustees of occupational pension schemes

By s.102 of the 1996 Act it is an automatically unfair dismissal to dismiss an employee who is a trustee of an occupational pension scheme and the reason or principal reason for the dismissal was that the employee performed or proposed to perform any of his functions as trustee.

Dismissal of an employee representative

By s.103 of the 1996 Act it is an automatically unfair dismissal if the reason or principal reason for the dismissal is that the employee is an employee representative or a candidate in an election for such a representative, and he performed or proposed to perform any functions or activities pertinent to his role.

Dismissal for acting as a companion

Section 12 Employment Relations Act 1999 renders it an automatically unfair dismissal if a worker is dismissed because he has acted as a worker's companion in a disciplinary or grievance hearing.

Dismissal for making a protected disclosure

By s.103A of the 1996 Act it is an automatically unfair dismissal to dismiss an employee who makes a protected disclosure under the Public Interest Disclosure Act 1998.

Dismissal on the grounds of assertion of a statutory right

Section 104 of the 1996 Act states that it is an automatically unfair dismissal if the reason is that the employee brought proceedings to enforce a relevant statutory right or alleged that the employer had infringed his relevant statutory rights. Relevant statutory rights for the purposes of the section are any rights conferred by the Employment Rights Act 1996 where the remedy for infringement is a complaint to an employment tribunal, minimum notice rights, and rights in relation to union activities and time-off rights conferred by the Trade Union and Labour Relations (Consolidation) Act 1992, including the new rights to time off for union learning representatives, rights conferred by the Working Time Regulations 1998 and rights conferred by the Transfer of Undertakings (Protection of Employment) Regulations 2006. In addition, under the Part Time Workers (Prevention of Less Favourable Treatment) Regulations 2000 (Regulation 7) and the Fixed Term Employees (Prevention of Less Favourable Treatment) Regulations 2002 (Regulation 6) it is an automatically unfair dismissal to dismiss a person exercising their rights. It is irrelevant for the purposes of the section and the Regulations whether the employee has the right or not, and whether it has been infringed, as long as the allegation or proceedings were made in good faith. As before, selection for redundancy for this reason is also an automatically unfair dismissal.

Dismissal in national minimum wage cases

Section 104A Employment Rights Act 1996 provides that it is an automatically unfair dismissal if the reason for the dismissal was that action was proposed or taken to enforcing or securing a right under the National Minimum Wage Act 1998, the employer was prosecuted for an offence under s.31 of the Act as a result of action taken by or on behalf of the employee, or that the employee qualifies or will qualify for the national minimum wage.

Dismissal in tax credit cases

Similar provisions exist in s.104B in respect of an employee enforcing a right etc under the Tax Credits Act 1999.

Dismissal for requesting flexible working

Section 104C makes it an automatically unfair dismissal to dismiss an employee who has requested, or proposes to request, flexible working or has brought proceedings against the employer in respect of such.

Dismissal for jury service

Section 98B of the 1996 Act renders it an automatically unfair dismissal if the reason or the principal reason for the dismissal was that the employee had been summoned for, or had been absent attending jury service. It will not be automatically unfair if the employer can show that the undertaking would suffer substantial injury if the employee was absent; he made this known to the employee and the employee unreasonably refused or failed to apply to be excused jury service or have service deferred.

Dismissal in breach of the statutory dismissal procedures

Section 98A Employment Rights Act 1996 provides that where an employer has dismissed but failed to go through the statutory procedures, the dismissal is automatically unfair, provided that the failure is wholly or mainly attributable to the employer. In addition, such a failure leads to an increase in compensation of between 10 and 50 per cent.

9.8 Dismissal During a Strike, Lock-Out or Other Industrial Action

When unfair dismissal was introduced by the Industrial Relations Act 1971, the legislature decided that tribunals should have a neutral position when the reason for the dismissal was that the employee was taking industrial action; thus tribunals had no jurisdiction to hear an unfair dismissal claim unless there were selective dismissals or selective re-engagement. This used to be the position in any situation, but the Employment Act 1990 took away the tribunal's jurisdiction in any circumstance where the action was unofficial, and the provision was re-enacted in s.237 Trade Union and Labour Relations (Consolidation) Act 1992. That section states that an employee has no right to complain of unfair dismissal if at the time of the dismissal he was taking part in an unofficial strike or unofficial action. Subsection (2) states that action is unofficial if it is not authorised or endorsed by the trade union. The meaning of 'authorised' or 'endorsed' is discussed later in Chapter 13. Thus, in relation to unofficial action, the employee now has no protection whatsoever.

In relation to official industrial action, the starting point is s.238A (as amended by the Employment Relations Act 2004). This provides that an employee who is dismissed for taking part in protected industrial action shall be regarded as unfairly dismissed if one of the set of circumstances below applies. Protected industrial action is action which under s.219 of the 1992 Act, the union has lawfully organised and which is therefore protected from liability in tort for inducement to break or interfere with contracts (s.238A(1)). The circumstances are:

- the dismissal takes place within a period of twelve weeks (the basic protected period) beginning on the day the employee first took part in the industrial action; or
- the dismissal takes place after the end of that period and the employee had ceased to take industrial action before the end of that period; or
- the dismissal takes place after the end of that period, the employee had not ceased to take part in industrial action before the end of that period and the employer has not taken reasonable procedural steps for the resolution of the dispute to which the industrial action relates.

Where the employee is locked out during the action, any days of lock-out do not count towards the protected period (s.238A(7C)) so if the employee is locked out for one week he is protected for a total of 13 weeks (the basic 12-week protected period plus the one-week of lock-out known as the 'extension period'). 'Dismissal' means the date on which the employer's notice was given (not the date it ended) and in other cases the effective date of termination.

In deciding whether the employer had taken reasonable procedural steps for the resolution of the dispute, regard shall be had to:

- whether procedures established by collective agreement, or any other agreement, had been complied with by the employer or union;
- whether either party offered or agreed to negotiate or resume negotiations after the start of the protected action;
- whether the employer or union unreasonably refused, after the start of the protected action a request for conciliation services to be used;
- whether the employer or union unreasonably refused, after the start of the protected action, a request that mediation services be used in relation to the procedures to be adopted for resolving the dispute. (s.238A(6)).

Where the parties have agreed to use the services of a conciliator or mediator, s.238B sets out further matters that the tribunal must have particular regard to:

▶ whether the conciliation or mediation meetings have been attended on behalf of the employer and union by an appropriate person;
▶ whether the employer and union have co-operated with the conciliator or mediator in making arrangements to set up meetings;
▶ whether the employer and union have carried out any actions agreed with the conciliator or mediator and whether such actions were done in a timely manner;
▶ whether the employer and union answered all reasonable questions asked of them in meetings with all the parties.

The normal continuity rules do not apply. A claim must be presented to an employment tribunal within six months of the dismissal. A tribunal cannot order reinstatement or re-engagement until after the conclusion of the protected industrial action (s.239).

If s.238A does not apply or there is a dismissal in relation to a lock-out by the employer, then s.238 comes into play. This states that a tribunal has no jurisdiction to hear an unfair dismissal complaint unless:

(a) one or more of the relevant employees have not been dismissed; or
(b) a relevant employee has before the expiry of three months beginning with the date of his dismissal been offered re-engagement and the complainant has not been offered re-engagement.

This leads to the questions of: what action is covered and what is the definition of relevant employee?

Action covered

The section talks of a lock-out, strike or other industrial action. None of these words are defined by the Act but there is a definition in ss.235(4) and (5) Employment Rights Act 1996. Lock-out means 'the closing of a place of employment, or the suspension of work, or the refusal by an employer to continue to employ any number of persons – in consequence of a dispute, done with a view to compelling those persons – to accept terms and conditions of or affecting employment'. A strike is defined as 'the cessation of work by a body of persons employed acting in combination, or a concerted refusal . . . to continue to work for an employer in consequence of a dispute, done as a means of compelling their employer – to accept or not accept terms and conditions of or affecting employment'. While such definitions are only relevant to that particular Act (*Express and Star* v. *Bunday* [1988] ICR 379) they can be used for guidance in the interpretation of other legislation. They indicate that it is important to look at not only the action but the purpose behind it. Nothing in the statute suggests that the action must be a breach of contract. While invariably a strike or a lock-out will involve a breach, other industrial action may not. This does not mean that the employee is not taking industrial action for the purposes of s.238. This is shown by *Power Packing Casemakers Ltd* v. *Faust* [1983] IRLR 117 where the employees were engaged in a voluntary overtime ban. The employees were threatened with dismissal and all but three employees lifted the ban. The three employees were dismissed and the Court of Appeal, confirming the Employment Appeal Tribunal, held that the employment tribunal had no jurisdiction to hear an unfair dismissal complaint as the employees were taking part in industrial action at the time of their dismissals. It was irrelevant that the employees were not in breach of contract if the object of the action was to apply pressure on the employer or disrupt the employer's business. The section talks about 'a cessation of work by a body of persons', however a wide definition was given to the phrase in *Lewis* v. *Mason & Sons* [1994] IRLR 4. In this case an individual driver was dismissed when he refused to do an overnight trip in an unheated van in December. Other workers threatened to go on strike and they were dismissed. It was held that they were all taking part in industrial action at the time of their dismissals even though the original driver was acting on his own when he was dismissed.

For s.238 to apply, the employee must have been taking part in a strike or industrial action. The meaning of the phrase 'taking part' has led to the courts deciding that it is the employee who must disprove that he is taking industrial action. In *Coates* v. *Modern Methods and Materials* [1982] IRLR 318 the employee was frightened to cross picket lines and after refusing to do so on the first day of the strike, she was then ill for the remainder of the action although she did attend strike meetings. Despite the fact that her illness was certified, the Court of Appeal held that she was taking part because she had not openly disagreed with the action. By not attending work there was a presumption she was taking part which she had failed to rebut. So too in *McKenzie* v. *Crosville Motor Services Ltd* [1989] IRLR 516 an employee and trade union member who had worked during a previous dispute but failed to show up for work during the dispute in question was deemed to be taking part and therefore excluded from unfair dismissal protection, the Employment Appeal Tribunal holding that it was an implied contractual obligation on the employee to maintain contact with his employer and disassociate himself from the action. In *Rogers* v. *Chloride Systems* (1991) EAT 67/91 the employee was sick throughout the period of the dispute. The employer, in seeking to establish the intentions of his employees, sent a letter to those not at work requiring them to sign undertakings that they would return on a specific date. Rogers was telephoned at home and asked her views on the strike. She stated that if she was not sick she would support her colleagues, and when she refused to sign the undertaking she was dismissed with the rest of the strikers. She sued for an unfair dismissal. While the tribunal in the case could not make a finding because the employee had not given evidence in person, the tribunal established how an employer should deal with the situation of sick employees during a strike. If only a few employees were sick, they should be visited and their views elicited. Where there were more than a few and their views were determined by letter, then specific questions should be asked where the employee is required to give 'yes' or 'no' answers. These questions should ask specifically if the employee would have returned to work by the due date if he or she had not been sick and if the employee is prepared to return to work as soon as he or she is fit to do so.

Relevant employees

The tribunal will have jurisdiction if one or more of the relevant employees is not dismissed or is re-engaged. The definition of 'relevant employees', however, differs depending on whether there is a lock-out, strike or other industrial action.

Lock-out

In relation to a lock-out, 'relevant employees' mean those employees directly interested in the dispute. This has been interpreted to mean all those employees who have been locked out at any time during the dispute. In *Campey & Sons* v. *Bellwood* [1987] ICR 311 the company wished to bring in new working conditions and because of the threat of industrial action, closed the factory on 18 October. On 22 October the employers sent notices to the employees telling them to return on 24 October. Those who did not return on that date were told to return or be dismissed, and eventually a group were sacked. It was held that the date of the lock-out was 18 October and the relevant employees for the purposes of the statute were those employees locked out at that date. As some of those employees were not dismissed, there had been selective dismissals and the tribunal had the jurisdiction to see if those dismissals were unfair.

Strike or other industrial action

In this case the definition of 'relevant employees' means those employees who at the date of the complainant's dismissal were taking part in the action. This means that if the situation in *Campey* (above) had been a strike, the tribunal would not have had jurisdiction. The date the tribunal must look to is that of the complainant's dismissal and it must then see if all the other employees taking part at that time have been dismissed. It appears, however, that as long as those employees have been dismissed by the conclusion of the tribunal hearing, the employer will have immunity. The reason for the dismissal of the other employees appears to be irrelevant. This must be the conclusion from *McCormick* v. *Horsepower* [1981] IRLR 217 when an employee who was taking part in the industrial action was dismissed for redundancy after the other strikers had been dismissed but before the hearing. It was held that because all the employees, including him, had been dismissed, the tribunal had no jurisdiction to hear the other strikers' claims. This interpretation obviously gives the employer a great deal of leeway as there can be a substantial time period between the date of the dismissals and the date of the hearing. In addition, the group of relevant employees is taken from the establishment at which the dismissed employee works. This means that if the employer owns two factories and employees at both go on strike, he can dismiss all the strikers at one factory while retaining those at the other, without losing the immunity from unfair dismissal proceedings.

While the majority of cases revolve around the interpretation of 'relevant employees', one case has concentrated on the interpretation of the phrase 'offered re-engagement'. In *Tracey* v. *Crosville (Wales) Ltd (No. 2)* [1997] IRLR 691, all 119 employees were dismissed when they went on strike. The employers then recruited replacement staff by placing advertisements in the local press and radio and in jobcentres. All applications were considered, including those from the dismissed strikers of whom 22 were re-engaged. Tracey was not re-engaged and claimed unfair dismissal. The employers argued that the tribunal did not have jurisdiction as the advertising campaign constituted an offer of re-engagement to all the dismissed employees. It was held that a general advertising campaign did not constitute an offer of employment to any individual. The advertisements were invitations to treat. As such there had been selective re-engagement of relevant employees for the purposes of s.153 and the tribunal had the jurisdiction to hear the claim.

Should the tribunal have the jurisdiction to hear a claim, the normal standards of reasonableness apply, however. Just because the employee has been dismissed during industrial action does not mean that the employer does not have to act as a reasonable employer. In *McClaren* v. *National Coal Board* [1988] IRLR 215 the employee allegedly committed an assault while taking part in industrial action. The employer reported the matter to the police and after the employee was convicted the employer dismissed him.

At no time had the employee been given a hearing or an opportunity to put his side of the case. The Court of Appeal held that the dismissal was unfair. The fact of industrial action did not justify failing to give the employee the opportunity of offering an explanation. The tribunal may, however, reduce the award for contributory conduct. While *TNT Express* v. *Downes* [1993] IRLR 432 suggests that in some cases the industrial action may be contributory conduct, the Court of Appeal in *Crosville* has stated that there has to be individual conduct over and above the collective industrial action, a decision confirmed by the House of Lords.

Again, if the tribunal does have the jurisdiction the time limit is different for the presentation of a claim. The limit in a normal unfair dismissal is three months after the effective date of termination of the contract, but the tribunal does have the discretion to allow a claim outside that limit in exceptional circumstances (see above). In relation to a claim under s.238, the time limit is six months (s.239) with the tribunal having the same discretion to extend.

9.9 Remedies for Unfair Dismissal

Apart from claims under s.238 or 238A above, a claim for unfair dismissal must normally be presented within three months of the effective date of termination of the contract. The tribunal, however, by s.111(2)(b) Employment Rights Act 1996, may hear complaints out of time if it is satisfied that it was not reasonably practicable to present the complaint in time. There may be a variety of reasons why the tribunal will allow a complaint to be presented outside the three-month period. In *Cavaciuti* v. *London Borough of Hammersmith & Fulham* (1991) EAT 246/91 the Employment Appeal Tribunal ruled that where the effective date of termination is ambiguous, the tribunal should take the date most favourable to the employee to see if the complaint is presented within the time period. Cavaciuti was dismissed on 4 July 1990. A letter of 6 July stated that he would be paid during his notice period but he did not have to work. After a series of letters, a final letter was sent on 19 July stating that his paid notice ended on 5 August 1990 and with his holiday entitlement he would be paid up to and including 22 August. His final pay slip showed the normal deductions as if he remained a local authority employee. The issue was whether his date of termination was 5 August or 22 August. The tribunal ruled that this was not a summary dismissal with payment in lieu as the employee had been employed during his notice period. The important letter was that of 19 July and the natural interpretation of that letter was that the employee remained employed up to and including 22 August. Likewise, if the employee has been given incorrect advice by a competent person such as a tribunal officer, the tribunal will allow a claim out of time. We have already seen in *London International College* v. *Sen* that the tribunal decides the cause of the applicant's failure to present the claim in time and that the Court of Appeal has stated that there is no cut-and-dried rule that advice given by a solicitor which is wrong does not necessarily prevent the tribunal from exercising its discretion.

In addition to erroneous advice or ambiguous termination letters, there are other situations when a tribunal will allow a late complaint. In *Rogers* v. *Northumbria Leisure Ltd t/a Border Travel* (1990) EAT 321/90 Rogers was informed that she would be made redundant in June but at the request of the employer began work on a temporary contract on 3 July. On 14 August she was informed that the office would close on the 31st of the month and she stopped work immediately, receiving a month's pay in lieu. In January 1990, she discovered that the business was still operating and presented a complaint to the tribunal in February 1990. She argued that it was only in January that she was aware and could reasonably be aware that the business was still trading. The tribunal, however, found that Rogers had visited the premises on 31 August and 12 September, therefore she knew the business was still trading on those dates and she should have enquired whether the business was actually closing down. As such, it was reasonably practicable for her to present her complaint in time. She appealed. The Employment Appeal Tribunal dismissed her appeal but considered the law in this area. In *Walls Meat Co Ltd* v. *Khan* [1979] ICR 52 it was held that it would be reasonably practicable to present a complaint in time if the fault lay in the complainant not making the enquiries that he reasonably should. In *Palmer* v. *Southend-on-Sea Borough Council* [1984] ICR 373 it was held that misrepresentations on the part of the employer were relevant and in *Machine Tool Industry Research Association* v. *Simpson* [1988] ICR 559 the tribunal held that the question to ask was whether the continuation of the business was something which was reasonably unknown to the complainant. In *Rogers*, the employee was a manageress and had been told by her employer on 31 August that he considered it worth while to continue trading. As such, it was reasonably practicable for Rogers to present her complaint in time.

Should the applicant be successful in his claim for unfair dismissal there are a variety of remedies that the tribunal can award.

Reinstatement

Reinstatement is an order that the employer shall treat the employee in all respects as if he has not been dismissed and must include all the benefits payable in the period since his dismissal including seniority and pensions (s.114(2) Employment Rights Act 1996). In exercising its discretion to make an order for reinstatement, the tribunal must have regard to:

(a) the wishes of the complainant;
(b) whether it is practicable for the employer to comply with the order;
(c) if there is contributory conduct, whether it is just to make the order (s.116(1)).

In *Coleman* v. *Magnet Joinery Ltd* [1974] IRLR 343 the Court of Appeal held that 'reasonably practicable' meant reasonably practicable in the industrial relations sense. A redundancy or reorganisation which has arisen after the dismissal will normally render it impracticable to order reinstatement, as will tension between the parties or the situation of a small employer who would have to work closely with the reinstated employee (*Enessy Co S.A.* v. *Minoprio* [1978] IRLR 489). The fact that the employer has appointed a replacement to do the employee's job does not make it impracticable to order reinstatement unless the employer shows that it was not practicable for him to arrange for the dismissed employee's work to be done without engaging a replacement, he waited a reasonable time before engaging the replacement without having heard from the dismissed employee that he wished to be reinstated, and when he engaged the replacement it was no longer reasonable for him to arrange for the work to be done except by a replacement (ss.116(5) and (6) Employment Rights Act 1996). While reinstatement is rarely ordered, if the tribunal exercises its discretion, failure to comply will lead to an additional award (see below).

Re-engagement

If the tribunal declines to award reinstatement it must then consider re-engagement. Such an order means that the employee is returned to a comparable job rather than his old job but the job must be as favourable as the old (s.115(2) Employment Rights Act 1996). The job must not be more favourable however (*Rank Xerox (UK) Ltd* v. *Stryczek* [1995] IRLR 568). In deciding whether to exercise its jurisdiction, the tribunal takes into account similar factors to those when considering reinstatement. In *Nairne* v. *Highland & Islands Fire Brigade* [1989] IRLR 366 the employee was found to be unfairly dismissed because of a procedural irregularity. The employee was a fireman where it was a contractual requirement that he was able to drive and his dismissal occurred when he had been banned from driving for three years. His contributory conduct was assessed at 75 per cent and given that it was so high and the fact that there was no suitable alternative work an order for re-engagement was unsuitable.

Financial compensation

Given that orders of reinstatement or re-engagement are made in fewer than 1 per cent of cases, this means that the main remedy for unfair dismissal is financial compensation. Until 1999 the various heads of award were increased annually (s.208 Employment Rights Act 1996, now repealed). While this is still the case, s.33 Employment Relations Act 1999 provides that the limits on such awards are index linked and thus they may rise considerably in any one year. As such, in the discussion below, the specific limits on the heads of awards will not be given. The compensation comes under a number of heads.

Basic award

The basic award is to compensate the employee for the loss of his job. It is calculated in the same way as redundancy pay and is based on the employee's age and years of service in the following way:

- service below the age of 22: half a week's pay for each year of service;
- service between 22 and 41: one week's pay for each year of service;
- service over the age of 41: one and a half week's pay for each year of service (s.119(2)).

The above is subject to a statutory maximum weekly rate and 20-years' service. In addition, the award can be reduced for:

- conduct (whether it contributed to the dismissal or not);
- unreasonable refusal of an offer of reinstatement;
- any redundancy pay received;
- any *ex gratia* payments.

The award cannot be reduced, however, as a result of conduct committed by the employee after his dismissal (*Soros* v. *Davison* [1994] IRLR 264).

Compensatory award

The award is to compensate the employee for the loss he has suffered as a result of the dismissal (s.123(1)). Until 1999 the maximum of this award was £12,000. This figure was unlikely to provide adequate compensation for a highly paid employee who had been unfairly dismissed. As such, the Employment Relations Act 1999 by s.34(4) raised this figure to £50,000, a figure which is now indexed linked and is raised annually. While the award should reflect the employee's loss, it must be just and equitable in the circumstances, therefore if the employee would have been dismissed even if the procedures had been followed, for example, he can claim nothing under this head (*British United Shoe Machinery Co Ltd* v. *Clarke* [1978] ICR 70). The tribunal will look at a variety of factors when assessing compensation under this head, such as immediate loss of earnings, future loss of earnings, loss of fringe benefits, expenses in looking for work, loss of pension rights, loss of employment protection and the manner of the dismissal. Immediate loss of earnings will involve the tribunal in a calculation as to the loss between the date of the dismissal and the date of the hearing, less any unemployment or other benefits received. Future loss of earnings involves the tribunal in an estimate of how long the employee is likely to remain unemployed, given the area and the prospects of future employment. In *James W. Cook & Co (Wivenhoe) Ltd* v. *Tipper* [1990] ICR 716 it was held that if the employee's dismissal arises from the closure of the employer's business, then the future loss element should not extend beyond the date of the closure of the business. In *Dunnachie* v. *Kingston upon Hull City Council* [2004] EWCA Civ 84 the Court of Appeal held that damages could be awarded under this head for non-economic loss such as damage to reputation or psychiatric injury, however this was overruled by the House of Lords ([2004] UKHL 36) which held that the word 'loss' in s.123 only covered pecuniary loss. The employee is under a duty to mitigate his loss under this head.

Additional award

Where the employer has ignored an order for reinstatement or re-engagement, the dismissal was discriminatory or the dismissal was for certain specified statutory reasons, the tribunal may make an additional award. In the case of refusing to comply with or to fully comply with an order for reinstatement or re-engagement, or if a discriminatory dismissal, the award will be between 26 and 52-weeks' pay (ss.117(5) and (6)) subject to the statutory maximum weekly pay rate. This limit does not apply where the award would not reflect the true loss of benefits (ss.124(3) and (4)), so reflecting the view of Donaldson MR in *O'Laoire* v. *Jackel International Ltd* [1990] IRLR 70 that the limit can discourage employers from complying with a reinstatement order and creates injustice to higher-paid employees. An additional award can also be made when the employer takes back the employee but on different terms from the tribunal order (s.117(1)(b)). In *Artisan Press* v. *Strawley and Parker* [1986] IRLR 126 the tribunal found that two security staff had been unfairly dismissed and ordered their reinstatement. The employer re-employed them on fundamentally different jobs involving very minor security duties. The Employment Appeal Tribunal held that there was no difference between an employer refusing to allow an employee back and an employer who did not give the employee his old job back when assessing the additional award. When assessing the award, however, the issue of practicability can be looked at again (*Port of London Authority* v. *Payne* [1994] IRLR 9). The monetary provisions of a reinstatement order cannot be enforced through court action (*O'Laoire* v. *Jackel International Ltd*, above).

Where the dismissal is due to membership or non-membership of a trade union or union activities, the complainant is entitled to a minimum basic award by s.156 Trade Union and Labour Relations (Consolidation) Act 1992. The applicant is also entitled to a minimum basic award where the dismissal is for health and safety reasons, because the employee is a trustee of an occupational pension scheme, or because the employee is an employee representative. This gives a minimum basic award plus, where reinstatement or re-engagement is not ordered, an award of 104-weeks' pay with a statutory minimum and maximum figure. Should the tribunal order reinstatement or re-engagement and the employer fails to comply, the award is 156-weeks' pay with a statutory minimum but no statutory maximum. The award can be reduced for conduct on the part of the complainant, the amount of the reduction being at the discretion of the tribunal and the reduction being what is just and equitable according to the circumstances of the case.

Furthermore, the Employment Act 2002 adds s.112(5) and s.120(1A) into the Employment Rights Act 1996 which provide that where an employee is regarded as unfairly dismissed because of the non-completion of the statutory dismissal and disciplinary procedure, and the non-completion is attributable wholly or mainly to the employer, the tribunal must award a minimum of four-weeks' pay to the employee, unless the tribunal feels that such an award would result in injustice to the employer. In addition, compensation can be increased by between 10 and 50 per cent.

Interim relief

If the dismissal is in connection with trade union activities, membership or non-membership of a trade union, or because the employee did certain actions in relation to recognition, an application may be made for interim relief under s.161 Trade Union and Labour Relations (Consolidation) Act 1992 and paragraph 161(2) of Schedule A1 of the same Act. Such an application may also be made if the dismissal is on health and safety grounds, or because the employee is a trustee of an occupational pension scheme, the employee made a protected disclosure or is an employee representative by s.128(1) Employment Rights Act 1996. In all instances an application must be made within seven days of the dismissal. In the case of a dismissal on trade union grounds, the application must be supported by a signed certificate from a trade union official that there are reasonable grounds to believe that this is the true reason for the dismissal. A tribunal, if satisfied that on the hearing of the unfair dismissal complaint it will find the complaint well-founded, can ask the employer if he will reinstate or re-engage the employee. If the employer so agrees, the tribunal will make an order to that effect. If the employer refuses, then the tribunal may make an order for continuation of employment. Such an order preserves the employee's benefits under the contract until the case is determined or settled. Failure to comply with any order under these provisions allows the tribunal to award compensation to the employee such that is just and equitable in the circumstances, reflecting the infringement of the employee's rights and the loss he has suffered.

Summary

1. Unless there is an automatically unfair dismissal, at present only employees with one-year's continuity who are not excluded by the legislation can claim unfair dismissal.

2. 'Continuity' means that a contractual relationship exists for the requisite time.

3. The law allows certain breaks in the continuity to count in the final computation.

4. Depending on what is being transferred, a change of employer may or may not break continuity.

5. The requisite period of continuity must exist at the effective date of termination of the contract.

6. In addition to employer termination recognised at common law, statute recognises two other situations where a dismissal will have occurred for unfair dismissal purposes: non-renewal of a fixed term contract and constructive dismissal.

7. The employer must prove he had one of the statutory five fair reasons to dismiss.

8. It is sufficient for the employer to prove that he had a genuine belief, based on reasonable grounds after a reasonable investigation.

9. 'Capability' can mean inherent incapability or incapability due to illness.

10. Qualifications can include aptitude tests.

11. 'Conduct' normally means conduct within the employment but, in some circumstances, conduct outside the employment can justify dismissal.

12. Redundancy can be automatically unfair or unfair because the employer has not acted reasonably when dismissing.

13. 'Statutory restriction' means it is a breach of law to continue to employ the employee.

Summary cont'd

14. 'Some other substantial reason' tends to fall into two categories: business needs and pressure from third parties.

15. Pressure from a union will be ignored when deciding the issue of fairness.

16. The tribunal must also be satisfied that the employer has acted reasonably. This involves looking at the fairness of the decision and compliance with statutory dismissal and disciplinary procedures.

17. 'Fairness of the decision' means looking at all factors and seeing if dismissal was within the band of reasonable responses that a reasonable employer would choose.

18. Procedural fairness will rely heavily on the statutory procedures which will be abolished during the currency of this text. However an employer's own procedures are also important.

19. Statute recognises some reasons are automatically unfair.

20. The remedies for unfair dismissal are reinstatement, re-engagement or financial compensation.

21. Financial compensation is divided into the basic award, the compensatory award and the additional award.

22. Certain employees may claim interim relief until the case is heard.

Exercises

1. Alf, Mike and Jack work for Coronation Products Ltd and have done so for four years. Five weeks ago, the company decided to streamline production. It therefore looked at the shopfloor workers and decided to ignore the redundancy selection policy of last in first out which had been agreed with the unions. The company dismissed for reasons of redundancy all workers over the age of 50, despite the fact that many younger workers had less continuity. If the policy had been observed, Alf would have been retained, but, because he is 52, he has been selected for redundancy. There is an internal appeals procedure which all employees can use to appeal against selection for redundancy. Coronation Products has refused to allow any of the selected men to use the procedure on the basis that nothing they could say would alter the decision. Alf has been told he may not use the procedure.

    Mike and Jack were caught fighting by Mr Ogden, the personnel manager. Red, the trade union representative, dislikes both men because they disagree with how he negotiates for his members. Mr Ogden investigates the fight, and having got Red's version of events (he was one of 10 witnesses) Mr Ogden dismisses Mike and Jack. There is an internal appeals procedure. Mike chooses not to use the procedure but Jack appeals. The appeal panel consists of senior managers. On the evidence they decide that as it is difficult

Exercises cont'd

to apportion blame for the fight, Jack's appeal against dismissal on that ground should be upheld. However, there has been a problem of stock shortages in Jack's department and Jack has been suspected of being responsible. The appeal therefore endorses Jack's dismissal on the grounds of the stock shortages.

Advise Alf, Mike and Jack in respect of unfair dismissal.

2. 'Unfair dismissal is perhaps a misnomer. It would be truer to call it unreasonable dismissal, since it is the concept of reasonableness which causes most employers to lose their cases. However, the new statutory procedures may render the common law concepts a thing of the past.' Discuss.

Further Reading

Anderman *The Interpretation of Protective Employment Statutes and Contracts of Employment* (2000) 29 ILJ 223.

Bennett *Practicability of Reinstatement and Reengagement Orders* (1994) 23 ILJ 164.

Bowers and Clarke *Unfair Dismissal and Managerial Prerogative: A Study of 'Other Substantial Reason'* (1981) 10 ILJ 34.

Bowers and Lewis *Non-Economic Damage in Unfair Dismissal Cases: What's Left After Dunnachie?* (2005) 34 ILJ 83.

Brodie *Fair Dealing and the Disciplinary Process* (2002) 31 ILJ 294.

Collins *The Meaning of Job Security* (1992) 20 ILJ 227.

Collins *Finding the Right Direction for the 'Industrial Jury'* (2000) 29 ILJ 293.

Davies *Taken to the Cleaners? Contracting Out of Services Yet Again* (1997) 26 ILJ 193.

Dolding *Unfair Dismissal and Industrial Action* (1994) 23 ILJ 243.

Elias *Fairness in Unfair Dismissal: Trends and Tensions* (1981) 10 ILJ 201.

Evans, Goodman and Hargreaves *Unfair Dismissal Law and Changes in the Role of Trade Unions and Employers Association* (1985) 14 ILJ 91.

McMullen *An Analysis of the TUPE Regulations 2006* (2006) 35 ILJ 113.

Morris *Fundamental Rights: Exclusion by Agreement?* (2001) 30 ILJ 49.

Pollard *Pensions and TUPE* (2005) 34 ILJ 127.

Reynold and Palmer *Proving Constructive Dismissal: Should One Be Concerned With What Was in the Employer's Mind?* (2005) 34 ILJ 96.

Sargeant *TUPE – The Final Round* (2006) JBL 549.

Vickers *Unfair Dismissal and Human Rights* (2004) 33 ILJ 52.

Chapter 10

Redundancy

10.1 Introduction

Compensation for redundancy was one of the first employment protection rights introduced into British law. The first piece of legislation was the Redundancy Payments Act 1965 and the law is now contained in the main in the Employment Rights Act 1996. The aim of a redundancy payment has never been to cushion a person over a period of unemployment, but rather to recognise an employee's stake in his job. This means that it is irrelevant if the employee has another job to go to once he has been made redundant, he is still entitled to a redundancy payment. In addition, the employee's stake increases the longer he has worked for the employer and as such his payment increases with age and years of service. A redundancy payment is calculated in the same way as the basic award in unfair dismissal.

10.2 Qualification to Claim

In order to claim a redundancy payment an employee must have two-years' continuous service and be dismissed for reasons of redundancy. The requirements and complications in continuity have been previously discussed. In addition, the same classes of employee are excluded from claiming a redundancy payment as are excluded from claiming unfair dismissal.

The definition of dismissal for redundancy purposes is contained in s.136 Employment Rights Act 1996. These situations are the same as unfair dismissal, that is employer termination with or without notice, a fixed term contract expiring and constructive dismissal. In addition, by s.139(4), if the employment is terminated by the death, dissolution or liquidation of the employer, or the appointment of a receiver, there is a dismissal for reasons of redundancy. Entitlement to claim, however, is dependent on the dismissal being because of redundancy and not for any other reason. In *Saunders* v. *Earnest A. Neale Ltd* [1974] IRLR 236 the employees conducted a work to rule. The employer sacked them and eventually the factory closed down. It was held that there was not a dismissal for redundancy; the work to rule had caused the dismissals which had in turn led to the factory closing down and not the other way round. There is a statutory presumption in s.163(2) that if an employee is dismissed and claims a redundancy payment the dismissal is for reasons of redundancy and it falls to the employer to rebut the presumption. In *Willcox* v. *Hastings* [1987] IRLR 298 two employees worked for an employer who sold the business to a married couple. The new owners only wanted one employee so that one of the existing employees would be redundant. However, the new owners intended that their son should work for them and so dismissed both of the original employees. They stated that one of the employees was redundant but did not specify which one. The Court of Appeal held that both were entitled to a redundancy payment. The presumption arose in respect of both employees and the new employers had not rebutted the presumption in relation to either of them.

The definition of redundancy is found in s.139(1) of the Act. This states that a redundancy has occurred if the dismissal is wholly or mainly attributable to:

'(a) the fact that his employer has ceased, or intends to cease, to carry on the business for the purposes for which the employee was employed by him, or has ceased, or intends to cease, to carry on that business in the place where the employee was so employed; or

(b) the fact that the requirements of that business for employees to carry out work of a particular kind, or for employees to carry out work of a particular kind in the place where he was so employed, have ceased or diminished or are expected to cease or diminish.'

This means that redundancy occurs in three situations: the employer ceasing business, the employer moving his place of business or the employer reducing his labour force.

10.3 Definition of Redundancy

Cessation of business

Where there is a close-down of the business there are few legal problems. The tribunal is merely required to see if in fact the business has been shut down and is not required to look at the reasons behind the closure (*Moon* v. *Homeworthy Furniture (Northern)* [1976] IRLR 298).

Moving place of business

Where the employer moves his place of business or closes down in one particular place but continues elsewhere, there is a redundancy for the purposes of the Act. Two points should be noted, however. First, the move must be substantial and affect the employee's travelling costs and so on. In *Managers (Holborn) Ltd* v. *Hohne* [1977] IRLR 230 the employee was employed at Holborn and the employers moved premises to Regent Street which was a short distance away. It was held that there was no redundancy situation. Both premises were in central London and neither the applicant's work nor travelling expenses were affected by the move. Second, before deciding whether the move constitutes a redundancy, it is necessary to see if the employee has a mobility clause in his contract. The phrase 'in the place where the employee was so employed' means the place where he can be required to work under his contract according to the court in *United Kingdom Atomic Energy Authority* v. *Claydon* [1974] IRLR 6. This means that if there is a clause requiring the employee to work at any of the employer's establishments, on the face of it the employee will be in breach of contract if he refuses to move and his dismissal will be for disobedience to lawful, reasonable orders rather than for redundancy. The contract must require the employee to move, however, in the particular situation. In *Provincial Insurance plc* v. *Loxley* (1990) EAT 161/90 the employee had been employed by the company in a variety of locations but in 1977 was moved to East Grinstead where he had settled. His son was to sit GCSE examinations in June 1989 and the employee was told that, because of a restructuring of the company, he would be required to move to Reading in July 1989. The employee's contract contained a mobility clause but with a provision that this would not be enforced against employees who produced evidence of hardship. Examples of hardship included children who were about to sit public examinations. The employee refused to move because his son wished to proceed to A-levels and so he resigned and took up employment elsewhere. The employee claimed a redundancy payment. The tribunal, relying on the case of *Marley* v. *Forward Trust Group Ltd* [1986] IRLR 369, held that where there was a mobility clause and a redundancy clause the two could not coexist and the redundancy clause predominated. The Employment Appeal Tribunal held that the tribunal had misdirected itself and while on the interpretation of the contract in *Marley* the redundancy clause had overridden the mobility provision, the Court of Appeal in that case did not say that as a matter of law this would always be the case. The tribunal had to decide whether the employee fell within the hardship provisions of the mobility clause to see if he was required to move or not. The case was therefore remitted back. The case demonstrates that even an express mobility clause may not be enforced against an employee in some circumstances. (See also *United Bank* v. *Ahktar*, Chapter 3.)

If there is no mobility clause in the contract, the courts will rarely imply one unless that is the way the contract has been worked by the parties in the past. In *O'Brien* v. *Associated Fire Alarms* [1968] 1 WLR 1916 the employee had always worked within commuting distance of Liverpool. His work was administered from the Liverpool office which was part of the north-western area of the employer's business. Because of a reduction in work in Liverpool the employer tried to move the employees from Liverpool to Barrow-in-Furness (some 120 miles away), arguing that Barrow was still within the region and that there was an implied term that they would work anywhere within the region. The Court of Appeal would only imply a term that the employee should work within daily travelling distance of his home. By contrast, in *McAndrew* v. *Prestwick Circuits Ltd* [1988] IRLR 514 the employee was taken on in 1975 and the employers acquired another factory some 15 miles away in 1983. All the contracts of new employees after that date contained mobility clauses, but in practice employees worked between the two factories regardless of whether there was a mobility clause or not. The Court of Session held that there was an implied mobility clause in McAndrew's contract.

Even if there is no mobility clause, express or implied, if the job at another site is deemed to be an offer of suitable, alternative employment and the employee unreasonably refuses it, he will disentitle himself to a redundancy payment (see below).

Excess labour

This is probably the most difficult provision within the statute. Section 139(1)(b) of the 1996 Act talks of the requirements of the employer for employees to carry out 'work of a particular kind', and it is this phrase which has caused the most problems. The first point to note is that the statute talks about the employer's requirements for employees. It therefore follows that if the employer no longer requires employees to do the tasks because, for example, he is putting out the work to self-employed people, then the requirements of the employer for employees has ceased (*Bromby* v. *Hoare & Evans* [1972] ICR 113). Apart from that obvious fact, the question for the tribunal is: what is the particular work for which the employee is employed and have the employer's requirements for that work ceased or diminished? In *Vaux Breweries Ltd* v. *Ward* [1968] ITR 385 the employer decided to replace barmaids with bunny girls. The question was whether the work of the bunny girls was of a different kind from that of Ward, an older barmaid who was dismissed. The answer had to be 'no'. The work had not changed, merely the type of person that the employer required to do that work. So too in *North Riding Garages* v. *Butterwick* [1967] 2 QB 56 the employee had been a manager of a garage for 30 years. He had always been heavily involved in the repair work of the garage, but the new owners wanted him to do much more paperwork and less of the practical work. The manager was not very good at the paperwork and after eight months he was dismissed. He argued that the employer now needed a different type of manager and that he was redundant. The court held that essentially the tasks of a manager had been reallocated but essentially the work remained the same. The new employer had merely introduced different methods of doing the same job and he was dismissed for reasons of incompetence (see also *Hindle* v. *Percival Boats* [1969] 1 WLR 174). In *Safeway Stores plc* v. *Burrell* [1997] IRLR 200 the Employment Appeal Tribunal stated that tribunals have to ask themselves three questions. Was the employee dismissed? If so, had the requirements of the employer's business for employees to carry out work of a particular kind ceased or diminished? If so, was this diminution in the requirement for employees the reason for the dismissal? This was applied when an employee was dismissed because the employer decided that he required someone with more experience, the Employment Appeal Tribunal holding that the dismissal was for redundancy (*BBC* v. *Farnworth* (1998) IDS Brief 624).

While normally a change in emphasis in the tasks comprising the job will not be a redundancy, in rare situations the court may find that the change in emphasis means that the employer does require different work. In *Murphy* v. *Epsom College* [1985] ICR 80 the employee was employed as a general plumber. The employer updated the heating system by introducing an electronic control system and Murphy was made redundant on the basis that the employer now needed a heating technician who could deal with both electrics and plumbing rather than a general plumber. The Court of Appeal upheld the tribunal's decision that Murphy was redundant. It has also been held that night-shift work as opposed to day-shift work is work of a particular kind and therefore moving night work into daytime hours is a redundancy (*Macfisheries Ltd* v. *Findlay* [1985] ICR 160).

The starting point to discover what kind of work the employee is employed to do will be his job duties under his contract. This could mean that if there is a wide flexibility clause the employee can never be redundant because there will always be work he is contracted to do. However, the courts have limited the application of flexibility clauses by stating that they must be interpreted by reference back to the main job duties (*Haden Ltd* v. *Cowan* [1982] IRLR 314).

At one time it was thought that a change in the terms of the contract meant that the employer now required a different type of work. In *Chapman* v. *Goonvean & Rostowrack China Clay Ltd* [1973] 1 WLR 678 seven employees resigned and claimed constructive dismissal by reason of redundancy when works transport which was provided by the employer was ceased when it became uneconomic to run. Although the terms of the contract had changed, this did not mean that the type of work required by the employer had changed according to the Court of Appeal. The employer still required seven employees and had taken on seven new employees to replace the ones who had resigned. This appears to be the test. Does the employer still need the same number of employees to do that particular type of work? If the work is increasing, but the employer requires fewer employees to do the work (for example, because of new technology) then there is a redundancy situation. Conversely, if there is a reorganisation, but overall the employer still needs the same number of employees to do that particular work, there is no redundancy. In *Johnson v. Nottinghamshire Combined Police Authority* [1974] IRLR 20 two women had worked as clerks working 9.30 a.m. to 5.30 p.m. The authority wanted them to work shifts of 8 a.m. to 3 p.m. and 1 a.m. to 8 a.m. Both women refused and were dismissed. The Court of Appeal held that there was no redundancy. The employer still required two employees doing the same amount of work, albeit at different times. It follows, therefore, that if a dismissed employee is replaced, the dismissal cannot be for redundancy because the requirements of the employer have not diminished. This is also the case if the employer takes on extra staff in the hope of increased production which never materialises (*O'Hare v. Rotaprint Ltd* [1980] IRLR 47). In *Shawkat v. Nottingham City Hospital NHS Trust (No. 2)* [2001] IRLR 555 the Court of Appeal held that the mere fact of a reorganisation, as a result of which the employer requires employees to do a different job, is not conclusive of redundancy. The tribunal must then decide whether there is a change in the requirements of the employer for employees to carry out work of a particular kind.

Finally, under these provisions, redundancy must be the whole or the main reason for the dismissal. Until recently, therefore, if the employer decided to redeploy the redundant employee and give him another employee's job, then the employee who was eventually dismissed could claim a redundancy payment as redundancy was the reason for his dismissal even though it was not his job which was made redundant (*North Yorkshire County Council v. Fay* [1985] IRLR 247). This is the situation known as 'bumping'. A recent case, however, has now placed doubt on this interpretation. As recently as 1997 in the case of *Safeway Stores plc v. Burrell* (above), the Employment Appeal Tribunal said that a bumped dismissal was a redundancy because the dismissal is caused by a diminution in the requirements of the employer for employees to carry out work of a particular kind and it was irrelevant that there was not a diminution in the kind of work the dismissed employee was employed to do. However, in *Church v. West Lancashire NHS Trust* [1998] IRLR 492 the Employment Appeal Tribunal reconsidered bumped redundancies and the meaning of the words 'work of a particular kind'.

In the case Church was employed in a particular department where the Trust decided that there had to be some redundancies. As no one volunteered for redundancy, the Trust decided to interview staff for the retained jobs and those who failed the interview would be made redundant. Church was told that he would have to attend interviews for two posts available to him, one of which was his own. The union was not happy at the way the redundancies were being handled and advised their members not to take part in the interviews. As a result, Church did not attend and was deemed to have failed the interview and was made redundant. He claimed that he had been unfairly dismissed. The employment tribunal found that although Church's post existed after the reorganisation, it was filled by an employee who would otherwise have been made redundant, therefore Church had been bumped out of his job and was therefore dismissed by reason of redundancy. The tribunal also found, however, that he had been fairly selected in that there had been proper consultation before his dismissal. Church appealed, arguing that he had not been dismissed by reason of redundancy.

The Employment Appeal Tribunal regarded the previous decisions on bumped redundancies and concluded that it was not bound by any Court of Appeal decisions in the area. In the tribunal's opinion, 'work of a particular kind' in s.139 meant work of the kind done by the employee being made redundant. The tribunal said that it was a matter of causation. The reason for the bumped employee's dismissal was not redundancy but the application of a procedure which required the dismissal of that employee in order for the employer to complete a reorganisation. Church's dismissal was not wholly attributable to a diminution in the employer's requirements but rather it was attributable to the method selected by the employer to handle the redundancy situation. The Employment Appeal Tribunal also stated that the test for deciding whether the employee was employed to do work of a particular kind was a mixture of a functional and a contractual approach, as stated by the Court of Appeal in *High Table Ltd* v. *Horst* [1997] IRLR 513. As such, Church's appeal was allowed.

The contractual test looks at the work specified in the employee's contract, the functional test looks at the work the employee was actually doing. While in *Burrell* the Employment Appeal Tribunal laid emphasis on the contractual test to establish the particular kind of work that the employee undertook, *Horst* and *Church* both talk of a mixture of the two tests, which is a more flexible approach. This has been endorsed by the House of Lords' decision in *Murray* v. *Foyle Meats Ltd* [1999] IRLR 562. In this case the employees worked as meat plant operatives. They normally worked in the slaughter hall but under their contracts could be required to work elsewhere and had occasionally done so. Because of a decline in business, the employers had decided that fewer employees were needed in the slaughter hall and the applicants were made redundant. The applicants argued that the selection pool was too narrow. As they were required to work elsewhere under their contracts, selection should have been across the whole of the business and not just the slaughter hall. The House of Lords upheld the original tribunal decision that the requirements of the employer for employees to work in the slaughter hall had diminished and that this was the reason that the applicants were redundant. The pool for selection was therefore correct. Lord Irvine LC, however, commented that:

> 'both the contract test and the function test miss the point. The key word in the statute is "attributable" and there is no reason in law why the dismissal of an employee should not be attributable to a diminution in the employer's need for employees irrespective of the terms of his contract or the function he performed.'

This, it is suggested, goes further than the previous decisions and looks to the cause of the employee's dismissal.

The main criticism of the decision in *Church* is that it leaves employees in Church's position with no redress. Church wanted to dispute the employer's redundancy claim to strengthen his complaint of unfair dismissal, but given the 'some other substantial reason' category of fair dismissal it is likely any dismissal of bumped employees would be found to be fair. Furthermore, the procedure used in Church's case to select for redundancy, that is getting employees to apply for their own jobs, is getting to be a more common way of selecting those to be dismissed. If they are not dismissed for redundancy and the dismissal is fair for 'some other substantial reason', this decision leaves those employees with no compensation for the loss of their jobs. The wider definition given by Lord Irvine in *Murray* can allow a bumping situation to constitute a redundancy. This appears to be confirmed by the later Employment Appeal Tribunal decision of *Leventhal Ltd* v. *North* EAT 0265/04. In this case the EAT said that in a redundancy situation employers should consider bumping a more junior colleague and offering the job to a more senior member of staff at risk of redundancy. The case concerned a publishing firm in severe financial difficulties and the quickest way of reducing overheads was to make the senior editor's job redundant. At no time did the company consider making the subordinate editor redundant and offering the job, with less pay, to the senior editor. The EAT held that the company had acted unfairly. While an unfair dismissal case, this clearly shows that bumping not only falls within the definition of redundancy, but also an employer may face an unfair dismissal claim if it fails to consider it.

10.4 Misconduct and Redundancy

Section 140(1) Employment Rights Act 1996 provides that in certain situations the employee will be disentitled to a redundancy payment. This occurs when the employer terminates the contract where:

(a) the employee commits an act of misconduct and the employer dismisses without notice; or

(b) the employee commits an act of misconduct and the employer dismisses with shorter notice than the redundancy notice; or

(c) the employer, when the redundancy notice expires, gives the employee a statement in writing that the employer is entitled, by virtue of the employee's conduct, to dismiss without notice.

In such cases the dismissal is for reason of the employee's conduct and not redundancy.

There are two exceptions to s.140(1). By s.140(2) where an employee, while under notice of redundancy, takes part in a strike or other industrial action subsection (1) does not apply. This allows employees to take industrial action to protest against the redundancies. If, however, an employee who is on strike is selected for redundancy, the tribunal will have no jurisdiction to hear the case unless it falls within the special provisions on unfair dismissal (*Simmons* v. *Hoover Ltd* [1977] QB 284). By s.143 the employer can extend the redundancy notice period and require the employees to work in order to make up the days lost by the industrial action, and if the employees refuse they disentitle themselves to a redundancy payment. By s.140(3) if an employee while under notice of redundancy commits an act of misconduct and is dismissed for this misconduct, the tribunal may award him such part of his redundancy payment as the tribunal considers just and equitable. The employee must have actually committed the misconduct however, a reasonable belief by the employer is insufficient. In *Bonner* v. *Gilbert (H.) Ltd* [1989] IRLR 475 an employee, while under notice of redundancy, was dismissed for suspected dishonesty. The tribunal held that as the employer genuinely believed in the employee's guilt, s.140(3) applied. The Employment Appeal Tribunal held that the test for the section was whether the employee was actually guilty and not the employer's belief in his guilt. Section 140(3) did not apply and the employee was entitled to a redundancy payment. Thus an employee who commits an act of misconduct during notice of redundancy may get some, if not all, of his redundancy payment ,whereas the employee who has committed misconduct before being given notice of redundancy and is then made redundant will get nothing if he is dismissed with short notice or the employer gives the necessary statement.

10.5 Suitable Alternative Employment

If the employer offers the employee his old job back or a different job which is suitable alternative employment, the new contract starts on the termination of the old or within four weeks of the old contract expiring and the employee unreasonably refuses the offer, he is disentitled to a redundancy payment by ss.141(2) and (3). The sections therefore mean that two questions must be asked: is the offer suitable alternative employment and is the employee's refusal of that offer unreasonable?

The first question is an objective one based on all the circumstances. Obviously, if the employer offers the employee his old job back it must be an offer of suitable alternative employment. If the employer offers a different job however, a variety of factors must be looked at together to see if the employment is suitable. For example, the alternative work may be at a lower salary but include a bonus which will offset the difference. It may involve extra travelling expenses but give a higher salary, or the employer is prepared to pay travelling expenses. A drop in status or responsibility will often mean that the offer is unsuitable even if salary is unaffected. In *Taylor* v. *Kent County Council* [1969] 2 QB 560 the headmaster of a boys' secondary school was, on its closure, offered a post in a pool of mobile staff at the same salary. It was held that the drop in status meant that the offer was unsuitable. (See also *Cambridge & District Co-operative Society Limited* v. *Ruse* [1993] IRLR 156.) The court said in *Carron Co* v. *Robertson* (1967) ITR 484 that all factors should be considered, such as the nature of the work, hours and pay, the employee's strength and training, experience and ability and status in the employer's premises. Thus in *Standard Telephones & Cables* v. *Yates* [1981] IRLR 21 an offer of unskilled assembly work was unsuitable alternative employment for a skilled card-wirer. One thing which is clear, however, is that the employer must actually offer alternative work and that work must be specific. In *Curling* v. *Securicor Ltd* [1992] IRLR 549 the employers lost a contract to provide security at a detention centre. The employees' contracts contained wide mobility clauses and after the loss of the contract at the detention centre, the employer circulated a list of alternative jobs and interviewed employees as to whether they were prepared to accept any of them. No attempt was made to invoke the mobility clause. Curling left to take up employment with the company who gained the contract at the detention centre and claimed a redundancy payment. The company argued that Curling had resigned because he had refused to comply with the mobility clause. The Employment Appeal Tribunal held that there was a dismissal. The employer had not attempted to invoke the mobility clause at the time and could not do so as an afterthought. As such, there was a dismissal and the employer had sought to offer alternative work. The offers, however, were not of suitable alternative employment. No specific offers had been made, merely a list distributed which contained a multiplicity of insufficiently specified jobs.

If the offer is unsuitable, that is the end of the matter and the employee is entitled to a redundancy payment. If the offer is deemed to be suitable, then the employee will still be entitled if his refusal is reasonable in the circumstances. While the court will look at features of the job to see if it is suitable, when looking at the employee's refusal it will look at broader issues, for example the employee's domestic circumstances. In *Paton, Calvert & Co* v. *Westerside* [1979] IRLR 108 the employee, who was under notice of redundancy, was offered his old job back when his employers got a Temporary Employment Subsidy from the government. The employee was 61 and had already found a new permanent job. His refusal was held to be reasonable. The offer was of temporary work and, given his age and the difficulty a person of his age had in getting work, the permanent nature of the job he had accepted was very important. On the other hand, a personal fad will not render the refusal reasonable. In *Fuller* v. *Stephanie Bowman Ltd* [1977] IRLR 7 the employer moved offices from Mayfair to Soho. The employee refused to move because the new office was above a sex shop. The tribunal found that the refusal to move was based on undue sensitivity and was unreasonable in the circumstances.

10.6 Trial Period in New Employment

If the terms of the new contract differ (wholly or in part) from the old contract, then by s.138 of the 1996 Act the employee is entitled to a trial period. By subsection (3) the statutory trial period is four weeks, but this can be extended by the employee's contract as long as the period is in writing and specified precisely. If the employee is dismissed during the trial period, he is treated as being dismissed for the reason his original contract ended, that is redundancy, and on the date his original contract ended, so entitling him to claim a redundancy payment. If the employee resigns, he is treated as dismissed for redundancy unless his resignation was unreasonable. The four weeks is interpreted strictly and means four calendar weeks whether the employee worked or not. In *Benton* v. *Sanderson Kayser Ltd* [1989] IRLR 19 four calendar weeks ended on 18 January. The employee resigned on 19 January when he had worked less than four weeks because of the Christmas break. It was held that he had lost his entitlement to a redundancy payment. If, however, the employer does not terminate the employee's old contract, but merely moves him to different work, then there is a variation which the employee can accept or reject. At common law, he will be entitled to a reasonable period of time to make up his mind and this may well exceed four weeks. In *Shields Furniture Ltd* v. *Goff* [1973] ICR 187 the employees were transferred because of lack of work in their own department and left after more than four weeks. Their employer had never terminated their old contracts. The Employment Appeal Tribunal held that at common law they were entitled to a reasonable period of time to see if they accepted the variation. After that acceptance they were entitled to the statutory four-week trial period and if they resigned before that period had expired, they were entitled to a redundancy payment. In *McKindley* v. *William Hill (Scotland) Ltd* [1985] IRLR 492 it was held that this meant that a resignation 12 months after the employee was moved to another job entitled him to a redundancy payment.

10.7 Lay-Off and Short-Time Working

In order to prevent redundancies, the employer may temporarily lay off his workers or put them on short time. By s.147 of the 1996 Act a lay-off is where no work or pay is provided by the employer. Short-time working is where less than half a week's pay is earned. By s.148 where the lay-off or short time has lasted for more than four consecutive weeks or six weeks in any 13, the employee can give notice to his employer that he intends to claim a redundancy payment. He must give the notice in writing and he must give the correct notice needed to terminate his contract. The employer has a defence if he can show that he reasonably expects to provide full-time work for the next 13 weeks and he raises this defence in written counter-notice served within seven days of the receipt of the employee's intention to claim.

10.8 Redundancy Compensation

A redundancy payment is calculated in the same way as the basic award for unfair dismissal (see Chapter 9) and is therefore based on age and years of service. Since the Employment Equality (Age) Regulations 2006 there are no upper or lower age limits for eligibility. Unlike the basic award, there is no deduction for contributory conduct.

To make a claim, the employee must have two-years' continuous employment at the relevant date. The problems involved with the calculation of the period of continuity have already been discussed in Chapter 9. Should the employee claim unfair redundancy and be successful, any redundancy payment is deducted from the basic award to prevent double compensation (s.122(4)). If the payment exceeds the basic award it is also set off against the compensatory award (*Roadchef Ltd* v. *Hastings* [1987] IRLR 142).

The employer must give his redundant employee a written statement setting out how his redundancy compensation has been calculated (s.158). Failure to do so renders the employer liable to a fine.

If the redundancy is caused by the employer's insolvency, the employee may make a claim for a redundancy payment to the Department of Employment under s.166 Employment Rights Act 1996. While the employee ranks as a preferential creditor in his employer's insolvency, this will not be much use if the employer has no assets, and therefore additionally the

Department can pay certain sums directly to the employee from the National Insurance Fund. The following payments can be made from the fund (s.184):

(a) up to eight-weeks' wages, including guarantee pay, medical suspension pay, maternity suspension pay, pay for statutory time off and a protective award, up to the existing statutory maximum weekly pay in a redundancy calculation;

(b) minimum pay during notice under s.86 Employment Rights Act 1996 (subject to statutory weekly maximum);

(c) up to six-weeks' holiday pay accumulated in the previous 12 months (subject to statutory weekly maximum);

(d) basic award issued by a tribunal;

(e) reimbursement of fees paid for apprenticeship or articles (subject to statutory weekly maximum).

10.9 Consultation

We have already seen in Chapter 9 that a failure to consult and warn the employee about his redundancy may render the dismissal unfair. In addition to the procedural requirements for unfair dismissal, statute creates an obligation on employers to consult with unions or elected employee representatives in certain cases of redundancy. The original legislative provisions were contained in the Employment Protection Act 1975 which was implemented to give effect to the EC Directive on the Approximation of Laws Relating to Redundancies (EEC/75/129). The relevant provision is now s.188 Trade Union and Labour Relations (Consolidation) Act 1992 (as amended). The amendments were enacted after *Commission for European Communities* v. *United Kingdom of Great Britain and Northern Ireland* [1994] ICR 664 which stated that the provisions on consultation did not fully implement EC Directives EEC/75/129 (above) or 77/187 (Acquired Rights Directive), in that they did not provide for consultation where there was not an independent recognised trade union. The original provisions created an obligation on the employer to consult with independent recognised trade unions before the redundancies occur. Amendments in 1995 and 1999 now provide that the employer is under a duty to consult with representatives of an independent recognised trade union, or employee representatives where there is no independent recognised trade union, where he proposes to dismiss as redundant 20 or more employees in 90 days or less. It should be noted that the government at the time of the amendments took the opportunity to remove from consultation provisions the situation where fewer than 20 employees are being dismissed for redundancy, a removal unsuccessfully challenged by the trade union movement (*R* v. *Secretary of State for Trade and Industry ex parte UNISON* [1996] IRLR 438). At the time of the amendments, protection from detrimental treatment and dismissal was introduced for employee representatives (see Chapters 7 and 9). The statutory definition of an independent trade union is given in s.5 Trade Union and Labour Relations (Consolidation) Act 1992. Recognised trade union is wider than a union recognised under the statutory procedure (see Chapter 12). Section 178(3) of the 1992 Act states that recognition means the recognition of the union by the employer, to any extent, for the purposes of collective bargaining, and collective bargaining is defined in s.178(1) as negotiations relating to or connected with one or more of a list of specified matters.

Where there is no written agreement, the question of recognition is a question of fact for the tribunal. In *NUTGW* v. *Charles Ingram & Co Ltd* [1977] IRLR 147 it was held that the tribunals should consider five points when deciding if a union is recognised for the purposes of the statute:

1. Recognition is a mixed question of law and fact.
2. Recognition requires mutuality.
3. There must be an express or implied agreement for recognition to exist.
4. If an agreement is implied, there must be clear conduct to establish the agreement, usually over a period of time.
5. There can be partial recognition for some purposes but not all.

Thus, in the case, the employer was a member of a trade association which bargained with the union, the manager over a substantial period of time had discussed terms and conditions with the union official and the firm had stated on a government form that the union was recognised. All of these factors indicated that the employer recognised the union for collective bargaining purposes. On the other hand, it would appear that, in the absence of a written agreement, membership of a trade association which has negotiated with the union is not sufficient for recognition (*National Union of Gold, Silver and Allied Trades* v. *Albury Brothers Ltd* [1979] ICR 84), likewise one-off negotiations on particular topics do not constitute recognition.

As noted above, if there is no recognised independent trade union, the employer is required to consult with elected employee representatives. Original amendments in 1995 did not specify the criteria for how the election of such representatives was to be conducted, it was up to the employer to choose. Further amendments in 1999 now require the employer to make suitable arrangements for the election and take reasonable steps to ensure that it is carried out sufficiently early enough for information to be given and consultation to take place in good time (s.188(7A)). While it is up to the employer to decide the number of representatives to be elected and the amount of time they serve, the number must be sufficient to represent all of the employees properly and the period of office must be long enough to complete the consultation (ss.188(A)(1)(b) and (d)). The representatives must be members of the affected workforce (s.188(A)(1)(e)) and no one who is a member of the affected workforce may be unreasonably excluded from standing for election (s.188(A)(1)(f)). Everyone who is a member of the affected workforce must have a right to vote and the voting must be in secret (ss.188(A)(1)(g) and (h)). In the event of a dispute as to the validity of the election, any of the affected employees may complain to a tribunal and the burden is on the employer to show that the election conditions were complied with (ss.189(1) and (1B)). The definition of 'affected employees' was also changed in 1999 and now includes any employee who may be affected by the redundancies and not only those who will be dismissed (s.188(1)). This amendment reflects the duty to consult in the event of a transfer of an undertaking.

The duty in s.188(1A) requires the employer who proposes to declare redundancies to begin consultation in good time. The original provisions required the employer to consult at the earliest opportunity and it remains to be seen if the change in wording leads to a different interpretation by the courts. This leads to two questions. When does the employer propose to make redundancies and what constitutes 'in good time'? In *Re Hartlebury Printers Ltd* [1992] ICR 559 (a case under the old provisions) the employer was experiencing financial difficulties in May 1990. Consideration had been given to declaring redundancies but the idea was rejected. On 25 June, a prospective buyer indicated that it would require some employees to be made redundant. The union was informed on 27 June and agreed the figures on 29 June although the redundancies were not implemented. On 3 July the company went into liquidation. The union sued. One of the arguments turned on when the duty to consult arose. The legislation talks of when the employer is proposing redundancies, however the Directive states it is when an employer is contemplating redundancies, which arguably is sooner. The court declined to pursue that argument and concluded that the legislation complied with the Directive until the European Court decided otherwise. The point then turned on when it could be said that this employer proposed to make redundancies. The court held that as no definite decision had been made until 25 June, the consultation had been at the time of the proposal. However, in *MSF* v. *Refuge Insurance* [2002] IRLR 324 the union claimed that the consultation period implemented by Refuge on planned redundancies following a merger was too short. Refuge argued that, under s.188, consultation did not have to begin until a proposal on redundancy had been made. The Employment Appeal Tribunal agreed but stated that the UK does not comply with the Directive.

Unless the minimum consultation periods apply (see below) the law until recently told us what was not in good time instead of stating what the time limit was. Consultation at the time of the issue of redundancy notices did not comply with the original provisions (*NUT* v. *Avon County Council* [1978] IRLR 55) nor did a meeting half-an-hour before such notices were issued. Likewise, two or three days before was held to be useless (*TGWU* v. *Nationwide Haulage Ltd* [1978] IRLR 143). In *Junk* v. *Kuhnel* [2005] IRLR 310 the ECJ held that an employer should begin the statutory consultation procedures when he intends to terminate contracts, and this was interpreted by the Employment Appeal Tribunal in *Leicestershire County Council* v. *UNISON* [2005] IRLR 920 that consultation must begin when the employer proposes to give notice of dismissal.

The time when the duty to consult begins has now been the subject of judicial discussion in the case of *UK Coal Mining Ltd* v. *National Union of Mineworkers and The British Association of Colliery Management* UKEAT 0397/06. The facts of the case are quite complicated. After debates about the viability of a colliery, the government in April 2004 gave the company £19 million to develop it, and the managing director announced, in May 2004, that the colliery would remain open as long as it met production targets and operating costs were kept to a minimum. On 12 January 2005, water began to rise at the face of the seam being worked and although pumps were installed, the water was rising more quickly than it could be pumped out and production had to stop. By 25 January the water-level was falling, however on 21 January the managing director had contacted the DTI (see below) and informed them that the company was close to announcing the closure of the colliery, stating that the economic and risk cases for developing a new face were not satisfactory. He also stated that for safety reasons they would not restart the damaged face. A number of meetings were held with the NUM and BACM representatives from 26 January until 26 February when the first compulsory redundancies were made. The company did not respond to any suggestions made by the representatives and although the company reiterated that the colliery would close on health and safety grounds, they produced no evidence of any surveys or reports they had commissioned to support this.

The employment tribunal found that the company had misled the unions as to the true reasons for the dismissals, which were economic rather than on health and safety grounds. This finding was not overturned by the Employment Appeal Tribunal. The EAT also upheld the finding that since *Leicestershire Council* v. *UNISON* the words 'proposing to dismiss' in s.188(1) must be interpreted as 'proposing to give notice of dismissal' and therefore consultation must be completed before notices of dismissal are given to the workforce. Since the number of redundancies were over 100 this meant that the required 90-day consultation period (see below) had not been complied with. However, the Employment Appeal Tribunal overturned the employment tribunal on one point. The tribunal had been bound by the earlier case of *R* v. *British Coal and Secretary of State for Trade and Industry ex parte Vardy* [1993] ICR 720 which stated that the then s.188 did not require an employer to consult over the reasons for the closure of the colliery. However, an amendment to s.188 introduced in 1995 was a definition of 'consultation'. This is found in s.188(2) and requires an employer to consult on ways of avoiding the dismissals, reducing the number of employees to be dismissed or motivating the consequences of the dismissals. The Employment Appeal Tribunal therefore held that, given this amendment, there must now normally be a duty on an employer to consult on the reasons for closure, otherwise it would make a mockery of s.188(2).

Where there are a substantial number of redundancies, s.188(1A) of the 1992 Act lays down minimum consultation periods. If 100 or more employees are to be made redundant within 90 days, at least 90-days' consultation must take place. If between 20 and 99 are to be made redundant within 90 days, at least 30-days' consultation must take place. The employer must disclose to the employee representatives in writing the reasons for his proposals, the numbers and descriptions of those employees affected, the total number of employees of that description employed, method of selection and the proposed method of carrying out the dismissals (s.188(4)). Consultation should be undertaken with a view to obtaining agreement with the representatives, and the definition of redundancy for consultation purposes is widened to include dismissal for reasons not related to the individual (s.195(1) of the 1992 Act), that is, it covers bumping. Representatives must also be told the method of calculation of redundancy payments other than those required by law (s.188(2)(f)).

The employer may plead special circumstances as a defence to a failure to consult. By s.189(6) if the employer can show that it was not reasonably practicable to comply with any of the consultation requirements and he took all steps towards compliance with the requirements as were reasonably practicable in the circumstances, he will reduce and may even extinguish his liability. The most common situation pleaded is that the business has suddenly gone into liquidation which was unforeseeable. If the employer continues to trade in the hope that he will avoid liquidation and this is a reasonable expectation, then special circumstances will exist. A foreseeable liquidation, however, will not constitute special circumstances and the employer will be liable. The employer who shuts his eyes to the obvious will have no defence (*Association of Patternmakers and Allied Craftsmen* v. *Kirwin Ltd* [1978] IRLR 318). Since 1993 there is no defence available to the employer that he failed to consult because information was not provided by a controlling employer (s.188(7)).

Where the employer has broken his statutory duty to consult, the union or the employee representatives can apply to a tribunal for a protective award which is payable to those employees in respect of whom the representatives should have been consulted (s.189(2)). The award is for the protected period, that is, beginning at the date the first dismissals took place and continuing for as long as the tribunal considers just and equitable, but in all cases subject to a statutory maximum of 90 days if 100 or more were made redundant, 30 days if 20 to 99 were made redundant (s.189(4)). In *Spillers-French* v. *USDAW* [1980] ICR 31 the Employment Appeal Tribunal held that as the section requires the tribunal to consider the seriousness of the employer's default, the purpose of the section is compensatory rather than punitive and if the employees had suffered no loss as a result of the failure to consult, no award should be made. However, in the case of *Smith and Another* v. *Cherry Lewis Ltd* [2005] IRLR 86 a later EAT has stated that the purpose of the award is punitive and intended to have a deterrent effect. In the case the employer went into receivership and told the staff to contact the DTI for payment arrears. There was no consultation. The employment tribunal held that it could not make a protective award as the employer could not pay, but the EAT made an award of 90-days' pay because of the employer's blatant breach of the requirements. It stated that the ability of the employer to pay was irrelevant when the objective was to punish and deter. How far this would help employees in the situation of a bankruptcy, however, may be more theoretical than real. Since 1993 the requirement on a tribunal to offset any award made against wages or payment in lieu of notice has been removed.

Similar provisions relate to consultation where there is a transfer of an undertaking under the Transfer of Undertakings (Protection of Employment) Regulations 2006. The issues of dismissal and liability for redundancy have already been discussed in Chapter 9. Where such a transfer takes place, Regulation 13 creates a duty on both the transferor and the transferee to inform the representatives. The representatives must receive information about the transfer and the legal, economic and social implications of it, the measures that the employer envisages it will take in relation to the employees and, if the employer is the transferor, the measures the transferor envisages the transferee will be taking. Furthermore, consultation is more strictly defined in that the employer must consult with the representatives, consider any representations they make and give reasons if they reject the ideas (Regulation 13(7)). By Regulation 6, where the transferor recognises a union then, when, after the transfer, the undertaking remains a distinct identity separate from the remainder of the transferee's undertaking, recognition is transferred so that the transferee is deemed to recognise the union which may, therefore, transfer a duty to consult. By Regulation 6(2)(b), however, the transferee may vary or rescind any agreement for recognition so transferred.

The remedy for failure to comply with the consultation provisions under the Regulations is found in Regulation 15. Again the employer can raise the defence of special circumstances. The maximum award which can be made under the Regulations is thirteen-weeks' pay. Regulation 15(9) states that the transferor and transferee are jointly and severally liable for a failure to consult.

Summary

1. Redundancy payments are a recognition of a worker's property right in his job.

2. To claim a redundancy payment, an employee must have two-years' continuity and be dismissed for reasons of redundancy.

3. 'Redundancy' is defined as the employer ceasing business, moving his place of business, or reducing the number of employees employed to do particular work.

4. If the employee has committed misconduct and is selected for redundancy, or commits misconduct during the redundancy notice, the dismissal is for misconduct if the employer so elects.

5. If the employee who has been selected for redundancy goes on strike or participates in other industrial action, the dismissal is still for redundancy.

6. If the employer offers suitable alternative employment which the employee unreasonably refuses, the employee becomes disentitled to a redundancy payment.

7. If the employee accepts alternative employment, he is entitled to a statutory trial period and if during this trial period he reasonably resigns, he may still claim a redundancy payment.

8. In certain situations of lay-off and short-time working the employee can claim a redundancy payment.

9. Redundancy compensation is calculated in a similar way to the basic award in unfair dismissal.

10. There is a statutory duty on an employer to consult with employee representatives when making a certain number of employees redundant and a statutory duty to inform the Department of Employment when making mass redundancies.

Summary cont'd

11. Failure to consult with the union or employee representatives, when there is no justification for the failure, entitles the affected employees to a protective award.

12. There are similar consultation duties on both the transferor and transferee when there is a transfer of an undertaking.

Exercises

1. Good Nosh Ltd is a contract catering company. One of the units they operate is Westshire Hospital where three weeks ago they changed all their food preparation to cook–chill. Cook–chill involves prepared food being delivered from a production kitchen 50 miles away. The food is then regenerated at the unit.

    Den has been employed for eight years. He was the chef at Westshire. As a chef, his duties included the preparation of 1,000 meals a day. As a result of cook–chill, he now only prepares 20 meals a day from their raw state for senior management at the hospital. His post has been renamed Kitchen Supervisor and his duties are the preparation of food for senior management and the supervision of the kitchen staff. His hours have been reduced by five a week with a consequent reduction in pay. Today Den handed in his notice.

    Ethel has worked there for four years. She is a general assistant. Before cook–chill her duties involved the preparation of vegetables and salads, but since cook–chill was introduced, her duties have been altered so that she now puts out the prepared food and serves it. Her hours and pay are the same, but she feels she is no longer using her creative skills.

    Pete is a delivery man for Good Nosh Ltd and has worked for the company for three years. Since the introduction of cook–chill his hours have radically altered. Before, he started at 8 a.m. and finished at 3.30 p.m. for five days a week. Now he works from 5 a.m. to midday for six days a week (the sixth day being Sunday). This is because the prepared chilled food has to be delivered for use within 24 hours. His pay has remained the same. He feels aggrieved because he feels that he is working unsociable hours which are disrupting his domestic life.

    Advise Den, Ethel and Pete.

2. What is the relationship between s.218 Employment Rights Act 1996 and the Transfer of Undertakings (Protection of Employment) Regulations 2006?

Further Reading

Armour and Deakin   *The Rover Case (2): Bargaining in the Shadow of TUPE* (2000) 29 ILJ 395.

Bourne   *Redundancy Law and Practice* (Butterworths, 1983).

Collins   *Transfer of Undertakings and Insolvency* (1989) 18 ILJ 144.

Eady   *Collective Dismissals, Consultation and Remedies* (1994) 23 ILJ 350.

Grunfeld   *The Law of Redundancy* (3rd edn, Sweet & Maxwell, 1989).

Hall and Edwands   *Reforming the Statutory Consultation Procedure* (1999) 28 ILJ 299.

McMullen   *Takeovers, Transfers and Business Reorganisations* (1992) 21 ILJ 15.

McMullen   *An Analysis of the Transfer of Undertakings (Protection of Employment) Regulations 2006* (2006) 35 ILJ 113.

Njoya   *The Interface Between Redundancy and TUPE Transfers* (2003) 32 ILJ 123.

Wedderburn   *Consultation and Collective Bargaining in Europe: Success or Ideology?* (1997) 26 ILJ 1.

Chapter 11

Duties of Ex-Employees

Introduction

In Chapter 4 we saw that the employee owes a duty of faithful service to his employer and part of that duty is not to divulge, or otherwise misuse, confidential information. This duty is either implied into the contract by the common law or it may be an express term in the contract. This raises the question, however, of the protection afforded to the employer once the relationship has come to an end. The damage that can be caused to an employer's business by a third party learning trade secrets or secret processes is just as serious whether passed on by a present or a past employee. We have already seen that the courts grapple with the problem of distinguishing what is confidential to the employer and what can be said to be part of the skills acquired by the employee during his period of employment. This problem becomes more acute once the employment relationship has ended, for the new employer will be buying the employee for his skill and knowledge. As such, the courts are wary of any attempt to restrict the employee after the termination of his contract. Having said that, some restrictions are allowed and there are two methods which can be invoked. These methods are discussed below.

11.2 Express/Implied Duty of Fidelity

While there is a term in the contract restricting the employee from divulging confidential information while he is employed, in some circumstances this duty will continue after the relationship has ended. It appears from *Faccenda Chicken Ltd* v. *Fowler* (Chapter 4), however, that the duty is limited when applied to ex-employees and will only extend to the divulgence of trade secrets and, possibly, customer connections. Furthermore, the contractual duty will only prevent the divulgence of information and will not prevent the employee from working for a competitor or setting up in competition. Whereas a blatant transfer of information, for example giving the new employer a formula, will be protected, other use of information will not be. What of the ex-salesman who visits his old customers rather than give the list to his new employers, as in the *Faccenda Chicken* case? He is not divulging any information, merely using his existing contacts. *Faccenda Chicken* demonstrates that such action is not a breach of the contractual duty. It is because of these limitations of the contractual duty in relation to ex-employees that employers rely on the second method of protection: restraint of trade covenants.

11.3 Restraint of Trade Covenants

A covenant is merely a promise. A restraint of trade covenant is a promise contained within a contract of employment whereby the employee undertakes that he will accept a restraint upon where he works and for whom, for a period of time after he has left the employment relationship. This may at first sight appear to be the panacea to all employers' problems in relation to the misuse of confidential information. Would it were that simple! The courts are notoriously wary of such covenants because they are required to balance conflicting interests – the interests of the employer on the one hand, who wishes to protect his business, and the interests of the employee on the other hand, who has a legitimate right to be free to pursue his career where and with whom he wishes.

The starting point will be whether the covenant is enforceable on contractual principles before the court will look at the validity of the covenant itself. If the covenant has been agreed at the end of the relationship, it is likely to be unenforceable as the employer is giving no consideration for the employee's promise to restrict his future employment. Likewise, a repudiatory breach on the part of the employer repudiates the whole contract, including the covenant, and therefore the covenant becomes unenforceable. In *Briggs* v. *Oates* [1990] IRLR 472 a solicitor had been employed by two partners. The partnership changed which meant that his contract terminated. This was done without notice and was thus a repudiatory breach of contract. It was held by the High Court that therefore he was no longer bound by the restraint clauses in his contract. The employer must commit a repudiatory breach of contract however. By contrast, in *Rex Stewart Jefferies Parker Ginsberg Ltd* v. *Parker* [1988] IRLR 483 the employee had been joint managing director of an advertising agency. There was a covenant in his contract which prevented him from soliciting clients of the agency for 18 months after his employment had ended. The employee left and set up his own agency. He argued that the employer could not rely on the covenant because he had been dismissed and paid wages in lieu of notice. The Court of Appeal held that paying wages in lieu of notice was not a breach of contract, therefore the covenant was valid and enforceable. The employer cannot, however, write into the covenant that it will be enforceable whether the termination of the contract is lawful or not (*Living Design* v. *Davidson* [1994] IRLR 69). The covenant does not have to be reiterated, however, every time the contract is varied. In *Marley Tile Co Ltd* v. *Johnson* [1982]

IRLR 75 the employee's original letter of appointment contained a number of restraints which prevented him from seeking employment with rival organisations, or competing with his employer, for a period of 12 months after leaving his employment. On promotion to area manager, his letter of appointment contained the same restraints, but when he was promoted a second time the letter made no reference to the restraints. The Court of Appeal held that the restraints in his original letter of appointment applied to any subsequent promotions. The court said that as the employee had remained with the same company, each time his contract varied the parties must have assumed that the same terms applied unless anything was said to the contrary. No reference was made, for example, to his company car or expense account because both parties assumed that they were still part of the contract. Thus the covenants were part of each successive contract. They were, however, too wide and therefore void.

Even if the clause is technically enforceable, the courts may still render it void if they feel it is not reasonable. Whereas the courts are prepared to protect an employer against the misuse of confidential information by existing employees, they are less happy in giving protection against ex-employees by upholding a provision that limits the employee's choice of future employment. The modern law on restraint of trade covenants is to be found in *Nordenfelt* v. *Maxim Nordenfelt Guns and Ammunition Co* [1894] AC 535. The case was not an employment case but involved the sale of a business. The contract contained a provision preventing the vendor from setting up in competition. The House of Lords established that a restraint of trade covenant is to be considered void unless the party alleging its validity can prove it is (a) reasonable as between the parties and (b) reasonable in the public interest. Since the later case of *Esso Petroleum Ltd* v. *Harper's Garage (Stourport) Ltd* [1968] AC 269 the courts have emphasised that both aspects are equally important and therefore both must be proved for the covenant to stand.

'Reasonable between the parties' has been interpreted to mean that the employer must have a recognisable interest to protect and is not merely attempting to prevent normal competition. 'Reasonable in the public interest' means that even if the employer has a legitimate interest to protect, he may only give himself the protection he needs. Therefore if the covenant is so wide in area or time that it gives more protection than is needed, it will be unreasonable in the public interest and will fall. If the covenant is not drafted as separate provisions, if one part offends the test of reasonableness the whole covenant will be void even if the rest is only giving the necessary protection that the employer needs.

11.4 Reasonable Between the Parties

To establish that the covenant is reasonable between the parties, the employer must show he has some proprietary right to protect. In other words, he must show that he has a trade secret, secret process or customer connections, the disclosure of which could damage his business. In addition, he must show that the ex-employee has knowledge of the trade secret or secret process, or be in a position where customers are likely to follow him to his new employment. The employer cannot restrain all his employees merely because he has a trade secret, secret process or customer connections to protect. He can only restrain those employees who have the necessary knowledge or connections to do harm to the employer's business. Further, the employer can only restrain the employee in relation to those aspects of the business in which the employee was employed and of which he thus has knowledge, and cannot impose a restraint covering all aspects of the employer's business (*Turner* v. *Commonwealth and British Minerals Ltd* [2000] IRLR 114). If, therefore, it is shown that the employee does not have the knowledge or connections, the covenant will be seen as a blatant attempt to prevent competition and void. In *Herbert Morris Ltd* v. *Saxelby* [1916] 1 AC 688 there was a provision in the employee's contract preventing him from working for a competitor for seven years after leaving his employment. The employee had no knowledge of the employer's trade secrets and had no personal contact with the employer's customers. All the employee had was his own technical skill and knowledge. It was held that the covenant was an attempt to prevent competition and void. Similar conclusions were reached in *Strange* v. *Mann* [1965] 1 All ER 1069 and *Faccenda Chicken Ltd* v. *Fowler* (Chapter 4).

A trade secret or secret process does not have to be patented to be able to be protected, but it must be confidential, that is, outside the sphere of public knowledge, and it must be more than the employee's knowledge of the trade which he has acquired through his employment. Valid restraints have covered secret processes and formulas (*Forster & Sons* v. *Sugget* (1918) 35 TLR 87), the design of a machine (*Ansell Rubber Co* v. *Allied Rubber Industries* [1967] VR 37) and detailed knowledge of the workings of a specialised business (*Littlewoods Organisation Ltd* v. *Harris* [1978] 1 All ER 1026).

The law is even more restrictive in relation to the employer's customers. The employer may only protect himself in relation to employees who have established a relationship with the customers so that there is a real danger that the customers will follow the employee when he leaves (*International Consulting Services (UK) Ltd* v. *Hart* [2000] IRLR 227). In *Strange* v. *Mann* (above), the contract of a manager of a firm of bookmakers included the provision that he was not to engage in a similar business to that of his employers within a 12-mile radius once his employment had terminated. It was held that, given that the manager had little influence over the customers, most of whom placed bets by telephone rather than face to face, the employer had no legitimate interest to protect. A similar conclusion was reached in *Bowler* v. *Lovegrove* [1921] 1 Ch 642 where a restraint against an estate agent who mainly dealt with customers by telephone was also held to be void. In addition, in the *Bowler* case the nature of the employer's business was relevant. Customers rarely build up long-term relationships with estate agents.

Sales people, in particular, will have built up relationships with customers and therefore the customers may follow the employee when he leaves. In unusual cases, the employee may have influence over customers that he has not had direct contact with and it will be legitimate to protect the employer against the possibility of the loss of such customers (*John Michael Design plc* v. *Cooke* [1987] ICR 445). Generally, however, the employer should only protect himself in relation to customers who have had direct contact with the employee. In the old case of *Mason* v. *Provident Clothing and Supply Co* [1913] AC 724 a restraint covenant purported to prevent the employee from competing with her ex-employers within a 25-mile radius of the centre of London. The employee had only had contact with customers in a specified area of London and, as such, the House of Lords stated that the covenant covered customers she had not met and was therefore too wide and void. More recently, in the complex case of *Office Angels Ltd* v. *Rainer-Thomas and O'Connor* [1991] IRLR 214, there were two restraint clauses which the employer sought to enforce. Relevant to this discussion was clause 4.5(a) which stated that the employees would not, for six months after the termination of employment, solicit custom from any person who had been a company client during the employees' employment. The Court of Appeal held that the clause was too wide in itself. It covered all clients (6,000–7,000), of which the employees had dealt with about 100. As such, the clause was void (see also *Scully UK Ltd* v. *Lee* [1998] IRLR 259).

11.5 Reasonable in the Public Interest

Even if the employer proves he has a legitimate interest to protect, the covenant will still be declared void if the court feels that it is not reasonable in the public interest. There are three ways in which a covenant may infringe public interest considerations.

First, the covenant may be drafted too broadly and give the employer more protection than he actually needs because, on construction, it prevents the employee from entering non-competitive employment. In *Fellowes & Son* v. *Fisher* [1976] 2 QB 122 a conveyancing clerk, employed by a firm of solicitors in Walthamstow, agreed that for five years after the termination of his employment, he would not be employed in, or concerned with, the legal profession anywhere within the postal district of Walthamstow and Chingford, or solicit any person who had been a client of the firm while he had worked there. The Court of Appeal held that, on construction, this prevented him from working in any part of the legal profession, including local government. As such, the restraint was wider than that needed by the employer and void. Likewise, in *Commercial Plastics Ltd* v. *Vincent* [1965] 1 QB 623, an employee's contract contained a restraint covenant which prevented him working in the PVC calendering field for one year after leaving his employment. The employee had only ever been employed in the adhesive tape side of the business and therefore the covenant, which prevented the employee from working in any aspect of the industry, was too wide and void. Second, the covenant may cover too wide an area and therefore give the employer more protection than he actually needs. This may be because there is no area limit and therefore the restriction is deemed to be worldwide or because the employer is preventing the employee from working in an area in which the employer has no interest and therefore does not need protection. In *Spencer* v. *Marchinton* [1988] IRLR 392 the restraint covered an area of 25 square miles, but the employer had not expanded into that area by the time the employee left. It was held that the clause was too wide and unenforceable. In the *Office Angels* case (above), clause 4.5(b) provided that the employees would not, within six months after the termination of their employment, 'engage in or undertake the trade or business of an employment agency' in Greater London within a one-kilometre radius of the branch at which they had been employed. The employees left and formed another employment agency within the kilometre limit. On interpretation of the clause, the Court of Appeal recognised that the employers did have a legitimate interest to protect – their clients and the temporary workers which the agency sent out to organisations. The employers, however, only specifically protected themselves in relation to clients in clause 4.5(a) (above), therefore clause 4.5(b) obviously also related to clients and was set up with the intention of preventing the employees from diverting business from their ex-employers by taking advantage of the influence they had over clients while they were still employed. Clause 4.5(b), however, did not do this. Although the branches of the employer's agency did have area boundaries, these boundaries were not absolute. Furthermore, whereas temporary workers were influenced by the location of the office, clients were not. They merely telephoned and the branch could be located anywhere. As such, all the clause did was to prevent competition and it did not protect the legitimate interests of the employer. It was therefore void. Whether the area is too wide will depend on a variety of factors. The fact that the employer has not expanded into the area will mean that he is overprotecting himself. While this may look like an attempt to prevent competition, it should be remembered that normally a covenant will be inserted into the contract at the beginning of the relationship, at a time when the employer may genuinely believe that he will expand. In *Greer* v. *Sketchley Ltd* [1979] IRLR 445 the employer, who operated a business in the Midlands and London, intended to expand nationwide and inserted a covenant preventing the employee from competing on a nationwide basis. It was held that as the employer had not yet expanded by the time the employee left, the clause was too wide and void. This demonstrates the problems if the employer thinks ahead. The decision in *Greer* left the employer with no protection at all in the areas in which he operated.

The density of population within the area will also affect the decision of the court. In the *Fellowes* case (above) the area was not particularly wide but was densely populated, which was a factor taken into account by the court when holding the clause to be void. On the other hand, in *Fitch* v. *Dewes* [1921] 2 AC 158 a lifelong restraint on a solicitor's clerk which prevented him from working within a seven-mile radius of Tamworth Town Hall was held to be valid. The House of Lords decided that it was a modest area which was not densely populated and so a lifetime restraint was not unreasonable.

The final way in which the covenant could offend public interest is that it is too long in time. To a large extent, however, the geographical and time factors are looked at together. Generally, the more extensive the area, the shorter the time limit should be. In *Commercial Plastics* (above) a one-year restraint was too long, given that the restriction was worldwide, and in *Scully* (above) a 24-month worldwide restriction was unenforceable. By contrast, in *Fitch* v. *Dewes* (above) the small area involved led the court to find that a lifelong restraint was reasonable. Note, however, that the Court of Appeal in *Beckett Investment Management Group* v. *Hall* [2007] EWCA Civ 613 stated that the mere fact that the duration chosen (in that case 12 months) is arbitrary does not prevent the clause from being enforceable.

In practice, all the factors are looked at together and each case turns on its own particular set of facts. As Pearson LJ said in *Commercial Plastics* v. *Vincent* (above): 'It would seem that a good deal of legal know how is required for the successful drafting of a restraint clause.'

11.6 Enforceability

It may appear from the above that it is difficult to draft a valid restraint of trade provision in a contract. To some extent this is right as the courts do not particularly like enforcing a provision which will restrict an employee's future job prospects for some time after leaving his employment, and we have already seen from the above that even the courts recognise that it takes a great deal of skill to draft a clause which the courts will enforce. Having said that, even if the clause does offend the principles of reasonableness, there are two methods that the court may use to save it.

First, the court may look at the reality and effect of the provision. The courts, however, will not allow an employer to try and get a covenant imposed 'by the back door'. For example, the employer may not disguise the covenant by providing that the employee must pay the employer a commission if he solicits customers after leaving the employment, for this is just another way of restraining him (*Stenhouse Australia Ltd* v. *Phillips* [1974] AC 391). Nor can the employer enter an agreement with another employer to prevent the employment of his ex-employees. In *Kores Manufacturing Co* v. *Kolok Manufacturing Co* [1959] Ch 108 two employers manufacturing similar goods entered an agreement that neither would employ a person who had been employed by the other in the preceding five years. The Court of Appeal held that as neither employer had a valid interest to protect, if such a provision had been in an employee's contract it would have been void as unreasonable between the parties. The employers could not do covertly what the courts would not allow them to do overtly, and the agreement between them was void. Furthermore, the employer cannot prevent the ex-employee from poaching the employer's employees (*Hanover Insurance Brokers Ltd* v. *Schapiro* [1994] IRLR 82).

However, given that the courts look to the effect of the provision, they have been prepared, in some cases, to interpret the provision in the way the parties intended and not in the way it strictly reads. This only happens rarely and will only occur where the clause is ambiguous. The courts normally will not go against a strictly worded clause. Should they interpret an ambiguous clause however, it may save the covenant. In *Home Counties Dairies Ltd* v. *Skilton* [1970] AC 403 there was a restraint clause in the contract of a milkman which stated that he should not 'serve or sell milk or dairy products' after leaving his employment. On a strict interpretation of the clause, this restricted his future employment beyond acting as a milkman. He would be in breach of the provision if he, for example, worked in a supermarket. As such, it was too wide and void because the employer did not need that amount of protection. It was obvious, however, that the employers wanted to restrict his future employment as a milkman only, and the clause was interpreted in this way and upheld. Similarly, in *White (Marion) Ltd* v. *Francis* [1972] 3 All ER 857 a restraint provision in the contract of a hairdresser prevented the employee from taking future employment in the hairdressing business 'in any way'. Again, the parties obviously intended the restriction to apply only to employment as a hairdresser and the covenant was interpreted as the parties intended and saved. In *Ward Evans Financial Services* v. *Fox* [2002] IRLR 120 there was a restraint clause in financial advisers' contracts preventing them from inducing customers to leave the company. Two advisers intended to leave the company and set up in competition and had purchased a dormant company for this aim. A client asked if it could transfer business to the new company and it was agreed that the business would transfer on the setting up of the new company. This eventually happened. The Court of Appeal held that although the advisers had not solicited the client, by saying that the business could transfer to the new company, they had failed to put the interests of the employer first and thus had to pay damages. In other words, the spirit of the covenant was upheld. Recently in the *Hall* case (above), the Court of Appeal rejected the literal interpretation of the words 'the company' and held that the words also protected the clients of subsidiary companies within a large corporate group. Maurice Kay LJ stated that the law would recognise the reality of big business and not take a 'purist approach to corporate personality'.

Perhaps the most surprising case is *Littlewoods Organisation Ltd* v. *Harris* [1978] 1 All ER 1026. In this case the employee had been employed as a director by Littlewoods. His employer's main competitor in the mail-order business was Great Universal Stores Ltd and there was a provision in the contract of employment that, for 12 months after leaving his employment, he would not be employed by Great Universal Stores Ltd or any of their subsidiaries. Littlewoods was, by this restraint, protecting confidential information relating to the preparation of its mail-order catalogue, in which capacity the employee had been employed. As Great Universal Stores operated all over the world and in businesses other than mail order, the ex-employee argued that the restraint was too wide and therefore void. He argued that Littlewoods only required protection in relation to mail order in Great Britain, but that the clause gave much greater protection. The Court of Appeal, however, said that, looking at the ex-employee's job and the employer's intention, the clause could be interpreted to relate only to Great Universal Stores' mail-order business in Great Britain. As such it was valid and enforceable.

While the court may interpret ambiguous clauses favourably, such cases are rare. We have already seen in the *Office Angels* case that the court felt that the employer had a legitimate interest to protect but that the wording of the covenant did not afford that protection and the court would not interpret it so that it could be saved. The Court of Appeal stated that restraint covenants totally restricting employment should only be used as a last resort and normally a non-dealing clause would be looked upon more favourably by the courts. Furthermore, it should be noted that in that case the Court of Appeal felt that the employer needed protection against the poaching of other employees. This had not been written into the covenant and the court was not prepared to imply that the restriction on setting up in competition related to other employees (which probably would have been valid) rather than clients. The clause was ambiguous and was therefore construed in favour of the ex-employees. This case could be seen as a change in attitude on the part of the courts to ambiguous covenants.

There is another way in which the court may save a potentially void covenant which does not involve issues of interpretation. This is known as the 'blue pencil rule' and involves the court severing the offending part of an otherwise valid covenant, so leaving one which is reasonable and enforceable. It must be stressed, however, that the courts will not rewrite a covenant and will only use this technique if the severance will leave a valid covenant. Therefore, a court cannot sever an area provision which is too wide, for to do so will leave a worldwide covenant which will still render the covenant void. The same would apply to the severance of a time limit which is void because it is too long. Severance would leave a lifelong restraint which will also fail the test of reasonableness. This means that there are only certain types of covenants where the rule can be used, that is, covenants which have individual clauses. In *Lucas (T.) & Co Ltd* v. *Mitchell* [1974] Ch 129 a salesman covenanted that for a year after the termination of his employment he would not:

(a) solicit orders within his trading area from present customers and those whom his employer supplied during the previous 12 months; and
(b) deal in the same or similar goods to those that he had sold.

The court held that the second clause was unreasonable and unenforceable. That clause could, however, be severed from the first clause and still leave a valid, enforceable covenant. A similar severance was performed in the *Stenhouse Australia Ltd* case (above). How the clause is drafted, therefore, can be the deciding factor in whether the covenant falls or is saved.

The cases discussed above have been confirmed in *TSF Derivatives Ltd* v. *Morgan* [2005] IRLR 246. In that case the High Court deleted part of a covenant it felt was excessive and enforced the remainder. It also stated that if a clause is capable of two interpretations, one too wide and the other reasonable, a court should always adopt the latter. Finally, a court should not rewrite a clause, but if part can be deleted and a enforceable covenant remains, a court should grant an injunction as long as the employer can show a legitimate business interest requiring protection.

11.7 Enforcement

Should a clause be upheld by the courts, the question to be asked by the employer is which is the best method to enforce the covenant against the ex-employee. Two remedies are available: those of injunction or damages; both, however, are fraught with difficulties.

If the employer chooses injunctive relief, he will wish to apply for an interlocutory injunction before the case is heard by the full court. This is obviously the quickest and most effective form of protection as it will prevent any immediate breaches of the covenant which could severely damage the employer's business by the time of the full hearing. The rules governing the granting of interlocutory injunctions were discussed at length by the Court of Appeal in the case of *Lansing Linde Ltd* v. *Kerr* [1991] IRLR 80. Kerr had been employed by Lansing Bagnall and had transferred when the company was taken over by Linde AG. His new contract contained a variety of restraint clauses. In contravention of those clauses, he left to work for a competitor. The employer sought an interlocutory injunction. The Court of Appeal looked at the guidelines laid down by *American Cynamid Co* v. *Ethicon Ltd* [1975] AC 396, that is, that before an interlocutory injunction can be granted there must be an arguable case and damages would not be an appropriate remedy. If both parties would be inconvenienced by the injunction and damages are an inadequate remedy for either party, then the injunction should be given to the party who would suffer the most inconvenience if it is not granted. In deciding this last point, the Court of Appeal in *Lawrence David Ltd* v. *Ashton* [1989] IRLR 22 stated that one of the most relevant criteria is whether or not the employer would have any real prospect of winning his case.

In the *Lansing Linde* case the court found that Kerr was in charge of marketing and although he did not regularly visit customers, he did have access to trade secrets in relation to the UK marketing operation. However, the company did not operate on a worldwide basis and the restraints were worldwide. The court felt this was giving the employer more protection than was needed and felt that a restriction on employment in western Europe would have been more reasonable. In relation to the balance of convenience test the court identified three situations which might apply. First, there would be the situation where only one party would suffer loss which damages could not compensate and in that case an injunction would be granted. Second, there would be the situation where there would be a rapid full trial and then the injunction would be granted to the party who would suffer the most loss before the trial. Third, there was the situation when a full trial would be unlikely, either because the interlocutory action would effectively decide the issue, or because, given time delays on a full hearing, the time period within the restraint would be exhausted. In the case in hand, the court thought it unlikely the parties would go to a full trial given that the time restraint was only 12 months and that it was unlikely that there would be a full hearing before that date. Even if there was such a hearing, the court thought it unlikely that the employer would succeed, given the geographical restraint. As such, the injunction was refused.

Given this ruling and that the majority of restraint covenants are not for long periods of time (indeed they may well fail the test of reasonableness if they are for too long a period) injunctive relief would seem to be difficult to obtain.

If the employer does not seek an injunction to prevent the breach of the covenant, he may seek damages to compensate the loss he has incurred as a result of the breach. While this is an easy proposition to state, in practice it may be difficult for the employer to quantify his loss in financial terms, which is why in practice the majority of employers will seek injunctive relief. Should the employer seek to claim damages, however, the House of Lords recently in *Attorney-General* v. *Blake* [2001] IRLR 36 has extended the damages for which an employer can claim. The case has established that a defendant can be required to pay to the employer the profit that he has received as a result of the breach, even if the employer has suffered no actual financial loss. It was envisaged by the court that the return of profits would only apply in exceptional circumstances where the normal remedies of specific performance or injunction are not compensation for the breach of contract.

One further point should be noted. We have already seen in Chapter 9 that if the employer's undertaking is transferred to another and the employees are taken on by the new employer, the contracts transfer with the employees. In *Morris Angel & Son* v. *Hollande* [1993] ICR 71 the Court of Appeal held that where there was a transfer of an undertaking and by Regulation 5 (now Regulation 4) all the employee's contractual terms were transferred to the transferee, this included the transfer of a restraint covenant entered into with the transferor. Thus the new employer could rely on the covenant.

Summary

1. A restraint covenant will only be enforceable if the employer can prove that he has a legitimate interest to protect, that is, that the clause is reasonable between the parties.

2. Even if the clause is reasonable between the parties, the employer must also prove that it is reasonable in the public interest, that is, it is not for too long a time period or for too wide an area.

Summary cont'd

3. A clause will be strictly interpreted and normally any ambiguity will be interpreted to the advantage of the employee.

4. If one part of the clause is unreasonable the whole clause will fall, unless the covenant contains severable parts and the courts, using the 'blue pencil rule', can sever the offending part and still leave an enforceable covenant.

5. If the employer commits a repudiatory breach of contract then the covenant is also repudiated.

6. Even if the covenant is upheld, effective enforcement by the employer may prove to be problematical.

Exercise

Tweedledum and Tweedledee work for Rooftec Ltd, a manufacturer of a revolutionary new roofing material with outlets throughout the United Kingdom. Tweedledum works in the laboratory which developed the new material, as a technician. He has the following provision in his contract of employment:

'The employee undertakes that for 12 months after leaving his employment, he will not work within the roofing industry anywhere in the United Kingdom.'

Tweedledee is a salesman. There is a provision in his contract which states the following:

'The employee undertakes that for 12 months after leaving his employment, the employee will not:
(a) work in the roofing industry anywhere in the United Kingdom;
(b) solicit any customers of Rooftec Ltd with whom he has dealt during his period of employment;
(c) set up in business in roofing anywhere in the United Kingdom.'

Both employees now want to leave and work for another roofing manufacturer. Advise Tweedledum and Tweedledee as to the likelihood of the court upholding the covenants.

Further Reading

Cabrelli   *Post Termination Covenants in the Spotlight Again* (2004) 33 ILJ 167.

Edwards   *Restrictive Convenants and Employment* [1991] BLR 3.

Hepple   *Employee Loyalty in English Law* (1999) Comparative Labour Law and Policy Journal (20) 204.

Jefferson   *Interlocutory Injunctions and Convenants in Restraint of Trade Affecting Employees* 133 SJ 232.

Further reading cont'd

Jefferson *Restraint of Trade: Dismissal and Drafting* (1997) 26 ILJ 62.

Korn *Losing Staff and Trade Secrets* 135 SJ 484.

Korn and Small *Confidential Information* [1991] 2 IPB 2.

Sales *Convenants Restricting Recruitment of Employees and the Doctrine of Restraint of Trade* 104 LQR 600.

Part V

Trade Unions and the Law of Industrial Action

Chapter 12

Trade Unions

Introduction

The idea of a group of people associating for mutual protection and benefit in relation to employment is a common enough one today but this was not always the case. The Industrial Revolution saw the birth of trade unions as we know them today, but that birth was met with hostility from both the legislature and the judges. The Combination Acts 1799–1800 made any agreement with the purpose of improving working conditions an offence and imposed criminal sanctions upon those who called or attended a meeting for that purpose, so essentially undermining the very essence of a union. The major legal obstruction to unions during the early part of the nineteenth century was that, as their main purpose was to improve the working conditions of their members, they were seen to be in restraint of trade and therefore illegal if they performed this function. The Combination Laws Repeal Act 1824 meant that unions were not criminal *per se* but after a series of strikes the Combination Act 1825 rendered unions criminal except where their sole purpose was the determination of wages or hours. Major advances were made by the introduction of the Trade Union Act 1871 and the Criminal Law Amendment Act of the same year. The former provided that trade union activity was not to be regarded as in restraint of trade and gave unions the power to enforce certain contracts and hold property. The latter modified the offences of intimidation, obstruction and molestation in relation to trade union activity, but this was thwarted somewhat by the judiciary's increased use of the offence of criminal conspiracy in relation to industrial action. The Conspiracy and Protection of Property Act 1875 defined the ambits of lawful industrial action and created immunity from criminal conspiracy where the act was done in furtherance of a trade dispute, and was not criminal if done by one person alone. So began the system of immunity from the law in certain circumstances, rather than the creation of specific rights.

The judiciary, however, was, and some would argue still is, hostile to the unions. Despite legislative intervention, judges found ways to find that industrial action was against the law by extending the common law and creating what have come to be known as the economic torts. We will see in Chapter 14 that this is not confined to the early part of the century but has continued. This development was limited, however, in that, as a trade union was not a body corporate, the union itself could not be sued, only the individual members, thus trade union funds were protected. This position, however, was overturned by the famous House of Lords' case of *Taff Vale Railway Company* v. *Amalgamated Society of Railway Servants* [1901] AC 246. In this case, their Lordships ruled that the Trade Union Act 1871 had enabled unions to be sued in their own name and as such the Amalgamated Society of Railway Servants was ordered to pay £23,000 in damages and £19,000 in costs. The implications of the judgement were far-reaching and meant that union funds were at risk. As a result, the Trade Disputes Act 1906 was passed. Rather than providing that unions could not be sued, the Act continued the theme of immunity from tortious liability. This immunity remained until the Industrial Relations Act 1971 was resurrected in the Trade Union and Labour Relations Act 1974 and was again removed by the Employment Act 1982. In addition, the 1906 Act gave immunity to individual members from conspiracy and inducing breaches of contract, provided such actions were done in contemplation or furtherance of a trade dispute, the so-called 'golden formula' which is present in modern-day legislation.

This battle between the judiciary and the legislature is one that has continued during various stages of trade union history, and will be referred to in more detail in this and the following chapter. What this brief introduction hopes to show is that a union is a strange hybrid, in that it is a separate entity for certain purposes only. In addition, the introduction lays down the basis on which a union or its members can take industrial action. Unlike in any other European country no one has the right to take action, he or she is merely immune from certain civil liability in certain situations, that is, when the action is within the golden formula. This means that successive governments can radically alter the protection enjoyed by both unions and their members simply by changing the statutory definition of a trade dispute.

12.2 Status of Trade Unions

The statutory definition of a trade union is now found in s.1(a) Trade Union and Labour Relations (Consolidation) Act 1992 which provides that a trade union means:

> 'an organisation (whether temporary or permanent) which consists wholly or mainly of workers of one or more descriptions and whose principal purposes include the regulation of relations between workers of that description or those descriptions and employers or employers' associations.'

The definition is wide and concentrates on the purpose of the body. Thus a body which had a subsidiary purpose of regulating relations between workers and employers would not be a trade union within the above definition. In *Midland Cold Storage* v. *Turner* [1972] ICR 230 a shop stewards' committee drawn from various trade unions was not a trade union within the definition since its purpose was to discuss whether industrial action should be taken and it did not engage in negotiations with employers. On the other hand, the body can have other purposes and still fall within the definition which says that the principal purpose must be the regulation of relations and so on, not the sole purpose. In *BAALPE* v. *NUT* [1986] IRLR 497, BAALPE was a small organisation representing the interests of advisers and lecturers in physical education. Its constitution stated that it was concerned with the professional interests of its members. As such, it fell within the statutory definition and was entitled to representation on a teachers' national negotiation committee.

The fact that the body is temporary will not prevent it from being a union if its purposes fall within the definition. In the *Midland Cold Storage* case (above), the committee had been set up during a particular dispute with no official status within the unions that the members came from. This was irrelevant when seeing if it was a union within the definition. From s.1(a) a body can be temporary and still be a union.

The definition talks of a union consisting of a group of workers. The definition of 'worker' is to be found in s.296 of the 1992 Act which states:

'In this Act worker means an individual who works, or normally works or seeks to work –
(a) under a contract of employment, or
(b) under any other contract whereby he undertakes to do or perform personally any work or services for another party to the contract who is not a professional client of his, . . .'

As such, professional bodies such as the Law Society are not trade unions within the definition (*Carter* v. *Law Society* [1973] ICR 113).

Section 1(b) of the Act widens the definition to include 'constituent or affiliated organisations which fulfil the conditions in paragraph (a)'. This means that federations of unions are to be regarded as trade unions themselves.

While s.1 helps to identify which groups are trade unions and which are not, it does nothing to explain the precise legal status of such a body. We have already seen that for many years a union as an unincorporated body could not be sued and that therefore union funds were protected. This protection ended with the House of Lords' decision in the *Taff Vale* case (above) when it was decided that as the Trade Union Act 1871 allowed unions to hold property and enter certain contracts, the union could be sued in its own name. But if a union can be sued in its own name, logically it can also sue in its own name. That this is clearly the case was established in *NUGMW* v. *Gillian* [1946] KB 81 where a union successfully sued the general secretary of another union for defamation.

This means that a union is a kind of hybrid organisation. Lord Parker in *Bonsor* v. *Musicians' Union* [1956] AC 104 called the union a 'near corporation'. In other words, it has many of the characteristics of a body corporate without actually having corporate status. The Industrial Relations Act 1971 tried to resolve this anomaly by giving corporate status to all unions who registered under the Act. For reasons well-documented elsewhere and which will not be rehearsed here, the unions were totally opposed to the Act and merely did not register, so thwarting the purpose of the provision. Unions opposed corporate status to avoid the scrutiny of accounts to which all companies are subject. While they have been successful in the former, they have not been so successful in the latter, as will be seen. The present position is therefore that unions are still unincorporated associations but they have certain advantages which corporate bodies enjoy. This statutory regulation began in the Trade Union and Labour Relations Act 1974 and is now contained in ss.10 and 12 of the Trade Union and Labour Relations (Consolidation) Act 1992. Section 10 provides that although a trade union is not a body corporate it is capable of:

(a) making contracts;
(b) suing and being sued in its own name;
(c) having criminal proceedings brought against it.

In addition, s.12 allows the union to hold property vested in trustees and by subsection (2) provides that any judgement or award made against the union is enforceable against its property to the same extent and in the same manner as if it were a body corporate. Furthermore, s.23 protects the personal property of members and trustees in the same way that shareholders within a company obtain protection through the concept of limited liability. The clarification of the law, however, does not mean that the union has a legal personality within the legal definition of such in certain circumstances. In *EEPTU* v. *Times Newspapers* [1980] 1 All ER 1097 the union sued for defamation. O'Connor J held that as the statute specifically states that the union *is not and is not to be treated as a body corporate*, then the union has not got a legal personality which must be protected through the law of defamation. It is because of the italicised words introduced in 1974 that *Gillian* (above) is no longer good law.

12.3   Listing

The concept of maintaining some kind of voluntary listing of trade unions was introduced in the Trade Union Act 1871. Such a list continued with the compliance of the unions until the Industrial Relations Act 1971 which introduced a very different system of registration. Under that Act, only unions who registered were entitled to statutory immunity against certain industrial action (something the unions had enjoyed, remember, since 1906). In addition, any unions who registered under the 1971 Act had to 'pay' for their immunity by subjecting their constitution, rules and accounts to outside scrutiny. Union opposition to the Act demonstrated itself by a policy of non-compliance and very few unions registered, indeed those that did were expelled from the TUC. The Trade Union and Labour Relations Act 1974, which repealed the Industrial Relations Act, reintroduced the concept of voluntary listing similar to that which existed under the 1871 Trade Union Act. The provisions are now in ss.2 and 123 Trade Union and Labour Relations (Consolidation) Act 1992. These provide that the Certification Officer shall maintain a voluntary list of trade unions and employers' associations. Any union can apply for inclusion on the list. A body can be removed from the list by the Certification Officer if at any time it ceases to fall within the statutory definition. An appeal against refusal to list or removal from the list lies to the Employment Appeal Tribunal.

While there are few advantages to being listed, it is the first requisite to obtaining a certificate of independence. It is this certificate which brings considerable advantages to both the union and its members.

12.4 Independent Trade Unions

The Certification Officer can issue any union on the list with a certificate of independence (s.6). Such a certificate is conclusive evidence that the union is independent (s.8). An independent trade union is one which is not under the control of an employer or liable to interference from an employer arising out of financial, material or other support (s.5). While financial support is easy to identify, the other aspects of the definition are more subjective and the Court of Appeal in *Squibb UK Staff Association* v. *Certification Officer* [1979] ICR 235 held that the test was whether the union was exposed to or vulnerable to the risk of interference rather than interference as a fact.

The *Squibb* case (above) demonstrates that the test for determining independence is not a clear-cut one and involves looking at a variety of factors. The Employment Appeal Tribunal in *Blue Circle Staff Association* v. *Certification Officer* [1977] ICR 224 approved the criteria listed by the Certification Officer in his 1976 annual report. The report states that the following should be considered:

1. *History*: The union's past links with the employer are relevant. The more recent those links, the less likely that the union is truly independent. In

Blue Circle's case, the association had been formed six months earlier with total employer control, one of the factors leading the Employment Appeal Tribunal to agree with the refusal of the certificate of independence.

2. *Finance*: Any direct financial assistance from the employer will mean dependency.

3. *Employer facilities*: If the employer provides facilities for the union such as a free office or telephone, this will be a factor considered and this was a major factor in the *Squibb* case in deciding that the union was not independent. It should be noted, however, that the *ACAS Code of Practice on Time Off for Trade Union Duties and Activities* suggests in paragraph 24 that management provide facilities such as accommodation and telephones to enable officials to perform their duties effectively.

4. *Membership*: If membership is limited to one company, this may raise the question of total independence from the employer. It has been pointed out, however, that members of the NUM used to be employed by one employer and yet it is unthinkable that the independence of that union would ever be challenged.

5. *Negotiation record*: The Certification Officer will take into account whether there is a 'robust attitude in negotiation'. In other words, regular compliance with the employer's wishes may indicate a lack of independence.

6. *Organisation*: One of the arguments against *Blue Circle* was that ordinary members had a restricted role. Only members of three-years' standing could be elected as area committee representatives and the employer nominated the chairperson of the Joint Central Council. In addition, members of management had originally been committee members and had helped draft the rules, which removed them as such in the bid for independence.

On an application for a certificate of independence, the Certification Officer will make such enquiries as necessary, including listening to representations from other unions. An appeal against the refusal of a certificate lies to the Employment Appeal Tribunal. A certificate may also be withdrawn if the nature of the union changes.

The certificate of independence gives certain rights to the members of the union. It will be seen below that members of independent trade unions are protected against dismissal and detriment on the grounds of trade union activities or membership (ss.146 and 152 of the 1992 Act). However, more rights pertain to both the union and its members if it is independent and recognised by the employer for collective bargaining purposes.

12.5   Recognition of Trade Unions

The major purpose of any union is to protect and promote its members' interests, and the way it will do this is by collective bargaining. Many workers in Britain still have their terms and conditions collectively agreed rather than individually. Obviously, however, for the union to perform this function the employer must accept it as the bargaining agent for the workforce. Prior to 1979, successive governments felt that collective bargaining was the best way to conduct industrial relations and as such it was supported. The Industrial Relations Act 1971 introduced a statutory procedure whereby if the majority wanted recognition in a workplace the employer had to comply and the National Industrial Relations Court had the jurisdiction to enforce the employer to do so. These rights, however, were only given to registered unions and, given that the majority of unions refused to register, the procedure was little used. A more complicated procedure was introduced by the Employment Protection Act 1975 whereby an independent trade union could refer a recognition dispute to ACAS who, after investigation, could then order the employer to recognise the union. These powers, however, were not enforceable and ACAS could not coerce the employer to comply, as demonstrated by the famous Grunwick dispute (*Grunwick Processing Laboratories* v. *ACAS* [1978] AC 655). As such, rather than give ACAS more teeth, the recognition procedures were abolished by the Employment Act 1980 and until recently nothing was put in their place.

Recognition, however, is still an important issue for the union. Apart from meaning that it can fulfil its primary purpose of regulating relations between its members and employers, recognised independent trade unions and their members have certain rights. We have already seen that only members of independent recognised trade unions are entitled to time off without pay for trade union activities and only officials of such unions are entitled to paid time off for trade union duties (see Chapter 7). Recognised independent trade unions are entitled to information for collective bargaining purposes. Thus recognition is vitally important for it to perform its functions. It is also important for individual members who will acquire extra rights.

The above discussion therefore raises the question of when is a union recognised. Since the Employment Relations Act 1999 there are two ways by which this can occur: where the employer recognises the union voluntarily or where the union has invoked the statutory recognition procedure and thus the employer has to recognise the union for collective bargaining purposes. Different consequences apply to the two situations. Where recognition is voluntary the employer can vary or withdraw recognition unilaterally (unlike where a union is recognised under the statutory procedure). Furthermore, an employer may recognise a union which only represents the minority rather than the majority of his workforce. By contrast, as will be seen below, once a union has gained statutory recognition it may not normally be derecognised for a period of three years and if recognition was granted because of a ballot of the majority of affected workers, derecognition may only occur after a ballot supporting derecognition has been conducted.

(a) Voluntary recognition

The starting point is s.178(3) of the 1992 Act which defines recognition as 'recognition of the union by the employer . . . to any extent, for the purposes of collective bargaining'. Collective bargaining means negotiations relating to or connected with one or more matters specified in s.178(2). These are:

(a) the terms and conditions of employment, or the physical conditions in which workers are required to work;

(b) engagement or non-engagement, or termination or suspension of employment or the duties of employment, of one or more workers;

(c) allocation of work or the duties of employment as between workers or groups of workers;

(d) matters of discipline;

(e) a worker's membership or non-membership of a trade union;

(f) facilities for officials of trade unions;

(g) machinery for negotiation or consultation and other procedures, relating to any of the above matters, including the recognition by employers or employers' associations of the right of a trade union to represent workers in such negotiation or consultation or in the carrying out of such procedures.

The phrase in s.178(3) that the union is recognised 'to any extent' for the purposes of collective bargaining means that an employer may recognise a union for only one of the matters listed above. Where there is no express agreement however, the section does not state what conduct constitutes recognition. We have already seen in Chapter 10 that recognition is a mixture of law and fact when looking at issues of consultation with recognised trade unions when declaring redundancies. Where there is an express agreement normally no problems arise, however the law may imply recognition from the parties' conduct. In *National Union of Gold, Silver and Allied Trades* v. *Albury Brothers Ltd* [1979] ICR 84 discussions between a union and an employer concerning whether a particular individual's wages came within agreed pay scales, where no agreement was reached, did not amount to recognition. Conversely, in *Joshua Wilson & Bros Ltd* v. *USDAW* [1978] IRLR 120 the cumulative effect of a number of contacts over a year with the employer led the Employment Appeal Tribunal to imply recognition. These contacts included allowing the union to put up notices detailing a pay rise negotiated nationally, allowing an official to collect union payments from workers during working hours and consulting the union over a reallocation of duties. The appeal tribunal stressed that separately none of the incidents would have led to a conclusion of recognition, it was the cumulative effect of all of the incidents which led the tribunal to its conclusion.

(b) Statutory recognition

The procedures outlined in brief below were introduced by the Employment Relations Act 1999 which inserted a new Schedule A1 into the Trade Union and Labour Relations (Consolidation) Act 1992 which itself has been amended by the Employment Relations Act 2004. The Central Arbitration Committee (CAC) cannot accept an application for recognition where there is already a collective agreement in force covering pay, hours and holidays, but can accept an application if the agreement only covers one or two of those issues (para 35). In *R (on the application of the NUJ)* v. *CAC and MGN* [2005] IRLR 28 the NUJ had been discussing recognition for sports journalists with MGN. MGN, however, accepted an approach from the British Association of Journalists, which had recognition for some MGN titles, but who only had one member in the sports area. The CAC refused to accept the NUJ application for recognition because there was a voluntary collective agreement with the BAJ covering pay, holidays and hours, even though BAJ did not have many members in the bargaining unit.

The steps described below are cumulative, that is if the first step is successful then that is the end of it; if not, step two applies and if that is not successful step three applies. Any application for recognition is made to the Central Arbitration Committee.

(i) Recognition by agreement

The process begins with a request for recognition which must satisfy certain conditions. First, the request must be received by the employer (para 5). Second, the request must be made by an independent trade union (para 6). The request can only be made to an employer who employs, on the day the request is received, 21 employees, or an average of 21 employees in the 13 weeks ending on the day the request for recognition is received. The number of employees includes those employed by an associated employer (para 7). In *Graphical Paper and Media Union* v. *Derry* [2002] IRLR 380 the majority of shares in two printing companies were owned by one person. The employees had the same contracts and one management, and workers employed by both companies had been used in calculating the minimum number of employees needed for a recognition claim. The union claimed that the companies were one bargaining unit and sought joint recognition. The CAC held that normally joint recognition could not be granted even where employees at the associate employer had been used to calculate the number of employees. However, in the particular circumstances the CAC concluded that there was one employer and the union claim was allowed. Third, the request must comply with the minimum criteria laid down by para 8, that is it must be in writing; it must identify the union or unions and the bargaining unit and state that it is made under Sch A1. If the employer refuses within 10 days but wishes to negotiate, then negotiation begins (which may involve ACAS). If after 20 days (or a longer period if the parties agree) there is still failure to reach agreement, then the steps below apply.

(ii) Recognition by application to the Central Arbitration Committee (CAC)

If the employer refuses a request for recognition, fails to respond in the time limits above or negotiations fail, the union may apply to the CAC. The CAC must decide whether the bargaining unit is appropriate within the terms of paras 19B(2) and (3) of the schedule. The CAC must try to help the parties reach agreement as to the appropriate bargaining unit within 20 days of receipt of the union's application, or a shorter period if both parties request or the CAC sees no reasonable prospect of the parties reaching agreement on the bargaining unit (para 18). The CAC can extend the period it has previously shortened at the parties' request if it feels this will allow the parties to reach an agreement (para 18(5)). In both cases (shortening or lengthening the period) the CAC must state the reasons for the action. A new para 18A requires the employer to provide information to the union and the CAC within 5 working days after the CAC gives notice of acceptance of the union's application. The employer must provide:

- a list of the categories of worker in the proposed bargaining unit;
- a list of the workplaces at which the workers in the proposed unit work;
- the numbers of workers the employer reasonably believes to be in each category at each workplace in the proposed unit.

The union can request the CAC to appoint an independent person to formally communicate with the relevant workers on behalf of the union, after the application for recognition has been accepted. Once appointed, the employer must within 10 working days give the CAC the names and home addresses of the relevant workers and the CAC must pass this information on to the independent person. Should an employer fail to give the information, the CAC can either issue a declaration that the union is recognised or order a ballot.

If the parties have not reached an agreement, the CAC must decide the appropriate unit within 10 working days, starting with the end of the negotiation period stated above (para 19). By para 19A if the employer has failed to give the information listed in para 18A, the union can ask the CAC to decide the appropriate unit before the end of the 20-day period in para 18 (above).

In addition, the CAC must decide whether the union is likely to have the support of the majority of the workers constituting the unit and must not proceed with the application if this is not the case. If the CAC is satisfied as to worker support it must issue a declaration that the union is recognised and is entitled to conduct collective bargaining on behalf of the workers constituting the bargaining unit.

(iii) Recognition after a secret ballot

A secret ballot must take place instead of a declaration in three situations:

- the CAC feels that the ballot will be in the interests of good industrial relations;
- a 'significant number' of union members in the bargaining unit inform the CAC that they do not want the union to conduct collective bargaining on their behalf;
- membership evidence is provided which leads the CAC to conclude that there are doubts whether a 'significant number' of union members within the bargaining unit want the union to conduct collective bargaining on their behalf (para 22).

The ballot must be conducted by a qualified independent person appointed by the CAC and must take place within 20 days of the person being appointed unless that period is extended by the CAC. An extension may be granted if both parties request, to enable them to voluntarily reach an agreement. The ballot may take place in the workplace or by post. The employer is under a duty to co-operate with the ballot and to give the union reasonable access to the workers constituting the bargaining unit. The *Code of Practice on Access to Workers during Recognition (and Derecognition) Ballots* gives guidance on this, as does para 26(4D). The employer must also give the CAC the names and addresses of the workers constituting the bargaining unit, any worker who later joins that unit and inform the CAC if a worker leaves the unit. In addition, the employer is under a duty not to induce workers not to take part nor take action or threaten to take action against workers taking part (para 26). If the employer fails to comply with these obligations the CAC may order the employer to remedy this or issue a declaration that the union is recognised. The costs of the ballot are met 50:50 between the employer and the union. If the ballot shows that the union is supported by a majority of the workers voting and at least 40 per cent of the workers constituting the bargaining unit, the CAC must issue a declaration that the union is recognised (paras 25–29). The Court of Appeal in *R (on the application of Ultraframe (UK) Ltd)* v. *CAC* [2005] IRLR 641 stated that where there has been a problem with a ballot (in the case the GMB and United Road Transport Union complained that not all staff had received ballot papers) the CAC can order a re-run. The statute refers to a 'ballot' and that means a ballot conducted in accordance with the statutory provisions. In the case not all relevant workers had received ballot papers and it was irrelevant that the qualified independent person had announced the result of the ballot. As it had not complied with the statutory procedures, the CAC could annul it and order a new ballot.

(iv) Consequences of recognition

The parties must within 30 days of the declaration come to an agreement as to the method by which they will conduct collective bargaining. Collective bargaining means bargaining in relation to pay, hours and holidays, although the parties can change this by agreement. If no such agreement is reached, the CAC must specify the method. Such a specified method is legally enforceable although the parties may agree in writing to vary or replace the method specified by the CAC and that agreement shall be legally enforceable (para 31). The remedy for breach of either of the above is specific performance, not damages. If the CAC has specified the method of bargaining the employer must invite (on at least a six-monthly basis from the date of recognition) trade union representatives to discuss:

- the employer's policy on training members of the bargaining unit;
- plans for training them in the next six months; and
- training which has taken place since the last meeting (s.70B(2) Trade Union and Labour Relations (Consolidation) Act 1992).

The employer must provide certain information to the union at least two weeks before such meetings take place. Failure to comply allows the union to apply to an employment tribunal which may make a declaration and award compensation to members of the bargaining unit which does not exceed two-weeks' pay (ss.70C(1), (3) and (4) Trade Union and Labour Relations (Consolidation) Act 1992).

(v)   Derecognition if fewer than 21 employees
If three years after the agreement or declaration to recognise, the employer has fewer than 21 employees on average, the employer may serve notice as required by para 99(3) on the union of derecognition and if the union does not apply to the CAC, the collective bargaining arrangement shall cease after 35 days. In addition, a union may be derecognised in the same way as it can be recognised, except that the CAC may not proceed with a secret ballot unless it decides that at least 10 per cent of the workers constituting the bargaining unit are in favour of ending the arrangement and there is *prima facie* evidence that the majority of workers constituting the bargaining unit would be likely to favour the ending of the bargaining arrangement. Such a ballot may be held on either the request of the employer or the workers falling within the bargaining unit (paras 112 and 128).

12.6 The Political Fund

The labour movement in the early years was reliant on a sympathetic Liberal government to give it legal protection. While this partnership worked well, it soon became apparent that the movement required working-class Members of Parliament who would fully understand the problems and provide truly representative views in parliament. As such, the movement decided to fund such MPs through union funds, and introduced the idea that part of each member's contribution to the union would support working-class MPs. This subsidy to promote political aims was declared illegal by the House of Lords in *Amalgamated Society of Railway Servants* v. *Osborne* [1910] AC 87 since under the Trade Union Act 1871 a union could only pursue those objects listed in the Act, that is, the regulation of relations between workers and employers. Pursuance of political aims was not subsumed within those objects. The Liberal government again came to the aid of the unions by the passage of the Trade Union Act 1913, which by s.3 allowed unions to pursue any object listed within its constitution, although insisting that such a fund supporting political objectives should be a separate fund and it should be called the political fund. Substantial amendments were made to the Act by the Trade Union Act 1984 although at the time the government renounced its original intention of reintroducing the contracting-in system and left the contracting-out system in place, but insisted that unions ballot their members every 10 years to see if the members wished the political fund to be maintained. The Trade Union Reform and Employment Rights Act 1993, however, introduced the contracting-in system by amending the 1992 Act. Section 68 of the 1992 Act provided that an employer should not deduct union subscriptions from a worker's wages (the so-called 'check off' system) unless the worker had authorised the deduction in writing within the previous three years, the employer had notified the worker of any increases at least one month before the deduction was made and the employer had notified the employee of his right to withdraw his authorisation at any time. The worker had a right of complaint in an employment tribunal in the case of unauthorised deductions. Since the Deregulation (Deduction from Pay of Union Subscriptions) Order 1998, new members need only give written authorisation once and it continues indefinitely, subject to the right to withdraw authorisation. Existing members may give notice in writing to the employer that they wish their authorisation to last three years. After that period, any further authorisation will be indefinite, again subject to the right to withdraw authorisation.

The 1993 Act also introduced stringent balloting provisions in relation to the maintenance of a political fund (ss.75–78 of the 1992 Act), requiring such ballots to be conducted in the same way as the ballot for the election of trade union officials.

The present law is contained in the Trade Union and Labour Relations (Consolidation) Act 1992. Section 71(1) lays down that payment for political purposes whether made directly or indirectly can be made only from a separate political fund. Political purposes are then defined in s.72(1) as the expenditure of money:

'(a) on any contribution to the funds of, or on the payment of expenses incurred directly or indirectly, by a political party;
(b) on the provision of any service or property for use by or on behalf of any political party;
(c) in connection with the registration of electors, the candidature of any person, the selection of any candidate or the holding of any ballot by the union in connection with any election to a political office;
(d) on the maintenance of any holder of a political office;
(e) on the holding of any conference by or on behalf of a political party or of any other meeting the main purpose of which is the transaction of business in connection with a political party;
(f) on the production, publication or distribution of any literature, document, film, sound recording or advertisement the main purpose of which is to persuade people to vote for a political party or candidate or to persuade them not to vote for a political party or candidate.'

Section 72(2) states that attendance at a conference as a delegate or participator falls within subsection (e) above.

A challenge on expenditure goes to the Certification Officer or the High Court with an appeal to the Employment Appeal Tribunal. Many cases have discussed the meaning of the present s.72(1)(f). In *Coleman* v. *Post Office Engineering Union* [1981] IRLR 427 the Certification Officer ruled that affiliation to the Canterbury District Trades Council Campaign Against the Cuts was not political activity since there was no expenditure on literature and the meetings were not held by a political party or directly or indirectly in support of a political party. It was also relevant that there was a great deal of support from unions not affiliated to the Labour Party. This decision can be contrasted with the cases of *Richards* v. *NUM* [1981] IRLR 247 and *Paul* v. *NALGO* [1987] IRLR 43. In *Richards*, the Certification Officer held that money spent on a march and a parliamentary lobby against government cuts should have come from the union's political fund. In *Paul*, NALGO distributed leaflets and posters highlighting cuts in public services and the effects of privatisation, urging people to use their vote in the forthcoming local elections. All the publicity stated that NALGO was not affiliated to any political party. Browne-Wilkinson VC decided that payment for the campaign should have been made out of the political fund. Given the closeness of the local election, he held that the purpose of the leaflets and posters was to dissuade people from voting Conservative. Contributions to funding Labour Party Headquarters is a political object and not a commercial investment (*Association of Scientific, Technical and Managerial Staff* v. *Parkin* [1984] ICR 127). The political fund can operate on an overdraft as long as the interest is charged to the fund (s.83 Trade Union and Labour Relations (Consolidation) Act 1992).

The 1992 Act lays down conditions for the establishment and maintenance of a political fund. A political resolution must be passed by a majority of members voting on a ballot conducted according to the provisions of the Act, that is, it must comply with the union's political ballot rules as approved by the Certification Officer (s.73). The Certification Officer cannot approve such rules unless they include the appointment of an independent scrutineer, entitlement of all the members to vote, voting complies with s.77 (that is, it is postal and secret) and the rules provide for a scrutineer's report. Additional provisions introduced by the 1993 Act include the requirement that the scrutineer sees a register of members and the requirement of an independent person to count the votes (s.77A). By s.73(3) the union must ballot its members every 10 years to maintain the fund. If it fails to do so or the resolution is lost, the fund lapses and any levy collected after that date must be returned to the members. The remaining fund can be transferred to any other union fund.

12.7 Trade Union Accounts

The Trade Union and Labour Relations (Consolidation) Act 1992 as amended by the Trade Union Reform and Employment Rights Act 1993 lays down stringent rules for the organisation of a trade union's financial affairs.

By s.32 Trade Union and Labour Relations (Consolidation) Act 1992 the union must make annual returns to the Certification Officer including a profit and loss account, a balance sheet, an auditor's report and any other documentation he may require. Following the case of *Taylor* v. *NUM (Derbyshire Area) (No. 2)* [1985] IRLR 65 the Employment Act 1988 placed a duty on unions to allow their accounts to be inspected for at least a six-year period after their creation and gave members the right to be accompanied by a qualified accountant (ss.29 and 30 Trade Union and Labour Relations (Consolidation) Act 1992). Failure to keep accounting records, failure to allow such records to be inspected, failure to allow a member to inspect the accounts, failure to submit an annual return and failure to keep a separate fund for members' superannuation are all criminal offences (s.45). Section 45A lists the penalties and prosecution time limits for such offences and s.45B allows for disqualification of offenders from union office (that is, a member of the executive, the president or the general secretary) for a period of up to 10 years. Failure on the part of the union to disqualify convicted persons from office allows a member of the union to complain to the Certification Officer or the court for a declaration that the union has failed to comply with s.45B.

Following allegations in the press of irregularities in relation to the NUM's funds, the union established an enquiry under the chairmanship of Gavin Lightman QC. The subsequent report was critical of some of the dealings of the senior officials of the union. Criminal charges were commenced by the Certification Officer under the now s.45, but the charges were subsequently dismissed. As a result of the Lightman Report, the Trade Union Reform and Employment Rights Act 1993 introduced more rights for members and gave greater powers to the Certification Officer. By s.32A of the 1992 Act information about the salary and benefits of each member of the union executive, the president and the general secretary must be included in the annual return. The trade union must take reasonable steps to ensure that all its members, within eight weeks of the submission of the annual return, are provided with a written financial statement of income and expenditure. A copy must also be given to the Certification Officer. Section 37A gives the Certification Officer new powers to order an investigation into the conduct of a union's financial affairs and publish a report after such an investigation. Failure to comply with such an investigation will be a criminal offence. In addition, new offences are created arising out of such an investigation and persons convicted of such offences can be disqualified from being a member of a union executive, or from being the president or general secretary of a union from between five and 10 years, depending on the gravity of the offence.

At first sight, it appears that the legislature is merely attaching the same rights to trade union members as are enjoyed by shareholders of a company, and making senior trade union officials responsible in the way that company directors are responsible, including imposing the sanction of disqualification. It should be noted, however, that the information available to trade union members under these provisions is much greater than that available to shareholders.

12.8   The Rule Book

The rules of a trade union form the terms of a contract between it and its members. They become part of the contract in the same way that collective agreements become part of the individual's employment contract between the employer and the employee. The rule book, however, will form the express terms in that contract and, as in every other type of contract, terms may be implied. Custom and practice may add to the rules and so too add to the terms in the contract of membership. In *Heaton's Transport Ltd* v. *TGWU* [1973] AC 15 the House of Lords held that shop stewards had customary power to call industrial action even though the express provisions of the union's constitution did not give this power. So too the 'Oh of course' test so common in other areas of contract can be used to imply terms into the contract of membership and amend the rules. In *MacLelland* v. *NUJ* [1975] ICR 116 the courts implied into the rule book of the NUJ the requirement of reasonable notice before important meetings.

Apart from contractual devices, other areas of law impact on the union rule book. Statute has now impacted in a variety of ways. By s.69 Trade Union and Labour Relations (Consolidation) Act 1992, for example, there is a rule in all union rule books allowing a member to terminate his membership on the giving of reasonable notice. Both the Sex Discrimination Act 1975 and the Race Relations Act 1976 render it unlawful to discriminate on the grounds of sex or race in relation to membership, access to benefits or subjecting members to a detriment on those grounds. The rules cannot be contrary to the common law, so that in *Drake* v. *Morgan* [1978] ICR 56 the House of Lords stated that a union policy to pay the fines of members convicted of unlawful picketing was illegal because such a policy supported the criminal actions of its members (now s.15 Trade Union and Labour Relations (Consolidation) Act 1992). By contrast, however, it appears that rules which support members in the commission of breaches of contract or torts are not unlawful. In *Porter* v. *NUJ* [1979] IRLR 404 the House of Lords held that the provision of funds to members on strike or taking other industrial action was not illegal. The distinction between supporting the commission of criminal and civil acts arose again in the case of *Thomas* v. *NUM (South Wales Area)* [1985] IRLR 136. In the case it was alleged that the strike was bound to result in the commission of both crimes and torts. Scott J stated that while it would be unlawful for the union to organise and support criminal activity, he was not clear what the position would be in relation to the organisation of tortious activity. Given that in the normal situation, the activity organised and supported by the union may result in torts or criminal acts being committed rather than such being inevitable, he did not feel that he had to decide the point.

The basis of the decisions above may be looked at in another way, however. Although the union is not a body corporate, in some ways it is treated as if it is, for example in the making of contracts and suing and being sued in its own name. This has led courts to impose certain company principles upon unions, more particularly the *ultra vires* doctrine, that is, that the union only has the power given to it by the rules and therefore has no power to act outside them. Thus, any payment of fines for criminal acts, for example, is *ultra vires*. The rule which allows such payment is unlawful and void, therefore the union has no power to act under its auspices. A strike, for example, must be called only after a proper ballot has been conducted. If the ballot is illegal, the union has no power to call a strike and if the union has no power to call a strike, it has no power to pay strike pay. Thus in *Taylor* v. *NUM (Derbyshire Area) (No. 3)* [1985] IRLR 99 Vinelott J ruled that payment of strike pay to members involved in a non-balloted strike was *ultra vires*. Similarly, in *Clarke* v. *Chadburn* [1984] IRLR 350 a resolution of the NUM conference to change the disciplinary rules was *ultra vires* because this could not be done without a prior meeting of the Nottinghamshire Area Council, and in *Hopkins* v. *National Union of Seamen* [1985] IRLR 157 the imposition of a levy on members by the National Executive Council was declared *ultra vires* and void as that body had no power to raise a levy. While many have argued that as unions are not corporations the *ultra vires* rule should not apply, the courts continue to use it to control the unions' exercise of their power under the rules. This means that, given the analogy with companies, on occasion the courts have also used the so-called rule in *Foss* v. *Harbottle* (1843) 2 Hare 461 which has implications for individual members who wish to sue for breaches of the rules. This will be discussed more fully in Chapter 13.

12.9 Inter-Union Disputes

Unions may clash over the organisation of workers or rights within a particular factory or industry, for example, as to which union has the right to organise a particular group of workers or as to which union should have recognition rights within a particular industry or workplace. In addition, disputes may arise between unions because of 'poaching' of members from one union to another. Such disputes can arise because in the UK there is no tradition of single-union workplaces, for example there were some 15 unions operating in Ford workplaces in 1969 and eight unions covering Austin Rover workers in 1985. Foreign companies establishing workplaces within the UK are more prone to try and reach a single-union deal – often offering recognition rights to one union in return for flexible working patterns or no-strike clauses. These trends mean that the risk of inter-union disputes remains high.

To prevent government intervention in this area, the Trades Union Congress polices such disputes. To do so it operates a series of principles known as the Bridlington Agreement, which was first adopted in 1939, in Bridlington. The agreement has been amended in subsequent years. Breach of the agreement is dealt with by the TUC Disputes Committee and the ultimate sanction for breach of the agreement is expulsion from the TUC.

To prevent dual membership of unions, Principle 2 laid down that on receipt of an application for membership, a union must check the record of the applicant. If the applicant is the subject of a disciplinary sanction or has outstanding subscriptions or there are other reasons why he should not be accepted, the union should reject the application. In addition, the existing union must agree to the transfer and if the agreement is withheld the new union should not take on the member unless it feels that permission is being unreasonably withheld, in which case the matter must be referred to the Disputes Committee. The principle, at one time, did cause problems when there was an abundance of closed shops operating, and cases often came before the Committee arising from the transfer of an employee who was the member of one union to another site where a different union was operating a closed shop. Changes in the law which have now rendered the operation of a compulsory closed shop illegal have alleviated the number of cases on this issue.

Apart from issues involving individual members transferring between unions, Principle 5 is designed to prevent unions from going into competition with each other in a workplace or industry in relation to membership or recognition. The principle provides that no union may organise at an establishment where another union has the majority of workers as members and engages in negotiations on wages and conditions for those workers, unless that union agrees.

It appears that in relation to the individual member, the principles are not implied as terms in his contract of membership but are merely a code of conduct (*Spring v. National Amalgamated Stevedores and Dockers Society* [1956] 2 All ER 221). However, even though the principles are voluntary self-regulation, the courts may still get involved in relation to their supervisory jurisdiction to ensure that the Disputes Committee acts within the law. This is demonstrated by *Rothwell* v. *APEX* [1976] ICR 211. The case arose after an attempt by the TUC to avoid the implications of the *Spring* decision (above). In *Spring*, the plaintiff had been enrolled as a member of NASDS contrary to the Bridlington Agreement and the TUC Disputes Committee ordered the union to expel him, which it did, despite the fact that there was no power to expel under its own rules. It was held that the expulsion was void. As a result, the TUC invited all affiliated unions to adopt a model rule (model rule 14) covering expulsion in compliance with a Disputes Committee ruling. In *Rothwell*, members of a staff association called SAGA voted to merge with APEX, but this amalgamation was objected to by the Association of Scientific, Technical and Managerial Staff (ASTMS). The Disputes Committee then ruled that ASTMS was the appropriate union for those workers and the General Council therefore called upon APEX to expel all those who had already joined under model rule 14. It was held that the expulsions were invalid for three reasons. First, ASTMS had less than 50 per cent membership and therefore under the Bridlington Agreement APEX was right to proceed with the merger. Second, the merger had been conducted in accordance with the relevant statutory provisions and the General Council had no power to undo what had lawfully been done by statute. It therefore followed that APEX had no power to expel because the decisions of both the Disputes Committee and the General Council were *ultra vires* and void. Section 174(4) of the 1992 Act now provides individuals with the right not to be expelled or excluded on the basis of membership of another union.

12.10 Trade Union Amalgamations

By s.97 Trade Union and Labour Relations (Consolidation) Act 1992 there are two ways in which unions can become one – either by an amalgamation or by a transfer of engagements. If there is a transfer of engagements (that is, the new union undertakes to fulfil all the engagements of the old), there must be an instrument of transfer submitted to the Certification Officer and approved by him and a resolution approving the instrument must have been adopted by a simple majority vote, after seven-days' notice, of the members of the transferor union (s.97(2)). In relation to an amalgamation, the requisite notice and vote must be conducted by both the transferor union and the transferee union (s.97(1)). The Trade Union Reform and Employment Rights Act 1993, amending s.100, requires that any vote on union mergers or transfers shall be fully postal and subject to independent scrutiny. A member of a union passing a resolution to approve an instrument of amalgamation or transfer may complain to the Certification Officer that the statutory provisions have not been complied with within six weeks of the application to register the instrument (s.103(2)), and the Certification Officer cannot register the instrument until he has investigated and determined the complaint or the complaint is withdrawn. The Certification Officer can make a declaration that he finds the complaint to be justified or order that the union take certain steps before the instrument can be registered. An appeal lies against the Certification Officer's decision to the Employment Appeal Tribunal on a point of law only (s.104). When the instrument of transfer takes effect, the property of the old union is immediately vested in the new union without the necessity for any conveyance (s.105). Further, by s.101A if the amalgamated unions are already listed, the Certification Officer must enter the name of the newly amalgamated union onto the list and remove the old names, and ss.101A(3) and (4) provide for the issue of a new certificate of independence if the amalgamating unions had such certificates prior to amalgamation.

12.11 Trade Union Elections

One of the tenets of recent legislation in this area has been democratising the trade union movement, and to this end the legislation has introduced the requirement of balloting in respect of many issues. We have already seen above that a ballot complying with the statutory requirements is required for an amalgamation or transfer and for the maintenance of the political fund. We will see in Chapter 14 that members must also be balloted before industrial action is undertaken and failure to hold a legal ballot before such action has severe consequences for the union. So, too, the law requires balloting of all relevant members in the selection of the officials of the union, but further requires that such ballots and elections must take place every five years.

The first piece of legislation to introduce the idea of full membership balloting for union officials was the Trade Union Act 1984. This required that all voting members of the principal executive committee, whatever it was called, be elected every five years. The principal executive committee is the main committee of the union exercising executive functions. The government obviously intended that this should prevent certain union officials, not least Mr Scargill, president of the NUM, from holding his job for life. Many union presidents however, including Mr Scargill, merely gave up their vote so that they were not caught by the legislation. As such, the Employment Act 1988 amended the 1984 Act by the so-called 'Scargill clause' so that the president, the general secretary and every member of the principal executive committee must be re-elected every five years. 'Member of the executive' includes any person who by the rules or practice of the union may attend and speak at some or all of the meetings of the executive except in the capacity of giving advice or information upon which the executive may act. These provisions have now been consolidated in s.46 Trade Union and Labour Relations (Consolidation) Act 1992. This has now been amended by the Employment Relations Act 2004 so that a union is allowed to appoint a president in accordance with its rule book and without the need for an election, if the president already holds the position of General Secretary or is a member of the executive and has been properly elected to that position. In other words, the union is not required in those circumstances to hold a second election. Section 47 of the 1992 Act further provides that no member of the trade union shall be unreasonably excluded from standing as a candidate and no candidate shall be required to be a member of a political party. In *Ecclestone* v. *NUJ* [1999] IRLR 166 the national executive committee refused to accept a candidate for election to General Secretary, because although he had held the post for 17 years, he had been dismissed following a dispute with the NEC which claimed it no longer had confidence in him. The court held that this was the same as saying the NEC could block anyone it did not want to stand and was thus a breach of s.47.

By s.50, all members of the union are entitled to vote, with three important exceptions – those who are unemployed, those who are in arrears with their subscriptions or those who are apprentices, trainees, students or new members. The union rules may restrict entitlement to vote to members of a class determined by occupation or geographical area, but may not do so if the effect is to disentitle a member from voting at elections for officials (s.50(4)).

By s.51 voting must be postal, however s.54 Employment Relations Act 2004 gives a power to the Secretary of State to widen the means of voting as long as it always includes postal voting. The statute also lays down the requirements which must be complied with on the ballot paper, for example the name of the independent scrutineer appointed and a number marked on the paper. At present, the union must provide the candidates with the opportunity of preparing an election address and if such addresses are prepared the union must distribute them to the voters (s.48(1)).

Section 49 requires the union to appoint an independent scrutineer. The functions of the scrutineer are listed in the section and he must prepare a report on the election to the trade union as soon as reasonably practicable after the last date for the return of the voting papers. The report must contain items such as the number of returned voting papers, the number of valid votes, the number of invalid papers and a statement that there are no grounds for believing that there was a contravention of the statute, that the arrangements for the election minimised the risk of unfairness or malpractice and that he was able to carry out his functions free from interference (s.52(2)). The union cannot issue the results of the election until the receipt of the scrutineer's report and must bring the contents of the report to the attention of its members. The union is obliged to maintain a register of the names and addresses of its members (s.24). By s.49 the union must require the scrutineer to inspect the register of members and the scrutineer must state in his report that an inspection has been requested and completed. In addition, s.51A requires an independent person to count the votes and if this person is not the scrutineer, the scrutineer must receive the voting papers once they have been counted and his report must identify the independent counter and whether the scrutineer was satisfied with his performance.

The Act provides two remedies for failure to comply with the statutory provisions. The first, contained in s.55, is an application to the Certification Officer. Any member or candidate, up to a year after the default, may apply to the Certification Officer for a declaration. The Certification Officer must make a determination within six months of the application and if a declaration is granted, it can state the steps that the union must take to remedy the declared failure. The second remedy is an application to the High Court (s.56). The advantage of turning to the court is that it has the additional power to make an enforcement order (s.56(4)) and this may be an order that the election be reheld within a specified time period. In addition, the court may grant interlocutory relief.

12.12 The Right to Information

The Employment Protection Act 1975 recognised that to be able to collectively bargain effectively, unions needed certain information from the employer and, as such, the Act introduced a right to receive certain information. This right has been retained and the provisions are now ss.181–185 Trade Union and Labour Relations (Consolidation) Act 1992.

By s.181 an employer who recognises an independent trade union is required to disclose certain information to representatives of the union at their request. 'Representative' means a trade union official or any other person authorised by the union to carry on collective bargaining. The information which must be disclosed is any information about the employer's undertaking or that of an associated employer without which the representatives would be materially impeded in carrying on collective bargaining, and such information which would be in accordance with good industrial relations practice to disclose (s.181(2)). The major limitation on this right is that by the wording in s.181, the employer only has to disclose information in relation to those matters for which the union is recognised for collective bargaining. Thus, if the employer only recognises the union for collective bargaining on pay, this is the only issue on which he is required to disclose information. In *R v. CAC ex parte BTP Tioxide Limited* [1982] IRLR 60 the company negotiated with the union on pay awards. It sought to introduce a job evaluation scheme without consulting the union although the company gave the union the right to represent workers who wished to appeal against their gradings under the scheme. The union sought information about the scheme. It was held that that information need not be disclosed as the union was not recognised and did not have negotiating rights on job evaluation.

Section 181 further limits the rights by restricting the information to topics within the statutory definition of collective bargaining found in s.178. This states that collective bargaining means negotiations relating to one or more of the following matters:

(a) terms and conditions of employment, or the physical conditions in which any workers are required to work;
(b) engagement or non-engagement, or termination or suspension of employment or the duties of employment, of one or more workers;
(c) allocation of work or the duties of employment between workers or groups of workers;
(d) matters of discipline;
(e) a worker's membership or non-membership of a trade union;
(f) facilities for trade union officials; and
(g) machinery for negotiation or consultation, and other procedures, relating to any of the above matters, including the recognition by employers or employers' associations of the right of a trade union to represent workers in such negotiation or consultation or in the carrying-out of such procedures.

ACAS has produced a Code of Practice (*ACAS Code of Practice 2: Disclosure of Information to Trade Unions for Collective Bargaining Purposes*) which in paragraph 11 lists the type of information it would be good industrial relations practice to disclose. This includes pay and benefits (including job evaluation systems, distribution of pay and total pay bill), conditions of service (including policies on recruitment, appraisal systems, and health and safety), manpower (including numbers, grades and labour turnover), performance (including productivity data, sales and return on invested capital) and financial (including cost structures, and gross and net profits loans). Paragraph 12 states that this is not intended to be a checklist nor is it intended to be exhaustive.

While the code provides a wide-ranging list it is important to remember that it is merely a code and therefore is not binding, although s.181(4) makes particular reference to it. Section 182, however, provides for restrictions on the general duty to disclose and therefore an employer does not have to disclose information:

'(a) the disclosure of which would be against the interests of national security, or
(b) which he could not disclose without contravening a prohibition imposed by or under an enactment, or
(c) which has been communicated to him in confidence, or which he has otherwise obtained in consequence of the confidence reposed in him by another person, or
(d) which relates specifically to an individual (unless that individual has consented to it being disclosed), or
(e) the disclosure of which would cause substantial injury to his undertaking for reasons other than its effect on collective bargaining, or
(f) obtained by him for the purpose of bringing, prosecuting or defending any legal proceedings.'

Section 182(2) further provides that the employer need not produce or allow an inspection of the originals or copies of any documents for the purpose of conveying or confirming information. Nor is the employer obliged to compile or assemble information if to do so would involve work or expenditure which is out of proportion to the value of the information in the conduct of collective bargaining. Given these restrictions, it is valid to question the value of the right to the information.

Section 183 provides a remedy for a trade union where the employer has failed to provide information or failed to confirm information in writing when the union has requested such. The union may complain to the Central Arbitration Committee (CAC). If the Committee feels the matter can be dealt with by conciliation, it will call upon ACAS to promote a settlement. If conciliation is unsuccessful or inappropriate, the Committee may make a declaration that the complaint is well-founded and require the information to be disclosed by a particular date. If the employer ignores the declaration, the union may make a further complaint by s.184. The union may present a claim to the Committee in writing in respect of one or more descriptions of employees that their contracts should contain the terms and conditions specified in the claim (s.185). If the Committee finds for the union it may make an award that the employer shall observe those terms and conditions which by the award become part of the individual employee's contract. No award can be made if the employer discloses the information which is the subject of the complaint.

The rights to information have been further enhanced by the Transnational Information and Consultation of Employees Regulations 1999 which were brought in to implement the European Works Council Directive (EC 94/45). The Regulations require a European Works Council (EWC) or an information and consultation procedure (ICP) to be established in every Community scale undertaking. A 'Community scale undertaking' is one which has at least 1,000 employees and at least 150 employees in each of two Member States (Regulation 2(1)). Central management is responsible for starting negotiations to establish an EWC or ICP and they must be initiated if at least 100 employees or representatives of at least 100 employees who represent employees in at least two Member States so request (Regulation 9). Employee representatives are either representatives of an independent recognised trade union, who represent the relevant employees, or elected employee representatives who are expected to receive, on behalf of employees, information relevant to terms and conditions of employment of those employees or information about the activities of the undertaking which may significantly affect the interests of those employees (Regulation 2). The scope, function, composition and term of office of an EWC or the implementation of an ICP are determined by a special negotiating body (SNB) in conjunction with central management (Regulations 16 and 17). The SNB must consist of a representative of each Member State where the undertaking is based and up to three additional members (Regulation 12). Central management must convene a meeting of the SNB to reach a written agreement on the arrangements for the information and consultation of employees (Regulation 16(1)).

There are default provisions. If central management refuses to begin negotiations within six months of a request from employees or their representatives, or if the parties are unable to agree information and consultation procedures within three years of such a request, an EWC can be established with between three and thirty members. The information and consultation that the EWC can receive is, however, limited to matters concerning the group of undertakings as a whole. This EWC has the right to meet with central management once a year and receive a report on the progress and prospects of the undertaking or group. Paragraph 7 of the Schedule to the Regulations specifies issues which should be covered at this annual meeting.

If the parties agree to establish an EWC or ICP, or the default provisions become applicable, and no EWC or ICP has been established because of a failure by central management, the SNB, a former SNB member or employee representative may complain to the Employment Appeal Tribunal. That tribunal can require central management to establish an EWC or ICP and also order the payment of a penalty to the Secretary of State of up to £75,000. This will be payable unless the failure resulted from a reason beyond the control of central management or there is other reasonable excuse for the failure (Regulation 4).

There are two important limitations on the information to be disclosed. First, members of an SNB, EWC or ICP representatives owe a duty not to disclose information which has been given to them on confidential terms.

Disclosure of such information is a breach of statutory duty unless it is a protected disclosure under the Employment Rights Act (Regulation 23). Second, central management do not have to disclose information which would 'seriously harm the functioning of, or would be prejudicial to, the undertaking or group of undertakings concerned'. A challenge to a decision by management that information falls within this category may be made to the CAC which may order disclosure if it feels the information is not protected (Regulation 24).

In addition to the Transnational Information and Consultation of Employees Regulations 1999, the Information and Consultation Directive (2002/14/EC) was agreed in 2002 and implemented by the Information and Consultation of Employees Regulations 2004. At the date of implementation the Regulations applied to employers with at least 150 employees, in March 2007 they applied to those employing 100 or more, and from March 2008 to those employing 50 or more.

The Regulations provide a fall-back statutory scheme if there are no voluntary arrangements in place. This will apply on a request in writing from 10 per cent of the workforce. The statutory procedure involves the establishment of an information and consultation committee consisting of one representative per 50 employees, up to a maximum of 50 members. The committee must be given information and be consulted about: the development of the undertaking's activities and its economic position; the state of employment in the undertaking and measures to be taken if there is a threat to employment; and any decisions likely to lead to substantial changes in work organisation where consultation must be with a view to reaching agreement. Where there are voluntary arrangements in place, the employer can ballot the workforce to see if new arrangements should be negotiated. If 40 per cent wish to change the arrangements, the employer has six months to negotiate with elected employee representatives as to the new arrangements. If negotiations fail, the statutory provisions apply. Where there are voluntary arrangements, the parties can decide the areas for consultation and information. Complaint on failing to release the information is to the CAC which may then refer a case to the Employment Appeal Tribunal if a penalty judgement is required. There is evidence that the courts are interpreting the Regulations against employers who drag their feet. In *Amicus* v. *Macmillan Publishers Ltd* [2007] IRLR 378 Macmillan had been before the CAC in 2005 for failing to provide information and was ordered by the CAC on its second appearance to give Amicus more precise information about employee numbers (a right granted by the Regulations so that a union can determine whether they have 10 per cent support for a request). Amicus therefore put in a second request in March 2006. Macmillan declined to ballot all employees to ascertain the level of support or start negotiations with employee representatives. Macmillan argued that the existing arrangements complied with the requirements for a pre-existing arrangement, but the Employment Appeal Tribunal disagreed. As such, the standard information and consultation procedures came into play within 6 months of a valid request. The standard procedures give timescales for negotiations which require an employer to ballot employees to assess support for the request, and then enter negotiations. Macmillan should have arranged for the election of employee representatives by September 2006 but failed to do so. The EAT assessed the award on the basis that there had been a significant failure 'because it must have been plain, reading the legislation, that the relevant provisions were being ignored at almost every stage' (Elias P) and decided that Macmillan should pay £55,000. The maximum possible award is £75,000.

12.13 Financial Assistance

The Employment Relations Act 2004 introduces a new s.116A into the 1992 Act. This lists five purposes for which the Secretary of State can give money to enable or assist a trade union to:

(a) improve the carrying out of any of its functions;
(b) prepare to carry out any new function;
(c) increase the range of services it offers to persons who are or who may become members;
(d) prepare for an amalgamation or the transfer of any or all of its engagements;
(e) ballot its members (whether as a result of a statutory requirement or otherwise).

The union must be independent (unless a federation of unions applies) and the Secretary of State can determine the way the assistance is provided and any terms relating to its disbursement. Section 116A(4) prohibits such assistance being added to the union's political fund and if there is a breach of this, the Secretary of State must take such steps as are reasonably practicable to recover such sums from the political fund.

12.14 The Closed Shop

A closed shop is the situation where in a particular workplace, or workplaces if the employer operates a multi-site operation, membership of a particular union is necessary in order to work. If there is a pre-entry closed shop, this means that the potential employee must be a member of the union before he can be offered a job and so essentially the union is controlling the pool of applicants. A post-entry closed shop means that employees must join the union after acquiring the job. The closed shop raises many emotional arguments. Those who defend it argue that it prevents free-riders from obtaining the benefit of union representation (for example, on wage rises) without paying any union dues. Employers too have argued that a closed shop makes collective bargaining easier and prevents the problems of many unions representing disparate groups of workers on one site. By contrast, opponents of the closed shop argue that it takes away freedom of the individual to choose the union to which he wishes to belong and also takes away the right of an individual not to belong to any union. Certainly, where a closed shop exists, the union will have a great deal of strength against the employer. When the Donovan Commission reported in the 1960s it found that industries where the closed shop was prevalent were more strike-prone than those where union membership was not compulsory, and many people believe that the existence of a closed shop inevitably leads to more industrial action.

There was no legal control over the closed shop until the Industrial Relations Act 1971. This Act introduced the concept of unfair dismissal and it was through this concept that the closed shop was controlled. It was an unfair dismissal to dismiss a worker who would not join a union, although certain approved closed shops (or agency shops) could exist if on a majority vote the workers wanted one.

The fall of the Conservative government and the repeal of the Industrial Relations Act by the Trade Union and Labour Relations Act 1974 brought with it statutory protection for the closed shop. The original Act defined a closed shop as a union membership agreement which required a group of workers to belong to a specified union or unions. Protection came in the form that it was a fair dismissal to dismiss an employee who refused to join a union when a union membership agreement had been signed, but allowed a worker to be protected from dismissal if he objected to joining the union on religious grounds. These provisions meant that the union could coerce employees to join and put pressure on the employer to dismiss those employees who refused.

The Thatcher government which was returned in 1979 made the closed shop one of the targets of its industrial legislation policy and began to slowly dismantle any protection. The Employment Acts 1980 and 1982 increased protection for those employees who did not wish to join the union by making any dismissal unfair, while retaining the idea of a fair dismissal for those employees who refused to join but who did not fall within the categories of protection. This, however, only applied where a legal closed shop was operating, that is, one that had complied with the complicated balloting provisions introduced in 1980 and extended by the 1982 Act. In addition, where there was a claim of unfair dismissal the union could be joined as a co-respondent in the claim and could be ordered to pay some if not all of the compensation awarded. While some would argue that this was a deliberate attempt to destroy the power of the unions, the European Court of Human Rights in *Young, James and Webster* v. *United Kingdom* [1983] IRLR 35 had ruled that the legislation which allowed for compulsory membership of a particular union was an infringement of Article 11 of the European Convention on Human Rights as it restricted the freedom of the individual to join the union of their choice.

Despite the ruling, it remained possible to enforce a legal post-entry closed shop until 1988, when the Employment Act of that year rendered any dismissal for union or non-union membership unfair in any circumstances (now s.152 Trade Union and Labour Relations (Consolidation) Act 1992). As such, while post-entry closed shops can still exist, no one can legally be compelled to join a union.

The legislation of 1988, however, did nothing to prevent pre-entry closed shops operating and while it was unlawful to dismiss or otherwise discriminate against an existing employee who refused to join the union, it still remained legal to discriminate against potential employees by insisting that they were union members before offering them employment. It was obvious that the government would not allow this situation to exist for very long and the Employment Act 1990 finally destroyed any protection which existed for the pre-entry closed shop by rendering any action to discriminate in the appointment of persons on the grounds of union membership or non-membership illegal (now ss.137–143 Trade Union and Labour Relations (Consolidation) Act 1992). It should be noted that it was not part of government policy at the time to give protection to union members who were refused work because the employer wanted a union-free workplace. The European Social Charter, however, recommended that Member States prohibited discrimination on the grounds of non-union membership or union membership and the government felt obliged to comply. This policy did not continue, however. Two Court of Appeal decisions (*Associated Newspapers Ltd* v. *Wilson* [1993] IRLR 336 and *Associated British Ports* v. *Palmer*, same reference), discussed below, decided that where an employer gave the employee the choice of a collectively bargained contract and an individual contract, the individual contract giving 4.5 per cent more pay than the collectively bargained one, then this amounted to discrimination on the grounds of trade union membership. While the decisions were reversed by the House of Lords ([1995] IRLR 258) the then government, in response to the Court of Appeal decisions, inserted a new clause in the Trade Union Reform and Employment Rights Bill (now s.148(3) of the 1992 Act) allowing employers to offer better terms to non-union members.

Section 17 Employment Relations Act 1999 reversed these decisions and amended the legislative provisions by redefining detriment as an act or any deliberate failure to act. This amendment, however, only applied in the context of collective agreements and pay. As a result of *Wilson* v. *UK* (see Chapter 7), the Employment Relations Act 2004 has provided protection against being offered an inducement or suffering detriment or dismissal for refusing to come out of collective bargaining (now ss.145A and B Trade Union and Labour Relations (Consolidation) Act 1992).

Summary

1. A union is not a body corporate but it has certain powers which are also given to incorporated associations.

2. The legal definition of a union is that it must be a body of workers whose principal purpose is the regulation of relations between those workers and an employer or employers' association.

3. A union may be temporary or permanent.

4. A union must be listed and obtain a certificate of independence to enable its members to acquire certain rights.

5. In addition to independence, it is important for the union to be recognised by the employer for collective bargaining purposes.

6. Maintenance of a political fund by the union must be the subject of a membership ballot.

7. Unions must comply with stringent statutory rules regarding their accounts.

8. While the rule book lays down the express terms of the contract of membership between the union and its members, such terms may be augmented by custom and practice or the officious bystander test.

9. Unions must act within their stated objects for their actions to be *intra vires*.

10. The unions have adopted voluntary regulation in the form of the Bridlington Agreement.

11. Unions must comply with the statutory balloting provisions if they wish to amalgamate. In addition, all voting officials must be elected by membership ballot every five years.

12. Recognised independent trade unions are entitled to certain information from an employer for collective bargaining purposes and independent trade unions are entitled to financial assistance from the Secretary of State.

13. A union can no longer enforce a pre-entry or post-entry closed shop by compulsory union membership.

Exercises

1. Why did it take unions so long in the UK to establish an ability to pursue their aims?

2. How far is the present legislation reminiscent of the Industrial Relations Act 1971?

3. Do you feel that the current legislation meets the present government's (2008) stated aim of democratising unions?

4. Good industrial relations should involve a balance of power between both sides. Many would argue that the balance has shifted in favour of the employer to the detriment of the unions. Do you feel that this is an accurate reflection of the present legislation?

Further Reading

Democracy in Trade Unions, Cmnd. 8778 (1983).

Trade Unions and Their Members, Cmnd. 95 (1987).

Bercusson   *The European Social Model Comes to Britain* (2002) 31 ILJ 209.

Ewing   *The Strike, the Courts and the Rule Books* (1985) 14 ILJ 160.

Ewing   *Trade Union Recognition and Staff Associations – A Breach of International Labour Standards?* (2000) 29 ILJ 267.

Ewing   *The Implications of Wilson and Palmer* (2003) 32 ILJ 1.

Ewing   *The Function of Trade Unions* (2005) 34 ILJ 1.

Gall   *The First Five Years of Britain's Third Statutory Recognition Procedure* (2005) 34 ILJ 345.

Hall   *Assessing the Information and Consultation of Employees Regulations* (2005) 34 ILJ 103.

Kidner   *Trade Union Democracy: Election of Trade Union Officers* (1984) 13 ILJ 193.

Simpson   *Trade Union Recognition and the Law: a New Approach – Parts I and II of Schedule A1 to the Trade Union and Labour Relations (Consolidation) Act 1992* (2000) 29 ILJ 193.

Wedderburn   *Collective Bargaining or Legal Enactment? The 1999 Act and Union Recognition* (2000) 29 ILJ 1.

Chapter 13

The Rights of Trade Union Members

Introduction

For many years the legislature adopted a non-interventionist approach in the area of trade union activity and apart from giving trade unions immunity from liability in certain situations, to enable them to take industrial action, very little legislation was passed. This meant, however, that while individual members were protected should they take industrial action, very few other rights accrued. The Industrial Relations Act 1971 showed a departure from the previous non-interventionist approach and although the Act was short-lived its successor, the Trade Union and Labour Relations Act 1974, introduced strong protection for the union and its members engaging in industrial action and gave legal protection to the closed shop. The Labour government which introduced that piece of legislation, however, saw it as part of a three-part plan in this field. The second part was the introduction of employment protection rights which were enacted in the Employment Protection Act 1975 and which also, for the first time, gave rights to trade union members *vis-à-vis* the employer. The final part was to be legislation on industrial democracy which did not get very far owing to the party losing power. The government which took office in 1979 was anxious to protect non-union members and democratise the unions, therefore, while retaining many of the rights union members had against an employer, it introduced rights for non-union members to protect them in situations where the union was putting pressure on the employer to either dismiss or discriminate against them because of their non-union membership. In addition, it introduced new rights for union members *vis-à-vis* the union, and a special Commissioner to enforce these newly created rights. While the post of Commissioner was abolished in 1999, jurisdiction passed to the Certification Officer. Thus, the trade union member now has two groups of rights – those against his employer to ensure that he is not treated less favourably than a non-unionist and that he is allowed time off to pursue his trade union activities, and those against his union to ensure that the union acts within the bounds of the rule book and that it does not unreasonably discipline or exclude him. Some of these particular rights have been discussed elsewhere. The time-off rights were more logically discussed with employment protection rights in general in Chapter 7. So too dismissal for trade union membership or activities was more logically discussed with unfair dismissal in Chapter 9. The discussion below deals with the rest of the rights that a trade union member is now granted by law.

13.2 Enforcement of the Union Rule Book

While there is special statutory protection for union members in relation to rules concerning discipline and exclusion or expulsion (see below), a member must rely on the common law to enforce any other rule in the rule book. Although the rule book forms the contract of membership between the individual member and the union, this will not always provide him with a remedy. Rather, the trade union member is treated in a similar way to a shareholder in a company and, as such, his remedies against the union are similar to those imposed against incorporated associations.

The simple proposition is that because a union as an entity only exists as a creation of statute, its legal capacity to act comes from its rules (and to some extent from statute when talking about industrial action, elections, amalgamations and so on). As such, if the rules or statute lay down when a union can act (for example, after a majority vote of members) then should the union act without fulfilling the requirements, it has no capacity to do so and hence its actions are *ultra vires*. *Ultra vires* actions, as we have already seen in Chapter 12, are void and a member may challenge the union. In certain cases the member may do this by application to the Certification Officer, a right introduced by the Employment Relations Act 1999. So, for example, a member may apply to the Certification Officer where a breach or threatened breach relates to the appointment, election or removal of a person from office, disciplinary proceedings, balloting of members on any issue other than industrial action and the constitution or proceedings of any decision-making body (s.108A Trade Union and Labour Relations (Consolidation) Act 1992). Should the complaint be upheld, the Certification Officer may make an enforcement order requiring the union to take steps to remedy the breach, withdraw the threat of the breach and abstain from action which would mean that the breach would occur in the future (s.108B). However, apart from the statutory specified actions, the member's right to enforce the rule book is a negative one and the member may only obtain a declaration stating that the rule has been broken rather than restraining a breach or compelling the union to observe it. This is well illustrated by the case of *Taylor* v. *NUM (Yorkshire Area)* [1984] IRLR 445. Although this case has now been superseded by the statutory requirements concerning balloting before industrial action (s.226 Trade Union and Labour Relations (Consolidation) Act 1992) the principle is important. The case arose out of the national miners' strike of 1984–85. Under the national union rules, a national strike could not be called without a ballot which obtained a 55 per cent majority vote in favour of such a strike. This rule was reiterated in the rules of each of the area unions. Taylor challenged the strike because there had been no national ballot. In relation to the Yorkshire branch there had been a ballot, but this had been held in 1981, although there was a vote in favour of a strike with a 85.6 per cent majority. The court held that the union's argument that the strike was a series of local strikes rather than a national strike was arguable. Even if that was the case, however, the ballot in 1981 in Yorkshire was too distant from the strike to authorise it and as such the strike was *ultra vires*. Taylor's remedy, on the other hand, was a declaration that the strike was unofficial; he could not obtain an injunction to prevent the strike continuing or insist that a proper ballot was conducted. Nicholas J held that a member's right under the rules was confined to being able to insist that a strike could not be lawfully held without the requisite ballot. In other words, the best a member can do is restrain *ultra vires* behaviour, not enforce the union to act *intra vires*.

Enforcement of the rules is further complicated by the introduction of company law concepts in this area. We have already mentioned in Chapter 12 that the rule in *Foss* v. *Harbottle*, on occasions, has been applied to unions. In simple terms, the rule states that if a breach of the rules controlling the organisation is really a wrong done to the organisation, only the organisation can sue. It therefore follows that if the wrongful act is capable of ratification, the individual member may have no action because the majority can override his wishes by ratifying the act. To prevent useless actions being taken against companies, therefore, the rule has developed that if the action is capable of ratification the individual loses his right of action whether it is ratified or not, unless there is a fraud on the minority members. By applying this rule to trade unions (unincorporated associations, remember) the individual trade union member may therefore be deprived of his right to challenge a breach if the court feels that, for example, the union had the power to do the act but performed it in an irregular way. A contrast with *Taylor* (above) is *Cotter* v. *NUS* [1929] 2 Ch 58 when an official challenged a resolution made by a Special General Meeting to make an interest-free loan to the Miners' Non-Political Movement. The basis of the challenge was that the delegates at the meeting had not been properly elected and the meeting had not been properly convened in accordance with the union rules. The Court of Appeal held that, given that such a loan could be made by such a meeting, the irregularities were minor and the loan was capable of ratification. As such, the member was prevented from challenging the loan by *Foss* v. *Harbottle*. On the other hand, if the union had no power to act in the first place, for example by calling a strike without first holding a ballot, the union has no power to call a strike and hence that act can never be ratified. It therefore follows that the rule in *Foss* v. *Harbottle* cannot apply and the member may take action, although his remedy may be limited. While the proposition may be easy to state it is far from easy to apply in practice and, although the rule in *Foss* v. *Harbottle* has only been applied infrequently to unions, the fact that it has been applied to unincorporated associations at all has been the subject of criticism.

13.3 Exclusion and Expulsion

We have already seen in Chapter 12 that essentially a trade union cannot legally enforce a closed shop and therefore it may appear that any discussion on exclusion and expulsion may be redundant. Closed shops still exist, however, in certain industries and whereas the employee may have a remedy against the employer for refusing to employ him because he is not a trade union member, that will not help him if the reason he is not such a member is that the union do not want him or have expelled him, particularly as other rights arise from trade union membership. In addition, there may be other reasons why a member is excluded or expelled, such as non-membership of a trade. While the principle of freedom of association is well-established and protects those who are union members, the question arises as to how far the law can intervene when an employee wishes to associate with a union which does not want to associate with him. Article 8(a) of the International Covenant on Economic, Social and Cultural Rights states that the freedom to join an association is subject to the rules of the association and the European Court of Human Rights in *Cheall* v. *United Kingdom* [1986] 8 EHRR 74 held that an expulsion did not infringe Article 11 of the European Convention for the Protection of Human Rights and Fundamental Freedoms (giving the right of freedom of association with others including the right to form and join a trade union) if the expulsion was conducted to comply with the Bridlington Agreement. Thus it appears that the organisation itself can regulate its membership.

You may feel that this should be the case, particularly when a union is a voluntary organisation. This ignores the fact, however, that unions are very powerful both politically and economically, and this is a fact which has not escaped the notice of the courts. The problem in this area is that the member is complaining that the union will not enter a contract with him rather than the more normal complaint that a contract has been broken. He is not complaining that he is deprived of a right but rather the complaint is that he has lost the chance of acquiring a right and, until fairly recently, such a complaint had no legal remedy in the English courts. The Court of Appeal, however, and Lord Denning in particular, has suggested that a right to work exists which may be infringed by exclusion or expulsion from a union.

(Discussion of whether there is a duty to provide work to enforce this right has already been given in Chapter 4.)

Lord Denning began to establish that a right to work may exist in the case of *Nagle* v. *Fielden* [1966] 2 QB 633. In the case the plaintiff, a woman, complained that she had been refused a trainer's licence by the Jockey Club because she was a woman. The importance of the licence lay in the fact that no horse could be entered for a race unless the trainer had a licence and Mrs Nagle's head-lad had to obtain the licence in his name. Lord Denning opined that given that the Jockey Club operated a monopoly, in that it was the only body to grant licences, and given that without a licence Mrs Nagle could not carry out her living of racing horses, a rule the operation of which unreasonably prevented Mrs Nagle from obtaining a licence was in restraint of trade and void. While the other judges did not go so far, they were prepared to concede that the point was arguable.

While the association in *Nagle* was not a trade union, it was operating a monopoly and it was not long before Denning used the analogy in a closed-shop situation. In *Edwards* v. *SOGAT* [1971] Ch 354, a case involving expulsion from a trade union, Denning said that he did not feel that a trade union could give itself an unfettered discretion to expel or exclude a member. He continued: 'The reason lies in a man's right to work . . . The courts . . . will not allow so great a power to be exercised arbitrarily or capriciously or with unfair discrimination, neither in the making of rules nor in the enforcement of them.' While the idea of a right to work may be questionable, the comments help to explain the reasoning for Denning's judgement. He decided that the union could not rely on its immunity from restraint-of-trade claims because the union's action destroyed the right of an individual to earn his living and so was *ultra vires*. Whereas a rule of a union cannot be unenforceable by the reason only that it is restraint of trade (s.11 Trade Union and Labour Relations (Consolidation) Act 1992) Denning's comments that a union cannot exercise its rules arbitrarily or capriciously have been adopted by statute. Originally, s.65 Industrial Relations Act 1971 made it unlawful to exclude 'by arbitrary or unreasonable discrimination' a worker from a trade union. When that provision was repealed in 1976, the TUC set up its own Independent Review Committee to hear complaints from people about exclusion or expulsion from unions who were members of the TUC. The government which came to power in 1979 was not happy with this self-regulation and in the Employment Act 1980 introduced the right not to be excluded or expelled from a trade union unless a person does not satisfy the membership requirements, he no longer qualifies on geographical grounds, he is no longer employed by a relevant employer, or the expulsion or exclusion is entirely attributable to his conduct. Protection is now found in s.174 of the 1992 Act as amended by the Employment Relations Act 2004.

By s.174(2)(d) a union can expel or exclude where it is entirely attributable to conduct and the conduct is neither excluded conduct nor protected conduct. There are no rights to expel or exclude where it is to any extent related to excluded conduct but there are limited rights to expel or exclude where such is attributable to some extent to protected conduct. However, s.174(4) (as amended by the Employment Relations Act 2004) specifies that excluded conduct is:

(a) current or former membership of a trade union;
(b) current or former employment by a particular employer or at a particular place; or
(c) conduct for which disciplinary action taken by a union would be regarded as unjustifiable (see below).

Protected conduct is found in s.174(4A) and is defined as being or ceasing to be, or having been or ceased to be, a member of a political party. Political activities of any kind are not protected conduct (s.174(4B)).

The relationship between s.174 and the European Convention on Human Rights was tested in the recent case of *ASLEF* v. *UK* [2007] IRLR 361 (ECHR). Lee, a train driver, joined ASLEF in 2002 and a few months later stood as a BNP (formerly the National Front) candidate in local elections. ASLEF had a formal policy to 'campaign vigorously to expose the obnoxious policies of political parties such as the National Front' and expelled Lee from membership. However, because of s.174 ASLEF was forced to take him back or face a huge compensation claim. ASLEF considered this to be a breach of Article 11 of the Convention which provides that the right to form and join a trade union can be subject to such restrictions 'as are necessary in a democratic society in the interests of national security or public safety, for the prevention of disorder or crime, for the protection of health or morals or for the protection of the rights and freedoms of others'. ASLEF claimed that s.174 was a breach of Article 11 and the European Court of Human Rights agreed. The Court held that forcing a private body to accept Lee as a member was an infringement of Article 11. The UK government was ordered to pay ASLEF's costs. Whether the case will lead to an amendment to s.174 has yet to be seen.

A claimant has the right to go to an employment tribunal and, if the complaint is well-founded, the tribunal may make a declaration and an award of compensation which, although it is based on unfair dismissal figures, exceeds the statutory maximum imposed in unfair dismissal cases (s.176(6)). Where a declaration is made, a tribunal must state the ground (that is, protected or excluded conduct) and a tribunal must also make a declaration if the breach of s.174 is because of conduct which is contrary to the rules of the union (ss.176(1A, 1B, 1C and 1D)). A tribunal must award the statutory minimum of, at present, £6,100 where, at the time of the decision, the claimant had not been admitted or re-admitted into the union. But the minimum does not apply where the tribunal has issued a declaration that the exclusion or expulsion was for excluded or protected conduct (ss.176(6A and 6B)). Compensation can be reduced for contributory conduct. An appeal lies to the Employment Appeal Tribunal.

An expulsion where there is no right to expel in the circumstances will be *ultra vires* and the tribunal will grant the complainant a remedy (*Bonsor* v. *Musicians' Union* [1956] AC 104) and likewise the refusal of an appeal where one is granted by the rules will render the expulsion invalid (*Braithwaite* v. *Electrical, Electronics and Telecommunications Union* [1969] 2 All ER 859). In addition, if the rules are vague, the courts will place their own interpretation upon them. In *Kelly* v. *NATSOPA* (1915) 84 LJKB 2236 the court held that an expulsion based on a rule which allowed such action if the member was guilty of conduct prejudicial to the union's interests had been misapplied when the union expelled the plaintiff when he obtained a part-time job. By contrast, in *Evans* v. *National Union of Bookbinding and Printing Workers* [1938] 4 All ER 51 the rules provided for expulsion of a member who acted contrary to the interests of the union. Evans was absent from work on a number of occasions contrary to an agreement between the union and employers. It was held that his expulsion was a valid exercise of the union's power under the rules.

While the above cases are examples of the common law rather than statute operating, the principles are the same when applying the statutory provisions. Furthermore, when dealing with exclusion cases, the Employment Appeal Tribunal has stated that the provisions should not be read in a restrictive way. In *Clark* v. *NATSOPA (SOGAT'82)* [1986] ICR 12 Clark had taken voluntary redundancy from the printing industry in 1976 as part of an agreement to reduce overmanning in the industry. Part of the agreement was that he should not seek work in the printing industry in the United Kingdom. Some years later, he wished to work again in the printing industry and tried to rejoin the union. His application was rejected and he complained that he had been unreasonably excluded. The union argued that as he had not applied for a job which required union membership he had no cause of action. The Employment Appeal Tribunal disagreed. It was sufficient that a person was seeking employment generally to invoke the protection. The complainant did not have to show that the exclusion had lost him a job before he could sue.

13.4 Discipline of Union Members

Although expulsion from the union may be imposed as a disciplinary sanction, it is not the only form of sanction imposed by a union on its members. As such, the court's powers are wide enough to control a union's use of its power when the sanction is something other than expulsion. The main form of control exercised by the courts is that the union must comply with the rules of natural justice. While these rules are normally applied to judicial or quasi-judicial bodies, it has been clear since *Lee* v. *Showman's Guild of Great Britain* [1952] 2 QB 329 that trade unions must abide by the rules when making decisions in relation to their members. Lord Denning stated in *Breen* v. *AEU* [1971] 2 QB 175 that although a union hearing was operating in an administrative way, it must still act fairly and the courts had the power to issue declarations and injunctions to enforce fair treatment. The rules of natural justice involve four elements:

1. *Notice* A person must be given adequate notice of the charge against him and the potential penalty so that he has an opportunity to answer it. In *Annamunthodo* v. *Oilfield Workers Union* [1961] AC 954 the plaintiff knew that he was charged with making allegations against the union president and knew he could be fined. He did not know that such conduct was treated as prejudicial to the union and that he could be expelled. It was held that his subsequent expulsion was void.
2. *Opportunity to put his case* A person must be given the opportunity to put his side of the case and to answer the charges against him.
3. *Unbiased hearing* The hearing should be unbiased. This is probably easier to state in theory than operate in practice as often the members of the hearing who are judging, for example, prejudicial conduct are union officials. Although the rule is stringently adhered to in judicial hearings, it is modified in the case of domestic tribunals and as long as there is no obvious bias, for example a person involved in the dispute is also involved in the hearing, the rule will not be offended. In *White* v. *Kuzych* [1951] AC 585 the plaintiff was expelled from the union because of his opposition to the closed-shop policy that the union had adopted. The fact that those who were involved in the hearing had spoken in support of the policy did not render the decision void for bias. On the other hand, in *Roebuck* v. *NUM (Yorkshire Area) (No. 2)* [1978] ICR 676 two union officials had given evidence to a newspaper in a libel action taken by the union president Arthur Scargill on behalf of the union. Mr Scargill presided over the hearing which recommended that the two officials be suspended from office for conduct prejudicial to the union, and then chaired the area council meeting which, not surprisingly, confirmed that decision. It was held that the suspensions were void. Mr Scargill had in reality been the complainant and had made up his mind on the matter before the first hearing commenced, let alone the second. So too in *Taylor* v. *NUS* [1967] 1 WLR 532 the union's general secretary dismissed an

official and then chaired the appeal against the dismissal. It was held that
the decision to dismiss was void.

4. *Representation*   The rules do not specifically state that a person should be
allowed legal representation and it appears from *Enderby Town Football
Club* v. *Football Association* [1971] Ch 591 that such representation can be
specifically excluded by the rules as long as some kind of representative
is allowed.

While the rules are the basis of the contract of membership between the
union and its members and as such the courts do not like to interfere in that
contract, a rule ousting the jurisdiction of the court is void. This was the
position at common law and it is now s.63(1) of the 1992 Act. A rule which
purports to postpone a member from seeking a remedy in the courts until
internal procedures have been exhausted is not void under this provision,
but by subsection (2) such a rule will be ignored by the court if a member
has asked for the matter to be dealt with by the union and six months after
such application the union has not completed the internal procedures.

In addition to the common law controlling the conduct of disciplinary
hearings and the statutory provision preventing the rules from ousting the
courts' jurisdiction, statute has further provided a right for all trade union
members not to be unjustifiably disciplined. The original right was
introduced by the Employment Act 1988 and is now contained in ss.65–67
Trade Union and Labour Relations (Consolidation) Act 1992. Section 64
lists the sanctions which are defined as discipline and includes expulsion,
fines, refusal of access to benefits or any other detriment. Section 65 then
defines what is meant by 'unjustifiably' which includes: failing to
participate in industrial action, failing to contravene a provision in the
contract of employment, asserting breaches of the legislation by an official
or union representative unless that allegation was made in bad faith,
making representations to the Certification Officer and encouraging a
person to perform their contract of employment contrary to union
instructions. In addition, five other paragraphs were inserted by the Trade
Union Reform and Employment Rights Act 1993 which are now
ss.65(2)(f)–(j). These additional grounds are: failing to agree or withdrawing
agreement to deduction from wages of union fees, resigning or proposing
to resign membership or proposing to join or refuse to join another union,
working with non-union members, working for an employer who employs
non-union labour and requiring the union to perform an act which by
statute it must perform on the requisition of a member. If the action
complained of is an exclusion or expulsion under s.174 and the reason is a
breach of s.65, the expulsion or exclusion is automatically unreasonable
(s.66(4)).

A breach of the provisions allows a member to complain to the employment tribunal which may make a declaration and award compensation. The amount of compensation is the same as that awarded under s.176 (that is, 30 times the maximum weekly pay in the basic award for unfair dismissal plus the maximum compensatory award, with a statutory minimum). The Employment Appeal Tribunal has held in *NALGO* v. *Courtney-Dunn* [1991] IRLR 114 that if a member is successful in obtaining a declaration and compensation, the union must put him in the position he was in before the unjustifiable discipline was imposed. The compensation awarded should, however, reflect the actual loss sustained by the member and not be punitive. In *Bradley* v. *NALGO* [1991] IRLR 159 the complainant was expelled for failing to take part in industrial action and claimed compensation. The union did not contest the declaration nor did it revoke the expulsion. The Employment Appeal Tribunal awarded the minimum award only. The expulsion did not affect his job prospects and would not affect his joining another union.

13.5 The Certification Officer

The office of the Commissioner for the Rights of Trade Union Members was created by the Employment Act 1988 as a body to give assistance to trade union members who wished to take action against their union for infringement of certain statutory rights. The post was abolished by the Employment Relations Act 1999 and jurisdiction over specified contractual matters passed to the Certification Officer. The Certification Officer can give assistance to an individual member to enforce certain rights discussed above and in Chapter 12. The provisions are now in the 1992 Act. The Commissioner may now give assistance in the following matters:

(a) failure to hold a ballot before industrial action;
(b) failure to permit members to inspect union accounts;
(c) unlawful application of union property by trustees;
(d) failure to maintain a register of members;
(e) failure to comply with balloting provisions in relation to the political fund;
(f) failure to bring or continue proceedings to recover property used to unlawfully indemnify an individual;
(g) failure to comply with the balloting provisions in relation to trade union elections;
(h) application of union funds for unlawful political purposes;
(i) alleged breaches of union rules in relation to appointment to any office, disciplinary proceedings, authorisation or endorsement of industrial

action, balloting, the application of the union's funds or property, the imposition or collection of levies for industrial action purposes and the constitution or proceedings of any committee, conference or body of the union (s.109 Trade Union and Labour Relations (Consolidation) Act 1992).

'Assistance' includes the funding of the costs of legal advice and representation, but these funds are recoverable where costs are awarded to the member (s.111). In deciding whether to grant assistance, the Commissioner must have regard to whether the case involves a matter of principle, whether it is reasonable for the applicant to deal with it unaided and whether it involves a matter of substantial public interest (s.110).

13.6 Action Short of Dismissal

So far this chapter has dealt with the rights of individual members against the union, but the law also affords a certain amount of protection against an employer. We have already seen in Chapter 9 that the law will protect an employee who is dismissed for trade union membership or non-membership or for taking part in trade union activities at the appropriate time. Protection against dismissal, however, is complemented by protection against action short of dismissal for one of the above grounds and is now found in s.146 Trade Union and Labour Relations (Consolidation) Act 1992. Should a tribunal find a complaint well-founded it can make a declaration to that effect and award compensation to offset any loss caused by the action (s.149(2)). In addition, either the complainant or the employer may join the union as a co-respondent if it was union pressure which induced the action, and the tribunal can order that some or all of the compensation be paid by the union (ss.150 (1) and (3)).

The original provisions were contained in the Employment Protection (Consolidation) Act 1978 and under that legislation, refusal to grant a benefit on these grounds was action short of dismissal for the purposes of protection. In *NCB* v. *Ridgway* [1987] ICR 736 it was held that refusal to give a pay rise negotiated with the UDM to NUM members was unlawful action short of dismissal. In other words, it is sufficient if the employer discriminates against members of a particular union and it is not necessary to show discrimination against union members as a whole. Whether there is protection against threats, however, is more in doubt. The Employment Appeal Tribunal in *Brassington* v. *Cauldron Wholesale Ltd* [1978] ICR 405 stated *obiter* that it felt that the threat to close down a factory, sack the workforce and open under a different name if the workers joined a union was not sufficient to be caught by the statute.

Despite earlier interpretations, the provisions on action short of dismissal came under scrutiny in a number of cases. In *Associated British Ports* v. *Palmer* and *Associated Newspapers Ltd* v. *Wilson* [1995] IRLR 258 an action arose in both cases as a result of 'sweeteners' paid to employees who agreed to give up their rights to have their wages determined collectively and to switch to individual contracts. The converse obviously applied, that is, those who still wished to have their wages collectively negotiated did not receive these payments. As such, the question in both cases was whether such payments were contrary to s.146 of the 1992 Act. The Employment Appeal Tribunal held in both cases that there was no breach of s.146 because it was not shown that the employer had the purpose of 'preventing or deterring [an employee] from being or seeking to become a member of an independent trade union, or penalising him for doing so' (s.146(1)). The Court of Appeal, however, decided that the necessary purpose was shown, that is, the purpose of the payments was to persuade employees to abandon their trade union representation and deter them from trade union membership. These cases went against the then government's stated policy of encouraging the development of individual contracts and, as such, the Trade Union Reform and Employment Rights Act 1993 amended s.148 by providing that such conduct is not action short of dismissal if it is intended to further a change in the employers' relationship with any class of employee, unless it is action that no reasonable employer would do. After this amendment, the House of Lords reversed the decisions in *Palmer* and *Wilson* and further restricted any protection by holding that action short of dismissal envisaged a positive act on the part of the employer and did not include an omission to act (for example, by not giving a pay rise). As such, the employers' conduct did not amount to action short of dismissal for the purposes of s.146. Wilson and Palmer took their case to the European Court of Human Rights and that court gave its decision. The court ruled ([2002] IRLR 568) that the UK was in breach of Article 11 of the European Convention on Human Rights by permitting employers to use financial incentives to persuade employees to relinquish their rights to trade union representation for collective bargaining purposes. The court said: 'It is the essence of the right (under Article 11) that employees should be free to instruct or permit the union to make representations to their employer. If workers are prevented from so doing the freedom to belong to a trade union becomes illusory.' While the Employment Relations Act 1999 overturned the House of Lords' decisions, the government felt that the amendments did not cover the judgement in *Wilson* and *Palmer* and the Employment Relations Act 2004 introduced further protection as discussed below.

Gallacher v. *Department of Transport* [1994] IRLR 231 was another case involving s.146. In this case, the applicant was a civil servant who was elected to a full-time union post in 1986. Until 1990 he had no management functions and was not fully under the staff appraisal system. In 1990 he applied for promotion but was rejected because there were doubts as to his management capabilities after a four-year gap. He was told that he would need more management experience which would mean a reduction in his union activities. The employment tribunal upheld the complaint of detriment but the Employment Appeal Tribunal held that the tribunal had erred in making that decision because it had failed to consider what 'action' had been taken and what the 'purpose' was behind it. The Court of Appeal upheld the decision.

In order to pursue a claim under s.146 the employee must be subjected to a detriment as an individual and therefore action taken against the union is not covered, although action taken against a group who are members of the union could be covered if it affects them as individuals. Cases like *Gallacher*, *Palmer* and *Wilson*, however, show a difficulty in the provision in that in order for a claim to be successful, the act or failure to act on the part of the employer must be for the purpose of preventing or deterring the employee from union membership or activities. Thus, in *Gallacher*, the purpose of not promoting him was not to deter him from trade union activities even though the effect was precisely that. This may now be subject to the later decision of *London Borough of Southwark* v. *Whiller* [2001] EWCA Civ 808 where the employer offered a promotion to a union official, but on the basis that she would only receive the higher rate of pay applicable to the grade when she was able to undertake the duties of the grade. The Court of Appeal held that the tribunal was entitled to conclude that the purpose of the employer was to deter her from union activities.

Given the problems with s.146, and the *Wilson* and *Palmer* decision, the Employment Relations Act 2004 inserted new sections 145A to F into the 1992 Act. Section 145A gives a worker the right not to have an offer made to him by his employer where the employer's sole or main purpose is to induce the worker not to be or seek to be a member of an independent trade union; not to take part in the activities of an independent trade union at an appropriate time; not to make use of the services of a trade union at an appropriate time and to be or become a member of a trade union. Section 145B gives a right to a worker who is a member of an independent union seeking recognition or recognised by the employer, not to have an offer made to him, where similar offers are being made to other workers, the sole or main purpose of which is to secure that the terms of the workers will no longer be determined by collective agreement. These new sections mean that, along with s.146, workers are now protected against detriment and inducement.

In addition to existing statutory protection, it has been seen above that the Human Rights Act 1998 impacts on this area. As noted in Chapter 12, in *Young, James and Webster* v. *United Kingdom* [1983] IRLR 35 (a case under the now repealed closed-shop provisions) the European Court of Human Rights ruled that legislation which allowed for compulsory membership of a particular union was an infringement of Article 11 as it restricted the right of an individual to join a union of their choice, and in *Ahmed* v. *UK* [1999] IRLR 188 the same court held that the threats of disciplinary action would also constitute an interference with the right to join a trade union and freedom of expression. The decision in *Wilson* and *Palmer* adds to this list of actions which constitute an infringement of Article 11.

Summary

1. The rule book forms the contract of membership between the trade union member and the union.

2. Enforcement of the rule book by a member is governed by the common law and not by statute.

3. The remedy for a member where a breach of the rules is alleged is the restraint of *ultra vires* behaviour. A member cannot force a union to act *intra vires*.

4. The rule in *Foss* v. *Harbottle*, which comes from company law, on occasions has been applied to trade unions.

5. *Foss* v. *Harbottle* can never be applied when the union acts *ultra vires*.

6. Statute provides individual members with a right not to be excluded or expelled from a union.

7. The common law rules of natural justice apply to trade unions and if they are breached, the decision is void.

8. Statute has also created a right for trade union members not to be unjustifiably disciplined by their union.

9. In addition to giving protection from dismissal on the grounds of non-membership of a trade union or union membership or activities, statute protects employees who have had action short of dismissal taken against them on these grounds.

Exercises

1. Do you consider that the rule in *Foss* v. *Harbottle* can legitimately be invoked against a trade union member and if not, why not?

2. The Domestic Bus Company was involved in a dispute with the Travel Union over proposed redundancies. The union had concluded a union membership agreement with the company which covered drivers only. The union decided

Exercises cont'd

to take industrial action and held a ballot of its members. A majority of 79 per
cent voted in favour of industrial action. The union then called on all its
members to strike, despite the fact that the union rule book stipulated in Rule
84 that 'all negotiating procedures should be exhausted before industrial
action is taken on any issue'. In a collective agreement concluded the
previous year between the company and the union, three distinct stages were
spelt out in a 'Grievance Procedure'. In this instance, only the first stage of
the procedure had been completed before industrial action was taken. Fred, a
conductor, was expelled from the union for failing to obey the union's
instructions to strike under Rule 9 which stated that: 'Any union member
acting contrary to the interests of the union is liable to expulsion.' He was
informed that the local committee had met and, after considering his refusal,
had decided to expel him.

Jim, another union member, wishes to challenge the Travel Union in
respect of two payments made from the union's general fund. One was a
payment of £10,000 to a strike committee to support pickets, where no rule
specifically authorised such payment, and the second was a payment of
£5,000 to support the 'Troops Out of Afghanistan' movement's meetings. The
union's political fund rules authorised funds to be made generally available
for political purposes.

Advise Fred and Jim.

Further Reading

Trade Unions and Their Members, Cmnd. 95 (1987).

Removing the Barriers to Employment, Cmnd. 655 (1989).

Bogg   *Employment Relations Act 2004: Another False Dawn for Collectivism?* (2005)
34 ILJ 72.

Corby   *Limitations on Freedom of Association in the Civil Service and the ILO's
Response* (1986) 15 ILJ 161.

Ewing   *The Implications of Wilson and Palmer* (2003) 32 ILJ 1.

Hendy and Ewing   *Trade Unions, Human Rights and the BNP* (2005) 34 ILJ 197.

Kidner   *Unjustified Discipline by a Trade Union* (1991) 20 ILJ 284.

Mead   *To BNP Or Not to BNP: Union Expulsion on the Ground of Political Activity –
A Commentary on ASLEF v. Lee* (2004) 33 ILJ 267.

Morris   *Fundamental Rights: Exclusion by Agreement?* (2001) 30 ILJ 49.

Wedderburn   *Freedom of Association and Philosophies of Labour Law* (1989) 18 ILJ
1.

Chapter 14

Industrial Action

Introduction

Since the growth of trade unionism after the Industrial Revolution, the strength of the employee has been in his freedom to associate with fellow employees and to negotiate collectively with the employer. This may seem to be a bold statement at first sight but its basis is the fundamentals of industrial relations. An employer has economic strength when compared to an employee. He has the job and if the employee does not comply with the employer's wishes then, unless the law prevents it, the employer can easily replace him. Any protest by the individual employee is unlikely to have much effect. If the employee, however, is one of a large group, all of whom protest against the employer, then the impact will be much greater and the possibility of such a protest could keep the employer from making unreasonable demands. Thus, simplistically, the power of employees to organise balances the economic power of the employer. This power to organise, however, is only half of the story. The body of workers must be able to protest in a way which will be effective and which will persuade the employer to see their point of view. Hence, industrial action in one form or another, be it a go-slow, a work-to-rule or ultimately a strike, gives the body of workers bargaining power. It is therefore the power to organise plus the power to take industrial action that is the balance to the employer's economic power. Good industrial relations policy tries to achieve an equal balance of power. Too much power on the part of the unions will shift the balance in their favour, too little power on the part of the unions will shift the balance the other way and increase the strength of the employer.

We have seen already in Chapter 12 that unions in the UK did not have a political base until the early part of the twentieth century and so were dependent upon political parties which did not consist of workers to support and help them. This fact, coupled with the fear in the UK caused by revolutions in Europe, led to protection for unions being developed in a strange way. In most European countries, workers have rights to take industrial action which are protected by a written constitution. In the UK, the law developed a series of immunities rather than rights. In other words, all industrial action will break the law, either civil or criminal, but the law gives immunity from civil liability in certain situations. This system of immunities has two important consequences. First, a right enshrined in a written constitution cannot easily be taken away once granted. On the other hand, an immunity can be widened or narrowed by merely redefining the situations where it will apply. To give an example, a union and its members have immunity when taking industrial action if they are acting in contemplation or furtherance of a trade dispute – the so-called 'golden formula'. In 1974 the definition of a trade dispute covered disputes between employers and workers, and workers and workers. In 1982 the definition was altered to a dispute between workers and their employer. By removing four words and inserting the word 'their' into the first part of this definition, immunity was removed from tertiary action, most forms of secondary action and inter-union disputes.

The second important consequence of immunities is that they create no rights. The media often talk about the right to strike but jurisprudentially this is wrong. If a person has a right to do something, there must be a corresponding duty on the part of someone else to allow that person to exercise their right. If someone has a right of way over my property, I have a legal duty to allow them to exercise that right and I can be sued if I refuse to do so. The law will protect the right. In the area of industrial action no such protection of rights exists. We will see below, for example, that while union members may peacefully picket their own place of work if it is in contemplation or furtherance of a trade dispute, and have immunity from civil liability if they commit any torts, the police can disperse pickets at any time if they fear a public order offence may be committed or they fear a breach of the peace. Thus the law only gives a freedom to picket which can be exercised at the discretion of the police.

The present law on industrial action has had a chequered history. For many years the law was, to a large extent, non-interventionist in this area. The main piece of legislation governing industrial action was the Trade Disputes Act 1906 which created the basic immunities, defined the golden formula and gave trade unions total immunity from civil liability in all situations. Apart from the odd statute to overrule judicial decisions which increased liability, the law kept out of industrial relations.

Change in this policy came with the Conservative government of the early 1970s. Despite the recommendations of the Donovan Report the government decided to alter the policy of non-intervention in this area at one fell swoop, with the introduction of the Industrial Relations Act 1971. We have seen already in Chapter 12 that this Act introduced a system of registration for trade unions and it was only by such registration that unions kept the immunity they had until then enjoyed. In addition, the Act attacked the closed shop which had been the basis of union strength for so long and introduced new concepts such as 'unfair industrial practices' and 'cooling off' provisions. In short, overnight the Act tried to alter totally the system of industrial relations which had been in force for most of the century.

The result of this and the consequent demise of the government are best recorded in history books. It is sufficient to say here that the unions at the time were very strong and the policy of non-cooperation they adopted did much to aid the government's downfall. The Labour government which came into power repealed the Act by the Trade Union and Labour Relations Act 1974 (amended in 1976) and tried to restore labour relations to their pre-1971 position. Conflict with the unions culminating in the 'winter of discontent' in 1979 meant the return of the Conservative government in that year.

That government had learned from its mistakes in the 1970s and so set about reforming the law by a 'softly, softly' approach. In other words, rather than introducing a one-off piece of legislation changing everything overnight, the government reformed step by step. This is evidenced by the amount of legislation it passed during its time in office – ten Acts of Parliament in 18 years. In addition to the approach, the policy basis of the legislation changed. It has already been stated that a good industrial relations policy should seek to balance the power between both sides. The Conservatives argued that this was their aim in 1971, when, alarmed by the growing number of strikes, they felt that the power had shifted too far into the lap of the unions. The 1979–97 government, however, had a totally different rationale behind its industrial relations policy. It saw employment legislation as part of a broader economic policy. That policy was one of market forces, that is, the market should be free to conduct itself. Legislation was needed, therefore, to remove obstacles to the market. Unions distort the market because, when strong, they can demand high wage rises and cause financial loss to an employer by taking industrial action. The costs caused by this are therefore put on to goods, so making Britain less competitive in the marketplace. Reduce the power of the unions and you remove one of the major obstacles to competitiveness.

This discussion is necessary to understand the law in this chapter and elsewhere. Increasing continuity periods for unfair dismissal, for example, was another way of increasing competitiveness by allowing an employer to dismiss more people without incurring the expense of legal compensation. Curbing the situations where a union's funds will be protected when it takes industrial action is another, so too is preventing a union from enforcing a closed shop. This policy, however, means that the balance of power is ignored because the policy predicates that the employer must have the greatest power. Many would argue that by the time the Trade Union Act 1984 was passed, the law was in the same position as in 1971. Since then the law went much further than the Industrial Relations Act. Many felt that the law had gone too far and indeed both the Confederation of British Industry and the Institute of Personnel Management felt that the Trade Union Reform and Employment Rights Act 1993 was unnecessary. The present Labour government which was elected in 1997 has enacted a number of legislative provisions introducing rights at an individual level, discussed elsewhere in this text. While the government introduced some collective provisions in the Employment Relations Acts, most particularly recognition rights, it has not yet indicated an intention to repeal much of the legislation brought in by the previous administration.

14.2 Industrial Action and the Contract of Employment

Virtually all forms of industrial action will constitute a breach of contract on the part of the employee. While often when talking of industrial action it is assumed that this means a strike, striking is only one type of industrial action and it will be useful at the outset to look at the common forms of industrial action and their effect on the contract of employment.

Go-slow

A go-slow is a breach of an implied term to work at a reasonable pace in the absence of justifying circumstances. In *General Engineering Services Ltd* v. *Kingston & St Andrew's Corporation* [1989] IRLR 35, a case on vicarious liability, the Privy Council held that fire officers operating a go-slow were not acting within the course of their employment. The go-slow was an unlawful act which repudiated their contracts of employment.

Work-to-rule

Prior to 1972 it was thought that such action could not constitute a breach of contract because the employee was merely doing what he was legally obliged to do, that is, carrying out instructions to the letter. However, the leading case of *Secretary of State for Employment* v. *ASLEF (No. 2)* [1972] 2 QB 455 decided that such action could constitute a breach of contract. The facts of the case have been discussed in Chapter 4. The reasons why the Court of Appeal held that was a breach of contract are important for our discussion here. First, the rule book which the employees were following was merely instructions from the employer and not terms of the contract. As such, they could be unilaterally altered by the employer. Second, the employees were in breach of an implied duty not to interpret orders in an unreasonable manner. Third, one of the rules stated that they should prevent avoidable delay, so the action was a breach of this rule and, finally, if the intention of the work-to-rule was to disrupt the employer's business, this made the action a breach of contract. Whichever reason is adopted, it would appear that any work-to-rule will result in breach and this is further supported by the later case of *Ticehurst* v. *British Telecommunications plc* (see Chapter 4).

Overtime ban

Whether this action constitutes a breach of contract depends on whether the overtime is compulsory or voluntary and involves looking at the terms of the contract itself. Even if there is no express term relating to overtime, there may be an implied term based on past practice. If the term talks of 'reasonable overtime' the courts will interpret the term 'reasonable'. In *NCB* v. *Galley* [1958] 1 WLR 16 the employee was required to do reasonable overtime and refused to work on Saturday mornings. It was held that he was in breach of contract. Even if overtime is purely voluntary, it is arguable that there may still be a breach of contract. *ASLEF* (above) shows that if the effect of the action is a disruption of the employer's business, a breach will have occurred. *ASLEF* also introduces the concept of intention so that a lawful act may become unlawful if the intention behind that act is unlawful (that is, a breach of contract). While the Court of Appeal in *Ticehurst* left open the issue of whether an act which did not disrupt the employer's business could be actionable, *ASLEF* seems to suggest, given the importance of intention, a ban on voluntary overtime which does not affect the employer's business will be actionable if the intention behind it was to so disrupt. However, in *Burgess* v. *Stevedoring Services Ltd* [2002] IRLR 810, a Privy Council case, Lord Hoffman said that intention alone would not make lawful conduct unlawful.

Blacking

Blacking may take a variety of forms. An employee may refuse to handle goods from a particular supplier or goods that are destined for a particular customer. If employees are instructed to handle such goods and refuse to do so, then they are refusing to obey a reasonable lawful order and are in breach of contract. Another form of blacking is refusing to work with particular employees, for example non-unionists. In *Bowes & Partners* v. *Press* [1894] 2 QB 202 miners refused an order to go down in a cage with a non-unionist. It was held that their refusal was a breach of contract.

Strike without notice

A strike is a situation where the employee is withdrawing his labour and refusing to work. As such, he is failing to perform his part of the work/wage bargain and therefore is committing a repudiatory breach.

Strike with notice

Traditionally the view is that if a strike takes place after due notice has been given, that is, the notice needed to terminate the contract, then the strike is legal (*Allen* v. *Flood* [1898] AC 1). This view means that the employee has effectively resigned. This, however, is not what the employee intends and the traditional view was questioned by Donovan LJ in *Rookes* v. *Barnard* [1964] 1 All ER 367 and Denning MR in *Stratford* v. *Lindley* [1965] AC 269. Both their Lordships considered that strike notice was, in fact, notice to break the contract of employment as the employees did not intend to terminate their contracts. While the traditional view may hold where the correct notice is given, a problem arises when the employee gives short notice or ambiguous notice. Does this constitute notice to terminate, notice to break the contract or notice to suspend the contract? If the notice is taken as notice to break the contract, it will amount to an anticipatory breach, the view taken by Lord Devlin in *Rookes* v. *Barnard* and by Lord Denning in *Stratford* v. *Lindley*. However, Lord Denning observed later in *Morgan* v. *Fry* [1968] 2 QB 710 that such a view would do away with the 'right to strike'. For this reason, in *Morgan* v. *Fry* Denning interpreted strike notice as notice to suspend the contract, focusing on the fact that there is no duty to pay wages during a strike. This was by no means the majority view in *Morgan*, however. Russell LJ considered strike notice to be notice of a breach of contract, Davies LJ thought it was notice to terminate and Denning MR thought it was notice to suspend. The Donovan Commission considered Denning's proposition but rejected it because of the difficulties which could arise from such an interpretation. For example, what happens if the strike never ends or if the employer dismisses the strikers? Despite this, the view that strike notice suspends the contract was adopted by the Industrial Relations Act 1971. After that Act was repealed, however, the view was rejected in *Simmons* v. *Hoover Ltd* [1977] QB 284 where the Employment Appeal Tribunal decided that a strike with or without proper contractual notice is a repudiatory breach on the part of the employee and the notice given is notice to break the contract, Phillips J stating that he did not think that *Morgan* v. *Fry* was intended to revolutionise the law in the area. Thus, the employer can choose to treat the repudiation as terminating the contract by dismissing the strikers, or can treat the contract as continuing. One other analysis is possible. This rests on the distinction between notice to terminate the contract, which is intended, and notice to terminate the employment, which is not. This was the view expressed by Davies LJ in *Morgan* v. *Fry* who saw strike notices as notice to terminate present contractual conditions coupled with an offer to work on new terms. This view can be questioned, however, since the House of Lords' decision in *Miles* v. *Wakefield Metropolitan District Council* [1987] IRLR 193 where their Lordships suggested that all industrial action is a repudiatory breach since there is an intention to harm the employer's business which goes fundamentally against the duty of loyalty and cooperation which the employee owes to the employer. If this view is correct and the intention behind the action is the test of legality, it would suggest that any strike notice, whether of correct length or not, is notice of a breach of contract and it will only be construed as notice to terminate if it is expressed to be so.

Fairness At Work considered that it is an anomaly that employees taking industrial action risk dismissal for a breach of their employment contracts, particularly as employees can lose the right to claim unfair dismissal in certain circumstances (Chapter 9). The government therefore reinstated protection against unfair dismissal for those involved in official industrial action by Schedule 5 Employment Relations Act 1999 (see Chapter 9).

14.3 Industrial Action and the Economic Torts

Inducement of a breach of contract

If a person induces or persuades a party to a contract to break that contract, the injured party may sue the inducer in tort for inducement of a breach of contract. For example, a trade union official persuading members to go on strike is inducing those members to break their contracts of employment, therefore the employer can take action in tort against the official. This form of inducement only involves the breach of one contract and is called a 'direct inducement' because the pressure is being exerted on the party who is in a contract with the person the inducer wishes to harm, in this case the employer. The tort is also committed if a person induces a party to break a commercial contract or a contract for services.

The tort of inducement first emerged in *Lumley* v. *Gye* (1853) 2 E&B 216. Gye, an impresario, induced an opera singer to break her contract with Lumley and sing for him for higher wages. The court found Gye liable as he had induced the breach of contract. Prior to the case, the only recourse was against the actual contract breaker. The principle was further extended in *Bowen* v. *Hall* (1881) 6 QBD 333 when the Court of Appeal held that it applied to inducement of breaches of all types of contract and not just breaches of contracts for personal services. In addition, *Allen* v. *Flood* [1898] AC 1 makes it clear that malice is not the essence of the tort. In *Thomson* v. *Deakin* [1952] Ch 646 Jenkins LJ stipulated the elements of the tort of inducement: the defendant knew of the existence of the contract and intended its breach; the defendant persuaded or procured employees to break their contracts with this intention; and the employees did break their contracts.

The requirements of the tort are therefore as follows:

Unlawful act

In order to be liable, the defendant must have induced an unlawful act. If the unlawful act is a breach of contract, the contract must exist and be valid in law at the time of the inducement (*Long* v. *Smithson* (1918) 118 LT 678). In recent years, however, liability has been extended to cover inducements of other unlawful acts. In *Cunard SS Co Ltd* v. *Stacey* [1955] 2 Lloyds Rep 247 the court granted an injunction preventing union officials from inducing seamen to break their duties under the Merchant Shipping Act 1894 (see also *Meade* v. *Haringey London Borough Council* [1979] 2 All ER 1016). Similarly, in *Prudential Assurance Co Ltd* v. *Lorenz* (1971) 11 KIR 78 a union instructed insurance agents to withhold payment of premiums that they had collected from their employer. It was held that the union was guilty of inducing breaches of contracts of employment and inducing breaches of the agents' fiduciary duties. Because it is necessary to induce an unlawful act, it therefore follows that if the inducement is to terminate the contract lawfully there can be no liability nor is there a tort of inducing a party not to enter a contract (*Midland Cold Storage* v. *Steer* [1972] Ch 630). This leaves the question, however: what if a breach would occur but for an exclusion clause? In other words, does the tort extend to interference with a contract rather than breach? Until 1969, it was clearly the case that an actual breach had to have occurred before the tort was committed, however in *Torquay Hotels Ltd* v. *Cousins* [1969] 2 Ch 106 the Court of Appeal extended the tort. In the case, the managing director of the Imperial Hotel at Torquay refused the TGWU recognition and as a result the union cut off oil supplies to the hotel by picketing and a series of strikes. The managing director told a reporter that the Hotel Association was determined to stamp out the TGWU's intervention in the hotel trade and the union reacted by placing pickets outside the hotel. Furthermore, a union official telephoned Esso, which supplied the hotel with oil, and informed them that an official dispute existed at the hotel and that the union would be calling on the delivery drivers, who were members of the TGWU, not to deliver the oil. In the hotel's contract with Esso, there was a *force majeure* clause, that is, a clause which exempted Esso from liability for breach if they were prevented from delivering because of an industrial dispute. All three members of the Court of Appeal held that the TGWU was guilty of the tort of inducement. Russell LJ and Winn LJ both stated that a breach had occurred and that the clause only prevented liability arising. Denning MR went further. He stated that despite the fact that there was no breach of contract, the tort was satisfied as there had been an interference with the performance of the contract. Despite this widening of the tort, there can be no liability if the act induced is not unlawful (*Patrick Stevedores Operation Pty Ltd* v. *ITWF* (1998) IDS Brief 613).

Knowledge

It is further necessary to show that the defendant knew that there was a contract between the parties and that he knew enough of its contents to realise that what he was doing involved the risk of its breach. It is unnecessary to prove that the defendant knew all of the terms of the contract, but if the inducement is to break one specific term, then knowledge of that term must be proved, although that knowledge may be implied. In *Bents Brewery* v. *Hogan* [1945] 2 All ER 570 a union official persuaded a brewery manager to obtain financial information about the company to aid the union in collective bargaining. This was a breach of the duty of fidelity implied into the contract of employment of the manager. It was held that as the official knew that the manager was an employee, he must have been aware of the duty of fidelity. This idea that the defendant must have known of the existence of the term has been developed through the cases. In *Stratford* v. *Lindley* [1965] AC 269 Lord Pearce stated that it seemed unlikely that the union would be ignorant of the commonplace terms that existed in a normal contract in the industry. In *Greig* v. *Insole* [1978] 1 WLR 302 Slade J stated that it would be sufficient to prove that the defendant knew of the existence of the contract, provided it was shown that the defendant intended the contract to be breached. Furthermore, if the defendant has deliberately turned a blind eye and disregarded the means of discovery, he will be deemed to have the requisite knowledge (see *Emerald Construction Ltd* v. *Lowthian* [1966] 1 All ER 1013 and *Merkur Island Shipping Co* v. *Laughton* [1983] IRLR 26).

Intention

Closely coupled with the requirement of knowledge is the need to intend to cause the breach. This means that the defendant must have foreseen the possibility of breach as well as wishing to achieve that end. If the defendant did not appreciate that there was a risk of breach, even though he knew a contract existed, there will be no liability. In *British Industrial Plastics Ltd* v. *Ferguson* [1938] 4 All ER 504 an employee left British Industrial Plastics and contacted a rival firm, telling it that he had knowledge of a particular moulding process. The rival thought that disclosure may be a breach of contract and told the ex-employee to get a patent before revealing the information, believing this would avoid the breach. It was held that there was no liability for inducement as the company honestly thought that they would not cause a breach of contract. Thus if the defendant intends that the contract be terminated lawfully, there is no liability. If, however, the defendant knew enough about the contract to realise that a breach was inevitable yet persists in what he is doing, the court will infer that he intended the breach.

The standard required was relaxed over the years and it appeared that recklessness was enough to establish intention in that if the defendant was indifferent as to whether the contract was terminated lawfully or not, he was deemed to have intended the breach. In *Emerald Construction* (above), Higgs and Hill were the main contractors on a site. Emerald were engaged as labour-only subcontractors. The union did not like labour-only contracts and tried to get Higgs and Hill to get rid of Emerald. In the union's experience such contracts were terminable upon short notice, but Emerald's contract needed longer notice than was usual. The union called a strike to pressure Higgs and Hill to end the contract. It was held that the union intended that the contract be terminated unlawfully if it could not be terminated lawfully. It had deliberately turned a blind eye to the specific terms and just wanted Emerald out. In other words, the union was reckless as to the actual term relating to notice. However, in the recent case of *Mainstream Properties Ltd* v. *Young* [2007] IRLR 608 the House of Lords has held that it is an essential prerequisite of the tort that the wrongdoer specifically intended to interfere with the contract. As such, it now appears that the wrongdoer must deliberately and not just carelessly or negligently induce a breach for the requirements of the tort to be met.

Inducement

The word 'inducement' implies pressure being put on an unwilling party, but what amount of pressure does the law require? In *Allen* v. *Flood* (above) it was held that communicating the view of employees to the employer was not an inducement. Similarly, a statement of the facts was not an inducement in *Thomson* v. *Deakin* (above). However, again the standard has been relaxed over the years and the line between communicating information and an inducement is now difficult to draw. In *Torquay Hotels Ltd* v. *Cousins* (above) it was held that the union had induced Esso to break the contract by telling them that there was a dispute at the hotel. The key factor appears to be the intention of the speaker and if the speaker intends that the contract be broken, then there is an inducement even if the speaker is merely communicating a set of facts to the recipient of the information. This, however, raises another issue. What if the recipient is willing to get out of the contract anyway? For example, what of the situation when the employee votes in favour of a strike and after the ballot is then called out on strike by the union? Is there an inducement? It is probably sufficient that there is an agreement to act inconsistently with the terms of the contract. This view is supported by *British Motor Trade Association* v. *Salvadori* [1949] 1 All ER 208 where the seller of new cars induced purchasers to resell to him in breach of a term of the purchasing contract. In fact the purchasers were willing to do this because they received a good price but it was still held to be an inducement.

Causation

There must be a causal connection between the inducement and the breach. Thus if the contract breaker intended to break the contract anyway and was not influenced by the inducement, there will be no liability. Lord Pearce in *Stratford* v. *Lindley* (above) said that the breach had to be a reasonable consequence of the inducement. This suggests that if the inducement is one of a series of factors which persuaded the contract breaker, there will be sufficient causation.

The discussion above has concentrated on direct inducement, that is, pressure being exerted on a party to a contract with the party that the inducer wishes to harm, the typical situation being a union official inducing an employee to break his contract of employment with the intention of harming the employer. Inducement, however, can also be indirect. This involves an inducement of someone who is not in a contract with the party that the inducer wishes to harm, but the consequence of the inducement is a breach of a further contract. For example, a union official may induce the employees at A (a supplier of X, the employer in dispute) to refuse to deliver goods to X. The result is that A cannot perform his contract of supply with X and so X suffers a loss.

A case which is a good illustration of the tort is *Torquay Hotels Ltd* v. *Cousins* (above). In that case the refusal of Esso drivers to deliver to the hotel resulted in the breach of the commercial contract. For an indirect inducement to be actionable, the conditions listed above must exist, but in addition there must be the use of unlawful means (*Middlebrook Mushrooms* v. *TGWU* [1993] IRLR 232). In the case of an indirect inducement, the unlawful means will be the original direct inducement, as in *Torquay* (above).

There is, in theory, a defence to an action of inducing a breach of contract, that of justification. I say in theory because it has only been successful in one case. In *Brimelow* v. *Casson* [1924] 1 Ch 302 chorus girls in the King Wu Tut Tut Review were paid so poorly that many of them turned to prostitution to increase their earnings. The union ordered a strike. It was held that the union officials were justified in inducing the girls to break their contracts in order to ensure that the employer was obliged to pay them a living wage. Russell J said that if justification did not exist he could hardly conceive the case when it would be present! The fact that no ill-will is intended towards the employer is not sufficient for the defence. In *Greig* v. *Insole* (above) the International Cricket Council was found to have induced breaches of cricketers' contracts with the Kerry Packer World Cricket Series. Slade J held that the fact that they acted from impersonal or disinterested motives did not justify the tortious conduct.

Procurement of a breach of contract

This tort is similar in its effect to inducement and, like inducement, can exist in direct or indirect form. In its direct form it involves the same three parties seen in direct inducement, but rather than persuading an employee to break a contract, procurement involves removing the means by which the contract can be performed. For example, if a union official persuaded a lorry driver not to drive, this would be a direct inducement. If, however, the official took away the driver's keys, so that he could not drive, this would be a procurement because the official has taken away the means by which the driver performs his contract; the driver himself has not made a decision to break his contract. As with direct inducement, there must be an unlawful act, knowledge, intention, procurement and causation. *Thomson* v. *Deakin* (above) recognised that such a tort existed and examples were given of removing essential tools or kidnapping an essential employee. The only decided case, however, would appear to be *GWK Ltd* v. *Dunlop Rubber Co Ltd* (1926) 42 TLR 376. In this case, GWK made cars and contracted with Allied Rubber that whenever their cars were displayed at motor shows they would be fitted with Allied's tyres. On the eve of a show, someone changed the tyres to Dunlop tyres. Dunlop was held liable to Allied and GWK, having committed the wrongful act of trespass intending to injure Allied. It appears therefore that a constituent part of the tort is that the procurement is by unlawful means.

Just as with the case of inducement, there can be an indirect procurement. Again, this involves four parties, as in indirect inducement, and occurs when the procurer takes away the means by which the contract can be performed. Perhaps the most common example is where a trade union official persuades the employees at a supplier of the employer in dispute to black supplies intended for that employer. Hence the supplier is in breach of his commercial contract, not because he has been persuaded to go into breach but because the action of his employees means that he cannot get supplies through. A case which affords a good illustration of the tort is *Stratford* v. *Lindley* (above). In this case Stratford was the chairman of Stratford Ltd and Bowker & King Ltd. The latter owned oil-carrying barges and employed 48 men, 45 of whom were members of the TGWU and three of whom were members of the Watermen, Lightermen, Tugmen and Bargemen's Union (WLTBU). The TGWU obtained recognition from Stratford Ltd and the WLTBU put pressure on the company to receive recognition also. Stratford Ltd owned barges which it hired to firms which employed their own crews. The crews were members of the WLTBU. The union told the crew members not to return the barges at the end of the hiring contract and as a result Stratford Ltd was unable to fulfil other contracts of hire. It was held that the WLTBU was liable for procuring breaches of contract between Stratford and the new hirers.

With regard to causation, it appears that the breach must be the necessary consequence of the procurement and not merely the reasonable consequence as in inducement.

Intimidation

The basis of this tort is the use of unlawful threats to induce a party to commit a lawful act which causes injury, classically threatening industrial action which causes the employer to lawfully terminate an employee's contract. It differs from inducement because there is no breach of contract. Until 1964 the tort had only been committed when the threat was a threat of physical injury, however in that year the House of Lords decided the case of *Rookes* v. *Barnard* [1964] 1 All ER 367 and considerably widened the operation of the tort. In *Barnard*, the branch chairman of the union and two other officials told BOAC that if they did not dismiss Rookes, who had resigned from the union, they would strike. Rookes was consequently lawfully dismissed, that is, he was given the correct contractual notice. Rookes sued on the basis that the threat of a strike was the threat of a breach of contract and therefore the threat of an unlawful act. The House of Lords upheld Rookes's argument and decided that the threat of a breach of contract was an unlawful threat for the purposes of intimidation.

The requirements of the tort are as follows:

(a) *Unlawful threat* There must be a threat. It is uncertain whether there is a distinction between a threat and a warning. There probably is not, as the basis of the tort is the intention to injure by unlawful means. The threatened act must be conditional, however, on action or lack of it. In other words, the threat must be, for example, that there will be a strike unless X is dismissed. There is no case law as to the position if the official merely threatens a strike and the employer works out that he can avoid it by sacking X, if this has not been said to him. Furthermore, the threatened wrong must be unlawful and actionable so that if the strike would not be actionable because a statutory immunity exists (see below), then no liability will occur.

(b) *Intention* The defendant who utters the threat must intend to harm the plaintiff. This was clearly the case in *Rookes* v. *Barnard* and will normally be evident as the victim will normally be named in the threat. Recklessness would appear to be insufficient.

(c) *Causation* While the threat must have persuaded the party to act and so harm the plaintiff, it is unclear whether the threat must be the sole cause of the action. If in *Rookes*, for example, the employer had already considered sacking the employee for bad workmanship so that the threat was not the sole cause of his action, it is unclear whether the tort would have been made out.

(d) *Loss to the plaintiff* The plaintiff must have suffered a loss which was caused by the unlawful threat.

It is possible that the defence of justification could apply to the tort. Lord Devlin suggested this in *Rookes* v. *Barnard* but it is difficult to envisage the situations when it might apply.

Conspiracy

This tort consists of two forms. The first is a 'simple conspiracy', sometimes called a 'conspiracy to injure', which is a combination to cause injury to a third party without justification. The second form is a 'conspiracy to use unlawful means'. In a simple conspiracy, no unlawful means are required.

The existence of a simple conspiracy was recognised in *Mogul Steamship Company* v. *McGregor Gow & Co* [1892] AC 25 when the House of Lords stated that the tort had three elements: a combination of at least two persons; intentionally causing loss; and the predominant purpose is not to further a legitimate interest. In addition, there must be an agreement to injure, not merely coincidental action. This is a question of fact and should not be inferred from common conduct. To found an action, the plaintiff must actually suffer loss. This is different from criminal conspiracy when the intention to cause loss forms the basis of the offence even if no loss occurs (s.1 Criminal Law Act 1977).

At least two persons, therefore, must agree to injure the plaintiff and intend to cause him loss. In *Quinn* v. *Leathem* [1901] AC 495 Leathem employed non-unionists. Officials of the union asked him to dismiss one of his non-union workers. Leathem refused and was told that one of his major customers would be warned not to place further orders with Leathem. Leathem offered to pay the fines and joining fees of all his non-union employees but the union refused and the customer withdrew his custom after the union threatened a strike should he fail to do so. It was held that although there was no unlawful action, the officials were guilty of conspiracy because their intention was to injure Leathem. The common law, however, has developed the defence of justification. In other words, relating back to the third element of the tort, if the purpose of the combination is to further the legitimate interests of the conspirators then there is no liability. In *Crofter Handwoven Harris Tweed* v. *Veitch* [1924] AC 435 yarn was imported from the mainland because it was cheaper than yarn made on the island of Lewis. The yarn was then woven by crofters. This meant that the cloth so produced was cheaper than cloth produced wholly on the island and, as a result, wages of the mill workers on the island were very low. The mill workers were members of the TGWU. Dockers, who were also members of the TGWU, placed an embargo on yarn from the mainland to ensure that price competition was eliminated, as this was keeping the wages of the mill workers down. It was held that the predominant purpose of the action was to protect the legitimate interests of the combiners and protect the livelihood of the union members. As such the action was justifiable and no liability arose. Thus action to enforce the legitimate interests of the union will never attract liability. Action where the predominant purpose is spite or vengeance will create liability however, even if it also furthers the aims of the union. In *Huntley* v. *Thornton* [1957] 1 All ER 234 the plaintiff was expelled from the union and hounded out of several jobs after he refused to comply with a union instruction to stop work and after he called the district committee of the union 'a shower'. It was held that the action of certain officials was motivated out of spite and vengeance with the aim of injuring the plaintiff, and hence their action was not justified. Two officials who were not taking action out of spite were not liable for the tort.

The tort of conspiracy to use unlawful means is more complex. As with a simple conspiracy there must be an agreement to injure, intention to cause loss but in addition there must be the use of unlawful means. Unlike a simple conspiracy, it is enough if damage to the plaintiff is likely to result even if that is not the defendant's predominant purpose. This was doubted by the House of Lords in *Lonrho* v. *Shell Petroleum (No. 2)* [1982] AC 173 but reaffirmed by a later House of Lords' decision in *Lonrho* v. *Fayed* [1991] 3 All ER 303. The most difficult question is: what kinds of unlawful means will be sufficient to constitute the tort? Certainly a conspiracy to commit a crime would suffice and Lord Wright in *Crofter* (above) thought that a conspiracy to commit an offence under the Conspiracy and Protection of Property Act 1875 would be sufficient. It is not clear whether a conspiracy to commit a breach of contract is enough although, as already seen, this will found an action for intimidation. One thing is clear, however. The illegal act must be integral to the aims of the conspirators and not peripheral so, for example, an agreement by two picketers to pilfer will not set up the tort.

Interference with a trade or business by unlawful means

It is sometimes argued that no such tort exists or it is merely an umbrella phrase to describe existing torts in this area, although immunity against such a tort was included in the Trade Disputes Act 1906 and later repealed by the Employment Act 1982. It would seem, however, that such a tort does exist although it is of recent origin. The tort was declared to exist by the Court of Appeal in *Hadmor Productions Ltd* v. *Hamilton* [1981] 2 All ER 724 (CA) and the House of Lords in the same case appeared to tacitly accept that such a tort existed ([1982] IRLR 162). The development of the tort can be explained given that since *Rookes* v. *Barnard* there is liability for threatening to use unlawful means to interfere in a person's trade, therefore, logically, the actual interference must also be tortious. In *Hadmor* it was alleged that ACTT officials threatened to persuade their members to refuse to transmit television programmes produced by Hadmor. Thames Television had acquired a licence to transmit the programmes but was under no contractual obligation to do so. Hadmor therefore had no contract which the action would interfere with, merely a commercial expectation. It was held, however, that a *prima facie* case that a tort had been committed had been made out. The essence of the tort is the use of unlawful means, which raises the question of what constitutes 'unlawful means'. It has always been the case that inducing someone to break their contract is unlawful means for the purposes of torts which have that requirement. Under the Trade Disputes Act 1906 there was immunity from liability for inducing breaches of contracts of employment if done in contemplation or furtherance of a trade dispute. Section 13(3)(b) Trade Union and Labour Relations Act 1974 stated that a breach which was not actionable could not constitute unlawful means. This provision was repealed by the Employment Act 1980 but the House of Lords in *Hadmor* stated that the provision had only stated the law and that a wrong which was immune from liability could not constitute unlawful means. Therefore, if statutory protection exists, the tort is not made out. Likewise, void acts do not give rise to legal rights or duties and, as such, cannot be unlawful means (*Mogul* v. *McGregor Gow*, above). Certainly, however, any tort which does not attract statutory immunity will provide the basis of the tort, for example trespass, deceit, intimidation, breach of statutory duty and so on.

From *Hadmor* it appears that in addition to unlawful means there must be an intention to harm the plaintiff and the plaintiff must sustain actual loss. The Court of Appeal expanded upon this in *Lonrho* v. *Fayed* (above) and stated that it was not necessary that the defendant's predominant purpose was to harm the plaintiff, but it must be shown that the defendant's unlawful act was directed against and intended to harm the plaintiff. The kind of interference which will create liability is still unclear. In *Fayed*, Lonrho claimed that the Fayed brothers had fraudulently deceived the Secretary of State for Trade in not referring their bid for the House of Fraser to the Monopolies and Mergers Commission, and therefore Lonrho had been wrongfully deprived of the opportunity to acquire Harrods. The Court of Appeal felt it was arguable that this constituted a tort and that the case should go to a full trial. The tort is therefore a developing one and one which could take over from the more common torts listed above, particularly as no immunity exists apart from the fact that inducement or intimidation cannot be unlawful means if they are not actionable because of statutory immunity.

Economic duress

All industrial action is intended to put economic pressure on the employer. In contract law, economic pressure can amount to duress and, if proved, the contract can be avoided and any money paid under it recovered. Normally, this argument is not used against unions because they have no contract with the employer, however in *Universe Tankships of Monrovia* v. *International Transport Workers' Federation* [1983] AC 366 such a contract did exist. The Federation, as part of its campaign against flags of convenience, insisted that employers paid a sum into the union's welfare fund as a price for lifting the blacking of a ship. As soon as the blacking was lifted, the employers sought to recover the money they had paid, arguing that payment had been made under duress and therefore was avoidable. The House of Lords said that if the action had been protected by the immunities, that is, it was in contemplation or furtherance of a trade dispute, the employer could not circumvent the protection by bringing an action for duress. However, since payment into a welfare fund is not a recognised trade dispute, there was no such protection and the employer's action succeeded. A similar conclusion has been reached in *Dimskal Shipping* v. *ITWF* [1992] IRLR 78.

14.4 Statutory Immunities

It can be seen from the above that unions can commit a great number of economic torts when they take industrial action, but we have already seen that in some circumstances there will be statutory immunity from liability for the commission of certain torts. The immunity is now contained in s.219 Trade Union and Labour Relations (Consolidation) Act 1992 which states:

'An act done by a person in contemplation or furtherance of a trade dispute is not actionable in tort on the ground only:
(a) that it induces another person to break a contract or interferes or induces another person to interfere with its performance, or
(b) that it consists in his threatening that a contract (whether one to which he is a party or not) will be broken or its performance interfered with, or that he will induce another person to break a contract or interfere with its performance.'

It will be seen therefore that protection is not afforded against the commission of any tort, and that torts such as libel, slander, trespass, breach of statutory duty and so on have no immunity. It can also be seen that immunity does not apply every time one of the protected torts is committed but only where it is committed 'in contemplation or furtherance of a trade dispute', the so-called 'golden formula'. It should further be noted that only torts can attract statutory immunity; a union or its members can never be immune from criminal liability.

This means that to discover whether the union and its members have statutory protection from liability, the starting point is to discover whether there is a trade dispute and whether they are acting in contemplation or furtherance of it.

Trade dispute

The definition of a 'trade dispute' is to be found in s.244(1) of the 1992 Act. This provides that a trade dispute is:

'a dispute between workers and their employer which relates wholly or mainly to one or more of the following:
(a) terms and conditions of employment, or the physical conditions in which any workers are required to work;
(b) engagement or non-engagement, or termination or suspension of employment or the duties of employment, of one or more workers;
(c) allocation of work or the duties of employment between workers or groups of workers;
(d) matters of discipline;
(e) a worker's membership or non-membership of a trade union;
(f) facilities for officials of trade unions; and
(g) machinery for negotiation or consultation, and other procedures, relating to any of the above matters, including the recognition by employers or employers' associations of the right of a trade union to represent workers in such negotiation or consultation or in the carrying out of such procedures.'

Workers and their employer

First, it should be noted that a trade dispute can now only exist between workers and their employer. Prior to the change in definition introduced by the Employment Act 1982, the dispute could be between workers and any employer, and workers and workers. Such a broad definition meant that secondary and tertiary action fell within the definition, as did inter-union disputes. This type of industrial action has no protection today. Therefore industrial action cannot be directed at an employer whose employees are not involved in the dispute. The employer, however, cannot change his identity to try and prevent the statutory immunity applying. In *Examite Ltd* v. *Whittaker* [1977] IRLR 312 the AUEW was in dispute with Baldwins Industrial Services. The company formed a second company called Examite Ltd which took over the entire business of Baldwins. Examite then argued that they were not the employers with whom the AUEW was in dispute. It was held that the court should look at the reality behind the facade. Lord Denning was prepared to raise the veil of incorporation, Roskill LJ and Shaw LJ found for the union on other grounds. The corporate veil will not be lifted, however, where long-established companies are involved. In *Dimbleby & Sons Ltd* v. *NUJ* [1984] 1 WLR 427 journalists employed by Dimbleby refused to send printing work to TBF Ltd rather than to their own associated printing house, T. Bailey Foreman Ltd, where the printers were on strike. TBF was also an associated company of T. Bailey Foreman. The journalists were taking sympathy action to support the printers. The NUJ argued first that they were employed by the same employer and second that the dispute was about the allocation of work under s.244(1)(c). While the House of Lords accepted that there was a dispute about the allocation of work, the journalists were not in dispute with their employer. All the companies were legitimate separate legal entities and the journalists were not employed by T. Bailey Foreman, who was the employer in dispute.

By s.244(2) a dispute between a Minister of the Crown and workers shall be treated as a dispute between those workers and their employer if the dispute relates to matters referred to him by a joint body on which he is represented or, broadly speaking, his approval is required before a settlement can be made. This provision was discussed in the dispute involving teachers and the boycott of national tests arising out of the National Curriculum. In *Wandsworth London Borough Council* v. *NASUWT* (1993) The Times, 26 April the question for the Court of Appeal was whether there was a trade dispute. On the issue of the parties, the court unanimously held that there was a dispute between workers and an employer, by the operation of s.244(2).

'Worker' is defined in s.244(5) of the Act. It must be noted that the protection is for workers and not merely employees. Section 244(5) gives a definition of 'worker' in relation to a trade dispute but the general definition in s.296 is wider. In *TGWU* v. *Associated British Ports* (2002) IDS Brief 705, ABP was the port authority for the Humber Ports. Under the Pilotage Act 1987 it had the power to authorise suitably qualified persons to act as pilots and a duty to arrange for the provision of the services of self-employed authorised pilots to be exercised on its behalf. In 1991 it entered an agreement with Humber Pilots Ltd for the provision of the services of self-employed pilots. HPL was the collective voice of pilots in the area and not their employer. In 2001, ABP decided that from January 2002 it would employ pilots directly. HPL declared a trade dispute involving the TGWU and threatened strike action. ABP sought an injunction arguing that self-employed pilots were not workers and thus there was no trade dispute. Section 296(1)(b) defines a worker as an individual who works, normally works or seeks to work 'under any other contract whereby he undertakes to do or perform personally any work or services for another party to the contract who is not a professional client of his'. At first instance an interim injunction was granted, Hunt J deciding that the pilots were not workers within the definition. On appeal, the Court of Appeal reversed the judgement. That court stated that the existence of a statutory duty imposed on ABP to provide pilotage services did not preclude the existence of a contractual relationship between the pilots and ABP. The pilots' authorisation was on terms and conditions on which the offer of authorisation was made and when a pilot accepted those terms and conditions he had entered a contract with ABP. As such, the pilots fell within the definition in s.296(1)(b). It should be further noted that the definition in s.244(5) not only covers those employed by the employer but also a person who has ceased to be employed where his employment was terminated in connection with the dispute or the termination of his employment was one of the circumstances giving rise to the dispute.

Dispute

The second question which must be determined is whether there is a dispute between the parties. In *Beetham* v. *Trinidad Cement Ltd* [1960] AC 132 Lord Denning said that a dispute exists wherever a difference exists between the parties. But the question arises of what is the situation if one party concedes to the demand made by the other. Is there a dispute? In the case of *Cory Lighterage Ltd* v. *TGWU* [1972] 1 WLR 792, a case under the Industrial Relations Act 1971, an employee had allowed his union membership to lapse and after pressure from the union, the employer suspended him on full pay. The employee was quite happy to do this and it was held that at the time no dispute existed between the employee and his employer but there was a dispute between the employee and the union. (Such a dispute did not have protection under the 1971 Act.) Buckley LJ said: 'if someone threatens me with physical injury unless I hand over my wallet and I hand it over without a demur, no one could, in my opinion, sensibly say that there had been any dispute about my handing over my wallet.' Such a decision obviously creates problems in relation to the statutory immunities and so the effect of the decision in *Cory* was reversed in 1974 and is now s.244(4) of the 1992 Act. This provides that:

> 'An act, threat or demand done or made by one person or organisation against another which, if resisted, would have led to a trade dispute with that other, shall be treated as being done or made in contemplation of a trade dispute with that other, notwithstanding that because that other submits to the act or accedes to the demand no dispute arises.'

Thus a threat of industrial action which causes the employer to, for example, dismiss someone, is action in contemplation of a trade dispute.

Related wholly or mainly to

The next step is that the dispute must relate 'wholly or mainly to' one or more of the statutory items in s.244(1) and it is important to note that it is the dispute which must relate wholly or mainly to those matters, not the action, which should merely further the dispute. This means that the dispute must be identified to discover what the quarrel is really about. If it is not about one of the statutory items in reality, it will not be sufficient to show some theoretical connection. For example, in *Stratford* v. *Lindley* (above) the reason for the blacking by the union was not to obtain recognition but to retaliate because the employer had recognised another union, hence there was not a trade dispute. Under the 1974 definition, the dispute merely had to be connected with one of the statutory items. This meant that as long as one of the items was part of the reason for the dispute, it did not matter that other non-statutory items were involved, although the courts would not afford statutory immunity to a dispute where the statutory items were peripheral to the main reason for the dispute. In *BBC* v. *Hearn* [1977] 1 WLR 1004 the Association of Broadcasting Staff, to which the majority of BBC staff belonged, objected to racial and political discrimination. The union felt that it would be wrong to broadcast the FA Cup Final to South Africa because of that country's apartheid policy and when the BBC refused to give an undertaking not to transmit the broadcast, the union instructed members televising the match not to work on the programme. It was held that there was no trade dispute as the real motive for the action was political and it was over-subtle to say that it was a dispute connected with terms and conditions of employment because there was an issue as to whether a condition should be inserted into the employees' contracts that they would not be compelled to transmit to South Africa.

Under the old definition, therefore, as long as a statutory item was one part of the dispute, a trade dispute existed. A contrast to *Hearn* can be seen in *NWL Ltd* v. *Nelson and Laughton* [1979] 3 All ER 614. In this case a ship was originally registered in Norway but the owners, to save money, decided to employ a Hong Kong crew and therefore reregistered the ship in Hong Kong although the ship never went near Hong Kong, that is the ship was flying a flag of convenience. The Hong Kong crew were content with their wages, but the ITWF blacked the ship when it docked at a British port. It was well known that the ITWF had a campaign against flags of convenience and the ship owners sought an injunction arguing that the dispute was political. The House of Lords, however, held that the dispute was clearly connected with terms and conditions of employment of seamen even if other purposes existed behind the dispute. The change in definition from 'connected with' to 'relating wholly and mainly to' was clearly an attempt to reverse the NWL decision and the effect of the change can be seen in the case of *Mercury Communications Ltd* v. *Scott-Garner* [1984] Ch 37. The dispute arose out of the government's licensing of operators other than British Telecom to operate telecommunications. Mercury planned to establish a communications network partly using the British Telecom network, and the Post Office Engineers' Union instructed their members not to connect Mercury. At first instance it was held that there was a trade dispute because the union was concerned with future job losses. However, when the case reached the Court of Appeal a different conclusion was reached because of the existence of a job security agreement between British Telecom and the union. Donaldson MR said that 'in this context the phrase wholly or mainly relates to directs attention to what the dispute is about and, if it is about more than one matter, what is it mainly about'. On this definition, the court held that the action related to 'a political and ideological campaign seeking to maintain the concept of public monopoly against private competition' (per May LJ).

Subject matter

The dispute must be wholly or mainly related to one or more of the items in s.244(1) listed above. This is demonstrated by the *Hearn* case (above). In subsection (a) the phrase 'terms and conditions of employment' is given a wide meaning. In s.244(5) 'employment' is defined as 'any relationship whereby one person personally does work or performs services for another', that is it is not confined to a contractual relationship. 'Terms of employment' obviously refers to all matters covered by the contract whether express or implied, for example hours, pay, holidays and so on. However, the expression has an even wider ambit. In *Hearn* Denning MR said that 'terms and conditions of employment' includes not only the contractual terms and conditions, but also 'those terms which are understood and applied by the parties in practice, or habitually, or by common consent, without ever being incorporated into the contract'. This phrase was approved by Lord Diplock in *Hadmor* (above) and by the House of Lords in *Universe Tankships* (above). Thus in *P* v. *NAS/UWT* [2003] IRLR 307 a union's action in instructing its members not to comply with an instruction to teach a disruptive pupil was held to be a trade dispute. The Court of Appeal held that a dispute regarding the reasonableness of an instruction from an employer could be regarded as a dispute about terms and conditions of employment.

Conversely, however, in *Universe Tankships* their Lordships considered that some things within the contract might not necessarily be part of the terms and conditions. Lord Diplock said: 'But wide as the expression "terms and conditions of employment" is, it is limited to terms which regulate the relationship between an employee and the person for whom he works i.e.

his employer. It does not extend to terms which regulate a relationship between an employer and some third party acting as principal and not as agent for the employee.' Thus a term that the employer would make a contribution to the union would not, in Lord Diplock's view, be a term or condition of employment even if it was a term in each individual employee's contract. Further interpretation can be seen in *University College London Hospitals NHS Trust* v. *UNISON* [1999] IRLR 31. In the case the union wanted the Trust to enter into a contractual agreement with a consortium who were taking over staff from the Trust, that the consortium would, for a period of up to 30 years, maintain the equivalent terms and conditions for all employees working for the consortium to those employees who had not been transferred. The Trust gained an injunction restraining the union from organising a series of strikes to support its demands. The Court of Appeal rejected the union's argument that the proposed industrial action was in furtherance of a trade dispute within the meaning of s.244(1)(a) because the sought-for agreement would not only guarantee the pay of existing staff but, given the 30-year period, would inevitably cover staff who had never been employed by the Trust. Section 244(1)(a) does not cover a dispute over terms and conditions of employees who have never been employed by the employer in dispute.

The problem that arises with the expression is shown in a situation, for example, where the employee is employed by the state and the state imposes a pay freeze to which the employees object. Is that a dispute about terms and conditions, that is pay, or is it a political dispute objecting to government policy? Without doubt, action which purely demonstrates against government policy is political and gains no immunity. The first determination of what constitutes a political dispute was the General Strike of 1926 which received no immunity (*National Sailors and Firemen's Union of Great Britain and Northern Ireland* v. *Reed* [1926] 1 Ch 536). Action taken to protest against the Industrial Relations Act 1971 similarly lost immunity. One factor in these cases is that the employer cannot concede the union's demands. Where the government is also the employer, however, s.244(2) can render the dispute a trade dispute even if the dispute does challenge government policy, provided the main objection to the policy is that it affects terms and conditions. We have already seen in the *Wandsworth* case (above) that the Court of Appeal held that the dispute between the local authority and the NASUWT fell within s.244(2), furthermore it was held to be a trade dispute relating to terms and conditions of employment because of the policy of testing increased teachers' workload and this had been emphasised as the purpose of the dispute in the strike ballot which had been conducted. So too in *Westminster City Council* v. *UNISON* [2001] IRLR 524 a ballot was held in relation to proposed industrial action in response to a council plan to privatise the housing assessment and advice unit. The Court of Appeal held that a proposal to transfer a unit and its employees to a private employer was a trade dispute within s.244(1) as it is a dispute about the identity of the employer. In other situations, however, the distinction between a trade dispute and a political dispute is not so easy to draw.

Section 244(3) states that a trade dispute exists even though it relates to matters outside Great Britain as long as the persons taking the action are likely to be affected in respect of one or more of the statutory items.

In contemplation of

The phrase attempts to place a chronological limit on legitimate industrial action. Two questions have to be answered: does a trade dispute exist or is one imminent? and when the persons acted were they contemplating the trade dispute? Thus this part of the 'golden formula' applies when a trade dispute exists or is imminent. Lord Loreburn LC said in *Conway* v. *Wade* [1909] AC 506: 'I come now to the meaning of the words "an act done in contemplation or furtherance of a trade dispute" ... I think they mean that either a dispute is imminent and the act is done in expectation of and with a view to it, or that the dispute is already existing and the act is done in support of one side to it.' In the case Conway had been expelled from the union for failing to pay a fine. He later rejoined the union at another branch. Wade discovered the earlier expulsion and told the employer (falsely) that there would be a strike if Conway was not dismissed. It was held that Wade was not acting in contemplation of a trade dispute. He may have decided subjectively that he would try to call a strike, but the dispute was all in his mind and it could not reasonably be inferred from the facts that a dispute was likely to occur.

It appears, therefore, that whether the dispute is imminent is an objective test and there must be evidence that there is or there is about to be a dispute. Furthermore, the dispute must be 'impending or likely to occur' according to Lord Shaw in the case. He went on to say, 'it does not cover the case of coercive interference in which the intervener may have in his own mind that if he does not get his own way he will thereupon take ways and means to bring a trade dispute into existence'. Likewise, action taken which may result in a trade dispute breaking out is not in contemplation of it (*Bents Brewery* v. *Hogan*, above). By contrast, *Heath Computing Ltd* v. *Meek* [1981] ICR 24 shows that a dispute may exist even though there has been no confrontation or direct discussions. In the case, NALGO had sent out a circular to its members in the NHS, instructing them not to cooperate with Heath Computing because it foresaw that, if the NHS gave computing work to Heath, the members' jobs would be in jeopardy. It was held that such action was in contemplation of a trade dispute which was imminent.

In furtherance of

Once again a dispute must exist or be imminent, and then the test is whether the action is in furtherance of it. Action which does not further the dispute will lose immunity. In *Beaverbrook Newspapers* v. *Keys* [1978] ICR 582 a trade dispute existed between the Daily Mirror newspaper and the union which resulted in a total stoppage in production. The Daily Express decided to print more copies to cater for the increase in demand but the union told its members not to handle the extra copies. It was held that the action was not in furtherance of the trade dispute at the Daily Mirror because it would do nothing to aid the dispute. It may appear that this introduces an objective test and that it is up to the court to decide if the action furthers the dispute. This, however, goes against the judgement of Lord Loreburn LC in *Conway* (above). He said:

> 'If however some meddler sought to use the trade dispute as a cloak beneath which to interfere with impunity in other people's work or business, a jury would be entirely justified in saying that what he did was done in contemplation or furtherance, not of the trade dispute, but of his own designs, sectarian, political, or purely mischievous, as the case may be. These words do, in my opinion, in some sense import motive, and in the case I have put, quite a different motive would be present.'

In other words, the intention behind the action is important. The Court of Appeal, in a series of cases from 1978 to 1980, chose to adopt an objective approach. The House of Lords, however, in reversing the Court of Appeal decisions reaffirmed the situation in *Conway* that the test is subjective and the test is whether the person honestly believed that his actions would further the dispute. In *Express Newspapers Ltd* v. *McShane* [1980] AC 672 the NUJ was in dispute with provincial newspapers. The NUJ called its members in the provincial newspapers out on strike, but the papers still received news from the Press Association teleprinter. The NUJ called out its members at the Press Association but not all members complied. The NUJ then instructed its members working on national newspapers to black any copy from the Press Association. The House of Lords, reversing the Court of Appeal, held that whether an act is done in furtherance of a trade dispute depends only upon whether the defendants honestly and genuinely believed that they were furthering the dispute, which was the situation in the case. Reasonableness is only a factor in determining whether the belief is genuinely held and if no reasonable person could possibly have thought that the action would further the dispute, then it calls into question whether the defendant really did so believe. Here, as the defendants genuinely believed that they were furthering the dispute, the action had immunity. The same conclusion was reached in *Duport Steels Ltd* v. *Sirs* [1980] 1 All ER 529 where, after the British Steel Corporation refused a pay claim, the steel unions in the public sector went on strike. As this seemed to have no effect, the unions instructed their members in the private sector to strike. This was designed to compel the government to intercede and make more money available to the Corporation to enable it to meet the pay claim. The House of Lords, reaffirming the decision in *McShane* (above), held that the subjective test applied and that, because the steel unions genuinely believed that they were furthering the dispute by their actions, the action had immunity. The House particularly regretted this result but decided that this was the correct interpretation of the law and that it was up to parliament to change the law if it so wished. Indeed, soon afterwards the Employment Act 1980 made the secondary action in *Duport Steels* illegal and further legislative intervention has now rendered most secondary action illegal.

While the subjective test prevails, it still remains the case that action taken in consequence of a trade dispute rather than to further it will have no immunity. Arguably, this was the situation in the *Beaverbrook* case (above) and the action there was in consequence of the dispute at the Daily Mirror rather than an attempt to further it. This means that action taken after the dispute has ended will have no protection. In *Stewart* v. *AUEW* [1973] ICR 128 the plaintiff, a haulage contractor, had defied pickets on strike at a shipyard. After the strike was settled, the plaintiff was blacked. It was held that the union had no immunity. The action was in consequence of a trade dispute, not in furtherance of it.

Secondary action

It will be noted from the discussion above that if employees at a supplier or customer of the employer in dispute take sympathy action by, for example, refusing to handle goods meant for that employer, as those employees are not in dispute with their employer they do not fall within the definition of a trade dispute and therefore have no immunity. Originally, s.17 Employment Act 1980 provided certain immunity for such action, known as 'secondary action', by providing what were known as the 'gateways' to protection. The section was complicated and as such was repealed by the Employment Act 1990, leaving only protection for picketing which has a secondary effect. In other words, if employees who are in dispute with their employer lawfully picket their own place of work, they are likely to turn back drivers from suppliers or customers. This means that they are inducing those drivers to break their contracts of employment with their employers, who are not parties to the dispute. This secondary effect of picketing, however, will still have immunity under s.219 Trade Union and Labour Relations (Consolidation) Act 1992. All other forms of secondary action will have no protection.

14.5 Trade Union Liability

The Trade Disputes Act 1906 introduced immunity from tortious liability for trade unions. This was brought in to reverse the *Taff Vale* decision (see Chapter 12) and was re-enacted in the Trade Union and Labour Relations Act 1974. This blanket immunity was removed by the Employment Act 1982 and now a union has the same immunity as its individual members, that is the union will be immune if the action is within the 'golden formula' and the acts committed are the torts listed in s.219 of the 1992 Act. There is, however, a statutory limit on the damages that can be awarded against a union, first introduced in 1982 and now contained in s.22 of the 1992 Act. The amount of damages depends on the number of members the union has. If there are fewer than 5,000 the maximum is £10,000. Between 5,000 and 25,000 the maximum is £50,000. Between 25,000 and 100,000 the maximum is £125,000 and over 100,000 members the limit is £250,000. Each separate action may result in the maximum being imposed, therefore if more than one employer takes action against the union each employer can be awarded the statutory limit. Furthermore, the limit only applies to damages and not to fines for contempt. Thus in the NGA dispute against the Stockport Messenger in 1984 the union was fined £675,000 for contempt.

This means that if the individual member is protected then the union, provided it complies with the balloting and other provisions below, will also have immunity. Furthermore, if the individual member has lost immunity or it was an act which did not have immunity in the first place, then the union may be liable also. This rider is added because the union will only be liable for action which when taken had been authorised or endorsed by the union. Section 20(2) states that action shall be taken as authorised or endorsed by the union if it was authorised or endorsed by any person empowered by the rules to do so: by the principal executive committee, the president or the general secretary or by any other committee or any other official of the union. Further by subsection (3) a 'committee' is any group of persons constituted in accordance with the rules of the union and an act is taken to be 'authorised or endorsed by an official' if it was authorised or endorsed by, or by any member of, any group of persons of which he was, at the material time, a member and where the purpose of the group included the organisation or coordination of industrial action. The number of persons who carry the authority of the union was greatly extended by the Employment Act 1990. The reason was that although previously the union had only been liable if it had given authority to a person or committee to authorise or endorse industrial action, a great many strikes were in fact called by shop stewards, who under the old provisions did not have such authority and, as such, the action was unofficial and the union not liable for torts committed. The government, however, felt that a great deal of unofficial action was tacitly supported by unions and hence extended the definition of official action to prevent unions from escaping liability. In effect these provisions resurrect the old case of *Heatons Transport Ltd* v. *TGWU* [1973] AC 15 where the House of Lords held that the custom and practice of the union gave shop stewards a general implied authority to institute blacking by their members.

The union can escape liability if it repudiates the action, but the provisions relating to repudiation are very stringent. Section 21 provides that an act shall not be taken to be authorised or endorsed by the union if it is repudiated by the executive, president or general secretary as soon as reasonably practicable after knowledge of the action has come to any of those bodies (s.21(1)). Subsection (2) states that to constitute a valid repudiation it must be written and given to the person or committee which instituted the action without delay, and the fact and date of the repudiation must be given to every member taking part or who might take part in the action and the employer of such members. Subsection (3) then states what the repudiation must say:

> 'Your union has repudiated the call (or calls) for industrial action to which this notice relates and will give no support to unofficial action taken in response to it (or them). If you are dismissed while taking unofficial industrial action, you will have no right to complain of unfair dismissal.'

Repudiation which does not comply with subsections (2) and (3) is ineffective and the action will be deemed official and the union liable. An act is also not treated as repudiated if at any time afterwards the executive, president or general secretary behaves in a manner which is inconsistent with the purported repudiation (s.21(5)). In *Express and Star* v. *NGA* [1986] ICR 589 the general secretary of the union had sent out circulars saying the action should cease but one official stated at a meeting that he had had a nod and a wink that they should not be distributed and another stated that he had been told that strike pay would be given. While this was not a case concerning repudiation, it gives an example of the type of conduct that the subsection is intended to catch. In addition, subsection (6) states that the executive, president or general secretary shall be treated as acting inconsistently with a repudiation if on a request made to them within six months of the repudiation, by a party to a commercial contract which is affected by the action and who has not received written notice of the repudiation from the union, the union does not give such notice.

14.6 Loss of Trade Union Immunity

It has already been noted that a union has the same immunity as individual members, thus if the member commits a tort for which there is no immunity, for example slander, then the union will be liable. The union will also be liable if the member, for example, induces a breach of contract but this is after the trade dispute has finished and is therefore outside the 'golden formula'. Even if the member is immune, the union will lose its statutory immunity if it fails to comply with the statutory balloting provisions. As such, it is inaccurate to say that the union's immunity reflects that of the individual member. Trade union immunity depends on the 'golden formula', the protected torts being committed and the balloting and notice requirements being complied with. Breach of any of these conditions will render the union liable for any tortious wrongs committed.

A ballot is required in respect of any act done by a trade union, that is, in respect of any action authorised or endorsed by the union. Entitlement to vote must be accorded to all members of the union which the union reasonably believes will be induced by it to take part in the action, and the ballot will be ineffective if this provision is not complied with (s.227). This section was amended by the Employment Relations Act 2004 after the case of *National Union of Rail, Maritime and Transport Workers* v. *Midland Mainline Ltd* [2001] IRLR 813 which showed a lack of clarity about which union members the union was required to give an entitlement to vote. The section now makes it clear that the union does not have to give an entitlement to those who may take industrial action, even though they have not been induced by the union. By s.226A the union must give, no later than the seventh day before the opening of the ballot, written notice to the employer of those members entitled to vote in the ballot, stating the opening day of the ballot and a description of the employees who will be entitled to vote. The Court of Appeal in *Blackpool and Fylde College* v. *NATFHE* [1994] IRLR 227 held that the union had not complied with s.226A when it had stated that it would ballot all staff who were union members. There were 288 union members in the college, but the employer could only identify 109 who had their union subscriptions deducted from their salary. This suggests that the names of those employees balloted should be given to the employer, in order for him to ascertain which employees are involved. This could obviously lead to employees being singled out by the employer. As such, the Employment Relations Acts 1999 and 2004 amended s.226A so that a union need only give information to the employer so that he can make plans and bring information to the attention of those of his employees involved. That information must contain a list of the categories of employees who the union reasonably believes will be entitled to vote and a list of the workplaces at which they work (ss.226A(2A to 2I)). Further, failing to name those employees entitled to vote will not be grounds for declaring that a union has not complied with the legal requirements. In addition, no later than the third day before the opening day of the ballot, the union must send to the same employers a sample of the form of the voting paper which is to be sent to those employees entitled to vote. Opening day of the ballot means the first day that a voting paper is sent to a member. Failure to comply with these provisions means the loss of immunity for the trade union.

Section 228 provides for separate workshop ballots for each place of work. A new s.228A, inserted by the Employment Relations Act, relieves the union of the duty to hold separate workplace ballots if one of the following applies: the workplace of each member entitled to vote is the workplace of at least one member who is affected by the dispute; if entitlement to vote is accorded to and limited to all members who according to the union's reasonable belief have a common occupation and are employed by a common employer or number of employers with whom the union is in dispute; if entitlement to vote is accorded to and limited to all the union members employed by a particular employer or number of employers with whom the union is in dispute. By s.229 the method of voting must be by ballot paper which must be framed in a way that the member can answer 'yes' or 'no' to the question of whether he is prepared to take part in a strike and whether he is prepared to take part in action short of a strike. It must specify who is authorised to call for industrial action and must also contain the following: 'If you take part in a strike or other industrial action, you may be in breach of your contract of employment.'

Amendments made by the Employment Relations Act make it clear that an overtime ban and a call-out ban are action short of dismissal (s.229(2A)). Further, the voting paper must also contain the following:

'However, if you are dismissed for taking part in a strike or other industrial action which is called officially and is otherwise lawful, the dismissal will be unfair if it takes place fewer than eight weeks after you started taking part in the action, and depending on the circumstances may be unfair if it takes place later.'

Section 230(2), which was amended by the 1993 Act, requires that such a ballot must be a postal ballot, the voting paper being sent to the member's address, and that all members should be given a convenient opportunity to vote by post. All those voting should be informed, as soon as reasonably practicable after the vote, of the number of 'yes' votes, the number of 'no' votes and the number of spoiled ballot papers (s.231). By an amendment in 1993, this information must also be given to all relevant employers (s.231A). The Trade Union Reform and Employment Rights Act 1993 amended the legislation so that all industrial action ballots must now have an independent scrutineer (s.226B) and the name and details of the scrutineer must be given on every voting paper (s.229(1A)). A copy of the scrutineer's report shall be available, on request, to any member entitled to vote or any relevant employer. Section 226C, introduced by the 1993 Act, excludes the appointment of a scrutineer where the total number of members entitled to vote is fewer than 50. If the vote supports industrial action, the union will again lose immunity if it is not called by the person specified on the ballot paper as being so authorised (s.233(1)). In *Tanks and Drums Ltd* v. *TGWU* [1991] ICR 1 the union had nominated its general secretary as having authority to call a strike. Negotiations with the employer had been conducted by a district official and, two weeks after a ballot in favour of industrial action, the official obtained permission from the general secretary to call a strike the next day if the employer did not come up with a better offer. The employer did not come up with a better offer and the official called a strike. The Court of Appeal held that the delegation of authority from the general secretary was so specific and related to such specific events, that it could be said that the general secretary had, in fact, called the action for the purposes of the legislation. This would suggest that a more general delegation of authority would mean that there had been an infringement of s.233 and the union's immunity would be lost.

If the ballot supports industrial action, it will cease to be effective after four weeks or after such longer duration not exceeding eight weeks as agreed between the union and the members' employer (s.234, as amended by the Employment Relations Act 1999). If during that time industrial action is prohibited or suspended by a court order or undertaking, the union can apply to the court for an order that the period of suspension or prohibition should not be counted as part of the four-week period, although the court shall not make such an order if it feels that the ballot no longer represents the views of the union members concerned. No application to the court may be made by the union after eight weeks has elapsed from the date of the ballot. The period between making an application and its determination is not counted in the calculation of the period but, in any event, the ballot lapses after 12 weeks. The notice periods can cause problems when the employer wishes to negotiate and so action is suspended and then negotiations break down. In *Post Office* v. *UCW* [1990] 1 WLR 981 a ballot which was held in September 1988 led to industrial action which continued until December 1988. There was no action between January and April 1989 but in May action started again, culminating in a strike in September 1989. The disputes were all over the same issue but the Court of Appeal held that the dispute which began in May was a new campaign and that a fresh ballot should have been taken before action commenced.

The Trade Union Reform and Employment Rights Act 1993 added s.234A into the 1992 Act which has since been amended by the Employment Relations Act 2004. This introduces the concept of notice of industrial action to employers. Failure to give such notice will result in the trade union losing its immunity for any torts committed during the subsequent action. The notice must be given to an employer whose employees the union reasonably believes will be taking part in the industrial action. By subsection (3) the notice must be in writing and give a list of the categories to which the 'affected employees', that is, those employees whom the union reasonably believes will be induced to take part in industrial action, belong and a list of the workplaces at which they work. The notice must also state whether the action will be continuous or discontinuous and the date when the action will commence, or, if discontinuous action is intended, the dates when any affected employees will take part. It must also state that the notice is being given for the purposes of s.234A. The notice period begins on the date that the union informs the employer of the ballot result and ends on the seventh day before the first of the days specified in the notice. The notice must cover all those employees falling within the notified categories and employed at a notified workplace (s.234A(5)). If the action ceases to comply with a court order or undertaking and the union then authorises or endorses the action again at a later date, the original notice lapses and the union must again give notice to the employer stating the date or dates on which the action will take place. This will not apply, however, where the union has suspended action to negotiate with the employer. In this case, the union and employer can agree that the action will cease to be authorised or endorsed from a date specified in the agreement (the suspension date) and that it will resume authorisation or agreement at a date specified in the agreement (the resumption date). This is stated in ss.234A(7A) and (7B), introduced by the Employment Relations Act 1999. This means that should negotiations fail, the union will not need to issue a fresh notice to the employer.

The Employment Relations Act 1999 inserted s.232B into the 1992 Act (as amended by the Employment Relations Act 2004) which now provides that minor procedural failures will be disregarded and will not render the union liable. The failures which will be disregarded are: s.227(1) (entitlement to vote accorded to all members who the union reasonably believes will be induced to take part in industrial action); s.230(2) (every person entitled to vote should have the voting paper sent to his home address and be given a convenient opportunity to vote by post); and s.230(2A) (voting provisions for merchant seamen). Such failures can only be disregarded if they are accidental and on a scale which is unlikely to affect the result of the ballot or, if more than one failure has occurred, then taken together they are on a scale which is unlikely to affect the result of the ballot (s.232B(1)(b)).

In addition to procedural requirements the legislation removes immunity where industrial action is taken over particular issues. In some ways this is strange as all of the issues fall within the statutory items which can be the subject of a trade dispute and, as such, the legislation removes them from the general definition. The first issue which may be the subject of industrial action and where immunity is lost is pressure to impose union membership and union recognition requirements. The provisions were first introduced in 1982 and are now contained in ss.144, 145, 186 and 187 Trade Union and Labour Relations (Consolidation) Act 1992. These sections render void any terms in a contract which require the other party to recognise a union or to maintain a closed shop among its workers. By ss.222(3) and 225 any industrial action for the purpose of persuading a party to insert such a clause in a contract will lose immunity. Section 222(1) removes immunity if one of the reasons for the action is to pressure the employer to discriminate against non-union members, that is, action to maintain a closed shop will lose immunity. Finally, protection against unfair dismissal was removed from strikers engaged in unofficial action in 1990 and is now s.237 of the 1992 Act. In addition, by s.223, any industrial action where one of the reasons for it is the dismissal of unofficial strikers loses immunity.

14.7 Picketing

Picketing is a method by which a trade union can strengthen a strike. It can prevent workers from entering the workplace and so increase the disruption to the employer. It can prevent supplies getting in, so that production is affected, and it can prevent goods leaving, so causing problems with any commercial contracts that the employer may have with his customers. In short, it is a very effective industrial weapon. The effectiveness of picketing was demonstrated during the miners' strikes in the 1970s when coal was prevented from reaching power stations, bringing industry to a halt. Mass picketing was seen at Grunwick in 1977 when workers from all over the UK joined the employees at Grunwick in their fight for union recognition.

The problem with picketing from a legal point of view is that inevitably it involves a consideration of both the criminal and civil law. The criminal law becomes involved not, by any means, because all pickets are violent, although a great many violent acts were committed on the picket lines during the miners' dispute in 1984–85 and the Wapping dispute in 1986, but because the fact that picketing involves a group of people standing around can create criminal liability. In addition, pickets will normally interfere with contracts, be committing a trespass and often commit private nuisance, so rendering them potentially liable in tort. As such, it is necessary to consider all the potential liability and then look at the immunity. This is also an area where the Human Rights Act 1998 is likely to have an impact. Article 11 of the Convention which guarantees the right to freedom of peaceful assembly and Article 10 which guarantees the right to freedom of expression may be applicable to individual employees who picket, particularly if the pickets are restricted to 6, as suggested under the Code of Practice discussed below.

Criminal liability

Obstruction of the highway

It is an offence to wilfully obstruct free passage along the highway without lawful authority or excuse (s.137 Highways Act 1980). Given that inevitably this is the intention of the pickets, it should not be surprising that this and the following offence are the ones most frequently levied against such activity. Lawful authority will exist if the picket has statutory immunity (subject to police discretion) and if the use by the picket is a reasonable exercise of a member of the public's right to pass and repass on the highway. In *Tynan* v. *Balmer* [1967] 1 QB 91, 40 pickets were walking around at the top of a service road to prevent lorries reaching the factory gates. The pickets argued that they were only exercising their right to pass and repass on the highway. It was held that their actions were an unreasonable exercise of that right. Thus the reason for the picket, where it occurs, how long it lasts, why it is done and whether it causes an obstruction are all relevant questions. The offence, if committed, is one of strict liability and it is irrelevant that the plaintiff genuinely believes he is exercising his rights. In *Broome* v. *DPP* [1974] AC 587 a picket failed to verbally persuade a lorry driver not to enter a site and so stood in front of the lorry and refused to move when asked to do so by the police. He was arrested and charged with obstructing the highway. The magistrates felt that as he had only delayed the lorry driver for about nine minutes this was a reasonable exercise of his right to picket. The House of Lords held that there is no such right, merely a freedom, and the fact that Broome thought he was exercising a right was irrelevant. The delay of the lorry driver was an unreasonable use of the highway, hence an obstruction and as the offence was one of strict liability, Broome should have been convicted.

Obstructing a police officer in the execution of his duty

Under s.51(3) Police Act 1964 it is an offence to obstruct a police officer in the execution of his duty. Thus refusal of a police order to stop obstructing the highway is an offence (*Tynan* v. *Balmer*, above). The police also have a duty to do what is necessary to prevent a breach of the peace where such a breach is a real possibility. This means that the police have a wide discretion to control pickets by limiting their number when they feel that a breach of the peace is likely. In *Piddington* v. *Bates* [1961] 1 WLR 162 a policeman told the defendant that two pickets were sufficient at a factory gate. The defendant pushed past the policeman, stated that he knew his rights and proceeded to picket. Unfortunately, his knowledge of his rights was limited as he was arrested and charged with obstruction! Lord Parker stated that the police are entitled to take any proper steps to prevent a breach of the peace, including limiting the number of pickets. In *Moss* v. *McLachlan* [1985] IRLR 77 it was decided that the police have a power to disperse pickets some way from their destination if they reasonably believe a breach of the peace will occur should they get to their destination. This gives the police control over flying pickets and is supplemented by s.4 Police and Criminal Evidence Act 1984 which gives police the authority to operate road checks for certain purposes which include ascertaining whether a vehicle is carrying a person intending to commit an offence which a senior police officer has reasonable grounds to believe is likely to lead to a serious public disorder. However, *R* v. *Chief Constable of Gloucestershire* [2006] UKHL 55 suggests that such a power only exists if an offence is imminent. In the case the chief constable knew of demonstrators moving by coaches into Gloucestershire. The chief constable had reasons to believe that the demonstration would not be peaceful and ordered his officers to intercept the coaches before they reached their destination and to search but not arrest the passengers. After the search the officers concluded that some but not all of the passengers intended to cause a breach of the peace at the demonstration. The officers therefore ordered all the passengers back onto the coaches and they escorted the coaches back to London. One of the passengers argued that the police officers' actions were an unlawful interference of her rights of freedom of expression and assembly under Articles 10 and 11 of the European Convention on Human Rights. The House of Lords agreed. It held that at the time the coaches were stopped and turned back there was no indication of an imminent breach of the peace and, since the chief constable did not think that, when the coaches were stopped, a breach was likely to occur, the action by the officers was an unlawful interference with Article 10 and Article 11 freedoms. As such, it seems that the power of the police is not as widespread as may at first seem.

Breach of the peace   In addition to obstruction of a police officer there is the common law offence of behaving in a manner likely to cause a breach of the peace. Thus stopping vehicles or shouting at employees trying to work can constitute the offence (*Kavanagh* v. *Hiscock* [1974] QB 600). Likewise, refusing to obey a police instruction to disperse can constitute the offence as well as the offence of obstructing a police officer.

Public nuisance   It is an offence to obstruct the public in the exercise or enjoyment of their common law rights, including the right to free passage along the highway. Originally, in *Lyons (J.) & Sons* v. *Wilkins* [1899] 1 Ch 255 it was thought that the picket *per se* constituted the nuisance; this was doubted by Denning MR in a dissenting judgement in *Hubbard* v. *Pitt* [1976] QB 142 but the rest of the Court of Appeal did not discuss the issue. In *News Group Newspapers Ltd* v. *SOGAT'82* [1986] ICR 716 the High Court held that the conduct of the pickets at the plant in Wapping amounted to an unreasonable obstruction of the highway and so constituted a public nuisance. A public nuisance is also actionable in tort if the plaintiff can show particular damage other and beyond that suffered by the general public.

The Trade Union and Labour Relations (Consolidation) Act 1992

Originally certain offences were created by the Conspiracy and Protection of Property Act 1875. These offences have now been consolidated into s.241 of the 1992 Act. The offences are committed by those who try and compel another to do (or not to do) something, without legal authority, by means of:

(a) using violence towards or intimidating that person, or his family or injuring his property;
(b) persistently following that person from place to place;
(c) hiding tools, clothes or any other property, or depriving or hindering the use of such;
(d) watching or besetting the person's home, workplace or the approach to either;
(e) following a person with two or more others in a disorderly fashion, in any road or street.

The most common charge is that of watching and besetting. In *Galt* v. *Philp* [1984] IRLR 156 workers were engaged in a sit-in during which they barricaded laboratories and prevented other employees from entering. It was held that they were besetting. In *Thomas* v. *NUM (South Wales Area)* [1985] IRLR 136 it appears that 'wrongfully and without legal authority' means that the act must be independently tortious or criminal for the offence under s.241. Thus if the picket has immunity, it would have to be shown that some wrong outside the immunity had been committed for the offence to be raised.

The Public Order Act 1986

This Act abolished the common law offences of riot, rout, unlawful assembly and affray and repealed provisions in the Public Order Act 1936 relating to threatening behaviour likely to cause a breach of the peace. The 1986 Act creates a series of statutory offences which may be invoked in an industrial dispute. These are:

1. *Riot (s.1)*: this is where 12 or more persons use or threaten to use violence for a common purpose which could cause a person of reasonable firmness to fear for his personal safety.

2. *Violent disorder (s.2)*: this is the same as riot but occurs where three or more persons threaten etc.
3. *Affray (s.3)*: this has the same element as riot but only one person is involved. Threats themselves are insufficient and there must be violence.
4. *Fear or provocation of violence (s.4)*: it is an offence to use threatening, abusive or insulting words or behaviour, or to distribute or display any visual representation which is threatening, abusive or insulting where the intention is to make a person fear immediate violence, or provoke immediate violence or the action is likely to do the above.
5. *Harassment, alarm or distress (s.5)*: this has the same elements as fear or provocation of violence but is committed within the sight or hearing of a person likely to be caused harassment, alarm or distress. It is a defence if the defendant can show he had reasonable cause to believe that a person was not in his sight or hearing.

Civil liability

There are four main torts which can be committed by pickets.

1. *Private nuisance*   This is an unlawful interference with an individual's enjoyment of his land. The tort was extensively discussed by Scott J in *Thomas* v. *NUM* (above) when he held that mass picketing constituted a nuisance because the sheer volume of numbers had an intimidatory effect which prevented the users of the land from exercising their rights over it. Furthermore, it has been seen that an unreasonable obstruction of the highway is also actionable as a private nuisance by the owner of the land whose right of access to the highway is being restricted by the picket (*News Group Newspapers Ltd* v. *SOGAT'82*, above).
2. *Trespass to the highway*   Using the highway for a purpose other than the exercise of the right to pass and repass is a trespass to the highway. The injured parties are the owners of the soil below the highway, either adjoining landowners or the local authority.
3. *Economic torts*   It has already been noted that invariably a picket will induce breaches of contracts of employment, procure breaches of commercial contracts, in fact cover the whole gamut of economic torts during the course of the picket.
4. *Protection from Harassment Act 1997*   The act has introduced a statutory tort which is relevant to pickets. By s.1 it is an offence to pursue a course of conduct which amounts to harassment of another and which he or she knows or ought to know amounts to harassment. 'Course of conduct' is defined as conduct on at least two occasions (s.7(3)) and 'conduct' includes speech (s.7(4)). 'Harassment' includes alarming a person or causing a person distress (s.7(2)). There is a defence if the person shows

that in the circumstances the pursuit of the conduct was reasonable (s.1(3)(c)). In this context the Human Rights Act may be relevant. A person who is the victim of such conduct may seek an injunction to restrain it and it is an offence, punishable by up to five-years' imprisonment, to breach the injunction without reasonable excuse (s.3). Damages may also be awarded.

Immunity for picketing

The immunity for pickets is contained in s.220 of the 1992 Act. This renders it lawful for a person, in contemplation or furtherance of a trade dispute, to attend at or near his own place of work for the purpose of peacefully obtaining or communicating information, or peacefully persuading a person to work or not to work. In addition, a trade union official may peacefully picket at or near the place of work of a member of the union whom he is accompanying and whom he represents. Unemployed employees are allowed to picket their former place of work if their employment was terminated in connection with the trade dispute or the dismissal gave rise to the trade dispute.

The limit of attending at or near the employee's place of work was introduced after public disquiet about flying pickets, that is, pickets travelling all over the country to support other workers in their disputes. Such attendance is now only lawful if done by a trade union official. In the *SOGAT'82* case (above), Rupert Murdoch had moved from Fleet Street to Wapping and when the unions refused the move and took strike action, all those who went on strike were dismissed. They picketed Wapping. It was held that their place of work was Fleet Street and therefore the picket was outside s.220. By contrast, in *Rayware Ltd* v. *TGWU* [1989] IRLR 134 the workplace was on an industrial estate which was private property. The roadway was about two-thirds of a mile from the premises and as the pickets would have committed a trespass if they had gone to the factory entrance, they picketed the entrance to the site instead. It was held that they were picketing near their place of work for the purposes of s.220.

According to the Code of Practice on picketing, 'place of work' means the entrance or exit of the factory, site or office. Even if the picket is lawful as to place, it should be noted that all that can be done is the peaceful obtaining or communication of information or peaceful persuasion of a person. *Broome* v. *DPP* (above) makes it clear that a picket has no right to stop a person. Furthermore, while there is no mention in the legislation as to the numbers which can lawfully picket, Scott J in *Thomas* v. *NUM* (above) thought that 50 or 70 miners picketing colliery gates fell outside the immunity on the basis that sheer weight of numbers contradicted the aim of peaceful picketing. He relied on the Code of Practice, which states that mass picketing is not lawful picketing in the sense of an attempt at peaceful persuasion and states that no more than six pickets should be allowed at each entrance to the workplace. Scott J thought that this provided a guide as to sensible numbers on a picket line so that the weight of numbers should not intimidate those who wish to work. The result of this decision seems to be that more than six pickets will be construed as intimidation and therefore not peaceful. As such, the picket will lose the protection of s.220.

14.8　Remedies

Obviously, although the individual member commits the tort, it is more beneficial for an employer to sue the union, hence the removal of blanket union immunity in 1982. The majority of employers, however, do not want damages but rather want to prevent the action from commencing or to stop it as soon as possible. Thus the most common remedy sought is that of injunctive relief. Often the relief sought will be for a interlocutory injunction, requiring those who organise the action to call it off until the matter comes to a full trial. This is an important remedy for the employer as often if an interlocutory injunction is granted and the action is suspended, the case never gets to full trial as support for the action has waned. The House of Lords in *American Cynamid Co* v. *Ethicon Ltd* [1975] AC 396 laid down the principles which must be applied by the court when considering whether to grant injunctive relief. The court must ask itself three questions. Is there a serious issue to be tried? Has the plaintiff shown that the defendant's conduct is causing him irreparable harm which cannot be remedied by a subsequent award of damages? On the balance of convenience, is the harm being suffered by the plaintiff greater than will be incurred by the defendant if he is ordered to cease his activities pending a full trial? This decision represents a relaxation of the previous law in *Stratford* v. *Lindley* (above) where the plaintiff had to show at least a *prima facie* case which was likely to be successful at full trial. The decision, however, works against unions (although see the Court of Appeal in *Viking Line ABP* v. *ITWF* [2006] IRLR 58) as the balance of convenience test is usually in favour of maintaining the status quo, that is, full production, as it is obvious that the employer will lose from the industrial action much more than the union. In *Mercury Communications* v. *Scott-Garner* (above) the plaintiffs succeeded in showing that there was a serious issue to be tried and that they had a real prospect of securing a permanent injunction at full trial. In considering the balance of convenience, the court held that the loss which would have been sustained by the plaintiff would have vastly exceeded the limit of £250,000 which could have been imposed as damages. On the other hand, even if the union did prove that the action was lawful, it would have suffered no loss as the temporary cessation in the industrial action would not hasten or cause any redundancies. The plaintiffs got their injunction. In an attempt to rectify this imbalance, s.221(1) provides that if there might be a trade dispute defence to an injunction, the court should not grant the injunction *ex parte* until all reasonable steps have been taken to inform the defendant and give him an opportunity to put his side of the case, and by subsection (2) the court must have regard to the fact that the defendant would succeed in a trade dispute defence at full trial. The House of Lords in *NWL* v. *Woods* [1979] ICR 867 has stated that if it is likely that the defence will succeed then an injunction should not be granted. Such a defence, however, will only apply to the torts for which there is statutory immunity.

If the union fails to comply with an injunction, the two methods of enforcement are committal for contempt or sequestration of the union assets. The court may imprison for contempt, fine or order security for good behaviour. The union may be held in contempt if it does not prevent its officials from acting in contempt by s.20(6) of the 1992 Act.

Sequestration is a discretionary remedy of the court and can be granted if the court is satisfied that the disobedience to the court order, be it an injunction or an award of damages or a fine, is intentional. The order sequestrates all the property of the union and commissioners move in to take possession of the property so sequestrated. It was ordered in cases during the miners' dispute of 1984–85 where one area branch was attempting to move money into officials' personal accounts to prevent paying a fine and when later the trustees of the union's assets were attempting to send money abroad to frustrate the sequestrators, the court removed them as trustees. The remedies against trade union funds mean that officials are less likely to risk unlawful industrial action because they run the risk of bankrupting the union.

Until recently, remedies against the union were given to employers and members only. The 1993 Act gave, for the first time, protection to an individual who suffered as a result of unlawful industrial action. Section 235A of the 1992 Consolidation Act creates a right for an individual, where the industrial action either prevents or delays the supply of goods or services to him, or reduces the quality of goods or services supplied to him, to apply to the High Court. This action arises where the act to induce a person to take part or continue to take part in industrial action is unlawful, that is it is actionable in tort or a union member would have a right to sue the union because the balloting requirements had not been complied with. It is immaterial whether the individual is entitled to be supplied with the goods or services. If the court finds an application well-founded, it may make an order requiring the inducer to stop the inducement and requiring him to take steps to prevent further industrial action (s.235A(4)). Any act of inducement shall be taken to be committed by the trade union if it has authorised or endorsed the action (s.235A(6)).

This section creates rights for members of the public to take proceedings when they are affected by unlawful industrial action. *P* v. *NAS/UWT* (above) is an example of the section being invoked, where a disputative pupil took action because teachers were refusing to teach him. This section particularly affects the unions in those industries which deal with members of the public, in particular the service industries.

Summary

1. The basis of the legal regulation of industrial action under some previous governments was the pursuance of a market forces economic policy rather than the balance of power between the two sides of industry. The present government has yet (in 2008) to indicate that it will change the majority of the law restricting unions in relation to industrial action.

2. Virtually all forms of industrial action will constitute a breach of the employee's contract of employment.

3. All forms of industrial action will involve the economic torts.

4. The range of economic torts has been extended since the reduction in the scope of the statutory immunity.

5. Unions and their members are immune from liability for certain economic torts only if they are acting in contemplation or furtherance of a trade dispute.

6. Because of the definition of trade dispute, all tertiary action and the majority of secondary action create liability.

7. Trade unions only have the same immunity as their members and will lose immunity if they fail to comply with the statutory requirements on balloting and notice.

8. A trade union is only liable, however, when it has authorised or endorsed the action and can escape liability if it repudiates the action.

9. There is a statutory maximum on the award of damages against a union in any one action. There is no such limit in relation to fines imposed for contempt.

10. Picketing can involve both criminal and civil liability; there is no immunity for criminal actions.

11. A person can now only lawfully picket at or near his own place of work and must be acting within the 'golden formula' to be protected from civil liability.

12. The police have a total discretion to disperse pickets if they reasonably fear a breach of the peace. This means that there is only a freedom to picket and not a right.

Summary cont'd

13. Employers normally seek an injunction to prevent or suspend industrial action. In addition, an individual may claim relief against the union if the action disrupts the supply of goods or services to that individual.

14. Breach of any court order by a union can lead to a fine or imprisonment for contempt or ultimately sequestration of union assets.

Exercises

1. At Groanwick Ltd a dispute exists with the employees represented by Bovver Union over pay. The workers refuse to handle goods from the company's suppliers, having also organised a sit-in at the company's premises, where they effected entry by force.

The company has existing contracts for the supply of goods from Conthem Ltd. The Bovver Union contacts the union representing the majority of workers at Conthem, the Aggro Union, and informs it of the dispute. Officials of the Aggro Union inform Conthem that its members will refuse to handle goods bound for Groanwick and the company agrees to stop the supplies to Groanwick.

Certain supplies are, nevertheless, still leaving Conthem, being handled by non-union labour. As a result, workers from Groanwick and Conthem mount a picket at the gates of Conthem to prevent supplies leaving the company.
Advise the employers.

2. 'The past 50 years have witnessed an enormous extension of the scope of the economic torts as they affect industrial action, while simultaneously seeing a significant contraction in the breadth of the golden formula, a combination of events which has considerably extended the scope of potential liability for individual participants in industrial action.'
Consider the accuracy of this statement.

Further Reading

Auerbach   *Legal Restraint of Picketing: New Trends; New Tensions* (1987) 16 ILJ 227.

Beardsmore   *Labour Disputes in 2005,* Labour Market Trends, June 2005.

Carty   *The Public Order Act 1986: Police Powers and the Picket Line* (1987) 16 ILJ 146.

Carty   *International Violations of Economic Interests: The Limits of Common Law Liability* (1988) 104 LQR 250.

Elias and Ewing   *Economic Torts and Labour Law: Old Principles and New Liabilities* (1982) 41 CLJ 321.

Further reading cont'd

Hendy *Caught in a Fork* (2000) 29 ILJ 53.

Howarth *Against Lumley v. Gye* (2005) 68 MLR 195.

Miller and Woolfson *Timex, Industrial Relations and the Use of Law in the 1990s* (1994) 23 ILJ 209.

Morris *Industrial Action in Essential Services: The New Law* (1991) 20 ILJ 89.

Sales and Stilitz *Intentional Infliction of Harm Caused by Unlawful Means* (1999) 115 LQR 411.

Simpson *A Not So Golden Formula: 'In Contemplation or Furtherance of a Trade Dispute' After 1982* (1983) 46 MLR 463.

Simpson *The Code of Practice on Industrial Action Ballots and Notice to Employers* (2001) 30 ILJ 194.

Wallington *Injunctions and the Right to Demonstrate* (1986) CLJ 86.

Wedderburn *Underground Labour Injunctions* (2001) 30 ILJ 206.

Index